# The Cinema of Soviet Kazakhstan 1925–1991

# Contemporary Central Asia: Societies, Politics, and Cultures

## *Series Editor:* Marlene Laruelle, George Washington University

At the crossroads of Russia, China, and the Islamic world, Central Asia remains one of the world's least-understood regions, despite being a significant theater for muscle-flexing by the great powers and regional players. This series, in conjunction with George Washington University's Central Asia Program, offers insight into Central Asia by providing readers unique access to state-of-the-art knowledge on the region. Going beyond the media clichés, the series inscribes the study of Central Asia into the social sciences and hopes to fill the dearth of works on the region for both scholarly knowledge and undergraduate and graduate student education.

### Recent Titles in Series

*Language, Literacy, and Social Change in Mongolia: Traditionalist, Socialist, and Post-Socialist Identities*, by Phillip P. Marzluf

*The Dialectics of Post-Soviet Modernity and the Changing Contours of Islamic Discourse in Azerbaijan: Towards a Resacralization of Public Space*, by Murad Ismayilov

*The European Union's Influence in Central Asia: Geopolitical Challenges and Responses*, by Olga Alinda Spaiser

*Central Asia in the Era of Sovereignty: The Return of Tamerlane?*, edited by Daniel L. Burghart and Theresa Sabonis-Helf

*State-Building in Kazakhstan: Continuity and Transformation of Informal Institutions*, by Dina Sharipova

*Tajikistan on the Move: Statebuilding and Societal Transformations*, edited by Marlene Laruelle

*Visions of Development in Central Asia: Revitalizing the Culture Concept*, by Noor O'Neill Borbieva

*The Nazarbayev Generation: Studies on Youth in Kazakhstan*, edited by Marlene Laruelle

*Modern Central Asia: A Primary Source Reader*, edited by Yuriy Malikov

*The Central Asia–Afghanistan Relationship*, edited by Marlene Laruelle

*The Cinema of Soviet Kazakhstan 1925–1991: An Uneasy Legacy*, by Peter Rollberg

# The Cinema of Soviet Kazakhstan 1925–1991

## An Uneasy Legacy

Peter Rollberg

LEXINGTON BOOKS
*Lanham • Boulder • New York • London*

Published by Lexington Books
An imprint of The Rowman & Littlefield Publishing Group, Inc.
4501 Forbes Boulevard, Suite 200, Lanham, Maryland 20706
www.rowman.com

6 Tinworth Street, London SE11 5AL, United Kingdom

Copyright © 2021 by The Rowman & Littlefield Publishing Group, Inc.

*All rights reserved.* No part of this book may be reproduced in any form or by any electronic or mechanical means, including information storage and retrieval systems, without written permission from the publisher, except by a reviewer who may quote passages in a review.

British Library Cataloguing in Publication Information Available

Library of Congress Control Number: 2020946693

ISBN 978-1-7936-4174-8 (cloth : alk. paper)
ISBN 978-1-7936-4175-5 (electronic)

∞™ The paper used in this publication meets the minimum requirements of American National Standard for Information Sciences—Permanence of Paper for Printed Library Materials, ANSI/NISO Z39.48-1992.

*To Marlène Laruelle*

# Contents

Acknowledgments ix

Introduction xi

1 The First and Second Birth of Kazakhstani Cinema 1
2 Heroic Interlude in Alma-Ata 31
3 The Third Birth 57
4 The Mid-1950s: A Cautious Emancipation 85
5 En Route to Complexity I: Capturing the Present 121
6 En Route to Complexity II: Capturing the Past 163
7 The Searchings of Shaken Aimanov 191
8 Hits and Anti-Hits 217
9 The New Status Quo 251
10 State Cinema and Its Subversion 283
11 Crisis and Reconstruction 325
12 From Perestroika to Katastroika 367

Conclusion 423

Glossary 431

| | |
|---|---:|
| Bibliography | 433 |
| Index | 441 |
| About the Author | 449 |

# Acknowledgments

I would like to offer my gratitude to the following filmmakers who granted me interviews: Asanali Ashimov, Bolat Sharip, Ardak Amirkulov, Darezhan Omirbaev, Satybaldy Narymbetov, Adilkhan Erzhanov, Ermek Shinarbaev, Zhanna Isabayeva, and Serik Abishev.

In Almaty, I enjoyed the help and hospitality of Olzhabai Musabekov and Aizhan Kassymbekova at Kazakhfilm Studio; Alla Seitova, director of the State Archive for Film and Photo Documents, and her colleagues; and Dr. Gulzhan Nauryzbaikazy at the Zhurgenov Institute for the Arts.

Sincere thanks are due to the following colleagues and friends who provided essential logistical and research support: Aitolkyn Kurmanova, Serik Jaxylykov, Dinara Nurusheva, Karlyga Hasen, Bota Ayasbaeva, Dinara Amreyeva, Ayush Dwivedi, and, last but not least, Omirbek. Ellen Powell and Emma Handel edited the manuscript with exceptional care and thoroughness—thank you!

I am grateful for the consistent lively interest that Erlan Karin, adviser to the President of the Republic of Kazakhstan, showed in my work. The encouragement I received from Ambassador Kairat Umarov, Ambassador Erzhan Kazykhanov, and Dana Masalimova meant a lot. Needless to say, that I alone am responsible for all possible inaccuracies in this book.

# Introduction

A few years ago, at a reception honoring the ambassador of Kazakhstan to the United States, some Kazakh students asked me about my current research. I replied that I am writing a history of Kazakhstani cinema. When the students asked about specifics, I mentioned the name of Shaken Aimanov. To my astonishment, they had never heard of it. An elderly Kazakh woman who joined our conversation was just as amazed: "Shaken Aimanov, our great actor and director! Have you not seen *Our Dear Doctor*?" The students had not. They were not so much embarrassed as surprised by the fact that the name of the founder of Kazakh national cinema had never crossed their path. A few months later, I talked to one of these students again, and she happily reported that she had watched *Land of the Fathers*, Aimanov's greatest directorial accomplishment, and was deeply touched by it. She added that after returning to Almaty, she intended to start a Kazakh film club in order to learn more about her nation's cinema and spread the word among friends.

The students' lack of knowledge of their country's film history was no coincidence. While Kazakhstani high schools provide youths with a solid survey of the nation's leading authors, cinema is not a focus. While this is typical of many countries where cinema is primarily viewed as a form of entertainment rather than an art form to be both enjoyed *and* studied, the degree to which many Kazakhs show indifference with respect to their own cinema is unusual. To be sure, it has not always been this way. The emergence of a national cinema in Kazakhstan in the mid-1950s was accompanied by enthusiastic reactions of millions of viewers to each new film coming from the Alma-Ata studio, and box office results of 12–15 million viewers in the first year of release throughout the Soviet Union was the rule. In the 1960s, millions of Kazakhstanis regularly flocked to movie theaters to watch the latest comedy or historical adventure, and even contemporary dramas attracted their fair share of viewers. Aimanov's *End of the Ataman* became a Soviet-wide superhit, with over 30 million viewers. These are numbers that today's directors even of plain commercial pictures can only dream of. However, by the mid-1970s, the trusting relationship between the country's filmmaking community and native audiences fell apart, and in the 1980s, Kazakhstani cinema was in full crisis mode, not so much artistically (although there was a decline as well) but with respect to the acceptance of Kazakhstani films by the republic's population. Then, the breakdown of Soviet society and its film industry opened the doors for an astonishing artistic revival, but those films were shown at festivals and remained unknown to regular audiences. Thus, for current international film connoisseurs, Kazakhstani cinema is synonymous with the films of Darezhan Omirbaev and Emir Baigazin. To regular viewers at home, these names mean little—instead, mass audiences associate the notion of "Kazakhstani cinema" with Nurtas Adambaev's *Kelinka* comedies and Akan Sataev's thrillers, which, incidentally, are unknown abroad.

Today, only relatively small groups of cineastes are aware of the achievements of Soviet-Kazakh cinema, and only a minority take pride in the achievements of the cinema of independent Kazakhstan.[1] The fact that recent Kazakhstani pictures have won prizes at prestigious international festivals makes for good media headlines, but the films themselves are watched and appreciated by few. This dilemma is also true with respect to the legacy of Soviet-Kazakh cinema, which is kept alive by television. However, there is an additional generational divide: many Kazakhs who grew up with cult films such as *My Name Is Kozha* and *The End of the Ataman* remember these films fondly, whereas younger viewers, whose taste has been shaped by Western commercial movies, have difficulty connecting with the legacy films' aesthetics and morality.

Several factors may explain why Kazakhstani cinema takes such a hard stance at home and why its history has been largely forgotten. For one, there have been no systematic efforts to establish an awareness of Kazakhstani cinema of the past. When legacy films are shown on television, they usually come without preface or any form of contextualization, which makes their appreciation by unprepared spectators a challenge. Second, the official attitude toward Soviet-Kazakh cinema as part of the nation's twentieth-century cultural legacy has been ambivalent since the nation's independence. The cultural efforts to modernize society are often viewed as synonymous with the need to westernize and implicitly or explicitly reject the Soviet heritage.

Apart from current political considerations, the manner in which Soviet film history was written in past decades has influenced the perception of Kazakhstani cinema as well. One such factor was the russocentric approach taken by Soviet film historians. Suffice it to look at the authoritative *Dictionary of Film* (*Kinoslovar'*, 1987), which affords even to the leading Kazakhstani filmmakers Abdulla Karsakbaev, Sultan-Akhmet Khodzhikov, and Mazhit Begalin merely a few lines, reducing their careers to the bare facts and not making even a minimal effort to define their specific accomplishments. This sad state of affairs was mirrored by Western literature about Soviet cinema, which often did not mention any Kazakhstani picture or director at all.

The emergence of the "Kazakh New Wave" in the late 1980s for the first time brought Kazakhstani filmmakers to the attention of international festival audiences. However, this did not cause a reevaluation of the previous decades, which were usually dismissed in a superficial and undifferentiated manner. Ever since, new pictures coming out of Kazakhstan have been given a fair chance on the festival circuit and in specialized media. Yet, the legacy of Soviet-Kazakh cinema is still left unaffected.

This book has been conceived with the intention to reconstruct the history of Soviet-Kazakhstani cinema to the fullest extent currently possible. This includes its inner dynamics, contradictions, artistic achievements and failures, and the many gradations in between. I do believe that this legacy is worth knowing, both at home and abroad. To prove my case, I have analyzed many Soviet-Kazakh pictures in depth, including those that were ignored by official Soviet sources such as the four-volume *History of Soviet Cinema* (1967–1975). This thoroughness and inclusiveness are based on my experience that certain judgments quickly turned into clichés that were repeated by critics and then wandered from one article or interview statement to the next. An actual viewing of such neglected or dismissed films can make for a genuine surprise! Particularly the first three decades of Kazakhstani cinema have often been irreverently mischaracterized by film critics and historians. Thus, after mentioning that Eisenstein [Eizenshtein] shot his *Ivan the Terrible* in Alma-Ata during the World War II evacuation of Mosfilm studio, one author commented on the following decades of Kazakhstani cinema: "But propaganda films of the past years, historical dramas stressing Communist views, or love stories with predictable endings, created a cinema with little human interest."[2] Even well-wishing critics opined that prior to "the recognition of the New Wave Kazakh cinema in the late 1980s, the Kazakhfil'm Studios in Alma-Ata had an undistinguished history," adding that the history of Kyrgyz cinema boasted far greater accomplishments. "Meanwhile, the Kazakhfil'm Studios remained in obscurity: the only native director working there to attract interest was Abdula Karsakbaev who produced two films: *My Name Is Kozha* (*Menia zovut Kozha*, 1964), a film of daily life (*bytovoi fil'm*) and *Journey into Childhood* (*Puteshestvie v detstvo*, 1970) which was devoted to similar themes."[3] Anybody remotely familiar with Kazakhstani cinema of the 1960s and 1970s would likely protest against such generalizations. After all, during these years Shaken Aimanov made remarkable pictures such as *Land of the Fathers* (1966), Sultan-Akhmet Khodzhikov created a sensation with

*Kyz-Zhibek* (1970), Mazhit Begalin helmed one of the best war films, *Song of Manshuk* (1969), and Abdula Karsakbaev made what is arguably the most subversive picture about the Civil War, *A Worrisome Morning* (1966). These masterpieces were accompanied by lesser known, yet remarkable films. It is one of the goals of this monograph to challenge baseless cliché generalizations about the legacy of Kazakhstani cinema which, unfortunately, have been internalized by some Kazakhstani film artists themselves.

From the very beginning, Kazakhstani filmmakers were facing an uphill battle. The centralized apparatus of the Soviet film industry systematically diminished national aspects, accusing studios and film workers of provincialism and nationalism. When the filmmakers of Central Asia gathered for a five-day festival in 1966 in Ashkhabad (Ashgabat), critics from the center handed out marks and even numerical grades. One of the major points of contention was that "local problems, even the most poignant ones, are often being treated and dealt with from positions that do not go beyond narrow national frameworks."[4] While this was considered a shortcoming, in hindsight the dogmatic critics may have diagnosed a feature of Soviet national film cultures that had surprising staying power and deepened, despite all careful monitoring and intrusions from the Soviet center, a national identity whose vitality came to the fore after these nations gained political independence.

When assessing the importance of individual films for this project, it was not decisive whether any one film is generally considered to be part of "the canon," for it can be assumed that there is not one generally recognized canon for all of Kazakhstani cinema. Furthermore, the critical recognition of a film during the time of its release is treated as a factor of film history itself, that is, its contemporary relevance, but not the basis of its importance in general. For example, *Blood and Sweat* (1979), the adaptation of a socialist-realist epic, and *The Taste of Bread* (1980), a coproduction between Mosfilm studio and Kazakhfilm, were hailed as huge achievements of Soviet-Kazakhstani cinema at the time and were just as safely forgotten during the post-Soviet decades. Both of these films are analyzed in depth because of the aesthetic and political norm-shaping role that they played in their days.

In this book, the terms "*Kazakh* cinema" and "*Kazakhstani* cinema"[5] will be used interchangeably, denoting "the cinema of Kazakhstan," despite the fact that these terms are not exactly synonymous. Recent attempts to ethnically narrow down the meaning of "cinema of Kazakhstan," to include only films made by ethnic Kazakhs as being "truly Kazakh," have not led to usable results and would ultimately lead to a falsification of the real history of this subject. Each chapter outlines the historical framework of a certain period of Kazakhstani film development, pointing out significant administrative and organizational events referring to the national studio, the union of film workers, governmental structures responsible for Kazakhstan's film industry, as well as congresses, official declarations, and media discussions. However, the largest space is afforded to the analysis of individual films. The thoroughness and degree of detail with which key pictures of Kazakhstani cinema are treated is essential for a profound understanding of the evolution of national Kazakh cinema as a whole. Feature films represent the main focus of this book, whereas documentaries and animated pictures are discussed in exceptional cases only. The film analyses include a discussion of the sociopolitical context, plot, peculiarities of direction, acting, camera work, music, and art direction, as well as critical reactions and box office returns. When dealing with individual directors, major elements of their personal biography are discussed, including ethnic background, since ethnicity was very much on people's mind in the film community and became an explicit political factor in the 1980s. The same is true for language issues: as early as in the 1950s, film workers at Kazakhfilm studio voiced their intention to shoot their pictures in Kazakh, although that decision was not consistently implemented.

The transliteration of names and film titles in this book is largely based on the Cyrillic alphabet. The main reason for that approach was practical considerations, namely, that the vast majority of documents are spelled this way. The film titles are provided in English translation, then, in parentheses, the Russian title under which the film was released in the Kazakhstani SSR and the USSR at large, and, whenever possible, the Kazakh title.

Researching the cinema of Soviet Kazakhstan means encountering a number of problems. First and foremost, many films are difficult to find, especially those from the 1950s. Archival documents, such as protocols of meetings, are also hard to come by. This is especially calamitous when a film was re-released in a newly edited version, which was a habit in the 1960s and early 1980s. Only in rare cases could both the original and the new version be located and compared. Of course, this is a lacuna and a challenge for future researchers.

The economic conditions under which cinema evolved was taken into consideration whenever possible. For industrial film production and distribution, these notions are fundamental. The terms "totalitarian" and "nontotalitarian," which became ubiquitous in the discussion of the Soviet-Kazakh legacy in the 1990s, merely established a narrow and not particularly helpful ideological framework that is subject to critical assessment in some chapters. Indeed, if one were to take the notion of totalitarianism in cinema seriously, one would have to move beyond mere political polemics, since very few Soviet films outside of the pure propaganda productions fit the definition of totalitarian cinema. Among Kazakhstani pictures, the one that comes the closest is arguably *The Golden Horn* (1948), a film that has been completely forgotten. The totalitarian framework of interpretation is most meaningful when applied to documentaries and newsreels. Feature films rarely fit into this procrustean frame, even when they deal with revolutionary events from a communist viewpoint.

Ludmila Pruner, one of the first American scholars to deal with the cinema of Kazakhstan, once wrote: "One of the most tragic consequences of the socialist regime had been the catastrophic loss of the republics' individual cultural heritage, traditions, diversity, imagination and creativity."[6] This is only partially true for the cinema of Kazakhstan, as will be shown on a number of examples. The national aspect of cinema was one that Soviet-Kazakhstani filmmakers had to struggle with for a long time. They were fully aware of their mentee role vis-à-vis the Russian professionals sent to Central Asia to build national film industries. Especially in times of crises (and there were several such periods in Kazakhstani cinema), directors from other studios came to realize their projects at Kazakhfilm studio, which often caused subliminal or open frictions. Closely connected with the national question is the dichotomy center/periphery, which is applied to the Soviet paradigm of film production and is important for the explanation of certain decisions made in Moscow or Almaty.

## NOTES

1. The *Memory of the World. National Cinematic Heritage* project, organized by the United Nations Educational, Scientific and Cultural Organization (UNESCO, Paris, 1995, pp. 38–39) lists the following Kazakhstani feature films of the Soviet period as part of Kazakhstan's national heritage: *Abai's Songs* (1945); *His Time Will Come* (1957); *My Name Is Kozha* (1963); *Traces Are Going Till Horizon* [sic!] (1964); *Aldar-Kose* (1964); *The Land of the Fathers* (1966); *Kyz-Dhibek* [sic!] (1970); *Shok and Sher* (1971); *The Needle* (1987); *The Last Stop* (1989); *Fish in Love* (1989); *The Touch* (1989); *Fall of Otrar* (1990); *Surzhekei* (1991); *Kairat* (1991); *Woman between Two Brothers* (1991). The 1970s are clearly underrepresented, as are the early 1980s. Conspicuously, only films by ethnic Kazakhs were included (with one exception, *The Songs of Abai*)—neither Efim Aron's *Botagoz*, nor Aleksandr Karpov's *Tale of a Mother* are listed.

2. Dönmez-Colin, Gönül, "Kazakh 'new wave': Post-perestroika, Post-Soviet Union," *Central Asian Survey*, 16 (1)/1997, p. 115.

3. Ludmila Zebrina Pruner, "The New Wave in Kazakh Cinema," *Slavic Review*, 51 (4)/1992, p. 792.

4. M. Zinov'ev, S. Markov, "Seredina potoka." In V. Golovskoi (ed.), *Kino 1966–1967*. Moskva: "Iskusstvo," p. 74.

5. The two terms have political connotations that are associated with issues of ethnicity, national identity, and statehood.

6. Pruner, "The New Wave in Kazakh Cinema," p. 793.

*Chapter 1*

# The First and Second Birth of Kazakhstani Cinema

Histories of national cinemas usually begin with accounts of the first screenings of the pioneer cameramen in charge of the earliest newsreel shootings in the capital city, and the roots of the national film industry. In the case of Kazakhstan, this part of the story is quickly told: screenings began in the town of Vernyi (the later Alma-Ata/Almaty) in 1904, the first movie theaters were built in 1910, and the first newsreel cameramen arrived from Moscow in 1924. A national film industry developed in the late 1940s. But this is merely the factual side of the development, which is essential for the creation of a national cinema culture, but not specific for its aesthetics.[1] Suffice it to say that numerous cultural factors shaped specific cultural sensitivities and preferences, the effects of which can be felt in Kazakhstani cinema both during its Soviet and post-Soviet period.

## LATE ARRIVAL

There is a curious irony in the fact that the appearance of cinema in Kazakhstan was associated with a man who later himself became the eponymous hero of the first Kazakh feature film: the legendary revolutionary Amangeldy Imanov. Imanov's friend, the Bolshevik Alibi Dzhangildin,[2] spent years on the road in Europe and Asia, and returned to Kazakhstan in 1913 with a portable projector and forty boxes of newsreels. Subsequently, Dzhangildin and Imanov traveled across the steppes screening these films, accompanying them with the appropriate propaganda verbiage. Their success was immense. Large crowds came from faraway places to watch the miraculous moving pictures and listen to stories about the oppression of people in other countries. Thus, early on, film became a political force. It was recognized as such by the military governor of Turgai who gave orders to have Dzhangildin arrested for his subversive activities. However, the Kazakh Bolshevik managed to escape and continued to screen documentaries in *auls* and towns across the country.[3]

Cinema arrived in Kazakhstan (then part of Turkestan) later than in other parts of Central Asia. The delay was due to the country's vastness and its socioeconomic peculiarities: the predominant nomadic lifestyle of the Kazakh people and the scarcity of urban environments that are a precondition for the emergence of film as an industrial form of cultural production and entertainment. Prior to the communist revolution, Russian Bolshevik activists were among the first to recognize cinema's subversive power, especially in the provinces at the peripheries of the Russian Empire. Thus, it is not surprising that film, as a new cultural phenomenon, subsequently was closely associated with Soviet power and Sovietization. In the center of Russia, the development of a film industry began in all major cities with the establishment of distribution companies and movie theaters in the first decade of the twentieth century. In the peripheral territories, including those that would later become Kazakhstan, given their lack of urban infrastructure, this process took considerably longer. The relationship between center and periphery regarding the cultural development would remain a problem in the Soviet era as well. Until the 1930s, cinema was a rare and precious attraction in Kazakhstan, especially for the rural population, that is, the vast majority.

One of the first screenings in Kazakhstan took place in 1904 in Uralsk. Since Uralsk had no electricity, the projector was operated with the help of an oxygen lamp. Initially, film shows were met with a dose of skepticism, which remained the predominant attitude in some quarters of the political and cultural establishment in the first decades of the twentieth century. As the projectionist Sergei Kuzmichev later recalled,[4] the educated elites despised cinema, regarding it as entertainment for the lower class, while religious communities viewed it as a temptation from the devil. However, regular folks enjoyed the movies and flocked to the "electric theaters" whenever there was a chance.

The first stationary movie theater in Kazakhstan was built in June 1910 in the town of Vernyi, which, just like Uralsk, did not have electricity at the time. The screening room in the movie theater "Mars" was illuminated by gasoline lamps.[5] The films had to be transported from Baku via Tashkent on postal carriages,[6] and tickets were relatively expensive. According to an eyewitness, screenings were held in the evenings and lasted for about 40–50 minutes, with interruptions for changing reels when new viewers were admitted into the auditorium and others could exit. The entrepreneur Fabri, who had moved from Omsk to Vernyi, was the city's first movie theater owner. Vernyi's second so-called electric theater was named "20th Century," its construction started on September 16, 1910. In December of that year, it was destroyed by an earthquake but was quickly rebuilt by February 1911.

Each screening started with a documentary or a newsreel, followed by a melodrama or a comedy.[7] The repertoire was international. For example, one session would begin with the weekly "Pathé News," after which viewers were treated to a comedy starring the popular Max Linder or a Russian thriller such as the infamous *Little Sonia, the Golden Hand* (Son'ka—zolotaia ruchka, 1914), or the risqué *Keys to Happiness* (Kliuchi schast'ia, 1915). The interior of the "20th Century" was adorned with paintings by a local artist. Also featured was a music automaton, "Symphonium," playing popular tunes, including classical music. The screen itself was framed by decorations resembling a forest.

Prior to 1917, there were altogether thirteen film projectors on the territory that would soon be named Kazakhstan, all of them privately owned. By 1925, that number had not changed. However, considering the enormity of destruction that the country had suffered from political turbulences and Civil War during the previous decade, the constancy as such can be viewed as a success. Subsequently, additional movie theaters were established in Vernyi, which counted a total of four projectors, as well as Semipalatinsk, Petropavlovsk, Perovsk (Kyzyl-Orda), and Uralsk.

After the demise of the tsarist regime in 1917 and a brief period of independence, the newly established revolutionary councils (*soviets*) were given the right to requisition all film theaters and projection equipment.[8] But in Kazakhstan, this measure did not provide an impetus to the movie business. Indeed, after the Bolsheviks seized power, the state-supported development of cinema on an industrial scale (fashionably called "cinefication" [*kinofikatsiia*][9]) did not take off as in other republics of the Soviet Union, although the Communist Party had recognized its huge political potential, especially in a country in which only 2 percent of the population was literate. One of the factors that slowed down the process of cinefication in Kazakhstan was the lack of qualified personnel: technicians had to be rehired from the old private businesses, even though they were considered politically unreliable.

Still, despite manifold setbacks, the administrative regulation of culture according to communist standards had begun. First and foremost, this was part of the process of centralization of the entire cultural sphere, which the communists pursued with great resolve, if not expertise. On October 24, 1921, the board of the Main Administration of Political Education (*Glavpolitprosvet*) of the People's Commissariat of Education of the Kazakh Autonomous Soviet Socialist Republic confirmed a decision regarding the work of the Department of Cinema and Photography (*kinofotootdel*), stipulating that the exploitation of movable film projection equipment be initiated and that the work of movie theaters be centrally regulated. Over the next few years, the number of stationary film theaters grew steadily.[10] By 1927, 131 stationary and mobile film projectors were operating in Kazakhstan.[11]

Despite the aggressive implementation of strict political guidelines, various forms of ownership in the emerging Kazakh film business continued to coexist. One variety of mixed ownership was described in a well-sourced article by Kabysh Siranov.[12] These so-called film artels (associations for joint labor, *kinotovarishchestva*) consisted of several members who owned shares in the leasing or acquisition of a mobile film projector; the revenue of their work benefited both the artel members as well as the state. Such small collective businesses were typical of the 1920s when the principles of New Economic Policy (NEP) yielded positive effects in the Soviet economy. Kazakhstan had forty-one film artels. They were obligated to ask for permission to conduct their business, that is, rent space for screenings, pay a projectionist, lease films, etc. The official "film and photo department," which monitored the artels' repertoire and received a percentage of the profits, was politically responsible for all such decisions.

In the relatively liberal context of the 1920s, the imposed political structures were just one factor relevant for cinema among others; indeed, the communist-run film organizations had to compete with the more commercial structures in the film business for the attention of the public. Thus, in May 1925, the Dzhetysai province committee for political education asked the Main Administration of Political Education of the People's Commissariat of Education of the Russian Federation to send them films that would support the propaganda work among the native population.[13] In October 1925, the same local committee founded a film department tasked with distributing documentary films.

One of the chronic problems faced by the film industry in Kazakhstan was the absence of mechanics who could handle the projection equipment. The few qualified specialists traveled from *aul* to *aul*, delivering not only screenings but also political commentaries, that is, they worked both as projectionists and propagandists. These men had to overcome deep-seated cultural prejudices of the native population. Thus, in the *kishlaks*[14] of Taranchinsk, special daytime screenings had to be organized for the local women, since their husbands would not allow them to attend screenings at night.

Whenever a new film was released, crews with their mobile projectors traveled for months across the vast Kazakh regions to bring the film industry to every *aul* they could reach. Although many viewers were exempt from having to pay for the tickets (e.g., children and the poor) and despite the general lack of coordination and planning, these expeditions were financially profitable. But the conditions in Kazakhstani stationary movie theaters were so deplorable that they even caught the attention of central Soviet media. In 1927, the journal *Kino* published an article, "Dirt and Darkness," opening with the statement: "The issue of cinefication in Kazakhstan leaves much to be desired." The author went on to describe film theaters in Chimkent and other towns as humid and unsanitary; of the three movie theaters in Alma-Ata, two had no foyer and one was only open in the summer. Other movie theaters were housed in regular apartment buildings; several lacked normal seating.[15] The article concluded that cinema in Kazakhstan was not taken as seriously as it should be and that substantial investments were called for in order to improve the situation.

A persistent problem was language. In the Kazakh mainland, few people understood Russian, and the projectionists had to summarize the content of a film prior to the screening, or simultaneously translate the Russian intertitles into Kazakh. Since Kazakhstan in the first years of Soviet power had no film studio of its own, politically important films were prepared by studios in the Russian Federation that provided the Kazakh intertitles. Such was the case with the feature films *The Moslem Woman* (Musul'manka, 1925) and *Under the Power of the Adat* (Pod vlast'iu adata), which negatively depicted the life of women under the tsarist regime and were considered valuable for communist propaganda.[16]

The first film shooting in Kazakhstan took place in 1924 when the cameraman E.E. Blekhman filmed the arrival of Red Army commander Semen Budennyi in the city of Orenburg. While this was a simple report, later documentary episodes were shot with an openly didactic purpose, for example, *Cooperation in the Aul*, which praised the principles of cooperative trade in the countryside. Such episodes were combined into so-called film journals (*kinozhurnaly*), including the *Soviet Film Journal* (Sovkinozhurnal) and *Film Week* (Kinonedelia). Following Lenin's mandatory instructions regarding movie screenings, every feature film had to be preceded by film journals, thus combining information and propaganda with entertainment.

Kazakhstan soon became an important subject of newsreels that informed Soviet viewers about the unfolding industrial revolution. Among the Kazakh issues included in the newsreel series *Sovkinozhurnal* and *Soiuzkinozhurnal* was the construction work in Kyzyl-Orda (1925), which was the capital of the Kazakh Autonomous Soviet Republic (part of the Russian Federation at the time); the opening of the Chirkeisk canal (1927); the collection of rubber in Southern Kazakhstan (1930); and the work of the Chimkent lead factory (1934).[17] The first documentary to focus solely on Kazakhstan was *The Fifth Anniversary of the KaSSR* (Piataia godovshchina sushchestvovaniia KASSR), produced by the Moscow studio Kul'tkino in 1925. This short film was the debut of cinematographer Iakov Tolchan,[18] who had filmed the fifth conference of the Kazakh soviets in the capital, Kyzyl-Orda.

In the first years of Soviet power, Kazakh movie theaters screened USSR productions such as Ivan Perestiani's *Little Red Devils* (Malen'kie d"iavoliata, 1923), Lev Kuleshov's *The Unusual Adventures of Mr. West in the Land of the Bolsheviks* (Neobychainye prikliucheniia Mistera Vesta v strane bol'shevikov,

1924), and Sergei Eizenshtein's *Battleship Potemkin* (Bronenosets Potemkin, 1925), along with commercial fare imported from the West.

The first feature film dealing with Kazakhstani subject matter was produced by the Leningrad film studio Sovkino: *The Skirmish* (Miatezh, 1928). Adapted from a novel by Dmitrii Furmanov and directed by Semen Timoshenko, it dealt with a Civil War conflict that took place in Vernyi in 1920, when a Red Army unit, the Dzharkent battalion, disobeyed the orders of commissar Mikhail Frunze to conquer territories held by anti-Bolshevik forces (the so-called *Basmachi*) and openly revolted. According to the movie, only a passionate speech by the emissary Furmanov and support from a Communist Party school changed the minds of the rebels who finally began the fight against the enemies of Soviet power.... The ambitious Timoshenko included stylized scenes with large numbers of extras, but critical reactions to his film were largely negative.

An event seemingly unrelated to cinema, namely, the founding of the first Kazakhstani professional theater on January 13, 1926, in Kyzyl-Orda, years later turned out to be of vital importance for the long-term evolution of Kazakhstani film: the vast majority of future film stars received their professional education on its stage, which in 1933 was split into a dramatic and a musical branch. This cohort of performers became essential for the creation of Kazakhstani sound cinema in the late 1930s–1940s, securing the *national* character of films that were produced with the help of Russian studios.

## KAZAKH CINEMA'S FIRST BIRTH IN NEWSREELS. *TURKSIB*

In 1928, the All-Russian trust *Vostokkino* (Eastern Cinema) was founded under the auspices of the Council of People's Commissars of the Russian Soviet Federative Socialist Republic (at that point the national republics were autonomous republics within the Russian Federation).[19] The trust was helmed by the influential communist leader Turar Ryskulov[20] and was "intended to represent the Asian peoples of Soviet Russia, to spread Soviet propaganda among the 'oriental population,' and to introduce them and their way of life to other parts of the Soviet Union."[21] Vostokkino's headquarters were located in Moscow. One of its primary practical tasks, besides the production of films, was the education of technical personnel in the Soviet peripheries. Kazakhstan was chosen as the subject of feature films that were made by non-Kazakh filmmakers, with some native performers among the cast. Vostokkino studio hired a native consultant, the young writer Sabit Mukanov, who later became one of the most prominent Kazakh authors working as a screenwriter.[22]

In 1929, a production office of the Vostokkino trust was established in Alma-Ata. The facilities of the branch were small, but at least some amount of film stock could be developed and cut, which made the work of film personnel sent from Moscow to faraway regions somewhat easier.[23] However, the importance of the Alma-Ata office went beyond technical tasks. Its mere existence was to demonstrate that the role of cinema was understood and that film production was growing in the republic. The office produced the short *Alma-Ata and Its Surroundings* (Alma-Ata is ego okrestnosti, 1929), followed by the documentaries *Cooperation in the Auls* (Kooperatsiia v aulakh) and *At the Dzhailiau* (Na dzhailiau).[24] The writer Ilias Dzhansugurov was appointed head of the branch's screenplay department and passionately propagated the cause of creating a national Kazakh cinema.[25] Other Kazakhs working at the branch permanently or temporarily were Iskander Tynyshpaev,[26] Serke Kozhamkulov,[27] and Hakim Davletbekov,[28] all of whom later had long and successful careers in Kazakhstani cinema.

One particular film from that early period left its mark on the history of world cinema: Viktor Turin's *Turksib*, aka *The Steel Path* (Stal'noi put', 1929).[29] A propaganda documentary by genre, *Turksib* is a sophisticated picture that elevates its ideological argument to an extraordinary level of cinematic expressiveness and artistry, making the viewer forget the loud rhetoric and falsification of reality that was an inseparable part of such productions. As the first moving picture with Kazakhstani subject matter to catch the attention of international audiences, it merits a closer analysis.

*Turksib* is 50-minutes long and consists of five chapters, each of which advances its central thesis toward the climactic conclusion. The film is structured as a logical line of arguments, characterized by a rational, mostly economic conceptual approach. Images and verbal messages alternate in a rhythmic manner, allowing the spectator to absorb and think through successive messages.

The opening chapter depicts the harsh climactic conditions in Central Asia, juxtaposing the chronic absence of rain in the steppe to the plenty of snow and ice in the mountains. The next part of the scene, continuing its underlying argument, shows melting water. As the water is channeled into the dry plains, it sets in motion the process of labor–irrigation, blossoming fields, harvest, and processing of the harvest.

At this point, the focus shifts to explicit verbal polemics, stating that the people of Central Asia traditionally had to make a choice between giving preference to grain or cotton. Since there are not enough resources for both, it is either one or the other. The Soviet Union thus was forced to import cotton from Egypt and the United States, paying for it in gold—an absurdity, considering that the country could, in principle, produce sufficient amounts of cotton itself if it so chose. Once the needed amount of grain would be transported to Central Asia, this would enable its people to concentrate their efforts entirely on the production of cotton. However, there was no infrastructure capable of facilitating the transportation of grain, and the only available means were camels and horses. This part of the argument is illustrated in the second chapter. All the trains filled with grain and wood must stop at the border to Central Asia. There can be only one conclusion: "Make way! The country needs a railroad!"

Chapter three begins with the exploration of the soil for the railroad. At this point, Kazakhstan proper finally enters the picture. One intertitle states: "The Kazakh *aul* is resting." People are shown sleeping in midday heat, their world is motionless. The immobility swiftly changes when trucks with workers arrive. The workers get acquainted with the native population, are treated to *kumys*, and begin to put their equipment to work. However, despite the friendly welcome, the nomads continue to view the trucks as "devil's carts." Meanwhile, in Alma-Ata, "the city of apples," the planned railway line is designed in spacious modern offices. This sequence includes animation: on maps of "Kazakstan" [*sic*!], the line runs from Semipalatinsk to Alma-Ata, comprising a length of altogether 1,445 kilometers.

Chapter four demonstrates how the grandiose plan is put into action: men are digging "the stubborn soil" (as the intertitles repeatedly call it) and huge rocks are blown up. When the first locomotive begins to move, hundreds of nomads who have come to witness the sensation, watch in a state of shock, while their horses and livestock run away in panic. The concluding fifth chapter shows the wider civilizational implications of the railway construction, targeting the illiteracy of the native population and introducing tractors to render the agriculture efficient. The intertitles leave no doubt: "This is a war against century-old primitiveness," and "The defeated land opens up its riches."

*Turksib* features several similarities with other medium-length Soviet documentaries praising industrialization and modernization, especially Mikheil Kalatozov's *Salt for Svanetia* (Jim Shvante/Sol' Svanetii, 1930). Most importantly, in all of them, nature is depicted as the largest obstacle on the path to communism; indeed, the "war against nature" was a fundamental thesis of Soviet cultural propaganda in the 1920s and 1930s. However, compared to Kalatozov's film, *Turksib*'s emotional tone is restrained and the rational argument is advanced without raising unrealistic hopes or making far-reaching utopian promises. The intertitles are far less pathos-filled than those in the Georgian film. Furthermore, *Turksib* avoids fictional micronarratives and staged scenes. True, when the urgent need for water is visualized, the intertitle "water" is repeated several times: a typical verbal tool of Soviet propaganda documentaries in that period. But such bombardments with emotional verbal messages are rare. Instead, the film emphasizes the logic of the underlying argument. There are only a few extreme camera angles, bringing *Turksib* visually closer to mainstream norms. In the context of visually more expressive documentaries, such matter-of-factness adds to *Turksib*'s persuasiveness, making it appear more technological than political.

In hindsight, the film's argument in favor of modernizing an infrastructural wasteland is hard to disagree with. Nonetheless, *Turksib*'s enthusiastic endorsement of cotton monoculture was dangerously shortsighted and proved disastrous in the long term. For their part, the native population is shown as friendly and open-minded throughout, albeit painfully backward. Having passively endured the tyranny of "stubborn nature" for centuries, as the film claims, Kazakhs are depicted as the quiescent recipients of a benevolent assault from the industrially advanced parts of the Soviet Union.

From a cinematic viewpoint, *Turksib* is remarkable for its structural stringency and clarity. Despite its dogmatic stance against the "senseless and cruel nature," the film's images of wind and dust, of clouds, fog, and glittering mountain springs convey a sense of living beauty, whatever the original denunciatory context of these images may have been.

*Turksib* premiered on October 15, 1929. It was screened to great acclaim in many countries around the world and was recognized as one the most innovative documentaries in world cinema. British critic Huntly Carter even called it the best Soviet film ever made.[30] For the first time, a moving picture brought Kazakhstan to the attention of moviegoers worldwide, albeit without explicitly focusing on the country as such. But it is significant that while the native people do appear passive, the film never points to them and their traditions as being part of the problem; as a matter of fact, the cultural "backwardness" of Kazakhstan is not included in the progressive argument that the film was advancing. In the words of Charles Musser, *Turksib* belongs to the films in which a "radically new *ethnographic* impulse can be found (emphasis mine, P.R.)."[31] Unlike other documentaries, where the lifestyle and habits of the native population of Central Asia (but also of the Russian peasantry) were shown with disdain and urban arrogance, *Turksib* grants the inhabitants of the steppe dignity. This is no small achievement, given the impatience and radicalness of political propaganda in Soviet cinema at the time.

## SILENT FEATURES ABOUT KAZAKHSTAN

The first feature film dealing with Kazakhstani subject matter produced by Vostokkino was *Songs of the Steppes* (Pesni stepei, 1930). Its screenwriter was Efim Aron, previously a contributor to *Turksib* who would eventually play a decisive role in the development of Kazakh cinema in the 1940s and 1950s; behind the camera was Aleksandr Lemberg, one of the most accomplished cinematographers of the silent period, who also directed. Dedicated to the tenth anniversary of Soviet Kazakhstan, *Songs of the Steppes* is an attempt to combine the individual story of a poor farmhand (Serke Kozhamkulov) with a general account of the profound socioeconomic transformations taking place in the country. The farmhand's evolution from exploited victim to an active administrator with wide-ranging responsibilities was intended as a symbolic account of successful Sovietization. However, the film became a critical failure. According to Kabysh Siranov, the main character "was faceless and represented neither himself, nor his people."[32] Siranov also pointed out that the film was dominated by extreme long shots, which were typical of "epic" movies, and that individual characters were lost in the stream of historical developments.[33]

*The Freeze* (Dzhut, 1931), a so-called agitfilm directed by Mikhail Karostin (other spelling: Korostin)[34] from a screenplay coauthored by Sergei Ermolinskii and the director, illustrated "the birth of class consciousness among Kazakhs."[35] According to contemporary accounts, it was more successful from a political viewpoint than *Songs of the Steppes*. True to its genre, *The Freeze* featured a clearly outlined conflict and straightforward characterizations. The story of a cunning exploiter, Satyr-bai, who poses as a poor man during official inspections, but in truth remains the most powerful owner of livestock in the region, was typical of the privileged class that pretended to have given up their riches while continuing their abuse of the vast majority of nomads who remained poor. The fact that Satyr-bai tries to flee with his herds across the border to China addressed a fundamental problem: the escape of hundreds of thousands of Kazakhs from the Soviet Union. The film interprets their behavior as the result of inherent class hatred. It takes the interference of a poor farmhand, Malai (Hakim Davletbekov), to stop Satyr-bai from carrying out his plan. Malai, who spent his entire life increasing his master's wealth, summons the other farmhands to prevent the escape and keep the herds in Soviet Kazakhstan.[36] The poor nomads will now begin a sedentary lifestyle.

Whatever the qualities of these early films may have been, a fair evaluation of *Songs of the Steppes* and *The Freeze* is no longer possible since no copies have survived. A third film dealing with Kazakhstan, *The Secret of Karatau* [or Kara-Tau] (Taina Karatau, 1932/1933), was directed by Aleksandr Dubrovskii from his own screenplay coauthored by him and El-Registan.[37] This thriller about the search for rubber in the mountains was produced by the Yalta branch of Vostokkino. Its main character, professor Shakhrov (Vladimir Gardin), actively sabotages the search and even plans to escape to the West, until the members of the expedition can prove that caoutchouc (unvulcanized rubber) does exist in these areas. One of the supporting actors, Hakim Davletbekov, who was cast in the role of a native guide, was a pioneer of Soviet-Kazakh cinema and later became one of Kazakhstan's leading documentary filmmakers.[38] Critics took *The Secret of Karatau*, indeed a veritable potboiler, to task for overemphasizing the exotic and adventurous aspects of rubber production and the film's insufficient attention to the working class, even though the need for caoutchouc was admittedly a huge problem for the Soviet economy, which gave the plot political significance.

The issue of the national authenticity of Vostokkino films is controversial. According to the Soviet-Kazakh film historian Kabysh Siranov, who represented the official ideological line, the fact that films such as *The Songs of the Steppes*, *The Freeze*, and later *Enemies' Paths* were made in and about Kazakhstan by non-Kazakhs did not diminish their value for the development of the country's film culture. While these movies were, in Siranov's words, "works by the brotherly Russian people about Kazakhstan, (they) gained historical significance for Kazakh national cinema. In essence, they prepared the birth of Kazakhstan's feature cinema, and one should certainly consider them the foundation of our national film art."[39] This was the official view in a book published in 1980. However, in 1958, he had expressed more skepticism as to the Kazakh elements in the early feature films about Kazakhstan.[40] Similarly, in the 1990s, several Kazakh film historians took issue with this argument, doubting the ingenuity and national authenticity of the early silent films.

The Alma-Ata branch of Vostokkino independently produced a series of newsreels under the title *The Latest News* (Poslednie izvestiia), featuring events considered newsworthy, ranging from the work of Karaganda miners to the harvest season and celebration of communist state holidays. The newsreels were politically selective and followed strict thematic guidelines. Not surprisingly, the catastrophic famine that befell Kazakhstan as a result of collectivization policies and the escape of hundreds of thousands of Kazakhs across the Soviet-Chinese border was omitted by these reports.

In early 1931, the administration of Vostokkino decided to close its Alma-Ata branch, despite its undeniable successes. The closure meant that from that point onward, the entire footage shot in Kazakhstan had to be developed, edited, and printed in Moscow. One of the reasons was the absence of qualified native specialists. Apart from Ilias Dzhansugurov, who served as the head of the screenwriting department, the only other local permanently employed at the branch was Iskander Tynyshpaev, an assistant cameraman. Another major reason cited was the underdeveloped state of Kazakh literature. Native authors failed to provide usable screenplays, or even drafts that could be developed for the production of feature films. For that reason, a planned project about the uprising of 1916, when the Kazakh people had revolted against being drafted by the Russian Imperial Army to serve in World War I, was abandoned. Neither official competitions for the best screenplay, nor the outsourcing of the scripts to Russian authors yielded acceptable results. Vostokkino had to admit that, despite the enthusiasm of regular viewers, communist intellectuals, and Kazakhstan's Communist Party leadership, the studio had put the cart before the horse. Thus, it was not the low level of technical equipment alone that prevented the emergence of a full-fledged national cinema in Kazakhstan, but the fact that the country's cultural foundation as such was ill-prepared.

The official solution was to abandon feature film production altogether and start on a smaller scale, with newsreels.[41] In 1933, the trust *Union Cinema Chronicle* (Soiuzkinokhronika) was founded and charged with the production of a regular newsreel series, *Soviet Kazakhstan*. It was also given the assignment to produce Kazakhstan-related episodes for the central Soviet newsreel chronicles. Experienced cameramen from Leningrad were sent to Alma-Ata to document Kazakhstan's industrialization and to train young Kazakhs eager to learn the craft of cinematographer. In 1935, the newsreel branch was transformed into the Alma-Ata Newsreel Studio.

According to cameraman Gennadii Novozhilov, the newsreel series *Soviet Kazakhstan* was released in two versions, one silent and the other equipped with sound; the silent version came with Russian or Kazakh intertitles. These "film journals" differed in length, each containing four to eight episodes. Their thematic focus was on the country's latest achievements, for example, the first Kazakh pilot or the first Kazakh machinist. Despite the general enthusiasm of both makers and viewers, at the end of his memoirs, the veteran cameraman shared an unexpected observation: "In retrospect, I now realize that we omitted a lot in those years. While shooting everything that was new and emerging, we did not shoot that which was disappearing. After all, there was so much of interest that today cannot be recreated by any means."[42] Of course, such preference in subject matter, celebrating the country's breathtaking modernization, was understandable. After all, cinema was viewed both as the chronicler and an active participant in this process. But the changing priorities in the Kazakh nation's search for identity brought with it the realization that the losses incurred in that process were irreplaceable and that hardly any documentation of those losses existed.

Thirty years later, Kazakhstan's best-known feature film director, Shaken Aimanov, defined the newsreel years of budding Kazakh cinema as its "first birth." In this, he was in full agreement with Gennadii Novozhilov who suggested that July 5, 1935, the day when the first issue of *Soviet Kazakhstan* was released, should be regarded the birthdate of Kazakhstani cinema.[43]

In respect to the primacy of newsreels, Kazakhstan was hardly an exception. The act of straightforwardly recording and chronicling events marked the initial phase of film production all over the world. However, Aimanov was convinced that for Kazakhstan, that phase held special meaning. Newsreels "had to become the first kind of cinema particularly in our country, because no other country in the world experienced such a cosmic flight from medieval backwardness to the heights of socialist power as did my Kazakh land."[44] The images of smokestacks and new schools, of the mechanization of agriculture, the opening of theaters and clubs were needed to help people realize the enormity of historical changes. Aimanov explicitly credited the enthusiastic first generation of cameramen (Gennadii Novozhilov,[45] Maulutkhan Sagimbaev,[46] Faizulla Absaliamov, Iakov Smirnov,[47] and Oraz Abishev[48]) who explored with their cameras the country's construction sites and its coal mines, with facilitating the emergence of Kazakh cinema.

Meanwhile, the number of film projectors in Kazakhstan continued to grow exponentially, from 170 in 1929 to 846 in 1937. Some of these projectors were equipped with sound: in 1932, there were only 2, but in 1937, the country counted already 279 sound film projectors. In 1929, there were 12 permanent (stationary) film theaters in Kazakhstan, in 1937 that number had increased to 40, in addition to 160 mobile devices.[49] The technical innovations were financed by a so-called Cinefication Fund, which, beginning in 1934, collected a percentage of the profits made from all screenings. These funds were administered by the trust "Kazkino" and invested in the construction of new movie theaters and equipment.

In 1938, the entirety of national film-related activities was centralized in the "Cinefication Administration" as part of the Council of People's Commissars of Kazakhstan. The following year, all film projectors and film facilities that were previously owned by the Commissariat of Education (Narkompros) were transferred to the Cinefication Administration of Kazakhstan.[50]

## RUSSIAN CLASS STRUGGLE IN KAZAKH NO MAN'S LAND: *ENEMIES' PATHS*

The introduction of sound technology in the late 1920s and early 1930s considerably slowed down the production of feature films all over the world. In the USSR, only the large, well-equipped central film studios in Moscow and Leningrad could cope with costly sound pictures. Thus, it is no surprise that the first full-length sound feature film with Kazakhstani subject matter was produced not in the country itself but by the USSR's largest studio, Mosfilm. *Enemies' Paths* (Vrazh'i tropy, 1935)[51] was directed by Ol'ga Preobrazhenskaia and Ivan Pravov from a screenplay by Ivan Shukhov,[52] who adapted his novel *Hatred* (Nenavist').

The picture intensely reflects the paranoid zeitgeist in the Soviet Union. As a matter of fact, its plot is a direct illustration of Stalin's thesis that class struggle in a socialist society will not disappear but become fiercer in the long run, a concept that was used as the theoretical justification for communist state terror in the 1930s.

In *Enemies' Paths*, the class enemy is represented by well-to-do peasants (*kulaks*) who in 1929, backed into a corner, see no other solution than to pretend that they voluntarily gave up their possessions. Epifan Okatov, the family patriarch (Mikhail Narokov), publicly confesses that his behavior in the past "was not always supportive of Soviet power." He claims to have undergone a deep change of mind and donates his huge house to the community, to be used as a school. Okatov's son, Innokentii (Andrei Abrikosov), also indulges in Soviet ideological clichés about the coming bright future, the importance of Karl Marx, and socialism. However, the viewer soon realizes that father and son have not given up their dream to reinstate the former class order. The *kulaks*' public pro-Soviet charade is but a cover-up of their undiminished hatred for the poor who had just organized a kolkhoz. But the stronger the Soviet community grows, the harder it becomes for the class enemies to continue their masquerade. In the end, dramatic clashes within the family leave father Epifan dead (shot by his own son!) and Innokentii arrested for sabotage.

Clichéd stories about cunning class enemies who must be exposed and annihilated could have been set anywhere in the Soviet Union. However, the location chosen for *Enemies' Paths* was Kazakhstan, as announced at the very beginning. The opening credits are followed by an intertitle informing the viewer that the following story takes place in the Kazakh steppe. But the village, referred to as *khutor*, not *aul*, consists almost entirely of Russians. Only one secondary character is Kazakh, Ablai (Hakim Davletbekov). He sides with the Russian kolkhoz activists, expressing his disbelief in the *kulaks*' confession and conversion. Ablai's political instincts are spot-on, and, while being ethnically different from the majority, the young man is an active contributor to community debates. Still, the Kazakh's role was designed as somewhat ambiguous: physically unimposing, Ablai's strangely agile body language and his heavy accent in Russian, which is further marred by countless grammatical mistakes, stand out and are sometimes ridiculed by Russian characters. As if to make up for the jokes, the film also demonstrates that this man, representing an ethnic minority within the village, can stand up for himself: when a supporter of the *kulaks* mocks him, Ablai pours a bucket of water over his head. Still, while Ablai is likeable in a somewhat clownish fashion, it is hard to take him seriously as a full-fledged representative of his nation. Instead, he appears like an exotic addition to a community whose members act as if they were living in an ethnically undefined space.

This approach to ethnicity is of decisive importance: the character of Ablai is not shown as a member of the nominal nation, that is, the Kazakhs, but of a minority. On the one hand, such a designation may reflect the

Moscow filmmakers' hubris vis-à-vis the Soviet periphery. However, the decisive argument is the primacy of the class agenda over all other aspects in the story. The film's spatial organization, primarily in the interiors, is marked by class, not ethnicity. As for the exteriors, the vast steppes appear as an empty, indistinct space, for anyone to take. There are no references to the history of this village. How and when did its Russian community settle in Kazakhstan? Interestingly, as if to compensate for such onesidedness, during the dramatic finale it is Ablai who captures the fleeing *kulak* Innokentii in the steppe with a lasso, earning him the gratitude of his fellow kolkhoz members and the presumed respect of the viewer. This ultimate achievement notwithstanding, within the political framework of the film, Ablai has a demonstratively subservient function, that of an ethnic alibi character.

Aside from the one native, *Enemies' Paths* contains remarkably few references to Kazakhstan or Central Asia. For example, the founding director of the kolkhoz, Roman, announces that "the builders of Turksib" had sent him to the village. Or, when the first tractor arrives and Roman plows the field, a group of enthusiastic Kazakh horsemen surround him, implying that they must live somewhere close; later, Roman embraces Ablai; and finally, a communal celebration marking the completion of the harvest features musicians with dombras and some extras in Kazakh national costumes. These details, while marginal, are meant to signal that the Kazakh population is in principle recognized and respected by the village's Russian majority. This respect stands in contrast to the past: at one point, during a heated exchange between Epifan and his son, the old *kulak* furiously exclaims: "I thought you knew how to deceive the Kyrgyz with forged money!" (Throughout the film, the Kazakhs are referred to as "Kyrgyz," which was indeed common at the time).

*Enemies' Paths* stands at the beginning of a conspicuous tradition: to treat Kazakhstan as a wide-open space for socioeconomic construction, a tabula rasa without any obstacles for building a communist society as soon as the class enemy has been eliminated. The question of how this construction meshes with Kazakh tradition and cultural values is never even posed. The inclusion of a few Kazakh elements serves a mere apologetic function. The fact that Russian to these Kazakh characters is a foreign language and their customs and costumes are different adds an exotic color at best, but mainly paints them as in need of education, that is, learning better Russian. At no point is the presence of Kazakhs in *Enemies' Paths* considered worthy of becoming a thematic focus. While this may be an expression of the filmmakers' unconscious, quasi-colonial condescension, their negligent attitude was also fully in line with the communist establishment's parameters, by which ethnic differences had to be deemphasized because they all would eventually dissolve in the communist melting pot.

*Enemies Paths* thus was the first in a whole series of Soviet feature films that use Kazakhstan as mere background with almost no national specifics: Kazakhstan without Kazakhs, so to speak. In the best case, the building of a communist society could be presented as a joined project involving Russians and Kazakhs alike. But even if this were true, Kazakhstan was chosen as a setting whose historical and cultural specifics mattered little. No other Central Asian republic was treated that way by the Soviet center. This nonchalant attitude toward a country as a culturally and historically undefined space is in itself significant and worth pondering.

For the development of Kazakhstani cinema, *Enemies' Paths* was inconsequential. The creation of a genuine Kazakhstani national cinema had to be based on other principles. Pseudo-Kazakhstani movies with their faux exotic native characters were unable to satisfy the need for national authenticity. But in the late 1930s, the industrial foundation for the production of more authentic films in the country itself was still absent.

## SECOND BIRTH: *AMANGELDY*

The one feature film that for many years was considered Kazakhstan's first, was, paradoxically, produced by Lenfilm studio in Leningrad: *Amangeldy* (1938). Its production was part of a Soviet cultural strategy by which the periphery was supposed to follow the center, that is, the national republics were encouraged to emulate the most successful examples of Socialist Realism in the Russian Federation, adapting them to their native conditions. In cinema, the cultural establishment, and Stalin personally, elevated the revolutionary potboiler *Chapaev* (1934) to the position of a prime orientation provider for Soviet cinema in its entirety. Directed by the Vasil'ev brothers, the entertaining Civil War swashbuckler had taken Soviet audiences by storm. Its popular appeal and ideological stringency rendered *Chapaev* the ideal choice for the beginning implementation of the socialist-realist dogma in Soviet cinema; the Russian blockbuster was declared to be the new norm.

Among the central features of *Chapaev* that would become normative, the presence of a so-called positive hero was of vital importance. To a large extent, the title character, commander Vasilii Chapaev, met the criteria of a positive hero, and so did his ideologically trained sidekick, commissar Furmanov. Cinema officials in the Soviet republics tried hard to come up with similar character constellations—bold revolutionaries whose adventurous lives could provide a smooth synthesis of entertainment and propaganda. The challenge for Chapaev's successors in other Soviet republics was to identify historical characters who had played a role similar to the Russian Civil War hero and spin a comparable cinematic narrative. In Kazakhstan's case, the logical choice was Amangeldy Imanov. As was to be expected, the result was not so much emulation as imitation,⁵³ beginning with the basic plotline that soon turned into a cliché: a man from the lower classes demonstrates his unusual leadership qualities and initiates a Civil War against the ruling class during which he is tragically killed, but his cause is triumphantly continued by others. The film itself, then, played the role of an immortalizer, serving both as monument and inspiration for subsequent generations.

Three decades later, Shaken Aimanov pointed to *Amangeldy* as the "second birth" of Kazakh cinema, following the aforementioned "first birth" in the newsreel genre. Aimanov recalled that at some point (unfortunately, he provides neither the exact date, nor even the year when this took place) the government of Kazakhstan summoned the country's leading artists and asked: "Can we make a film about the legendary Amangeldy Imanov—our Kazakh 'Chapaev'?" There was enthusiasm for the idea, but not the necessary equipment and professionalism. "But brothers are called brothers because they help out in a difficult moment." Here, Aimanov was alluding to the fact that Lenfilm studio sent an entire crew to enable the Kazakh artists to create their Chapaev clone.⁵⁴

The screenplay was authored by the prominent Russian author Vsevolod Ivanov, a specialist on Civil War narratives, and the Kazakhs Beimbet Mailin⁵⁵ and Gabit Musrepov;⁵⁶ it was published in Russian in the journal *Novyi mir* (11/1936). The authors picked Amangeldy Imanov (1873–1919),⁵⁷ because this historical figure shared with his Russian counterpart social origins—both came from peasant families and had charisma, as well as a natural talent for military strategy and tactics. Unlike Chapaev, however, Imanov's main claim to fame was not a career in the Red Army but his leadership role during the 1916 Kazakh uprising in his native Turgai region, an event that the film interprets as essentially proto-Bolshevik. The screenplay was then considerably abridged, securing greater narrative stringency but also simplifying some of the characters.⁵⁸

*Amangeldy* depicts Russian tsarism and imperialism as the archenemies of the Kazakh people. In the opening episode, a government official visits Kazakhstan, eagerly expected by colonial military and skeptically eyed by the native population. Large groups of nomads arrive to meet the official. The widely respected Amangeldy (Eleubai Umurzakov) appears, too; the locals greet him by shaking his hand, unlike the officials who keep a safe distance. There can be no doubt that Amangeldy belongs to the "common folks," not the kowtowing native "elites." The visiting Russian general gives a speech in which he calls upon "his children, the Kyrgyz" to take up arms and fight for the Tsar against the enemies of the Russian Empire in World War I. Amangeldy immediately confronts the pompous demagogue, causing a scandal. He is arrested, chained, and taken into custody.

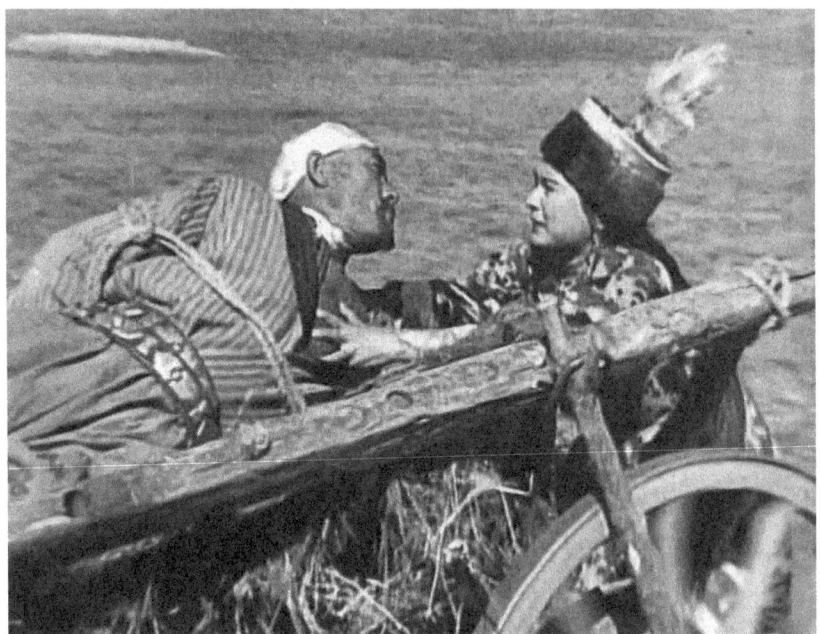

**Figure 1.1 Amangeldy Arrested; Eleubai Umurzakov in the Title Role, with Shara Zhienkulova as His Wife.** *Amangeldy* (1938, Moisei Levin)

Amangeldy's first opportunity to demonstrate his leadership talent is his outspoken opposition to the imperialist war, stating that the Kazakh people had no desire to serve as cannon fodder in the ongoing slaughter. Amangeldy is arrested, but a group of fighters frees him. Amangeldy then picks a drafting station as the target of his first attack, destroying the name lists of men to be forced into military service. The attack ignites a wider revolt against tsarist power, to which Russian troops respond by destroying several auls, killing the civilian population, and burning down their yurts.

A typical feature of the early Soviet biopic was its heavy-handed focus on the leader himself. The prevailing cultish, personalist view of history was one of the cornerstones of Stalinist ideology and a modification of certain basic Marxist-Leninist assumptions regarding the prevalence of class dynamics over individual agency. In *Amangeldy*, the title hero is the object of either admiration or hatred, with no gradations in between. The presence of the leader is essential in every scene; without him, as the viewer is compelled to conclude, the upheaval would have no chance to succeed.

*Amangeldy* is a film about recent history, illustrating events that numerous viewers either participated in or observed. Many episodes are devoted to the tsarist police trying to find Amangeldy's whereabouts, eliciting suspense. The exposition introduces the title character as an authentic rank-and-file man, poor,

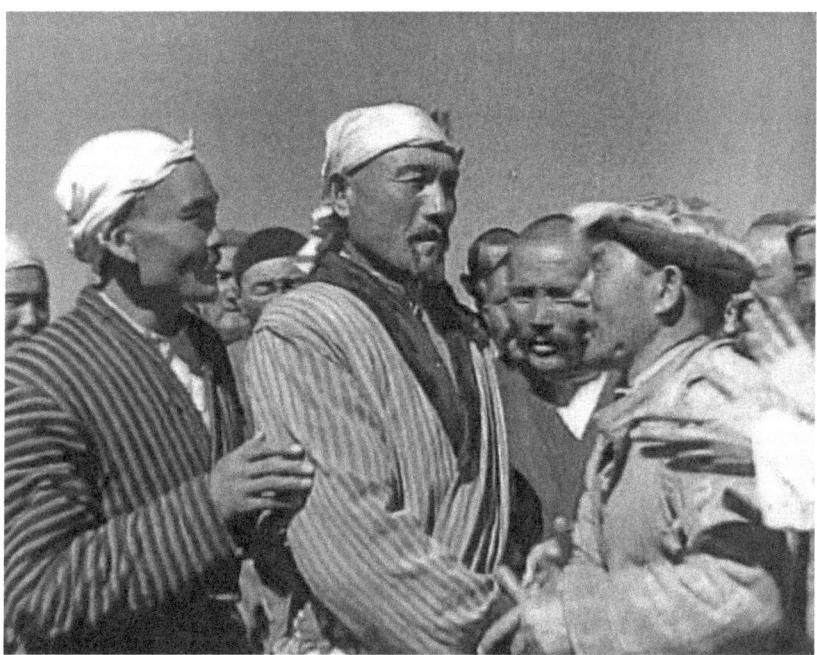

**Figure 1.2 The Natural Leader.** *Amangeldy* (1938, Moisei Levin)

yet admired for his fearlessness and intelligence.[59] While he is ideologically still somewhat naïve (just like his filmic predecessor Chapaev was), Amangeldy's main talent lies not in ideological or theoretical deliberations, but in military tactics: he knows how to organize troops, where to place the cannons, and when to attack to fight most efficiently. This ability endows him with natural authority and makes him an indispensable factor for the success of the uprising. Once the tsarist troops flee in panic, Amangeldy's competence and his right to leadership are confirmed for good.[60] Similar to Chapaev, Amangeldy displays a softer side when the mutineers gather in a yurt to plan further action: the leader takes a dombra and sings, pensively, and visibly loved by the people sitting around him. His wife dances, enchanting the guests at a wedding ceremony (*toi*).

The most complicated issue for the makers of *Amangeldy* was how to deal with the Alash-Orda. Without pronouncing the term, the film contains clear references to this Kazakh national independence movement at the end of World War I.[61] In 1919, when the tsarist administration was gone, Amangeldy is shown in a debate with a man portrayed as a demagogue who proclaims the need to establish a national Kazakh society, securing peace as its main priority. This, according to the film, is unacceptable to Amangeldy who already envisions the Kazakh people within a Soviet avant la lettre family of nations.

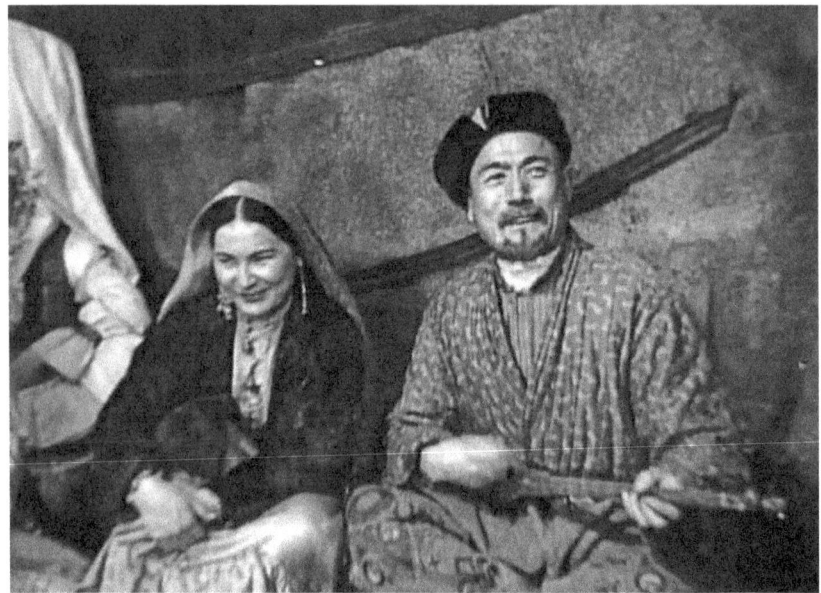

Figure 1.3  **Amangeldy Relaxed.** *Amangeldy* (1938, Moisei Levin)

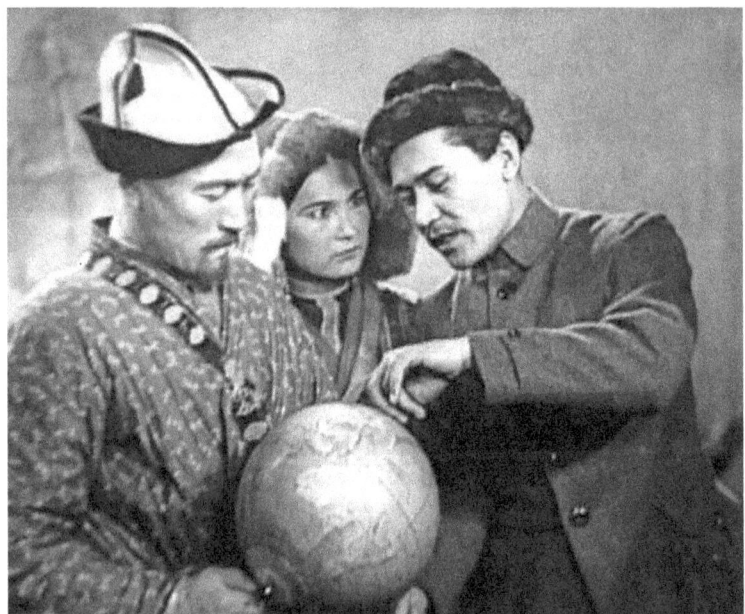

Figure 1.4  **Global Perspectives.** *Amangeldy* (1938, Moisei Levin)

His fight is motivated by a future whose description sounds exactly like the Soviet Union of the 1930s. Amangeldy's wife, Balym (Shara Zhienkulova), is enthused by Amangeldy's vision and reveals that he will soon become the father of a son, the greatest blessing that a man can experience. Tragically, and again reminiscent of *Chapaev*, this moment of triumph is followed by sudden denouement: enemies entrap Amangeldy. Armed Kazakhs come to his rescue, and he can proudly march in front of a unit of freedom fighters, but soon thereafter, he is shot and killed during a skirmish. His death comes precisely in the moment when his wife exclaims "Victory!"

The purges of the late 1930s that severely affected Kazakh intellectuals, did make an impact on the production of *Amangeldy*. One of the three screenwriters, Beimbet Mailin, was denounced as a sympathizer of Alash-Orda, arrested, and executed. His name was erased from the credits and never mentioned in any review. (It is worth mentioning that Mailin's name was absent even in Kabysh Siranov's 1958 monograph *The Film Art of Kazakhstan* where only Musrepov and Ivanov are listed as the authors of the screenplay). A 1938 newspaper report about the production contained an indirect reference to these events. After mentioning difficulties in the filmmaking process due to language issues, the journalist wrote: "These difficulties were further complicated by the sabotage activities of enemies of the people, the national-fascists who did their utmost to distort the image of the people's beloved hero and to slow down the development of Kazakh art, which is national in form and socialist in content."[62]

Apart from the shadows cast by Soviet state terror, the production of the first Kazakh feature film was nothing short of sensational. "I remember well," wrote Shaken Aimanov, "that the entire acting world of Kazakhstan immediately split into 'the lucky ones' and 'the unhappy ones.' The former were those who made it into the picture, the latter were those who were not cast."[63]

*Amangeldy* was directed by Moisei Levin,[64] a Leningrad painter who had worked as a stage designer in the 1920s, acquired some directorial expertise in the 1930s, and moved to Kazakhstan in the late 1930s. When *Amangeldy* was released on January 25, 1939, the film was touted as one of the success stories of Soviet cultural policies that began many years before the production of the first Kazakh feature film. Budding critic Rostislav Iurenev stated in a brochure that was published for the film's Soviet-wide release: "(. . .) this is the first film about Kazakhstan that was made with the creative forces of Kazakhstan. All Kazakh performers who appear in the film are genuine offspring of the socialist October revolution. They entered the artistic world in the time of Soviet power, which firmly and consequently embodies the nationalities policy of Lenin and Stalin."[65]

*Amangeldy*'s status as the first Kazakh feature film remained undisputed until the late 1980s.[66] However, after the end of the Soviet era, in the first phase of Kazakhstan's independence, the issue of *Amangeldy*'s "Kazakhness" and thus its status as the first national feature film became a politically sensitive subject. The film critic Bauyrzhan Nogerbek [in earlier publications Nugerbekov] called the claim that *Amangeldy* was the first Kazakh feature film "a myth," pointing to the undeniable fact that it was produced by Lenfilm "with the assistance of Kazakh writers and artists."[67] Although Nogerbek was downplaying the creative contributions of the Kazakh cast members somewhat, the question to what degree his claim is accurate is certainly worth examining.

In the debate on whether *Amangeldy* is a truly Kazakh picture or an artificial implant, two basic criteria were applied. The first was ethnic: several crew members were not Kazakh, including the director, the cameraman, and one of the two composers (Mikhail Gnesin, who worked together with Akhmet Zhubanov).[68] For those adhering to an ethnocentric viewpoint, this means that the film itself cannot be called Kazakh. The other criterion is geographic: the fact that *Amangeldy* was produced by Lenfilm studio in Leningrad, thousands of miles away from Kazakhstan, was used as another argument corroborating the case against the film's Kazakhness.

However, there are counterarguments that weaken the "implant" thesis. First, the film's subject matter is purely Kazakh: Amangeldy Imanov was a revered popular hero, still remembered by many contemporaries at the time of the film's production and popular throughout the Soviet and post-Soviet era. Second, two of the screenwriters were Kazakh: Beimbet Mailin was already an established Kazakh author, while Gabit Musrepov was viewed as a young hopeful in Kazakh literature.[69] Third, the film's cast consists of Kazakh stage performers who all made their screen debut, which for many marked the beginning of a successful film career. Indeed, these performers *define* the film. Eleubai Umurzakov in the title role brings an impressive energy to the screen, his body language is natural and self-confident and his face conveys genuine passion. The other performers, including Kalibek Kuanyshpaev (Baibol), Kurmanbek Dzhandarbekov (Dzhakas), Serke Kozhamkulov (Beket), Kanibek Baiseitov (Dzhafar), Shara Zhienkulova (Amangeldy's wife), and Kapan Badyrov (Karatai), ensure *Amangeldy*'s largely believable image of Kazakhstan and its social relations. On the visual level, the film is remarkably realistic: both the interiors and the exteriors are atmospherically precise, as are the group portraits of nomads young and old. The exteriors were all filmed in Kazakhstan.

Of course, *Amangeldy* was a product of *Soviet* Kazakhstan and typical of the late 1930s, which by definition prevented it from positively emphasizing too many civilizational specifics. Furthermore, while dealing with Kazakhstan, the film was not made for Kazakhstani spectators alone but for a multinational Soviet audience. Indeed, *Amangeldy* was produced in two versions, one in Kazakh and another in Russian. As a genuinely Soviet picture, the film does its utmost to preclude any ethnocentric or nationalist interpretation: the enemy of the Kazakhs are not "the Russians" per se but Russia's ruling class, allied with sellout Kazakh elites. Thus, one satirical scene mocks the Russian general (G. Stanislavskii) feasting with Kazakh leaders who are willing to unconditionally follow his orders, trying to suggest a commonality between the two nations. In another episode, one of Amangeldy's fellow prisoners, a Russian, tells him that the Russian people are being exploited just as mercilessly as are the Kazakhs. "There is but one enemy—the common one," states a rear-projected slogan (*Vrag odin—obshchii*). Amangeldy's class-conscious Russian sidekick named Egor Ponomarev (F. Fedorovskii), later returns to Kazakhstan as an emissary of the Bolshevik Party, educating Amangeldy and his Kazakh freedom fighters on the class nature of their struggle and its strategic goal: the creation of a communist society. Ponomarev's role is the equivalent of commissar Furmanov in *Chapaev* who also enlightens the spontaneous revolutionary about the true essence of his fight.

Obviously, the 1990s controversy over the Kazakhness of *Amangeldy* was an inevitable part of the nation's search for identity after achieving independence. At heart, the eagerness to demystify the history of Kazakhstani cinema was also an expression of the deeper drive to de-Sovietize Kazakh culture in its entirety. One art historian formulated the new iconoclasm polemically: "Kazakh national cinema, during the period of the 'cultural revolution' in the Land of the Soviets was born periodically: organizationally in the form of all kinds of studios, trusts, branches, and creatively, as fictional and non-fictional movies made by cinematographers sent from Moscow and Leningrad. The explanation for such manifold 'births' of national cinema is easy: cinema, just like our entire social and personal life, was forcibly ideologized and filled with legends and myths serving the regime."[70] But for the sake of historical objectivity, such a discussion should take into account the fundamental principles of nationhood and class that were espoused by the Soviet establishment at the time and were endorsed by the Kazakh communist elites. Given the profound contributions of Kazakh performers and writers and considering the specific ideological framework of the 1930s as well as the underdeveloped state of the Kazakhstani film industry, *Amangeldy* can legitimately be considered the country's first feature film, rendered with substantial assistance of film artists from outside Kazakhstan. The non-Kazakh director, cameraman, and composer did not make this film with the intention to enhance their own individual filmography, but as *enablers* performing a political and cultural assignment. And, judging by numerous memoirs, for the Kazakh crew members, *Amangeldy* was a labor of love.

On a deeper conceptual level, the communist establishment of the USSR and its republics promoted projects such as *Amangeldy* with the purpose to ingrain in people's minds the idea that revolutions were not artificial imports but born organically on native soil. In the post-Soviet period, when most former Soviet republics initiated a process of self-distancing from the revolutionary communist movements, controversies about the national character of films such as *Amangeldy* served as a vehicle to support the idea of the alienness of the communist movement to the respective native society and culture. This explains the radical assessment of films such as *The Skirmish*, *Turksib*, *Songs of the Steppes*, and *Amangeldy* as "'assigned' totalitarian films on Kazakh themes" by formerly Soviet, then post-Soviet critics.

Neither *Amangeldy*'s obvious propaganda purpose nor its lack of artistic originality prevented it from becoming a groundbreaker for Kazakhstan itself. "It is hard to express the feeling of gratitude to the masters of Russian cinema for the enormous help that they provided, and indeed are still providing, to the cinema of Kazakhstan," wrote Shaken Aimanov, who had played a minuscule episodic role in the film.[71]

Due to its openly imitative nature, the contribution of *Amangeldy* to the advancement of Soviet cinema as a whole was negligible. Indeed, despite being officially proclaimed the first Kazakh feature film, it did not become part of the all-Soviet socialist-realist canon, not even in its narrow Stalinist formulation.[72] In addition, despite the film's canonization in Soviet Kazakhstan, its aesthetic weaknesses were openly discussed, for example, by Kabysh Siranov who pointed to a lack of compositional exactitude and to many inaccuracies in editing and lighting.[73] This probably was the reason why the film was ignored when Stalin Prizes were awarded for the first time in 1941, even though other non-Russian pictures were recognized on that occasion. However, despite such neglect, within the framework of Kazakh national cinema, *Amangeldy* represented an indubitable step forward, indeed a foundational accomplishment. It clearly demonstrated that Kazakhstani subject matter could be authentically represented in a feature film by native actors with whom audiences were eager to identify. The film was popular at the time of its release and decades later,[74] so much so that it was rereleased in a redacted version in 1966. For the millions of viewers of *Amangeldy* in Kazakhstan, the ethnicity of the director or cameraman was of little relevance: what really mattered were the people on screen. And, unlike other national republics, it was Kazakh performers who represented Kazakhstani characters, not professionals from other nationalities in heavy makeup posing as natives, as was the case in many Soviet films of the 1930s–1950s. This, too, is a reason why *Amangeldy* was accepted and ultimately embraced by Kazakh audiences as *theirs*.[75]

The latter aspect was understood by the republic's leadership that repeated time and time again that *Amangeldy* was the first Kazakh feature film.[76] Despite their relative youth, in 1936 the main cast members had been awarded the title "People's Artist of the Kazakh SSR," the highest title within each Soviet republic, only one step short of "People's Artist of the USSR." Indeed, from the viewpoint of Kazakhstani film history, *Amangeldy* supported the formation of a foundational cadre of performers who early on internalized the fundamental difference between acting for the screen and acting on stage. These performers, while continuing their successful theater careers, became the core of Kazakhstani film actors in the following decades. This alone makes *Amangeldy* a thoroughly Kazakh accomplishment whose impact on national film history should be neither denied nor diminished.[77]

Most importantly, for regular Kazakh audiences, the character of Amangeldy became the first native superhero on screen. The virtues that made him appealing for millions were his fearlessness and pride, his strategic intelligence and wit, as well as his natural egalitarianism. The film's long-term acceptance by rank-and-file viewers as a product of their own culture renders all debates about the genuineness of its national pedigree scholastic.

## NOTES

1. For an understanding of the deeper roots of the cinema of Kazakhstan, it would be useful to look at its culture before cinema appeared on the scene, especially the art of the minstrels with their highly developed poetic improvisation, satirical verve, and musical expressiveness.

2. Alibi Dzhangildin (sometimes transliterated as Jangildin) (1884–1953) hailed from a poor family and became acquainted with Marxist ideas in Moscow in 1915. He joined the Bolshevik Party in 1916 and was among the leaders of the anticolonial uprising in Kazakhstan in 1916. Dzhangildin fought against the Provisional government of Aleksandr Kerenskii and, after the October Revolution, was one of the Bolshevik leaders in the Civil War in Central Asia. In Soviet Kazakhstan, he was appointed to high-ranking government positions.

3. Shoinbaev, S.T., *Alibi Dzhangil'din*. Alma-Ata, 1957, pp. 19–22.

4. *Novyi fil'm*, 10/1973, quoted in Kabysh Siranov, "Nachalo bol'shogo puti." In *Ocherki istorii kazakhskogo kino*, Alma-Ata: Izdatel'stvo "Nauka" Kazakhskoi SSR, 1980, p. 14.

5. Michael Rouland, Gulnara Abikeeva, and Birgit Beumers (eds.), *Cinema in Central Asia*. London: I.B. Tauris, 2013, p. 3.

6. Proskurin, V., "Volshebnyi fonar' Vernogo." *Vecherniaia Alma-Ata*, 18 August 1979.

7. T.Z. Turchak in *Alma-Atinskaia pravda*, 21 September 1957.

8. Siranov, "Nachalo bol'shogo puti." In *Ocherki istorii kazakhskogo kino*. Alma-Ata: Izdatel'stvo "Nauka" Kazakhskoi SSR, 1980, p. 16.

9. Cf. "Kinofitsiruem Kazakhstan" in *Kino Front*, 2-3/1926.

10. Siranov cites data for various cities such as Semipalatinsk, which had three movie theaters before the revolution and nine by 1 November 1923; see "Nachalo bol'shogo puti," p. 18.

11. This number was provided by the newspaper *Sovetskaia step'* (18 January 1928), quoted in Siranov, ibid., p. 25.

12. Kabysh Siranov (1914–1978) was the first and for many years most influential Kazakh film critic and historian. He graduated from the Soviet State Film School VGIK in 1943 when it was temporarily located in Alma-Ata and subsequently authored screenplays, monographs, and numerous articles on Kazakhstani cinema.

13. Cf. Kairbaev, Amangel'dy, *Vstrechi na ekrane: Rasskazy o kazakhskom kino*. Alma-Ata: Zhalyn, 1979, pp. 3–4.

14. *Kishlak*: winter settlement in Central Asia.

15. "Griaz' i temnota," *Kino*, 33(205)/1927, p. 1.

16. Siranov, "Nachalo bol'shogo puti," p. 24.

17. Kairbaev, *Vstrechi na ekrane*, p. 4.

18. Iakov Tolchan (1901–1993) was one of the pioneers of Soviet documentary cinema. Long after he retired, in the early 1990s, Tolchan gained international prominence when he was interviewed in a number of Western documentaries about the history of Soviet cinema.

19. The announcement of the film company's establishment was made in 1926, "but the organization effectively began to work only two years later, after the first shareholders' meeting in Moscow on 26 March 1928." Gabrielle Chomentowski, "Vostokkino and the Foundation of Central Asian Cinema." In Michael Rouland, Gulnara Abikeeva, and Birgit Beumers (eds.), *Cinema in Central Asia*, London: I.B. Tauris, 2013, p. 33.

20. Proskurin, "Volshebnyi fonar' Vernogo."

21. Chomentowski, "Vostokkino and the Foundation of Central Asian Cinema," p. 33.

22. Sabit Mukanov (1900–1973), Kazakh prose writer, famous for his novel *Botagoz* (1938), which was adapted for the screen in 1957.

23. "Cameramen and directors came to Alma-Ata with assignments given to them by the trust administration. They filmed episodes in the republic or objects that were needed for films in production, developed them in the department, and then returned home." Siranov, "Nachalo bol'shogo puti," p. 30.

24. Cf. Siranov, Kabysh. *Kazakhskoe kinoiskusstvo*. Alma-Ata: Kazakhskoe Gosudarstvennoe Izdatel'stvo, 1958, p. 3.

25. Iliias Dzhansugurov (1894–1937) hailed from a peasant family. He joined the Communist Party in 1924, studied in Moscow at the Communist Institute of Journalism in 1925–1928, and became one of the most influential Soviet Kazakh authors. Dzhansugurov excelled in all literary genres, including satire, and authored a novel, *Comrades* (1933), about the transformation of Kazakh society. During the Stalinist purges, he was arrested and executed. In 1973, Bulat Mansurov adapted *The Funeral Feast* from Dzhansugurov's poem "Kulager;" the film remained shelved for fifteen years.

26. Iskander Tynyshpaev (1909–1995), Kazakh cameraman and documentary director. He was born into the family of Kazakhstan's first professional engineer, Mukhamedzhan Tynyshpaev, who fell victim to the Stalinist purges in 1931. Iskander Tynyshpaev studied in the department of cinematography at VGIK when Turar Ryskulov assigned him to the Alma-Ata branch of Vostokkino studio in 1928. Tynyshpaev was arrested in the early 1930s and spent ten years in the GULAG. Released in 1943, he was able to continue his career and became one of Kazakhstan's leading cinematographers both in documentary and feature film. In 1994, he was honored with the title People's Artist of Kazakhstan.

27. The actor Seraly (Serke) Kozhamkulov (1896–1979) fought with Alibi Dzhangildin during the Civil War and was one of the founders of the theater in Kyzyl-Orda in 1926. Kozhamkulov created an entire gallery of memorable characters of simple Kazakhs in cinema, from *Songs of the Steppes* (1930) and *Amangeldy* (1938) to *Daughter of the Steppes* (1954) and *Tale of a Mother* (1964). His natural comedic gift made him an all-time favorite of Kazakhstani audiences. Kozhamkulov was honored with the title People's Artist of the Kazakh SSR in 1936.

28. Hakim Davletbekov began his career as an actor but later became a documentary filmmaker. Cf. endnote 43.

29. Viktor Aleksandrovich Turin was born in St. Petersburg in 1895 and studied engineering at the Massachussetts Institute of Technology in 1912–1916, before working in Hollywood for Vitagraph and other studios as a screenwriter and assistant director. After returning to Russia in 1922, he directed feature films and documentaries. *Turksib* made a major impression internationally. The screenplay was authored by Turin, Viktor Shklovskii, and Aleksandr Macheret. Several of Turin's later projects remained incomplete; he died in Moscow in 1945.

30. Huntly Carter, *The New Spirit in the Cinema*. London: Harold Shaylor, 1930, p. 335.

31. Geoffrey Nowell-Smith, *The Oxford History of World Cinema*. Oxford, New York: Oxford University Press, 1997, p. 94.

32. Siranov, "Nachalo bol'shogo puti," p. 40.

33. Siranov, *Kazakhskoe kinoiskusstvo*, p. 5.

34. Mikhail Karostin (1895–?) directed both feature films and documentaries beginning in the 1920s; *The Freeze* (Dzhut) was his only film based on Kazakh subject matter.

35. *Istoriia sovetskogo kino*, vol. 2. Moskva, "Iskusstvo," p. 484.

36. As Gabrielle Chomentowski wrote, "much of the famine in Kazakhstan was due to the collectivization of agriculture and the forced settlement of nomadic Kazakh herdsmen." Chomentowski, "Vostokkino and the Foundation of Central Asian Cinema," p. 41.

37. El Registan later gained fame as one of the authors of the Soviet national anthem.

38. Hakim Davletbekov was born March 22, 1910, in the Akmolinsk region into a wealthy family. Following his education at a madrasah, he became a teacher. In 1929, director Mikhail Karostin cast him in the lead role of *The Freeze*. Davletbekov then studied at VGIK in 1931–1934 and was cast in supporting roles in a number

of Russian pictures, including Vsevolod Pudovkin's *Victory* (Pobeda, 1938). After military service in World War II, he worked as a documentary director at Kazakhfilm studio. Davletbekov was named Merited Artist of the Kazakh SSR in 1959. He died in Almaty on January 11, 1983.

39. Siranov, "Nachalo bol'shogo puti," p. 42.

40. Siranov, *Kazakhskoe kinoiskusstvo*, pp. 8–9.

41. According to one source, the Alma-Ata branch of Vostokkino produced a newsreel, *The Latest News* (Poslednie izvestiia) beginning in 1929. Cf. *Novyi fil'm*, 12/1986, p. 5.

42. Siranov, "Nachalo bol'shogo puti," p. 49.

43. Shaken Aimanov, "Tri rozhdeniia," *Novyi fil'm*, 1/1969, p. 5. Bauyrzhan Nogerbek, writing from a post-Soviet viewpoint, vehemently disputes this concept, although without naming Aimanov as his opponent. According to Nogerbek, "the 1920s and 1930s cannot be considered birth periods of Kazakh national cinema" since neither local facilities nor a cadre of national film workers existed. (cf. Nogerbek's article in Smailova, T.K., ed. *Kinoentsiklopediia Kazakhstana*. Almaty: Kazakhfil'm, 2010, p. 12.)

44. Aimanov, "Tri rozhdeniia," p. 5.

45. Novozhilov, Gennadii Nikolaevich (1910–1996), Kazakhstani cameraman and documentary director; graduated from the All-Soviet Cinema Institute in Moscow in 1932. Novozhilov moved to Alma-Ata in 1938 and became one of the most influential documentary directors in Kazakhstan. His memoirs were published in 1987.

46. Maulutkhan Sagimbaev (1916–2007), Kazakh documentary cameraman who learned his craft at the Alma-Ata Newsreel Studio beginning in 1936. Among other assignments, he assisted Dziga Vertov on *To You, Front* (1942) before embarking on a long career as a cinematographer in documentary films.

47. Smirnov, Iakov Konstantinovich (1906–2000), Kazakhstani cinematographer and director. Born in Russia, he graduated from the All-Soviet Cinema Institute (VGIK) in 1937. Smirnov was evacuated to Alma-Ata during World War II and worked as a newsreel cameraman at the frontlines and later made numerous documentary shorts about Kazakhstani subjects, especially agriculture.

48. Abishev, Oraz (1916–2013), arguably the best-known Soviet-Kazakh documentary filmmaker. After working as an assistant for Moisei Levin and Roman Karmen, Abishev was an intern at Mosfilm studio and Lenfilm studio (1939–41) and became one of the most productive documentary directors of Kazakhstan with a career spanning over five decades. In 1966, he was honored with the title "People's Artist of the Kazakh SSR."

49. Chomentowski, "Vostokkino and the Foundation of Central Asian Cinema," p. 38.

50. Siranov, "Nachalo bol'shogo puti," p. 38.

51. According to Gabrielle Chomentowski, *Enemies's Paths* (translated as *Accursed Trails*) was produced by Vostokkino studio, which was closed the same year. Cf. Chomentowski, "Vostokkino and the Foundation of Central Asian Cinema," p. 41.

52. Ivan Petrovich Shukhov (1906–1977) was born into a Russian family in Kazakhstan. He became a journalist in the 1920s and later a writer of fiction. His novel *Hatred* (Nenavist', 1931) was praised by Maksim Gor'kii. Shukhov played an important role in the development of Kazakh and Kazakh-Russophone literature during his tenure as editor-in-chief of the literary journal *Prostor* (1963–1974).

53. The similarity between *Amangeldy* and *Chapaev* was recognized immediately; some of the borrowings were criticized as excessive upon the film's release. Thus, even the otherwise well-meaning Rostislav Iurenev observed that some similarities could have been avoided, citing the character of Serik, the parallel to Chapaev's adjutant Pet'ka. Cf. R. Iurenev, *O fil'me "Amangel'dy."* Moskva: Goskinoizdat, 1939, p. 23. In later years, Soviet film historians tried their best to give the imitation a positive spin: "The inner connection and the external similarity between 'Chapaev' and 'Amangeldy' does in no way minimize the artistic merits of the film about the Kazakh batyr." (Kairbaev, *Vstrechi na ekrane*, p. 10.)

54. Aimanov, "Tri rozhdeniia," p. 5.

55. The author Beimbet Mailin (1894–1938 or 1939) was a country teacher who published poetry with a strong social component; one of his poems was devoted to the 1916 protests against the tsar's attempt to draft Kazakhs into the army. Mailin joined the Communist Party in 1926 and began a career in journalism while continuing to write poetry, prose, and plays. After his arrest in 1937 and subsequent execution, his name was removed from the credits of *Amangeldy*. In Rostislav Iurenev's booklet devoted to the film, only Vsevolod Ivanov and Gabit Musrepov are listed as screenwriters (Iurenev, *O fil'me*, p. 15).

56. Gabit Musrepov (1902–1985) had previously written a play, *Amangeldy* (1936), coauthored with Mailin.

57. In Rostislav Iurenev's brochure about the film, the date of birth is given as 1877. Cf. Iurenev, *O fil'me*, p. 7.

58. Siranov, *Kazakhskoe kinoiskusstvo*, p. 10.

59. The historical Amangeldy was educated at a madrasah and knew three foreign languages: Persian, Arabic, and Turkish. For the film, his image was simplified and intellectually lowered, perhaps to make him more similar to Chapaev, who was depicted as witty but largely uneducated in the 1934 cult film.

60. The true scope of the upheaval was not shown on screen. In reality, Amangeldy's army counted about 50,000 men and was very well organized. The clashes with Russian troops lasted until early 1917; later that year, Amangeldy joined the Bolshevik movement.

61. Echoing the official version of Kazakhstani history as defined in the 1930s, Iurenev calls them "the hirelings of the bays—the Alash-Orda members, the traitors of the Kazakh people . . ." (Iurenev, *O fil'me*, p. 10.

62. Kasym Toguzakov, "Pervyi kazakhskii fil'm." *Kazakhstanskaia Pravda*, 17 May 1938.

63. Aimanov, "Tri rozhdeniia," p. 5.

64. Moisei Zelikovich (or Zeilikovich) Levin was born February 28, 1895 in Vilno (Vilnius). He studied painting and subsequently worked for various theaters in Leningrad in the 1920s; in 1934, he joined the First Artistic Workshop under Sergei

Iutkevich, a filmmaker whose career had also begun as art director and who became one of the leading Soviet directors. Levin made his directing debut with the Pushkin biopic *Sojourn to Arzrum* (Puteshestvie v Arzrum, 1936) at Lenfilm Studio and was then assigned the direction of *Amangeldy* and *Raikhan* (1940) for Kazakhstan, a country where he continued to live during the Great Patriotic War. In 1944, he returned to Leningrad; his last contribution to cinema was the art direction on *The Sons* (Synov'ia, 1946). Levin died on August 19, 1946, in Leningrad.

65. Iurenev, *O fil'me*, p. 12.

66. The designation as "the first Kazakh film" began immediately after its release; cf. Toguzakov, "Pervyi kazakhskii fil'm."

67. Cf. Nogerbek, Bauyrzhan, "The Various Births of Kazakh Cinema." In M. Rouland, et al. (eds.), *Cinema in Central Asia: Rewriting Cultural Histories*. London and New York, I.B. Tauris, 2013, p. 59. The first version of this article appeared under the title "Pervenets li kazakhskogo kino fil'm 'Amangel'dy'?" in *Izvestiia Akademii nauk Kazakhskoi SSR* (seriia filologii), 4/1990, pp. 63–67.

68. The other film composer was Akhmet Zhubanov (1906–1968), one of the leading Kazakh composers and founder of the Kurmangazy National Orchestra.

69. B. Ramazanuly points out that in the volume *Stsenarii natsional'nykh fil'mov* (Moscow, 1939), only Vsevolod Ivanov is listed as the author of the screenplay and even Musrepov's name was omitted. Cf. Ramazanuly, B. "Kto pervyi kazakhskii kinorezhisser?" *Madeniet*, 18/1992, p. 10.

70. Ramazanuly, "Kto pervyi kazakhskii kinorezhisser?" p. 10.

71. Aimanov, "Tri rozhdeniia," p. 5.

72. In Grigorii Roshal''s article on the Soviet biopic, *Amangeldy* is not mentioned at all. Cf. Roshal', G., "Sovetskii biograficheskii fil'm." In Eremin, D. (ed.), *Tridtsat' let sovetskoi kinematografii. Sbornik statej*. Moskva: Goskinoizdat, 1950, pp. 219–224. The only Kazakhstani film listed is Roshal' and Efim Aron's *The Songs of Abai*, strangely under the incorrect title *Pesnia Abaia* (The Song of Abai), cf. p. 223.

73. Siranov, *Kazakhskoe kinoiskusstvo*, p. 11.

74. The release date was 25 January 1939.

75. Even the revisionist art historian B. Ramazanuly concedes that "the myth" of *Amangeldy* as Kazakhstan's first feature film is ingrained in mass consciousness. Cf. Ramazanuly, "Kto pervyi kazakhskii kinorezhisser?" p. 10.

76. Cf. the article "Pervyi kazakhskii fil'm" by Nurtas Undasynov, the chairman of the Council of People's Commissars of the Kazakh SSR, in *Iskusstvo kino*, 5/1939.

77. The political scientist Rico Isaacs commented on the debates about the birth of Kazakh cinema: "The fixation (. . .) on pinpointing when Kazakh cinema began overlooks a more important issue. What matters is not so much when Kazakh cinema begins, as this rests on the contested assumption that we can disentangle an essential Kazakh identity from its Russian and Soviet history and legacy, but rather the way in which different forms of Kazakh identity and nationhood have been realized through the cinematic lens." Isaacs, Rico. *Film and Identity in Kazakhstan*. London, New York: I.B. Tauris, 2018, p. 67.

*Chapter 2*

# Heroic Interlude in Alma-Ata

The regular production of newsreels and documentaries, together with the coproduced feature film *Amangeldy*, integrated Kazakhstan into the rapidly growing apparatus of the Soviet film industry. However, compared to other republics of the USSR, which had already established national studios, Kazakhstan was lagging behind. While local activists' enthusiasm for advancing Kazakh cinema was beyond doubt, the decision to build a national film studio in Alma-Ata could only be made in Moscow.

The administrative model of Soviet cinema that had evolved in the 1930s was profoundly centralist. Since cinema was considered an ideologically and economically significant part of the Soviet cultural sphere, the government regulated it directly, and the film administration networks were branches of the complex governmental hierarchy and its *nomenklatura*. The hierarchical relationship between center and periphery was a guiding and controlling one. What "Moscow" decided was the law for the entire Soviet film industry. This relationship was maintained until the end of the Soviet system, albeit with certain temporary modifications. The centralist model of cultural governance also implied constant personal interferences of the highest echelons of leadership in all matters concerning the film industry, ranging from the macro- to the micro-level. The simultaneity of numerous levels of decision-making and answerability rendered the administration of Soviet cinema clumsy, distrustful of individual creativity, and prone to political and personal schemes.

These problems were reflected in the emerging film branches in the Soviet republics. The mentor-mentee relationships between the Moscow center and the national peripheries were thus primarily structural, although their perception was often national and ethnic. In other words, the many difficulties caused by the Soviet system of administration were sometimes interpreted as the result of Russian arrogance toward other ethnic groups in the USSR, even though their causality was organizational and managerial, not necessarily prejudicial. The undeniably advanced position of the film industry of the Russian Federation was another factor contributing to the long-term mentor-mentee relationship between central and national studios. This relationship was reinforced by the education of all creative personnel at the Soviet State Film School VGIK in Moscow, from which almost all filmmakers of the national cinematographies graduated until the 1950s. The cinema of Kazakhstan had to struggle with centralist attitudes throughout its Soviet phase. Only during World War II did the relationship undergo an unexpected reversal.

One of the chronic malaises of the Soviet film industry in the 1930s and 1940s was its inability to produce the number of quality feature films demanded by the communist establishment. Before Ivan Bol'shakov was appointed head of the Committee of Cinema Affairs of the Council of People's Commissars in 1939, his predecessors as leaders of Soviet cinema were unable to solve this problem, which caused endless quarrels among various branches of the cultural bureaucracy and among the hacks assigned to this task. Stalin expected that the correct administrative decisions would eventually lead to a qualitative and quantitative enhancement of Soviet film production. He, like the establishment overall, failed to see that his and his minions' systematic intrusions in the creative and production processes were among the very reasons for the industry's inefficiency.

On April 22, 1940, Film Minister Bol'shakov presented to Viacheslav Molotov, head of the Council of People's Commissars, the adjusted thematic plan of Soviet feature films for 1940 and 1941. Most of the planned movies were assigned to the central studios in Moscow and Leningrad; films in the national studios were clearly in a minority position. Among the thirty-three titles listed, one was from Kazakhstan (albeit administered by Lenfilm studio): *Raikhan*, from a screenplay by "A.O. [*sic!*] Auezov."[1] The director assigned to the project was Moisei Levin, who had helmed the first significant feature film on Kazakh subject matter, *Amangeldy*. While that picture did not become a sensation in the USSR at large, it did earn its makers considerable national honors. Among others, Levin was awarded the title Merited Artist of the Kazakh SSR three months after the official release of *Amangeldy*, on April 29, 1939.[2]

## A SOVIET-KAZAKH EMANCIPATION TALE

Film Minister Bol'shakov's aim was to accelerate production throughout the USSR as much as possible in order to meet the ambitious goals laid out in the plan; after all, the failure to do so had cost one of his predecessors, Boris

Shumiatskii, his life. In the Kazakh SSR, just ten days after the presentation of the plan for the entire Soviet film industry, on May 3, 1940, the production of *Raikhan* began.[3]

One year earlier, in February 1939, the Central Committee of the Communist Party of Kazakhstan and the Council of People's Commissars of the Kazakh SSR had issued a decree, "On the Further Development of Literature and the Arts in Kazakhstan," that included a plan for the creation of a national film industry.[4] The implementation of the decree was assigned to a film committee that was part of the Kazakhstani government. It was to ensure that professionals of the "root nationality" (i.e., native Kazakhs) would be provided with a proper education. At the Moscow animation studio "Soiuzmul'tfil'm," a Kazakh department was established, which dubbed films such as *The Thirteen, Lenin in October, Lenin in 1918, Member of the Government*, and *Iakov Sverdlov* into the Kazakh language. Several Kazakh stage artists and painters were sent to Mosfilm and Lenfilm to enhance their professional qualification in the leading Soviet film studios.[5] The first film project to be conceived on the basis of the 1939 decree was *Raikhan*. Its production model, namely, the combination of creative personnel from Lenfilm studio and Kazakhstan under the auspices of the former, was the same as for *Amangeldy*.

In August 1940, the Soviet film industry transitioned to an eight-hour workday and a seven-day work week. These quickly implemented changes allowed the overall production time for *Raikhan* to be significantly reduced. Levin and his team rose to the challenge and managed to deliver the film by the end of September: the Kazakh version was accepted by the Film Committee on September 30, 1940. In terms of production efficiency, the Russian-Kazakhstani production left nothing to be desired.

However, in a manner resembling *Amangeldy*, *Raikhan* was deliberately non-innovative, treading both cinematically and thematically safe ground. The most talented Kazakh writer of his generation, Mukhtar Auezov,[6] had won a national screenplay contest with *Raikhan* in 1939. The contest had been organized jointly by the Communist Party and the Kazakhstani government. Thirty authors took part in it. Auezov's victory meant that his story had already been scrutinized and ideologically purified on numerous levels. Indeed, the plot followed a pattern that had been tested in earlier Soviet films: an oppressed young woman overcomes the resistance of the class enemy and is enabled by the Soviet state to start down a path toward personal and professional self-realization.

During the early sound period, a typical feature of ideologically sensitive Soviet films was the inclusion of an explicatory intertitle at the beginning. *Raikhan* was no exception: "The October Revolution liberated the Kazakh people from feudal oppression. But in the remote mountains, the power of

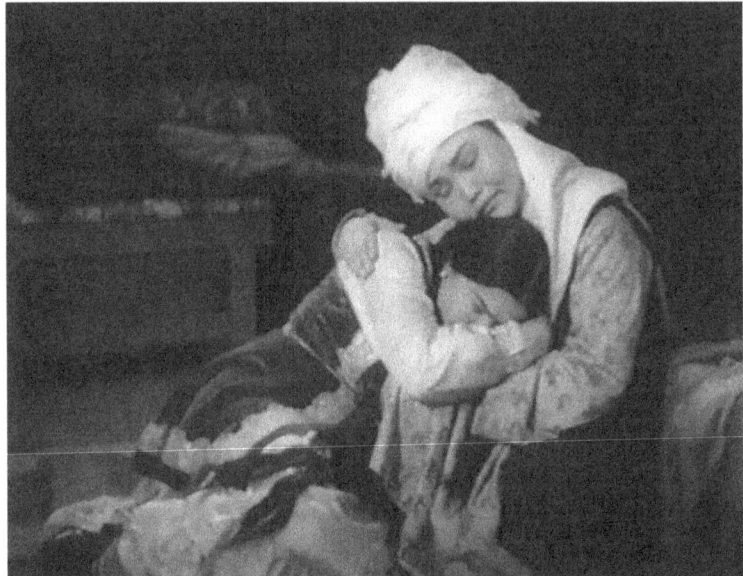

Figure 2.1 Unhappy Daughter and Complacent Mother. Hadisha Bukeeva and Rakhia Koichubaeva. *Raikhan* (1940, Moisei Levin)

the *bays* persists. In the Bala-Shakpak region, the *bay* Zhaksen is in charge." The still influential Zhaksen (Eleubai Umurzakov) forces young Raikhan (Hadisha Bukeeva) into marriage because her mother is indebted to him and is interested in obtaining a wealthy son-in-law.

But Raikhan loves another man and is appalled by Zhaksen's advances.

During the wedding night, she flees from the *bay*'s yurt and goes to the city where she studies agriculture and later returns to her aul as a specialist and steadily earns professional authority among shepherds, thanks to her competence and fearlessness. The film culminates with an encounter between Raikhan and her nemesis, Zhaksen, who has never forgiven her for the shame that she brought upon him. After escaping from the Soviet state, he secretly crossed the border to commit acts of sabotage to his former community. He captures Raikhan and almost kills her; in the last moment, shepherds come to her rescue and the perpetrator falls to his death.

Stories about women acquiring equal rights were always in high demand in the Soviet Union. One of the best emancipation films, *Member of the Government* (Chlen pravitel'stva, 1939), directed by Iosif Kheifits and Aleksandr Zarkhi at Lenfilm studio, depicts the personal and professional growth of a Russian peasant girl who rises to occupy a high-ranking administrative office in Moscow. Such inspirational tales of women's upward social mobility in communist society were imitated by other studios, with

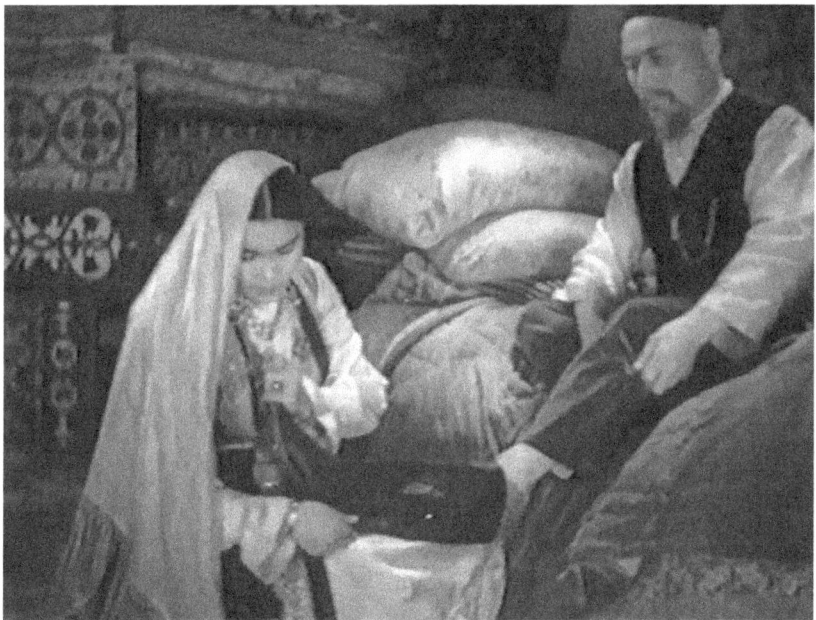

**Figure 2.2** Conjugal Humiliation. Hadisha Bukeeva and Eleubai Umurzakov. *Raikhan* (1940, Moisei Levin)

adjustments to national specifics. In all such stories, the main obstacle to the desired freedom and equality is a patriarch who cannot fathom any other role for a woman than the one defined by the ancient social order. The methods used by these angry patriarchs easily crossed the line to become criminal acts.

Some elements of the plotline in *Raikhan* resemble an earlier emancipation film, Grigorii Kozintsev's and Leonid Trauberg's *Alone* (Odna, 1934), also produced by Lenfilm, in which the endangered young woman is an activist for Sovietization, literally a messenger of modernity. Unlike her Russian predecessor, however, the Kazakh heroine was not born in the city: she is the offspring of the mountains and retains close ties to her *aul* community. Raikhan's innate strength and intelligence convince the local men of her respectability. Thus, in this derivative Kazakh emancipation tale, the patriarchal community is not presented as unconditionally resisting reforms. After all, the only uncompromising retrogrades are the *bay* and two community members, one of whom is a two-faced bureaucrat (Shaken Aimanov). In other words, the traditional Kazakh *aul* is shown to be teachable, open to innovation, and essentially healthy in its attitudes, except for the class enemy within.

Concentrating all negativity in a cluster of overt and covert anti-Soviet characters reflects the official concept of the omnipresence of "enemies of the people" who were purported to sabotage progress at every opportunity.

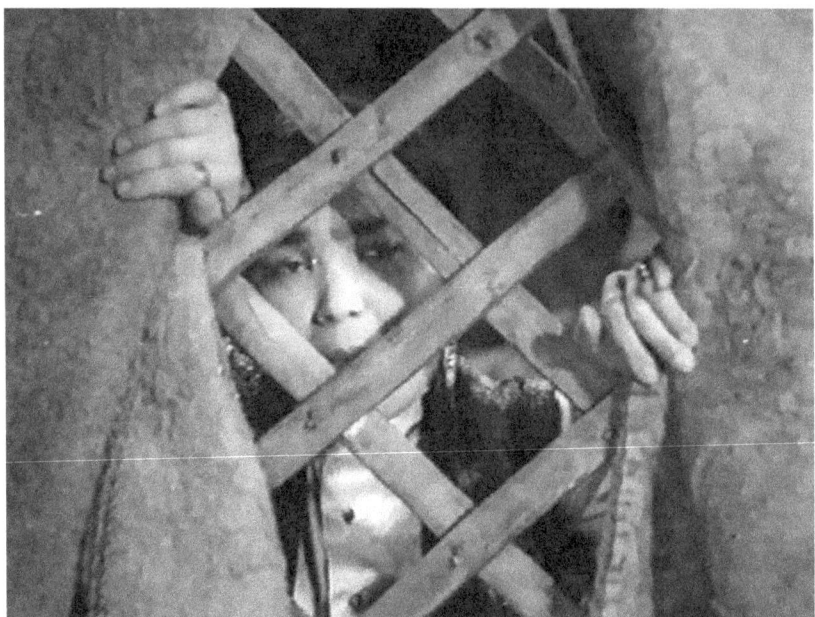

**Figure 2.3 The Yurt as Prison. Hadisha Bukeeva in the Title Role.** *Raikhan* (1940, Moisei Levin)

This scheme leaves no room for differentiation. Indeed, *Raikhan* juxtaposes "the people" and "the enemy" in an utterly black-and-white fashion. Once the enemy is exposed and eliminated, harmony and openness to innovation are secured, and the heroine can continue her path toward social and professional advancement.

It is obvious that *Raikhan*'s central conflict and almost all its characters are clichéd. However, this does not mean that the film lacks any merit. One of its genuine accomplishments is Hadisha Bukeeva's performance in the title role. Just like Eleubai Umurzakov in *Amangeldy*, Bukeeva brings to the screen a vital freshness and energy that make the viewer forget the story's inherent and at times grotesque simplifications. A virtuoso equestrian, Bukeeva is convincing in both physically challenging and psychologically intense episodes. Just as in *Amangeldy*, Khecho Nazariants was responsible for the cinematography.[7] His camerawork, too, must be counted among *Raikhan*'s accomplishments: the mountains of Kazakhstan are shown in rare, crisp beauty, breathing life into an otherwise predictable story. Once again, the cast was entirely Kazakh, not only bringing back many of the performers from *Amangeldy* but also introducing some new names.

Most importantly, *Raikhan* showcased a new Kazakhstan that had shed the legacy of ancient prejudices and practices. The title heroine appears in

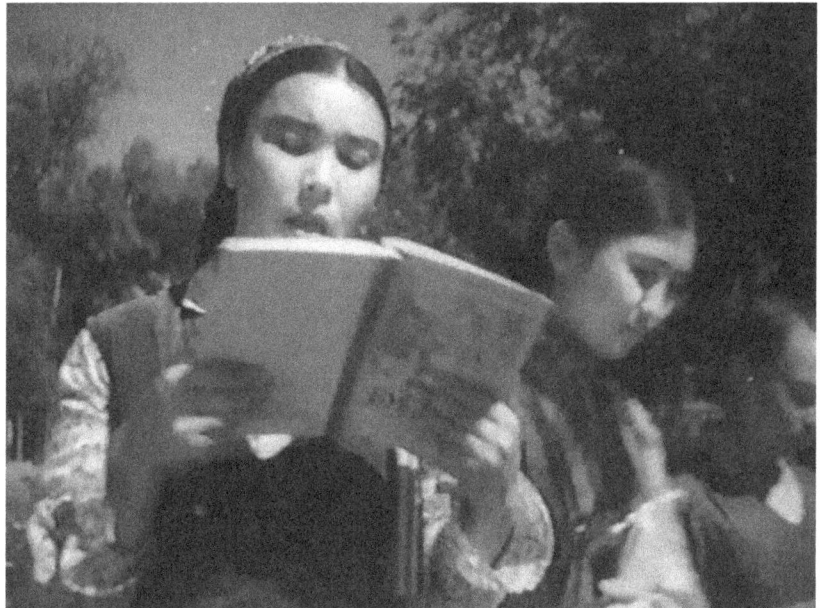

**Figure 2.4 Liberation through Education.** *Raikhan* (1940, Moisei Levin)

trousers and an attractive blouse and feels just as confident in the city as on horseback in the mountains. Whenever she needs a helping hand, the Communist Party secretary is there to offer advice.[8]

It would seem that the crew had demonstrated its ability to transfer an ideologically safe plot onto Kazakh soil in a satisfactory manner. Nevertheless, the film, despite complying with virtually all criteria of socialist realism, did not receive the official recognition enjoyed by comparable Soviet movies. Why did *Raikhan* not become the breakthrough that would have given Kazakhstani cinema legitimacy and a consistent presence in Soviet movie theaters?

Indeed, *Raikhan* remained a phenomenon significant for the history of Kazakh cinema, but not beyond, repeating the fate of *Amangeldy*. Auezov's script and Levin's direction brought a good deal of national authenticity to the screen; the performances were interesting enough, and the camera work solid. But *Raikhan* followed the already established pattern of communist emancipation tales all too transparently, and the resolution of the conflict was too easy even by Stalinist standards. Perhaps the role played by Lenfilm's infrastructure and creative personnel was viewed as an impurity of sorts, although films from Central Asia that won Stalin Prizes were often made with input from the center during the 1930s–1950s. Thus, paradoxically, a picture from a Soviet republic fell victim to its own excessive obedience to ideological guidelines. Conspicuously, *Raikhan* was not rediscovered and rehabilitated by film historians in later years either. The failure to make an impact on Soviet cinema as a whole had far-reaching consequences for the evolution of Kazakhstani film: it continued to exist below the radar and played a largely subservient role.

These consequences extended to the careers of individual performers. A telling example is that of Hadisha Bukeeva: despite her outstanding talent and clear star potential, there was hardly any work for her in Kazakh cinema in the decades thereafter. For Bukeeva, the only way out was to focus on her stage work and teaching. Thus, this immensely gifted actress received few worthwhile offers in cinema over the course of a very long career, finding true national appreciation as a declamation artist rather than on screen.

Of course, the problem of excessive ideological subservience was not limited to Soviet Kazakhstan. The essential dilemma of Soviet cinema was its demand that filmmakers both stick to ideological clichés and simultaneously display creative originality. To make matters worse, film artists in the national republics were subject to even more scrutiny than their colleagues in Moscow or Leningrad, since the latter were often personally connected with central Soviet cultural institutions and political power structures. The administrations of the national republics, too, were more easily frightened by critical signals coming "from Moscow." Being accused of insufficient attention to their republic's cultural production was no trivial matter and could cost politicians their career, if not worse. Thus, in the 1930s–1950s, the tense relationship between the Soviet center and the national periphery served to impede the emergence of truly significant films. Each project had to pass numerous committees before the final product could be sent to Moscow for approval. This made the production process arduous and lengthy: the average production time for a feature film was two years; *Raikhan*'s ultra-efficient production was an exception. Once again, the communist system proved to be its own worst enemy, as strict ideological supervision and production efficiency were mutually exclusive. When under pressure, cultural bureaucrats preferred to err on the side of production volume rather than ideology; on the whole, the punishments for a low number of completed films were less drastic than those for political inattention.

But it was not just ideological commitment or the number of films that bothered the Soviet leadership. Those in the upper echelons of power were quite aware of the deplorable artistic quality of many films made in the USSR. As usual, the solution of choice was harsh administrative measures. Ignoring the real reasons for Soviet studios' inefficiency, Film Minister Bol'shakov introduced strict "quality controls" by tightening the criteria for the formal professional accreditations of film directors. Those who delivered inadequate films received a lower professional category. On November 27, 1940, Bol'shakov presented a list of demoted directors; it included Moisei Levin, the man who had helmed *Amangeldy* and *Raikhan*. The order went into effect on December 12, 1940.[9] As a consequence, Levin, despite the undeniable regional success of his two feature films, could no longer direct and, if he wanted to stay in the profession, could merely be appointed as "second director," working under the supervision of someone else. Understandably, Levin preferred to return to his first vocation: painting. Thus, the filmmaker who had once been the leading light of Kazakhstani cinema earned scorn instead of recognition for his efforts and never helmed a feature film again.

And yet, *Raikhan* avoided the fate of a dozen other films during that period, that is, of being harshly criticized by various party hacks. A number of films taken to task by chief watchdogs Dmitrii Polikarpov and Andrei Zhdanov at a meeting of the organizational bureau of the Communist Party about the work of the Film Committee on March 3, 1941, were withdrawn from distribution altogether. This did not happen to Levin's films. On the contrary, *Amangeldy* and *Raikhan* enjoyed continued popularity within Kazakhstan and evoked pride in the fact that genuine Kazakh narratives had come to the country's screens. Lukewarm reactions outside Kazakhstan did not mean that the experiment of setting up national feature film production (even if only partially) was considered a failure.

The Soviet government continued to make financial investments in the film industries of the "national republics." In May 1940, Bol'shakov presented a plan to the Central Committee of the Communist Party for the construction of national film studios in a number of Soviet republics, including one in Kazakhstan, which was intended to be capable of producing three to four feature films per year and was to be completed in 1943. On December 14, 1940, the State Film Committee issued an order to begin the systematic dubbing of feature films into the Kazakh language. And on April 2, 1941, the Film Committee issued a follow-up decree on the creation of a dubbing department at the Alma-Ata Newsreel Studio.[10] At the time, 1,270 film projectors were operational in Kazakhstan, of which 969 (including 872 mobile projectors) serviced rural locations.[11]

But the war put an end to this positive development and all other plans. On June 22, 1941, the day Germany and its allies attacked the Soviet Union, the repertoire of Soviet cinemas was changed: those movies that had previously been hidden so as not to provoke the Nazi government, including Sergei Eizenshtein's *Aleksandr Nevskii*, Vsevolod Pudovkin's *Suvorov*, and Gerbert Rappaport's *Professor Mamlock*, were rereleased. Under the conditions of mobilization, Kazakhstan's trajectory toward self-sufficient film production was no longer a priority. However, the harsh reality of the war gave Kazakhstani cinema an unexpected impulse that became apparent a few months later.

Two days after the war began, on June 24, 1941, the Central Committee of the Communist Party and the Council of People's Commissars of the USSR formed an evacuation committee that instructed all ministries to prepare plans for the relocation of their enterprises. In early July, the USSR Film Committee was evacuated by train to Novosibirsk. Numerous cameramen were sent to the frontlines to document developments on the battlefields. Screenwriters and directors conceived short propagandistic feature films that could be produced efficiently and distributed immediately. The first *War Film Almanac* (Boevoi kinosbornik), consisting of several shorts, was released on August 1, 1941.

## THE CENTRAL UNITED FILM STUDIO IN ALMA-ATA

On August 19, 1941, Bol'shakov informed the director of Lenfilm, Ivan Glotov, that the studio was to be evacuated to Alma-Ata.[12] Amid chaos and panic, and despite setbacks, the film industry was among those branches that were relocated relatively quickly and efficiently. Initially, Mosfilm, the Soviet Union's largest studio, was to be evacuated to Novosibirsk, where the Main Administration of Cinema had been relocated; indeed, it would have made sense for Bol'shakov and his team to have Mosfilm nearby.[13] However, on November 3, the Film Committee decided to move Mosfilm, like Lenfilm, to Alma-Ata. The ultimate choice of the Kazakhstani capital was based on a number of considerations, for example, that Alma-Ata and its surroundings have a relatively stable climate with a high percentage of sunny days, a factor that would allow prolonged location shooting without the need for extensive artificial lighting equipment.[14] Moreover, Kazakhstan consists of regions with vastly different natural conditions that would enable crews to shoot films set in geographically diverse areas.

The first train carrying equipment and personnel from Mosfilm and Lenfilm studios left Moscow in October 1941; it reached Alma-Ata after two weeks. The overall number of evacuated Soviet film workers was about 3,000. Not all of them came from Moscow and Leningrad; some were from the studios in Kiev and Minsk.[15]

Already on September 7, 1941, the Council of People's Commissars of the USSR had granted permission to organize a studio for the production of feature films in Alma-Ata. The following week, on September 12, 1941, the Council of Ministers of the Kazakh SSR (then called the Council of People's Commissars) officially decided to organize a film studio in the city of Alma-Ata on the premises of the Palace of Culture and the film theater "Alatau." (In the 1990s, the 12th of September, the day the decree #762 was issued, was declared *Day of Kazakh Cinema*.) Back then, under war conditions, these plans were fused with the establishment of a temporary studio bringing together most of the evacuated film personnel. On November 14, 1941, Bol'shakov as head of the Soviet film industry officially proposed to the State Defense Committee (GKO) that Mosfilm and Lenfilm studios be merged with the Alma-Ata Feature Film Studio. That same day, the Council of People's Commissars issued a decree that the three studios be united into The Central United Film Studio (*Tsentral'naia Ob"edinennaia Kinostudiia*, or TsOKS).[16]

From that point onwards, the abbreviation TsOKS became the key term for a unique phenomenon in world film history, an improvised production conglomerate that managed to churn out war propaganda narratives and entertainment on an unprecedented scale. Three years later, when all was said and done and the studio's components had been separated again and returned home, it became clear that among its films were some genuine masterpieces. Although TsOKS existed only for a relatively short period, it is an important part of the Soviet film legacy and one of the rarely disputed positive achievements of the Stalin period in Soviet culture.

In addition to the Central United Film Studio, an All-Soviet Screenplay Department, which supplied the scripts for all TsOKS films, was organized. Another affiliated organization was the Seminar for Film Dramaturgy and Direction, founded on January 10, 1942. The artistic council of TsOKS read like a Who's Who of Soviet cinema: Eizenshtein, Pudovkin, Kozintsev, Aleksandrov, Pyr'ev, Raizman, and the Vasil'ev brothers represented the directors (by far the largest group within the council); Boris Volchek was the sole cameraman; Boris Chirkov represented the actors, and Boris Dubrovskii-Eshke[17] (a professor at VGIK since 1938) the art directors.

Despite inevitable turbulences and hiccups, TsOKS quickly became an efficient studio, producing 80% of Soviet feature films. Its productivity can only be explained by the quasi-military discipline in all its branches and by the high level of motivation among its personnel. Of course, forcing two formerly competing studios to work together under one roof could not but cause a certain degree of friction. Adding to the stress were frequent tensions among egotistical filmmakers, performers, and their spouses. But during the Great Patriotic War, military structures commanded the highest authority in the film industry: no movie could be released without their consent, and subordination ruled the day. Still, despite military order, the communication between filmmakers and film officials, on the one hand, and colonels and generals, on the other, was often difficult.

The living conditions for the evacuated artists were harsh compared to their privileged lifestyle in Moscow and Leningrad prior to the war. However, film professionals and their families continued to belong to the upper echelons of the Soviet establishment and lived on a better level than the mass of Soviet population, even in wartime conditions. In hindsight, it is often difficult to distinguish between real and perceived hardships. When prominent director Mikhail Romm and administrator Konstantin Polonskii, who were in charge of the Main Administration for the Production of Feature Films, visited the TsOKS premises for an official inspection on January 17, 1942, they concluded that there were serious shortcomings in all vital areas of film production and living conditions, with housing among the most severe problems.[18] The less privileged among the film workers suffered the most, but diseases such as typhus affected prominent artists, too. Typhoid fever claimed the lives of actor Boris Blinov, a star since his portrayal of commissar Furmanov in *Chapaev*, and the actress Sofia Magarill, wife of director Grigorii Kozintsev; altogether, 215 TsOKS employees died of typhoid fever during the war years. One of the rising stars of Soviet cinema, Vera Maretskaia, received the news of her husband's death at the front while celebrating the premiere of *She Defends Her Motherland* (1942), the first full-length feature film produced during the war. Just a month after arriving in Alma-Ata, one of Sergei Eizenshtein's most valued students, the young director Valentin Kadochnikov, died from exhaustion as a result of being compelled to carry out heavy physical tasks.[19]

Still, there can be no doubt that the conditions of film evacuees in Alma-Ata were better than those in most regions of the USSR. Even the students of the State Film School VGIK, who had likewise been evacuated to the Kazakh capital (by decree of October 25, 1941; the institute began to move into its temporary space on November 5, 1941), had access to bread, pasta, and apples. In the summer and early autumn, they worked in agricultural communities around the Kazakhstani capital, helping with the harvest. Prominent filmmakers and their families lived in a newly built three-story apartment complex flippantly called "laureatnik" (the laureates' barn), a Russian pun derived from the word *kuriatnik* (chicken house). After the war, among the most common memories was that even celebrities were inundated with trivial duties such as selling or buying household items on the black market.[20] Eventually, Bol'shakov was granted permission for the organization of a supply department for TsOKS that helped provide those working in the film industry with food. On top of that, twenty-five Stalin Prize winners and ten leading Soviet actresses were given special access to the cafeteria of the Council of People's Commissars of the Kazakh SSR.[21]

While the management of relations between the evacuees and their Kazakh colleagues could be complicated at times, even more complex were the relations among native film workers themselves. One of the few experts on Kazakh cinema, Kabysh Siranov, benefited from the new situation in major ways. While in his twenties and still studying at the evacuated Soviet film school, he was assigned the position of deputy director of the entire TsOKS. However, his sizeable influence was not to everybody's liking. On January

19, 1943, Nurgali Beisekov,[22] a young theater director, submitted an official grievance to Film Minister Bol'shakov and his deputy, Lukashev, in which he described the rampant corruption under Siranov's leadership.

Beisekov emphasized that he, together with many other Kazakhs, saw the arrival of Lenfilm and Mosfilm professionals in Alma-Ata as a real chance to create a national Kazakh cinema. Although he was a member of the Communist Party, the Central Committee and the Council of People's Commissars of the Kazakh SSR had sent him to the studio in a subservient capacity, as assistant director, and he had to agree to a hefty pay cut that represented nearly 50% of his previous salary—from 2,100 rubles per month to 1,200 rubles. But this sacrifice was worthwhile since now Beisekov was given the opportunity to work with legendary director Vsevolod Pudovkin and cameraman Boris Volchek. However, according to Beisekov, as soon as Kabysh Siranov joined the studio, things changed: Beisekov was drafted and sent to the front; six months later, when he was brought back to Alma-Ata, Siranov did everything in his power to prevent Beisekov from getting work, while aggressively pushing his own projects, including the comedy *The White Rose* and the concert film *To the Sounds of the Dombras*. Claiming to be the representative of the Central Committee and the Council of People's Commissars at the studio, Siranov, according to the grievance, used his position to undermine any other Kazakh, including the writer of the letter. Seeing no way out, Beisekov decided to resign, pointing to the machinations of the deputy studio director and his friends: under the pretext of preparing the studio's new project, *Dzhambul*, Siranov, the producer Esbatyrov, and the assistant cameraman, Absaliamov,[23] were enriching themselves. As if that was not enough, Siranov had convinced the film director Grigorii Roshal' to hire the actress Amina Erguzhinova,[24] arbitrarily increasing her salary, and receiving from her a precious overcoat in return. Other details reported by the informant are politically more precarious: in the concert film *To the Sounds of the Dombras*, Siranov had replaced an episode from Auezov's play *Honors Guard* featuring Stalin and Zhukov with a speech by the Kazakh leader Undasynov.

Letters such as this shed light on the less savory aspects of the conditions at TsOKS, the petty schemes, and interpersonal tensions. Regardless of whether the information provided by Beisekov was accurate, exaggerated, or simply made up, letters such as this could have the gravest consequences for the targeted individuals. Interestingly, Lukashev reacted with caution, merely encouraging the studio boss, Tikhonov, to have a conversation with Siranov, because "his development is going the wrong way and he will not become an administrative leader for national film cadres." Beisekov's most damning accusation is Siranov's alleged drive to become a coauthor on any project involving Kazakhstan to the exclusion of any other qualified candidate. Be this as it may, Nurgali Beisekov ultimately remained at the studio and worked as an assistant director on Aleksandr Stolper's *Wait for Me* and Grigorii Roshal's *The Songs of Abai* (1945). It is not clear whether Siranov's arrest in 1946 and his long prison sentence had anything to do with Beisekov's letter.[25]

Despite countless internal conflicts, which reflected the specific conditions in Soviet society, Nazi Germany's attack on the Soviet Union consolidated the emerging communist nation with unprecedented force. The film industry was no exception. From the beginning of the war, national unity was emphasized as a supreme value, while the class differences that had dominated Soviet film plots of the 1930s were downplayed or eliminated. Of course, ideological criteria were not forgotten, but they were applied differently, with a modicum of practical common sense, inclusiveness, and even forgiveness. Many authors who had been victimized in the 1930s now got a chance to express patriotic sentiments and help mobilize the population to make sacrifices for victory over Germany.

At TsOKS, when the production of a film made it necessary to summon an actor or a technical specialist from a GULAG concentration camp, such efforts had a realistic chance of success, whereas before the war, they would have been unthinkable. An example was screenwriter Sergei Ermolinskii who had been arrested by the NKVD in spring 1942 and sentenced to three years of exile in the Kyzyl-Orda region of Kazakhstan. Ermolinskii, who was living in a provincial town, was summoned to Alma-Ata a year later by Sergei Eizenshtein and Nikolai Cherkasov, officially because of the urgent need for qualified screenwriters.[26] Thus, TsOKS secured the writer's survival.

In the decades after the war, a considerable number of articles were written by Kazakh film professionals, who had been employed at TsOKS, and by film workers from Moscow and Leningrad, who had spent the war years in Kazakhstan. The tenor of these texts is one of mutual gratitude: the evacuees emphasize the hospitality of regular Kazakhs in those trying times, while early-career Kazakh film professionals appreciated the opportunity to study and partner with leading specialists. Several Kazakh memoirists describe their work with celebrated directors and their crews as the chance of a lifetime. Thus, young Mazhit Begalin, severely injured in the war, was admitted to the directing class taught by Sergei Gerasimov. However, Begalin was the only Kazakh in his class. Overall, about 300 Kazakhs worked at the TsOKS studio, predominantly in technical jobs. Many of them learned their craft during short courses taught by specialists from the evacuated studios. Thus, the cutters were trained by VGIK pedagogue G. Shirokov (about fifteen of his students were later employed as cutters at Kazakhfilm studio), while those working in the development labs were taught by VGIK professor Evsei Iofis,[27] a leading specialist on the chemical treatment of film stock.[28] Another educational initiative was an acting studio for native performers that enlisted around twenty budding actors who were selected in a competition; the studio was headed by Grigorii Roshal'. Luminaries such as Eizenshtein, Pudovkin, and Pyr'ev were among the pedagogues; students included Abdulla Karsakbaev and Zamzagul Sharipova.

Soviet publications about the TsOKS years emphasize time and time again how beneficial the cooperation was for native Kazakhs. However, the concrete role of TsOKS in the individual careers of Kazakh film artists has not been sufficiently studied. Sometimes it appears as if the role of native specialists was predominantly auxiliary. Were Kazakh artists members included in mixed crews on projects that did not involve Kazakh themes, or did the professionals from Moscow and Leningrad prefer to work within their established groups? Did the guests perceive a genuine need to reach out to the budding film workers native to the area, or was the cooperation mainly motivated by political pressures?

Several films produced by TsOKS reveal that the studio administration was sensitive to ethnic questions. After all, what had not changed in Soviet cinema was the assignment of projects to specific filmmakers based on ideological parameters. One such parameter was to praise the friendship among all nationalities that were part of the Soviet Union. In the context of the existential challenge of a world war, that aspect was even more vital.

## *Son of a Fighter*

Among the short films produced by TsOKS that feature strong Kazakhstani motifs was *Son of a Fighter* (Syn boitsa, 1942), part of *War Film Almanac 12* (the other film in that almanac was Gerbert Rappaport's *Van'ka*).[29] *Son of a Fighter* was directed by Vera Stroeva from a screenplay by Sergei Mikhalkov, Iosif Prut, and Gabit Musrepov (who had won accolades for his contribution to *Amangeldy*) and released on August 12, 1942.

*War Film Almanac 12* opens with a powerful photo montage featuring atrocities committed by Nazi troops in the occupied territories. The ensuing fictional story further develops the theme of civilian suffering. In the opening scene, a Red Army sniper, Petr Vorob'ev (Oleg Zhakov), talks to a Kazakh soldier named Aimanov (Kapan Badyrov) about children. The Kazakh proudly describes his three daughters, to which his Russian comrade responds, much to Aimanov's astonishment, that he does not like children and is not interested in having them. A subsequent German infantry attack puts Vorob'ev's view to the test: the attackers use hundreds of civilians (mothers with their children, as well as old men and women) as human shields. The Soviet soldiers are baffled: how can they shoot at women and children? When one of the Soviet women cries out "Shoot at us!" it is a German who shoots her in the back. The woman's baby clings to her motionless body and cries for help. Aimanov crawls out of the trenches to rescue the child but is wounded; Vorob'ev, after getting permission from the commander, pulls both Aimanov and the baby to safety and then participates in the triumphant Soviet counterattack.

Back in the trenches, soldiers and officers discuss what should happen to the rescued baby. Vorob'ev volunteers that it could be sent to his mother, and he himself would later adopt it. But Aimanov interferes: "I know that Vorob'ev does not like children—let me adopt the baby instead." However, something has changed in the mind of the Russian sniper. He insists that the baby be registered under his name.[30]

*Son of a Fighter* shares with other *War Film Almanacs* narrative linearity and conceptual simplicity. But it uses the studio's limited resources to its advantage. The camera work (Semen Sheinin) is solid throughout and extraordinary at times. The opening scene consists of several panoramic shots featuring a chaotic, mud-filled foreground, a few thorny bushes, and barbed wire near the trenches—a torn landscape that anticipates the cinematography of Soviet lyrical war films in the late 1950s and early 1960s. The appearance of hundreds of civilians on the horizon is likewise powerfully visualized and supported by ominous tunes, forming a truly horrific sight that gains in pathos as soon as the extreme long frames are complemented by close-ups of individual women and children.

The experienced Oleg Zhakov gives the character of sniper Vorob'ev a believable harshness necessary to survive the tribulations of trench life.[31] The conversation with his Kazakh comrade exposes a side of his soul that he normally would not have disclosed, but the incident with civilians used as human shields leaves him no option but to change his attitude toward children.

Interestingly, the film does not deny, hide, or downplay ethnic differences. In one of the dialogues, Aimanov, who is pointing proudly to his seven years of marriage, comes across as more emotionally candid and appealing than his Russian counterpart. He sings in his mother tongue and explains that his song is about his hatred of the German tanks. His spontaneous singing is fresh and lively. The film describes it as a peculiarity of the Kazakh people, one that Russians lack but admire. The differences between the two men are slight and do not seriously threaten their unity in combat, but they are noticeable nonetheless. Only at the end are Vorob'ev and Aimanov emotionally in agreement. Conspicuously, the film's original title was *A New Feeling* (Novoe chuvstvo). When Vorob'ev discovers his "new feeling" of a desire for fatherhood, his restraint in expressing it is touching, especially when he asks the commander, "May I consider myself the father of this child?" To which Aimanov responds by singing about the proud spirit of the Soviet people that cannot be crushed by the Nazi bandits.

Given the circumstances of its conception and production, *Son of a Fighter* is remarkable for its emphatic respect for the Kazakh character. To be sure, Aimanov's attitude toward the enemy is similar to that of his Russian counterpart, but he expresses it in a more forward, optimistic way, through singing and talking about his early marriage and three children. Such positive emphasis on a Kazakh character as opposed to a Russian was not common: in many films, when relations between Russians and other Soviet nations were depicted, Russian characters often were assigned the role of mentor, although cultural differences were usually described benevolently and with a dose of humor. *Son of a Fighter* can legitimately be viewed as a film reflecting the experience of the evacuated filmmakers in Kazakhstan, reversing clichés about non-Russian people and even depicting them as emotionally stronger in certain respects.

## Giants of the Steppe

The second feature film about Kazakhs fighting in World War II was *Giants of the Steppes* (Batyry stepei, 1942, aka *Kazakh Novellas*/Kazakhskie novelly, aka *Song of a Giant*/Pesn' o velikane). The screenplay was initially titled *Kazakhs Are Fighting* (Kazakhi voiuiut). The dominant motifs of the film are water as the source of life; the soldier's love for his mother; and heroic self-sacrifice for the greater good.

As a Red Army unit marches through a swampy area, its soldiers suffer from thirst because the abundant water surrounding them is unfit for human consumption. The conversations revolve around their mothers and wives. During a moment of rest, the Kazakh soldier Kuregen (Kapan Badyrov) talks about Tolagai, a *batyr* who saved his people by sacrificing his life. "Was he a member of our unit?" asks one of the soldiers. "He was," answers Kuregen, "one thousand years ago." The legend he relates is impressively visualized: Tolagai (Zhagda Oguzbaev), a veritable giant, ten times taller than his fellow nomads, lives among regular folks and is revered by them. When a drought strikes, Tolagai removes an entire mountain and carries it away, thus eliminating the obstacle that had prevented clouds from reaching his *aul*. The film emphasizes that it is Tolagai's deed that brings water to his kin, not the disparate prayers of the frightened nomads. "A hero is a man unafraid to die," concludes one of the listeners.

The following scene (back in the present) portrays the dangerous operation of crossing a strategically important river. Kuregen is ordered to go behind enemy lines and destroy a machine gun unit. After his two comrades are killed, Kuregen is left alone in the fight to keep the attacking Germans at bay. Despite being severely wounded and through sheer willpower, he continues to operate his machine gun; his body language resembles that of the legendary Tolagai. Finally, the Soviet attack ends in victory, a victory made possible by Kuregen, who dies with the word "Apa" (mother) on his lips. Later, far away, Kuregen's wife gives birth to his child while his mother reads a letter from her son's comrades: "Dear mother of our Kuregen! We love you as if you were our own mother!"

The 40-minute-long film, directed by Grigorii Roshal[32] from a screenplay by Abdilda Tazhibaev and Leonid Zhezhelenko, was inspired by a real-life soldier, Tulegen Tokhtarov, who was posthumously honored with the title Hero of the Soviet Union. *Giants of the Steppes* suffers from the weaknesses typical of most war films in that early period: a cartoonish depiction of the Nazi enemies as inept and easy to kill and grandiose gestures accompanying the theatrical, unrealistic fighting. But the special effects created by Aleksandr Ptushko for the Tolagai episode are nothing short of astonishing, considering the state of the studio equipment after evacuation. The use of slow motion and sound effects enhances the majestic quality of this episode, making the overall pathos believable. That episode alone renders *Giants of the Steppes* a worthwhile part of Kazakhstani film history.[33] The two main performers, Zhagda Oguzbaev (other spelling: Ogizbaev) as Tologai and Kapan Badyrov as Kuregen, earned critical praise for making the legendary hero believable.[34]

The war film almanacs played a significant role in the ideological mobilization of the Soviet population and in motivating the rank-and-file at the front. Production efficiency was particularly important: short films such as *Son of a Fighter* or *Giants of the Steppes* could be completed within two to three weeks. While production facilities in Alma-Ata were limited in size and technical sophistication, the various crews worked round the clock to make use of electricity whenever it was available, mostly at night. Screenwriters adjusted their scripts to the circumstances and limitations, coming up with plots that could be filmed in the Kazakhstani steppe.

After the war, the almanacs disappeared into archives until the end of the Soviet era and only reappeared on television in the new millennium when patriotic sentiments made a powerful comeback in post-communist Russia.

## *The White Rose*

A largely forgotten feature film with Kazakh subject matter made during the Great Patriotic War at TsOKS studio was *The White Rose* (Belaia roza, 1943), directed by Efim Aron from a screenplay by Kabysh Siranov and Valentin Morozov. A medium-length film of about 40 minutes, it depicts the life of Kazakh youths in the hinterlands, their hard work supporting the fighters at the front, and their competition for the love of a beautiful young woman, Sabira (Nursulu Topalova). Several men hope to receive Sabira's formal promise to wait for them while they are at the front. Because she respects their sacrifice, she gives each of them a white rose. An injured officer, Zhakan[35] (Shaken Aimanov in his first lead role), comes to his village for a few days to get some rest. He is still weak and walks with a cane, but this does not prevent him from likewise falling in love with Sabira. She tells the four suitors that she loves them all yet gives Zhakan a red rose as the sign of true love. To be sure, the competition between Sabira's admirers is not overly passionate: all of them are friends, and one of them says to Zhakan: "You are the one who has shed his blood for our *aul*, for our homeland." Sabira's grandfather, Dzhakpar (Serke Kozhamkulov), meanwhile, takes her to task for thinking about love. After all, there is a war to be fought.

The film's depiction of the Kazakh *aul* is idyllic, as if to convey to viewers the importance of protecting the motherland. Aimanov's performance, characterized by manly restraint, earned him praise. However, following a short release, *The White Rose* was prohibited in December 1943.[36] Fifty years later, in a reassessment of the possible reasons for this verdict, the Soviet State Film Fund (*Gosfil'mofond*, GFF) noted that no official documents regarding the film's shelving could be located and concluded that "The (war) theme merely served the authors as a pretext for using a traditional plot—the competition of several young men who are in love with the same young woman."[37] Another possible objection may have been that this little comedy was seen as too apolitical; indeed, films by Leonid Trauberg and others were severely criticized for the same reason. Conspicuously, the only time a Stalin portrait appears in the entire film is during the farewell meeting. In later years, Kabysh Siranov, who coauthored the screenplay, credited director Efim Aron with having created the first Kazakh national musical comedy, *The White Rose*.[38]

A fourth TsOKS production with Kazakh motifs was *To the Sounds of Dombras* (Pod zvuki dombr,[39] 1943), a so-called concert film (*fil'm-kontsert*). This genre was very popular during the Great Patriotic War, as it was easy to produce and filled with spectacular performances by the most celebrated singers and actors. *To the Sounds of Dombras*, directed by Lenfilm evacuees Semen Timoshenko and Adol'f Minkin[40] from a screenplay coauthored by Kabysh Siranov and Timoshenko, consists exclusively of performances by Kazakh artists, held together by a narrator, Kalibek Kuanyshpaev. He presents a medley ranging from highbrow to lowbrow, including arias from Evgenii Brusilovskii's operas *Silk Maiden* (Kyz-Zhibek) and *Er-Targyn*, folksongs played by the Kurmangazy orchestra, and Oskar Sandler's war song "To Battle, Kazakh Brothers!" (V boi, brat'ia kazakhi!). Also included was a scene from Gogol's *Inspector General*, the monologue of general Panfilov from Mukhtar Auezov's play *The Honor Guard*, and a poem by legendary *akyn* Dzhambul Dzhabaev (other spelling: Zhambyl Zhabaev). In an article written many years later, Siranov observed that a formally innovative aspect of *To the Sounds of Dombras* was the avoidance of theater decorations; instead, the filmmakers decided to build film-specific sets that allowed for a mobile camera with numerous points of view and a variety of shot types.[41] On the one hand, the film was a living testimony to the achievements of Kazakh music and theater; on the other, it was a gesture of gratitude for the hospitality of a nation that had enabled the Soviet film industry to continue its work under dire circumstances. Sixty years later, Rustam Khamdamov's highly stylized picture *Vocal Parallels* (Vokal'nye paralleli, 2005) was made at Kazakhfilm studio as a peculiar homage to the TsOKS concert film, demonstrating that the genre had not lost its peculiar aesthetic fascination.

The Alma-Ata Newsreel Studio remained separate from TsOKS. During the war years, it hosted the most prominent Soviet documentary filmmakers, including Roman Karmen, Aleksandr Medvedkin, and Iakov Poselskii. The now marginalized film pioneer Dziga Vertov continued to work on his full-length documentary *Kazakhstan—to the Front*; its limited release under the title *To You, Front!* (Tebe, front!) started on May 15, 1943.[42]

## To You, Front!

*To You, Front!* begins with a sequence of five static shots, from medium to close-up, moving closer and closer to a seated *akyn*. Although one can hear the loud explosion of bombs, the old man remains strangely stoic, as if he did not notice anything or the violent noise did not concern him in the least. He then sings a song featuring the story of a Kazakh couple, Dzhamil' and Saule. Dzhamil' works in a lead-mine, dutifully shouldering his heavy workload every day, achieving results like nobody else. But when Nazi Germany attacks the Soviet Union, he volunteers for the front. Saule bids him farewell in a gorgeous mountain setting, only to take up her husband's job in the mine, wishing that the lead ore she is unearthing help defeat the aggressor. One day she and her colleagues hear from a public radio loudspeaker about a Kazakh fighter's heroic deed. It is none other than Dzhamil' who killed several German machine gunners and captured two high-ranking officers. In the evening, Saule writes Dzhamil' a letter; we see him reading it and associating his wife's words with memories of Kazakhstan's industrial awakening, of which he himself was part. From oil fields to the rich variety of minerals that are found in Kazakhstan and the intensive agricultural production: it all goes toward the cause of victory, as a choir sings "We are beating the fascists with grain." When Saule comes home from work, she looks at her husband's portrait, which changes to a live shot of him.

Vertov, who was assisted by his wife Elizaveta Svilova, focuses on the close connection between homefront and battlefield. He also praises the multinational nature of Soviet society which is embodied by the two central characters. Their faces regularly appear in close shots: both are young, handsome, and pure like children, yet dead serious in their commitment to the cause of defending the Soviet motherland. Another visual motif is the sky, shown in numerous low-angle shots denoting the lofty idealism that inspires the Soviet-Kazakh people. The fictitious frame narrative is presented in a deliberately naïve, almost fairy-tale-like manner. In accordance with Vertov's principles of using live sound, we can hear the characters speak a few times, conspicuously, in Russian.

The reasons why *To You, Front!* was not widely shown and soon withdrawn from screens are hard to assess. There is certainly nothing subversive in subject matter or imagery that could have caused any official misgivings. Perhaps some montage sequences resembled Vertov's early work that had been denounced as "formalistic," an accusation that would haunt him until the end of his days. Still, these elements are too rare to have subverted the overall clarity of narration. The score by Gavriil Popov strikes one as dissonant and gloomy at times, but these moments are outweighed by many conventional marches and choir songs that were indistinct from Soviet mainstream. *To You, Front!* went through numerous changes, as a number of screenplay variations document.[43] Although its intentions are undoubtedly patriotic and in tune with official ideological guidelines, this 40-minute film did not bring about Vertov's rehabilitation as a filmmaker and was a marginal phenomenon among Alma-Ata productions at the time. The official view of its significance only changed in the 1960s when Vertov was finally recognized as a classic of Soviet cinema and his work in Alma-Ata was integrated into the overall narrative of proud cinematic achievements of the Great Patriotic War.

Assessing the legacy of the Alma-Ata years for Soviet cinema, film historians generally depict it as positive. Despite enormous material and logistical restrictions, TsOKS managed to produce more than two dozen full-length feature films during the three years of its existence. Several of them established Soviet narrative norms in films about the Great Patriotic War for decades to come, particularly Fridrikh Ermler's *She Defends Her Motherland* (Ona zashchishchaet Rodinu, 1942, released in the United States as *No Greater Love*). Others became popular hits, providing much-needed optimistic entertainment, such as Gerbert Rapapport's comedy *The Air Chauffeur* (Vozdushnyi izvozchik, 1944). Several feature films were shelved by military censors; for the most part, these were attempts to analyze Nazi ideology and its societal manifestations. The most intriguing among these prohibited pictures is Vsevolod Pudovkin's *Murderers Are on Their Way* (Ubiitsy vykhodiat na dorogu, 1942) from Bertolt Brecht's play *Fear and Misery of the Third Reich*. While the exact reasons for its shelving have not been established, it is fair to assume that its sharp depiction of the inner workings of a totalitarian society, in which children inform on their parents, evoked inconvenient associations with Soviet reality. To some degree, the sensibilities of military censors who had the final say in what could or could not be released during wartime differed from those of their civilian counterparts, as various directors, including Kozintsev, Romm, and Trauberg, had to learn the hard way. Still, despite the shelving of some films, all reprimanded directors continued to work and some won prizes for their subsequent projects.

From an artistic standpoint, by far the most significant achievement of TsOKS's was Sergei Eizenshtein's *Ivan the Terrible* (Ivan Groznyi, 1944). Its first part won a Stalin Prize; the second part was shelved in 1946 and only released in 1958. None of its episodes reveal the incredible difficulties that its crew had to overcome. Although this was admittedly a prestige project eagerly awaited by Stalin himself, and despite enjoying preferential treatment by Soviet authorities, filming took place mostly at night in icy studio facilities. Yet *Ivan the Terrible* has the look of a lavish super-production, making it hard to believe that it was completed by an improvised studio during a war that threatened the very existence of the Soviet Union.

The years of TsOKS, when almost the entire Soviet film industry was concentrated in the capital of Kazakhstan, must have seemed like a dream to those Kazakhs who were eager to create a film industry for their nation. When the last trains with evacuated personnel and their studio equipment left Almaty for Moscow and Leningrad, the awakening was rough. Shortly before their departure, as a gesture of gratitude to Kazakhstan for its hospitality, luminaries of Soviet film had participated in a five-day conference about the future of Kazakhstani cinema. The conference, attended by Eizenshtein, Pudovkin, Pyr'ev, Ermler, Vertov, Ptushko and other prominent filmmakers, was part of a festival of Kazakhstani cinema held from January 8–14, 1944. During that week, All Alma-Ata movie theaters screened feature films and documentaries dealing with the host republic. At the conference, Sergei Vasil'ev, of *Chapaev* fame, the erstwhile artistic director of TsOKS, spoke about "Kazakhstan as the Basis of Soviet Feature Film in the Years of the Great Patriotic War," calling on his colleagues to provide help to the budding filmmakers of Kazakhstan.[44] Mukhtar Auezov devoted his presentation to the kinship between literature and film, and expressed his belief that a synthesis of folklore and modern literature would lead Kazakhstan's cinema to success. Grigorii Roshal' pointed to the need to educate an entire generation of native young film artists. Several panelists repeatedly warned the film workers of arrogance (*zaznaistvo i kinochvanstvo*)[45] toward the other arts: cinema can only be successful in synthesis with literature, music, and the fine arts. The final resolution of the conference includes the demand that Kazakhstani film workers must remember "that their task is not only the creation of films, but the creation of the national cinema art of the Kazakh people with its own style and traditions, which requires the critical appropriation of the century-old national culture of Kazakhstan, its courageous enrichment, as well as the constant learning from the advanced Russian culture and from the masters of Soviet cinema."[46]

The Kazakhstani government showed its gratitude toward the prominent guests in various ways. For example, director Vera Stroeva, who helmed *Son of a Fighter* and assisted her husband on *Giants of the Steppes*, was rewarded with the title Merited Art Worker of the Kazakh SSR on January 13, 1944. Young directors Efim Aron and Boris Iurtsev,[47] along with other film professionals, chose to stay in Alma-Ata, planning projects that would address Kazakh subject matter. At a meeting on September 9, 1944, the State Film Committee decided that the Alma-Ata Newsreel Studio was to be combined with the Alma-Ata Feature Film Studio.[48] The order for the reorganization was issued on September 26, 1944. In May 1945, the Committee on Cinema of the Council of People's Commissars of the USSR appointed Iurtsev as the director of *The Enchanted Sergeant* (Ocharovannyi serzhant), a feature film project at the Alma-Ata Film Studio. However, in 1946, when a third of the film had been shot, Iurtsev was arrested and the project terminated.[49] Following the Soviet victory over Nazi Germany, the cultural and political atmosphere in the Soviet Union had become harsher than ever before, and Kazakhstan was hardly immune.

## NOTES

1. V.I. Fomin, ed., *Letopis' rossiiskogo kino 1930–1945*. Moskva: "Materik," 2007, p. 664.

2. The honorary title, Zasluzhennyi deiatel' iskusstv Kazakhskoi SSR, sometimes translated as "Merited Art Worker," came with privileges but was the lowest in the nomenclature, followed by People's Artist of the Kazakh SSR and, beginning in 1936, People's Artist of the USSR. Moisei Levin, who was head of the Union of Artists of Kazakhstan, was awarded a higher title in 1944, People's Artist of Kazakhstan.

3. *Letopis' rossiiskogo*, p. 666.

4. Smailova, *Kinoentsiklopediia Kazakhstana*, p. 447.

5. Siranov, *Kazakhskoe kinoiskusstvo*, p. 14.

6. Auezov, Mukhtar (1897–1961), the most important Kazakhstani author of the 20th century, showed a life-long interest in cinema. Apart from writing screenplays, many of Auezov's short stories were adapted for the screen, as were parts of his magnum opus, *The Path of Abai* (1942–1956).

7. Khecho M. Nazar'iants (b. 1906) was later drafted, sent to the front, and killed in action in 1942.

8. Bauyrzhan Nogerbek wrote in 2010 that "the ideological norms and aesthetic canons of Soviet totalitarian cinema left their shining mark on the film dramaturgy,"

claiming that "Raikhan kills people with surprising ease because they are class enemies." (In Smailova, *Kinoentsiklopediia Kazakhstana*, p. 13) However, the latter statement is factually inaccurate: Raikhan does not kill anybody, end even the bay who tries to kill her is thrown off a cliff by another person. Still, the critic admits that, despite the "harsh model of the totalitarian film" which *Amangeldy* and *Raikhan* followed, the screenwriters were able to insert a number of national motifs into the structure of these films (ibid.).

9. Letopis' rossiiskogo, pp. 687–88.
10. *Letopis' rossiiskogo*, p. 703.
11. Smailova, *Kinoentsiklopediia Kazakhstana*p. 447.
12. Letopis' rossiiskogo, p. 720.
13. Fomin, V.I., (ed.), *Kino na voine. Dokumenty i svidetel'stva*. Moskva: "Materik," 2005, p. 229.
14. Kabysh Siranov, "V sem'e edinoi." In: *Ocherki istorii kazakhskogo kino*, Alma-Ata: Izdatel'stvo "Nauka" Kazakhskoi SSR, 1980, p. 52.
15. In addition to filmmakers, technical personnel, administrators, and their families, the Soviet State Film School, VGIK, was also evacuated to Alma-Ata; it was housed in two large buildings assigned to educational purposes and a dormitory for its students. Cf. Siranov, "V sem'e edinoi," p. 54.
16. *Letopis' rossiiskogo*, p. 726.
17. Boris Vladimirovich Dubrovskii-Eshke (1897–1963) was a prominent Soviet art director.
18. *Letopis' rossiiskogo*, p. 735.
19. Kadochnikov died on March 9, 1942. Cf. Eizenshtein's very emotional obituary in Sergei Eizenshtein, *Izbrannye proizvedeniia v shesti tomakh*, vol. 5. Moskva: "Iskusstvo," 1963, pp. 451–53.
20. For an assessment of TsOKS's achievements, the living conditions in Alma-Ata, and the studio's significance in the history of Soviet cinema see Neia Zorkaia's article in *Iskusstvo kino*, 7/1999, pp. 125–39, reprinted in Fomin, *Kino na voine*, pp. 229-45.
21. The order and list of participants were confirmed on December 28, 1942; cf. *Letopis' rossiiskogo*, p. 752.
22. Nurgali Beisekov (1908–1959) graduated from the State Institute for Stage Art in Moscow in 1940 and directed a number of plays at the Kazakh Drama Theater in Alma-Ata. He was an assistant director at TsOKS working with Eizenshtein, Pudovkin, Roshal', and Aron; in later years, he specialized in documentary films.
23. Faizulla Absaliamov (1911–1993) became one of the leading Kazakh documentary cinematographers.
24. Erguzhinova was the birth name of the famous actress Amina Umurzakova.
25. The letter is archived in the Russian State Archive for Literature and Art (RGALI) and was published in Fomin, *Kino na voine*, pp. 511–13.
26. Ermolinskii was later assigned to the Tbilisi film studio for a project on Georgia. He was allowed to return to Moscow in 1949, his official rehabilitation followed in 1956; cf. *Letopis' rossiiskogo*, p. 687. Ermolinskii made a significant

contribution to Kazakh cinema as the author of the screenplay of *His Time Will Come* (Ego vremia pridet, 1957).

27. Evsei Abramovich Iofis (1905–1978) was Soviet cameraman and pedagogue.

28. Siranov, "V sem'e edinoi," p. 61.

29. There is confusion about the content of this almanac. Some sources claim that *War Film Almanac 12* consisted of *Son of a Fighter* and *Batyrs of the Steppes* (Batyry stepei); even an overall title, *Kazakh Novellas* (Kazakhskie novelly), can occasionally be found. However, the extant copies of the twelfth war film almanac show that its second part is not Kazakhstan-related, while *Batyrs of the Steppes* did not become part of an almanac but was released separately. Cf. *Letopis' rossiiskogo*, p. 753.

30. Curiously, the authoritative *History of Soviet Cinema* grossly misrepresents the story: "[The film] praises the noble deed of the fighter Aimanov who saves a Russian child during a battle with the fascists and adopts it." *Istoriia sovetskogo kino*, vol. 3, 1941–1952. Moskva: Izdatel'stvo 'Iskusstvo,' 1975, p. 226. Similarly, Kabysh Siranov in his synopsis leaves out that Vorob'ev at first is not fond of children, thus depriving the story of its most important psychological element. Cf. Siranov, "V sem'e edinoi," p. 52.

31. Vorob'ev's demonstrative coldness (likely meant to signify a feature that is typical of snipers) nonetheless seems strange and unnatural.

32. There is conflicting information about the director of this film. For example, Siranov 1958, p. 16, ascribes the film to Vera Stroeva. However, the official catalogue of Soviet feature films names Roshal' as the director and Stroeva as his assistant.

33. The reason why *Giants of the Steppe* was categorized as a "film almanac," even though there was no other film attached to it, is unclear. One possible explanation is that it was initially meant to be paired with *Son of a Fighter*, which would indeed have resulted in "Kazakh Novellas." Perhaps in order to not single out Kazakhs, as opposed to other nationalities, that plan may have been dropped altogether. Cf. the film's entry in Macheret, Aleksandr, and Nina Glagoleva, eds. *Sovetskie khudozhestvennye fil'my. Annotirovannyi katalog Gosfil'mofonda SSSR.* 5 vols. Moscow: Iskusstvo, 1961–1979, vol. 2, pp. 290–91.

34. Siranov, "Nachalo bol'shogo puti," p. 64.

35. Other sources: Dzhakpan.

36. It was not included in the comprehensive catalogue *Sovetskie khudozhestvennye fil'my. Annotirovannyi katalog*. Moskva: Iskusstvo, 1961.

37. Evgenii Margolit, Viacheslav Shmyrov, *Iz"iatoe kino*. Moskva: Double D, 1995, pp. 86–87. No documents outlining the film's prohibition could be found. Moreover, according to one source, there is no copy of the film in the Soviet State Film Archive. However, Kulshara Ainagulova claims that Gosfil'mofond does own a copy (Ainagulova, K., "Kak sozdavalas' 'Belaia roza'," *Kazakhstanskaia Pravda*, 13 April 1975).

38. Siranov, *Kazakhskoe kinoiskusstvo*, p. 17.

39. Its alternate title was *Kazakh Film Concert* (Kazakhskii kinokontsert).

40. One of the assistant directors was Karl Gakkel, who a decade later played a crucial role as Shaken Aimanov's codirector on his first Kazakh feature films.

41. Siranov, "Nachalo bol'shogo puti," p. 65.

42. Other sources list the release year as 1942: cf. *Dziga Vertov, Iz naslediia. T. 1 Dramaturgicheskie opyty*. Moskva, Eizenshtein-tsentr, 2004, p. 505.

43. These manuscripts were published in *Dziga Vertov, Iz naslediia. T. 1 Dramaturgicheskie opyty*. Moskva, Eizenshtein-tsentr, 2004, pp. 370–411. The differences between various versions are considerable. Closest to the actual film is *Kazakhstan—frontu* (pp. 401–410). Vertov's frustrations during the war years are reflected in his diaries; cf. *Kino-Eye: The Writings of Dziga Vertov* (ed. by Annette Michelson). Los Angeles and London: University of California Press, 1984, pp. 244–248. The screenplay that is published in that volume under the title *To You, Front!* is not identical with the film.

44. Siranov, "Nachalo bol'shogo puti," p. 68.

45. Siranov, *Kazakhskoe kinoiskusstvo*, p. 20

46. Ibid.

47. Boris Ivanovich Iurtsev (1900–1954) was a screenwriter, director, and actor who began his career in Eizenshtein's Proletkult theater in 1922; in 1935, he was arrested and spent several years in the GULAG. His attempt to make a comeback in the Alma-Ata studio in 1946 failed.

48. *Letopis's rossiiskogo*, p. 805.

49. *Letopis' rossiiskogo*, p. 821.

*Chapter 3*

# The Third Birth

When the world war was over, there could be no doubt that Soviet culture had done its utmost to help achieve the victory over Nazi Germany. It seemed that now the Communist Party should be able to trust writers, composers, painters, and filmmakers, whom it had patronized so aggressively in the years prior to the war. Alas, the opposite happened. As if to demonstrate that only the communist leadership had the ability to determine who was worthy and who did not pass muster, the ideological and terror campaigns of the 1930s were reignited. None of the wartime accomplishments counted anymore, and the artistic intelligentsia, exhausted from war deprivations and administrative hyper-control, was harassed with one ideological assault after another. Merely a year after the great victory, Soviet cinema, too, became a major target of the political establishment's wrath.

On May 20, 1946, the secretary for ideology of the Communist Party, Andrei Zhdanov, together with Grigorii Aleksandrov (no relation to the director) and film minister Ivan Bol'shakov sent a memo to Stalin, declaring that not only had the production volume of feature films decreased twofold during the Great Patriotic War, but the artistic quality had diminished as well.[1] The memo triggered a debate in the upper echelons of the Soviet cultural administration about the best strategies for increasing film production without compromising artistic and ideological standards. The resulting policies were inconsistent, meandering from one extreme to another and imposing a draconian set of rules that was eventually replaced by no less draconian, but equally inefficient measures. The main victims of this administrative hyper-activity were individual directors such as Grigorii Kozintsev and Aleksandr Dovzhenko whose projects dragged on for years, undergoing revision after revision and driving their makers into a state of desperation and creative stupor.

Even worse were the effects of these interminable intrusions into the filmmaking process in the national film studios. While the major studios in the Russian Federation, Mosfilm and Lenfilm, could maintain at least a minimal output of mostly unremarkable, formulaic, and dogmatic pictures, feature film production in the national studios practically came to a halt.[2] To be sure, in 1946, the situation in Alma-Ata still seemed stable. In March, thirty-two-year-old Kabysh Siranov, now the director of the Alma-Ata Feature Film Studio (the new official name established by governmental decree on January 25, 1944) gave an interview to the Communist Party newspaper *Kazakhstanskaia Pravda*, titled "Kazakhstani Cinema in 1946."[3] He announced that *Semetei, the Son of Manas*, a large-scale production with 2,000 extras, was currently being shot in Kyrgyzstan and Kazakhstan. The second project was *The Enchanted Sergeant*, directed by Eduard Pentslin, whose cast consisted of the graduates of the first Kazakh film acting school. (Originally, on May 13, 1945, the Film Committee had assigned Boris Iurtsev to the Alma-Ata studio to direct *The Enchanted Sergeant* [Ocharovannyi serzhant]).

However, Siranov's pride in these two projects proved to be premature. The production of *The Enchanted Sergeant* was stopped late in 1946, after about one-third of the film had been completed,[4] and the large-scale *Semetei* was also shut down. Now the studio was without any project presentable to the authorities. The crisis was particularly obvious because the situation stood in such sharp contrast to the productive TsOKS years.

On July 31, 1946, the Council of Ministers of the USSR issued a decree about the creation of new Ministries of Cinema in the Azerbaijani SSR, the Georgian SSR, the Belarusian SSR, and the Kazakhstani SSR.[5] Such official measures to restructure the hierarchy and nomenclature of the film industry were intended to give the impression that a solution was being implemented, but what difference could it make? How could the renaming of the Administration for Cinefication at the Council of People's Commissars of the Kazakh SSR, which had been established in 1938, as the Ministry of Cinema of the Kazakh SSR (*Ministerstvo kinematografii Kazakhskoi SSR*) really improve the situation? Perhaps the fact that Kazakhstan's first film minister, Valiia Iakubov, would be a permanent member of the highest executive body of the Kazakh Soviet Socialist Republic, which, at least formally, increased the status of cinema, setting it apart from the other cultural branches overseen by the Ministry of Culture. But in reality, such changes yielded no measurable effect as long as the stiff and paranoid bureaucratic management remained the same, turning the postwar period into one of the least noteworthy in the history of the Alma-Ata studio. Surely, Kazakhstan now had its own national studio, yet only one director, Efim Aron, worked there on a permanent basis, while others were hired from the outside for select projects before returning to their Russian home studios. The inadequate personnel situation alone made continuous project development and the actual production of feature films impossible, to say nothing about the demoralizing effect of ongoing ideological interferences.

As previously demonstrated with *Amangeldy* and *Raikhan*, in response to external pressure, Kazakh film officials usually chose the path of maximal thematic and political safety. Thus, it is no coincidence that they resorted to the biographical picture, the Stalinist genre of choice, which combined national themes with cinematic formulas.

## THE SONGS OF ABAI

Grigorii Roshal' and Efim Aron's *The Songs of Abai* (Pesni Abaia), which was released on January 20, 1946, was the first completed feature project at Alma-Ata film studio after the end of TsOKS.[6] Mukhtar Auezov, whose multi-volume epic about nineteenth-century enlightener Abai was to become the greatest achievement of Kazakh prose in the twentieth century, had written a screenplay that was both poetic and melodramatic, and also offered the necessary space for the ideological messages that any biopic in the 1940s had to include. But Auezov was too much of an artist and the towering figure of Abai Kunanbaev too much of a sacred topic to allow for a simple application of preapproved formulas. Thus, with an implicit mild deviation from Stalinist standards, Auezov proposed an unusual plot structure, depicting the Kazakh renaissance man as a living human being with genuine feelings, an individual who does not stand alone on a pedestal but lives in the very midst of his people. Abai is shown as a wise and revered intellectual who deeply empathizes with the poor and disenfranchised. To bring this empathy to life was the main purpose of a fictitious love drama that Auezov combined with the biographical portrait proper. As a result, *The Songs of Abai* became a noteworthy variation of the Stalinist biopic, avoiding a simplistic outline of the life of an outstanding creative individual. Instead of a didactic illustration of biographical facts, the film provides a portrait of Abai in his time, focusing on his conflicts with contemporary society: both Russian colonial rule and the Kazakh clan system.

To be sure, the opening images do convey the grandiose monumental spirit typical of Soviet biopics. Following introductory shots of the majestic landscape, Abai is shown walking with a book in his hand, touching a *kurgan*.[7]

His first conversation is with a Russian archeologist named Dolgopolov, who opines about an unearthed human skull. This scene is supposed to convey Abai's materialist worldview and his openness to modern science. Then, some regular Kazakhs ask him to recite his poetry, which he readily agrees to do; the camera illustrates his words with beautiful images. Thus, Abai's

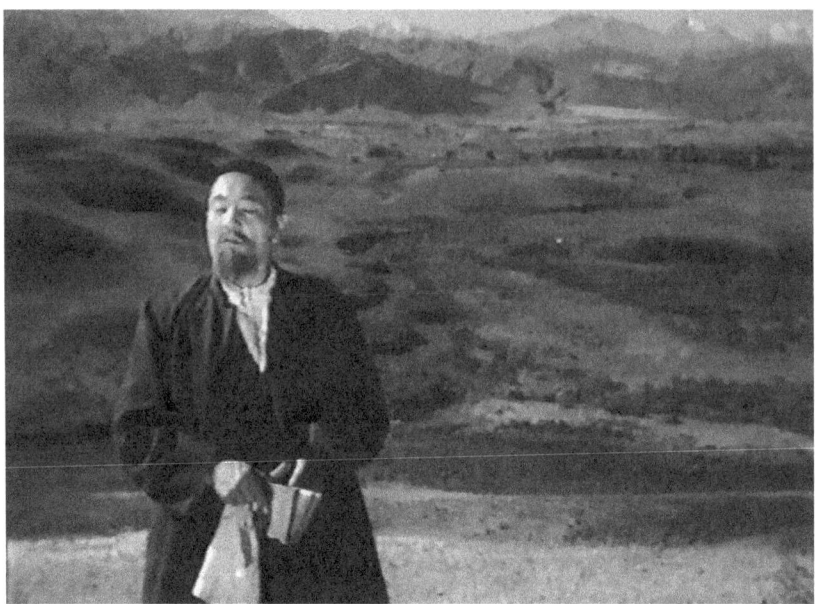

**Figure 3.1  Kalibek Kuanyshpaev in the Role of Abai.** Source: *The Songs of Abai* (1945, Grigorii Roshal')

second sphere of creativity, poetry, is brought to the fore. The sudden appearance of horsemen interrupts that idyll. The men are chasing two young lovers whose story demonstrates the cruelty of the traditional patriarchy. Ancient law demanded that the young woman, Azhar (Amina Erguzhinova), marry the brother of her deceased husband, the old Narymbet, but she resisted, wishing to marry the man she really loved, Aidar (Kapan Badyrov), a young poet who also happens to be Abai's favorite disciple. Not surprisingly, Abai sides with the lovers against the law and his authority is powerful enough to initiate court deliberations about the case. Abai's disciple, the ambitious yet insecure Sharip (Shaken Aimanov), fails to make a convincing case against Narymbet's lawyer (a so-called *bii*), and Abai has no choice but to become the defender himself.

Here, Auezov's strategy of combining biopic and melodrama pays off: the love story generates human interest, much more than even the most appealing portrait of a genius ever could. Conceptually, the story of the two lovers conveys the necessity of modernization: ancient moral rules are depicted as inhumane, and to implement them literally would be both heartless and reactionary. Not surprisingly, the militant Kazakh traditionalists in the film are allied with the Russian tsarist authorities. Colonialism is depicted as the safest framework within which to secure the harsh order of sharia law. Abai's eloquent interference saves the two lovers, even though the judge admits that,

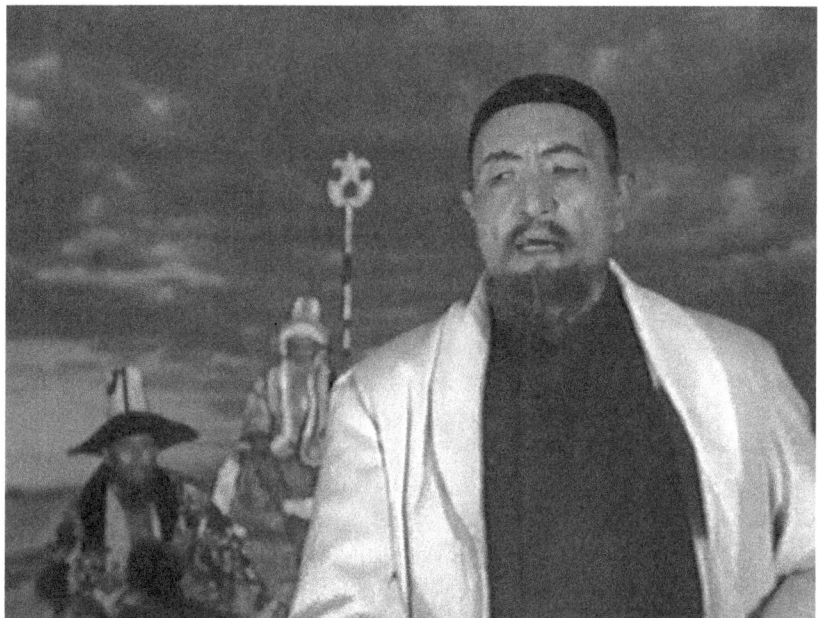

**Figure 3.2  The Defender of Justice.** *The Songs of Abai* (1945, Grigorii Roshal')

according to formal rules, they are guilty. Abai is shown as a talented lawyer and rhetorician who skillfully uses the audience's reactions to gain support for Aidar and Azhar. The lovers eventually became the main characters of Abai's famous poem "Spring."

Despite its unusual plot structure, which transformed the more linear Soviet genre clichés, *The Songs of Abai* remains within ideologically safe territory, endorsing a number of Stalinist dogmas.[8] Thus, Dolgopolov lends Abai books on science and aesthetics (Darwin, Chernyshevskii), pointing to the role of Russian progressive intellectuals as educators and mentors of developing peoples. In turn, the Russians recognize Abai's extraordinary stature; indeed, Dolgopolov writes in a letter about the "Republic of Abai," a renaissance island in the middle of the steppes. Heavy emphasis is placed on the rootedness of Abai's creativity in the world of rank-and-file people, a must for all Stalinist biopics. But this is not just a nod to cultural officialdom: the film vindicates Auezov's own concept of Abai as a man whose genius sprang from the very depth of the Kazakh people and whose poetry was nourished by an intense interaction with commoners. The fact that this concept coincides with the communist dogma of culture (namely, that genuine art stems from the people, denoting the principle of populism/*narodnost'*), legitimized it ideologically.

Abai is shown composing his music while listening to singing girls, that is, folklore serves him as direct inspiration. This points to another ideological rule: only music inspired by the people and comprehensible to everyone can be considered genuine art. This was a core motif in all Stalinist biopics about composers such as Glinka (1946, 1953) and Musorgskii (1951).

And, of course, there is always an enemy lurking in the shadows who must be exposed and neutralized. In *The Songs of Abai*, it is Abai's jealous disciple, Sharip, whose personal ambition outweighs all ethical considerations, although he does stop short of killing the master himself. To mobilize viewers' emotions against this evil individualist, the film has him poison his competitor, the dashing Aidar, who just defeated Sharip in a poetic competition. The presence of a ruthless mortal enemy, who tries to undermine Abai's connection with the Kazakh people, projects Stalinist hatred and paranoia onto the nineteenth century. Indeed, the film's ideological frame is profoundly Soviet and, as a result, ahistorical in several respects.

It would be easy to blame the two non-Kazakh directors for the film's conceptual opportunism, which diminishes its persuasiveness, but it is hard to imagine what native Kazakh filmmakers could have done differently at the time. After all, the screenplay was written by the greatest Kazakh writer of the twentieth century, who incorporated required Stalinist dogmas, albeit reluctantly. In other words, the problematic aspects of *The Songs of Abai* cannot be explained by the mixed ethnicity of its cast; its dilemma was in many ways unavoidable, whether the filmmakers were Russian or Kazakh. Considering the many pressures under which cinema found itself in the mid-1940s, *The Songs of Abai* certainly is not the worst imaginable picture about Abai. The film's indisputable qualities include artistic aspects such as the performances. To be sure, the acting is generally theatrical and declarative, no different than in other Soviet Stalinist biopics. However, certain performances are exceptional, particularly Kalibek Kuanyshpaev's portrayal of Abai that often manages to overcome the prescribed stale monumentality.

One point of criticism raised against the film was the abundance of secondary plotlines, which purportedly renders the plot brittle.[9] Indeed, Auezov's screenplay included an episode that later became significant for his novel *Abai*, namely the attack of a neighboring clan, led by the *bay* Erden, on Abai's *aul*. Abai, always a man of peace and reconciliation, risks his own life to prevent bloodshed. However, rather than taking away from plot cohesion, such episodes transcend the formulaic framework of Stalinist biography and add important facets to the depiction of Kazakhstan, demonstrating the Kazakh nation's complex history.

The fact that Soviet-Kazakh cinema chose the greatest nineteenth-century Kazakh intellectual for its second biopic after *Amangeldy* is remarkable in and of itself. After all, most of this thinker's rich and multifaceted legacy is as far as can be from Marxist theory, a circumstance that the film carefully avoids. Despite a clear selectiveness regarding the biographical facts (Abai's religious and spiritual views, as well as his existential pessimism, are not mentioned at all), the film's philosophical one-sidedness is outweighed by its genuine respect for this exceptional representative of Kazakh culture and the believable depiction of the Kazakh people's love for Abai.[10] Within its historical paradigm, *The Songs of Abai*, despite many shortcomings, remains a worthwhile picture to this day.

## IMPLEMENTING STALINIST NORMS

While Kazakhstan celebrated the release of its third full-length feature, and the first to be completed by its national studio on its own, the Soviet cultural establishment continued its experiments designed to render film production more efficient. Essentially, and in addition to thematic priorities and aesthetic parameters, the relations between center and periphery had to be defined in unambiguous terms; thus, the document establishing ministries of cinema in several Soviet republics outlines the responsibilities of these ministries and the terms of their subordination to the central ministry of film. However, subordination and control mechanisms do not stimulate creativity but rather stifle it, as the late 1940s demonstrate.

At a meeting of the "all-Soviet film workers," where the Communist Party Central Committee's decision to prohibit the second part of Leonid Lukov's miners' saga *A Great Life*, was discussed, Film Minister Ivan Bolshakov aimed sharply worded remarks at all Soviet studios, including Kazakhstan's. "The Alma-Ata studio in 1945 made one picture, *Abai*. In 1946, due to the cancellation of the production of *The Enchanted Sergeant* and *Semetei, the Son of Manas*, the studio is currently doing nothing at all."[11] He went on to criticize the studio's artistic director, Grigorii Roshal': "The local government likes him, but comrade Roshal' spends three-quarters of the year in Moscow. What kind of work is that? The artistic director has to manage the studio, not live in Moscow and visit the studio only as a kind of tourist." Bol'shakov's broadside yielded no effect. The following year, not one feature film was released by the Alma-Ata studio, and the Soviet press took notice.[12]

Scathing criticism notwithstanding, the creation of administrative structures that were assigned responsibility for Kazakhstan's fledgling film industry was in itself noteworthy. The vital question was: How could the production of feature films be stimulated? According to the Soviet film minister, the most pressing problem was the lack of good screenplays, especially stories dealing with contemporary issues. Bol'shakov opined: "The excessive indulgence of national studios in the depiction of life in the past and the absence of films about the present has had a very negative effect on the situation of national film cultures. The Soviet people do not wish to see how tsars and khans lived, they want to see the contemporary life of their republics, they want to see what Soviet power has given the people of these republics, how their culture and their economy have grown."[13] A direct consequence of that strong criticism was *The Golden Horn* (Zolotoi rog, 1948), a film about scientists working in Kazakhstan. For several years, it remained the only feature film completed at the Alma-Ata studio.

The inner workings of the studio in those years are difficult to assess. Documents shedding light on the production process, decision-making, and Party meetings have yet to be unearthed. For unknown reasons, the administration discarded a number of screenplays that had already been approved, and assigned new projects to leading authors such as Mukhtar Auezov and Gabit Musrepov.[14] In March 1948, a department of film dramaturgy was organized as part of the Union of Kazakh Writers,[15] designed to encourage the creation of screenplays by both established and budding authors. At the same time, the leadership of Kazakhstan's film production once again became the target of harsh criticism. On April 4, 1948, a collective complaint about the "unhealthy situation" at Alma-Ata Film Studio was sent to *Pravda* and the secretary for ideology of the Central Committee of the Communist Party, Andrei Zhdanov. The authors pointed to specific problems, such as nationalism, corruption, the suppression of criticism, and moral degeneracy among leading studio administrators.[16]

*The Golden Horn* was released on June 24, 1948. It is the most explicitly Stalinist film in the history of Kazakhstani cinema. Its production was keenly observed by the press; for example, the newspaper *The Altai Bolshevik* reported about the shooting and the screenplay.[17] The film addresses a topic that was considered cutting-edge in the 1940s: genetics, its ideological underpinnings, and its economic effects. Once again, a Kazakh feature film followed ideological paths established by the central studios. Prominent film directors in the Soviet center, such as Abram Room and Fridrikh Ermler, had devoted officially acclaimed dramas to the purported "class struggle" in the sphere of genetics, which was viewed as part of the global geopolitical confrontation between advancing communism and degenerating capitalism. The screenplay of *The Golden Horn*, written by the Shatrov brothers, gave the issue a Kazakh coloration. Its central character is one of Kazakhstan's most qualified scientists, young Zhakan Dasanov (Shaken Aimanov). He strives to create a perfect hybrid by combining the features of regular sheep and mountain goats. This hybrid would be able to withstand the cruel weather conditions in winter and would not require the traditional and laborious translocation from the mountains to warmer regions every year.

*The Golden Horn* follows the patterns of plot development that were obligatory in Stalinist cinema: the young enthusiast has supporters (in this case, his beautiful assistant Saule, as well as regular workers from the neighboring

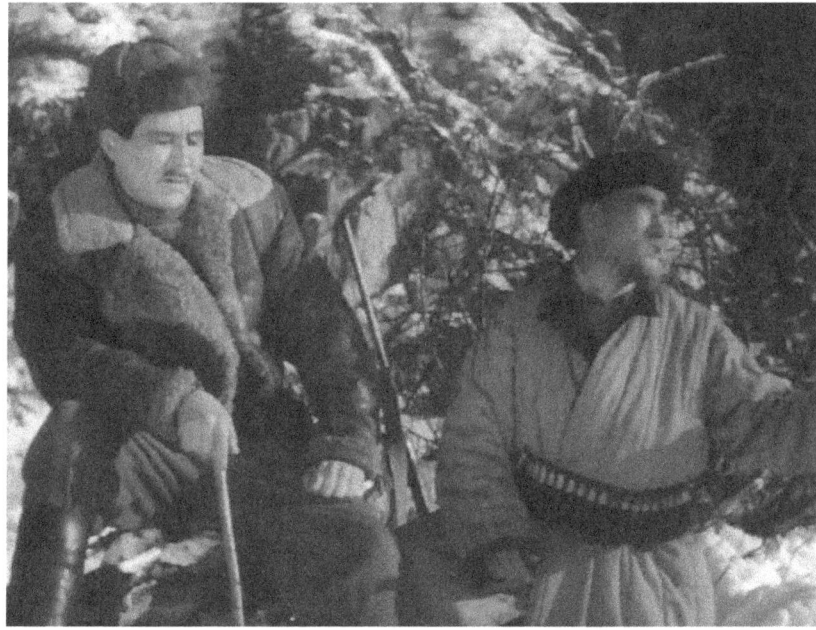

**Figure 3.3** **Shaken Aimanov (left) in the role of Zhakan.** *The Golden Horn* (1948, Efim Aron)

kolkhoz) and antagonists (mostly careerist scientists, who declare the hybridization scientifically impossible because it contradicts Western theories of genetics). As might be expected, the antagonists are eventually proven wrong, and the Party leadership, which had trusted the innovators all along, offers its generous encouragement and protection.

Director Efim Aron and cameraman Aleksandr Petrov present Kazakhstan as an idyll of wondrous beauty (the film takes place in the Zailiisk Alatau mountains). The gorgeous peaks shine as if waiting to be conquered, as do the proud Arkhar goats whose horns shimmer like gold in the sunlight—hence the film's title. Shaken Aimanov in the lead role imbues the character of the young scientist with unrelenting, at times excessive physical mobility.

Whether hunting a male goat to initiate the insemination of a mother sheep or begging the kolkhoz for more of the rare animals, Zhakan is always jumping, running, yelling. For him, nothing is done fast enough, and his tone toward colleagues is often rude. However, Zhakan's coworkers do not seem to mind, as this kind of loudmouth authoritarian impatience had become a cliché of Stalinist culture and a marker of innovative drive, whereas thoughtfulness and skepticism were denounced as defeatist, if not symptoms of clandestine sabotage altogether. From a modern standpoint, to place this type of

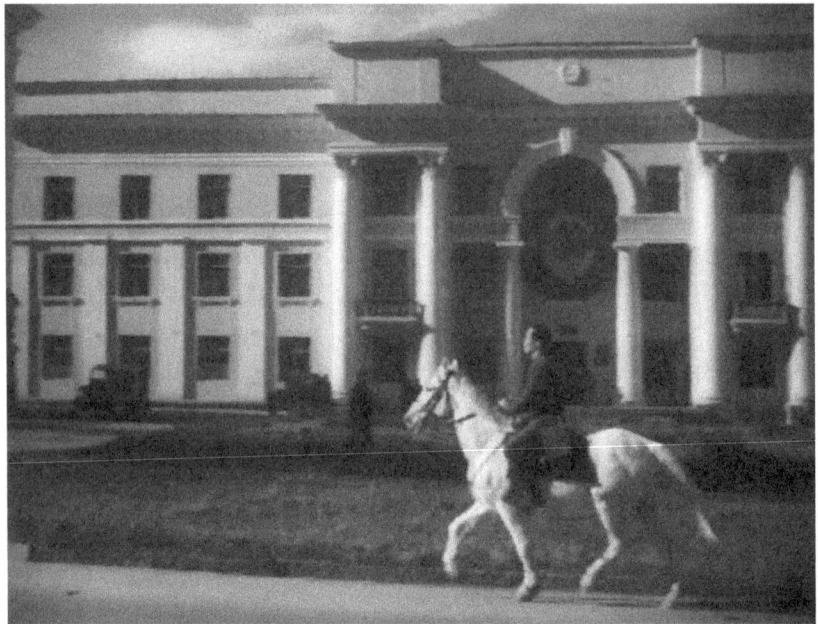

**Figure 3.4 On Horseback to the Capital.** *The Golden Horn* (1948, Efim Aron)

blind enthusiasm in the milieu of scientists and endorse it as exemplary was particularly precarious, indicating that any scholarly debate was unnecessary as long as the ideologically correct arguments were voiced. The suspicion that Zhakan's boisterous disorganization and refusal to consider alternative arguments may have been the actual cause for the terrible losses of rare sheep suffered at the institute may enter the viewer's mind (after all, four out of five inseminated merino sheep die, while the fifth escapes and is shot by an unsuspecting Russian hunter), but such rational arguments are never entertained by any of the characters. Aimanov's acting supports this questionable endorsement of a high-risk, hothead leadership style in the sciences. No matter how severe the resulting catastrophes, the project is being pursued with even greater stubbornness, making ever larger investments in a questionable cause. The viewer must conclude that Zhakan's ultimate success is based not so much on rational arguments, but on faith.

In hindsight, that which was meant to convey innovative decisiveness appears as obsessive impulsiveness and thoughtless endangerment of life and precious resources. Although unintentionally, *The Golden Horn* de facto exposes the incompetence at the root of the Soviet economy during the Stalin period, its shameless willingness to turn any defeat into victory by means of mere rhetoric. To make this concept work on screen, the characters had to be reduced to ideologically defined "goodies" and "baddies." Only on rare occasions are some real human features allowed to break through the cardboard characterizations. Thus, Zhakan's young assistant Saule (Liailia Galimzhanova) clearly suffers from his lack of personal attention—she wants to be more than just a devoted subordinate and at one point complains to her boss that he talks about her as if she was already dead. Besides the devoted Saule, who conveys warm femininity and care, another performance stands out: Raisa Koichubaeva's portrayal of a kolkhoz chairwoman. This character has an authentic natural humor that stands in noticeable contrast vis-à-vis the many bloodless constructions and their endless speechifying.

The official *History of Soviet Cinema* criticized *The Golden Horn* for its faux conflicts and the ease with which they are resolved. "From the very beginning, the majority sides with the main character: the old professor and mentor, the kolkhoz members who assign sheep for the experiment, the wise herdsman, and the student intern, Saule. Regarding the retrogrades, they are not particularly threatening either: the pseudoscientist-cum-schemer, who remains in pitiful isolation, and the director of the institute (. . .), who immediately sides with progress after the minister's explanations."[18] These characterizations are largely accurate, although the film never exclusively focuses on conflicts between scientists (as did Room's and Ermler's pamphlets about genetics). The real issue at the heart of *The Golden Horn* is one that has long tormented the Kazakh people—the need to take hundreds of thousands of sheep to safer pastures in the wintertime using an ancient approach that comes with huge dangers and losses. Zhakan is motivated by the urge to find a solution to this age-old dilemma; after all, he is a passionate scientist and a true Kazakh-Soviet patriot.

The main foe in *The Golden Horn* is not the off-putting, scheming Professor Turdukulov (Eleubai Umurzakov) who has no better argument than to quote Western authorities ad nauseam, but nature itself. This is one of the major differences between *The Golden Horn* and its Russian predecessors, in which the ideological debates about genetics constituted the films' substance. While nature is generally depicted as harmonious and even idyllic in the Kazakh film, storms and avalanches continue to cause problems for the economy by destroying livestock. According to *The Golden Horn*, it is up to inventive scientists such as Zhakan Dasanov to outwit nature's powerful destructiveness and create a breed of sheep that can withstand frost and snow. In the end, when the newly created herd of "arkharo-merino"[19] sheep emerges unharmed from a severe storm, Zhakan, who almost perished in an avalanche, has made his case to the country and to the viewer.

*The Golden Horn* features many elements typical of Soviet films in the late 1940s: artificially designed and ideologically correct characters; the constant virtual presence of leaders (Stalin and Lenin portraits adorning the walls); bombastic music; and the absence of any believable humanity in the conflicts. But would it be fair to say that *The Golden Horn* is nothing more than a mechanical application of Stalinist thematic and aesthetic principles to Kazakh subject matter?

Not entirely. As a matter of fact, inside the predictable shell of a Stalinist ideological drama hides a small cinematic gem that, regrettably, has been ignored by film historians. In this particular episode, Zhakan talks to a teenage boy who is enthralled by the novels of Jules Verne and dreams of traveling to faraway places. The scientist encourages the boy to imagine himself on a legendary magic horse that will take him to a country with beautiful cities and gigantic factories. The boy and the viewer begin to realize that Zhakan is referring not to some foreign place but to Kazakhstan itself and how it will look in the future. Here, in the middle of the film, the authors risked inserting something extraordinary: Zhakan's story is illustrated by combined animation/live action in which the boy is seen on a flying horse above the mountains and rivers, dams, and power stations.

Psychologically, this three-minute insert is plausible, showing Zhakan as a dreamer whose powerful imagination can inspire others. Moreover, the episode slightly lowers the criteria of realism for the film as a whole, moving it in the direction of utopia rather than claiming to be a realistic contemporary

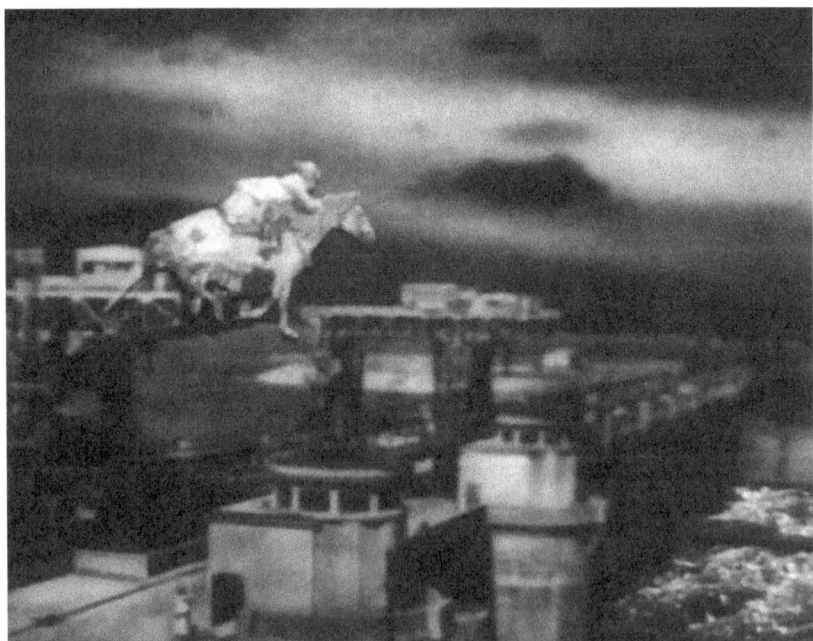

Figure 3.5 **The Flying Horse—combined animation and live action.** *The Golden Horn* (1948, Efim Aron)

*The Third Birth* 69

drama. But the most important aspect of this brief episode is its cinematic innovativeness—it uses a special effect in an unexpected but plausible manner. Equally significant is its national relevance: in invoking an ancient myth, the bland contemporary story suddenly acquires an element of "Kazakhness."

Another small episode continues this line of genuine national values, although without visual effects. When Saule lectures the old shepherd, who will take the arkharo-merinos to the mountains, he interrupts her and asks, "How long have you studied, girl?" She answers, "About fifteen years." To which he responds, with a sheepish smile, "And I have studied a thousand years: I learned from my father, and he from his father, and so on." Then he sings a joyous folksong in Kazakh, while his traditionalist argument goes undisputed.

Despite such snippets of ancient dream and wisdom, the most fundamental concept proposed by *The Golden Horn* is the enmity between man and nature, which is a profoundly Soviet idea. On the one hand, this enmity is treated in the film as a given; on the other, it is framed as something that should not be accepted with humility, but rather warrants heroic and intelligent resistance. Zhakan is conceptualized as a quasi-promethean hero who refuses to bow to nature's unforgiving laws. Instead, he uses the advances of Russian and Soviet biology to defeat nature and come out on top. Of course, this resolution

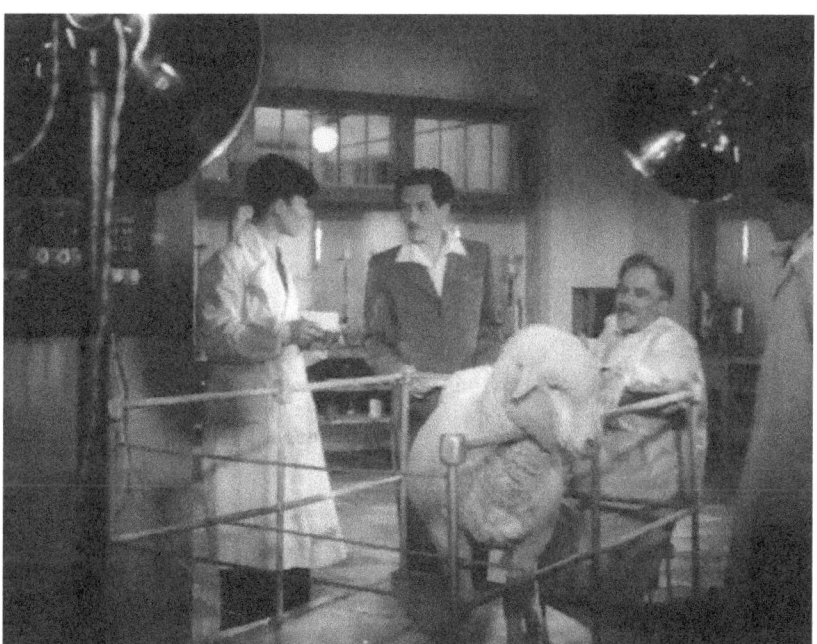

**Figure 3.6  The New Breed in the Lab.** *The Golden Horn* (1948, Efim Aron)

is problematic insofar as a radical juxtaposition of man and nature is not part of the Kazakh tradition. On the contrary, the assumption of nature's wisdom is axiomatic for the national heritage. Thus, Zhakan himself, much like his "arkharo-merino sheep," comes across as an artificial creation, planted in the Kazakh mountains for reasons of ideological servitude and dogmatism. This may be the deeper reason for Shaken Aimanov's failure to portray Zhakan in a persuasive manner.

*The Golden Horn*, announced as a major cultural event in its day,[20] was safely forgotten in the decades thereafter. However, as an illustration of Stalinist ideology and aesthetics in Kazakh culture, the film is priceless.

## BACK TO THE BIOPIC: *DZHAMBUL*

Meanwhile, the organizational problems surrounding the emerging Kazakhstani film industry continued. On August 2, 1948, Stalin personally rejected a request from the Council of Ministers of the Kazakh SSR to declare losses in the amount of 242,310 rubles incurred during the construction of the film theater "Kazakhstan" in Alma-Ata; his advice was to find and punish the administrators responsible for the loss.[21] Also in August 1948, the film acting school in Alma-Ata was shut down. However, later that year, the Council of Ministers of the USSR gave permission to open a school for film projectionists in Alma-Ata for 200 students. As of 1949, the number of stationary and mobile film projectors had returned to prewar levels, with 1,257 projectors total, of which 1,157 were servicing the countryside.[22]

In a manner resembling the 1940 campaign that had cost Moisei Levin his professional certification, in 1949, the personnel department (*upravlenie kadrov*) of the Ministry of Cinema of the USSR launched a campaign to professionally test all specialists working in Soviet cinema. As a result, a considerable number of film workers were fired. At the Alma-Ata film studio, eighteen people lost their jobs.[23] Repressive measures against writers and artists continued as well. Thus, one of the most promising screenwriters and administrators at Kazakhfilm studio, Kabysh Siranov, was arrested in 1946 and spent eight years in the GULAG. The director of the Kazakh National Philharmonic, Ilias Esenberlin, was also arrested and sentenced to ten years of hard labor.[24]

At the same time, the efforts of the Kazakhstani film bureaucracy to please central authorities by emulating normative Soviet productions yielded no demonstrable effect. Conspicuously, in terms of official recognition, neither *The Songs of Abai* nor *The Golden Horn* were awarded Stalin Prizes, unlike feature films made at other Central Asian studios. In 1952, the cast of the *theater* production of Auezov's drama *Abai*, including Shaken Aimanov,

Kapan Badyrov, Kalibek Kuanyshpaev, and Hadisha Bukeeva, received Stalin Prizes.[25] But Kazakhstani feature films had yet to receive any prize at all!

After *The Golden Horn*, it took the Alma-Ata studio four years to release another feature film: *Dzhambul* (aka *Zhambyl*, 1952), a biopic about the famed *akyn* (or *aqyn*) Dzhambul Dzhabaev,[26] who had passed away in 1945 after becoming an all-Soviet celebrity in the prior two decades. Unlike Auezov and Aron with *The Songs of Abai*, the film's director, Efim Dzigan, made no attempt to push the envelope aesthetically but did his utmost to follow the norms of the biographical genre that had been established in the mid-1930s to late 1940s. The depiction of the title character as a near-perfect human being was mandatory; no weaknesses, however minor, were permissible. The ideological scrutiny to which all Soviet biographical feature films were subjected was thorough and petty. Time and time again, directors were forced to rewrite and reshoot entire episodes due to criticism from the highest offices, especially from Stalin himself, who had very specific ideas about how great men of the past should be presented on screen.

The choice of Dzhambul as the subject of a biopic was no accident. The art form of improvised singing was highly respected in Kazakhstan, and *akyns* often enjoyed a nation-wide authority that far surpassed their actual position on the socioeconomic ladder. However, Dzigan's film claims that their true recognition came only with the advent of Soviet power, whereas in the nineteenth century class-based bias and repression hampered the native minstrels and their art. Be this as it may, the traveling bards always formed an order of their own, with an internal hierarchy that was based in part on seniority, but mostly on individual artistic prowess.

The film reconstructs Dzhambul's life from the Soviet point of departure, when the octogenarian singer-poet who improvised his lyrics and accompanied himself on the dombra, was elevated to a living legend and surrounded by Soviet state care and cult. He demonstrated his appreciation in numerous poems and songs devoted to Stalin's leadership, the sacrifices of the Soviet people in the Great Patriotic War, and the expectation of a bright communist future for his homeland.

*Dzhambul* opens with a scene showing the dying *akyn* Suinbay,[27] who chooses Dzhambul as his successor. This high honor is symbolically presented by the senior artist handing over his dombra to the junior, a gesture that outrages older contestants for this recognition. Dzhambul, youthful and strong, sings on horseback and quickly gains popularity with his satirical wit. Fearlessly addressing social ills, he is adored by the oppressed Kazakhs, while the *bays* and the Russian colonial administration distrust and resent him. For example, Dzhambul is forced to ask a *bay*'s permission to marry the woman he loves, enduring humiliation as a result. Many *akyns* viewed themselves as entertainers whose clowning and joking was most welcome at weddings and folk festivities; Dzhambul, however, adds a distinct social dimension to his art. The respect afforded this form of artistry was such that even powerful officials had to comply. Discrimination or aggression in response to a satirical song would violate a powerful, albeit unwritten law. Thus, the arrogant *bay* Kadyrbai, who tries to insult Dzhambul by telling him to sing a song in honor of his dead dog, is ridiculed when Dzhambul makes him the target of a satirical assault and gets away with it. Worried about the dangerous political effects of Dzhambul's art, the Russian tsarist authorities try to bring the unruly artist under control. One day, the governor-general orders all *akyns* to sign a document obliging them to never stir up the people or challenge the Russian administration. Dzhambul, pretending to be illiterate, acquiesces by signing with his thumb. His face, though, expresses the deepest contempt for the procedure.

When the victory of the October Revolution is announced, Dzhambul's son, Algadai, tells him about the new nationalities policy issued by Lenin. The aging minstrel not only sympathizes with the declared goals of the revolution but joins the fight, preventing a *bay* from escaping with his huge herd of horses. Moreover, the old singer makes himself useful to the nascent communist culture: he travels from kolkhoz to kolkhoz, telling their members how successful the neighboring kolkhoz is, thus inspiring competition for the best production results. In one of the concluding episodes, Dzhambul visits a high school and realizes that a new era has begun: children study in sparkling clean classrooms featuring pianos and globes. He tells the children about the horrors of the past, about freezes and starvation. The government honors the artist, to which he responds with unconditional loyalty, praising communist construction efforts.

The screenplay by prominent Russian playwright Nikolai Pogodin and Kazakh author Abdilda Tazhibaev was rendered with well-advised caution, avoiding the many pitfalls facing a film about a national artist who specialized in social satire. The project had been discussed in 1949 and the debate had been reported by the Communist Party newspaper.[28] Furthermore, excerpts from the screenplay had been published in the same newspaper: a sure sign of its ideological safety.[29] Several episodes emphasize the Russian-Kazakh progressive alliance even before the revolution; that, too, was an unwritten norm of Stalinist biopics. For example, one of the tsarist officers is democratically inclined and releases the old man from prison after witnessing how revered he is by his people. Another Russian returns Dzhambul's precious dombra to him.

In later years, Efim Dzigan was taken to task for his film's loose narrative structure, which left many episodes unrelated to one another (this argument was first formulated by the director Vera Stroeva in an article published in the journal *Iskusstvo kino*, 5/1953). However, Soviet biopics of the 1940s and early 1950s were never meant to reflect a great individual's unique development in a cohesive manner. Rather, they were supposed to follow the law of historical development in Marxist-Leninist interpretation: from oppression under the tsar to liberation in the new communist society; from enforced isolation between artist and people to unity, making creative individuals truly "people's artists." Shaken Aimanov, in the third lead of his career, does his utmost to enrich the formulaic material and breathe life into ideological clichés, believably portraying Dzhambul both as a young minstrel and as an octogenarian. His performance is one of the film's saving graces. Indeed, Kulshara Ainagulova's (1990) praise is not exaggerated: "If one could erect a monument through acting, Aimanov did just that in the film 'Dzhambul'."[30] At the time of its release, Dzhambul was reviewed by virtually all Kazakhstani periodicals and received unequivocal praise.

Today, a historically fair analysis of *Dzhambul* is difficult to provide since the film was reedited in 1968 and the original version has disappeared. One can assume that all references to Stalin (who in the original version was portrayed by Mikheil Gelovani) and his nationality policies were eliminated from the redacted version. When *Dzhambul* was released on May 25, 1953, the canonical straight jacket for biopics was still in place but, with Stalin no longer in charge, it was clear that it would not take long for the genre scheme to crumble. Remarkably, with Mazhit Begalin's *His Time Will Come* (1957), Kazakhstan's cinema played a pioneering role in the process of redefining the Soviet biopic.

*Dzhambul*, however, firmly belongs to the outgoing model. For Soviet cinema as a whole, and for the genre of film biography in particular, *Dzhambul* is of minor interest, certainly less so than the more original *Songs of Abai*. However, for the cinema of Kazakhstan, Dzigan's picture (the first Kazakhstani feature film shot in color!) represents the completion of a distinct period, the end of an era during which the country's sole studio had to rely on nonnative artists and specialists to create feature films with Kazakh subject matter within the framework of Soviet genre conventions. The following decade was defined by an intensive search for a cinema that was national both in content and form and that opened the gateways for native film artists.

Looking at the meager output of the Alma-Ata film studio, it is obvious that by the early 1950s, the Stalinist phase of Kazakh-Soviet cinema had arrived at a dead end. It is telling that the full-length documentary *Soviet Kazakhstan* (Sovetskii Kazakhstan, 1950), directed by Muscovite Lidiia Stepanova, was officially recognized as the country's highest cinematic achievement: it was awarded a Stalin Prize in 1952, the first (and last) Kazakh film to be honored in this manner. Kazakhstanis Gabit Musrepov and Ivan Shukhov had contributed to its screenplay, and Mikhail Aranyshev[31] belonged to its team of cameramen, but for the most part, the film was a nonspecific, ultra-Soviet product, rendered according to the same aesthetic principles as dozens of other celebratory documentaries. Its picturesque images feature the most presentable industrial, agricultural, and cultural aspects of the Kazakhstani SSR: the Irtysh hydroelectric power plant, the Karaganda coal mines, cotton harvesting in Chimkent, the singer Kuliash Baiseitova, the writer Sabit Mukanov, and the president of the Kazakhstani Academy of Sciences Kanysh Satpaev, as well as prominent workers and kolkhoz farmers. In the postwar period, Stepanova had made this kind of film her specialty; for similar fare, she received a total of five Stalin Prizes.[32] In later years, though, her films were forgotten and her name eliminated from Soviet film encyclopedias. Thus, what was celebrated as a victory of the Alma-Ata film studio at the time, became a negligible quantity shortly thereafter.

As of 1952, however, the deputy film minister of the Kazakhstani SSR, Sabrasov, still publicly boasted about the government's enormous plans for Kazakh cinema, citing a number of screenplays that had been accepted or were already in pre-production: *Kazakh Steelworkers* by Gabit Musrepov; *The Expatriation*, also by Musrepov, about the struggle of Kazakh coal miners before the October revolution (this script was apparently later turned into the film *In Those Days*, 1970); *Energy* by Abdilda Tazhibaev[33]; and *Stars of the Steppe*, a comedy about the competition between two kolkhozes by Shakhmet Khusainov.[34] The titles promise ideologically normative fare, neither entertaining, nor aesthetically ambitious. Also on the list is a screenplay by Mukhtar Auezov about Abai, a theme that numerous directors were eager to take on.[35]

Few if any of these screenplays ever made it to the big screen. With Stalin's death on March 5, 1953, Soviet cinema in its entirety underwent a profound reorientation. On April 23, 1953, the Presidium of the Supreme Soviet of the Kazakh SSR issued a decree about the transformation of the republic's ministries. One of the outcomes was the abolition of the national film ministry, which was replaced by the Main Administration of Cinema within Kazakhstan's Ministry of Culture. One year later, it was renamed the Main Administration of Cinefication and Film Distribution of the Ministry of Culture of the Kazakh SSR.

However, much more important was one man's personal decision: the star of Kazakhstani theater, Shaken Aimanov, turned a unique historical opportunity into a veritable rebirth for Kazakhstani cinema.

## A NEW BEGINNING: *POEM ABOUT LOVE*

In the early 1950s, Shaken Aimanov decided to abandon the stage and devote himself entirely to cinema. His radical step raised eyebrows: nothing in the short history of Kazakhstani film suggested much potential that could attract an established mime whose theater career had been outstanding, while his appearances on screen were often unsatisfying, as he himself was the first to admit. Was Aimanov motivated by the realization that Kazakhstan would never see its own genuine national cinema art if it had to rely on non-Kazakh artists forever? Was he frustrated by acting in other people's films, the faults of which he clearly recognized? Whatever the case may be, Aimanov, a man in his late thirties, brought unprecedented energy and an abundance of ideas to Kazakh cinema, creating a multifaceted oeuvre, a fair and detailed assessment of which is still wanting. Although his directorial career lasted only seventeen years, the long-term effects of his decision to devote himself to film direction shaped Kazakhstani cinema for decades.

Aimanov's first directorial project was *Poem About Love* (Maxxabat turaly dastan/Poema o liubvi, 1953), a historical drama based on a Kazakh *Romeo and Juliet* that had been successfully adapted for the stage. The acclaimed theater production was the source of the movie, and in many ways it shows: *Poem About Love* is a work of transition. From the beginning, Aimanov reveals his film's theatrical origins with utmost candor: the credits state that the following is an adaptation of a stage production of *Kozy Korpesh and Baian Slu* at the National Kazakh Theater, directed by Moisei Goldblatt in 1953.

As the two halves of a transparent silken curtain open, a stage-like decoration appears, showing two yurts and an old man delivering a monologue. The man is the rich and stingy Karabai (Serke Kozhamkulov), who is worried about the impending marriage of his beautiful daughter, Baian. Inside one of the yurts, two women talk to him about Kozy, a young man to whom Baian was promised when both were children. Then, a group of horsemen appears. The group's leader is Kodar (Nurmukhan Zhanturin), a fierce warrior who wants Baian for himself. Baian, too, is surrounded by a group, but of girls. The female and the male cohorts engage in sometimes witty, sometimes serious verbal exchanges. Later, Kozy is hunting in the mountains, where a chance encounter with Baian takes place. Both are struck by the realization that they are strongly attracted to each other. Learning about the promise made seventeen years earlier by their fathers seals their fate: not only are they meant for each other by tradition, but they are also in love. Yet Kodar and his evil advisor do everything in their power to undermine the sacred vow. Besides, after his father's death, poor Kozy is no real match for the wealthy Baian. Kodar and his men meet Kozy and his friends in the steppe and challenge them to a fight; Kozy wins and takes his tied-up rival to his beloved's yurt. Later, however, when Kodar and Kozy fight again, the resentful Kodar repays Kozy's magnanimity by stabbing him in the back.

Gabit Musrepov's play puts strong emphasis on the story's class aspect: Kozy represents the strong and noble underdog, while Baian's father, Karabai, and Kodar stand for the wealthy establishment. However, this modern, quasi-Soviet reading of the legend can only go so far: the law of the steppe was valid for both rich and poor, and the vow made at one point between Kozy's and Baian's fathers can be invalidated neither on a whim nor for economic considerations. Furthermore, for the jealous Kodar, it is not so much the lower status of his rival that drives him to commit a heinous crime, but his own inability to accept fate and the mutual love of others. His aggressiveness is a character flaw rather than a symptom of his class status.

Conspicuously, both rich and poor characters support Baian and Kozy in their pursuit of love. Thus, the story's class dimension ultimately proves to be secondary. The lovers' tragedy is caused by human selfishness and male pride that cannot acquiesce to the inevitable. This became a recurring motif in Kazakhstani cinema: the betrayal of traditional rules and the fundamental envy that marks the inability or unwillingness of some individuals to tolerate the happiness of others. The motif would reappear in later groundbreaking works of Kazakh cinema such as Sultan Khodzhikov's *Kyz-Zhibek* (1971) and Akan Sataev's *Zhaurzhurek Myn Bala* (2011). It is noteworthy that class aspects are largely irrelevant to both of those pictures.

Ever since *Poem About Love* was released to film theaters, film critics and historians have derided it for its theatricality.[36] This is a rather convenient criticism that fails to take into account the historical situation in which the film was made. In defense of *Poem About Love*, it must be said that adaptations of theater productions, the so-called performance films (*fil'm-spektakl'*), were a respected and popular genre in the USSR in the early 1950s. Produced quickly and economically, they were featuring top stage performers, many of whom rarely appeared on screen, and brought high-caliber theater art to all corners of the country. These arguments apply to *Poem About Love*, too, as the film was appreciated by millions and continuously screened for years after its first release.

Most importantly, film historians overlooked the fact that many segments of Aimanov's film were not theatrical at all.[37] A number of episodes were filmed in the Kazakhstani steppe, showing large herds of horses caught in dusty winds against a backdrop of majestic mountains. The first duel between Kozy and Kodar, fought with lancets on horseback, was shot entirely on location. Mikhail Aranyshev's camera works miracles, delivering the crisply accentuated nature shots that became his trademark and skillfully using the entire range of shot types, especially extreme long shots and close-ups. In several episodes of *Poem About Love*, the artificiality of the decoration is suddenly interrupted by a realistic location shot. For example, in the beginning, a group of horsemen is approaching the *aul* in a location shot and entering the set in the following studio shot. Such transitions from living nature to artificial construction positively define the film's style. As a matter of fact, this alternation between internal studio scenes with static stage lighting and external extreme long shots is one of the most aesthetically productive elements of *Poem About Love*, one that keeps the picture alive to this day and makes it not only watchable but enjoyable.[38]

It is ahistorical to point to the studio scenes as symptomatic of Kazakh filmmakers' lack of experience. After all, even many Hollywood films of the early 1950s were shot partly or entirely in the studio and betray the artificiality of decorations every step of the way. Stylistic conventions during the 1950s made filming in studio conditions acceptable to viewers, while producers appreciated the fact that it was less expensive and risky than location shooting. The one element that is indeed questionable and reflects negatively on the film is the predominant acting style: in almost all scenes, it is declarative, excessively controlled, and distinctly uncinematic. As a result, the emotional effect of this heartbreaking love story remains limited. Another problem is the film's cast. The star of the Kazakh National Theater, Sholpan Dzhandarbekova, could pass as a youthful ingénue on stage, but not on screen. While she performed her character's long monologues and mood swings flawlessly, she was simply too old for the role of Baian, especially opposite the boyish T. Argimbekov in the role of Kozy. As for the latter, the actor's rather tender features make it hard to believe that Kozy could defeat the violent Kodar. On the other hand, Nurmukhan Zhanturin's Kodar is spot-on: always tense and resentful, his body language resembles that of a stern samurai. Zhanturin delivered a performance that provides the perfect counterpoint to the romantic sweetness of the two lovers. Kodar's final appearance, as a wandering outcast surrounded by merciless sand dunes, reveals the enormous potential of Zhanturin who became a mainstay of Kazakh cinema in the four decades that followed this picture.

For Shaken Aimanov, one of the all-time stars of Kazakh theater, *Poem About Love* was not just his debut as a filmmaker, but a labor of transition in his artistic evolution, a work synthesizing features of theater and cinema. True, these features often coexist in his film and are not always in agreement. But the criticism that Aimanov's first attempt at film direction (together with Karl Gakkel[39] as second director) reflected the "learning process" he was undergoing, while the chosen genre of performance film was an expression of the Alma-Ata studio's lack of resources, as Kul'shara Ainagulova and others have argued, is misplaced.[40] As a matter of fact, all of Aimanov's subsequent pictures contain episodes whose studio character and theatrical features are hard to deny, revealing either its maker's pedigree or, more likely, his preference for clearly organized misc-en-scènes that allow for a fuller appreciation of the performers' artistry. *Poem About*

*Love* remains a worthwhile film, and not merely for historical reasons. Its capturing of the steppe atmosphere as an active space for an eternal love story is exemplary and certainly prepared the ground for later pictures such as *Kyz-Zhibek*.

## THE FIRST EPIC

In his second project, Aimanov was able to show the full range of his ambitions as a filmmaker. *Daughter of the Steppes* (Doch' stepei, 1954) became one of his best pictures, although it contains transitory elements as did his debut. Its wide historical range and diverse set of characters suggest that Aimanov's goal was to create an epic, a large-scale production reflecting Kazakhstan's development from the 1920s to the 1950s through the eyes of one character. Aimanov again worked with Karl Gakkel as co-director; the screenplay was written by Roman Fatuev. The plot resembles *Raikhan* from fifteen years earlier, as *Daughter of the Steppes* focuses on a female character whose individual biography symbolizes the evolution of the entire Kazakh nation in the first Soviet phase. In its emphasis on individual and national development, *Daughter of the Steppes* could be called a biopic, with the difference that it is devoted to a fictitious rank-and-file person still living in the present, not a historical celebrity.

The opening episode shows a conflict illustrating the lawlessness of pre-communist Kazakhstan with regards to women. The rich Aktambai (Eleubai Umurzakov), fearing the approaching Bolsheviks, attempts to smuggle his huge herds across the country's border. But only the poor shepherd Molbagar (Zhagda Oguzbaev) knows the secret paths across the mountains to China. To secure Molbagar's goodwill, Aktambai gives him the teenage Nurzhamal as a wife, ignoring the girl's fierce resistance. The decent Molbagar feels sorry for the orphan and allows her to leave. She departs on horseback and manages to reach a Bolshevik community.

While the first episode reveals the degree to which Aimanov learned to adjust pacing, the characterizations remain politically and psychologically schematic. To be sure, the film is directed with dramatic verve, but the characters are depicted in accordance with their position in the officially confirmed class configuration. Both experienced performers such as Umurzakov and newcomers such as the young Zamzagul Sharipova (in the title role) visibly struggle with the stock nature of their roles.[41] However, the schematic acting is compensated for by Mikhail Aranyshev's camera work, which blends majestic vistas of the steppe with dynamic dolly shots in more intimate settings. Evgenii Brusilovskii's tunes convey a sense of authentic Kazakh tradition. Images and music thus act as counterweights to the ideological dryness of the film's underlying ultra-Soviet conception of twentieth-century Kazakh history.

After her liberation from the patriarchal yoke, Nurzhamal embarks on a medical career. A Russian doctor who saved Nurzhamal's life during her escape encourages the native young woman to study with her in Alma-Ata. Nurzhamal turns out to be an excellent medical student, respected and liked by all. Her only problem is the pushiness of Kerim (Nurmukhan Zhanturin), an arrogant peer who uses shameless deceit in an effort to win her heart and ward off the truly decent Murad, whom she loves. However, Nurzhamal decides to put her personal problems on the back burner and quickly grows as a professional. Her ideological firmness becomes obvious when the ambitious Kerim talks about the need to "pursue one's career" (*kar'era*) and she angrily responds, "I cannot stand that word. It's not our word." Indeed, Nurzhamal herself bases her decisions primarily on societal needs and picks a provincial hospital for her first deployment.

Of special significance in *Daughter of the Steppes* is the guiding function of the Russian characters. Nurzhamal's first encounter with a Russian, the physician Liubov' Petrovna Lunina, takes place in a communist settlement. Everybody greets the Russian woman as "comrade doctor," and someone explains, "These people have come from far away to teach us literacy; they were sent by the Soviet government." But the Russians' intentions go further than that: they are missionaries preaching the new communist values, including the equality of the sexes. This is the main theme of a lecture to which only women are admitted. Indeed, the motif of female emancipation is primary among the film's explicit ideological messages. A secondary motif deals with native Kazakh-Soviet science as opposed to foreign sources that must be treated with distrust. Not coincidentally, the arrogant Kerim constantly quotes from Western articles, whereas Nurzhamal refers to the nineteenth-century Russian surgeon Pirogov as the decisive authority. Such motifs are late echoes of the 1940s campaign against cosmopolitanism; one may assume that the change of priorities in culture and science after Stalin's death had not yet made its full impact.

Another secondary motif deals with alternative healing methods, a rare topic in Soviet cinema. Early on, Nurzhamal expresses an interest in herbal medicine. In *Daughter of the Steppes*, herbal healing signifies an organic connection between the intelligentsia and ordinary people, respect for national tradition, and skepticism toward Western-style modernity that values technology as an end in itself, at the expense of what is simple, efficient, and natural. However, Nurzhamal's strong case for herbal healing notwithstanding, the film takes a stance against other ancient methods such as witchcraft, illustrating its negative consequences in a drastic episode, in which superstition results in the death of a child.

It is easy to recognize remnants of Stalinist cinema in Aimanov's second film. While portraits of Stalin are much rarer than in films of the 1940s and verbal references to the late leader are completely absent, several conflicts are obviously connected with the previous historical epoch.

After the film's release, one of the reviews criticized *Daughter of the Steppes* for historical inaccuracies, noting that military personnel did not wear epaulettes at the beginning of the war and the dorms in which students lived were far from the lavishness that the film portrays. These points are not nitpicky: they signal the emergence of new quality criteria centered on truthfulness for Soviet films.[42] Kabysh Siranov delivered a rather strict verdict as well: he found Nurzhamal's story too superficial and insufficiently motivated.[43] However, a few years later, he formulated a fairer assessment and acknowledged that *Daughter of the Steppes* appealed to huge audiences in Kazakhstan and Central Asia.[44] Indeed, despite certain embellishments and ideological bias that do belong to the 1940s, the central plotline of a previously enslaved girl whom the new society gives a chance to apply her professional potential and gain recognition, is far from falsehood, and the tragedies that doctor Nurzhamal Bulatova has to go through (including the death of a little girl for whom her treatment comes too late, as well as the death of her husband Murad in World War II) are believable.[45] For all her awe of her Russian teachers, the film's title character embodies a feminine strength and endurance that are deeply Kazakh. Nurzhamal's personality and love for her native land are related to Raikhan from the 1940 picture. Her social advance can be compared to the Russian-Soviet female characters of Vera Maretskaia and Tamara Makarova. Just like them, she addresses the audience directly in a concluding shot, saying emphatically, "You are our hope, you are our future."

The association of female emancipation with national modernization became a mainstay of Soviet cinema, especially in the national film cultures of Central Asia. *Daughter of the Steppes* occupies a worthy place among those films, despite its undeniable historical limitations.[46] It also proved Shaken Aimanov's ability to helm a major picture with numerous complicated episodes and a multifaceted cast. Whether deliberately or unconsciously, Aimanov had followed Auezov's advice from the film conference in 1945: his first picture drew on national folklore directly, while the second conveyed contemporary sociopolitical concepts about the path of the Kazakh nation in the twentieth century, yet also contained deep mythological layers. The fact that millions of viewers were attracted by this film demonstrates that Aimanov was on the right path.

## NOTES

1. V.I. Fomin, ed., *Letopis' rossiiskogo kino 1946–1965*. Moskva: Izdatel'stvo Kan N-Plius, 2010, p. 18.

2. Roza Abdulakhatova, who divides the postwar years in Kazakhstani cinema in one period from 1946 (rather than 1945) to 1953 and a second period from 1954 to 1960, acknowledges the low production numbers in the first phase but points out that the studio's dubbing department became very active, releasing films such as *The Oath* (Kliatva), *The Young Guard* (Molodaia gvardiia, 1948), *Alisher Navoi*, and others in Kazakh. Cf. *Ocherki istorii kazakhskogo kino*. Alma-Ata: Izdatel'stvo 'Nauka' Kazakhskoi SSR, 1980, p. 103. She does not address the political problems at the studio and the arrests of leading administrators.

3. "Kazakhstanskoe kino v 1946 godu," *Kazakhstanskaia Pravda*, 13 March 1946.

4. *Letopis's rossiiskogo*, p. 821.

5. *Letopis' rossiiskogo*, 2010, p. 24.

6. The credits list the production year as 1945 and the studio as Alma-Ata Film Studio (Alma-Atinskaia kinostudiia).

7. *Kurgan* is a Turkic word denoting a grave monument.

8. Bauyrzhan Nogerbek's claim that *The Songs of Abai* was "quite far from the ideologically nascent themes of Soviet cinema" is based on a reductionist view of Stalinist biopics. In reality, concepts such as that of populism (*narodnost'*) were fundamental for Soviet cinema and found their expression in films about artists and their rootedness in the depth of the people. Cf. Smailova, *Kinoentsiklopediia Kazakhstana*, p. 14.

9. *Istoriia sovetskogo kino*, p. 229.

10. Bauyrzhan Nogerbek, who undertook a detailed comparison of Auezov's original screenplay and the director's reduced version, regarded *The Songs of Abai* the first feature film of the Kazakh republic (as opposed to *Amangeldy*). Cf. Nogerbek, Bauyrzhan. *Na ekrane 'Kazakhfil'm.'* Almaty: RUAN, 2007, p. 14.

11. "Vsesoiuznoe soveshchanie rabotnikov khudozhestvennoi kinematografii po obsuzhdeniiu resheniia TsK VKB (b) o kinofil'me 'Bol'shaia zhizn'' (2 seriia). 14-15 oktiabria 1946 goda." In L.A. Parfenov, ed. *Zhivye golosa kino*. Moskva: "Belyi bereg", 1999, p. 335.

12. Cf. the editorial "More Feature Films of High Artistic Quality!" (Bol'she vysokokhudozhestvennykh kinofil'mov!), *Kul'tura i zhizn'*, 10 October 1947.

13. L.A. Parfenov, ed. *Zhivye golosa kino*. Moskva: "Belyi bereg," 1999, p. 322.

14. *Ocherki istorii kazakhskogo kino*, p. 106.

15. *Letopis' rossiiskogo*, 2010, p. 95.

16. Ibid., p. 85.

17. "V Alma-Atinskoi kinostudii," *Bol'shevik Altaia*, 8 July 1947.

18. *Istoriia sovetskogo kino*, vol. 3: 1941–1952. Moskva: Izdatel'stvo "Iskusstvo," 1975, p. 231.

19. The Arkhar race that is found in the mountains of Central Asia is regarded the predecessor to domesticated sheep; hybridization with Merino sheep from the Caucasus resulted in the *Kazakh Arkharomerinos*.

20. See, for example, Bragin, A., "Novyi fil'm Alma-Atinskoi kinostudii khudozhestvennykh fil'mov," *Kazakhstanskaia pravda*, 5 September 1948.

21. *Letopis' rossiiskogo*, 2010, p. 94.

22. Smailova, *Kinoentsiklopediia Kazakhstana*, p. 448.

23. *Letopis' rossiiskogo*, 2010, p. 129.

24. Esenberlin was accused of embezzlement; he was released in 1953 and worked as the redactor of the collegiate for screenplays of Kazakhfilm studio in 1958–1967. He later became the most famous Kazakh author of historical fiction.

25. Cf. the official announcement in *Kazakhstanskaia Pravda*, 18 March 1952.

26. Other spellings: Dzhambul Dzhabayev, Zhambyl Zhabayev, Jambyl Jabayev.

27. Suinbay Aron-uly (1815–1898).

28. "Obsuzhdenie kinostsenariia 'Dzhambul,'" *Kazakhstanskaia pravda*, 20 November 1949.

29. Nikolai Pogodin, Abdil'da Tazhibaev, "Dzhambul v Moskve," *Kazakhstanskaia pravda*, 4 July 1950.

30. K. Ainagulova, K. Alimbaeva. *Tendentsii razvitiia kinoiskusstva Kazakhstana*. Alma-Ata: "Gylym," 1990, p. 8.

31. Aranyshev, Mikhail Fedorovich (1912–1989), one of the leading cinematographers of Kazakhstan. He graduated from the Soviet State Institute of Cinema (VGIK) in 1937 and was assigned to the Central United Film Studio (TSOKS) in 1942. Staying in Alma-Ata for the next five decades, Aranyshev worked on some of the best Kazakh feature films and, beginning in 1970, also contributed to animated films.

32. Lidiia Stepanova (1899–1962) received Stalin Prizes for *Soviet Estonia* (1947), *Moscow, the Capital of the USSR* (1948), *Democratic Hungary* (1949), *The 1 of May 1949* (1950), and *Soviet Kazakhstan* (1952). In 1953, Stepanova's career as the most decorated Soviet documentary director ended abruptly; in her last years, she directed shorts on scientific topics.

33. Tazhibaev, Abdilda (1909–1998), Kazakh poet and screenwriter. He began his career in the 1930s; in the 1960s, Tazhibaev also made a name for himself as a scholar in the humanities.

34. Khusainov (other spelling: Kusainov), Shakhmet (1906–1972), Kazakh playwright and screenwriter who studied at the Soviet State Theater Institute in Moscow in 1935–1937. His first plays, which dealt with life in Soviet-Kazakh kolkhoz farms, were published in the 1930s. In the 1950s, Khusainov coauthored (with Vladimir Abyzov) three successful screenplays (*The Djigit-Girl*; *We Live Here*; and *On the Irtysh's Wild Beach*) but discontinued his work in cinema thereafter, for unknown reasons. Khusainov was married to the prominent actress Biken Rimova.

35. Iakubov, V., "Za bol'shoe kinoiskusstvo," *Kazahstanskaia pravda*, 13 February 1948.

36. Ainagulova and Alimbaeva. *Tendentsii razvitiia kinoiskusstva*, pp. 8–10.

37. A good example is Kabysh Siranov's assessment in his monograph *Kazakh Cinema* (1958), where he voiced the suspicion that Aimanov was still too much under the influence of the stage (Siranov, *Kazakhskoe kinoiskusstvo*, p. 65). He repeated his arguments in his next monograph (Siranov, K., *Kinoiskusstvo sovetskogo Kazakhstana*. Alma-Ata: Izdatel'stvo "Kazakhstan," 1966, p. 131), but added that the

film's failure was a blessing in disguise, serving as a school for the budding filmmaker and his team.

38. Bauyrzhan Nogerbek defended the film's achievements and saw in it "the historical coming together of objective and subjective factors," when societal expectation and subjective will coincided. Nogerbek. *Na ekrane 'Kazakhfil'm,'* " p. 30.

39. Gakkel, Karl Al'fredovich (1906–1966), Soviet film director who worked as an assistant director at Lenfilm studio in the 1930s and at TsOKS in 1941–1945. Gakkel is best remembered for his codirection, with Shaken Aimanov, of *Poem About Love* and *Daughter of the Steppes* at Alma-Ata film studio in the 1950s, before he moved to Moscow, to work at Mosfilm studio.

40. Thus, the writer Dmitrii Snegin criticized that the film was shot in black-and-white and some performances were bland, including Koichubaeva's. Snegin, D., "Poema o vsepobezhdaiushchei liubvi," *Kazakhstanskaia pravda*, 30 May 1954.

41. One reviewer found her performance to be too emotionally restrained. Cf. Nurmagambetova, O., "Verno i ubeditel'no" *Kazakhstanskaia pravda*, 23 April 1955.

42. Cherkesov, V., "Volnuiushchaia pravda," *Kazakhstanskaia pravda*, 23 April 1955.

43. Siranov, Kabysh, *Kazakhskoe kinoiskusstvo*. Alma-Ata: Kazakhskoe gosudarstvennoe izdatel'stvo, 1958, p. 38

44. Siranov, *Kinoiskusstvo sovetskogo*, p. 155.

45. Cf. the positive reassessment of this film by Gulnara Abikeeva: Abikeeva, G. Natsiostroitel'stvo v Kazakhstane i drugikh stranakh Tsentral'noi Azii i kak etot protsess otrazhaetsia v kinematografe. Almaty: TSTSAK, 2006, pp. 74–75.

46. The film was certainly viewed as a significant national event. Thus, the Communist Party newspaper *Kazakhstanskaia pravda* published an entire page filled with reviews and letters. Cf. Nurmagambetova, "Verno i ubeditel'no" and Cherkesov, V., "Povest' o schast'e kazakhskoi zhenshchiny. Volnuiushchaia pravda." *Kazakhstanskaia pravda*, 23 April 1955.

*Chapter 4*

# The Mid-1950s
## *A Cautious Emancipation*

Shaken Aimanov's earliest features, *Poem About Love* and *Daughter of the Steppes*, were underappreciated by contemporary critics and later by film historians. Even though Kazakh audiences responded well to them at the time of their release, most Soviet critics viewed them as works of *regional* importance, as products of a fledgling film culture with little relevance for Soviet cinema as a whole, and even less international significance. However, Aimanov did not allow critical skepticism to slow him down. Passionate, driven, and artistically flexible in a way that few other Soviet filmmakers were, he turned to contemporary subject matter, a thematic focus that the Communist Party always demanded but that was rarely delivered in acceptable quality by any studio, central or peripheral. The topic to which Aimanov turned for his contemporary drama was unfolding in front of viewers's eyes: the Virgin Lands Campaign.

 The Soviet establishment chose Kazakhstan for its first major economic initiative after Stalin's death, namely the exploration of untilled (so-called virgin) lands (*tselina*). Of extraordinary proportions, the project was fraught with hyped expectation and promise: to establish a major new source of grain production that could compensate for the unreliable and inefficient agricultural output in the USSR's northern regions. As an economic super-project, the Virgin Lands Campaign was also an enormous test of post-Stalinist communist management methods. Any movie addressing this topic was considered "hot," but also politically sensitive. A possible motivation for Aimanov in tackling this issue may have been the fact that a non-Kazakh director had been the first to bring the *tselina* campaign to Soviet screens, before any native filmmakers did. The outside view left a lot to be desired, especially in respect to its understanding of the country in which the campaign was unfolding: Kazakhstan.

## THE VIRGIN LANDS CAMPAIGN I: MEDVEDKIN'S VIEW

The first director to make a feature film about the *tselina* was the legendary Aleksandr Medvedkin. In the early 1930s, Medvedkin had acquired the reputation of a highly inventive film pioneer with a sharp social agenda who cleverly used documentary cinema as a tool to contribute to the latest socioeconomic trends promoted by the Communist Party. His "film train," which traversed the country as a mobile studio-cum-viewing-facility, became an important part of Soviet silent cinema's legacy. Medvedkin's record as a feature filmmaker was more controversial: on the backdrop of Soviet mainstream, he remained a maverick with a style and sense of humor that noticeably differed from aesthetic norms. While his full-length feature debut, *Happiness* (Schast'e, 1934), was applauded by Eizenshtein and Dovzhenko, it found little appreciation among Soviet film administrators. Another comedy, *The New Moscow* (Novaia Moskva, 1938), was shelved altogether, even though Medvedkin displayed his loyalty to Communism in the picture that left no room for doubt. During the Great Patriotic War, he reestablished his reputation by serving as a reliable operative whose military cameramen units brought impressive footage from the battlefields.

In 1954–1956, Medvedkin headed a group of cinematographers assigned to chronicling the *tselina* campaign in Kazakhstan. One of the results was the documentary *The First Spring* (Pervaia vesna, 1954, co-directed with Iakov Posel'skii). Medvedkin's familiarity with the subject of the newly cultivated soil in Kazakhstan enabled him to propose a feature film that would approach the same topic, but in an entertaining fashion. The timing could not have been better: in the mid-1950s, when the end of the period of limited feature film production (the so-called *malokartin'e*) meant that many directors suddenly had the chance to realize their projects, Medvedkin's screenplay about the untilled soil had the potential to inaugurate his return from documentary to feature filmmaking. With good instincts, he chose the genre of comedy, as the post-Stalin years were marked by a craving for light-hearted fun, and the temporarily disoriented and divided communist leadership was willing to leave that window of opportunity open for a while. Moreover, the subject matter itself, featuring tens of thousands of young people moving into the vast steppe to render it useable for grain production, called for optimism, romance, song, and dance. As early as the 1930s, Medvedkin had evolved a deft, folklore-inspired humor unlike that of any other filmmaker. However, at that time it had found the approval of neither officials, nor audiences. The beginning of the Thaw seemed to be the right moment to reintroduce this populist, politically clean-cut variety of Soviet joie de vivre.

Interestingly, the plot of Medvedkin's screenplay *A Restless Spring* (Bespokoinaia vesna, 1956) did not initially have any national specificities. Only when its production was assigned to the Alma-Ata Studio of Feature Films was the story adjusted accordingly and secondary Kazakh characters added. But these changes were merely pro forma, since Medvedkin neither knew the country nor its people particularly well and apparently assumed that they were "Soviet" like everybody else.

The film's main protagonist is a young man, Zhenia Omega (Sergei Gurzo), who aspires to become a tractor driver and a "hero of the *tselina*." His other reason for moving to Kazakhstan is his infatuation with a young beauty, Olga. But from day one, Zhenia's abilities do not match the physical challenges of the cultivation work. He is lazy and vain, causing more harm than good in the newly established *sovkhoz* Mai-Balyk. His supervisor relegates him to the position of a water supply operative, a primitive and monotonous task that turns the young man into a driver on an old-fashioned horse cart with a large water keg. Zhenia must learn many hard lessons, including one from a fallout with Olga who is attracted to the Kazakh Idris (Idris Nogaibaev), before he becomes a conscious and disciplined worker. At the end, he is entrusted with a powerful tractor, with which he goes on to forcefully plow the dark, "virginal" soil, the virgin land.

Medvedkin uses numerous established *tselina* clichés, including the half-ominous, half-joyful arrival of a convoy carrying hundreds of young men and women into the middle of nowhere, emphasizing the pioneering and adventurous aspects of their task; setting up a post in the wide steppe with the name of the new settlement on it; and addressing severe problems related to basic needs, from heating and cooking to hygiene. Another cliché is the triumphant finale, featuring long rows of newly erected homes on both sides of an asphalt street in the wide steppe. In the mid-1950s, Soviet audiences were fed such images of the communist spirit at work ad nauseam in documentaries and newsreels. Alas, in *A Restless Spring*, Medvedkin simply rehashed them without deepening their meaning. He also inserted elements that were characteristic of his 1930s films, including slapstick jokes that do not always blend organically with the quasi-documentary parts of the film. Most interesting are the satirical broadsides against so-called negative social types, usually bureaucrats who are not part of the enthusiastic group of *tselina* conquerors. These include a propaganda official who indulges in pathos-filled announcements and a supply administrator who only does what he is ordered and misunderstands all his assignments, forgetting to bring salt and other staples to the settlement. The latter, a man with the telling last name of Borodavka (warts), is clearly akin to stock bureaucrats not only from the 1930s comedies of Grigorii Aleksandrov and Ivan Pyr'ev, but also to those from Medvedkin's own silent satirical shorts, which had earned him the reputation of an inventive social critic.

In Medvedkin's worldview, the rank-and-file, the *narod* (literally "the people"), was always right, for they were endowed with the correct political and social instincts and could therefore make fun of outsiders such as Borodavka and Filia. It is these rank-and-file people who see the good core in Zhenia and reeducate him. While the educational process may seem cruel at times,[1] it proves to be efficient in the end. Zhenia's ultimately successful transformation is part of an overall trend toward peaceful resolutions, be they local or global. Conspicuously, when a unit of former tank troops arrives to help with the harvest, someone says, "That's because the armed forces are being reduced in size now."

However, despite Medvedkin's obvious goodwill and inventiveness, the film, nominally a comedy, turned out to be unfunny. True, the director pushes the narrative along quickly enough to render *A Restless Spring* youthful and dynamic, and the score by Evgenii Brusilovskii and Bakhitzhan Baikadamov does imbue it with a certain energy. Yet in many episodes, the eccentric humor seems anachronistic, while the problems experienced by various characters are unspecific and have nothing to do with the hardships of cultivating faraway lands in a rough climate. The film's male star, Sergei Gurzo, one of the most beloved Soviet actors of the 1940s and 1950s, appears bland, and his first-person narration comes across as overly soft and conflict-averse.[2] Medvedkin had never seriously worked with actors; as a result, his characters seem to be left to themselves and often indifferent to their own story. Furthermore, within the realistic context of his film, the insertion of musical elements appears forced: it is unnatural for a young woman standing next to a tractor to suddenly begin to sing with orchestra accompaniment or for all the characters in a frame to form a choir circle and perform a song about "the conquerors of the new lands." In a more stylized production, such scenes requiring strong suspension of disbelief might have worked, but not in a film that has a deliberately quasi-documentary design.

An important aspect that contributed to the film's failure is Medvedkin's obvious lack of interest in Kazakhstan itself. True, ethnic Kazakhs do appear on screen from time to time, but they might as well be Russians, Ukrainians, or Armenians. This does not mean that Medvedkin intended to discriminate against the native population. Rather, for him, as a true believer in communist internationalism, the ethnic and cultural peculiarities of Kazakhstan were secondary and inconsequential for the *tselina* campaign. The Kazakhs in his film are treated neither with the condescension of a visiting Muscovite, nor with the curiosity of an ethnographer—they simply come across as unspecific and boring. The fact that the campaign to cultivate untilled soil is taking place in a country with a peculiar past and cultural heritage is treated as irrelevant. Even when there is a natural opportunity to create some friendly competition between the Russian newcomers and their Kazakh colleagues from "the legendary Atabaev" brigade, no hint of interethnic friction is forthcoming.[3] Had Medvedkin had the courage, or the interest, to devote some parts of the story to the encounter of different cultures, with all the serious and humorous side effects this would have entailed, it might have given his comedy some much-needed gravitas and originality. In all likelihood, though, any ethnic profiling, however benevolent, would have been considered undesirable at the time.

However, for film buffs and Medvedkin devotees, *A Restless Spring* does hold a certain interest: Zhenia Omega on the water cart, with a dappled horse in front of him, seems to come right out of *Happiness* from two decades earlier, as does much of the physical humor. But even in the most generous estimation, the film is a strange, fish-out-of-water product, making the director's subsequent decision to abandon comedy and turn to feature-length polemical documentaries seem wise.

## THE VIRGIN LANDS CAMPAIGN II: KHODZHIKOV'S FIRST STEPS

In 1955, Sultan-Akhmet Khodzhikov, war veteran and budding director, was given the chance to make his debut with a Virgin Lands story. The medium-length *Mother and Son* (Mat' i syn), shot in Kazakh and dubbed into Russian, consists of two chapters, "Grisha" and "Maksimovna." The first chapter features a young man, Grigorii Orlov, who dreams of becoming a tractor driver. However, the *aul* has a logistical problem: tractors are located on the left side of a wild river, while gasoline is stored on the right side. The gas is transported through a narrow tube hanging above the river. In early spring, when the ice is breaking, repairing the leaking tube is extremely dangerous. Grisha is courageous enough to try, and thanks to his acrobatics, the tube is repaired in mid-air, securing the gas supply for the tractors.

The second part of the film describes the trials and tribulations of Grisha's protective mother, who hears about her son's heroic act and arrives by train to take him home. But when Maksimovna realizes that she, too, might be able to contribute to the epic task of *tselina* cultivation, she decides to stay and work as a cook for the virgin soil workers. At the end, Grisha sits confidently on a tractor ploughing the fields while his mother walks happily alongside him.

*Mother and Son* is narratively even simpler than Medvedkin's comedy, and its forced optimism rings hollow. But the film does have a few noteworthy aspects. First, the division into two chapters is a literary device rarely used in cinema; this literariness is further emphasized by voiceover narration. The son's viewpoint, which dominates the first part, is replaced by the mother's viewpoint in the second part, and in the end the two come together, which in itself makes for an interesting structure. Second, Khodzhikov uses montages to create suspense in the dramatic repair episode, somewhat schematically, perhaps, but it nevertheless adds visual dynamics to an otherwise linear story. Third, the cameraman, Iskander Tynyshpaev, creates an image of *tselina* everyday life that is more grittily realistic than romantic. He and Khodzhikov prove that they have an eye for detail enriching the didactic storyline with curious observations, for example, a lady from the city who is forced to change her shoes because of the mud and the puddles. But most remarkable is the absence of any Kazakh element whatsoever. The community of workers is shown to be both tight-knit and multiethnic. Grisha and his mother are Russian, and the environment in which they come together is ethnically and culturally indistinct; it is Soviet and nothing else. This demonstrates that the filmmakers' own ethnicity alone was no guarantee of national framing. After all, Khodzhikov was Kazakh, yet his film was as nationally neutral as was Medvedkin's.

It would be easy to criticize the young director, who also coauthored the screenplay, for this ethnic-cultural neutrality vis-à-vis his own homeland. However, *Mother and Son* reveals the normative view of the Virgin Lands Campaign as an all-Soviet enterprise meant to attract predominantly young people from all over the USSR, whereas the location (the Kazakh SSR) was viewed as a negligible aspect. Khodzhikov acquiesced to this transnational view because this was the communist, internationalist norm. It is essential to be aware of this norm, which was given form in the works of both Medvedkin and Khodzhikov, to fully appreciate Shaken Aimanov's response to the *tselina* challenge.

## THE VIRGIN LANDS CAMPAIGN III: AIMANOV'S VERSION

Medvedkin's politically accurate but entirely disinterested view of Kazakhstan in *A Restless Spring* and Khodzhikov's echoing of this view in *Mother and Son* undoubtedly made an impact on Shaken Aimanov. Whether the implicit polemics against Medvedkin and Khodzhikov in his own treatment of the Virgin Lands Campaign were designed as an response to the Russian director and the young Kazakh debutant or purely a coincidence is hard to elucidate, but the contrast between the two arch-Soviet movies and the Kazakh film could not be sharper, despite the fact that all three were made at the same studio. Aimanov's feature (his third) was released under the title *We Live Here* (My zdes' zhivem). The screenplay was written by Vladimir Abyzov[4] and Shakhmet Khusainov, with additional input from the accomplished Mikhail Bleiman.[5] The film premiered in November 1956 in Alma-Ata and, in a dubbed version, in March 1957 in Moscow.[6]

The title has a polemical sound to it, or at least an ambiguous ring. At first, *We Live Here* simply seems to allude to the fact that the millions of acres of untilled land in Kazakhstan that were cultivated at an unprecedented rate during the *tselina* campaign were sparsely inhabited, and that a major problem facing the Soviet administration was the creation of minimally acceptable living conditions for tens of thousands of people who were supposed to not only cultivate these "virgin lands," but stay and make their homes there. The finale of Aimanov's film seems to confirm this interpretation with unequivocal clarity: after the resolution of all major conflicts, the members of a Komsomol brigade greet the arriving busloads of newcomers from various cities—"Leningrad, Pskov, Stalingrad [not yet renamed—P.R.], Voroshilovgrad." When the newcomers ask, "And where are you from?" one of the brigade members states, "We are from Komsomolskii settlement, *we live here*." In other words, the film concludes with an affirmative statement of belonging to this land: the "conquerors" of these territories, the so-called *tselinniki*, have turned them into their home for good.

However, the title can also be interpreted as referring to those native Kazakhs who *already* live on these territories and have lived in their villages for centuries. Taken this way, the title would sound like: "It is *us* who live here!" In other words, rather than turning "virgin land" into "native land" in one fell swoop, the emphasis would be on the rights of those who have considered this their homeland since time immemorial. Given Aimanov's lifelong loyalty to the communist cause and to the Party of which he was a member, such an outright political provocation may be hard to imagine. But the choice of an ambiguous title is certainly thought-provoking, especially since conflicts between natives and newcomers do shape the major plotlines in *We Live Here*. Based on numerous statements one can safely assume that Aimanov did not want to see his Kazakh homeland represented as a neutral, denationalized territory. Therefore, the semantic ambiguity of the title could plausibly have been intentional. In light of a statement made ten years later, a subversive interpretation makes sense.

In a 1965 article for the journal *Iskusstvo kino*, Aimanov discussed the "virgin land" theme from a national point of view, asking polemically:

> Did the cattle-breeding Kazakhs not roam for centuries the lands where new sovkhozes were built? Did the local population not welcome the youths from other places who came to Kazakhstan following the call of the Party? Were the Kazakhs in the Virgin Lands Campaign nothing but outside observers? And how was all this reflected in cinema?[7]

Applying these qustions to his own 1956 picture, Aimanov has nothing to be ashamed of: he did address the ethnic and cultural shifts that the influx of tens of thousands of new inhabitants brought to his Kazakh homeland.

The film's narration is fast-paced from beginning to end, with very few lyrical interludes. Thematically, Aimanov's primary focus is the disagreements between those administrators who rule by bureaucratic decree and those who pursue realistic goals, always keeping in mind the wellbeing of the workers entrusted to them. The former type is represented by Kuanysh Korkutov (Idris Nogaibaev), a man in charge of a consortium of new *sovkhozes*, and the latter by Il'ia Kudriash (Konstantin Bartashevich), the director of one such *sovkhoz*, named "Komsomol'skii". Kudriash, a Ukrainian, is a transitory leadership figure with both authoritarian and democratic features. He often takes decisions on a whim and is generally difficult to get along with. Yet, when it comes to his workers, he defends their interests, grants them higher salaries to keep them on the project, and gives his all to organizing modestly civilized living conditions. Korkutov, who is Kazakh, is authoritarian, too, but in the old way and, unlike Kudriash, he rejects any common-sense arguments and badmouths those who disobey his orders to the higher-ups.

Shaken Aimanov himself plays the role of a regional administrator, Beisov, an open-minded man who sees through Korkutov's schemes and encourages Kudriash's pursuit of pragmatic solutions. The juxtaposition of "good" and "bad" managerial methods was typical of Soviet cinema, both during the Stalinist period and thereafter. What is unusual in *We Live Here* is that the supervisors side with the more democratic administrator, not the authoritarian schemer. These conflicts are not just expressed through statements; they are psychologically motivated. Aimanov succeeds in establishing plausible links between individual personalities and their management style. It turns out that Korkutov not only informed on those who disagree with him, but he also abandoned his girlfriend when she was pregnant, a behavior that not even his doting parents can forgive. The explicit critique of this type of opportunism marks the film as a product of the evolving Thaw period with its call for honesty and integrity.

To be sure, *We Live Here* does contain elements of the virgin lands romanticism that was so fashionable in Soviet literature and cinema in the mid-1950s, but Aimanov did not indulge in them. There are visual *tselina* clichés such as spectacular sunrises in the steppe that bathe the workers' physical hardships in romantic light.[8] However, unlike other *tselina* films, the exotic, adventurous aspects remain secondary. After all, why should a Kazakh wonder about the climatic conditions in his native steppe? Rather, Aimanov shows the cultivation of new land to be a trying but normal civilizational process that, when handled responsibly, will benefit everybody involved. Thus, it is not so much the economic goal that defines the director's vision as the wellbeing of the participants, that is, those who arrive in Kazakhstan and those who already live there. This communist humanism is likewise a sign of Thaw sensitivities.

Completely new is the representation of Kazakhstan and its people as indispensable and *nationally distinct* partners in this process, confirming the intentionality of the title's semantic ambiguity. Indeed, in *We Live Here*, the sensitive ethnic issue is not covered up but addressed head-on. One of the brigade members, Khalida (Lola Abdukarimova), falls in love with the Russian Sergei. Both want to get married as soon as possible, but Khalida is afraid of her parents' conservative views. And indeed, her mother argues against marrying a man "who is not of our faith and does not speak our language." In the end, however, it is Khalida's father who persuades his wife to attend the wedding and endorse the interethnic marriage, after which the converted wife insists on the newlyweds' moving into their house, as tradition demands. The scenes involving Khalida's mother are among the most intriguing in the film, as they touch upon a subject that heretofore had been either largely taboo or thoroughly politicized in Soviet cinema. Had the issue of interethnic relations been shown as a problem in a film in the 1930s or 1940s, views such as the mother's would have been ridiculed or denounced as reactionary "enemy propaganda" that had to be aggressively confronted and eliminated. In Aimanov's treatment, however, mutual understanding and acceptance win the day, and a compromise is shown to be possible and desirable.

Most Soviet film historians did not write about *We Live Here* in a way that would have done it justice. However, in his 1958 monograph about Kazakhstani cinema, Kabysh Siranov gave a lengthy, positive assessment of Aimanov's picture, stating that the public recognized it as the best of the tselina films.[9] Ten years later, though, he accused Aimanov's film of resolving conflicts with too much ease. Interestingly, the critic discusses the relatively minor tensions between the Komsomol and the Party functionaries opposing those who came to the *tselina* project for easy money and little work, but omits the clashes between the pragmatist Kudriash and his narrow-minded supervisor Korkutov.[10] Kul'shara Ainagulova, from a late Soviet viewpoint, underlined the "positive hero" Kudriash, who is undergoing a learning process that takes him from shortsighted authoritarianism to more flexible, goal-oriented methods. She also emphasized Aimanov's realism in describing tensions arising from the clash between traditional and modern views on interethnic relations.[11]

The film's main weakness, however, was never addressed, perhaps because it is more aesthetic than thematic: the narrative pace is excessive and inconsistent to the point of causing confusion. *We Live Here* consists of numerous snippet-like episodes that are in desperate need of more screen time to give the characters a chance to evolve. The relatively large cast can sometimes be disorienting to the viewer, too, as the distinction between primary and secondary characters is insufficiently marked. This impression may have been intentional; perhaps Aimanov wanted to create an image of cheerful collectivism, presenting a community of equals and rejecting identification with just one or two major characters. This would be justified insofar as the Virgin Lands project did rely on large-scale collective efforts. But the miniportraits of various characters move by too fast for the viewer to appreciate, and many scenes end too abruptly to be fully grasped. Had *We Live Here* been given the regular 90 minutes running time instead of its actual 70 minutes, the performers would have had a greater chance to engrave themselves in spectators' minds. This might also have prevented the impression of overly fast conflict resolutions to which Siranov objected. Thus, Aimanov's third film, and the first dealing with contemporary issues, became an innovative, albeit narratively problematic experiment. However, despite its shortcomings, it stands as a worthwhile Kazakh response to an unspecific Soviet view of a joint socioeconomic experience. As such, *We Live Here* reveals the existence of a yearning for the expression of national identity on the legitimacy of which Aimanov self-confidently insisted, regardless of its Soviet framework.

## THROUGH THE EYES OF NEWCOMERS: *BIRCHES IN THE STEPPE*

Russian director Iurii Pobedonostsev[12] approached the *tselina* theme in an unexpectedly realistic manner that was superior to the typical inspirational fare at the time. Although his film was produced at Kazakhfilm studio, he portrayed conflicts that arose during the cultivation of new lands from the viewpoint of the arriving Russians. First and foremost, the director was honest about the terrible living conditions and the interethnic tensions experienced by the newcomers. Like many *tselina* films, *Birches in the Steppe* (Berezy v stepi, 1956), based on a screenplay by B. Tetkin and Budimir Metal'nikov, begins with the arrival in the middle of nowhere of a train full of settlers, but there is no enthusiasm among them. When one of the women emerges from the train and looks around, she begins to weep.

Not only are the Kazakhs in Pobedonostsev's film different in looks and outlooks (most of them do not understand a word of Russian), but the Russians themselves are marked as ethnically distinct and not just "average Soviets." Many of them cannot get used to the barrenness of the steppe and complain about missing the Northern forests. Since no housing had been prepared for the Russian workers, their spouses and children, they are forced to live with Kazakh families. While some of the natives are hospitable and invite the newcomers to their table, Kazakh bureaucrats prevent the Russians from obtaining even elementary food. When the chairman of the kolkhoz finally agrees to provide each new family with a cow, this enrages his superiors and almost costs him his job.

But the most important plotline in Pobedonostsev's film is devoted to gender relations. The main character, Maria (Raisa Kurkina), views her move to Kazakhstan as a necessary sacrifice that she is making for her Soviet homeland. Hardships are to be endured, and she wants it no other way. Her husband, Stepan, however, was only looking for quick money when he agreed to join the *tselina* campaign. Confronted with physical burdens and everyday frustrations, he decides to leave. The portrayal of Stepan as a choleric naysayer whose negativity borders on sabotage is somewhat excessive. Upon getting up in the morning, the man is already in a bad mood and harasses his environment with his complaints and threats. What distinguishes Maria and Stepan's marriage is the systematic abuse to which the husband subjects his wife, first verbally, then physically. Although deeply hurt, Maria is willing to accept Stepan's abuse, both in the name of their little son and because she was raised to make sacrifices. But when she meets Dmitrii, a man who treats her with respect and care, she finally decides to leave Stepan.[13]

A secondary conflict is that between Dmitrii and his domineering mother who immediately takes a dislike to Maria whom she views as a threat. This is a character constellation rarely seen in Soviet cinema. Overall, the film gives far more room to psychological developments than to the economic issues that normally dominated *tselina* movies. *Birches in the Steppe* stands out in its treatment of everyday Soviet social life, too. The first episodes show large groups of adults not as the carefree youth that usually populated *tselina* films but in a crammed train compartment. Noteworthy is the physical closeness of women and men, which does not seem to bother anybody. Later, in a scene portraying a communal holiday, the same women and men are shown dancing wildly and with clear erotic undertones. By this time, the Russians and Kazakhs, who have become accustomed to each other, are no longer separate groups. Interestingly, Kazakh men and women are shown drinking vodka and eating pork without a word ever being said about it.

*Birches in the Steppe* is valuable as a realistic everyday-life drama that neither hides nor denies the difficulties of forced togetherness as an essential part of the *tselina* campaign. The political macro-perspective is rarely mentioned, and the Russian workers are far from the singing enthusiasts that other films claimed to be the norm. Instead, the prevailing attitude is one of sober rationality and dignity. The depiction of the communist bureaucracy even adds some satirical tones, pointing out that the higher-ups often have nothing to offer but slogans and empty promises. Maria and Dmitrii represent humble average Russians, willing to wait for gratification as long as their sacrifice is meaningful. Their natural loyalty and sense of duty helps the Russian newcomers deal with the most severe obstacles and turn the alien land into their homeland. This process is what the title refers to: Maria plants the birches that she misses so much. She will stay to see these birches grow, together with her son and with Dmitrii, who offers her a partnership of equals.

Mikhail Aranyshev's camerawork masterfully captures both emotionally charged landscapes and psychologically intense interiors, the latter with dramatic chiaroscuro tones during the clashes between Maria and Stepan. Evgenii Brusilovskii's score[14] matches these contrasts, with strong dissonances in episodes of adversity and lyrical tunes inspired by Kazakh folklore in scenes of harmony.

The Virgin Lands Campaign was an extrinsic phenomenon; as a theme, it was forced on Kazakhstani cinema for political and propagandistic reasons.[15] The different artistic responses to this phenomenon demonstrated that underneath a surface of perfect Soviet homogeneity, a multitude of perceptions were at work. In the future of Kazakh cinema, national sensitivities would play a decisive role, regardless of the shared multinational communist ideology.

Conspicuously, documentary cinema continued to emphasize the Soviet nature of economic progress in Kazakhstan. Thus, in the 20-minute *Morning of Kentau* (Utro Kentau, 1956) by Aleksandr Karpov, the construction of a miners' town in the steppe is presented as a multinational endeavor, featuring a Moldovan husband with a Chuvash wife among the founding citizens of a city established in 1955. The film explicitly celebrates the happiness of "being a builder of the endless *Soviet* land [emphasis mine—P.R.]."

## THE FIRST HITS OF KAZAKHSTANI CINEMA

The Thaw period in Soviet cinema that began after the death of Stalin was, among other things, marked by the appearance of comedies with increasingly sharp satirical edges. The most famous of these was El'dar Riazanov's Mosfilm production *Carnival Night* (Karnaval'naia noch', 1956), whose memorable characters and utterances became part of Soviet folklore. Early on Kazakhstan made an important contribution to this trend with a very popular (albeit not quite as satirically daring) comedy, *The Djigit Girl* (Devushkadzhigit, 1955), based on a screenplay by Vladimir Abyzov and Shakhmet Khusainov. It preempted several elements of Riazanov's feature debut and of similar comedies that were churned out by national studios, including a strong female title character; a combination of harmless jokes and moderate social satire; the inclusion of romantic songs; and an overall atmosphere of festive joie de vivre that ultimately unites all the characters. The importance of this Kazakh film comedy and another one made by Shaken Aimanov soon thereafter lies in their successful building a relationship of trust with Kazakh audiences and establishing a positive reputation for Kazakhstani cinema with viewers throughout the Soviet Union.

*The Djigit Girl* is clearly marked as a Kazakh film, from its title to the milieu in which it takes place: a rural community whose horse-breeding kolkhoz is named after the revolutionary Amangeldy (the title character of the first Kazakh feature film). The film's main spatial motifs are spectacular vistas of vast and beautiful mountainous landscapes, which provide a majestic background to many episodes. Yet these mountains are more than picturesque: in a scene in which several characters are involved in a large horse race unfolding in front of the mountains, it is clear that the peaks denote a space that the Kazakh people visibly own and embrace. The open landscape in which the characters interact is conquered aurally as well, through joyful, passionate singing, which is presented in a non-diegetic manner, that is, not for real listeners, but as a means of self-expression toward the spectators. The harmony between people and nature and the exuberance with which this harmonious relationship is expressed is an element of authentic national culture in a film that otherwise may come across as sociopolitically timid. The many images showing the kolkhoz horses and sheep being herded in the mighty mountains are not simply visually impressive but radiate national pride, the pride of a people living on and with this land. The dynamic mobility of the film's characters in the vastly open space suggests a sense of freedom and sovereignty that is both individual and national, even though the ethnically mixed cast precludes any direct nationalist or ethnocentric associations.

The love triangle in *The Djigit Girl* is more of a pretext for situational comedy than a genuine conflict. Galiia, the title heroine, loves Aidar. Their professional closeness (she is the senior horse shepherd, while he works as a horse breeder) creates an ideal frame for their partnership. Aidar's competitor Angarbai, a salesman in charge of the local store, never stands a real chance of winning Galiia's heart, and his efforts and amorous hopes appear more ridiculous than threatening. However, the reason that Angarbai dares to harbor any illusions of marrying Galiia is rooted in Kazakh customs. Aidar is dissatisfied with the horses in the collective farm. His father, the kolkhoz director, Doskhan, stubbornly refuses to make expensive acquisitions. In order to prove that quality horses are vital for the kolkhoz, Aidar deliberately underperforms during a race. Of course, Galiia wanted Aidar to win so that she could give him the traditional reward, a kiss. Pointing to his loss, Aidar succeeds in persuading his father to buy new horses but loses Galiia's respect, thus giving Angarbai reason to believe that he might be able to take Aidar's place. An additional obstacle for the lovers is the administrator Zhurabaev, whose abysmal singing exposes him as the quintessential Soviet bureaucrat and represents one of the mildly satirical elements in the film. After many noisy deliberations, the misunderstanding between Aidar and Galiia is cleared up, and in the spirit of reconciliation, the defeated Angarbai generously sponsors their wedding.

Pavel Bogoliubov's direction[16] was visibly shaped by the traditions of Soviet musical comedy of the 1930s. *The Djigit Girl* echoes the latter's unabashedly pro-Soviet populism, its demonstrative faith in simple folks as the positive foundation of society, and anti-bureaucratic stance. Bogoliubov obviously favored Grigorii Aleksandrov's dynamic pacing over Ivan Pyr'ev's more sentimental slowness. Most importantly, he embraced the optimistic enthusiasm that Russian directors had prioritized in the 1930s and tried to continue into the 1940s and 1950s, proving that this type of comedy could be transplanted to the Kazakh cultural space. But Bogoliubov's film is exceptional because of its atmosphere that was unique at the time: its exuberance, distinct from the more lyrical joyfulness of Shaken Aimanov's later comedies, anticipates the positive, overwhelming energy of Abdulla Karsakbaev's *My Name Is Kozha* (1963) and subsequent children's films of the 1960s and 1970s that would become staples of Soviet-Kazakh cinema.

The acting in the film is predictably simple. As befits a kindhearted comedy, almost all the characters are likeable, designed as social and national stock types rather than unique individuals. One of the few critical points raised by reviewers was the performance of Kenenbai Kozhabekov in the role of Aidar: he was seen as too serious for the comedic genre.[17] Meanwhile, Galiia, as portrayed by twenty-year-old Lola Abdukarimova[18] in her debut role, was a sensation. Not only is she pretty and smart, as the female leads in these comedies typically are, but she is also strong-willed and makes legitimate claims on a leadership role. The film's title signals this claim by connecting a term that traditionally denotes virility (*djigit*) with the noun "girl." In her strength of character, Galiia resembles Raikhan of fifteen years prior, who also sang on horseback high in the mountains. Another line connects Galiia with Nurzhamal from Aimanov's *Daughter of the Steppes*. Unlike the latter, however, Galiia is devoid of tragic features; she never once looks to the past, only to the future, with unshakeable confidence and optimism. It is important to note that these heroines' strength does not contradict their femininity and desirability in the eyes of the male characters, but presents a positive challenge, to which only the strongest men are able to adequately respond.

*The Djigit Girl* became an enormous hit. It was welcomed by tens of millions of viewers throughout the Soviet Union, has been favorably remembered, and is still regularly shown on television. The reviews, too, were overwhelmingly positive, although the few points of criticism bear mentioning. The flagship newspaper *Kazakhstanskaia pravda* opined: "For some reason, the lyrics for the songs were first written in Russian, not in Kazakh. For a national film comedy, this is hardly justified. In the same way as the score, the songs were deprived of any national distinctiveness."[19] These are new tones in Kazakhstani film criticism, all the more significant for coming from the mouthpiece of the Communist Party itself. Vasilii Solov'ev-Sedoi, who wrote the music for *The Djigit Girl*, was one of the most prominent Soviet composers. To express dissatisfaction with the lack of national coloration of his tunes demonstrated an unprecedented self-consciousness on the part of representatives of the national periphery toward the Soviet center, an attitude that would remain a cultural factor, whether visibly or invisibly, in the following decades. Arguably the most negative response to Kazakhstan's first film comedy came from Kabysh Siranov, whose unforgiving analysis lists a whole range of transgressions, from unmotivated jokes to silly situational humor and the absence of a credible conceptual line.[20] However, such unfriendly attitude was the exception; as a matter of fact, the morose criticism itself seems comical.

Shaken Aimanov responded to the smashing success of *The Djigit Girl* with a comedy of his own, *Our Dear Doctor* (Nash milyi doctor, 1957), with which he finally turned out the all-Soviet hit that he so desired. It was the first of his career.

The title hero, Doctor Lavrov (Iurii Pomerantsev), works tirelessly for his patients in a beautiful spa, "The Mountain Rose," located near Alma-Ata. When the popular doctor's sixtieth birthday approaches, some of his supervisees decide to organize a concert in his honor. However, the bureaucrat Filkin (Evgenii Diordiev) refuses to release the necessary funds. The loyal Bibigul, responsible for culture and entertainment, therefore engages numerous prominent artists who agree to sing free of charge. After some confusion about the exact date of the concert, all the participants arrive on time and present their artistic gifts to the beloved physician.

Conscious of genre like few other Soviet directors, Aimanov decided to lay bare the revue character of his story from the very beginning, not even pretending to have a realistic plotline that would somehow justify the characters' constant singing. To be sure, neither *The Djigit Girl* nor *Our Dear Doctor* are musicals. The songs in the former are not important enough to the evolution of the plot, while those in the latter are too stylistically diverse to justify such a designation. However, both films are built on the assumption that viewers (especially Kazakhs, with their known passion for music and performance) would accept the artificiality of the situation and refrain from critically applying criteria of verisimilitude to deliberately semi-realistic entertainment. This assumption turned out to be accurate: of all of Aimanov's films, *Our Dear Doctor* has remained the most loved in Kazakhstan.

Compared to *The Djigit Girl*, *Our Dear Doctor* makes even fewer attempts to conceptually burden its plot by introducing sociopolitical motifs. For Aimanov, directing this film seems to have been a work of joy. Not coincidentally, the director himself appears in a scene from Shakespeare's *Much Ado About Nothing*.

*Our Dear Doctor* was conceived as a crowd pleaser. The scenery is picturesque, the colors are bright, and the mood stays optimistic throughout. In a move that would have been risqué in the still prudish 1950s, Aimanov included scantily clad people congregating in and around a pool, displaying the newest swimsuit fashions, elaborate hairdos (no less attractive than those in Italian movies), and generally beautiful and talented women and men. As if to polemicize against the lifeless asceticism of Stalinist culture, Aimanov advocates a relaxed and joyful attitude toward life: in his film, attractive physicality is not hidden but proudly displayed, portrayed by a local painter, and even ironically discussed. The humor is mostly situational and good-natured, but the artists involved are so friendly to each other and to the audience that the absence of social references or satire does not come across as a deficiency. The few sourpuss characters who refuse to share the overall good mood are turned into objects of collective laughter.

Most importantly for non-Kazakh viewers, *Our Dear Doctor* presents a genuine Who's Who of Kazakhstani culture in the 1950s. For that reason alone, it is worth watching today. In various circumstances and decorations, spectators can indulge in the singing of Bibigul Tulegenova and Ermek Serkebaev,[21] the acting of Hadisha Bukeeva and Kauken Kenzhetaev, the dancing of Shara Zhienkulova, and many other stars.

It also features (without ever making an explicit point about it) a natural unity between Kazakhs and Russians. After all, the title character, portrayed with comical brio by Iurii Pomerantsev, is Russian. Together, they are forming a well-functioning community. This harmony notwithstanding, most of the featured artists are Kazakh, a visible cause of national pride. Aimanov never hides the fact that the doctor's birthday element of the plot is but a pretext for the musical revue. In several episodes, the story loses pace when the singing takes center stage, and sometimes the lineup of songs is not motivated by any story element at all. There are numerous harmless inside jokes, including when Kapan Badyrov states that "the next song is from the film *Our Dear Doctor*." There are also subtle allusions to the Stalin years, as when a hairdresser who messed up a haircut is denounced as a "saboteur" (*vreditel'*) with pretended outrage.

Like never before in Kazakh cinema, Aimanov demonstrated a penchant for playfulness, beginning with the animated opening credits. A later episode featuring a lullaby is rendered in animation as well. While such devices may have been inspired by the classical 1930s comedies of Grigorii Aleksandrov,[22] the tone of *Our Dear Doctor* is completely modern; its protagonists are self-confident and belong to another epoch than those of Aleksandrov or Pyr'ev. It seems fair to say that with *Our Dear Doctor*, Aimanov demonstrated a directorial sovereignty that is both modern and national, yet never nationalistic, just like the culture that this light comedy celebrates.

Arguably the most important quality of Aimanov's film is one that, alas, went largely unnoticed by critics and film historians: the insistence on bridging the gap between highbrow and lowbrow culture, classical music and folklore, western-inspired *Estrada* and homegrown patriotic song.[23] The fact that Aimanov included a scene from Shakespeare in an entertaining revue says it all: for him, there was no insurmountable contradiction between the popular and the elitist, and listeners and viewers shown in the film do not make that distinction either. Such synthesis may seem forced today, but in the 1950s it offered a workable approach to culture by ignoring the existing hierarchy of its components and legitimizing them all equally, with emphasis on their enjoyable togetherness.

The film is so demonstratively apolitical that it must have been perceived as a provocation at the time. Moreover, *Our Dear Doctor* is energized by the new post-Stalinist civility of Soviet society and the degree of national self-confidence that the Soviet center afforded to the peripheries. Aimanov reacted sensitively to these signals and made a film not for critics or ideological administrators but for viewers: both in Kazakhstan, in the Soviet Union, and internationally.

It is significant that two largely apolitical crowd pleasers, *The Djigit Girl* and *Our Dear Doctor*, for the first time placed Kazakhstan on the map of Soviet cinema, bringing its people and culture to the attention of millions of viewers. Aimanov's increasing self-confidence as his country's first native film director and the production of two comedy hits within two years signaled that Kazakh cinema had been born once again. It was, by Aimanov's own count, a third time, this time for real.

## EPIC EXPLORATIONS OF NATIONAL HISTORY

The year 1957 turned out to be a good one for Kazakhstani cinema, bringing audiences a musical comedy, two historical dramas about the country's role in the Bolshevik revolution and subsequent Civil War, and a biopic about a famous Kazakh intellectual. Never before had the cinema of Kazakhstan made such a concerted effort to speak about national issues, specific historical experiences, and collective traumas, and rarely would it be able to repeat such multifaceted success in the following decades. To be sure, the quality of these films was uneven, but their thematic and stylistic variety was praiseworthy.

*Botagoz*, helmed by Kazakhfilm studio's longest-serving director, Efim Aron, became a milestone in the evolution of Kazakhstani cinema. This historical drama about early twentieth-century events was adapted from a 1948 novel by Sabit Mukanov, one of the leading adherents of Socialist Realism in Kazakhstan. It is the story of a young woman who experiences the oppression and abuse endured by millions of poor people, and particularly by women. The screenwriters considerably condensed the novel's plot, focusing on three aspects: class relations among Kazakhs prior to 1917, especially the exploitation of the majority by rich *bays*; the complex relations between Kazakhs and Russians, in which the local tsarist administration plays a particularly reprehensible role; and womens' chances of achieving self-fulfillment in a patriarchal society that denied them even an elementary education. In *Botagoz*, these three aspects do not compete but rather condition each other. After all, the Bolshevik approach assumed that it was pointless to fight against the oppression of women or the abuse of the Kazakh natives independently, as both phenomena were rooted in the same systemic injustice permeating imperial Russia.

*Botagoz* opens with a New Year's Eve celebration in the villa of a Russian official. The Kazakh guests swear loyalty to the tsar, while a boorish young Russian officer, Kulakov, vows to "bring culture to the primitive inhabitants of the steppe." It is Kulakov who later forces the young title heroine to kiss him.[24]

The following episode counters the opening by showing an exiled political activist who is telling natives about class injustice and Lenin's struggle against it. To mark the 300th anniversary of the "House of the Romanovs," a local *aksakal* invites Askar, a young teacher who loves Botagoz, to accompany him. In Askar's absence, the powerful *bay* Itbai tries to win over the young woman for himself, using wealth and violence. Botagoz's refusal to give in not only earns her the old man's wrath, but also alienates her from the community, whose members refuse to understand her "false pride." Meanwhile, Askar, who has escaped from the imperial army, joins a group of Kazakh draft-dodgers hiding in the forest. But he cannot tolerate the nationalists and Muslims who view their fight either as a purely Kazakh or as a religious cause. These inner disagreements notwithstanding, Botagoz is freed by the outlaws and joins them in the forest. And despite the odd mix of diverse political forces, they manage to defeat the *bay* and his Russian allies and free the *aul*. Finally, Askar and Botagoz can marry. The outlaws' leader, Amantai, unites with the army of Amangeldy Imanov in the major anti-tsarist uprising of 1916. Later, as news arrives that the Winter Palace in St. Petersburg has been stormed, Botagoz is in the hands of the enemy. She barely manages to flee but joins the revolutionary troops in the forest just in time. Finally, the revolutionaries succeed in conquering the town and bringing the oppressors to justice.

Aron's main directorial accomplishments in *Botagoz* are an energetic narrative pace and the poignant characterization of various milieus. The wealthy

Russian homes radiate atmospheric authenticity, as do the dwellings of the poor and the forest outlaws. Aron's detail-oriented direction is supported by solid camerawork (Isaak Gitlevich, B. Siglov), creating atmospherically rich images of life in Central Asia prior to the demise of the tsarist order. The characters' political and psychological differentiation is likewise noteworthy: the arrogant young Russian officer embodies imperial hubris, whereas his decent, humble sister Liza stands for the decency of the intelligentsia; she is disgusted by her brother's behavior and supports Botagoz. Even more multifaceted are the representatives of various political factions in the revolutionary camp. History is thus shown as complicated and contradictory: not everything can be reduced to the fight of the poor against the rich. While the filmmakers' loyalty to the Marxist-Leninist conception of history is never in doubt, it is this willingness to provide a differentiated picture of the various forces in Kazakhstan at the time that saves *Botagoz* from becoming a one-dimensional pamphlet of which there were so many in Soviet cinema. Compared to movies devoted to the same historical period released by Mosfilm and Lenfilm in the mid-1950s, Aron's film is distinguished by humanity and openness to the strengths and weaknesses of individuals. The film's epic breadth, its persuasive performances (including that of Gulfairus Ismailova, a nonprofessional, in the title role[25]) and visual authenticity could not but impress contemporary viewers.[26]

Some critics felt uncomfortable about the rich historical canvas being presented in Kazakhstan's cinema for the first time, although it was not easy for them to precisely enumerate the film's faults. The authoritative *History of Soviet Cinema*, while acknowledging Aron's accomplishments, charged *Botagoz* with "not fully realizing its underlying idea." In the spirit of such fuzzy criticism, the critic claimed that the screenwriters did not know how to select the most substantial elements of the novel's plot. Another critic made a similar point and opined, "This made it hard to follow the connections between the episodes and perceive the film as one whole (*tselostnoe*) work."[27] It almost seems as if Soviet critics simply did not expect to see a film of such caliber emerge from Kazakhstan and were looking for excuses not to give it the high marks it deserved. One aspect of *Botagoz* that was criticized at the time of its release was the character of Askar, a native intellectual who inspires the female heroine just as much as the pauper Amantai. Never before had Kazakh cinema featured a village teacher as a major character, but the fact that he was a man who had doubts and hesitated in certain situations contradicted typical clichés about revolutionaries.

In hindsight, *Botagoz* stands as a serious historical epic that meets high professional standards. Its ideological take on Kazakh history from 1913 to 1917 avoids overly dogmatic concepts, while its portrayal of a strong female character who grows from unconscious passivity to active involvement is persuasive. *Botagoz* became the second Kazakh epic about the nation's recent history after *Daughter of the Steppes*. Conspicuously, both films depict Kazakhstan's historical experiences through the eyes of a woman. Most importantly, these large-scale productions explored Kazakh identity in a new, nationally conscious manner. Compared to Aimanov's film, however, Aron's is less edgy in its characterizations and allows for more psychological nuance.

A thematically related picture, *We Are from Semirech'e* (My iz Semirech'ia, 1957), features not one central character but three. They are soldiers returning from the battlefields of World War I to their native Semirech'e (literally "the country of seven rivers"), a region in which Kazakhs and Cossacks had lived together for centuries. The Cossacks had been granted special privileges by Catherine II in exchange for protecting the Russian Empire's borders. They had also traditionally been used to suppress local unrest, whether at the empire's margins or in its centers. This "policing for hire" during critical periods of Russian history defined the Cossacks' reputation, even though there was another side to them: Cossacks were fiercely independent and freedom-loving and played a crucial role during such events as the Pugachev revolt (1773–1775).[28] Addressing interethic issues was a minefield, especially in the still dogmatic context of the 1950s, and compromising the truth was almost inevitable.

*We Are from Semirech'e* opens on a didactic note, with explanatory intertitles referring to the years 1914, 1916, and 1918, that is, the beginning of World War I, in which Cossack units fought in the tsarist army; the year when Kazakhs were ordered by the Tsar to support the war efforts, a decree that resulted in violent protests; and the year when the reverberations of the Bolshevik revolution in Russia's mainland caused turbulences in Central Asia. The three friends are Kazakh, Uighur, and Russian and come home with the same dream of rejoining civil life. But the war years have left the country in tatters: Nartai, the Kazakh (Kenenbai Kozhabekov), discovers that his fiancée, Raikhan, has been officially promised to a rich old man who paid a huge *kalym*[29] for her; Pavel, the Russian (Grigorii Karnovich-Valua) finds his little son in agony from hunger and disease; and Amir, the Uighur (Ahmed Shamiev), although overjoyed when kissing his seven sleeping children, discovers that his family only survived due to the support of a smithy who casts Orthodox crosses. The Cossack leadership, under ataman Dutov, plans to turn their units against the local Bolsheviks and later joins the White Army attacking Moscow and Petrograd. For them, it is imperative to prevent any kind of alliance between Kazakhs and Cossacks. However, the Bolsheviks skillfully use propaganda to convince both groups that their situation is similar: the Cossacks have been cynically abused as cannon fodder during World War I and have no desire to continue fighting, while the Kazakhs see no reason to trust those who want to turn them against the Bolsheviks, their liberators. The revolt itself is triggered by the initial blatant indifference of the Cossacks to the plight of the Kazakhs: they shamelessly feed their horses with buckets of grain as the native population starves.

Though *We Are from Semirech'e* did not become a breakthrough for Kazakh cinema, it would be unfair to call it a failure. The film contains disturbing images of ruins, hunger, and despair; indeed, many episodes in *We Are from Semirech'e* are, thanks to the cinematography of Iskander Tynyshpaev, visually powerful. The film's main problem is its plot. Multilinear and confusing, it switches from one character to another without rhyme or reason, alternating between psychological drama (Nartai/Raikhan), scenes of street clashes, and lengthy, pathos-filled political debates. The three friends hardly evoke any sense of identification in the viewer.[30] The main culprit for this regrettable outcome is the screenplay by the well-known writers Dmitrii Snegin and S. Ulanovskii. Written without an understanding of the specific needs of cinematic narration, it often makes the film tedious viewing. The performers have a hard time delivering more than poses and loud revolutionary pathos. Thus, on the one hand, *We Are from Semirech'e* clearly falls short compared to *Botagoz*, which manages to maintain human interest in the title heroine almost throughout. On the other hand, *We Are from Semirech'e* does feature some superb camerawork, showing the interiors of Amir's home and the beauty of the region's landscapes (this was one of the first films in which Askhat Ashrapov, soon to join the ranks of Kazakhstan's leading cinematographers, worked as second cameraman). But even on the visual level the film is incoherent: some episodes appear realistic, whereas others reek of studio artificiality.

Among the film's innovative aspects (and one specific to Kazakhstan) is the depiction of the provisional government, which was in 1918 dominated by members of the Alash-Orda, an organization subsequently defeated and destroyed by the Bolsheviks and then largely taboo in the 1920s–1940s. To be sure, *We Are from Semirech'e* denounces Alash-Orda and the national government because they favored independence from Russia and the creation of a sovereign Kazakh nation-state. Its members are depicted as sellouts betraying the interests of their own people. At the same time, the Alash-Orda leaders are shown to be politically inept, unable to channel the social energies unleashed by the mutiny in a manner that would benefit their own political goals. Even less efficient are the imperial Russian officers: whether because the actors chosen for these roles were weak or because the characters' weakness was true to historical reality, the atamans and their minions can at no point muster genuine resistance against the clever and determined Bolsheviks. Ultimately, the fact that the class enemy is so strangely passive also makes the clashes between the two sides less absorbing for the viewer.

For the history of Kazakhstani cinema, *We Are from Semirech'e* is of interest as the full-length feature debut of Sultan Khodzhikov who was to become one of the country's most interesting directors. Despite all its aforementioned shortcomings, the film's national elements are remarkable, especially when expressed through songs and rituals, although these elements are insufficiently integrated with the plotline of social unrest; the two seem to run separately, as if taking place in parallel worlds. This failure to mold an organic cinematic space featuring class aspects and national cultural elements can be observed in the acting as well: the Kazakh performers are noticeably more energetic and physically present than the Russians, who seem to be following the clichéd patterns of revolutionary and Civil War potboilers. Thus, unlike *Botagoz*, *We Are from Semirech'e* leaves the ambivalent impression of a film that wants too much, falling short of its intention to become a large-scale national historical epic.

## An Innovative Biopic: *His Time Will Come*

The most surprising (and certainly most daring) Kazakh picture of the 1950s was *His Time Will Come* (Ego vremia pridet, 1957). Formally, it continued the line of Kazakh biopics begun with *Amangeldy*, *The Songs of Abai*, and *Dzhambul*. But its philosophical complexity set it apart from all of its predecessors. Directed by the young Mazhit Begalin, the picture deals with a fascinating character in Kazakhstan's history, Chokan Valikhanov (1835–1865), an ethnographer, geographer, and cultural explorer.

Valikhanov has always been a popular but also controversial figure. While his status as a scientist was beyond reproach, he was at times suspected by Kazakh nationalists of overly pro-Russian leanings. There is no doubt that Valikhanov saw the best chances for the evolution of the Kazakh nation as being alongside Russia. At the same time, he was a genuine patriot, a man passionately devoted to his Kazakh homeland, its people, culture, and nature. Today, Valikhanov is revered as the first secular intellectual of the Kazakh nation. In Begalin's film, he is shown as feeling comfortable in various milieus, whether with fellow officers of the tsarist army, with fellow Kazakhs at a *bazar*, or with Russian colleagues in a salon. But Valikhanov is a torn man, and his meandering between two worlds also signifies his lifelong dilemma. Where should his primary loyalty lie: with the Russian state or with the Kazakh people that Russia has colonized?

When the Imperial Geographical Society assigns Valikhanov on a mission to an unexplored land near the Chinese border, the Kashgar plain, he is filled with doubts about the Russian officials' true motives. Do they really want to know about an ancient culture or rather about the armed forces stationed there? These are questions that define the film's central character, his inner tension.

The project of a Valikhanov biopic was first announced in 1948; the screenplay was authored by two of the most accomplished Soviet screenwriters, Sergei Ermolinskii and Mikhail Bleiman, who knew Kazakhstan from the war years. Both had gained considerable recognition by the Stalinist establishment, and both had encountered ostracism during repressive ideological campaigns. Thus, it seems safe to assume that their attitude toward the Soviet Union's nationality policies was not unconditionally positive and that they were open to an unconventional approach to Kazakh culture. The explicit depiction of Russian arrogance toward Central Asian peoples as a constant could, of course, easily be extrapolated by contemporary spectators to imply that these attitudes had not disappeared during the Soviet era.

It is important to note that while the film's explicit criticism is directed against tsarist imperialism as such, not all members of the tsarist elite are shown in a negative light. Overall, *His Time Will Come* is not an anti-Russian film, although it was accused of nationalist overtones already at the screenwriting stage. Conspicuously, the film avoids some more controversial episodes such as the brutal attacks of Russian troops under General Cherniaev against the local population, after which Valikhanov was no longer willing to participate in the Russian military campaign. The fact that such an important decision was not shown was criticized by the influential Kazakh author Anuar Alimzhanov.[31]

When Valikhanov rides into his native *aul* on a white horse, his family expresses pride in him as a *Russian* officer. At the table, he praises Russian civilization which taught him justice and humanity. In turn, several Russian officials display genuine respect and sympathy for the young Kazakh researcher. He is admitted to the Imperial Geographical Society, a prestigious membership. Tsar Aleksandr II himself talks to Valikhanov and commends him on receiving the Vladimir medal. Such differentiation notwithstanding, however, condescension toward other peoples is depicted as a chronic malaise among the Russian elites. "There are two Russias," concludes Valikhanov as an already well-known scholar.

The film's primary focus is the existential dilemma of a Kazakh intellectual representing a scattered nation on the imperial periphery vis-à-vis central administrative restrictions and geopolitical ambitions. Valikhanov was seen in some quarters of the tsarist establishment as a troublemaker. His activities were observed by the secret police, which duly noted his self-confidence and his closeness to Dostoevskii, a man officially labeled a terrorist and exiled in the 1850s.

Begalin's approach to Russian civilization as the deliverer of education and modern values to colonized territories and as the guarantor of security from external aggression, which was usually the official pretext for conquest and colonization, was not new to Soviet biopics. The novelty of *His Time Will*

*Come* was how it captured the intrinsic, cohesive power of Kazakh culture for its people, whether nomads in the steppes, urbanites, or exiles. Whenever Valikhanov encounters his native culture, he cannot but reconnect with his roots, as if there are "cultural genes" at work inside him. When the tsarist official, Baron Federiks, sends the sickly Valikhanov to his native village he suddenly feels an influx of positive emotions: observing a horserace (*kokpar*), he cannot help but get on a horse himself. This theme is addressed from the opening when Valikhanov inquires about ancient drawings on rocks and an old man sings verses from the epic *Manas*. One of the most lyrical scenes shows Valikhanov sitting in the steppe with his beloved Aizhan; this scene is accompanied by a folksong sung by a young Kazakh woman.

A central theme of *His Time Will Come* is that of modernization. Indeed, the title itself should be understood in this vein. In one episode, Valikhanov clashes with a man by the name of Sadyk, who proclaims the need to defend the old nomadic lifestyle and resist modernization, an attitude entirely unacceptable to the scientist.

Summoned to St. Petersburg by Petr Semenov-Tian-Shanskii,[32] Valikhanov is full of apparent contradictions: at one point, he demonstratively speaks in Kazakh, but also criticizes Islam and calls upon Russia to bring civilization to Central Asia. But the Russian Empire, too, is depicted in an ambiguous light: the tsar surely values Valikhanov's services, but he is completely oblivious to the hardships suffered by the native population of Central Asia. However, members of the intelligentsia with whom Valikhanov communicates are sincerely democratic in their approach to other nations. This ambiguity creates a dilemma for Valikhanov: there is no question that the Kazakhs could not survive on their own at the time, but is the Russian Empire the best framework within which to tread this part of their long path toward sovereignty?

Valikhanov's decision in favor of Russia is made with its main geopolitical rival, Great Britain, in mind. A British diplomat who knows about the problems caused by Russian imperial hubris and who calls the Russians "barbarians" comes to meet the Kazakh scientist. He invites Valikhanov to Britain, praising him as "the Columbus of Asia." However, the Kazakh sees through the foreigner's intentions, slyly quipping "the London fog will not be beneficial for my health." Valikhanov fully understands that in the context of competing empires, exploration is synonymous with conquest and colonization. To Russian imperialists, as to their Western counterparts, Asia means natural and human resources and little else. "I know now who my friends are," Valikhanov states. "Not the Emperor's [Russia], but this one, not yet free but already full of strength, that's our Russia. Her ideals are my ideals."[33]

The profound conceptual ambiguity in its depiction of Russia made *His Time Will Come* a new phenomenon not just in Kazakhstani cinema, but in Soviet cinema. Before it, the biopic genre, as developed in the 1930s and

1940s, had been one of the most normative and stale, in which larger-than-life characters voiced ideological dogmas that forced Soviet ideologemes in a line of continuity with imperial pre-Soviet values. A prominent figure such as Valikhanov, with his persistent doubts about Russia as the lead nation within the multiethnic empire, would have been unimaginable in the Stalinist framework of a genre dominated by conceptual linearity, grandiose gestures, and sloganeering. Contemporary criticism of the film, which charged that characters such as Dostoevskii, Aleksandr II, and Chernyshevskii appear only in passing and do not experience genuine development, missed the point: the prominent figures whom Valikhanov encountered in his short life could hardly be portrayed in transformative stages, even more so given that the film only shows the last period of Valikhanov's life. Instead, Begalin's direction represents an implicit argument against normative official historiography. His Chokan Valikhanov is and remains a searcher who suffers from the many contradictions he encounters, including his image of Russia.

It would be an understatement to say that Begalin's innovative directorial approach is *supported* by Nurmukhan Zhanturin.[34] In reality, it is directly conveyed by the manner in which this exceptional actor portrays Valikhanov. Avoiding declamatory exaggeration and theatrical posing, he brings to the screen a modern, nuanced character analysis profoundly different from the type of acting that characterized the biopics of the 1930s–1940s.[35] Indeed, in terms of acting, *His Time Will Come* was a very modern film for its time. Generally, the narrative pace gives the impression of a certain rush, as if the director was trying to express as many of the ideas driving him as possible. This, of course, is similar to Valikhanov's own perception of life. Thus, although the criticism of "hurriedness" voiced by Begalin's teacher Sergei Gerasimov, is to some degree legitimate, the fast pace is conceptually justifiable.[36]

Valkihanov's dilemmas proved irresolvable in the historical context of the nineteenth century. This included his personal life: at some point, he sees Aizhan, his love interest, who has been promised to his old foe Sadyr. Escaping with Aizhan gives him a short time of happiness, but he is tormented by tuberculosis and becomes increasingly exhausted. His final monologue is that of a rational yet deeply tired man. This avoidance of loud pathos in the end is yet another instance of implicit polemics against standard Soviet biopics. What truly triumphs in the finale is Kazakh native culture: Valikhanov, bedridden and coughing, intends to follow the warrior's tradition and asks for a horse so that he can die in the steppe. This ultimate reconnection with his native land is the film's lasting vision, not the dream about a happy future in a classless society that marred so many earlier Soviet films. *His Time Will Come* is profoundly Kazakh, not so much politically but culturally and spiritually.[37] Indeed, many viewers perceived it as a film about the spirit of contemporary Kazakhstan.

The *intellectual* appeal of *His Time Will Come* was a novelty for Kazakhstani cinema. So was the media controversy after its release. At times, the same newspaper could publish diametrically opposed views, which used to be an anomaly during the Stalin years. An example is the authoritative *Kazakhstanskaia pravda*, where Mukhtar Auezov praised the screenplay stating that "the Kazakhstani public must be grateful to the authors" (October 23, 1952), followed a month later by the scholar Nurusheva who accused that same screenplay of "bourgeois-nationalist views" (November 23, 1952).[38] The debates echoed all the way into the 1990s. For the critic Bauyrzhan Nogerbek, Nurmukhan Zhanturin's portrayal of Valikhanov marks an achievement that was misunderstood by contemporary viewers. Indeed, at the time of the film's release, the influential writer Anuar Alimzhanov doubted that this role was within Zhanturin's range, a view supported by Kabysh Siranov.[39] Writing from a post-Soviet perspective, Nogerbek vehemently disagreed. For him, the tormented features, the gestures and behavior of Valikhanov/Zhanturin express the experiences of the Kazakh people as a whole, indeed, their painful history.[40] Nogerbek submits that Zhanturin's portrayal of Valikhanov reflected the perception of his entire generation. If this was indeed so, and not just a retroactive projection, then *His Time Will Come* contained more than a message about Kazakhstan's modernization. It was complemented by a message of chronic discomfort with the state of de facto colonization and a yearning for future national liberation, distant though it may have seemed.

## THE DECADE'S PROMISING CONCLUSION

The 1950s ended with a contemporary drama that managed to attract viewers by aptly combining industrial and private conflict with a dosage of ideology. Politically and visually, *On the Irtysh's Wild Beach* (Na dikom brege Irtysha, 1959) presents an utterly modern Soviet Kazakhstan. Its energies are directed toward the completion of the Bukhtarminsk hydroelectric power plant on the Irtysh River, a gigantic construction site to which the film's characters are related in one way or another. Arguably the most interesting subplot deals with the director of the enterprise, Uralov (Kanabek Baiseitov), and his son, Zhamal/Zhanai (Asanali Ashimov). Zhamal leaves the university without a degree and displays an arrogant personality, expecting his influential father to rectify all his financial problems. The elder Uralov is so outraged by his son's behavior that at one point he resorts to physical punishment, literally whipping the young man. However, what changes Zhamal is not this drastic action, but taking a regular job. For the first time, he is part of a collective of workers who treat him with the same rough egalitarianism as everybody else. This kind of social healing through physical labor proves to be effective and returns the young snob (the term *stiliaga* is used) to the communist community. Efim Aron's surefooted direction manages to weave together the father-son yarn, another story about the chief engineer's lost old love, and an experiment to stabilize the foundation of the dam. This was Socialist Realism in textbook perfection.[41]

Most interesting in historical perspective is the film's take on Kazakh-Russian relations: members of both ethnicities are depicted working, celebrating, and philosophizing as a close community. At a birthday party, Uralov's wife sings a Kazakh folksong that deeply moves all guests, Russians and Kazakhs alike, as a sequence of close shots demonstrates. This interethnic symbiosis is further strengthened by their shared vision of the future. When the Russian engineer remarks on how he envies future generations, a senior character, played by Hadisha Bukeeva, responds, "I don't envy them. They will live in Communism, while we are building it"—to which Uralov says, "Let them envy us." *On the Irtysh's Wild Beach* depicts a Soviet-Kazakh society that experiences occasional turbulences, but whose foundations are unshakeable. Yet despite positive responses from viewers and some praise at the USSR film festival in 1960, Aron's efforts to create a Kazakhstani film that would be simultaneously ideologically safe, party-minded, and popular went without official appreciation, echoing the experience of *Botagoz*.[42]

The mid-to-late 1950s were decisive for the evolution of Kazakhstani cinema because, for the first time, three native directors had the chance to express genuine Kazakh sensitivities in films that offered thematic variety and courage in exploring important issues of the country's past and present while maintaining a fine balance between specific native perceptions and an accepted Soviet sociopolitical framework. *We Live Here* and *Our Dear Doctor*, both directed by Shaken Aimanov, Kazakhstan's first native filmmaker, can legitimately be viewed as responses to thematically similar films helmed by nonnative directors. This quasi-dialogue is particularly remarkable since all these films were produced at the same studio. Another interesting development took place in terms of language policy in cinema: at a meeting of the Communist Party members of the Alma-Ata film studio in 1958, a majority voted in favor of shooting all feature films in Kazakh, beginning in 1959.

The debate around the issue of language, namely, in which language should a Kazakh film be shot, Russian or Kazakh? carried considerable emotional weight. Critic and film historian Kabysh Siranov was a strong proponent of shooting Kazakhstani pictures in Kazakh and only then dubbing them into Russian, or, alternatively, shooting a Russian version simultaneously with the primary Kazakh one. His argument pointed to the effect that acting in a foreign language had on the performers: rather than focusing on intonation and body language, Kazakh actors and actresses were forced to direct most of their attention to simply remembering the text and to accurately pronouncein the Russian words. This could have a detrimental effect on the quality of acting. Furthermore, Kazakh performers who spoke Russian with a noticeable accent distorted the image of the characters they were trying to create by making them sound uneducated; thus, the intended effect of providing a scene with "authentic national color" was turned on its head. Another issue was the synchronicity of lip movements in dubbed versions: When a film was shot in Russian and then dubbed into Kazakh, native viewers noticed that sound and lip movement did not coincide, which seemed especially unnatural since the characters portrayed were Kazakhs!

While the resolution adopted by the personnel of Kazakhfilm studio expressed the dominating sentiment, it was not binding. In the following decades, much depended on whether the director was a native Kazakh or Russian. Interestingly, there were exceptions. For example, Efim Aron made several films in Kazakh before dubbing them into Russian (usually with the same actors speaking the Russian text), while some Kazakh directors chose to shoot their films in Russian. One can safely assume that the political ramifications of this question could be significant as well. Whenever there were official suspicions of "nationalism," the pressure to shoot films in Russian rather than in Kazakh became stronger.[43] It should be noted that after Kazakhstan gained its independence, many Kazakhstani producers gave preference to making films in Russian because it was easier to market them profitably in post-Soviet territories. And in Kazakhstan, the majority of urban viewers spoke Russian more often than Kazakh, a situation that has only begun to change in recent years.

Along with movies that were welcomed by Kazakh viewers and Soviet audiences alike, some feature films flopped both critically and financially, for example *It Happened in Shugla* (Eto bylo v Shugle, 1955), Mazhit Begalin's full-length feature debut from a screenplay by Abdilda Tazhibaev. The film dealt with problems of agricultural management in a period of transition, featuring a seasoned kolkhoz director, Telgara Temirbekov (Idris Nogaibaev), who no longer listens to the members of the community, ignores the decrease in production, and prefers to socialize with yes-men. Young kolkhoz workers start a campaign against Temirbekov; the fact that a regional Communist Party hack supports their criticism makes the outcome predictable. What is surprising, however, is Temirbekov's ultimate acceptance of the criticism. Even more surprising is the kolkhoz members' wish to keep the shamed leader in his old position, although he himself had intended to resign. While the management crisis reflected the transition from Stalinist methods to more participatory approaches, the harmonious ending seemed to indicate a specific Kazakh preference for leadership continuity rather than radical changes. In an all-Soviet context, however, this conflict resolution seemed anachronistic. *It Happened in Shugla* was taken to task by the influential newspaper *Izvestiia*, which even publicized the embarrassing fact that, based on its low artistic quality, the film was only given permission for release in the Kazakh SSR, not in the entire USSR.[44] A similarly weak film was *The Squall* (Shkval, 1958), directed by Kuat Abuseitov. The original screenplay dealt with the life of fishermen of Lake Baikal. However, when Kazakhfilm studio acquired it, the plot was transferred to the Caspian Sea—in later years, film historians attributed the film's failure to this artificial "import."[45] But it must be said that Abuseitov's other films were not much better either; thus, the real issue seems to have been a lack of directorial prowess, not the lack of genuine "Kazakhness."[46]

The issue of national authenticity was at the center of heated debates, most of them unofficial. Kabysh Siranov reported that some critics and viewers were dividing the entire production of Kazakhfilm studio into "Kazakh" and "non-Kazakh" films. The former could be distinguished by their depiction of certain lifestyle peculiarities, including ethnic music, whereas stories about contemporaries living in modern urban conditions were dismissed as lacking national flavor. Subliminally, these debates continued until the 1980s and and could never be fully controlled by the Soviet state or the Communist Party.[47]

There are some indications that the atmosphere at the Alma-Ata studio was far from harmonious in those years. The State Archive of the Republic of Kazakhstan (Novozhilov Collection) holds the proofs of an article by the deputy head of the department of propaganda of the Alma-Ata Regional Party Committee, Bekmuratov, that was to be published in *Kazakhstanskaia Pravda* under the title "Bringing Order to the Alma-Ata Film Studio" (Navesti poriadok na Alma-Atinskoi kinostudii). The article talks about a "desperate need for screenplays," even though the studio had signed seventeen contracts with various authors. A competition for best screenplay ended without awarding a first prize. The second prize went to *On the Wild Beach* (Na dikom brege); the third prize was given to Liailia Galimzhanova and S. Ulanovskii for *A High Position*. The article's most embarrassing revelation was that members of the jury were also participants in the competition, which ended up disbursing 50,000 rubles in prize money! Bekmuratov mentions the names of the well-known writers cum administrators, Abyzov and Galimzhanova, among others. When the latter's screenplay was reviewed negatively, it was simply sent to a different reviewer who gave it positive marks. Only Gabit Mustafin had the courage to conclude that "all contributions were of low artistic quality." The articles states, "The competition did not achieve desirable results because a small group of unscrupulous people used it for their own selfish gain." Apparently, the facts exposed in the article were so shocking that its publication was cancelled at the last moment, when the proofs were already to go to print. This turn of events suggests that the problems at Kazakhstan's national film studio were viewed as serious but that information about the rampant corruption in some of its quarters would be either suppressed or only addressed behind closed doors.

Despite various setbacks, in the second half of the 1950s, Kazakhstani cinema appeared increasingly surefooted, moving forward with energy and self-confidence. Young professional directors such as Sultan-Ahmet Khodzhikov and Mazhit Begalin, who had graduated from the Soviet State Film School VGIK, found employment at the Alma-Ata studio, beginning their careers with shorts, assisting senior colleagues, and eventually progressing to larger projects. Despite ethical and management issues and some undeniable flops, by the late 1950s Kazakhstani cinema had demonstrated artistic potential that was often overlooked by the center and rarely officially acknowledged. Most significantly, the studio had shown its ability to connect with native audiences and achieve solid (and, in some cases, hit-level) box office results. *The Djigit Girl* attracted 27.8 million viewers during its first year of release; *Our Dear Doctor*—17 million; *On the Irtysh's Wild Beach*—16 million; *Botagoz*—15 million, and *We Live Here*—12 million. On the low end, *We Are from Semirech'e* ended up with a dismal 2.2 million viewers, an exception in the context of the excellent results for most Kazakhstani feature films during this early period. The nonnative traditionalists among the directors (Aron and Bogoliubov) were clearly in line with viewers' preferences, but Aimanov's films were strong competitors. As for Khodzhikov and Begalin, both displayed artistic ambition but were less concerned with attracting and pleasing large crowds.

The first monograph on Kazakhstani cinema was published in 1958. With its seventy pages, *Kazakh Cinema* (Kazakhskoe kinoiskusstvo) gives a selective survey of the development of feature filmmaking in Kazakhstan. Its author, Kabysh Siranov, was himself an active participant of many events he described: he had studied at VGIK during the war, authored screenplays, and simultaneously served in various administrative roles at TsOKS. After his arrest in 1946, Siranov spent eight years in the GULAG, returning to Alma-Ata in 1954. There, he resumed his work on screenplays, but without much success. The area that brought him the most recognition was film criticism, in which he displayed a unique expertise and passion for his subject, but also a tendency to express strong, sometimes one-sided opinions. *Kazakh Cinema* is a good example for his approach.

The monograph begins in the late 1920s, leaving out the pre-Soviet period and the early Soviet years and the dominance of the newsreel genre, where the careers of many Kazakhstani film workers began. While the Vostokkino productions that addressed Kazakhstani themes in 1928–1932 are analyzed in detail, the first sound film made about Kazakhstan, *Enemies' Paths* (1935), is merely mentioned in passing. The significance of *Amangeldy* for the evolution of Kazakhstani cinema is fully recognized, whereas *Raikhan* (1940) is not mentioned at all. Likewise, the history of the Central United Film Studio (TsOKS) is given the appropriate attention, especially the films for which Siranov himself had written the screenplays (*The White Rose* and *To the Sounds of Dombras*), but nothing is said about Dziga Vertov's seminal *To You, Front!* Such selectiveness is complemented by a clear preference for the films of Efim Aron as opposed to those of Shaken Aimanov. Considering the year of its publication, the monograph could at least have hinted at the effects of Stalinism on Kazakh cinema, for example, providing an analysis of Aron's ill-conceived *The Golden Horn* (1948). Likewise, the cultural misery of the post-war years is not addressed at all. Thus, the critic's subjectivity and excessive caution ultimately produces a distorted picture when he chastises at great length the nationwide superhit *The Djigit-Girl* but does not address real flops such as *It Happened in Shugla*. Still, Siranov's booklet was the first attempt to view Kazakhstani cinema as a phenomenon deserving of critical and scholarly attention. Its emphasis on the need to find a nationally specific film aesthetic is remarkable.

Film criticism appeared regularly on the pages of the Communist Party press, particularly *Kazahstanskaia Pravda*. In some cases, the center (that is, Moscow-based newspapers and journals) took note of Kazakhstani films, especially the most solid or artistically original works, such as *Botagoz* and *His Time Will Come*. The fact that the leading professional journal, *Cinema Art* (Iskusstvo kino), devoted long reviews to films from Alma-Ata was a clear indication that Kazakhstani cinema had become an entity to reckon with. In several reviews in regional newspapers, one can sense a spirit of *ownership*, signaling that this is *our* cinema; we, Kazakhstani viewers, have certain expectations and are proud of its accomplishments. Such identification of Kazakhstani audiences with their films boded well for the coming decade.

On June 9, 1958, the Council of Ministers of the Kazakh SSR issued a decree establishing a blue-ribbon committee (*orgkomitet*) charged with the preparation of a Union of Kazakhstani Film Workers. Among its nine members were the directors Shaken Aimanov and Mazhit Begalin, the cinematographer Mikhail Aranyshev, and the composer Evgenii Brusilovskii. It would be almost five years before the founding congress of the union took place. By that time, Kazakhstani cinema would not only have a full-fledged studio, but a professional organization that could represent the interests of its members.

When Moscow hosted a ten-day festival (*dekada*) of Kazakh art from December 12 to 21, 1958, Kazakhfilm studio included three pictures in its program: *His Time Will Come*, *Our Dear Doctor*, and *We Are from*

*Semirech'e*. At this all-Soviet forum, the selected films were often discussed in a critical manner, perhaps at times even condescendingly. But the newfound self-awareness and self-confidence of Kazakh filmmakers could no longer be ignored or suppressed. These attitudes were the most vital condition for the foundation of a national Kazakh cinema that fully emerged in the 1960s.

During the rest of their relatively short careers, neither Shaken Aimanov nor Sultan-Ahmet Khodzhikov nor Mazhit Begalin were able to fully realize their artistic potential. But their oeuvres contain examples of artistic experimentation that justify considering these directors as emerging auteurs. The process of serious critical recognition of their best pictures would begin only after their passing, when Kazakhstan gained its national independence. In this sense, their time, too, would come.

## NOTES

1. In one episode, Zhenia and a notorious womanizer are placed in the middle of a circle; the improvised "show trial" resembles the ancient ritual of putting evildoers at a pillory. The two chastised men suffer visibly when they are shamed in front of everybody.

2. For a fair critique of *A Restless Spring*, cf. Katesh Alimbaeva in Siranov, *Ocherki istorii kazakhskogo kino*, pp. 120–22.

3. A Kazakh administrator, who comes for an official visit to the new settlement, states, rather awkwardly: "We are happy that you have come! Everything was empty, but now you are here, and we are happy." Statements such as this demonstrate the Soviet establishment's insecurity regarding nationalities' policies after 1953. During the Stalin years, humorous references to ethnic peculiarities, including specific accents in Russian, were common and accepted, especially in comedies.

4. Abyzov, Vladimir Ivanovich (1925–1986), Russian author; graduated from the screenwriting department of the Soviet State Film Institute (VGIK) in 1951. Abyzov then moved to Alma-Ata where he authored screenplays for several documentaries and, together with Shakhmet Khusainov, three successful feature films. In 1959, he moved to Yalta film studio.

5. Matvei Volodarskii is listed in the credits as Aimanov's co-director, but nothing could be established about his credentials or his specific contribution to this film.

6. The 2014 version, which Darezhan Omirbaev redacted, featured a new Russian voice-over.

7. Shaken Aimanov, "Obrashchaias' k druz'iam," *Iskusstvo kino*, 10/1965, p. 19.

8. This was Aimanov's first film in color; its cinematographer, Mark Berkovich, became one of the director's most trusted partners on several projects.

9. Cf. Siranov, *Kazakhskoe kinoiskusstvo*, pp. 41–49, the quote is on p. 48

10. *Istoriia sovetskogo kino*, vol. 4 (1952–1967). Moskva: "Iskusstvo," 1978, p. 235.

11. Ainagulova, Alimbaeva, *Tendentsii razvitiia kinoiskusstva*, p. 13.

12. Pobedonostsev, Iurii Sergeevich (1910–1990), Russian-Soviet director, graduated from the Soviet State Film Institute (VGIK) in 1950. *Birchtrees in the Steppe* was his second feature film and the only one produced in Kazakhstan.

13. The unusual degree of realism in the depiction of the tselina in Pobedonostsev's film, which distinguishes it from so many others, was rarely addressed; instead, some critics analyzed the film as a sociopsychological drama. However, the attempt to make Mar'ia a part of the tradition of Russian women emancipating themselves from patriarchal bonds is not entirely convincing since *Birchtrees in the Steppe* does not show any professional growth. Cf. Siranov, *Ocherki istorii kazakhskogo kino*, p. 134.

14. Brusilovskii, Evgenii Grigor'evich (1908–1981), Russian composer who worked most of his life in Kazakhstan. He composed the first Kazakh operas and a number of film scores, including the music for Begalin's *His Time Will Come* (1957).

15. Among later efforts of Kazakhstani filmmakers dealing with the Virgin Lands campaign was Emir Faik's *Once at Night* (Odnazhdy noch'iu, 1959), which was criticized for its lackluster performances and general artistic weakness.

16. This is the only film of note by Bogoliubov, who died soon after the premiere. The assistant director was Sultan Khodzhikov, who became one of the leading Kazakh filmmakers of the 1960s and 1970s.

17. Siranov, *Ocherki istorii kazakhskogo kino*, p. 110.

18. Lola Abdukarimova (b. 1935) graduated from the school of choreography in Tashkent in 1952 and became a popular singer and actress; she was married to well-known Kazakh cinematographer Askhat Ashrapov.

19. Buketov, E., "Zhizneradostnaia kinokomediia," *Kazakhstanskaia pravda*, 5 May 1955.

20. Siranov, *Kazakhskoe kinoiskusstvo*, pp. 39–41.

21. Tulegenova, Bibigul (b. 1929), famous Kazakh opera singer (soprano) who appeared in several feature films, most recently in the Nursultan Nazarbaev biopic *The Sky of My Childhood* (2011) as the grandmother of the main character. Serkebaev, Ermek (1926–2013), one of the most influential opera singers of Kazakhstan (baritone) who was cast in five feature films in the 1950s–1970s.

22. Katesh Alimbaeva points to similarities with the groundbreaking Russian comedy *Carnival Night* (Karnaval'naia noch', 1956) by El'dar Riazanov, especially the role of the spoiler-bureaucrat, Fil'kin. However, Fil'kin in *Our Dear Doctor* is harmless in comparison to his Russian counterpart Ogurtsov who, in Igor' Il'inskii's masterful interpretation, acts as the principal opponent to everything free, creative, and original. Aimanov's Fil'kin is far from this kind of conceptual weight.

23. Cf. the very critical review by E. Khan, "Bez skidok na molodost'," *Leninskii put'*, 15 July 1959, p. 3, which points out that the screenplay lacks compactness and a distinction between essential and secondary lines. The score of *Our Dear Doctor* was written by Aleksandr Zatsepin, one of the most prolific Soviet film composers who authored numerous melodies that were popular throughout the Soviet Union; Aimanov later worked with him on two other comedies, *A Song Is Calling* (1961) and *Angel in a Cap* (1968).

24. In her detailed analysis of *Botagoz*, the film historian Roza Abdulakhatova praises the principle of inner montage in this episode, with the camera closely following the main characters, registering their changing psychological state while in motion. Abdulakhatova also points to the insecurity of the Russian officer behind a mask of bravado and arrogance, an insecurity caused by Botagoz's natural strength and purity. Cf. Siranov, *Ocherki istorii kazakhskogo kino*, pp. 115–16.

25. Ismailova, Gulfairus (1929–2013) was an accomplished painter, art director, and non-professional actress who excelled in films such as *Botagoz* and *Kyz-Zhibek*; in the latter, she was both art director and portrayed the title heroine's mother, Aigoz. Her acting debut in cinema was in Mark Donskoi's *Alitet Leaves for the Mountains* (Alitet ukhodit v gory, 1947).

26. For a generally positive review of *Botagoz* in a central newspaper see S. Antonov, "V perelomnyi moment istorii," *Sovetskaia kul'tura*, 13 December 1958.

27. In a later text, Roza Adulakhatova wrote more positively about the film, stating that it leaves the impression of an integrated whole (*tselostnoe*) work. Cf. Siranov, *Ocherki istorii kazakhskogo kino*, pp. 113–14.

28. The late 1950s were marked by a renewed interest in the 1918-20 Civil War and the role that Cossacks played in it. Sergei Gerasimov's trilogy *And Quiet Flows the Don* (Tikhii Don, 1957), adapted from Mikhail Sholokhovs epic, one of the greatest box office hits of Soviet cinema, defined the relatively differentiated way in which Cossacks would be depicted henceforth.

29. *Kalym* denotes the traditional bride price that had to be paid by the groom's family and was obligatory in Central Asian societies; during the Soviet period, it was illegal.

30. Siranov, *Ocherki istorii kazakhskogo kino*, p. 92.

31. Cf. Alimzhanov, Anuar, "'Ego vremia pridet.' Zametki o kinofil'me." *Kazakhstanskaia pravda*, 23 November 1958. In his review, Alimzhanov accused the two screenwriters of ignoring the criticism that had been launched against their screenplay some years before.

32. Petr Semenov-Tian-Shanskii (1827-1914), prominent Russian geographer.

33. Siranov, *Ocherki istorii kazakhskogo kino*, p. 95.

34. Zhanturin, Nurmukhan (1928-1990), one of the leading actors of Kazakhstan who worked with prominent directors such as Mark Donskoi, Larisa Shepit'ko, Shaken Aimanov, and Sergei Urusevskii. Not all of his more than 80 roles in cinema were worthy of his talent, but in his best films, Zhanturin achieved an intensity of transformation that was unique even within the generally strong Kazakhstani school of acting. Zhanturin also directed three feature films, including *Forest Ballad* (Lesnaia ballada, 1972), which contains an insightful depiction of fascist ideology.

35. Siranov, *Ocherki istorii kazakhskogo kino*, p. 91.

36. Cf. Abyzov, V., Mart"iamov, S., "Iarko, pravdivo otobrazhat' zhizn'." *Izvestiia*, 12 May 1957.

37. Anuar Alimzhanov was one of the few critics who did not accept the film; among other points, he criticized its image of Kazakhstan as consisting of nothing but deserts. Cf. Alimzhanov, "'Ego vremia pridet.' Zametki o kinofil'me." *Kazakhstanskaia pravda*, 23 November 1958.

38. Quoted in Siranov, K., *Kinoiskusstvo sovetskogo Kazakhstana*. Alma-Ata: Izdatel'stvo 'Kazakhstan,' 1966, p. 9.

39. Cf. Siranov, K., *Kinoiskusstvo sovetskogo Kazakhstana*. Alma-Ata: Izdatel'stvo ,Kazakhstan', 1966, p. 291, quoted in Nogerbek, B., "Chokan Nurmukhana Zhanturina," *Madeniet*, 17/1992, p. 13, reprinted in Nogerbek, *Na ekrane 'Kazakhfil'm,'* pp. 8–13. Zhanturin had portrayed Chokan Valikhanov on stage, but this performance was controversial as well. See Alimzhanov, "'Ego vremia pridet.' Alimzhanov charged that Zhanturin's Chokan comes across as "obtusely arrogant, self-confident, narcissistic."

40. Nogerbek, *Na ekrane 'Kazakhfil'm,'* p. 11.

41. "There can be no doubt that the new Kazakhstani film *On the Irtysh's Wild Beach* has opened the path to the screen for the positive hero – the human being from the people, the creator of communism, whose grandeur and beauty lies in his creative, daring work." Pinchukova, L. "Fil'm o krasivykh liudiakh," *Alma-Atinskaia pravda*, 12 August 1959.

42. A particularly critical review was published in *Kazakhstanskaia pravda*. The author finds fault in the abundance of underdeveloped conflict lines, which had already burdened the screenplay, as well as logical flaws, and unrealistic elements. However, he praises the accomplishments of the young actors and juxtaposes the film as a whole to *We Live Here*, which he calls "colorless." Cf. Nikolaev, K., "Na podstupah k znachitel'noi teme." *Kazakhstanskaia pravda*, 13 August 1959.

43. Siranov, *Kazakhskoe kinoiskusstvo*, pp. 20–2.

44. Cf. Abyzov, V., Mart"iamov, S., "Iarko, pravdivo otobrazhat' zhizn'." *Izvestiia*, 12 May 1957.

45. Cf. Siranov, *Ocherki istorii kazakhskogo kino*, p. 108.

46. Kuat Abuseitov (1925–2003) belonged to the first generation of native Kazakh film directors; his name and films have been largely forgotten. He worked at TsOKS and graduated from the Alma-Ata school of film acting in 1947. In 1952-58, Abuseitov studied acting with Sergei Iutkevich at VGIK. He dubbed Russian films into Kazakh and directed four feature films and a number of documentaries, ending his career in the 1970s.

47. Cf. Siranov, *Kinoiskusstvo sovetskogo Kazakhstana*, p. 307.

*Chapter 5*

# En Route to Complexity I
## *Capturing the Present*

Within a relatively short time span, Kazakhstani cinema had acquired the ability to produce blockbuster comedies, historical epics, and biopics that could stand up to competition from other Soviet studios and even pursue pioneering aesthetic approaches. Such rapid development was nothing short of astonishing. The Soviet central cultural institutions would *de jure* maintain a mentor/mentee attitude in dealing with the rapidly growing filmmaking community in Kazakhstan, but the cultural periphery was de facto set to continue on its path toward national cinematic emancipation. Thus, Shaken Aimanov's strategy of actively engaging in a native film culture turned out to have been the right choice. The dynamically developing national cinema, which included both feature films and documentaries, became a factor within Kazakh culture that had to be taken seriously.

In November 1959, the 1,000th issue of the newsreel series *Soviet Kazakhstan* was released, an occasion that was widely acknowledged in the republic and celebrated as a gesture of respect of Kazakhstani cinema. The renaming of the republic's center of film production to *Kazakhfilm studio* on January 9, 1960, by the Ministry of Culture was obviously based on a growing recognition of its national significance.

However, there were also signs of discontent and downright resistance to this successful development. In September 1961, the Alma-Ata correspondent of the newspaper *Izvestiia* published an article that described conditions at the Kazakh film studio in the darkest possible tones. Regarding the reasons for the purported crisis, the journalist identified one main factor: Shaken Aimanov and his ambition to act, direct, write, and contribute to as many films as possible, even though the results, according to the journalist, were not much to write home about. The article's title, "Two Melons in One Hand," pointed to the inevitable consequences of an artist's drive to be involved in too many things at the same time. The author characterized Aimanov's early works (*Poem About Love*, *Daughter of the Steppes*, and *We Live Here*) as films that "have not brought him or the studio any fame," while his latest picture, *In One District*, is said to have evoked harsh reactions from viewers for being "far from the truth of life."[1] Aimanov, who was at that time the head of the studio's artistic council, was also criticized for overestimating his own writing and directing abilities. The article's second target is Kabysh Siranov, formerly head of the screenplay department, who purportedly accepted numerous manuscripts and paid their authors handsomely, even though the acquired screenplays were neither complete, nor of good quality. In contrast, established writers had little desire to work at Kazakhfilm studio because of the prospect that people like Aimanov would push to become their coauthor.

These harsh attacks, voiced by the second most influential newspaper in the USSR, caused shockwaves. The collegium of the Ministry of Culture of the Kazakh SSR held a special meeting and concluded that the criticism was justified and timely. "The studio 'Kazakhfilm' has indeed lowered the intellectual and artistic quality of its films. . . . Weak pictures such as *Silence*, *In One District*, and *A Song Is Calling* appeared because the leaders of the studio did not take into account the opinion of the artistic council." The new studio leadership was assigned the task of eliminating these mistakes and weaknesses.[2]

The fact that the internal problems of Kazakhstan's film production were made the subject of a Soviet-wide debate indicates that a power struggle in the highest echelons of the Kazakhstani cultural-political elite had begun.

A few months earlier, Kazakhstani cinema had likewise hit the headlines, that time in an unexpected and tragic way. The actors Nurmukhan Zhanturin, Idris Nogaibaev, and Kenenbai Kozhabekov became the targets of a knife attack carried out by thugs in broad daylight. Although the perpetrators (three young men) were arrested, the investigation dragged on, and it was six months before the court finally sentenced them to prison terms. The real scandal was the indifference of the police to resolving the case. Not only did security officials attempt to muddy the waters, but they even accused the victims themselves of having provoked the attack. Finally, it became known that the three accused were the sons of high-ranking government officials; the father of one was the Minister of Trade of the Soviet Socialist Republic of Kazakhstan. But the actors' injuries were too severe to be ignored. After all, Kenenbai Kozhabekov remained partially paralyzed until the end of his life. National and Soviet media got involved, and even *Izvestiia* published an article about the corruption of Kazakhstan's police and judiciary.[3] This scandal not only shook up the artistic world, but it also pointed to the emergence of a new social stratum of seemingly invincible officials and their "golden youth" offspring who deemed themselves above the law. There was something ominous about this crime, a traumatic event for the entire Kazakh theater and film community in which members of the nomenklatura clans assaulted well-known film artists.

The strategic debates to which the afore-mentioned 1961 *Izvestiia* article pointed concerned the direction in which the national film industry was supposed to move. One of the methods used in this fight was deliberate negligence of the specific requirements of different genres. This was particularly unfair in respect to *A Song Is Calling*, which became one of the favorite objects of official scorn. Demanding outstanding artistic qualities from a lighthearted musical comedy was preposterous and showed the underlying intent to discredit Aimanov, the studio's most authoritative and popular artist. Interestingly, the *Izvestiia* article mentions only Aimanov's films, not those of other directors. This indicates not only that the attack was strategically placed and ad hominem, but also that the aggressor faction likely had supporters in the highest ranks of the Party and the government.

One year later, Aimanov, who still commanded enormous authority, got his chance for revenge. The newspaper *Sovetskaia kul'tura* published an account of the inner struggle at Kazakhfilm studio, once again bemoaning the insufficient authority of its artistic council, but to completely different effect. According to the article, a screenplay by one A. Galiev was accepted and paid for by the studio administration, although Shaken Aimanov and Gabit Musrepov had advised against it. As a result, the studio incurred serious losses that could have been avoided.[4] Of course, disagreements between administrators, producers, and artists are a normal phenomenon in all film industries. However, in the case of Kazakhfilm studio, a complicating factor was the undeniable fact that national cinema was still in a fledgling state and that the production of feature films was monitored by too many local and central institutions, including the Central Committee of the Communist Party of Kazakhstan, with its department of culture; the Council of Ministers, with its committee on cinema; and Goskino in Moscow. In addition, there were the invisible structures of the secret service, the KGB, whose real impact on Soviet cinema has yet to be assessed. The fact that some excellent pictures were produced despite these many pressures, speaks to the talent and willpower of their cast (the performers were generally considered the strongest asset of Kazakhstani cinema), cameramen, composers, designers, and directors.

The mid-to-late 1950s had revealed the enormous potential of cinema in Kazakhstan. The national film studio's portfolio in 1954–1959, with its diversity of themes, aesthetic approaches, and creative personalities, marked Kazakh cinema's first real blossoming. Building on these accomplishments, the following decade turned into a period when Kazakhstani cinema underwent overall organizational consolidation, despite the accompanying patronizing ideological guidance and attacks on various levels. Several Kazakh filmmakers, including Aimanov, Begalin, and Khodzhikov, as well as newcomers Aleksandr Karpov and Abdulla Karsakbaev, came into their own with themes and stylistic approaches that would define the nation's cinema for the next two decades. The 1960s also saw the emergence of a more distinct genre configuration that included contemporary social drama, children's films, war and revolutionary drama, and comedy. Biographical films and literary adaptations, which featured prominently in the production of the USSR's central studios, Mosfilm and Lenfilm, as well as studios of other Soviet republics, during that period took a back seat in Alma-Ata.

In hindsight, it is hard to discern whether the choice of certain genres was made strategically, based on conscious preferences, or ad hoc, determined by the availability of acceptable screenplays and qualified directors. Statements delivered during official meetings of Kazakhstani film workers at the time suggest that specific genre decisions at Kazakhfilm studio were based primarily on the availability of resources rather than on long-term planning. Indeed, a studio with an average output of three to four feature films per year (although the official assignment was to produce seven films per annum) had limited room for broader thematic and genre diversity. While prominent artists such as Shaken Aimanov exercised considerable influence in establishing thematic priorities, the overall direction was determined by the Communist Party of Kazakhstan, especially the department of culture of its Central Committee, and the republic's Ministry of Culture. They provided the film industry with political and ideological guidelines, which could in turn impact the choice of genres.

## THE UNIONIZATION OF KAZAKHSTANI CINEMA

At the beginning of the new decade, the founding congress of the Union of Kazakhstani Film Workers formulated marching orders and set the tone for the next years. The congress took place in Alma-Ata on January 8 and 9, 1963. It emulated the typical pattern of Soviet officialdom: delegates were treated to a report by the founding committee's chairman, followed by discussions, speeches by invited guests, the approval of a letter to the Central Committee of the Communist Party, and the election of the administration of the Union of Film Workers.[5]

Shaken Aimanov, Kazakhstan's first native and by now most prominent feature film director, delivered the opening remarks, which contained a fair amount of criticism. He discussed the predominance of unremarkable and mediocre films in Kazakh cinema and identified the lack of quality screenplays as the main culprit. He also focused on the responsibility of the studio redactors, a position that was obscure to the outside world and rarely mentioned in film reviews or reports from the set. The redactor's responsibility was to accompany the production of a film from the formulation of the initial idea and the writing of the screenplay all the way to the shooting and post-production process. In Aimanov's words, the redactor "must be able to find a new turn in a difficult moment of life, suggest a correct solution, straighten the dialogues, and determine a film's political direction, not allowing the authors to get trapped by some mistake."[6] Aimanov's description makes clear that the studio redactors were the de facto onsite censors assigned to each project. His report proposed more trusting cooperation between filmmakers and redactors as early as the conceptualizing stage.

As usual, individual examples were more telling than the common-places and generalities that filled most speeches. Thus, Mark Berkovich, a cinematographer who worked closely with Aimanov, spoke about a documentary commissioned by Kazakhstan's Ministry of Agriculture. Berkovich described how, after the film's completion, the ministry demanded changes, but even when these changes were implemented, the final product was shelved because it was considered overly critical. As a result, the 8,000 rubles that the project had cost went to waste. "Are we really not supposed to speak about shortcomings, using the language of cinema?" Berkovich asked rhetorically. His testimony was one of few to provide insight into the highly opaque production process in Soviet-Kazakh cinema and its political implications.

Among the prominent guests from Moscow were Aleksandr Medvedkin, who gave high marks to Aimanov's just released *Intersection*, and Iulii Raizman, who also approved of Aimanov's new picture and emphasized the need for truthful films, unlike the ones that were produced during the "period of the cult of personality" (i.e., the Stalin period). But Raizman's words were not echoed by other speakers: none of the Kazakh delegates made any reference to the Stalin era or gave a critical assessment of the films of the 1940s and 1950s. Instead, Kazakhstan's minister of culture, the erstwhile actress Liailia Galimzhanova, pointed to the gap between many films' lofty intentions and the actual results when they appeared on screen.

The main practical charge of the congress was to finalize the creation of a national professional union. This goal was accomplished. The new union had eighty-seven members, of whom seventeen were elected to the board (*pravlenie*). However, official reports also allow insight into internal studio problems. Thus, Aimanov criticized the arrogance of certain directors, albeit without naming names, as preventing the development of collegial relations; he particularly pointed the finger at young filmmakers.[7] The lack of trust among directors was addressed again at a later point. This suggests that the atmosphere at the studio could be tense at times, obviously fueled by individual attitudes and ambitions. Also noteworthy is the wording in the official letter sent by the delegates to the Central Committee of the Communist Party. Its first sentence expresses a feeling of "deep gratitude and filial love" toward the "Party of Lenin"; a few paragraphs later, the communist leadership's "fatherly care" for cinema and its cadres is praised. Such verbal paternalism certainly reflected the typical kowtowing to the country's political establishment, despite a decade-long grassroots democratic process that had been named in the West "the Thaw" (a term that was never adopted in the Eastern bloc) and would continue for another two years. One may justifiably conclude that the founding congress of the Union of Kazakh Film Workers signaled to its members that socio-cultural experiments and liberal reforms such as those conducted in Moscow were out of the question in their republic. Here, the gap between center and periphery was one of ideological caution, which was the preferred approach of Kazakhstan's reform-adverse leadership.

Interestingly, at the founding congress the country's most senior film director, Efim Aron, was neither honored nor assigned any significant role. Likewise unmentioned were Aleksandr Karpov's *Silence* and Aimanov's *In One District*, two of the most sociopolitically relevant and provocative recent pictures produced by Kazakhfilm. Ultimately, the congress revealed internal problems in Kazakhstan's film industry not so much by what was discussed, but by what was omitted. Thus, no critical assessment of the country's recent past was intended or encouraged. Still, missed opportunity notwithstanding, in the end, the film workers of Kazakhstan had for the first time a professional organization, which would simplify many tasks both within the production process and in the film workers' everyday lives.

## TAKING THE BULL BY THE HORNS: *IN ONE DISTRICT*

Throughout the 1960s, Shaken Aimanov continued to act as the most powerful force of innovation in Kazakhstani cinema. Energetic and fearless, Aimanov was always on the lookout for new ways to bring issues to the screen that could engage audiences both in his native republic and in the Soviet Union at large. It was Aimanov who stood at the cradle of *civic cinema* in Kazakhstan, a trend that would really flourish much later, in the mid-1980s.

Aimanov started the new decade with a contemporary drama, *In One District* (V odnom raione, 1960). Its central character is a leading Soviet administrator, the first secretary of a large agricultural region, Sava Baianov. He is introduced as a man frustrated by something that he cannot share with anyone else. We see Baianov walking aimlessly in the city, forlorn among happy dwellers, casually talking to a depressed young man who is complaining about his lack of love. But this is not Baianov's problem. At home, his wife and daughter surround the seasoned communist functionary with affection. When Ryzhov, his old friend and supervisor, arrives, Baianov is happy, but the appearance of his daughter's fiancé, Bektasov (Asanali Ashimov), brings his inner frustrations to boiling point. A rising Communist Party official, Bektasov just published an article in *Pravda* sharply criticizing Baianov's administrative methods, which is a bad omen for their cooperation and for family harmony. The birthday party turns into a fiery debate.

Both Krylov and Bektasov argue for an aggressive modernization of Kazakhstan that includes agricultural diversification: Baianov's district should produce more sheep, but also ducks and even pigs, since the required natural conditions for such production are present. This, however, would contradict national traditions: raising pigs, for one, would go against Islamic law. Baianov accuses Bektasov of not knowing his own people and "thinking in a Russian manner." That argument is dismissed by Bektasov, who accuses Baianov of being possessed by "grandfatherly romanticism." The young man declares, "We should reject everything that prevents us from becoming richer and more cultured."

The next morning, the three men embark on a tour to assess the situation in Baianov's district first-hand. A truck driver, unaware of Baianov's rank, complains to him about the awful roads. A herdsman praises Kazakhstan's fertile lands and says that he could never imagine another life than his. However, his own son has no desire to become a herdsman. The young do not want to live in yurts anymore, preferring modern urban buildings with running water. When the Party functionaries go out on a hunt, Baianov is the only one who manages to shoot a duck, which convinces him that his connection with the land and its traditions is closer than that of his comrades. But it turns out that the duck was a runaway bird from a local farm, making Baianov a laughing stock. Clearly, the region's supreme representative is himself no longer in touch with the times and must rethink his ways.

What at first seems to be a conflict between communists of different generations soon reveals a fundamental disagreement regarding Kazakhstan's path to the future. Baianov, who emphasizes that his district is populated by a Kazakh majority, sees no need to introduce new methods. From his point of view, things are going well and will continue to do so, as long as the country's leadership respects certain national peculiarities and traditions. However, Bektasov, representing a new generation of Communist Party cadres, reminds him of General Secretary Nikita Khrushchev's slogan to "surpass America," which in his view means growing corn and buying motorcycles to replace horses. Shepherds, too, would like to have radio, TV, and bathrooms. But only when Baianov meets with Krylov one-on-one will he admit that the situation in his district is pathetic, that the roads are in bad shape and the living conditions of the herdsmen horrible. Baianov also visits the neighboring district, where ducks and pigs are raised, bringing in high profits. His thinking begins to change, and when two hacks come to him to complain about having been fired, he takes Bektasov's side for the first time, calling himself a retrograde and pondering about leaving "his" district where he has held the leadership role for twenty-five years.

*In One District* is a Soviet debate drama. Typically for Aimanov, who was always open with his audience, the peculiarities of this subgenre, that is, lengthy dialogues on ideological subjects, visual monotony—are openly displayed. The film's central characters are carriers of sociopolitical ideas and attitudes that are first verbalized and then illustrated with examples from everyday reality. The genre-specific suspense is ideological by nature and results from the taboos that are broken. In Soviet cinema, and even more in theater, schematic dramas about the right and the wrong way of building communism were a regular part of the repertoire. Indeed, the genre was a favorite of the Soviet establishment during the 1930s–1950s, albeit with a discriminating undertone, exposing those who held politically "incorrect" views as "enemies." The Thaw period triggered a moderate transformation of the debate genre, allowing for a somewhat more complex and even-handed treatment of nonconformist or anachronistic characters.

Aimanov clearly prefers the Thaw approach. His Baianov is a true communist, not a corrupt abuser. He is convinced that his administrative methods are time-honored and efficient because they take into consideration regional factors such as widespread religious beliefs. Of course, in his living room hangs a portrait of Lenin, and he makes a point of maintaining a trusting, warm relationship with higher officials such as Krylov: after all, they are old comrades who have been through a lot together. Conspicuously, the friends mention that it has been "25 years," that is, they have known each other since 1935, a period that includes the Stalinist purges and the World War, although none of those past traumas are explicitly discussed.

What is striking about *In One District* is Aimanov's candor regarding contemporary issues and his willingness to openly debate Kazakhstan's situation, including sensitive aspects such as the role of Islam. Furthermore, the explicit and repeated mentions of the general secretary of the Communist Party, Nikita Khrushchev, and his policies were an anomaly not just for Kazakh cinema, but for Soviet cinema as a whole. This detail alone is sufficient to explain the film's controversial status and its complete disappearance after Khrushchev's ouster in 1964.

Playing the role of Baianov himself, in addition to coauthoring the screenplay and directing, suggests that Aimanov's intentions were more empathetic than denunciatory. He did not want to point fingers at an entire generation of leaders just because changes in the upper echelons of power came too quickly for them to adjust. He also shows that Baianov's "conservative" arguments, in favor of retaining certain peculiarities of Kazakh life, were supported by many Kazakhstani Communist Party members. The generational divide, personified by Baianov and his soon-to-be son-in-law Bektasov, was a nationwide phenomenon.

*In One District*, a self-conscious contribution to the debate about Kazakhstan's present and future in a changing Soviet Union was certainly not intended as a vehicle for sophisticated artistry. Its purpose was to trigger debates. With exceptional honesty, Aimanov expressed that Kazakhstan had to make choices, some of them hard. The entire industrialization and modernization complex consisted of interconnected socioeconomic and cultural factors. It was impossible to change one without transforming the others. With his trademark energy, using his unrivaled national authority in overcoming ideological restrictions, Aimanov voiced the pros and cons of Kazakhstan's development as an integral part of the rapidly modernizing, post-Stalinist Soviet Union. He did so as a loyal communist who confided his convictions and doubts to his comrades and the audience at large. His film can also be viewed as a message to the other republics of the USSR: this is how Kazakhstan is dealing with its current problems.

Kazakhstan's political establishment, however, was not impressed, and Aimanov's debate drama was barely released. It was not screened in Almaty at all (!) and was reviewed by newspapers in an utterly dismissive tone. This uncompromising, undifferentiated rejection was not caused by the film's lack of realism, as some reviews falsely charged, but by the abundance thereof. The reviewer for *Kazakhstanskaia Pravda* claimed that Aimanov's performance lacks "love for the character" and his role is far from "the truth of life."[8] This is patently untrue, but of course the review could not talk about the socioeconomic and cultural taboos that the film had violated. Aimanov's authority was still huge enough to protect him from ad hominem attacks in the national press. Thus, critics pointed to the film's screenplay as the culprit for "the failure" of *In One District*, a common practice where the national film studio was concerned. It was suggested that its coauthor, the journalist Igor' Savvin, was not a professional screenwriter.

From a post-communist distance, it is easy to dismiss *In One District* as ideological hackwork featuring communist talking heads and their internal competition for power and influence. Within such a framework, the film, rather naïvely, puts forward arguments in favor of a harmonious transition from Stalinist administrative principles to slightly more democratic Khrushchevian ones. Such a reading would afford the film mere historical importance. However, viewed in its Soviet context, Aimanov's civic debate drama represents a rarity. As a matter of fact, its directness in verbalizing and visualizing problems had no equal in Soviet cinema at the time. This was the most likely reason why it was virtually ignored by the Soviet press. Normally, a feature film with such relevant subject-matter would have been reviewed by all the leading Soviet newspapers. Instead, it was hardly ever mentioned.[9]

To be sure, debate dramas became a hot commodity in the mid-1970s and 1980s, when plays by Aleksandr Gel'man and Ignatii Dvoretskii and their screen adaptations were promoted as national events. In comparison to those Russian films, Aimanov's was downright pioneering. Had it been a product of the Soviet center and released by Mosfilm or Lenfilm, it would have been a political and cultural sensation. But this cinematic pamphlet was produced on the Soviet periphery and thus habitually ignored. Furthermore, while the genre of Soviet debate drama was never given much attention by critics or film historians and nowadays has been largely forgotten, *In One District* certainly deserves a reevaluation as a snapshot of Kazakhstan's socioeconomic situation in the early 1960s. It also represents an experiment, testing the degree to which viewers could be attracted to films in which the political and ideological focus is primary while psychological or melodramatic elements are secondary. The experiment failed, but this was nevertheless a noteworthy result and a lesson for Aimanov and his colleagues.

## CONTEMPORARY SOCIAL DRAMA

Aleksandr Karpov, a war veteran and recent VGIK graduate, moved to Kazakhstan in the mid-1950s. During his fifteen years in Almaty, Karpov made a considerable impact on Kazakhstani cinema. However, even though his legacy is impressive, it has never been given a fair overall assessment. After several documentary shorts, Karpov helmed *Far in the Mountains* (Daleko v gorakh, 1958), a conventional historical drama about an *aul* where the poor fight their local *bays*. The ideological focus of this Kazakh-Kyrgyz coproduction was the need to distrust the class enemy; the main character, the horse-herd Nazarkul, dies at the end.

Judging by his subsequent lyrical contemporary dramas and historical films, Karpov was free of the national identity searches that haunted Aimanov and Begalin. For him, identity was never an issue: he was a *Soviet* filmmaker first and foremost, and this may have been his assigned role at the studio, too. While Karpov's films receive much less attention today than during the 1960s, it is safe to say that he helped maintain a close connection between the emerging Kazakhstani national cinema and the Soviet mainstream.

Karpov's black-and-white drama *Silence* (Tishina, 1960), released the same year as Aimanov's *In One District*, is set in the railway milieu, an excellent tool to showcase Kazakhstan's breathtaking vastness, as well as its fast-paced modernization. The film's main character, Akim Ostanov, is an aging locomotive machinist who unexpectedly gets reassigned to a distant railway station. That station's name is "Silence" (hence the film's title) which to Ostanov, who has never worked as an administrator before, sounds like a bad omen. A grumpy but deep down good-hearted man, Ostanov initially perceives the appointment as an injustice. He protests but ultimately acquiesces, albeit with great bitterness. He soon learns that the people living at Silence station are normal human beings and Soviet citizens just like him. A blend of ethnic Kazakhs and Russians, many of them are in need of help. The aging Ostanov immediately finds himself in the midst of various social conflicts that require his leadership qualities: he assists a single mother whose sick child must urgently see a doctor; he sets up a school for adults in which he himself teaches; and he mentors the operator Nartai, encouraging him to pursue a career in journalism that will allow him to write about heroes, not invented ones, but heroes taken from reality. To be sure, Silence is a quiet, isolated place, despite all the changes that Ostanov introduces, but its literal silence will soon end, since the construction of a new ultramodern factory is about to begin. To facilitate this megaproject, eight freight trains must be unloaded, something for which the station is not equipped. But when Ostanov is given the order to make it work, the viewer can be sure that he will.

The primary plotline of *Silence* follows a pattern common in the early 1960s, describing the inner struggle of a professional (an engineer, a teacher, or a doctor) who is being reassigned to a new, faraway place. This type of conflict signaled an increased degree of individual choices in the Thaw period that sometimes clashed with economic necessities.[10] The lesson to be learned from Karpov's film is that the main character's perception is wrong: the peripheries of the Soviet Union are just as dynamic as capital cities, and industrial progress will eventually arrive even in the most godforsaken locales.

Secondary plotlines, such as the insecurity of a female teacher vis-á-vis her adult pupils or the anxieties of a disabled war veteran, were recognizably rehashed from groundbreaking Russian Thaw pictures such as Marlen Khutsiev's *Springtime on Zarechnaia Street* (Vesna na Zarechnoi ulitse, 1956) and Grigorii Chukhrai's *Ballad of a Soldier* (Ballada o soldate, 1959).[11] The depiction of the noble mission of a teacher who has the magic touch with children resembles the pathos of Mark Donskoi's pedagogical dramas. Many of these borrowings give *Silence* a feel of imitation: conventional themes were transplanted from mainstream Russian-Soviet cinema to a Kazakhstani environment. But Karpov's work does develop a certain charm of its own. After all, the most important element of *Silence* is not plot-related but lies in the atmosphere. Captured by cameraman Mikhail Aranyshev with exemplary poetic sensitivity, the mood in this picture rivals the best examples of Soviet cinema of the late 1950s, in which communal apartments and offices are depicted as repositories of personal safety and mutual trust, while living nature serves as a mighty correcting agent to human relations and as a provider of health.[12] More nationally specific in *Silence* is the contrast between the windy, wintry exteriors and the cozy interiors, evoking an image of Kazakhstani reality that is at once authentic and poetic. Given that the film was shot in black-and-white, the overwhelming beauty of the transition from winter to spring is nothing short of spectacular. While the plot itself is admittedly often imitative and somewhat incoherent, the depiction of everyday life is original and appealing.[13]

*Silence* also boasts some excellent performances, particularly Kanabek Baiseitov in the lead and the film director's own turn in the role of the blind pedagogue Safonov who is doing everything he can to hide his disability.[14] Safonov, who dabbles in sculpture in his sparetime, offers a curious interpretation of the station's name: to him, silence means that there have been no accidents for many years. Maintaining this exceptional security record gives meaning to the lives of all those who have kept the railway station safe and functional. The teacher's uplifting words are typical of the film as a whole, a story that reassembles quite a few Soviet clichés of the late 1950s, including the theme of Komsomol brigades arriving for a big construction project.[15] Karpov manages to achieve some degree of originality by applying Thaw motifs to authentic Kazakh circumstances. The country's cultural specifics thus acquire primary importance.

In the years that followed, Karpov's career at Kazakhfilm studio demonstrated that his emphatically Soviet approach to Kazakhstani reality held genuine artistic potential, but also considerable risks. His next film, *The Fusion* (Splav, 1961), about the life of young Kazakh scientists working on a complex technical problem, was virtually ignored by audiences. However, when Karpov was assigned with an emotionally charged story about World War II, he created a masterpiece and one of the best films of Kazakhstani cinema, *Tale of a Mother* (Skaz o materi, 1963).

## *If Every One of Us*

Throughout his career, Sultan-Ahmed Khodzhikov remained somewhat outside Soviet mainstream cinema and continued to pursue his own artistic path with peculiar narratives. *If Every One of Us* (Esli by kazhdyi iz nas, 1961), from a screenplay by A. Tokmagambetov and the director, explores contemporary Kazakhstani reality from a similar point of departure to Karpov in *Silence*, yet the result could not be more different. His main character, Serkebai, a seventy-year-old shepherd (Akhmed Shamiev), is eager to contribute to building a socialist society yet insists on living by the old patriarchal ways. His stubbornness puts him, his family, and his herd in mortal danger. Only after arriving at a dead end is he willing to listen to and accept support from the state. To be sure, the old man is not some isolated retrograde. Serkebai is well-informed, he approves of the international steps being taken toward disarmament ("It would be best to forget the word 'war' completely"), and he is proud of the Soviet Union's success in space exploration ("Soon our people will land on the moon!"). But at home, he is a harsh tyrant, telling his obedient wife "to know where her place is." When his innovative proposal of shearing the herds twice per year instead of once is rejected by the *kolkhoz* chairman, Serkebai angrily jumps into the river, with the lead ram following him and the flock following the ram. Later, the well in the desert Kyzylkum on which he had pinned all his hopes literally implodes, and with it Serkebai's attitude of proud self-reliance.

Visually, Khodzhikov focuses intensely on exotic landscapes, chief among them the deserts along the Syr-Darya river that are crossed by railway tracks (Askhat Ashrapov was the director of cinematography).[16] The broad river, in particular, and the huge skies above it signify the might of nature and its unassailable constancy. These extreme long shots alternate with expressive close-ups and extreme close-ups of the shepherd, who sometimes noisily pontificates and sometimes quietly philosophizes. Khodzhikov's ambition was a visualization of Kazakhstan's current state, contrasting the ancient nomadic lifestyle with modern technology. The shepherd's daughter, Marzhan (Lola Abdukarimova), is torn between love for her father and the attraction of emerging urbanity. The ultimate synthesis comes when drilling technology is used to create a source of water for Serkebai's lifestock, helicopters rescue hundreds of his sheep, and he himself is saved by a medical truck.

Serkebai, who often addresses a divine power, abandons his religious faith after he sees that Allah leaves his prayers unanswered while human creativity brings about solutions to existential problems. A hat made of synthetic fur convinces the old man that a new age has begun, one in which animals no longer have to be slaughtered to satisfy human needs; now, chemistry can take care of that. In its naïve embrace of modern technology, *If Every One of Us* resembles Aimanov's *In One District* and Karpov's *Silence*, although this is one of the few elements that these films have in common.

There can be no doubt that *If Every One of Us* is visually original and often powerful, which makes the predominantly theatrical acting all the more regrettable. Creating memorable mise-en-scènes, establishing strong conflictual situations within clearly defined spaces, had been Khodzhikov's forte from early on. Yet it seems that the price of compositional stringency is declarative, artificial dialogues and unnatural body language by many characters.

Khodzhikov's manner of poeticizing Kazakh life did not find followers.[17] What is most interesting about his approach, and what sets him apart from other Kazakhstani directors, is his almost exclusive emphasis on national elements leading the country to modernity. In *If Every One of Us*, the depiction of the flock of sheep and its lead ram, of Serkebai's desire to fly, and of the appearance of technology in a quasi-miraculous way resemble the prose of Andrei Platonov, particularly his novella *Dzhan*. Kazakhstan's integration into the modern world is described as a fundamentally *existential process*. And the greatest miracle is not the production of crude oil but the drilling for water in the desert, which brings an age-old dream of nomadic people to life.

## *The Intersection*

Despite the fiasco he experienced with *In One District*, Shaken Aimanov continued his two-pronged strategy of developing Kazakhstani cinema as a forum for national self-determination and a tool for the representation of its culture to the Soviet Union as a multinational addressee. Judging by some accounts, the lack of proper recognition for his efforts seems to have depressed him at times, but without ever slowing him down or paralyzing his artistic drive. Indeed, Aimanov's contemporary drama *The Intersection* (Perekrestok, 1962) was as fearless in naming the issues that Kazakhstan was facing as was *In One District*, with the difference that Aimanov's new film was a melodrama, a genre that viewers preferred to the drier and more verbose debate drama.

The film's central character is Galiia Ismailova, a physician whose dedication to her profession, as well as her civic forthrightness, are depicted as exemplary. Dr. Ismailova works in the emergency departments of an Almaty hospital, making house calls day and night and putting her own life at risk to save others.

Farida Sharipova portrays Galiia with delicate grace and a nervous intellectual energy previously unseen in Kazakhstani cinema.[18] The plot provides her with ample opportunities to explore her character's complex, sometimes contradictory personality. Professionally, Dr. Ismailova gives her utmost and demands the same from those working with her; in her private life, however, she is vulnerable, looking for a partner whom she can both love and respect.

The first episode features a strange coincidence: a medical emergency call takes Galiia to a hotel room, where a man who complains about severe chest pain turns out to be her own estranged husband, a severe alcoholic. Galiia manages to overcome her initial confusion and acts with calm professionalism, warning the man of the dire consequences should his self-destructive behavior continue. The husband's self-righteous response is to attack Galiia for her perfectionism, which, according to him, has made her a lonely woman. These words open a deep wound. The doctor's private life clearly suffers from the stress of her job, including the daily clashes with self-absorbed patients and their rude relatives, as well as with supervisors who are indifferent to the needs of patients and physicians alike. But we soon learn that there is a new man in her life, Iskander (Asanali Ashimov), a young judge who adores her and her toddler daughter, Bakhisha. Both Galiia and Iskander share modern attitudes toward society, rejecting (and actively fighting) bribery and bureaucratic incompetence. When it comes to Galiia's child, however, the two young professionals overlook the little girl's needs, so engrossed are they in their discussion of daily problems. The girl protests by escaping and hiding: a dramatic reminder to adults of their indispensable duties.

*The Intersection* is an excellent picture in several respects. Its screenplay skillfully weaves psychological and social aspects into a captivating story. The performances are convincing throughout, with little L. Tastanova a veritable scene stealer in her role as Bakhisha. Mikhail Aranyshev's camerawork is dominated by soft black-and-white tones, especially impressive in the night scenes, and by a distinct closeness to the performers, capturing their most subtle mood swings in well-rendered close-ups. Sydyk Mukhamedzhanov's score has a beauty and dynamic elegance that corresponds to the alternation between dramatic and pensive episodes. Stylistically, one can discern in some episodes the influence of the French *nouvelle vague*, especially François Truffaut's *Les 400 Coups*. Of course, the film's conceptual framework and message are utterly Soviet, calling upon viewers to engage in difficult social processes, have faith in the power of progress, and work together for the improvement of living conditions in Soviet-Kazakh society. Remarkably, Aimanov succeeded in making the positive characters look truly attractive and beautiful, while the immoral ones come across as off-putting without being clichéd. In its civic openness, *The Intersection* is reminiscent of the films of Iosif Kheifits, Grigorii Chukhrai, and Iulii Raizman in the mid-1950s and 1960s that defined a brand of post-Stalinist Soviet humanism characteristic of the Thaw period.

Compared to *In One District*, *The Intersection* is less explicitly political. Its characters are fascinating as human beings, not merely as carriers of certain sociopolitical attitudes or concepts. One of the film's obvious strengths is its ensemble cast, in which even episodic roles are played by first-rate performers such as Raisa Koichubaeva who appears as the influential mother of a juvenile delinquent whom she tries to save from prison, meandering between maternal despair and proud arrogance. (Incidentally, this episode may very well be an allusion to the afore-mentioned scandal surrounding the three young thugs who attacked Kazakh actors, and their parents who tried to save them from justice.)

*The Intersection* features a number of scenes involving children, which is a risk factor for any director. The execution of these episodes demonstrates Aimanov's ability to elicit authentic, powerful performances even from non-professional actors. For example, the scene in which little Bakhisha teaches the intimidated Iskander how to calm her mom down when she is angry, is delightful in its warm humor. In *The Intersection*, Shaken Aimanov demonstrated that he had become a mature filmmaker who could easily hold his own in the genre of social melodrama; the psychological nuances are particularly remarkable. As in Aimanov's previous pictures, the narrative rhythm of *The Intersection* is fast-paced, but in a more balanced manner than, for example, in *We Live Here*.

From a Western viewpoint, the film's social didactics may seem overly explicit. But such was Soviet cinema's habit and identity. Indeed, that was its raison d'être: to entertain and to educate. Regarding his civic duty as a filmmaker, Aimanov once again took no prisoners. The episodes involving the city administrators demonstrate exceptional candor. It is these bureaucrats, after all, who are responsible for the acquisition of state-of-the-art emergency cars and equipment and are forced to openly admit their delayed decision-making and abundant red tape that prevent the doctor from doing her job successfully.[19]

The film's title points to one of its main theses, namely that all members of a society are connected to each other and that, because of this interconnectedness, they share the responsibility for one member's failure. Just like at an intersection, human beings interact in ways requiring responsibility and considerateness. Without this, the results can be tragic. Toward the end of the film, a car accident that costs the life of a pedestrian is analyzed as a conflation of many individual failures. Galiia's maximalist approach, blaming herself first, seems incompatible with that of Iskander, who believes that Soviet law is all it takes to achieve justice ("Justice is more humane than pity," he claims). The accident endangers the family happiness of Galiia's driver, one of the film's most appealing, down-to-earth characters.

The concluding episodes in the court are of programmatic significance. Indeed, the question of what constitutes justice is central to the culture and spirit of Kazakhstan. It is no coincidence that its greatest intellectual, Abai, was a highly respected authority on law; so was his father, Kunanbai. Many Kazakh films feature court episodes in which the ultimate finding of a fair solution yields a cathartic effect. Without considering this quest for justice, an understanding of Kazakhstan and its people's worldview and world perception are impossible.

Another aspect of *The Intersection* worth mentioning is the character of Galiia's estranged husband. Educated and eloquent, he is also a deeply immoral man, a cynic who does not believe in a higher purpose of human existence and who despises all human beings, himself included. The issue of faith in moral principles was, of course, always a sensitive one for atheist Soviet society: how could moral, unselfish behavior be rationally encouraged without invoking transcendental authority? From the husband's ramblings one can conclude that he must have read too much nihilistic literature. Galiia, however, reacts emotionally rather than rationally to his cynical sophistry. Through this character, Aimanov conveys a moral and spiritual concern that goes to the very heart of a communist society: why does a person like Galiia Ismailova behave in a selfless, socially conscious, and humane manner, whereas her estranged husband refuses to do so and manages to get away with it?

Axiological nihilism is deeply alien to the Kazakh socio-cultural tradition. In Aimanov's subsequent pictures, the danger emanating from this phenomenon is repeatedly addressed. One of the answers lies in the characters' yearning for family harmony. The newly emerging Galiia/Iskander/Bakhisha triangle points to stable harmony as a realistic possibility. Indeed, this little family's private happiness and social engagement condition each other almost in a textbook manner. However, Galiia's former husband has made his self-destructive choice, which leaves open the question of whether the others are justified in excluding this nihilist, and people like him, from their lives. Will this type of thinking disappear as part of historical progress?[20] The issue of the origin and sustainability of socially responsible, humane behavior is one that Kazakhstani filmmakers would continue to raise both during the Soviet period and in the first decades of independence.

One of Shaken Aimanov's directorial fortes was picking the right performers. A particular success in *The Intersection* is Farida Sharipova[21] as the female lead. Graceful and strong, intelligent and tender, her portrayal of Dr. Galiia Ismailova brought a new kind of modern Kazakhstani woman to Soviet screens. Sharipova's chemistry with Asanali Ashimov is remarkable: intellectually intense and clearly erotically charged, but without ever crossing the line to risqué exploitation. This chemistry was not lost on Mazhit Begalin, who cast Sharipova and Ashimov as husband and wife in another signature film of the 1960s, *The Traces Go Beyond the Horizon*, albeit within a very different psychological constellation. Unfortunately, Sharipova's enormous potential was virtually ignored in the following decades, just as that of Hadisha Bukeeva from *Raikhan* or Zamzagul Sharipova (no relation) from *Daughter of the Steppes* had been. The main problem seems to have been the virtual absence of stardom-building strategies within the national film administration and the lack of screenplays that would focus on these actresses. Aimanov himself, however, intuitively understood what a unique treasure his best performers represented, especially in building a Kazakh national identity! Thus, he regularly cast certain actors and actresses, even if only in supporting roles, throughout his career.

A curious footnote on *The Intersection*: at the beginning of independence, when Kazakhstan's film industry was in a moribund state, the country's first soap opera, which offered numerous writers, directors, and performers the chance to make a living, was titled *The Intersection* (Perekrestok, 1996–2000). Was this an allusion to Aimanov's earlier film, which had captured the optimism of a modernizing society, or a mere coincidence?

## CONTROVERSIAL EMANCIPATION TALES

Like Aleksandr Karpov, Mazhit Begalin had returned from the Great Patriotic War severely injured. A student of Sergei Gerasimov, Begalin's education at the Soviet State Film School VGIK began in 1943, after his discharge from the military. It provided him with a sense of thematic daring and aesthetic ambition, regardless of how strong the cultural bureaucracy's resistance to his projects often was.[22] With *His Time Will Come* (1957), Begalin joined the ranks of the most promising Kazakh directors. He then delivered a contemporary comedy, *Return to Earth* (Vozvrashchenie na zemliu, 1959), about a herdsman who dreams of becoming a cosmonaut and later, because of his looks, works as a stand-in for a famous actor, only to realize that his original vocation is just as honorable as those urban professions. While this contrived story did not make much of an impression on critics or viewers, Begalin's next film was of high quality. As an original and controversial picture about contemporary Kazakhstan, *The Traces Go Beyond the Horizon* (Sledy ukhodiat za gorizont, 1964), deserves a closer look, since it reveals the immense artistic originality displayed by a young native filmmaker in the early 1960s.[23]

Avoiding the psychological linearity and convenient simplification that were so common in Soviet cinema, Begalin introduces in *The Traces Go Beyond the Horizon* a complex character constellation whose individual participants must redefine and reposition themselves as the story unfolds. From the outset, when the insecure young heroine, Zhaukhaz, looks in the mirror, her eyes convey painful obedience: her marriage to the self-confident farmer Turar has been arranged against her will. Neither the following festive rituals nor Turar's demonstrative tenderness can relieve the young woman's doubts. However, after arriving in her husband's home, she develops affection for him that seems to offer both spouses a chance to build genuine trust. Working daily with Turar's parents who strictly follow traditional rules and duties and behave respectfully and even affectionately toward their daughter-in-law, Zhaukhaz begins to accept her destiny and adjust her feelings accordingly, until the day when the young chauffeur Tanabai arrives to deliver a radio to the farm. Tanabai immediately senses Zhaukaz's repressed loneliness and quiet frustration. His cheerful and generous nature suggests that he possesses all the qualities that the young woman is missing in her husband.

Soon enough, Turar's and Tanabai's personalities are put to the test. When a snowstorm breaks out, they ride together to save the livestock, managing to rescue a large number of animals. But a lot of sheep are still out in the freezing cold, likely to perish, which would mean an immense loss for the farm. When the men go out on horseback again, Zhaukhaz gives them a long rope so that they won't lose each other in the blinding hurricane. Then, in the most dangerous moment, when the storm prevents any orientation, Turar cuts the rope and returns to safety by himself. In the following hours and days, he exaggerates the cold that he caught, but Zhaukhaz now fully understands that Turar has betrayed Tanabai. Fearlessly, she calls him "a pathetic coward," refusing to apologize for the insult despite her husband's threats. Even Turar's parents realize his shameful transgression and are embarrassed. Zhaukhaz finally leaves Turar for good, moving toward the horizon of newly gained freedom—hence the title.

A psychological drama shot in ascetic black-and-white, *The Traces Go Beyond the Horizon* tackles the problem of modernity vs. tradition in a mature, forthright manner, without ever falling into self-righteous lecturing or ideological sermonizing. Indeed, the characters are forced to make decisions for which they lack ready-made solutions; they are exploring new social terrain.[24] Surely, Tanabai's characterization as a selfless, skillful, and loyal man smacks of the "positive hero" dogma, an indispensable part of socialist realism. This is corroborated by his heroism in saving the collective farm's lost sheep: he risks his life for the wellbeing of the community. However, the superb acting in *The Traces Go Beyond the Horizon* softens the underlying ideological or psychological schematics. The ensemble cast is strong, from Asanali Ashimov as the selfish Turar to Hadisha Bukeeva as his mother. Most impressive, though, is Farida Sharipova as the female lead. The way in which her initial insecurity and doubts about her feelings are transformed into a clear understanding of right and wrong, culminating in outrage over the cowardice of her husband, is shown with flawless precision. Expertly supported by Askhat Ashrapov's camerawork, which alternates dynamic, wide exteriors with a sensitive distribution of light and shadow in the interiors, the ambiguities of personal relationships within the family are rendered tangible. The characters' inner doubts and torments are visualized through dutch-tilt shots: the old world as it was known is literally out of order; the habitual points of orientation can no longer offer any guidance.

However, the most effective cinematic element in *The Traces Go Beyond the Horizon* is audial: the film gains enormous tension from prolonged periods of silence. Several episodes go on for minutes without a word being spoken. Perhaps Kaneto Shindo's masterpiece *The Naked Island* (1962) made an impact on Begalin: the scenes of silent physical labor, shown in detail, are just as constitutive as in Shindo's picture, which enjoyed world-wide fame at the time.[25] Due to the sparsity of words, the acting relies heavily on facial expressions and body language. Even when dialogues do take place, they avoid addressing the conflicts. These long silent sequences generate an atmosphere of tension that increases until it seems unbearable. This is precisely the tension that results from the status quo arrangement between Zhaukhaz and Turar.

In the end, even the husband's parents realize that Zhaukhaz's decision to leave is inevitable. Their son was so sure of the inviolability of traditional law that he did not make any effort to justify himself and his behavior to his wife. He never built trust, simply relying on the agreement made by his parents with Zhaukhaz's stepmother. Turar believes that all his wife needs is a secure life, and he promises her that. Within the framework of the triangle conflict, he interprets his wife's suffering as having to choose between him and another man. He therefore repeatedly challenges Tanabai to resolve the issue in the traditional way, not realizing that it is the patriarchal framework in its entirety that is being questioned and is ultimately neutralized by Zhaukhaz's emancipation.

A noteworthy detail in *The Traces Go Beyond the Horizon* is the spouses' visit to a monument to Chokan Valikhanov, the hero of Begalin's earlier groundbreaking picture. At the beginning, when the newlyweds travel to Turar's home, the caravan makes a stop at that monument and pays homage to the great scientist and enlightener. The inscription on the plinth, engraved both in Kazakh and in Russian, appears clearly legible. Later, when Zhaukhaz attends her father's funeral, another stop at the monument takes place. Both times, the heroine's solemn encounter with Valikhanov goes far beyond formality and suggests a deeper meaning. What were Begalin's intentions in giving these two scenes the significance of cornerstones? Valikhanov stands for the modernization of Kazakhstan. Regardless of the tyranny that came with Russian imperial rule and reinforced native clan despotism, Valikhanov saw no other way to develop his country's potential than in an alliance with its mighty northern neighbor. The significance attributed to this moment could be an indicator that Zhaukhaz's longing for the wider world, for modernity, culture, and education, as symbolized by the radio that Tanabai repairs, is in tune with the trajectory that Chokan Valikhanov had outlined for Kazakhstan.

*The Traces Go Beyond the Horizon* is a highly innovative modernization drama whose thematic daring and stylistic peculiarities betray Mazhit Begalin's wide-ranging directorial ambitions. In the Soviet context of the 1960s, this was an innovative picture, although Soviet critics virtually ignored it and it quickly disappeared from screens. Just like Begalin's earlier *His Time Will Come*, this film was ahead of its time.

Thematically and stylistically related to Begalin's film is Sultan-Akhmet Khodzhikov's *The Plane Tree on the Rock* (Chinara na skale, 1965). Once again, the young Askhat Ashrapov was director of cinematography, demonstrating a fascination with daring viewpoints and dynamic lighting: both

Begalin's and Khodzhikov's films were made in black-and-white, and both deal with contemporary issues. Just like Begalin's picture, Khodzhikov's is a chamber drama. Indeed, the director reduces the space in which the conflicts unfold even more radically than Begalin. In *The Traces Go Beyond the Horizon*, the narrowness of Turar's house stands for the restrictions of the traditional lifestyle, especially for the young woman. In *The Plane Tree on the Rock*, the narrowness of a cave, which provides shelter for three men who accidentally meet during a snowstorm, creates the compulsive need to communicate and open up to each other: there is nowhere to escape from that protective/restrictive space and, figuratively, from the pressing moral issues.

As if to make the claustrophobia in the main body of the film even more tangible, Khodzhikov begins it with a sequence of extreme long shots. A small plane carrying a high-level administrator flies over the vast, snow-covered steppes, assessing the dangers to the huge herds of sheep. A major problem is the transportation of hay to the livestock lost in the freezing steppe, but Karpov, the silver-haired, strong-willed first secretary, manages to resolve it. After finding a severely injured shepherd, he sends him on his plane to a nearby hospital, himself waiting for the plane's return in a cave. This is where he meets the convict Sagit, whose threatening presence and disrespectful behavior suddenly challenge the self-confident administrator in an unforeseen way. Soon, a third man joins them: Ilias, a doctor whose car broke down. The three men's different moral values become obvious when Sagit mindlessly burns pieces of a yurt in the little fire that Karpov had started. The criminal and the state functionary begin to compete for authority, while Ilias is struggling with problems of his own.

Karpov mentions the name of the location: the rock is named after Aisulu, a young woman who, according to lore, sacrificed her life to save her clan. The name Aisulu brings back the memory of another young woman whom Ilias met as a student and later as a young doctor; he still feels guilty because he betrayed her. In a quasi-confession to his two accidental acquaintances, Ilias admits that he cannot overcome a feeling of guilt for his cruel treatment of that exceptional woman. Then it turns out that Sagit, the criminal, also knew Aisulu: after Ilias let her down, he aggressively pursued her, driving her to despair. It is not clear whether Sagit raped her or not; flashbacks reveal that during subsequent court deliberations he denied any wrongdoing. But he did take revenge on her for refusing to give in to his advances by smearing the young woman's name. Back then, the community sided with Sagit, deeply traumatizing Aisulu. Sagit, who was convicted after all, now also confesses his guilt and expresses his deep regret. Only Karpov, who was present at the trial, can share good news: Aisulu is alive and studying at the Timiriazev Academy.

*The Plane Tree on the Rock* gains its tension from the stark contrast between the three very different personalities trapped in the cave: the political administrator, the intellectual, and the convict and erstwhile truck driver. The three actors who portray them (S. Popov as Karpov, Nurmukhan Zhanturin as Ilias, and Idris Nogaibaev as Sagit) deliver convincing enough performances to make up for the plot, the constructed nature of which is plain to see. The male perspective dominates the film, whereas Aisulu, portrayed by the young Gulbakhram Adilova, never gets a chance to evolve in any depth. Her character is meant to embody feminine purity, appearing more as an ideal than a real person. The many close shots showcasing her beautiful face with dark sensual eyes serve as reminders of this function.

Visually, the somewhat theatrical drama in the cave is deliberately cinematic, interspersed with flashbacks illustrating the men's stories: we witness Ilias flirting with Aisulu in a café, her attempt to follow him when he leaves the faraway place to which he has been delegated, and her escape from Sagit's aggressive pursuit. In between, in the present, the three men passionately debate the meaning of their decisions and their consequences, expressing regret and making accusations against each other. A remarkable element in Khodzhikov's film is Sagit's disrespect toward Karpov, the high-ranking administrator, pointing to a relaxation in social hierarchies in Soviet Kazakhstan in the 1960s. In earlier years, such provocative and violent behavior by a convict toward a communist administrator would have been denounced as that of an enemy. However, in Khodzhikov's picture, Sagit is not irredeemable. Instead, his mood oscillates between anger and friendly humor. Once viewers suspend their disbelief regarding the narrative framework, the extraordinary situation in which the three characters find themselves, having been forced together by "destiny" itself, allows for deep moral probing and, ultimately, for closure. The film seems to encourage further philosophical speculation about the location, that is, the cave, if the viewer assumes the presence of a Platonic fundament in this contemporary film.

Surely, the coincidence that three men happen to meet in a cave under the Aisulu rock, finding out that all of them knew a woman named Aisulu who turns out to be one and the same person, is implausible. But primarily the overall impression of a certain dissonance results from the film's overt appearance as a social parable that fails to achieve a synthesis with the underlying mythical roots to which it alludes. Can myth and parable be forced together in a contemporary social drama, as Mukhtar Auezov himself had predicted at a conference in 1945? Khodzhikov certainly tried his utmost. At a certain point, he even visualizes the Aisulu legend, the relevance of which seems to lie in the deprivation of the Kazakh people in the past, particularly the pitiful lot of women. The film's focus on women's plight in a patriarchal society connects it with *The Traces Go Beyond the Horizon*, although Khodzhikov's story has a more complicated structure, insofar as it tries to establish a causal link between the recent past in which the three men were involved and the mythical past that comes to life in the unfolding moral drama. That association remains weak, however. One might imagine a link between the modern present and the mythical past by pointing to the existential sacrifice that women were forced to make in ancient times, whereas in modern-day Soviet Kazakhstan, despite some degree of discrimination, a woman is free to make her own choices. But such a link would still be deliberately constructed.

A legitimate conclusion from comparing these two significant Kazakh pictures of the mid-1960s is that both in Begalin's *The Traces Go Beyond the Horizon* and in Khodzhikov's *The Plane Tree on the Rock*, modern Kazakh women are given the chance to shape their own destiny: they just need to realize it. Thus, the mythological dimension is one of departure, not of repetition. Unlike her legendary predecessor, the modern Aisulu does not die, even though the viewer may at first expect such a parallel outcome.

Most importantly, these are two films about Kazakh machismo. In *The Plane Tree on the Rock*, the men's attitudes are rooted in patriarchal tradition, but the consequences of these habits are no longer seen as acceptable by the same men who previously practiced them. Their encounter in the cave gives them the chance to revise their attitudes, which they do dialogically, forcing each other to face inconvenient truths. This strong anti-patriarchal stance was ignored by contemporary viewers, reviewers, and later by film historians.[26]

Neither *The Traces Go Beyond the Horizon* nor *The Plane Tree on the Rock* fared well with film critics, who refused to notice, let alone embrace, their radical novelty. *The Plane Tree on the Rock* was adapted from motifs of Mukhtar Auezov's unfinished novel *The Young Kin* (Plemia mladoe). However, the credits in the Russian version do not mention that. Auezov, who by the mid-1950s had been elevated to Kazakhstan's supreme author and who was officially canonized after his grandiose epic *The Path of Abai* won a Lenin Prize in 1959, was apparently not supposed to be associated with a controversial, uncomfortably dissonant movie, the main point of which was either critically ignored or misunderstood. At least some contemporary critics seemed to have agreed with Khodzhikov's artistic approach, however: he was awarded the prize for best director at the 1966 Central Asian Film Festival in Ashgabat. *The Plane Tree on the Rock* is loyal to the legacy of Auezov's oeuvre and Abai's stance on women and their role in Kazakh society. An ambitious, albeit ill-fated cinematic experiment, Khodzhikov's picture explored new ground.

## THE FIRST KAZAKH CULT FILM

Arguably the most unexpected Kazakhstani movie of the early 1960s was intended for young audiences but ended up endearing itself to millions of viewers from all generations: *My Name Is Kozha* (Menin atym Kozha/Menia zovut Kozha, 1963). The secret of its surprising and lasting success lies in its irreverent humor, its non-authoritarian approach to childhood and children's behavior, and its deep, optimistic trust in the wisdom of life. This film was not promoted by any official campaign that would force Kazakh viewers to movie theaters and to watch Kozha's adventures, yet come they did, embracing the picture and its title hero in a manner that justifies the term "cult film."

Earlier, Kazakhfilm studio had made some attempts to produce children's films, but the reactions were largely negative or indifferent. *A Winged Gift* (Krylatyi podarok, 1956) was devoted to children and wildlife, while *Your Friends* (Tvoi druz'ia, 1960) told an adventurous story of kids helping adults to fight poachers. The screenplay was written by a Moscow author, the film was directed by an outsider,[27] and the final product was devoid of any national features. One reviewer bemoaned that, "as paradoxical as it may sound, in a film made by the Kazakh studio there is no Kazakhstan!"[28] *My Name Is Kozha* is the exact opposite: it is Kazakh to the core, and viewers could recognize themselves in its characters. Since then, many Kazakhstani films dealt with the life of children, but *My Name Is Kozha*, directed by Abdulla Karsakbaev, an assistant on *A Winged Gift*, from a novella by Berdybek Sokpakbaev[29] (who also coauthored the screenplay), is still the best known. It opened a goldmine.

The boy Kozha (an abbreviation of his full name, Karakozha Kadyrov) is a bright and vivacious high school student who constantly gets in trouble with classmates and teachers. It seems that the label "ne'er-do-well" will remain attached to him forever, no matter how hard he tries to adjust to common behavioral norms. In the opening scene, Kozha looks at himself in the mirror and does not approve of what he sees.

Nor does he like his first name, which he interprets as "nincompoop." Kozha's best buddy is Sultan, a slightly older boy who dropped out of school and now leads the carefree life of a junior shepherd. Sultan challenges Kozha to follow his example, and for a while Kozha seriously considers that option, especially when problems at school get out of hand. A Huckleberry Finn-like character, Kozha finds solace in dreams, which are visualized in a hilarious manner. Thus, when Kozha returns from an imaginary flight into space, all those who had chastised him realize their mistake and ask his forgiveness.

Interestingly, the real official meeting at which some children denounce Kozha yields an unexpected outcome: instead of judging and marginalizing the outsider, most classmates unite against his critics, believing the repentant Kozha, not his detractors. The teacher, who served with Kozha's father in the

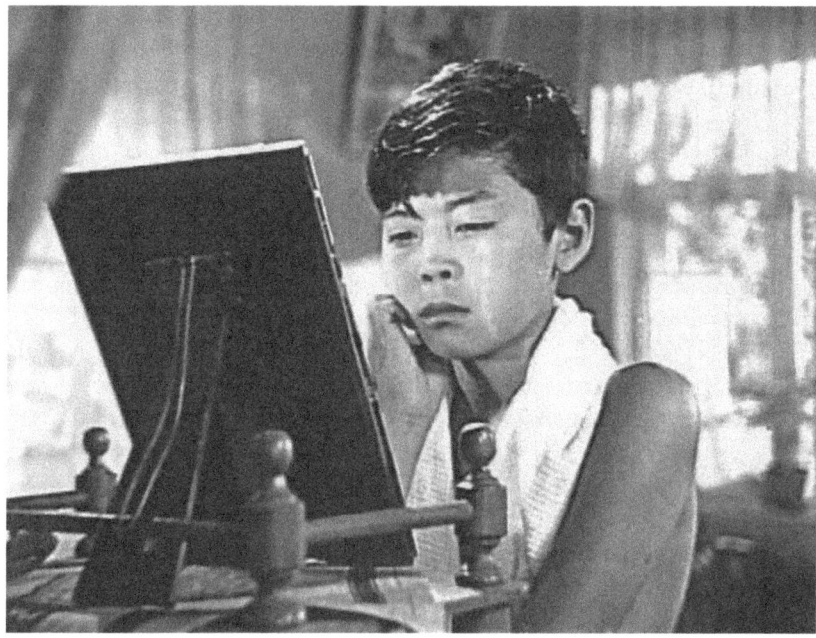

**Figure 5.1   Kozha in the Mirror. Nurlan Segizbaev in the title role.** *My Name Is Kozha* (1963, Abdulla Karsakbaev)

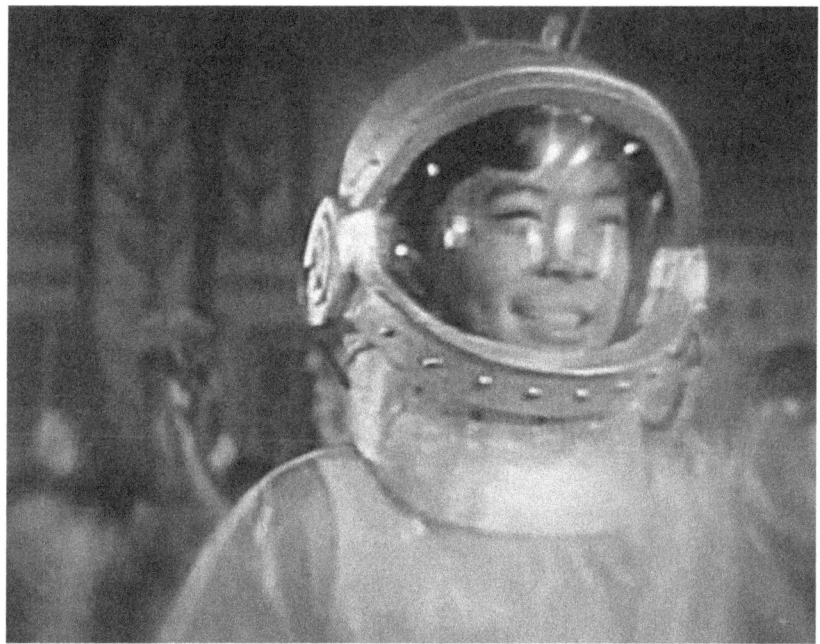

**Figure 5.2   Kozha's Cosmonaut Dream.** *My Name Is Kozha* (1963, Abdulla Karsakbaev)

military, also demonstrates a kind of empathetic pedagogy in which protecting the dignity and self-respect of the child is of primary importance. Rather than imposing his own judgment, he entrusts the kids with making their own decisions. And he is proven right!

Kozha's fundamental challenge is that he must come to terms with himself and his environment. At the same time, he musters resistance against peer pressure and opportunism. This challenge is the main point of viewer identification. Indeed, the most unusual aspect of *My Name Is Kozha* is that the film encourages the audience to identify with a nonconformist who is denounced by many as a misfit.

Karsakbaev's film is not only refreshingly anti-authoritarian, but also highly cinematic (the cameraman was the experienced Mikhail Aranyshev). As a matter of fact, endorsement of Kozha is expressed as much through cinematic means as it is verbally. When the boy runs to school, exuding overwhelming excitement, the camera runs with him, capturing his reflection in the river along with that of the shining sun. The film's fundamental approval of Kozha's personality is further expressed by Nurgisa Tlendiev's high-energy score,[30] which combines national themes and instruments with traditional orchestration. The music conveys Kozha's triumphant optimism, profound kindness, and a wild sense of humor.

The luckless boy acts as a first-person narrator, sharing his insights and frustrations with the viewer. Kozha is unhappy about the fact that the other children form groups while he is by himself, yet he will not allow his outsider status to force him to give in. Rather, he insists on his own specialness and self-confidence and makes fun of those classmates who act opportunistically. Kozha always stands up for himself, openly admitting his faults but never letting this admission hamper his self-respect. This creates a perspective on the young generation that is essentially nondidactic.[31] Kozha will only accept norms if he understands their meaning, never because adults impose these norms on him. In this approach, where the emphasis is on individual sovereignty, *My Name Is Kozha* is unique among Soviet films about children.

Karsakbaev takes Kozha seriously as a personality, emphasizing his complexity rather than diminishing it. Indeed, the book *My Name Is Kozha* represents a certain discontinuity with normative Soviet children's literature. Arkadii Gaidar, the classic author of the genre in the 1930s, was most successful in defining the official norm of exemplary children characters who actively engage with society, helping the weak and fighting all sorts of saboteurs, lazybones, and even undercover foreign agents and their unsightly homegrown allies, which guarantees the adventurous excitement of this type of pro-communist youth literature. In the framework established by Gaidar and his followers, children who have problems fitting in can at best serve as secondary personae but are never allowed to represent the center of the character constellation within a socialist-realist narrative.

Movies based on Gaidar stories and their imitations dominated the Soviet repertoire for decades, favoring children who fight the good fight together with the adults, be it during the Civil War or in the present. Children with socially deviant behavior served as warnings, as they were shown to be more susceptible to the influences of "enemies," especially to evil, materialistic temptations. In many of those status quo films, behavioral problems were resolved in the same way as in the adult world: at an official meeting, where the misfit is publicly criticized, regrets his wrongdoing, and promises betterment. *My Name Is Kozha* violates all these normative clichés. It is precisely this nondidactic approach that makes it so refreshing even today.

Another unusual element is Kozha's relationship with his grandmother. A kind and pious woman, she repeatedly refers to her religious faith, but neither the boy nor other characters relativize or neutralize these utterances in any way. Furthermore, the grandmother is completely unworried about Kozha's disciplinary issues. When neighbors mention them to her, she makes light of his maladjustment, simply saying, "He's got character, just like his father."

This generous endorsement of a juvenile with a free spirit has contributed to the film's lasting success. But *My Name Is Kozha* has an even deeper dimension that appealed specifically to Kazakhstani viewers. Of great significance is the juxtaposition of the unbound, quasi-nomadic lifestyle represented by Sultan with the strict regulation of Kozha's and the other youngsters' everyday life. Obviously, Sultan is free in many ways, and nobody can force him to do anything. However, one of the consequences of this freedom is the teenager's isolation and absence of deep social ties. He knows no loyalty except to himself: stealing, breaking promises, and even lying to his friend Kozha. Ultimately, Kozha is smart enough to realize that the price of Sultan's freedom is the absence of attachments and responsibilities, both of which Kozha desires.

The film's spatial organization reflects the difficulties experienced by the title character. Kozha lives in an *aul* surrounded by endless mountains, signifying the promises of the freedom of nature, whereas all restrictions and conflicts unfold inside buildings. When Kozha follows Sultan to live like a free *djigit*, they ride out into the mountains to live high above the repressive civilizational space. The film does not deny how beautiful that free mountain space is. But society's laws extend to it as well. Sultan's antisocial behavior is noticed by adults, and he gets caught and punished for his transgressions. A fundamental difference between Kozha and Sultan is that the former has a strong sense of honor, which the latter completely lacks. When Sultan takes advantage of the naïveté of a toddler whose parents are away on business, Kozha is ashamed of his friend.

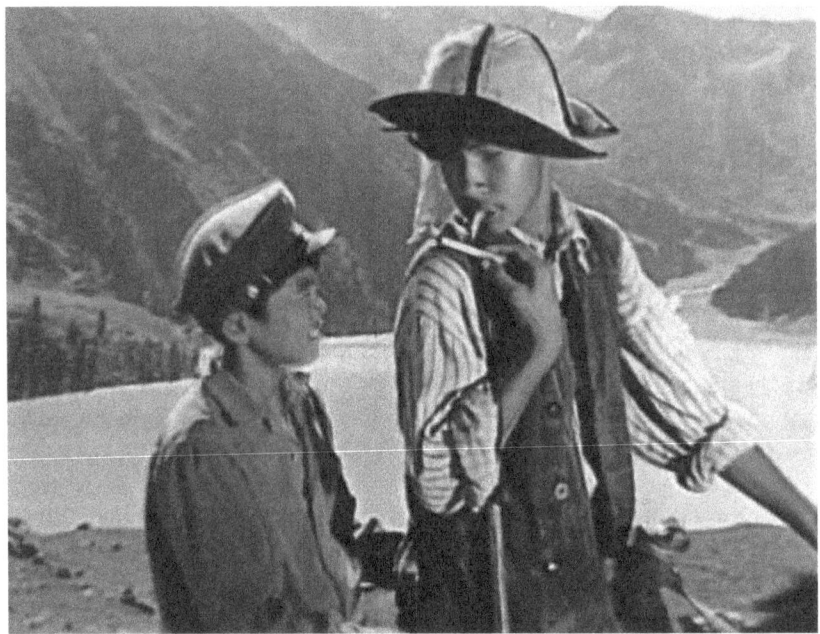

**Figure 5.3 Kozha and the Tempter Sultan.** *My Name Is Kozha* (1963, Abdulla Karsakbaev)

In the end, Kozha just laughs out loud when the older Sultan once again challenges him to join him in living in the mountains: Kozha now understands that the rejection of civilization, restrictive as it may be, is no solution for his problems, regardless of how romantic the mountain life may seem. Ultimately, Kozha is depicted as a young man whose heart is in the right place and whose difficulties arise from his clumsiness, dissatisfaction with parts of himself, and sometimes a stroke of bad luck. Indeed, the film is more optimistic about Kozha's chances of leading a successful life than is the boy himself, just like the wise grandmother, who fully trusts Kozha's inner values and understands that his rascal behavior is a temporary phenomenon and a natural phase of development.

Karsakbaev depicts life in provincial Soviet Kazakhstan as safe and harmonious. The usual attributes of Soviet civilization, with portraits of great Russian writers adorning the classroom walls and red flags and slogans decorating public buildings, are treated as commonplace, neither with awe nor with disdain. *My Name Is Kozha* is not subversive with respect to the Soviet civilizational framework, but it is assertive with respect to Kazakh values.

It is telling that the 2010 deluxe edition of the best Kazakhstani feature films opened with *My Name Is Kozha*, a film with which most Kazakhs

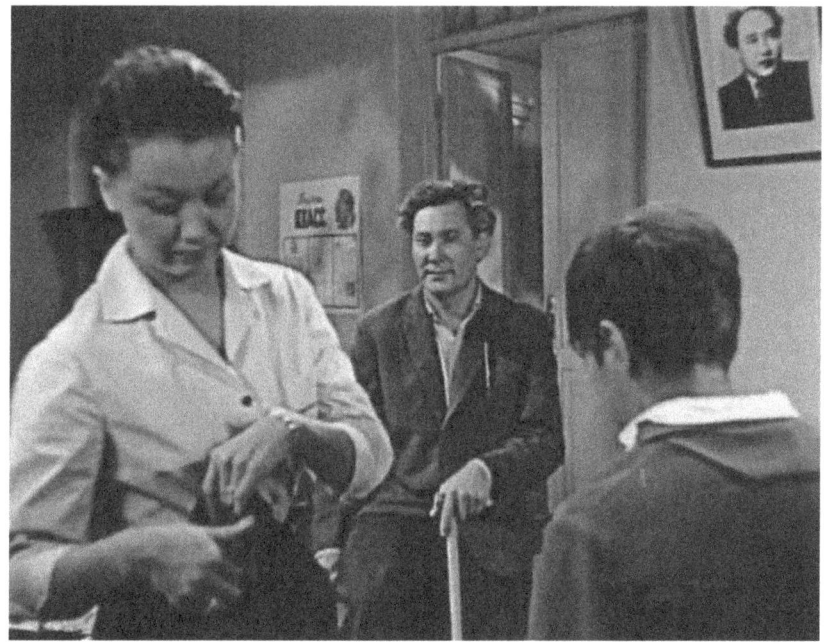

**Figure 5.4   Kozha, His Teachers, and a Portrait of Mukhtar Auezov.** *My Name Is Kozha* (1963, Abdulla Karsakbaev)

are familiar. It became a genuine sleeper hit, that is, one whose fame was unexpected and lasted over several generations. However, while *My Name Is Kozha* holds a special place in Kazakhs' memory, it is little known outside of Kazakhstan. How did that come to be? The answer lies in the film's national specifics. Kozha's problems can be viewed as consequences of his "Kazakhness," the free *djigit* spirit refusing to be tamed by authoritarian urban civilization. Yet the title character's ultimate choice is one in favor of urbanity and progress. And that is precisely the film's point: while the traditional quasi-nomadic life in the midst of nature is appealing, it cannot replace the advantages of modern civilization. Thus, Kozha's maturation is symbolic, implying a conscious farewell to the past. It is a farewell in good humor, not bitterness. Fundamentally, the film signals agreement with the pro-modern direction that Kazakhstani civilization had been taking in the Soviet era.

*My Name Is Kozha* initiated a line of films about Kazakh children who are finding their place in society. Not surprisingly, subsequently the topic was sometimes given a political coloration, which it did not have in Karsakbaev's picture. *Sound the Tomtom* (Zvuchi, tam-tam/Arman-Ataman, 1967), directed by Sharip Beisembaev[32] from a script by Akim Tarazi, was arguably the most explicit in its political agenda. Its main characters are boys who dream of going to Africa to support the liberation struggle of exploited peoples. In high school, children show an unusual interest in international affairs. Their environment is dominated by Lenin pictures and red flags. When they play "war," one of the boys criticizes the division between "us" and "the Germans": "We don't play correctly [*nepravil'no my igraem*]; there are our Germans, too, the democratic ones."

Young Arman, the first-person narrator, has read more books than anyone else, including *The USSR Is the Friend of Exploited People*. The boys examine each other on their knowledge of African politics and dream of participating directly in the anti-colonial fight, throwing grenades at the colonizers. Such political proficiency would have seemed strange coming from Kozha, whose problems were domestic and who lacked a global perspective. To be sure, Beisembaev's film is not a Soviet-style lecture on world politics. The boys are hard-to-tame little rascals, and the film, especially its first part, features some exciting episodes, like pursuing a wolf in the steppe and fighting for leadership of the gang (who has the right to be the *ataman*, or in another context, the commander of the liberation army). The family intimacy in a yurt is described with warmth, as are the relations between the kids. But the yearning for international heroism, with names such as Patrice Lumumba's quoted in the children's dialogues, gives this movie a distinct air of political correctness, and the score supports its propagandistic dimension. From the beginning, when a teacher reads aloud a letter in French, Kazakhstan is presented as an informed country fully integrated into world affairs, not as a country in state of modernization.

Apart from its heavy-handed political message, *Sound the Tomtom* is a well-acted ensemble movie whose political messages are pleasantly wrapped in comedic episodes. At every turn, the film makes visible efforts to breathe life into stale officialdom. The children's indoctrination is depicted as something natural. Thus, when Arman and his buddies learn English, they practice sentences such as "The capitalists deceive the people" and "Yankees go home!" It would be interesting to compare the 1967 original to the 1987 redacted version, with changes reflecting the altered international priorities of Soviet politics. Whatever these changes may be, however, the plot, with an African delegation arriving in Kazakhstan in the finale and children singing songs about "Lumumba's hot heart" and "the Black brothers in the trenches," is a visible construct compared to *My Name Is Kozha*. It should not come as a surprise that *Sound the Tomtom* did not leave as deep a mark as its 1964 predecessor. The same must be said about other Kozha derivatives that appeared in the 1970s. While they did satisfy a deep-seated need for children's adventure stories, they rarely dared to display the irreverent humor of the original that started it all.

Unfortunately, this is also true of Abdulla Karsakbaev's attempt to synthesize the children's film and the historical genre in *Voyage to Childhood* (Puteshestvie v detstvo, 1968). Just like *My Name Is Kozha*, it was adapted from a story by Berdybek Sokpakbaev, but the tone is considerably more serious. The sojourn of a man named Baktas to his native *aul* triggers memories of the 1930s and the campaign for the collectivization of agriculture. But the topic is so severe and was such a strict taboo throughout the Soviet period that an even halfway realistic depiction of the reality of that time was simply impossible. The horrendous famine, the escape of hundreds of thousands of desperate families across the border to China, and the systematic destruction of the nomadic lifestyle by the communist administration could not be visualized in a feature film. Not surprisingly, *Voyage to Childhood* failed to leave a deep mark in Kazakhstani viewers' memory. Only Karsakbaev's last film about children, *The Salty River of Childhood* (1983), which dealt with tragic experiences in the hinterlands during World War II, achieved a high level of truthfulness and was artistically convincing.

Sharip Beisembaev continued the theme of politically engaged children with another adventure, *At the "Red Brick" Fortress* (U zastavy "Krasnye kamni," 1969). The summer encounter of three teenagers (two Kazakh boys and a Russian tomboy) at a border fortress of which the girl's father is the commander, at first generates interest by describing the relationship between Kabysh, Olia, and Tanat in the exotic wilderness of the mountains, then involves the kids in the hunt for genuine spies, where they manage to demonstrate their mental and physical aptitude in practice. The conversations often revolve around foreign agents; consequently, the kids try to arrest a suspicious creature—which turns out to be a cow. But the danger of enemy infiltration does exist, and the children are happy to help bring the perpetrators to justice.

Movies such as *Sound the Tomtom* and *At the "Red Brick" Fortress* were assigned a function in the communist and patriotic education of Soviet children, but they did not ingrain themselves in viewers' minds as did Kozha. Indeed, they trivialized the innovations of Karsakbaev's masterpiece for political gain.

## BORDERS

The previous pages may give the impression that, with minor exceptions, the output of Kazakhfilm studio in the 1960s consisted exclusively of innovative masterpieces. However, such a conclusion would be incorrect. Along with thematically daring pictures, Kazakh cinema featured conventional movies without aesthetic ambition. Among these films are some that deserve a closer analysis, for example, Efim Aron's *Where the Edelweiss Are Blooming* (Tam, gde tsvetut edel'veisy, 1965). This film is noteworthy on two levels. Firstly, it was extremely popular: with 27 million viewers, it belongs on the list of the all-time greatest hits of Kazakhstani cinema. Secondly, it addresses a topic that would remain significant for Kazakhstan during the Soviet period and the independence era: the country's borders, a highly sensitive issue of Kazakhstani identity.

Because of its geographic specificities, the border with China was always hard to monitor, giving hundreds of thousands of Kazakhs the chance to escape from Soviet state terror in the 1920s and 1930s. Communist propaganda treated this mass exodus as an act of treason. In films such as *Raikhan* (1941) and *Daughter of the Steppes* (1954), the violators of the border were invariably the rich *bays* who either intended to steal the people's collective property and take it abroad or who came back to commit sabotage. Thus, violating the Soviet Kazakh-Chinese border was declared to be the consequence of class differences, not economic failure or political terror on the part of Soviet power.

The border security narratives produced their own set of clichés in Soviet cinema, and not only in Kazakhstan. Especially in the 1950s, numerous espionage thrillers featured shady characters entering the Soviet Union illegally. In their antagonism to Soviet heroic patrols, these intruders were the negative parts of an easily recognizable "goodies vs. baddies" pattern that made for adventurous entertainment, especially for young audiences. Interestingly, for a long time, it was the borders with Islamic countries that caused Soviet authorities the greatest unease; many movies in the 1940s and 1950s feature Muslim provocateurs who were paid and guided by their Western masters.

In Kazakhstani cinema, the border is not just a legal entity separating states from each other. It is also depicted as a protective line that guarantees civilizational stability within Kazakhstan. It is no coincidence that the aggressors in films dealing with the border issue are Islamists, revealing a continuity between the 1920s, the 1960s, and the 2000s. Indeed, the Kazakhstani cinematic discourse about the nation's borders is implicitly a discourse about secularism and its domination of Kazakhstani society.

Soviet border adventures such as Konstantin Iudin's *Fortress in the Mountains* (Zastava v gorakh, 1953) and Dmitrii Vasil'ev's *At the Tissa River* (Nad Tissoi, 1958) were huge hits, but were also considered trivial and found little reflection in contemporary reviews or in the critical literature. The same is true of Aron's *Where the Edelweiss Are Blooming*: although one of the most successful Kazakh movies, it was hardly reviewed in the official Soviet mainstream press or in post-Soviet film history. The reason for this critical neglect is not that espionage and border adventures were viewed as politically dangerous, but that the genre itself was considered "low" and not worthy of thorough critical assessment.

*Where the Edelweiss Are Blooming*, a latecomer to the border patrol subgenre, appealed to viewers throughout the Soviet Union. It was the last feature film directed by veteran Efim Aron, the only permanently employed filmmaker at Kazakhfilm Studio in the 1940s and early 1950s. The story unfolds in the high regions of the Pamir Mountains, in a garrison located directly at the border with an unfriendly country, the name of which is never made explicit. The viewer learns early on that the mother of the fortress commander was killed in that region in 1932 and that a monument has been erected in her honor. What the film leaves out is the historical background of that event, namely the mass escape from Kazakhstan of thousands who were starving due to the coercive collectivization campaign. In all likelihood, the commander's mother died as a result of clashes between fleeing Kazakhs and border patrols.

The opening episode takes place in the present day when a woman and her small child travel on a truck that routinely overcomes the most dangerous passes. The woman, Vera, is a physician and wife of the new fortress commander, Petr Solov'ev; the girl is their daughter, Tania. Both have agreed to give family life in a military framework a try, sharing the commander's hardships. The personnel at the fortress seem to be a friendly bunch, with only one bad apple, Pushkarev, who is eager to impress his comrades with cynical jokes and demonstrative indifference to any moral issues. When this arrogant Muscovite is sent on a mission with the Kazakh corporal Sutenbaev, he deliberately hides the truth about his comrade's harmlessly plucking an Edelweiss, causing a major disruption. The reason for Pushkarev's duplicitous game is simple envy: he is resentful because Sutenbaev and not he was chosen by a Moscow journalist for the cover photo of a magazine. His vanity puts him on a path of revenge that ultimately endangers the border guards' mission. Indeed, this is the film's main message: for a military unit to function, human relations among the servicemen and with their loved ones must be intact. Egotism and unhealthy competitiveness can hamper the unit's ability to carry out its mission.

In the context of human relations, gender roles are of decisive importance. The opening scene, in which the commander, Lieutenant Solov'ev, welcomes his wife, points to this aspect, which unfolds as a separate plotline. The military personnel display certain unease about the presence of a woman, but later behave like perfect gentlemen. When Solov'ev almost loses his life in an avalanche, Vera is not informed about the incident so as to spare her the shock. In contrast to the chivalry with which most of the soldiers treat Vera, Pushkarev indulges in cynicism and makes indecent allusions to her as a woman. He refuses to listen to her stories about the Edelweiss flower, the symbol of eternal loyalty, whereas the other soldiers are eager to learn more about it. However, the tensions between the spouses eventually take a toll. At the beginning, the two enjoy a happy partnership, kissing each other under the New Year's tree. But the isolation and monotony of life in the border fortress prove too much for Vera. As a doctor, she feels useless because the soldiers refuse to be treated for occasional minor injuries; as a wife, she misses her husband's attention, as his around-the-clock service leaves little time for private life. Solov'ev eventually accepts a separation from his wife but will not give up his daughter. This domestic dispute is the reason why Solov'ev leaves his post. As luck would have it, he violates his duty precisely in the moment when a group of saboteurs assaults the border. However, the plot makes an unexpected and symbolic, albeit highly improbable turn when the saboteurs' leader, Beishembek, is captured and confesses to the murder of Solov'ev's mother thirty years earlier! He has come back accompanied by two Islamist drug dealers, pretending to lead them into Soviet territory, but in truth handing them over to Soviet authorities as a gesture of repentance so that he can die in peace. Doctor Vera finally has the professional challenge she craves and successfully removes a bullet from the body of the injured Sutenbaev.

Considering the specific needs of the genre, Aron's handling of the material is surefooted and economical. This, together with an adventurous story and a complementary plotline about private relations that could satisfy multiple audience segments, turned *Where the Edelweiss Are Blooming* into one of the highest-grossing Soviet feature films of the year. While its ideological framework remains linear throughout, the characters are not without subtleties; there is even room for occasional irony. The causality connecting the private and the professional sphere is one of the noteworthy didactic elements of this film; another is the surprising tolerance in its treatment of human weaknesses such as Vera's frustration. The only character who is shown in an entirely negative light is the Russian Pushkarev, whose arrogance can be easily associated with his status as a Muscovite, whereas the Kazakh characters are depicted as modest and dutiful throughout.

To be perfectly clear, from an artistic point of view, *Where the Edelweiss Is Blooming* is negligible and belongs to a different sphere than the films of Aimanov, Begalin, and Khodzhikov. However, as part of the genre spectrum in Kazakhstani cinema of the 1960s, it is a noteworthy outlier in its insistence on traditional Soviet patriotic values, the depiction of Kazakh-Russian symbiosis, and its implicit allusion to mass starvation and escape in the 1920s and 1930s.

## A DEAD END ROUTE

While *Where the Edelweiss Are Blooming* represents conventional Soviet movie production, for Kazakhstani cinema overall the 1960s were a time of testing the stability of thematic and aesthetic conventions. Karpov's *Silence*, Begalin's *The Traces Go to the Horizon*, Khodzhikov's *The Plane Tree on the Rock*, and Aimanov's *Intersection* marked the beginning of a serious exploration of contemporary Kazakh reality. The responses from the political establishment, critics, and viewers, however, were not positive enough for filmmakers to continue on this path. The atmosphere at the studio apparently was often tense and fraught with conflict. In the mid-1960s, a new studio administration took a proactive stance on the production of quality screenplays, the chronic sore spot of Kazakh cinema from the beginning. But the problems did not end there. "One wished that the relations among the studio personnel were defined by greater mutual understanding, warmth, and care," wrote the newspaper *Leninskaia smena* in December 1965. "There are prominent masters working at Kazakhfilm studio. They are often offended because their films were not judged and not understood in the way they had hoped for."[33] Does the author allude to Aimanov? To Aron? The article leaves that question open.

The widening gap between Kazakhstani filmmakers and native audiences had become a worrisome problem, too. Iconoclast poet Olzhas Suleimenov took up the issue in his own provocative manner. In an article he published in *Leninskaia smena*, he described a Russian comedian, Il'ia Nabatov, who was on tour with his troupe in Alma-Ata. Their jokes were old, and the entire performance was shamelessly lackluster. When someone in the audience shouted, "Nabatov, this is crap (*khaltura*)!" the audience became agitated, but the performance continued as if nothing had happened. Suleimenov likens this shameless routine to the behavior of Kazakhstani film officials: when mediocre and downright bad movies were released, official reactions signaled "business as usual." Even if viewers left the movie theater, the film went on unperturbed. Flops produced by Kazakhfilm, such as *My Boy* (Mal'chik moi, 1962) and *Seriously and in Jest* (I v shutku i vser'ez,1963), certainly were met with criticism. However, "nobody is held responsible for a bad film."[34]

Despite such interjections, the overall output of Kazakhfilm studio was stronger than generally recognized or admitted. One might expect that by the mid-1960s, with the appearance of such diverse pictures as Karpov's *Silence* and *Tale of a Mother*, Aimanov's *In One District*, *The Intersection*, and *Beardless Swindler*, Begalin's *The Traces Go Beyond the Horizon*, Khodzhikov's *The Plane Tree on the Rock*, and Karsakbaev's *My Name Is Kozha*, Kazakhstani cinema would have been perceived as increasingly robust. It seemed undeniable that the country had an evolving original film culture with the potential to grow far into the future. Alas, the reactions were quite different. After young celebrity Olzhas Suleimenov was the first to express unease about the state of Kazakh cinema, painting an utterly negative view of its achievements in his afore-mentioned article, others followed suit. The screenwriter Lev Varshavskii reacted with an article in the Communist

Party newspaper *Kazakhstanskaia Pravda*, pointing to the recent successes of Kazakh cinema in the USSR and abroad. However, his praise was strangely backhanded: he only cited Aimanov's 1952 performance in *Dzhambul* and Karpov's direction in *Tale of a Mother* as positive examples and avoided all references to the controversial films of Begalin and Khodzhikov, let alone Karsakbaev.

Still, Varshavskii offered some practical suggestions.[35] Indeed, his article is not so much polemical as it is analytical; its matter-of-fact tone was to demonstrate that the author knew what he was talking about. He singled out three major weaknesses from which Kazakhfilm was suffering: screenwriting, direction, and acting. According to Varshavskii, these three aspects were interconnected. Even the best screenplay can be mishandled by lackluster direction, and incompetent performers can render a film unwatchable for audiences. Varshavskii revealed interesting specifics. Apparently, Kazakhfilm studio kept some thematically worthwhile screenplays on its shelves, as no director was willing to pick them up. He cites previous cases when directors had been pressured into accepting projects without being fully convinced of their intrinsic value, resulting in films of low quality (*My Boy*/Mal'chik moi; *Ask Your Heart*/Sprosi svoe serdtse; *The Fusion*/Splav; he also included *A Song Is Calling*/Pesnia zovet which will be discussed in chapter 7).

Varshavskii blamed the former two weaknesses on the lack of regular contacts between screenwriters and directors and the insufficient number of qualified directors at the studio. How could the number of native filmmakers be increased? At the root of this question lay a dilemma: the majority of Kazakh applicants to the Soviet State Film School (VGIK) were rejected due to their insufficient education. Indeed, when Varshavskii's article was published, not a single Kazakh applicant had been able to pass the entrance exams to VGIK! The Kazakhstani state and the studio should therefore help by taking practical measures. Of the three problems discussed by the author, the lack of qualified directors seemed to him the gravest.

Last but not least, the studio had no cadre of skilled performers. While theaters could rely on a good number of accomplished actors and actresses, they had their own schedules and often simply could not release performers for the period of shooting a movie. To fill the roles of young people, directors were forced to resort to nonprofessionals, which entailed serious risks. Varshavskii proposed bringing back the actors' studio (*akterskaia kinoshkola*) that had existed in the 1940s and boasted such graduates as Nurmukhan Zhanturin.[36]

The author's suggestions were heeded in part: the screenwriting department of Kazakhfilm was supplemented by preparatory courses, in which applicants to VGIK underwent intensive training to increase their chances of enrollment. Among those to benefit from these measures was one of the leading directors of the post-independence era, Damir Manabaev. But

Varshavskii's article indirectly also exposed a general problem of cinema in Kazakhstan: the impatience and often unfairly negative attitude of critics and viewers. It took decades for the Kazakh nation to better appreciate her leading film artists. Full recognition of the oeuvres of Begalin, Karsakbaev, Khodzhikov, and even Aimanov came only after their passing. Indeed, an even-handed assessment of their legacy is still underway.

Suleimenov and other intellectuals represented a vocal faction in the communist establishment that fought for serious cultural reforms. But their opponents in the Kazakhstani administration remained strong and waited for their chance to take revenge. Very often, the criticism of weaknesses in Kazakhstani cinema was a veiled attack on a certain group of artists and intellectuals. Indeed, while the Communist Party, to which most film workers belonged, constantly demanded more films about modern Kazakhstan, in reality these demands were pure lip service. As soon as a filmmaker risked tackling contemporary issues, the same authorities put up one ideological roadblock after another, stifling any creative desire to deal with modernity. Not surprisingly, leading directors of Kazakhfilm studio, such as Begalin and Khodzhikov, turned to historical subjects. An outlier in the second half of the 1960s is *The Blue Route* (Sinii marshrut, 1968), a rare example of contemporary social drama that demonstrated the enormous potential of that genre when used in a fresh, unconventional manner.

*The Blue Route* tells the story of two hydrogeologists, Omirzek (Adilbek Ismailov) and Zhol (A. Nurmakhanov), who travel across the endless steppe to check the state of water resources, measuring the depth of wells and taking probes. They hire a student, Korik (Marat Duganov), to perform low-level tasks. The dramatic tension between the three men arises from their distinct personalities: Omirzek, the expedition leader, is bossy and choleric; Zhol, the truck driver, spent time in prison and remains generally quiet but has sudden outbreaks of anger. Korik is obviously intellectually superior but also thin-skinned and cocky, showing disrespect to both Omirzek and Zhol. Korik also appears to have a highly developed sense of social responsibility: when the boss wants to use the precious water probes—the result of many weeks of drudgery—to cool the truck's motor, Korik threatens him with a rifle. More than once, the verbal exchanges between the three men turn almost physical, and their threats seem real. However, these constant frictions somehow enable the group to achieve the desired results: they manage to rescue the truck from a swamp and preserve the bottles containing water samples, despite a desperate need for cooling water. During the violent finale, when a trio of escaped convicts drags the men into a brutal robbery, it is the student, Korik, who defeats the gang leader.

Olzhas Suleimenov's screenplay tells this story with a keen eye for the complex relations between men in contemporary Kazakh society. The character constellation and issues of machismo resemble *The Plane Tree on the Rock*, although Korik, the young intellectual, represents an entirely new phenomenon, and the constellation evolves in dramatic mobility, not in forced stasis as in Khodzhikov's cage. The relations between the men are determined by differences in age, education, and social position. All three indulge in macho postures. In addition, the elderly administrator and the driver like alcohol, whereas Korik does not drink at all. Along the way, *The Blue Route* discloses unsightly aspects of Kazakhstani everyday life as no film before or after had or would.

The director, Zhardem Baitenov, who made his full-length feature debut, opted for a style so gritty that the previous social dramas produced by Kazakhfilm studio look tame in comparison. The three main performers seem not to act at all, appearing completely natural. The banality of everyday Kazakh life, its customs and jargon are captured with almost documentary-like precision. Unlike *A Plane Tree on the Rock*, which preempted the claustrophobic constellation "authoritarian Soviet administrator vs. primitive brute," Baitenov's film does not integrate the characters into a parable and does not confront them with a female foil; the implicit goal is not the disclosure of a hidden mythical truth. Rather, Baitenov strives to capture the social truth that is in plain view.

The three men are put in situations that reveal their character flaws, but they are then given a chance to prove their profound decency. With maximum candor, Suleimenov and Baitenov reveal the challenges and opportunities of being a man and a citizen in contemporary Soviet Kazakhstan, especially with respect to public self-representation and social duty. More so than in Begalin's and Khodzhikov's social dramas a few years prior, Kazakhstani society is shown in flux, with the difference that *The Blue Route* does not focus on a female character to demonstrate the male protagonists' disorientation. In this respect, Omirzek, Zhol, and Korik appear as though they were designed as quasi-antagonists to Begalin's and Khodzhikov's confused characters. They tend to act impulsively, provoking each other and competing against each other, but as soon as they are exhausted by their horseplay, their rational faculties take over and they draw constructive conclusions. In the end, their task to secure the water supply in their vast homeland is accomplished. Thus, *The Blue Route* is primarily a film about the Kazakh male mentality in the present, its peculiar aggressiveness, and its ability to revise and correct thoughtless decisions. When the social fabric connecting the three men is tested in a life-and-death situation, it holds firm. This is a lesson for the viewer who tends to overestimate surface tensions and to overlook the deep-seated positive values to which the protagonists adhere.

*The Blue Route* was extremely controversial at the time of its release. Two decades later, Katesh Alimbaeva criticized both the young director for his failure to stand up for his film and the administrators of Kazakhfilm studio for not understanding its significance.[37] It seems that the high moral standards expressed by Suleimenov and Baitenov pushed the envelope of social criticism to a degree that the Kazakhstani establishment, along with large segments of society, was unable to accept. Moreover, the fact that it is a young intellectual (the student Korik) who defends and implements moral standards against the indifference and cynicism of the older generation must have been viewed as a provocation.

Initially, not all reviews of the film were negative. For example, the Communist Party newspaper *Kazakhstanskaia Pravda* discussed *The Blue Route* in an empathetic manner, albeit as a thriller directed against cowardice and opportunism.[38] But soon the overall tone of assessments became utterly hostile. Arguably, this was part of a backlash against Suleimenov, who had become an irritant to parts of the Soviet-Kazakh political establishment. As a result, the kind of cinema he proposed—a blend of social and psychological analysis with a muscular, conflict-prone contemporary plot—was eliminated from Kazakhfilm's output until the 2000s. Only then did Akan Sataev, deliberately or unknowingly, take up the tradition of violent, hyperrealistic contemporary drama and about the rules of Kazakh machismo, which featured in his first thrillers.

## NOTES

1. Baiderin, V., "Dva arbuza v odnoi ruke." *Izvestiia*, 13 September 1961.
2. "Posle togo kak vystupili 'Izvestiia.'" *Izvestiia*, 4 December 1961.
3. Garina, E., Turovskii, F., "Sud ne skoryi i ne pravyi." *Izvestiia*, 14 October 1960, p. 4.
4. Khusainov, Shakhmet, "Chtoby zhizn' ne otstavala ot ekrana." *Sovetskaia kul'tura*, 3 October 1962.
5. The original term, *soiuz kinematografistov*, has often been translated as "union of cinematographers;" however, the term "cinematographer" in English usually denotes "cameraman," whereas *kinematografist* is much broader than that; hence the translation as "film workers."
6. "Krepit' sviaz' s zhizn'iu naroda, sozdavat' vysokokhudozhestvennye proizvedeniia. S uchreditel'nogo s"ezda kinematografistov Kazakhstana." *Kazakhstanskaia pravda*, 11 January 1963.
7. According to one of the interviews that I conducted in Almaty in October 2017, he may have had in mind Sultan Khodzhikov, whose relationship with Aimanov was known to be tense.
8. Kosenko, P., "Kuda idet karavan?" *Kazakhstanskaia pravda*, 11 May 1961, p. 3. Kosenko writes that he felt „pity for a great actor whom the screenwriter and the director forced to play a role that is void of the truth of life." The implicit irony is that

Aimanov himself was that actor, screenwriter (coauthor), and director. The journalist also shares that he was denied access to the director's script and that the whole project was clouded in secrecy during its production. In respect to the primary screenwriter, I. Savvin, Kostenko compares him to other "paraliterary" authors who had written weak screenplays and were paid an honorarium, but ultimately the films could not be made because of the screenplays' low quality. Some of these charges preempt the *Izvestiia* article that came out in September, indicating that this was an organized campaign against Aimanov.

9. A later reassessment of *In One District* revealed that the first versions of the screenplay was more interesting than the one ultimately produced. In it, Sabur Baianov is fired after being criticized in the newspaper and looks back at his career from the viewpoint of that traumatic experience. Cf. Siranov, *Ocherki istorii kazakhskogo kino*, pp. 158–60.

10. In an ironic way, it reflected the director's own biography, when he was given an assignment to Kazakhfilm Studio instead of Mosfilm or Lenfilm.

11. Petr Kosenko wrote an enthusiastic review of *Silence*, juxtaposing its plot and performances to previous Kazakhstani films whose weaknesses he saw in the mixture of too many styles due to an overabundance of creative staff from other studios. *Silence*, according to Kosenko, conveys a "stylistic unity" and thus raises hopes for a higher quality of forthcoming Kazakhstani films. Cf. Kosenko, P., "Rozhdenie stilia?" *Kazakhstanskaia pravda*, 22 July 1960. Three years later, his assessment looked considerably bleaker.

12. One of the best examples is *The House in which I Live* (Dom, v kotorom ia zhivu, 1957) by Lev Kulidzhanov and Iakov Segel'.

13. In a review of Karpov's following film, *Tale of a Mother*, P. Kosenko repeats one of the points of criticism launched against *Silence*, namely, that the many realistic details found by the director bury the "poetic truth." One may conclude that Karpov's film offered more verisimilitude than the average Soviet film at the time. Kosenko, P. "Mat' soldata." *Kazakhstanskaia Pravda*, 11 August 1963, p. 3.

14. While the immediate critical responses to *Silence* were contradictory, later assessments of the film were generally positive, especially with respect to the performances. Cf. Siranov, *Ocherki istorii kazakhskogo kino*, pp. 155–56.

15. In the generally positive assessment of *Silence* in volume 4 of the *History of Soviet Cinema*, the introduction of the gigantic construction project is interpreted as an artificial addition by the screenwriters. Cf. *Istoriia sovetskogo kino*, vol 4 pp. 236–37. The author of that assessment, Kabysh Siranov, had called *Silence* "weak" just a few years earlier. Cf. Siranov, *Kinoiskusstvo sovetskogo Kazakhstana*, p. 12.

16. Ashrapov, Askhat (1931–2008), leading Kazakh cinematographer in the 1960s–1980s. He graduated from the Soviet State Film School (VGIK) in 1955 and quickly became recognized for his poetic handling of color, particularly in films such as *Kyz-Zhibek* and *Protect Your Star*. His black-and-white camerawork in *The Traces Go Beyond the Horizon* betrays an unusual perceptiveness for chiaroscuro that reveals the characters' inner conflicts.

17. In a collection of articles on the history of Kazakhstani cinema, *If Every One of Us* was listed among the weak films coming out of Kazakhfilm studio; this assessment

was based solely on the screenplay, whereas the visual elements were completely neglected. Cf. Siranov, *Ocherki istorii kazakhskogo kino*, p. 191.

18. This was the debut of Farida Sharipova in cinema. Alas, only a few of her later roles could match the complexity of Galiia Ismailova.

19. The critic Petr Kosenko wrote that he would have preferred for the main conflict line to be the opposition between indifferent administrators and idealistic citizens such as Galiia. As Aimanov's film only mentions that opposition in passing, Kosenko regards the entire plot development as misconceived. His approach is clearly based on "thaw" priorities that were dominating the discourses on cinema, not artistic considerations. Cf. Kosenko, P., "Konflikty 'Perekrestka.'" *Kazakhstanskaia pravda*, 9 March 1963.

20. One reviewer expressed her frustration over the lack of authoritarian control in regards to such antisocial characters; she suggested that the film should have shown tough measures applied to Galiia's husband. Cf. Kalashnikova, T., "'Perekrestok.'" *Zapadnyi Kazakhstan*, 4 August 1963.

21. Sharipova, Farida (1936–2010) eventually became one of the most prominent Kazakhstani stage and film actresses; she was named People's Artist of the USSR in 1980.

22. Mazhit (or Majit) Begalin (1922–1978) was the son of a prominent author of children's books, Sapargali Begalin. After a severe injury in the Great Patriotic War, Mazhit Begalin was admitted to the highly competitive film school VGIK, which at the time had been evacuated to Alma-Ata. He served as an assistant director on his teacher Gerasimov's war tragedy *The Young Guard* (Molodaia gvardiia, 1948). In 1950, Begalin joined the staff of Kazakhfilm studio.

23. Begalin's drama was preceded by a somewhat similar film about a woman who realizes that her husband is petty und does not meet her standards: *Once at Night* (Odnazhdy noch'iu, 1959), directed by Emir Faik from a screenplay by A. Gintsburg). However, due to its low artistic quality, that film did not leave a mark in the annals of Kazakhstani cinema.

24. *The Traces Go Beyond the Horizon* also marks a historical step as the first feature film shot in Kazakh. Cf. Nogerbek. *Na ekrane 'Kazakhfil'm,'* p. 50.

25. Bauyrzhan Nogerbek alluded to Shindo as a possible source of inspiration in his book *Na ekrane 'Kazakhfil'm,'* pp. 50–51.

26. In a survey of recent films, the authors accused the filmmakers of merely offering the "trivial idea that women must be treated in a humane manner and old prejudices must be overcome (. . .)." Zinov'ev, Markov, "Seredina potoka," p. 74.

27. The author of the screenplay was L. Listov, the director V. Voitetskii.

28. Berggrin, A., "Kinozrotelei nado uvazhat'." *Leninskaia smena*, 11 April 1961.

29. Sokpakbaev, Berdybek (1924–1991), Kazakh author of children's and youth fiction.

30. Tlendiev, Nurgisa (1925–1998), Kazakh composer who began his career with the Kurmangazy orchestra of folklore instruments. In 1968–1981, Tlendiev was the chief musical redactor of Kazakhfilm studio. He wrote the scores to many of the best Kazakhstani feature films and also worked in animation.

31. There is a certain kinship with Astrid Lindgren's series *Pippi Long Stockings*, whose adaptations were very popular in the USSR in the 1960s and 1970s. However,

in the Swedish movies, the juxtaposition of the stiff adult world and an anti-authoritarian girl results in countless jokes, many of them slapstick, whereas a moral dimension is less palpable than in the *Kozha* film.

32. Beisembaev, Sharip (1926–1989), Kazakh film director who graduated from the Supreme Courses for Screenwriters and Directors in Moscow in 1959 and subsequently excelled in a variety of genres in the 1960s-1980s, including children's adventures and contemporary dramas.

33. L. Nazirov, "Khoroshie fil'my delaiutsia ne tol'ko v Moskve." *Leninskaia smena*, 19 December 1965.

34. Suleimenov, O., "Razmyshleniia na temu. . . (Zritel' ukhodit, a deistvie idet)." *Leninskaia smena*, 11 April 1965.

35. Varshavskii, L. "Tri problemy kazakhskogo kino." *Kazakhstanskaia pravda*, 27 May 1965.

36. Ibid.

37. Alimbaeva writes about Korik's moral strictness: "Such a high social burden put on a character is a rather rare phenomenon in Kazakh cinema." Ainagulova, Alimbaeva, *Tendentsii razvitiia kinoiskusstva Kazakhstana*, p. 88.

38. Reznikov, Iu., "Vybor marshruta." *Kazakhstanskaia pravda*, 5 December 1968, p. 2.

*Chapter 6*

# En Route to Complexity II
## *Capturing the Past*

The early 1960s were marked by Kazakhstani cinema's continuing fast maturation. Shaken Aimanov as the country's first native filmmaker opened the door for younger talents such as Mazhit Begalin, Sultan Khodzhikov, and Abdulla Karsakbaev; non-Kazakh directors such as Aleksandr Karpov found a new home at the quickly growing Kazakhfilm studio. An increasing number of performers became skilled screen actors and gained prominence as movie stars, including Farida Sharipova and Asanali Ashimov. Cinematographers such as Mikhail Aranyshev and Askhat Ashrapov brought visual brilliance to Kazakhstani pictures. These positive achievements were countered, however, by an increasing resistance of segments of Kazakhstan's political establishment against filmmakers' thematic daring, making it clear that addressing contemporary social problems would be met by repressive measures such as limited release and negative media campaigns. As a result, the second half of the 1960s shows a decrease in contemporary drama and a focus on history.

## THE KAZAKH "EASTERN"

The second genre to become a mainstay of Kazakhstani cinema, after the children's film, was the Civil War drama. These action-filled pictures, which became known, somewhat ironically, as "Easterns," acquired particular importance for all Central Asian cultures in the 1960s. Kazakh filmmakers made some distinct contributions to this subgenre, emphasizing the tragic turbulences of the 1920s for their nation in a way that went beyond the simple fight between Bolshevik forces and their enemies.

Prior to the 1960s, Soviet cinema depicted any anti-Bolshevik character, whether politically ultra-left or ultra-right, as evil, sadistic, greedy, and hopelessly anachronistic. Among the few exceptions, albeit halfhearted in their execution, were two adaptations of Boris Lavrenev's short story *The Forty-First* (Sorok-pervyi). A silent version was directed by Iakov Protazanov in 1927 and a sound version by Grigorii Chukhrai in 1956. Both demonstrated remarkable artistic prowess and were released to critical controversy. Lavrenev's master plot itself represented a test of a quasi-humanistic concept: a Bolshevik sniper falls in love with a White Army officer but, despite her passion, she ultimately shoots her lover out of political loyalty to the communist cause. The story conveyed an uncompromising message, namely, that class considerations must, and will, override individual affection. Yet even to acknowledge that there could be a romantic relationship between a Red and a White was daring. In most Soviet movies, in particular those targeting children and youth, the class enemy was not even granted the doubts that Mariutka in *The Forty-First* entertained. Anti-Soviet forces were depicted with cartoonish hyperbole as diabolical, stupid, and even physically inferior, a laughing stock rather than a serious opponent.

In historical action films produced in the national studios, a variety of anti-Soviet movements served as the negative targets of adventurous Civil War lore and ultimately became clichés. Conspicuously, however, major impulses for a more even-handed, differentiated picture of societal struggle beyond the imposition of predictable ideological schemas also originated from the Soviet peripheries, not from the center. Thus, it was Lithuanian director Vytautas Žalakevičius's seminal *Nobody Wanted to Die* (Nekas nenorejo mirti /Nikto ne khotel umirat', 1965) that raised eyebrows with its intense psychological and ethical differentiation among characters, whether they were anti- or pro-Soviet. Since the mid-1960s, especially the transition from Khrushchev to Brezhnev, were a period of political and cultural uncertainty within the Soviet establishment, such attempts to push the envelope had a real chance to gain recognition; Žalakevičius's film even won a USSR State Prize. In *Nobody Wanted to Die*, the tragic antagonism between the characters was so harsh and the conflicts so irreconcilable that the appropriate genre framework to capture them was the thriller. Because many revolutionary and war films had used that genre as a framework before, it seemed safe from the censorial viewpoint and did not experience such thorough scrutiny as did films in other genres, such as satirical comedy or debate drama in which literally every word counted. The new element that Žalakevičius introduced was psychological and axiological ambiguity: characters fighting against Soviet power were not necessarily evil, and those fighting for it were not inevitably good. Most importantly, all those involved in the struggle were shown to be part of one family, one nation. The film's ability to undermine the common "goodies vs. baddies" scheme, historically taken for granted in class struggle thrillers, suddenly revealed the genre's artistic potential.

Within this Soviet framework, the 1960s gave Kazakhstani filmmakers new opportunities to take a closer look at their country's history and move beyond ideological and narrative clichés that had dominated the previous decades. Thus, Abdulla Karsakbaev, who had made a name for himself with his debut film, *My Name is Kozha*, opted against remaining in the children's film genre, turning instead to the Civil War events that had led to Kazakhstan's incorporation into the Soviet Union. The result of this decision was nothing less than groundbreaking.

In just as innovative a way as he had renewed the Soviet children's film, Karsakbaev gave the genre of revolutionary thriller an unprecedented depth. The "Eastern," which evolved in the mid-1960s as a variation of the Soviet Civil War adventure, had quickly developed clichés: the noble native communist commander; the Russian ideological instructor-cum-friend-and-mentor; the impressionable native ingénue; the sadistic, fanatical anti-Soviet mutineers, etc. It seems worthwhile to ask why it was in Kazakhstan that a young filmmaker such as Karsakbaev broke those convenient clichés and shed critical light on many assumptions that the typical Eastern took for granted.

Karsakbaev's *A Worrisome Morning* (Trevozhnoe utro, 1966) begins with the usual Bolshevik perspective: a border patrol unit of Secret Service troops (aka Chekists, from *ChK—Chrezvychainaia komissiia*) under commissar Tokhtar Baitenov is pursuing anti-Bolshevik fighters led by a man named Zhunus. At the beginning, Baitenov (Idris Nogaibaev) seems to be the very image of the ideal Bolshevik leader that so many Soviet Civil War flicks had elevated to superhero status. When one of his men refuses to ride a white horse because it stands out as a target and brought its previous owner bad luck, Baitenov gives him his own horse and rides the "cursed" animal himself. The commissar displays no such tolerance toward the enemy, however: he interrogates imprisoned anti-Bolshevik mutineers with the kind of mercilessness required by communist ideology (and by the genre). But the further the story unfolds, the more the pro-Bolshevik viewpoint becomes uncertain and unreliable. Baitenov acts more as a Kazakh than a communist: he trusts regular Kazakh folks even when their political position is shaky; moreover, he respects traditional rules of behavior, including religious ones. When inhabitants of an *aul* invite the Chekist unit to a wedding where an old Muslim makes a speech praying for peace, Baitenov does not object. Only when the time and location of Zhunus' next attack are suddenly disclosed are the fighters ordered to leave the festivities. However, the fact that Baitenov has not yet been able to catch the leader of the anti-communist uprising raises the suspicions of some Bolshevik supervisors, who begin to question his intentions. The investigator Shcrin (Asanali Ashimov), who has been sent to clarify the matter, insinuates that in the not so distant past, Baitenov was part of the Alash-Orda movement. Although Baitenov's Russian friend Kostroma defends him and the commissar eventually manages to capture Zhunus, the Soviet secret police (*ChK*) subsequently arrests him.

Karsakbaev's film differs from typical Easterns primarily in its character constellation. The most striking difference is the absence of a senior Russian educator who helps the Kazakh characters understand the political significance of their struggle. Instead, it is the Kazakh Baitenov who defines the film's intellectual-political center, whereas his Russian sidekick is merely a loyal comrade who is killed off early in the film. The main hero is shown to be increasingly lonely among those who should be closest to him: his comrades in the Communist Party, which he joined in 1917. Baitenov can only rely on himself and on rank-and-file Kazakhs. After his arrest, alone in his cell, this harsh commander breaks down in tears, so deep is his despair. Ironically, he is incarcerated in the same cell as his opponent, Zhunus.[1] The ensuing dialogue between the communist and the class enemy is key to grasping the principal novelty of Karsakbaev's approach. It turns out that Zhunus had been the leader of the local 1916 uprising against "the white tsar," at which time Baitenov had fought alongside him. They only parted ways when Baitenov, in Zhunus' words, began to turn "against the people, together with the usurpers [i.e., the Soviets—P.R.]." Karsakbaev thus moves the focus of his narrative from the characters' attitudes toward the establishment of communist power in Kazakh territory (called "Turkestan" at the time and in the film), which was usually the main way of distinguishing the "goodies" from the "baddies," to their attitude toward the Kazakh people, the Kazakh nation, and the nation' future.

The second unusual element is Baitenov's personality: he is depicted as an intellectual. Whenever the commissar has a free moment, he searches for ancient monuments of nomadic culture, studying and copying symbols and drawings on stone. Apparently, he has even written books on the subject, as Sherin states with disdainful suspicion.

Almost twenty years after its initial release, in 1983, a redacted version of *A Worrisome Morning* was prepared by Kazakhfilm studio; it was released in 1984. Abdulla Karsakbaev was a member of the team that produced this version, although it is unclear under what circumstances he agreed to the changes, since their impact is profound. For example, the original 1966 version shows Baitenov beating a young, cocky prisoner in order to force him to reveal Zhunus' plans. The young man then asks that his father not be beaten, to spare him the humiliation. This statement, which gives the class enemy an air of honor, was removed from the later (redacted) version. In another scene, one of Baitenov's fighters sees the commander copying motifs from an ancient stone monument. In the original version, the befuddled fighter asks Baitenov why he was doing that, to which he responds, "These are the traces left by our ancestors. . . . There can be no future without the past. . . . He who remembers is alive." In the redacted version, this dialogue was modified as follows: the fighter states, "Our ancestors used to hunt animals, whereas we are hunting humans," to which Baitenov replies, "We are hunting those humans who have turned into animals." In other words, the national and cultural dimension of Baitenov's studies was completely removed from the dialogue and replaced by a claim that associates the communist fight with a brutal evolutionary claim. With these changes, the redacted version utterly transforms the original concept. In the 1966 original, Baitenov is a carrier of *both* communist and traditionalist ideas, while the 1983 version eliminates his traditionalism. Although no documents regarding the redaction have been published to date, it can be assumed that these changes were part of the "struggle against nationalism" conducted with renewed intensity by the Communist Party apparatus in Moscow and Alma-Ata in the 1980s.

Compared to popular Civil War flicks such as Mosfilm studio's adventurous comedy *The Uncatchable Avengers* (Neulovimye mstiteli, 1966) and similar fare, released around the same time as Karsakbaev's picture, *A Worrisome Morning* is considerably deeper in several respects. First, Baitenov experiences a personal tragedy when he realizes that a synthesis between Kazakh patriotism and loyalty to the communist state is no longer possible. Second, the Civil War is depicted as a catastrophe for the people who crave peace. Recurring images of devastated, empty settlements convey the sheer horror of war, which cannot be compensated for by victory or faith in a bright future. Thirdly, Karsakbaev alludes to the coming political repressions, when solidarity and trust were replaced by scheming and informing on one's comrades. In the original 1966 version, the shadow of the Stalin-era purges is already visible, and even if patriots like Baitenov manage to survive the 1920s, the viewer knows that they will almost certainly fall victim to the state terror campaign of 1937–1938.

On the surface, *A Worrisome Morning* meets the expectations of the typical Soviet Civil War action film, including a tough commissar in a leather jacket, skirmishes between pro- and anti-Bolshevik units, and a hunt for a clever enemy leader. In reality, though, Karsakbaev's picture subverts all the conventions of the Eastern genre: the commissar is a thinker haunted by doubts; he is marginalized and arrested by his own comrades; and even the skirmishes are not a reason for joy, since they add to the horrendous death toll of the Civil War. Most importantly, the class enemy is not a cartoon figure: a noble opponent with his own ideas, he lets Baitenov go free and even returns his sabre to him.

Another major subversion of the genre was related to the target audience, as children and teenagers were hardly able to make sense of the complexities of this film, and even adult viewers looking for easy entertainment would have found *A Worrisome Morning* to be an intellectual challenge. The original screenplay by Zinovii Shashkin, titled *The Stars Do Not Go Out* (Zvezdy ne gasnut), depicted the tragic life of the Communist activist Tokash Bokin, who was killed in 1918. But soon after the film went into production, it was halted and the screenplay rewritten by Shashkin, I. Savvin, and Olzhas Suleimenov.[2] Now the main character was given a depth that rendered him radically different from the historical Bokin—the reason that he was maligned by his own comrades was not the enemies' viciousness but the distrust among the Bolsheviks themselves!

How such a profoundly subversive picture ever came to be released in the first place is truly a mystery. One of the reasons may be the brief period of cultural liberalization after the end of the Khrushchev era in 1964, when a number of controversial projects were given the green light. Indeed, two critics who wrote about the 1966 festival of Central Asian films in Ashgabad criticized many Turkmen, Uzbek, and Tajik films' simplistic approach to the class enemy of the 1920s:

> In [the Basmachi movement], especially right after the revolution, not only landowners, rich people, and clergy participated, but also many teachers and craftsmen who were deceived by nationalist and religious, Islamist slogans. This is a very complicated, multifaceted phenomenon. In cinema, the Basmachi are far more primitive than they were in reality. They are almost always shown in the same way, as a group of horse-riding bandits, dumb, stupid, brutal, and seemingly unable to seriously resist. . . . Meanwhile, how much more interesting and useful would it be if an artist were to try the opposite perspective (. . .).[3]

Obviously, the nonconformist approach used by Karsakbaev was encouraged in some critical quarters. To be sure, *A Worrisome Morning* is not a political pamphlet. Its spirit is that of tormenting doubt, of a search for answers. Artistically, Karsakbaev achieved a remarkable synthesis of psychologically persuasive acting, precise camerawork (Abiltai Kasteev), and a powerful soundtrack, with Nurgisa Tlendiev's pensive score as its foundation.

The film's finale is far from triumphant. Rather, it continues the exploration of Kazakhstan's national destiny, ending in a symbolic but ambiguous image. Tokhtar Baitenov, injured and exhausted, walks slowly toward the mountains and begins to climb. The landscape is dominated by white and gray rocks; the sky is harshly blue. He slips and slides back down, gets up and climbs again. The cinematography alternates between extreme long shots conveying his utter forlornness, and low-angle medium-close shots that give his struggle a monumental dignity. Baitenov is depicted as Sisyphus, the ancient hero who will not give up even after learning that he will never reach the desired apex.

Only in the post-Soviet era did the artistic caliber of *A Worrisome Morning* and its philosophical daring receive long-overdue recognition, when Karsakbaev's artistry was appreciated much more than it had been in the 1960s. In the framework of national film history, his discovery of specific Kazakh approaches to genres such as the children's film and the Civil War drama helped define the essence of Kazakh cinema. It marked a quiet revolution, prepared in the mid-1950s and executed in the 1960s.

## A VARIATION OF THE DEEP EASTERN

The subgenre of Civil War action flick flippantly known as the "Eastern" lent itself to various conceptions of history, ranging from the dogmatic Leninist (the one preferred by the communist establishment) to the ambivalent and even nostalgic. Although originally intended as an entertaining adventure movie populated by stock characters, in the hands of sensitive artists the Eastern could become a work of cinematic originality and artistry. One such unusual Eastern variation is *A Shot at the Karash Pass* (1968), adapted from Mukhtar Auezov's short story "An Occurrence at the Karash Pass" (1927). This co-production by the studios Kazakhfilm and Kyrgyzfilm was the feature debut of Kyrgyz director Bolotbek Shamshiev, who would become one of the most interesting Central Asian filmmakers.[4]

The plot of *A Shot at the Karash Pass* focuses on the complicated relationship between the poor horse thief Bakhtygul (Suimenkul Chokmorov) and the wealthy, intelligent elder of the *volost*,[5] Zharasbai (Sovetbek Dzhumadylov). Bakhtygul displays a manly stoicism that is independent of status or wealth. In a society with a strict class hierarchy, such a disposition appears foolish and cannot help but cause frictions. Stealing horses is Bakhtygul's way of protesting against the murder of his brother. Prior to becoming an outlaw, he had worked dutifully as a herdsman for twenty years, but there was no reward for his service, which was taken for granted, and he himself was viewed as little more than a slave.

Zharasbai, who is not only *volost* elder but also the leader of his entire kin, behaves as a proud dignitary, fully aware of his power. He senses the intelligence and potential in Bakhtygul and, rather unexpectedly, strikes up a friendship with him. For Bakhtygul, this is a chance to reconcile his fury about social injustice with his yearning for a meaningful authority that he can accept and serve; likely, it is his last chance. But his trust in Zharasbai proves to be naïve: the powerful leader uses the proud pauper for his own schemes, which serve exclusively to consolidate his position in society.

Shamshiev's film presents Kazakh society prior to the Bolshevik revolution (it takes place in the early 1910s, although no concrete date is given) as fundamentally immobile. There is no room for development nor for alternatives; there is only the ancient, self-perpetuating hierarchical order that turns the law into a mockery from which the rich (both natives and Russians) profit. In essence, the law of the land is the law of the jungle, and the only way to resist it is vigilantism, to which Bakhtygul once again resorts in the finale. Indeed, the roots of lawlessness are one of the film's major themes. Conspicuously, *A Shot at the Karash Pass* begins with uninvited horsemen entering Bakhtygul's yurt. As though this intrusion were not humiliating enough, it is followed by the father being beaten in front of his wife and children.[6] The inviolability of the *shanyrak*[7] turns out to be an illusion. Bakhtygul defends his home with a dagger, but the forces of injustice are overwhelming.

Zharasbai initially gives the impression that he is different from other powerful *mirzas*. He listens to the poor who approach him and, unlike Russian administrators, can relate to their plight. Compared to another rich man, the cruel and corrupt Salmen, Zharasbai seems downright enlightened. But when push comes to shove, he, too, betrays Bakhtygul and has him exiled to Siberia. At that culminating point, Bakthygul escapes and brings his previously admired patron to justice: he shoots him in broad daylight, execution-style.

An intriguing aspect of *A Shot at the Karash Pass* is its treatment of Russians. On the one hand, there is the case of a Russian businessman wishing to buy land from Zharasbai. This land is sacred, since the ancestors are buried there. But the businessman is supported by military authorities and ultimately pressures the *volost* elder into selling it. In these episodes, Russians are depicted as colonial exploiters, insensitive and indifferent to native values and traditions. On the other hand, there is the poor Russian family of the farmer Fedor (Viktor Ural'skii), who saves Bakhtygul in a moment of urgent need and is himself later saved by the Kazakh. The Russian farmers' fields are recklessly destroyed by a group of native *djigits*, and when the farmers come to Zharasbai for justice, he has them flogged. Thus, the film's approach to the question of ethnicity is differentiated, applying class-determination instead of ethnicity alone. Indeed, the Kazakh Bakhtygul has more in common with the Russian Fedor than with Zharasbai, a fellow Kazakh who shares his language, culture, and belief system. Bakhtygul and Fedor both are subject to the same oppression and exploitation, factors that determine the outcome of the film.

The most interesting aspect of *A Shot at the Karash Pass* is Zharasbai's ultimate realization that, despite his flexibility and adaptability, the upper class is doomed, the days of his own power are numbered, and he deserves to be punished. However, the film leaves open what he recognizes as his main moral transgression: having sold the sacred land or having misled and betrayed the loyal Bakhtygul. Unlike Zhunus in *A Worrisome Morning*, Zharasbai has no future and does not fight for one. When it becomes clear that Bakhtygul will take revenge, Zharasbai rides toward his certain death in an upright manner, as though this were not a de facto execution but an act of liberation.[8]

*A Shot at the Karash Pass* analyzes the spontaneous awakening of class consciousness among the Kazakh people, an awakening that evolved on a mass scale in the mid-1910s, paving the way for the revolutionary unrests of 1916 and thereafter. It shows that the patriarchal order betrayed the poor who adhered to it, ultimately delegitimizing traditional society as such. But Shamshiev's interpretation also points to inalienable rights of all human beings, regardless of the type of society in which they live. This makes *A Shot at the Karash Pass* worthwhile beyond its class-focused narrative.

Suimenkul Chokmorov, a young painter with no background in acting, was cast in the lead role,[9] a choice that turned out to be one of the film's major accomplishments. With his ascetic features and restrained body language, Chokmorov's Bakhtygul resembles the samurai characters of Toshiro Mifune. Together with other formidable characterizations and impressive black-and-white cinematography (M. Turabekov), *A Shot at the Karash Pass* once again demonstrated the depth of which the "Eastern" was capable. In practical terms, its success also opened the door for future cooperation between the film studios of two neighboring republics, Kyrgyzstan and Kazakhstan, which would result in a number of quality co-productions in the 1970s and 1980s.

## THE KAZAKHSTANI LEGACY OF THE GREAT PATRIOTIC WAR

The 1960s brought new attention to the legacy and memory of the Great Patriotic War of the Soviet Union (1941–1945). Officially, the war experience was viewed as an all-Soviet cause. At the same time, each of the Soviet republics developed and cultivated its own collective memory of the events. For Kazakhs, the war was a historical experience that affected their nation in a profound way. While Kazakhstani cinema in the 1950s was largely silent about this topic, at the beginning of the 1960s, filmmakers made significant contributions to the nation's efforts to come to terms with the experience of hundreds of thousands of Kazakhs who fought in the Soviet army and of millions of their relatives in the hinterlands. These films were not just thematically groundbreaking but also aesthetically remarkable.

There can be no doubt that the Soviet sociocultural context played a major role in the emergence of the Kazakhstani war film. One source of inspiration for these innovatively told stories were Russian-Soviet pictures that were made during the Thaw and brought new, worldwide attention to Soviet cinema, from Mikheil Kalatozov's *The Cranes Are Flying* (Letiat zhuravli, 1957) to Sergei Bondarchuk's *Fate of a Man* (Sud'ba cheloveka, 1959) and Grigorii Chukhrai's *Ballad of a Soldier* (Ballada o soldate, 1960). Another significant factor was the literary works of Kyrgyz author Chingiz Aitmatov, which began to resonate throughout the Soviet Union in the 1960s. Aitmatov's moralistic and romantic approach to the war inspired authors and directors across Central Asia, including in Kazakhstan. With the (albeit limited) relaxation of ideological standards during the Thaw, the memory of the tragedies experienced by millions of Soviet people could now be addressed in a manner both honest and humanistic, reawakening a sense of moral legitimacy and pride in the legacy of the war. Moreover, Soviet cinema rediscovered the language of pathos through formal innovation and experimentation: the three aforementioned masterpieces by Kalatozov, Bondarchuk, and Chukhrai were all shot in black-and-white, using a richness of angles, chiaroscuro, and camera mobility to entangle the viewer in an intense emotional experience that contrasted sharply with the hollow pathos of Stalinist cinematic officialdom. To many filmmakers of the post-Stalin period, the rediscovery of expressive means of classical montage cinema brought an aesthetic liberation.

The increasing artistic freedom of the 1960s was tolerated by the political establishment because the filmmakers who were exploring new aesthetic grounds remained outspoken communist loyalists and Soviet patriots. In other words, their films did not challenge the ideological status quo of the period, only the Stalinist aesthetic norms of the 1940s and early 1950s.

The new expressiveness and open emotionality that began in Russian cinema had a noticeable impact on the cinema of the national republics. In Kazakhstan, Aleksandr Karpov was the first director to deliver a war story of great emotional power, *Tale of a Mother* (Skaz o materi, 1963). Its effect was profound, albeit with one caveat: Karpov's film clearly betrays the influence of other Soviet directors. However, while Chukhrai in *Ballad of a Soldier* had told a story about the hinterlands during the Great Patriotic War, he had done so from the viewpoint of a young soldier and his encounters with numerous Soviet citizens during a brief vacation, whereas Karpov's film focuses on an elderly Kazakh woman. Waiting for her son to return from the front, she meets various people during this tormentuous time.[10]

Stories of young men eager to get to the frontlines and of their mothers who try to hold them back and then wait expectantly for their return are common in humanist war films. The one element that sets *Tale of a Mother* apart from other such films is the title heroine's illiteracy. It becomes an issue when the local mailwoman can no longer bear the burden of delivering death notes to people's homes and the film's title character, Zhulpan, volunteers to take over the job. Since Zhulpan cannot read the addresses on the incoming letters, she must ask other people, mostly children, to read them to her so that she can deliver each letter to the right house in the *aul*.

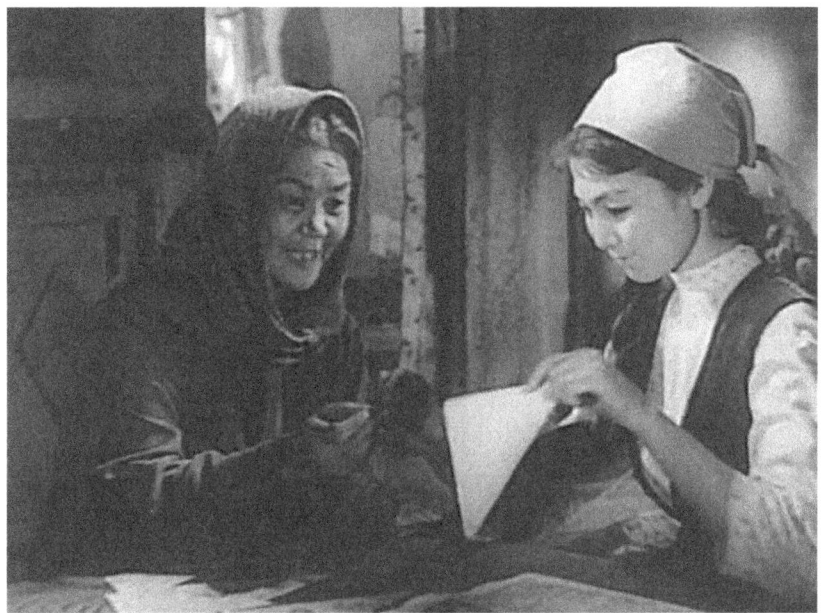

**Figure 6.1   Amina Umurzakova in the Title Role.** *Tale of a Mother* (1963, Aleksandr Karpov)

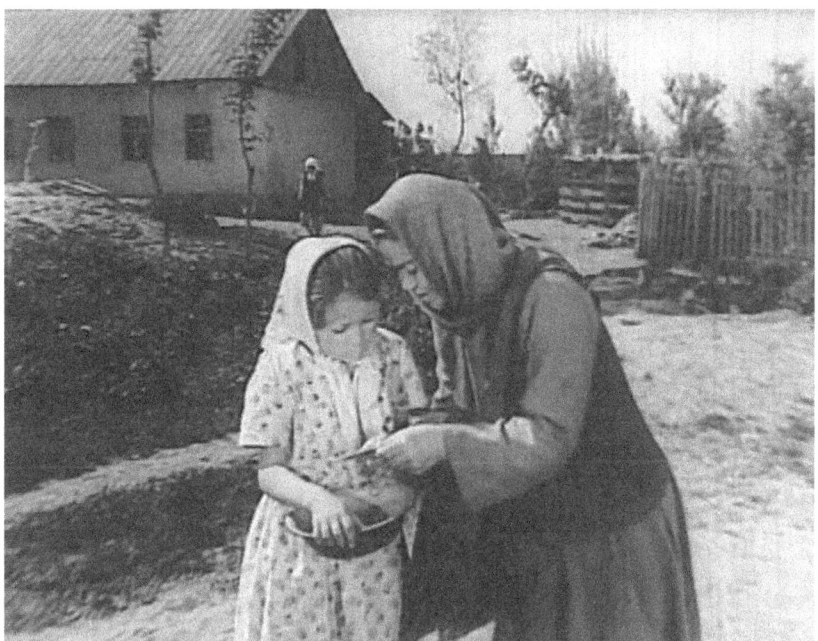

**Figure 6.2   Asking Children for Help.** *Tale of a Mother* (1963, Aleksandr Karpov)

174                    *Chapter 6*

The more familiar Zhulpan becomes with her job, the more she learns to decipher addresses, ultimately gaining the ability to read and write. Overcoming illiteracy in an emotionally trying situation represents a key element of the plotline and a deeply touching and truly novel motif in this Kazakh picture.

*Tale of a Mother* replicates certain pathos-filled devices that had been used by other Soviet films, for example, an omniscient narrator's stern vibrato voice at the beginning; low-angle shots of people wandering through the fields in expectation of war news, filmed against the backdrop of an ominous cloudy sky; and double exposure to indicate parallel actions or thoughts. But alongside such examples of visual pathos, Karpov's film contains moments that are truly unique.

One of the finest is a scene in which Zhulpan learns to spell her son's name, Asan (spelled in Cyrillic letters—*ACAH*). She forms it with hay straws on the road, but the wind begins to blow, pushing the straws around and destroying the name, predicting tragedy and suggesting to Zhulpan that her son may no longer be alive.

Throughout the film, Karpov emphasizes the selflessness of the civilian population, for the most part children and very young and elderly women. One episode, in which people refuse to interrupt the harvest even during a

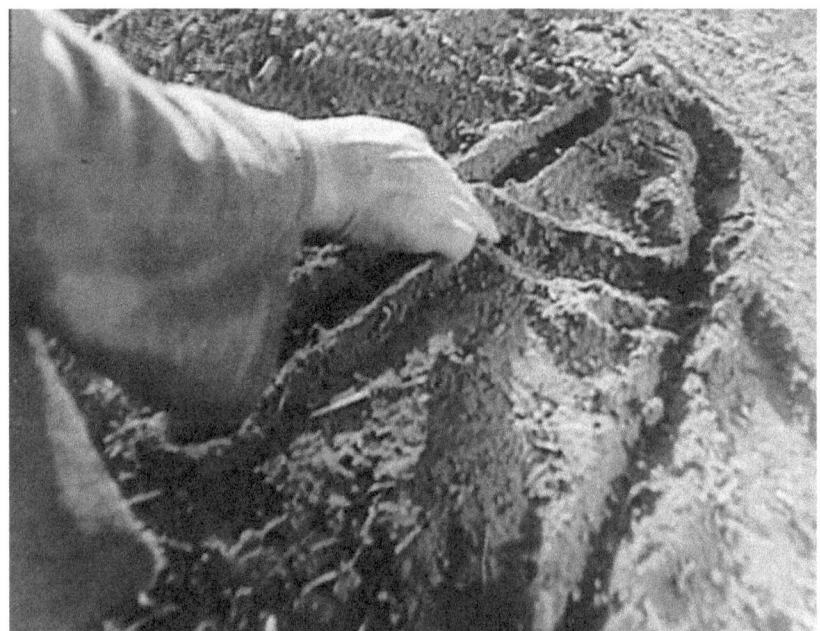

**Figure 6.3   A First Attempt to Write.** *Tale of a Mother* (1963, Aleksandr Karpov)

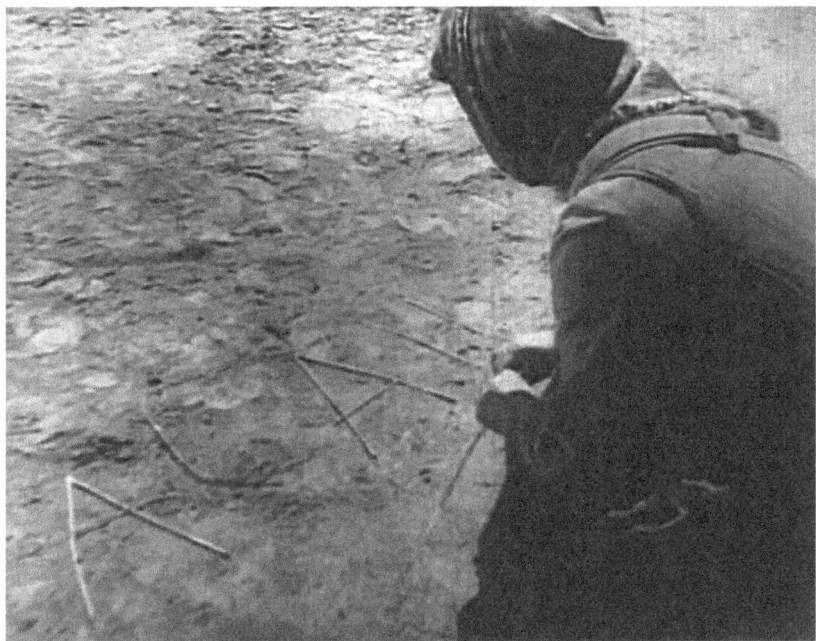

**Figure 6.4** **The Son's Name in the Dust.** *Tale of a Mother* (1963, Aleksandr Karpov)

thunderstorm, features an innovative element in the soundtrack, as the diegetic sound of thunder increasingly blends with the nondiegetic sound of machine guns and cannons. While the meaning of this device is clear, namely, that the war is fought both by the soldiers on the frontlines and by the civilians in the hinterland, the execution is inventive and engages the viewer with its simple yet unexpected originality. Karpov also shows people's changed perceptions during wartime, for example when children rejoice that their father lost a limb because this means that he will come home soon. Furthermore, the director repeatedly uses the audience's advanced knowledge as an emotional tool, as when the viewer already knows that a woman's husband has perished yet she herself does not, continuing to believe in dreams that show him to be alive.

A dream also plays a key role in the portrayal of Zhulpan. Exhausted from work, she stumbles and falls in the field. At this moment, an imaginary Asan tells her, "Had I stayed home, I would not have been able to defend you, mom!" Zhulpan awakens, gets up, and soldiers on, overcoming her physical weakness.

Amina Umurzakova gave the title role exceptional depth and authenticity and deservedly won accolades both nationally and internationally, adding a genuinely Kazakh heroine to Soviet cinema's time-honored line of heroic mothers. As a mail carrier, Zhulpan is a harbinger of both[11] sorrow and joy, someone who helps maintain the community's inner cohesion. Umurzakova's performance emphasizes the tact and restraint of her character, traits that allow her to fulfill this vital role. Zhulpan is full of quiet knowledge and wisdom; her utterances are never declarative. The unusual aspect in the mother's evolution is her growth from a woman absorbed by concern for her faraway son into a citizen who begins to transcend her personal grief and increasingly cares about the grief of others. As a result of this transformation, she does not reveal the news of her own son's death but, with incredible willpower, claims that he received a medal. She is motivated by the need to maintain the community's fighting spirit and prevent sorrow from paralyzing their efforts to achieve victory. Through this act of emotional selflessness, Zhulpan finds sufficient comfort to deal with her personal tragedy.

*Tale of a Mother* contains an interesting silent episode that echoes a key moment in *Fate of a Man*. Bondarchuk's title hero, a prisoner of war who is transported to Germany, encounters members of the Nazi military face-to-face on a train taking them to the frontline in Russia; the Germans sing with obnoxious self-confidence, fully convinced of their legitimacy and victorious advance. In *Tale of a Mother*, the heroine has a similar encounter at a train station. The only difference is that she observes young German prisoners of war. The mother deliberately makes eye contact with one of them, as if trying to penetrate his stone face and comprehend the motivations behind his behavior. The situation clearly makes the young man uncomfortable (his gaze turns in different directions, he begins to whistle), but nothing can overcome the force of Zhulpan's piercing gaze, which is deeply inquisitive, not hateful. No words are needed to convey the meaning of this psychological and spiritual confrontation between the wise Kazakh woman and the foolish, arrogant intruder. Later, there is a positive variation of this episode when the mother adopts an orphan boy from the besieged city of Leningrad and makes eye contact with other children on a train of evacuees: this exchange of glances is mutually encouraging, almost cheerful.

One day in the spring, someone exclaims "A soldier is coming!" and all the women in the *aul* run toward the arriving man in uniform. This is where the film ends. We will never know whose son has come home.

For many years, *Tale of a Mother* was a cause of pride for Kazakhstani filmmakers and was invariably listed among the highest achievements of national cinema. Three years after its release, in 1966, the director, Aleksandr Karpov; the cameraman, Askhat Ashrapov; and the female lead, Amina Umurzakova, were awarded a State Prize of the Kazakh SSR. Umurzakova also won the accolade of "best female lead" at the 1964 USSR film festival in Leningrad. However, after the breakup of the Soviet Union, the film disappeared and was not included in any of the DVD anthologies of Kazakhstan's cinema that were released during the post-independence period. Was this because of the plot's similarity to Russian films, which may have been perceived as clichéd? Did the director, who left Kazakhstan a few years later, part with Kazakhfilm on bad terms, overshadowing his contributions to the country's culture?[12] Whatever the case may be, *Tale of a Mother* stands as a powerful picture telling a deeply humane story and featuring outstanding performances and unforgettable images of Kazakhstan during World War II. Its unconditional endorsement of the Soviet system within a Kazakh framework was never denounced or relativized after the country gained its independence.

## A DIFFERENT PERSPECTIVE ON THE WAR

It took another war veteran at Kazakhfilm studio over twenty years from his discharge to address the war in a feature film. In *Behind Us Is Moscow* (Za nami Moskva, 1967), Mazhit Begalin chooses a more polemical approach than *Tale of a Mother*, conveying the pathos of the Thaw, a period when the legacy of the war was revisited as a test of the vitality of Soviet society's ethical principles. More explicitly than Aleksandr Karpov, Begalin emphasized the decisive *Kazakh* role in to the Soviet victory over Nazi Germany. Both thematically and aesthetically, Begalin's film stands as a highly original contribution to the Soviet memory discourse, responding to films such as Marlen Khutsiev's *I am Twenty* (Mne dvadtsat' let, 1964).

*Behind Us Is Moscow* features a contemporary frame narrative,[13] which is key to its concept of memory. Documentary footage of people laying flowers at the monument to the Unknown Soldier near the Kremlin wall is presented in disturbing silence. Later, groups of mostly young people visit a museum exhibition about the Great Patriotic War.[14] The visitors look at photos of Hitler, Stalin, and Zhukov, as well as historical artifacts. The scene is accompanied by modern jazz music, as if to suggest an audible disconnect between the reality of the past and its perception by later generations. One old man (Kauken Kenzhetaev) walks through the exhibition alone, on a cane. He is a war veteran, a character inspired by Bauyrzhan Momysh-uly, the legendary battalion commander whose unit defended Moscow in the winter of 1941 under the command of General Panfilov.

The film's historical episodes describe how this defense unfolded. At a later point, the contemporary exhibition is featured again, with a young couple discussing a picture of General Panfilov. The young man says, "No atmosphere at all, just medals!" This remark offends the old veteran, who perceives the man in his twenties as disrespecting his and his comrades' sacrifices. But then the young man apologizes to the veteran, adding that his generation does not want war, to which the elder replies, "We did not want war either." Begalin thus introduces a discourse about the nature of war, which is complemented by images of nuclear weapons seen by the former battalion commander in a documentary.

*Behind Us Is Moscow* describes the war experience in uncomfortable closeness, from within the trenches. Just a few miles from the Soviet capital, the German troops behave brazenly. After all, for the last five months, they had encountered little resistance, leaving them convinced that victory over the USSR was near and they could afford to march without precautions in the middle of the road. All of a sudden, the Germans encounter Soviet fighters who are holding out against all odds and throw the aggressors' plans into disarray. But the price these fighters pay is huge: when a counterattack is launched, the heroism of the first to storm into battle (under the slogan "For the Homeland!") lasts for a mere 10 seconds before they are killed. The battalion commander (Asanbek Umuraliev) then takes charge of the attack, and his men succeed in stopping the Nazi advance.

Even during his lifetime, General Panfilov was a famous commander. Movingly portrayed in Begalin's picture by Vsevolod Sanaev, Panfilov's fatherly style, his care for human beings ("Protect the people, protect them!"), and his common-sense tactics of retreat and attack are depicted as exemplary and are favorably juxtaposed with those of commanders whose recklessness alienates both the rank-and-file and civilians. Panfilov explains to Momyshuly the difference between a demanding attitude (*trebovatel'nost'*) and cruelty (*zhestokost'*). The former is necessary, the latter detrimental to achieving the goal. Conspicuously, Panfilov's own death in action is not marked as a special moment by dramatic music or slow motion. Rather, it is shown in passing, as if to say that in this early phase of the war even high-ranking commanders could lose their lives just as suddenly as regular fighters. What the protagonists miss the most after Panfilov's sudden death is his everyday humanity: only then does it become clear why his name was legendary. At the end of the film, images of flags bearing the Nazi swastika, shown to cheerful tunes, are "pushed out," through double exposure, by images of marching Soviet soldiers.

Begalin's treatment of casualties as a common and unspectacular occurrence is as realistic as it is shocking, since it goes directly against movie conventions for dealing with death and dying. But the most noteworthy feature of *Behind Us Is Moscow* is its emphasis on the outstanding role played by Kazakh fighters in the 1941 operations defending the Soviet capital. This emphasis is historically justified but has not always been sufficiently acknowledged in official Soviet historiography. Begalin uses sound motifs such as dombra tunes to mark the Soviet troops' ethno-cultural diversity.[15] Conspicuously, while Kazakhs and Russians fight shoulder to shoulder, the Kazakhs form a distinct group with their own communicative codes. They are shown as bilingual, often speaking Kazakh with each other. There is an air of quiet dignity in this emphasis on the Kazakhness of these men, whose contribution was decisive for the victorious outcome of the Battle for Moscow. And yet Begalin never romanticizes war, just the opposite. The battles are not triumphant but depressing; the countless bodies lying in the streets and the fields testify to an immense death toll. Action evolves within a very limited space, which adds to the claustrophobic urgency to fight and win. Long panoramic shots capture the apocalyptic destruction everywhere; many shots are dominated by fire and smoke, without drums or other ominous accessories. The film's ending, too, is deliberately anticlimactic, not joyful or celebratory as in mainstream war films. Indeed, the abruptness of the ending adds another degree of unspectacular verisimilitude, honesty, and quiet sadness. *Behind Us Is Moscow*, with its polemical contemporary frame narrative, is, de facto, an antiwar film.

In all Begalin's pictures, sharp cuts from present to past and vice versa are essential to his narrative style. When the veteran remembers his experiences, the film switches from peaceful contemporaneity to wartime history without a smooth visual transition. Close-ups are used in a conspicuous manner, suggesting introspections, as if the main character has the ability not only to look back, but also to look into the future. The editing technique, which is both associative and contrasting, combined with the contoured black-and-white winter landscapes and the sparse music give the film an atypical brittleness, avoiding pathos and indicating that the filmmaker knew war first-hand and was unwilling to follow cinema clichés.

Begalin emphasized the significance of the Kazakh sacrifices in World War II in a manner that no Soviet film had done before. The importance of the fact that it is Kazakhs who defend and save the capital of the USSR is hard to overestimate. After all, during the first year of the Great Patriotic War, Moscow was proclaimed to be more than the nation's capital in an administrative sense; it was the very heart of the country, which could not be surrendered under any circumstances. Begalin's focus on Moscow also implied that the Soviet leadership was residing in the Kremlin and coordinating the war efforts. In other words, Kazakhs played not just a significant but a crucial role in winning the Great Patriotic War by preventing the German troops from conquering the Soviet capital at a point when a defeat was viewed as a realistic possibility by many. This would again become a controversial issue in the new millennium, when a revisionist Russian film, the crowd-funded *Twenty-Eight Panfilov Fighters* (2016), deliberately downplayed the Kazakh contribution to the Soviet victory in the Battle for Moscow.

Begalin's next picture, *The Song of Manshuk* (Pesn' o Manshuk, 1969), once again addressed the theme of World War II, or, as it is known in Soviet canonical historiography, the Great Patriotic War. In a manner resembling his earlier contemporary drama, *The Traces Go Beyond the Horizon*, *The Song of Manshuk* features an outwardly weak yet internally strong human being whose enigma is never fully decoded. Manshuk Mametova was a real person; after her death in action, her heroism was recognized with the accolade Hero of the Soviet Union.

Like most survivors of the world war, Begalin viewed it in a manner that was far-from-hurray patriotism. Likely, the film's original title, *One Day of a Heroine* (Odin den' geroini), was implicitly polemical: Manshuk's heroism is undeniable, but far more complex than the poster-like representations of conventional movies. Indeed, just like in *Behind Us Is Moscow*, Begalin conveyed a deep aversion to war as such, regardless of its political justifications and concrete circumstances. At the same time, the enormity of the sacrifice that his generation made is never downplayed or relativized. To combine the awareness of the horror of war and the celebration of those who won it was the true challenge facing the director. Both of his war films demonstrate that his artistic search was too serious to allow him to settle for treading down paths already explored by others. Begalin's deliberately anti-cliché approach differs profoundly from mainstream Soviet war pictures.

From the outset, *The Song of Manshuk* confronts the viewer with the dark side of war: a long dolly shot shows a woman slowly walking across a muddy field covered with corpses, destroyed weaponry, and barbed wire.

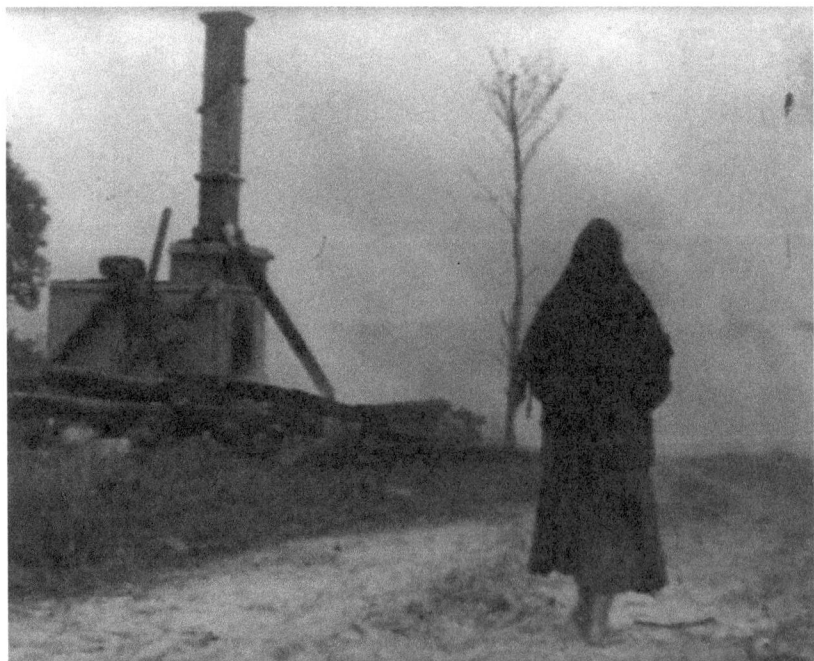

**Figure 6.5** **Devastation of War.** *The Song of Manshuk* (1969, Mazhit Begalin)

This woman, a marginal but conceptually important character, will later briefly reappear, searching for her family. The smoke-filled gloominess of the first shots introduces one of the dominant visual characteristics of the film: the absence of clear vision. There never seems to be clean air; the characters are constantly struggling to figure out what direction they should go in next.

The title character, Manshuk Mametova, is a master sergeant in charge of a machine gun unit. Her will to fight is so fierce that she ignores all orders to retreat. Indeed, a fellow Kazakh soldier literally must carry her back to the trenches, with her resisting all the while. Manshuk's physique is petite, and her haircut is extremely simple, as if to deemphasize her gender. This aspect becomes central in Manshuk's interactions with her foil, the youthfully handsome and annoyingly flirtatious Lieutenant Ezhov (Nikita Mikhalkov). A lighthearted jester, he is genuinely fascinated by Manshuk's serious personality. Ezhov's constant teasing of the heroine has clear sexual connotations: he offers to "teach her how to kiss" and mocks her bashfulness, provocatively indicating his openness to starting an affair. However, step by step, the morose female sergeant wins the lieutenant's respect and he begins to understand

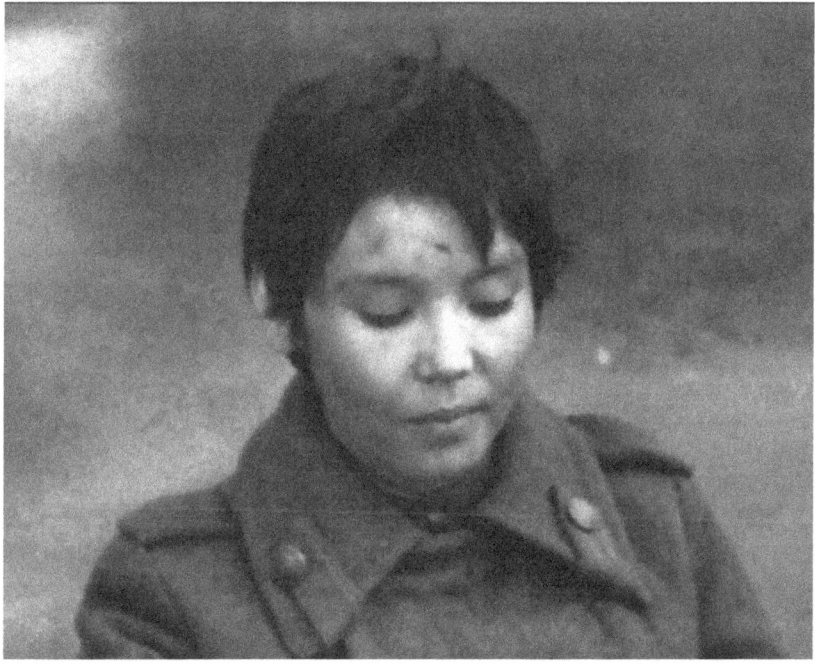

**Figure 6.6 An Unlikely Hero; Natalia Arinbasarova in the Title Role.** *The Song of Manshuk* (1969, Mazhit Begalin)

why the members of Manshuk's team adore her and how she in return treats them with comradely affection. More than anything, Manshuk wants to be a regular fighter who is taken seriously, hence her rejection of making light of gender relations in war, which is both touching and awe-inspiring.

The issue of Manshuk's femininity constitutes one of the film's central motifs. "Here's a real woman [*baba*]," exclaims Ezhov, pointing at Manshuk, to which she quickly retorts "At war, it is usually men who act like women," an allusion to the other meaning of *baba* (whiner) that reveals her wit and a conspicuous self-awareness. When one of the officers resentfully says, "I don't trust women," Manshuk replies, "My father taught me not to distinguish between men and women," adding, "The most important thing is to be a human being," a statement that receives the approbation of an elderly commander. Later, however, during a debate between two senior officers, one of them angrily states how unnatural it is to have a female fighter on the battlefield, as destroying life contradicts a woman's true calling, namely: creating it. This fundamental question, to what degree it is a violation not just of tradition, but of nature itself, for women to engage in actual warfare, remains a point of debate throughout the film. While the question is never explicitly answered, the deep respect that the filmmaker harbors for Manshuk is obvious throughout.

Those characters who like and admire the young sergeant try to downplay the fact that she is female. This is sometimes difficult, since Manshuk demonstrates a sensitivity that is absent in the male members of her unit. For instance, when Ezhov brings a sheep for slaughter, Manshuk is the only one to recognize that the animal is pregnant; she later skillfully assists in the birth process and dries the tiny newborn lambs.

The image of this awkward, modern-day Joan of Arc holding a lamb once again emphasizes her innocence in an archetypal manner, as if to say that Manshuk Mametova does not participate in the war against Nazism *despite* the fact that she is a woman, but *because* of it.

Begalin did his utmost to avoid turning *The Song of Manshuk* into a cinematic monument. The title heroine is not larger than life and is never removed from the rank-and-file surrounding her. To enhance the character's depth, the director uses a number of introspective flashbacks, visualizing Manshuk's dreams about her late father, an incarnation of decency and manliness to whom she looks up. Thus, when the film concludes with an image of a Soviet star and the official text announces that the title "Hero of the Soviet Union" was awarded to Manshuk Mametova after her death in action, this appears more like a formal appendix than a logical culmination of the preceding story. Yet this unspectacular element of Soviet officialdom does retroactively demonstrate the kind of human truth standing behind war medals and titles.

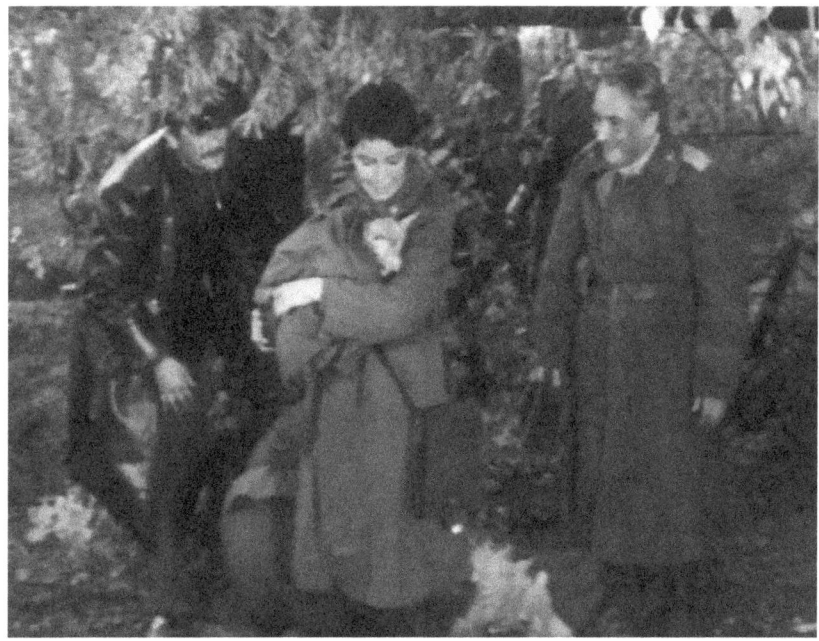

Figure 6.7  Holding the Lamb. *The Song of Manshuk* (1969, Mazhit Begalin)

Andrei Mikhalkov-Konchalovskii's screenplay provided Begalin with an artistically sophisticated, self-conscious, and intelligent foundation, the kind of exploration of the nature of heroism and self-sacrifice that had rarely been featured in Soviet cinema before. Begalin's direction recreates a harsh and believable battlefield environment in which every step can be the last and in which characters lose their lives one after another, with no internal logic, just as happens in war. However, it is Natal'ia Arinbasarova's extraordinary performance that renders the title character plausible: her face conveys a wealth of subtle emotions, from awkwardness and deep pain to decisiveness and courage, which may suddenly slip into a childlike vulnerability. Arinbasarova's portrayal is unique among female heroines in Soviet cinema.

The film's conceptual kinship with Andrei Tarkovskii's *Ivan's Childhood* (Ivanovo detstvo, 1962), a groundbreaking new chapter in Soviet filmmaking about the war in which Mikhalkov-Konchalovskii was also involved (as screenwriter and supporting actor), is undeniable. Ivan, the boy-cum-scout who gives his life for the success of one small operation, is motivated by strong emotions, just as is the twenty-one-year-old machine gunner Manshuk, whose girlish innocence Begalin consistently emphasizes. Another feature shared by both films is their focus on military personnel rather than the technicalities of the military operation as such. The various relationships that are depicted in *Ivan's Childhood* and *The Song of Manshuk* serve as means to bring out the title characters' specifics, their values and convictions. Ivan's and Manshuk's unconditional devotion to the Soviet patriotic cause and their military skills stand in uneasy contrast to their age and, in Manshuk's case, gender. A major difference from Tarkovskii's Ivan is that Manshuk never expresses hatred, however justified this feeling may be.

Like *Behind Us Is Moscow*, *The Song of Manshuk* has a strong Kazakh dimension.[16] As was mentioned earlier, Manshuk and her fellow Kazakh soldiers often speak to each other in their native tongue; Manshuk's dreams are accompanied by dombra tunes and her father singing in Kazakh. National identity does not defy the political and moral logic of this war, which takes place far from Kazakhstan, but is meant to serve as a source of motivation: Kazakhness and Sovietness complement each other. Manshuk is unabashedly Kazakh, but she is also a member of the Soviet Communist youth organization, the Komsomol, as she proudly states. Her fight is primarily value-based: one of the characters even speaks of the "ideological war" against Nazism. In this context, Manshuk's natural humane disposition plays the role of a positive ethical marker to the cause for which she is fighting and giving her life.

Another similarity with Begalin's previous picture is the anticlimactic ending of *The Song of Manshuk*: one by one, Manshuk's comrades are killed in

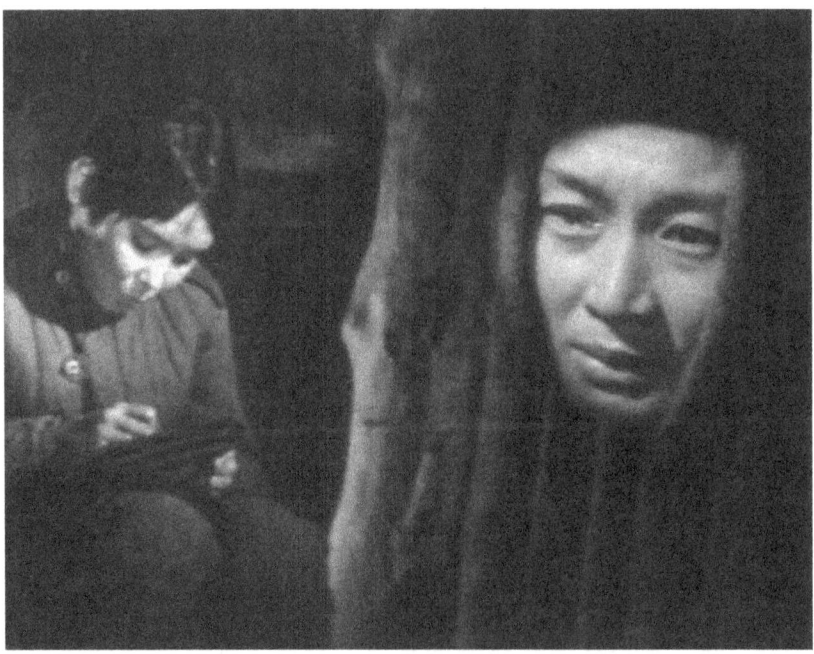

**Figure 6.8  A Letter to Mother.** *The Song of Manshuk* (1969, Mazhit Begalin)

the battle for a tactically decisive hill, the conquering of which will enable the Red Army to retake an unnamed Soviet city from the Germans. Then Manshuk herself is shot, without dramatic orchestral accompaniment and without visual emphasis such as slow motion. Instead, the fact that the title heroine looks genuinely helpless in this moment adds to the film's realism and to her humanity. *The Song of Manshuk* honors an unlikely hero and, in this way, does represent a cinematic monument after all: a monument without monumentality.

Begalin's *The Song of Manshuk* was received positively by critics and viewers; though its success was not sensational, it was solid. The director's next picture, *Steppe Sounds* (Stepnye raskaty, 1974), originally titled *Ural'sk in Flames* (Ural'sk v ogne), was devoted to the revolutionary events in a town near the Russian-Kazakh border.[17] The film was shelved because it purportedly gave an inaccurate picture of the Civil War in Kazakhstan. Some sources indicate that this traumatic experience led to Begalin's premature death.

## *Wings of a Song*

One of the strangest cases of posterior oblivion in the history of Kazakhstani cinema is *Wings of a Song* (Kryl'ia pesni, 1967). I am using the word "strange" because upon its release, this film was prominently honored by the Kazakh state. Helmed by Azerbaijan Mambetov,[18] a theater director who had just finished an internship at Mosfilm studio, it is filled with Kazakh cultural specifics like few other films of the 1960s.

*Wings of a Song* tells the story of a young *akyn* named Musa (Anuar Moldabekov). Together with his friend, the communist Kaimen (Asanali Ashimov), the minstrel entertains the countless nomads attending a loud and lively bazaar. Being in constant need of money so as to impress his love interest, Musa strikes up a friendship with an entrepreneur, Nurtaza (Kauken Kenzhetaev), who lends him a large amount of cash. But Musa will soon pay dearly for compromising his class conscience: not only does Kaimen accuse him of being a sellout, but Musa also witnesses how the enemies of the new Soviet order burn the haystacks of the collective farms and murder Kaimen. Musa is heartbroken; he feels that as an *akyn* he will always be unhappy and that his life is over.

At this point, the film introduces an episode from the history of Kazakhstani theater. Kapan, the giant martial artist who acted as a protector to the emotionally unstable Musa throughout his career, suggests that the *akyn* join the first dramatic theater of Kazakhstan, which had opened in the then-capital, Kyzyl-Orda, in 1926. It is the stage that brings closure to Musa and points to a productive future for him in communist society: in a drama about the killing of Kaimen, Musa plays himself, confessing in a long, emotionally charged monologue to his guilt vis-à-vis his dear friend. Musa's acquaintances and companions, including the woman he unhappily loves, all sit in the auditorium, watching in awe. Thus, tragedy is transcended by catharsis.

*Wings of a Song* features a number of cameos, including an appearance by Hakim Davletbekov, one of the surviving Kazakhstani film pioneers, and Serke Kozhamkulov, the great comedian of Kazakhstani theater and cinema, who had in real life directed the first play at the Kyzyl-Orda theater forty years earlier.

Anuarbek Moldabekov portrays an artist with a complex personality. His Musa displays a propensity for alcohol and a general bent toward self-destructiveness. The real-life inspiration for the character of Musa was the prominent *akyn* Isa Baizakov (1900–1946). However, while the film as a whole pays homage to this legendary singer, actor, and cultural activist, it did not risk a rehabilitation of Baizakov in his entirety. In 1936, the *akyn* was denounced as a supporter of Alash-Orda and exiled to the Arkhangelsk region: this part of Baizakov's life the film leaves out. *Wings of a Song* only shows how Musa is forced to make a choice between the world of capitalist greed and the world of communist equality; the severe contradictions of the latter are omitted. Such simplification gives *Wings of a Song* an air of propagandistic naïveté. However, the reductionist social framework is outweighed by the realism of the interpersonal conflicts, Gaziza Zhubanova's excellent score, and the dynamic camerawork of Mark Berkovich.

With respect to its depiction of milieus (the world of the poor hobos, the vibrant markets, the entertainment establishments for the wealthy) the film strongly resembles Maxim Gorky's canonical narratives and their cinematic adaptations, especially those helmed by Mark Donskoi. The application of these neorealist principles to the depiction of Kazakhstan at the beginning of the twentieth century creates an authentic atmosphere that was unmatched by any other Kazakhstani picture. Mambetov's ability to elicit solid performances from his cast betrays the experienced stage director. Visually, the film is not theatrical due to Berkovich's highly mobile camera featuring fast-paced dolly shots and hand-held camera shots that dominate the visual level from the onset. What is also remarkable about the film is its synthesis of dramatic action and song. While the number of songs is too limited for the film to be described as a musical, music is prominent enough to soften the harsh realism and add a note of romantic melancholy. Shaken Aimanov, who acted as the project's artistic supervisor, always sensed the importance of music for Kazakhstani cinema: his own pictures *Our Dear Doctor* and *Angel in a Cap* are ample proof of that. However, the only director who dared to develop this synthesis further was Sultan-Akhmed Khodzhikov in *Kyz-Zhibek*. Likely, the inclusion of songs in a film was regarded as too much of a challenge to verisimilitude, thus violating one of the normative criteria of socialist realism.

Mambetov and Moldabekov were honored with a State Prize of the Kazakhstani SSR in 1967 for *Wings of a Song*. The main reason for that distinction is the film's successful synthesis of basic Marxist concepts, especially the antagonism between profit-orientation and genuine art, and its strong endorsement of Kazakh national art.

Unfortunately, the director had no followers who would continue that synthesis. After the success of *Wings of a Song*, Mambetov left cinema for more than a decade to pursue a highly successful career in stage directing, only to return in 1977 as studio director for Kazakhfilm. Thereafter, he helmed two more feature films, both historical epics: *Blood and Sweat* (1978) and *Heralds Hurry* (1979). Alas, neither of them reached the level of quality of his debut.

For one of the stars of Kazakhstani cinema in the 1960s, the decade ended in disaster. Aleksandr Karpov, whose *Tale of a Mother* had won national and international laurels, tried out a genre that was new to him, the "Eastern," and failed miserably. *Path of a Thousand Miles* (Doroga v tysiachu verst, 1968) turned into an embarrassment for Kazakhfilm studio and became Karpov's last film in Kazakhstan, a country where he had spent a decade and a half and was honored with the title Merited Artist of the Kazakh SSR. He left for Belarus, never to return to Almaty.

At its conception, *Path of a Thousand Miles* appeared to be a failsafe project. Devoted to a dramatic Civil War episode in the life of one of Kazakhstan's leading communists, Alibi Dzhangildin, its screenplay was written by a senior native author, Kalikhan Iskakov, who had just attended special screenwriting courses in Moscow. The plot was ideologically correct and filled with action and suspense. Why, then, did the film flop so badly?

The problems started with Karpov's choice for the male lead. Satimzhan Sanbaev was a young writer, not a professional actor. And while other directors had fared well casting non-professional performers (for example, with Gulfairus Ismailova in the title role of *Botagoz* in 1957 and Atageldy Ismailov as the male lead in *Angel in a Cap* in 1968), Sanbaev never managed to fit into the ensemble of professionals. His delicate and pensive features were obviously intended to create the image of an intelligent Bolshevik leader rather than a gun-happy attacker. But Sanbaev was too much of an introvert to believably convey the emotions and reactions of a military commander in ultra-violent times.[19] As a result, the suspenseful story never takes off, the tense relations between the Kazakh commissar and his Czech sidekick are rarely tangible, and the search for the traitor within the Bolshevik unit lacks traction. While Mikhail Aranyshev's camera undeniably succeeds in capturing the horrors of a hundreds-of-miles-long march through a deadly desert and bizarre mountains, human interest in the people experiencing these tortures is not established. It is also true that Karpov's "Eastern" continued the line of Kazakh films featuring class enemies with a human face, a contradictory personality, and an opaque agenda, a tradition begun by Abdulla Karsakbaev and Bolotbek Shamshiev. The character of the cunning Sardarbek, who offers the Bolsheviks a deal and intends to betray them, but changes his mind when the White Army destroys his native *aul* was portrayed by Nurmukhan Zhanturin, a powerhouse of Kazakh cinema. Yet neither he nor the other supporting actors were able to save the film from its inherent flaws.[20]

In theory, the national center of film production of the Kazakh SSR, named Kazakhfilm studio in 1960, had the capacity to produce seven feature films, fifty documentaries, and twenty-four issues of the newsreel journal *Soviet Kazakhstan* per year. In addition, it could dub up to seventy films into the Kazakh language. However, in reality these goals were rarely achieved. As a matter of fact, in some years only two feature films were completed. A steady production flow was the exception, not the rule. This jeopardized the functionality of Kazakhfilm studio as an industrial enterprise: If there were no films in production, salaries could not be paid out and film stock could not be purchased. After all, the studio was financially autonomous (an early form of the so-called *khozraschet*). Under pressure to secure production continuity, directors were willing to accept low-quality screenplays.[21] The state addressed this problem by changing the supervisory structure in cinema.

On May 28, 1963, by decree of the Supreme Soviet of the Kazakh SSR, the State Film Committee was established as part of the Council of Ministers. In other words, the republic now had its own branch of Goskino. This administrative structure had greater longevity than its predecessors: it existed until 1988.[22] However, its significance changed over the course of its twenty-five years of existence, depending on the contemporary political and cultural situation in the Soviet Union. In the 1970s, the Kazakh Goskino (literally "state cinema") often acted as a force of ideological control and restriction, whereas in the early 1980s, it turned into a factor promoting reform and innovation. A detailed analysis of its archives, which is still wanting, is a necessary precondition for a differentiated assessment of its effect on the development of Kazakhstani cinema.

## NOTES

1. Because of the complex character of the bay Zhunus, Bauyrzhan Nogerbek defined Karsakbaev's film as "non-totalitarian": "The opponents of the Soviet system are no longer depicted in a cartoonish manner, with openly negative judgment, as was the case in the films *Amangeldy* and *Raikhan*. They appear as characters of a complex and tragic destiny who, just like the commissars, love their people, their homeland." In Smailova, *Kinoentsiklopediia Kazakhstana*, p. 15. However, this argument cannot

neutralize the fact that *A Worrisome Morning* is fundamentally pro-Soviet and pro-communist. While Nogerbek's statement was surely intended as a compliment to the filmmaker, the "non-totalitarian" criterion is not productive for the analysis of complex narratives.

2. About the film's prehistory cf. Siranov, *Ocherki istorii kazakhskogo kino*, pp. 198–99.

3. Zinov'ev, Markov, "Seredina potoka," pp. 76–77.

4. The film critic Gulnara Abikeeva considers *A Shot at the Karash Pass* a Kyrgyz film (Abikeeva, *Natsiostroitel'stvo v Kazakhstane*, p. 50); I happen to believe that, because of the literary source and the creative input of Kazakh artists, this film should be analyzed as part of the history of Kazakhstani cinema as well.

5. A *volost* was a rural administrative district in the tsarist empire.

6. This humiliation is echoed in Darezhan Omirbaev's *Killer* (1998), in which a man is transformed into an outlaw by unjust social conditions.

7. *Shanyrak*: literally, the peak of the yurt; the term denotes the home as such.

8. In her analysis that clearly denotes a radical post-Soviet and anti-Soviet viewpoint, Gulnara Abikeeva interpreted the finale of the film as tragic because it marks "the end of the free epoch, of the precolonial epoch," and Bakhtygul as "the last Kyrgyz hero, the last warrior of a free people." Abikeeva, *Natsiostroitel'stvo v Kazakhstane*, p. 67.

9. El'ga Lyndina pointed out: "Few professional actors are able to demonstrate their essence as performers through the interpretation of one role as did this non-professional." Cf. Lyndina, E., *Suimenkul Chokmorov*. Moskva: "Iskusstvo," 1985, p. 28.

10. P. Kosenko begins his overall positive review by pointing to Karpov's "creative teachers," Grigorii Chukhrai and Sergei Bondarchuk, describing several episodes that were clearly inspired by *Destiny of a Man*, *Ballad of a Soldier*, and *Clear Sky*; he concludes that these repetitions "cannot be considered accomplishments." For Kosenko, *Tale of a Mother* is even some kind of sequel to *Ballad of a Soldier*. Cf. Kosenko, "Mat' soldata," p. 3.

11. Gulnara Abikeeva emphasized that the image of heroic mothers was always strongly supported by Soviet propaganda but that Amina Umurzakova's performance went far beyond common ideological standards and impressed viewers by its emotional power and truthfulness. Abikeeva, *Natsiostroitel'stvo v Kazakhstane*, pp. 41-42.

12. As soon as Communist Party archives and other documents become accessible, it would be worthwhile to explore anew Aleksandr Karpov's fifteen years in Kazakhstani cinema. If the space afforded to him in the *Film Encyclopedia of Kazakhstan* (2010) is any indication, the general attitude toward Karpov's oeuvre seems to be one of indifference (his entry is about one-tenth that of other directors, with seven lines of text and a minute undocumented filmography).

13. The screenplay was written by the experienced Vasilii Solov'ev (the author of Bondarchuk's Tolstoi adaptation *War and Peace*) and the director; it was based on books and articles written by Bauyrzhan Momysh-uly who himself was a member of the division of General Ivan Panfilov.

14. The scene takes place at the Museum of the Soviet Army.

15. At one point, the commander of the battalion recalls a poem by Aleksandr Blok, the text of which is accompanied by a dombra.

16. Bauyrzhan Nogerbek went as far as to claim that Begalin's *The Traces Go Beyond the Horizon* and *The Song of Manshuk*, together with the works of Shaken Aimanov and Sultan Khodzhikov, represented protest-films [*fil'my-protesty*] against the Soviet-Communist humiliation of the dignity of the Kazakh people as "uncultured" and "backward."Cf. Nogerbek, *Na ekrane 'Kazakhfil'm,*" p. 46.

17. A lively portrait of Mazhit Begalin and the history of his last project, including statements by the production designer Idris Karsakbaev, can be found in the article "Begalinskii svet" by Ol'ga Khrabrykh in *Ekspress K*, 33 (16419), 22 February 2008 (http://old.express-k.kz/show_article.php?art_id14903).

18. Mambetov, Azerbaijan (1932–2009), Kazakh stage and film director. While Mambetov devoted most of his career to the theater, he accepted the position of head of Kazahfilm studio (1977–1980) and directed three feature films.

19. For a critical assessment, see Siranov, *Ocherki istorii kazakhskogo kino*, p. 97.

20. Matskevich, Oleg, "Karpov protiv Karpova." *Kazakhstanskaia pravda*, 20 September 1968.

21. Cf. Siranov, *Kinoiskusstvo sovetskogo Kazakhstana*, pp. 334–335.

22. Smailova, *Kinoentsiklopediia Kazakhstana*, p. 448.

*Chapter 7*

# The Searchings of Shaken Aimanov

Shaken Aimanov's status as the foundational figure of Kazakh cinema is undisputed and symbolically represented today: the country's national film studio is named after him, as are streets and an international festival. Aimanov's directorial legacy boasts a wide range of genres, from musical comedy to historical thriller. Several of his pictures belong to the classical heritage of Soviet cinema. Still, some voices maintain that Aimanov's genius found its greatest expression in acting on stage and not on screen, and that his move from theater to film direction in the early 1950s was an ill-advised sacrifice that deprived Kazakh art of its greatest interpreter of Shakespeare. Be this as it may, Aimanov's art both in the theater and in cinema was profoundly appreciated by audiences and the Kazakh-Soviet state alike. A lifelong political loyalist and member of the Communist Party from 1940, Aimanov received a Stalin Prize in 1952 for his stage work and was named People's Artist of the USSR in 1959, by which time he had four pictures under his belt and had established himself as a viable filmmaker.

Shaken Aimanov was born on February 15, 1914, in Bayanaul, in the Pavlodar region in Eastern Kazkahstan, near the river Irtysh. As a student in Semipalatinsk in the early 1930s, his goal was to become a teacher, but he, along with other gifted young laymen artists, was invited by theater activists Gabit Musrepov and Kalibek Kuanyshpaev to join their troupe. These enthusiastic performers would form the core of the Kazakh National Theater, of which Aimanov would become one of the leaders, both as an actor and director.

Initially, cinema was of marginal interest for Aimanov. This is understandable, given the state of film in Kazakhstan in the 1930s and 1940s, when visiting directors from Leningrad and Moscow used the local talent and landscapes to shoot movies on officially assigned topics. Although these films paid some attention to the Kazakhstani atmosphere, Kazakh film artists were long treated as junior partners. Aimanov appeared in a minute role in *Amangeldy* (1938) and in a supporting role as the treacherous bureaucrat in *Raikhan* (1940). His first lead was as the officer in the medium-length TsOKS comedy *The White Rose* (1943), but the film was withdrawn from screens shortly after its release. Only when Grigorii Roshal' cast Aimanov as the traitor Sharip in the biopic *The Songs of Abai* (1945) did viewers and critics take notice, thanks to the unusual complexity of his portrayal. His next on-screen role was the lead in Efim Aron's *The Golden Horn* (1948), a largely formulaic movie about Soviet genetics and its application to Kazakhstan's economy. Alas, not even Aimanov's energy could bring that ideological construct to life. Just a few years later, however, came a genuine highlight in his career as a film actor: his portrayal of Kazakhstan's national *akyn* in *Zhambyl* (aka *Dzhambul*, 1952), a biopic directed by Efim Dzigan, that showed the title hero from youth to old age.

Nevertheless, Aimanov's greatest accomplishments to that point were his celebrated Shakespeare interpretations at the Kazakh National Theater. Whether in comedy or tragedy, as Petruchio or as Othello, his abundance of transformative power imbued each new role with a vitality that made these performances groundbreaking events in Kazakhstani culture. Thus, many contemporaries could not understand why, at the pinnacle of his theatrical success, Aimanov decided to abandon the stage and devote himself to film direction. A novice without any formal education in this field, he learned from practical experience, beginning as co-director of *Poem about Love* (1954).

The ability to reach millions of viewers was certainly one of the motivations behind Aimanov's decision, and his musical comedy *Our Dear Doctor* (1957) gave persuasive proof of his talent for connecting with native audiences and spectators around the world. Of Aimanov's later comedies, *Beardless Swindler* (1964) contains the most national flavor. Portrayed by Aimanov himself, the title character, whose real name is Aldar Kose, is a mainstay of Kazakh folklore, a fearless jester in hard times who inventively fights the arrogant establishment. Tajik director Bension Kimyagarov later wrote that the character of Aldar Kose with his joyfulness, wit, and sense of justice was in many ways a self-portrait of Aimanov, a view echoed by other contemporaries and film historians.

Prior to *Beardless Swindler*, Aimanov had created a very modern film, the first psychological drama in Kazakh cinema, *The Intersection* (1963). This was followed by his best film in artistic terms, which, alas, had the greatest difficulties finding a receptive audience: *Land of the Fathers* (1966), from a script by Kazakhstan's leading poet Olzhas Suleimenov. The story of an old man traveling to Russia to find and bring home the remains of his son who had perished in the Great Patriotic War, the picture is rendered with rare elegiac solemnity and tact. While critics immediately recognized the caliber of this film as one of the true classics of Kazakhstani cinema, contemporary viewers were largely uninterested, a reality that thrust Aimanov into a veritable creative crisis. Likely in an attempt to overcome his self-doubts, he followed it with a musical comedy, *Angel in a Cap* (1968), before conceiving his all-time greatest hit, the Civil War spy thriller *The End of the Ataman* (1970). The story of a covert operation to kill one of the militant enemies of the Soviet state, Ataman Dutov, was intriguing, but overall not so much an artistic success as a crowd-pleaser. Aimanov would not live to bask in this achievement, however; on December 23, 1970, the very day that the picture was successfully screened for Goskino officials in Moscow, Aimanov was fatally hit by a car.

There can be no doubt that Shaken Aimanov's legacy as a filmmaker is that of an explorer and pioneer who gave his all to building the foundation of Kazakh national cinema. Aimanov's main goal was to explore Kazakh culture and the Kazakh mentality within the framework of different film genres. In this endeavor, he became a true leader, even though his attempts show undeniable imperfections. Indeed, the ambition to explore new territory with each new film prevented him from perfecting his skills in any one particular genre. This, too, was a sacrifice that he made for Kazakhstani cinema.

Aimanov's untimely passing prevented him from tackling his most cherished project: a large-scale adaptation of Mukhtar Auezov's epic *The Path of Abai*, which the director discussed with friends for years. Had it been produced and released in the 1970s, the entire development of Kazakhstani cinema would have taken a different direction.[1]

## *A SONG IS CALLING*

Following the controversies surrounding the debate drama *In One District* (1960), Aimanov turned to an inconspicuous genre that had previously brought him huge success: musical comedy. By the time he agreed to direct this film, which was originally titled *The Singing Aul*, the project had already gained notoriety for its inherent difficulties. According to one account, the screenplay had been reworked eight times, and an equal number of directors had tried to tackle it! That was when Aimanov signaled that he was willing to come to the project's rescue. The credits also list him as one of the screenwriters, indicating that he must have insisted on changes to the plot before signing on to the project.

*A Song Is Calling* (Pesnia zovet, 1961) is hardly ever mentioned in discussions of Aimanov's films. At best, it is treated as negligible; at worst, it is viewed as a stroke of bad luck or an embarrassment that stains Aimanov's directorial record. However, this musical comedy provides some important insights into Aimanov's professional and artistic principles. First, the cause of developing Kazakhstani cinema *as a whole* was a matter of personal importance to Aimanov. He viewed cinema primarily as a popular art that could only thrive when audiences responded to it on a massive scale. Therefore, the entertainment function of movies was not to be disdained but to be embraced wholeheartedly. Cinema lived and grew in a variety of genres, all of which had their own legitimacy and should not be played off against each other. Aimanov's choices demonstrate that he respected the variety of genres available and tried out as many as possible, encouraging others to do the same. Aimanov did not make the elitist distinction between high and low genres that became second nature to many Soviet directors and ultimately cost them the trust of viewers, making Soviet cinema unable to compete with foreign films that were always genre-conscious and unbiased with respect to audience expectations. Whatever administrators, ideologists, and critics in Moscow might decree, Aimanov would stand his ground, doing his utmost to deliver movies that were visually and technically as attractive as foreign fare and could endear themselves to native viewers with their intimate knowledge of local culture. Aimanov's democratic, egalitarian approach to cinema explains the "ups" and "downs" of his filmography, when a historical epic or an auteur film would be followed by a funny (or, in the case of *A Song Is Calling*, silly) musical. Aimanov's vision was to make films for the people. In addition, he was loyal to his home studio, caring deeply about its overall state and its particular projects. He would not tolerate financial waste or chaotic conditions on the set, for example. This professional loyalty is another reason why Aimanov accepted a project that other directors considered beneath them.

With its opening images of a car that has got stuck in the middle of a river and is rescued by a truck driven by an attractive young woman, *A Song Is Calling* signals to the audience that this film will deliver situational comedy and is primarily intended as entertainment. That purpose is supported by a modern, upbeat score. The realism of the movie's plot and the societal issues upon which it touches are secondary considerations; what counts are funny confrontations, witty dialogues, and attractive performers, all of which the film delivers. Why, then, was the critical reaction to this charming lightweight so fiercely negative? After all, the story of the young truck driver who falls in love with a famous tenor from Almaty is no less believable than that of a physician in a spa whose birthday is celebrated by the country's most famous artists, which was the core plot of the critically endorsed *Our Dear Doctor* four years earlier.

Let us look at the logic of *A Song Is Calling*. A famous singer gets stuck on the way to a concert in a faraway rural area; a female truck driver helps him out but first takes him to her home *aul*, where the seventy-fifth birthday of an *aksakal* is celebrated; the singer sees the dilapidated state of the *aul*'s house of culture and promises help, declaring himself to be the new supervisor; the young woman follows the singer to the city to remind him of his promise; and after numerous mix-ups and widespread skepticism regarding the star's commitment, the singer does show up at the *aul* for a rehearsal. On this optimistic note the movie ends. The story is improbable, but not entirely impossible. More importantly, its improbability is constantly debated within the picture itself: the social divide between famous artists and their audiences is an explicit thematic focus.

Indeed, the issue of the connection between producers and consumers of culture defines the film's conceptual center. The star cult surrounding the singer Nurlanov is shown as an ambiguous phenomenon. On the one hand, crowds of young women knocking on his apartment door are portrayed with mild irony; on the other hand, the inhabitants of the *aul* where Nurlanov accidentally makes a stop, recognize the artist and feel honored that he sings for the birthday of the local *aksakal*. Nurlanov appreciates the admiration of his listeners, and his respect for this audience and for the occasion is genuine. This includes his attention to Aigul, the young truck driver who cannot deny the fact that she is erotically attracted to Nurlanov, but who also insists on being respected, just like her fellow ensemble members who call themselves "the Singing Aul."

While the initial situation, featuring a fan getting personally close to a star, is typical of similar musical comedies in the West, Aimanov does not pretend that groupie fantasies about serious private relations between fans and their idols are realistic. Instead, he uses this unlikely situation to probe the true nature of the relationship between artists and their admirers in a communist society in general and in Kazakhstan in particular. The findings, as presented in the film, are significant: there is a broad, spontaneous cultural movement encompassing all strata of the population, indeed *uniting it*. Nurlanov gives solo concerts that are attended by thousands and listened to on the radio by hundreds of thousands. But he also sits on the jury of a folklore festival and uses his authority to help a provincial collective of singers. In one of the final scenes, when it seems that the star tenor will not show up in the singing *aul* after all, there is a dialogue that is key to the film's underlying message. In response to a casual statement that famous artists such as Nurlanov do not have the time to deal with local talent, one layman artist says: "Then why is it that we award them the title 'People's Artist'?! Rather, we should call them 'artist of the capital city' or 'artist abroad'!" It is at that very moment that Nurlanov arrives and corrects the misperception: he truly is a people's artist.

The issue of establishing and maintaining a close connection between the nation's cultural elite and regular audiences was essential for Aimanov, in cinema and everywhere else. *Our Dear Doctor* took this connection for granted, whereas *A Song Is Calling* diagnoses a potential crisis in mutual trust.

Of course, these discussions are relatively brief and do not take away from the film as a musical comedy in which characters sing at every possible turn, mostly as part of a concert but sometimes to come to terms with their own feelings. Aigul was portrayed by Raisa Mukhamediarova, a rising star of Kazakhstani cinema who won a prize for her performance. Yet the film's main star is Ermek Serkebaev, a hugely popular tenor whose range included all genres, from opera to *Estrada*. The film features eleven performances, including a potpourri of three solo appearances by Serkebaev that constitute a noteworthy mix: an aria from Tchaikovsky's *Eugene Onegin*, one from Rossini's *Barber of Seville*, and one from a Kazakhstani opera, *Abai*. The film as a whole is a light comedy, resembling Italian and American movies about popular singers with a comparably broad profile, such as Mario Lanza, movies in which the plot and the acting are secondary to the star power of the main protagonist and the celebration of his popular artistry. *A Song Is Calling* was meant to give its star as many opportunities as possible to display his talents. And audiences went to such films to see the star, not indulge in subtleties of acting or social criticism.

But Aimanov would not be Aimanov had he not used this entertaining movie to express some concerns about contemporary society. These concerns are not artificially inserted but an organic outcome of the plot, which, needless to say, does require a certain suspension of disbelief. The latter, however, does not justify the critical anger that the film encountered. Rather, Aimanov had profoundly different ideas than certain film critics about the purpose of cinema. A genre-based view, which was the norm and condition for commercial effectiveness in the West, was never fully legitimized in the Soviet Union, and even the efforts of great artists such as Aimanov were unable to change that prejudice. The maintenance of this normative view was also rooted in the center-periphery dynamic of Soviet cinema. With respect to evaluative norms and aesthetic hierarchies, the Soviet cultural center imposed an authoritarian worldview. Interestingly, other cinema cultures on the Soviet margins, such as Georgia's, permitted a combination of "low" and "high" genres in the profile of a studio or a director. Thus, Giorgi Shengelaia was able to direct a historical adventure film (*He Did Not Mean to Kill*, 1965) followed by a complex artist biopic (*Pirosmani*, 1969) and a musical (*Melodies of the Verigskii Quarter*, 1973). The Kazakhstani cultural administration, alas, followed the rules prescribed by Moscow more literally, and only someone with the authority of Aimanov could challenge them. It is telling that after his passing, no other Kazakh director ever dared venture into the dangerous territory of musical comedy, despite its popularity among native viewers and broader Soviet audiences alike.

## THE PARABLE OF THE ETERNAL JESTER

After the unfriendly critical reactions to both *In One District* and *A Song Is Calling*, Shaken Aimanov rehabilitated himself with *The Intersection*. Yet that film's success did not induce him to ever make another psychological urban drama. Instead, he continued to explore other genres. In his cinematic engagement with Kazakhstani culture, he turned to a mythological figure, the popular Aldar Kose, a Kazakh rogue trickster (*Ulenspiegel*) and character in many anecdotes and legends. This choice was of special significance for Aimanov. Despite his unquestionable devotion to the communist cause and the Soviet state, he continued to struggle with the issue of the "Kazakhness" of his art. How could he square the circle of connecting with native audiences in a way that was unique to them while at the same time reaching viewers in the other Soviet republics and possibly even internationally?

During the short period after Nikita Khrushchev's ouster and before the Brezhnev period began in earnest, when a relatively high degree of openness was possible, Aimanov shared his worries about the national character of culture at a meeting of the leadership of the Union of USSR Film Workers, which took place in May 1965 in Alma-Ata. His radical view that the national character of cinema is primarily defined by a nation's folklore was seconded by many filmmakers and did not even cause controversies. Furthermore, some Kazakhstanis believed that this statement, coming from the leading film artist of Kazakhstan, expressed the marching orders for the national film industry for years to come.[2] In the prestigious journal *Iskusstvo kino* (Film Art), he opened his article with the observation that whenever he traveled abroad in the company of other Soviet filmmakers, he and his colleagues, whether they came from Georgia, Uzbekistan, or Russia, were viewed first and foremost as *Soviet* artists united by their Marxist-Leninist worldview. This unity raised the question of whether there was even a need for national specifics in their Soviet films. And here Aimanov says something that would have been unthinkable a few years earlier: "Remember the whole series of 'positive Russian characters' who appear in our Kazakh films at the moment when a character experiences hardship. According to the authors, they were meant to express the idea that the great Russian people help Kazakhs, yet because such characters were not living human beings but abstract schemes, they gave nothing to the viewer's heart or mind."[3] Aimanov proposes to contribute to the treasure trove of Soviet cinema with deep images of the life of one's own people. Capturing the national features of the characters in one's films is thus elevated to a task of primary importance.

According to Aimanov, a common mistake is to assume that the synthesis of nations in Soviet society has already been accomplished and that a Kazakh engineer is in no way different from a Russian one. The second mistake is that the need to capture national peculiarities is seen as important only for directors in the national studios. However, directors from Mosfilm and Lenfilm should likewise view this as a worthy challenge: "I have the impression that the masters of cinema in Moscow and Leningrad are convinced that this task is irrelevant to them. . . . Why even in famous films such as *Taras Shevchenko* and *The Forty-First* are the depictions of Kazakhs helpless and blurry?"[4] Aimanov then complains about the Moscow exhibition devoted to the fortieth anniversary of Soviet cinema, from which the film studios of the national republics were almost completely absent!

If there was ever any doubt, Aimanov's *Crix de Coeur* proves that one of his major motivations for devoting himself to film was his desire to create a *Kazakh cinema* that was Soviet in its ideological direction but national in its core. He saw this goal as far from being achieved in the present (i.e., the 1960s). This motivation also explains his turn to folklore.

Aimanov not only directed *Beardless Swindler* (Bezborodyi obmanshchik, 1964), but also played the male lead. A friend of the poor and foe of the rich, Aldar Kose (literally "swindler without beard") sides with the underdogs and the victims of injustice, using no weapon but his wit and street smarts. The jester's greatest talent is his ability to tell stories that attract crowds of listeners. While entertaining them, he exposes social ills. His inventiveness knows no bounds, but most important is his common sense, which so many of the vain and powerful have lost. For example, he persuades a *Murza*[5] that his own old and thin rags keep him warmer than regular clothes, and the flabbergasted rich man gives him a fur coat in exchange for those magic rags, which Aldar Kose then exchanges for a sheep, which he then sells. Whenever the fooled and offended people punish the jester for his pranks (usually by giving him a beating) he quickly recovers and continues his mischief. He convinces an unsightly rich lady that she is beautiful, getting a ring as a reward for his lie; then he pairs her up with a vain *akyn*. Aldar Kose also mocks the overly pious and ridicules shamanistic rituals, but he is kind to a shaman who saves his life.

While the plot of *Beardless Swindler* is composed of loose episodes linked by the presence of the title hero, one character to whom the film returns time and time again is a beautiful girl, Karashash. Abducted by the rich Orazbai who wants her as his seventh wife, she is freed by Aldar Kose who plays a trick to make it seem as though she is dead. He then asks for her body as the price for him to leave town and never come back—a price that the exasperated townspeople are more than willing to pay. Having managed to get Karashash out of town, he awakens her so that she can be with her beloved, Taken. Thus, what began as a Romeo-and-Juliet story ends happily thanks to the interference of the compassionate jester.

*Beardless Swindler* was labeled a comedy, but it is dominated by serious and sometimes sad tones, even though several episodes are openly comedic and satirical. The overall atmosphere is rather gloomy, perhaps Shakespearean, resembling medieval darkness more than cheerful joie de vivre. Aimanov's face mostly appears somber: witnessing the overwhelming poverty and injustice around him obviously depresses the jester, who knows full well that his jokes and pranks can only provide temporary relief.

Aimanov treats the legend of Aldar Kose as an allegory of the artist, whose position in society is and will always be precarious and ambivalent if he wants to remain true to his calling. This view of the mythical figure allows for an evaluation of the filmmaker's own career. Shaken Aimanov was an artist who wanted to provide entertainment but also point to social ills, a combination that no society fully appreciates. In *Beardless Swindler*, Kazakhstan is depicted as a country of majestic natural beauty ruled by an arrogant and cruel establishment that is supported and legitimized by hypocritical priests. Aldar Kose's sadness about the state of affairs in his country is also expressed by a melancholic musical leitmotif (the score was composed by Sydyk Mukhamedzhanov). Conspicuously, the jokes, which are at times openly blasphemous, do not attack faith as such but only those who use faith as an instrument to maintain their power. It would not have taken too much effort to extrapolate this portrayal of Kazakhstani society to the Soviet present.

Despite its stylistic novelty, *Beardless Swindler* neither became a hit, nor satisfied critics,[6] although it ended up winning some official recognition. At the film festival of the Republics of Central Asia and Kazakhstan that took place in Almaty on September 19–26, 1965, Aimanov was honored with a diploma. One film historian complimented him for making the title character "a man who is comprehensible and close to us, a contemporary."[7] But did Aimanov really achieve that? And was this even his intention? The most unexpected feature emphasized by the director is Aldar Kose's isolation. Even when surrounded by sympathetic listeners and in moments of triumph, the witty prankster remains a deeply lonely man whose artistic inventiveness and antiauthoritarian wit appear more like a burden or a curse than like a gift. Aldar Kose manages to bring justice to some and even happiness to young lovers, but he cannot find salvation for himself. This tragic aspect of Aimanov's film may be indicative of the artist's identification with the title character: Aldar Kose is part of Aimanov the living legend, and Aldar's sadness is his own. In this regard, *Beardless Swindler* can be interpreted as a credo picture for its creator. Indeed, the title character's melancholy, wisdom, and resignation are presented as features both of the artful jester and of any true artist.

This approach renders Aimanov's picture subversive in an unexpected manner. Including the critique of dogmatic arrogance as part of the image of a free-spirited medieval artist made perfect sense and was fully in accord with Soviet ideological norms. But who would dare to apply the same critique to Soviet contemporaneity? The consequences would be more radical than anyone could imagine. Of course, Aldar Kose is portrayed as both knowing and powerless; his interferences put him at risk and never remedy social ills as such. At best, the subversive artist can bring individual fulfillment to select individuals. It would be worthwhile to explore the extent to which Aimanov's own passionate and exhausting struggle to create a national culture for his country had contributed to this sense of melancholic resignation. *Beardless Swindler* can also be viewed as a bitter reaction to the mean-spirited campaigns that had been unleashed against Aimanov just a few years earlier. Whatever the various allusions may suggest, the film is a parable, concluding that being loved and maligned is the destiny of any true artist.

## A CROWNING ACHIEVEMENT: *LAND OF THE FATHERS*

Arguably the most significant Kazakhstani picture of the 1960s was Shaken Aimanov's *Land of the Fathers* (Atameken/Zemlia ottsov, 1966). It is generally considered one of the highest achievements of Kazakhstani cinema and is certainly the most artistically original picture in Aimanov's multifaceted oeuvre.

While Aimanov's comedies, contemporary dramas, and the Civil War adventure *The End of the Ataman* are usually interpreted within the framework of their respective genres, *Land of the Fathers* is a standalone film. Both a postwar drama and a parable, it is also a deeply-felt reflection of Aimanov's search for the place of Kazakhness within the framework of Soviet civilization. The story of its making and unsatisfactory reception by Kazakh viewers has become a well-known and oft-repeated part of Aimanov's biography, in which the director's ongoing struggle to establish a meaningful dialogue with Kazakh and non-Kazakh audiences plays a fundamental role.[8] *Land of the Fathers* reflects many of the dilemmas faced by an artist loyal to the communist idea and the Soviet Union, but just as deeply committed to his Kazakh motherland. How was Aimanov to tell a story that was at once profoundly national and fundamentally internationalist?

The point of departure is a tradition described at the very beginning of the film. An elderly Kazakh man, whose name the viewer never learns, goes on a long sojourn to find the remains of his son, who was killed in action near Leningrad in 1943. According to an ancient Kazakh rule, the family must bring its member's remains home and bury them in native soil: literally, in the land of the fathers. The old man embarks on this journey with his grandson, Baian, who also acts as the voiceover narrator, reminiscing about his experience many years later.

Thus, the significance of the title and the narrative framework of *Land of the Fathers* are both made clear early on. However, the story's implications are far more complex than it may seem from the simple plot synopsis, and even the title holds a degree of ambiguity: the Russian word *zemlia* can mean both "soil" and "land." In other words, it can refer literally to the intended burial in native soil, but also to returning the soldier's remains to his homeland in a more general sense. The old man's son was ethnically Kazakh, but he was also a Soviet soldier who fought in a war that was waged against the Soviet Union as such. Thus, what was, and what is, his homeland? What is the land of his fathers?

The opening dolly shot of a grave monument (*mazar*) and the vast steppe surrounding it begins the visualization of this semantic ambiguity, while the monument near Leningrad under which the son is buried represents the other semantic pole, namely, the "Soviet land," which marks the end of the journey.

The long and arduous sojourn to fetch the soldier's remains represents both senses of "zemlia," the one that refers literally to the land of the ethnic ancestors and the one that refers to a much broader notion. Aimanov's picture, featuring a seemingly endless journey from one region of the Soviet Union to another, widens the semantic field of the term "fatherland," both for the protagonists and for the viewer. At the same time, the validity of the ancient rule remains intact. The latter is one of the aspects of this story that was largely overlooked by critics.

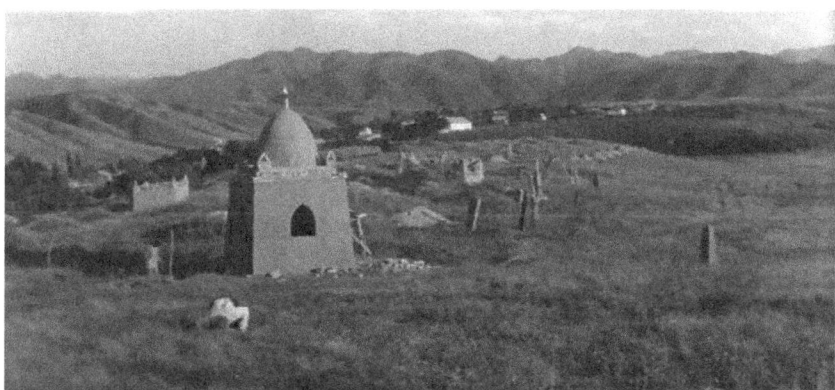

**Figure 7.1** **Remembering the Ancestors.** *Land of the Fathers* (1966, Shaken Aimanov)

In the first episodes, Baian and his grandfather are accompanied for several days by four fellow travelers on a primitive freight wagon. These people could not be more different in their views and customs. A peculiar old archeologist, Vitalii Iakovlevich (Iurii Pomerantsev), expresses a worldview that alienates and offends the old Kazakh. The professor carries with him a bag of bones from an expedition and shows the impressionable Baian the skull of a boy who died 3,000 years ago. To the Kazakh grandfather, such science is sheer blasphemy from which his grandson must be protected. In his outrage, he verbally attacks the Russian intellectual as a fool, asking him where he is from. The scholar's answer ("Leningrad, Moscow, Berlin") confirms the Kazakh's worst suspicions: this man has no homeland and no concept of it; Baian should avoid listening to him and his teachings. The grandfather does not mince his words in addressing the old professor: "You are a bad man. A human being must know the place where he is from, the place where the ghosts of his ancestors live."

These verbal attacks baffle and depress the kindhearted archeologist, who sincerely regrets his inability to establish a mutual understanding with someone whom he respects despite their incompatible worldviews. Those initial frictions notwithstanding, the journey, which lasts many days, brings the people in the wagon closer to each other, and the grandfather's attitude eventually softens.

During a stopover, when young Baian takes the professor to an ancient cave, the old scientist realizes that this may be the discovery of a lifetime, perhaps even a legendary lost city. Over all objections, the archeologist and his daughter-in-law decide to stay in the middle of the steppe and begin

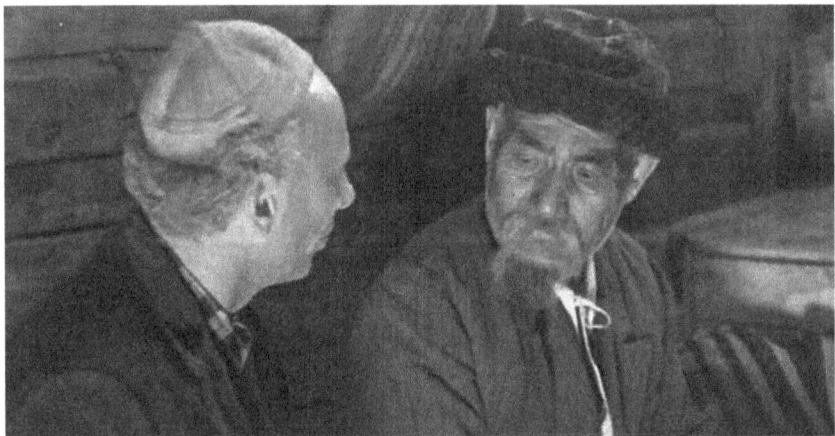

**Figure 7.2 The Scholar and the Grandfather.** *Land of the Fathers* (1966, Shaken Aimanov)

excavating the ruins. At this point, the scientist's passion impresses the grandfather; he brings him a bag filled with food before bidding him farewell. The viewer may assume that the experience has widened the old Kazakh's horizon, too: people can differ profoundly in their outlook on life and still respect each other. Moreover, the archeologist's fascination with, and respect for, ancient civilization, that is, the human beings who once inhabited this land, is not so different from the traditional respect for the ancestors, which the old Kazakh represents.

In accordance with the title and concept, nature plays a profound role in many episodes of the film. The characters' reactions to the landscapes seen through the wagon's wide open door indicate their differences. Thus, the happy-go-lucky soldier Egor exclaims "Farewell, Asia!" with obvious relief. Yet the sheer grandiosity of the steppe leaves a deep impression on all travelers, be they Russian or Kazakh. When a group of horsemen rides up alongside the train and shout happily about the birth of a son, the camera emphasizes their dynamic speed in parallel motion. Then, the landscape outside the train begins to change; the steppe gives way to fields and rivers.[9] For the first time, Baian sees the Volga, and its enormity makes him shout with joy. Without ever verbalizing this, the images of nature in the film indicate that members of different nations can appreciate landscapes (i.e., "the land") that are not their own in a narrow sense, recognizing and acknowledging their beauty.

Stylistically, *Land of the Fathers* is shaped by neorealist principles that were particularly influential in Soviet cinema in the late 1950s and early 1960s. The postwar reality is unembellished, with poverty, dust, and dirt dominating the background of almost every scene. The farther the journey takes the two travelers into Russia, the more are the scenes dominated by traces of the war. Since the film's main events take place far away from Kazakhstan, nothing can make up for the overall austerity of the impersonal spaces in which the grandfather and Baian find themselves: they are without a home. Perhaps the interior of the train car was intended as the equivalent of a shelter, improvised and inhabited by unrelated Soviet people, but atmospherically, this improvised space never conveys coziness or protection, even during episodes of joint eating and sleeping. During the long stopovers, the railway stations do not offer any shelter either. Rather, they expose the travelers to the inhospitable world of unpredictable railway traffic, as it is not clear which train will move when and to what destination. The Soviet postwar world is presented as frightening and at times apocalyptic, a space in which people's movements and decisions are uncoordinated, dependent on whims. Relationships are thus placed under enormous stress, and relatives and friends can easily lose each other.

This sense of forlornness only begins to wane when Baian, all alone because his grandfather did not make it to the train on time after a stopover, tries to find

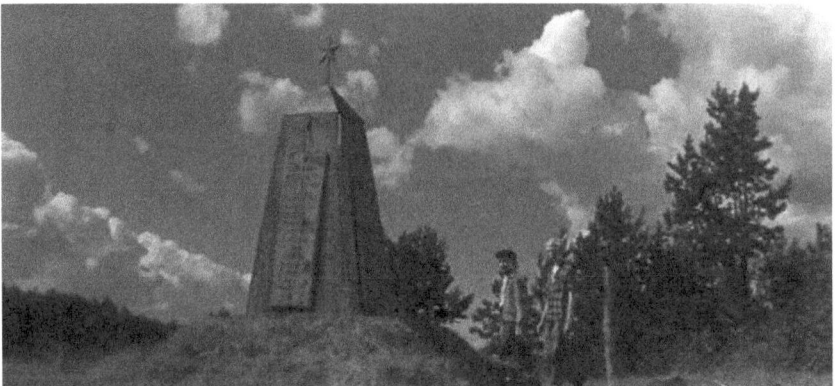

**Figure 7.3** **The Soviet Monument.** *Land of the Fathers* (1966, Shaken Aimanov)

the village of Nosakino, where his father is said to have been buried. The deep Russian forest, densely filled with trees and bushes, is unknown to the boy, but, surprisingly, not in a scary way. Only the anti-tank fortifications and other scars of the recent carnage resemble the apocalyptic atmosphere of the railway stations. The Russian village, meanwhile, is an entirely different matter: its inhabitants invite the Kazakh boy into their neat wooden houses, offering him shelter and nourishment. Vasilii, a boy his own age, immediately becomes a likeminded friend to Baian, sharing cigarettes and stories with him. Finally, when Vasilii takes Baian to the monument for fallen warriors who perished during the defense of Leningrad, the story comes full circle: Baian's father, in death, is part of a multinational community whose members are listed on the stone. This moment marks the film's philosophical culmination. It is the exact counterpoint of the *kurgan* shown in the film's opening.

Suleimenov's screenplay, which was based on his poem "One War Was Finished by Another" (Odna voina okonchilas' drugoi), derives a philosophical concept from a believable story in an almost ideal manner, without ever forcing its conclusion on the audience. It leads the viewer from a hypothesis (that the ancient law of burying a Kazakh's remains in the land/soil of his ancestors must be honored) through subsequent implicit arguments for and against that law, to an ultimate synthesis in which the semantics of "land" are widened to include both Kazakh *and* Soviet. The ultimate concept of the *Soviet world* conveyed in Aimanov's picture is neither nationalist nor internationalist. The film reflects the productive tensions between the two notions within the Soviet paradigm, tensions that defined Soviet-Kazakh life for seven decades.

What Suleimenov and Aimanov tried to do was propose a synthesis that would allow Kazakh and Soviet patriotism to form a harmonious unity.

At the time of the film's release, this synthesis found official recognition, although the reviews failed to mention the plot's sharper edges.[10] The confrontation between the Russian archeologist and the old Kazakh, in particular, would have merited a thorough discussion. After all, this is a confrontation between rationalist materialism and metaphysical spirituality, a debate that, according to Soviet officialdom, should long ago have been settled in favor of the former. Under Marxist-Leninist norms, an old man adhering to ancient mythical beliefs should have been denounced as absurd, an anachronism. Yet Suleimenov and Aimanov afford the grandfather and his convictions unconditional respect throughout. This respect for the elder is part of the film's authentic Kazakhness, its unmistakable national dimension.

In a peculiar way, the old man is *Kazakh but not Soviet*, as if he had been left untouched by the historical turmoil since the Bolshevik takeover twenty-five years earlier. The character of the grandfather is the true discovery of Aimanov's film, and there is a special irony in the fact that this *aksakal* (an honored old man) is portrayed by none other than Eleubai Umurzakov of *Amangeldy* fame. It is doubtful if Aimanov's film would have been released during the Khrushchev years, with their aggressive antireligious campaigns. However, after 1964, when official attitudes toward religion temporarily softened, *Land of the Fathers* seems to have met Soviet ideological standards to a satisfactory degree. The film resolves the verbal conflict between materialism and spirituality in a peaceful manner: the old man retains his beliefs as his grandson moves forcefully toward a new age, while his grandfather puts love for him above traditionalist dogma. But whatever the synthesis, or compromise, may have been at the time, it is clear that Suleimenov and Aimanov endowed the carrier of tradition with a dignity previously unseen in Kazakh cinema.

The old man, whom Baian always addresses as *ata*, represents the sternness of ancient rules, the law of the forefathers. His judgments about people are principled and harsh, his methods authoritarian. When Baian reacts with visible fascination to the Russian professor's tale about the ancient skull, the grandfather slaps the boy in the face. Whenever he talks to other people, there is not the slightest doubt in his voice. His degree of identification with the Kazakh homeland is absolute. Thus, he disapproves when someone points to a province outside the train that had been affected by the plague, remarking that it is wrong to tell foreigners about such national catastrophe. However, the guiding principle of his life is not the strict letter of the law but love. His devotion to his grandson is unconditional, and he risks his life to reunite with him at the end.

The plan to bring back home his son's remains, too, is primarily an expression of paternal love rather than of adherence to dogma.

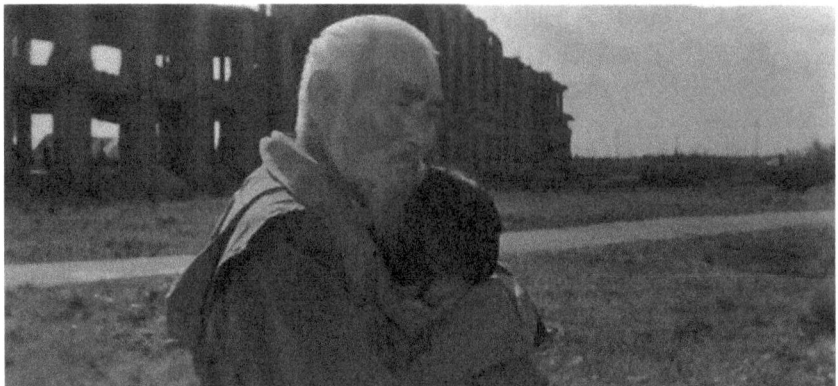

Figure 7.4   **Reuniting among Ruins.** *Land of the Fathers* (1966, Shaken Aimanov)

For Baian, his sojourn to Leningrad in 1945 (the first summer after the end of the war, as he notes at the beginning) is an initiation in more than one sense. He has been told that bringing home the remains of an ancestor is a deed of the highest order, one that will make him an adult and even a hero. Successfully completed, the journey will turn Baian into a man. And Baian is conscious of the meaning of this journey into manhood. That is why he asks Sofia, the professor's daughter-in-law, if a husband can be younger than his wife, revealing that he is in love with a girl who is four years his senior and that he intends to marry her, the sooner the better. Various encounters during stopovers force him to prove his courage and street smarts but, most importantly, give him a sense of legitimate citizenship when he is welcomed into the homes of Russians/fellow Soviets. Baian's journey both reaffirms his Kazakhness and allows him to discover his Sovietness: such is the true meaning of his trip.

Baian is thus a child of his ancestors, literally, an offspring of the "land of the fathers," and at the same time belongs to modernity. He has great curiosity about books, something that the archeologist immediately notices and encourages, even predicting that Baian will become a scholar one day. Unlike the boy Kozha from Karsakbaev's 1964 film, with whom he shares a natural inner strength and openness to the modern world, Baian is not playful but serious about his future. The pensiveness of his features and the sternness of his facial expression reveal that he and his grandfather have a lot in common.

While displaying a high degree of philosophical and artistic originality, *Land of the Fathers* does suffer from certain weaknesses. One of them is the score. Unlike other Soviet films, in which the depiction of the war experience is emotionally supported by a powerful leitmotif structure, in *Land of the Fathers* music only appears occasionally and negligibly; Erkegali Rakhmadiev's score remains colorless and does not play the cohesive role that it could have. This might be one of the reasons why regular viewers largely remained detached from the story. On another level, the different acting styles fail to form a dynamic unity. Umurzakov's consistent understatement contrasts with Pomerantsev's clowning, to the detriment of the latter. The camera work, which marked the debut of Aimanov's son Murat,[11] is often inventive and has moments of brilliance, but overall lacks stylistic consistency. Of great importance are montage sequences with numerous extreme close-ups of the grandfather and the grandson, emphasizing the centrality of their mental and spiritual transformations. However, the remarkable visual concentration of the beginning, with a silent dolly shot capturing both the grave monument built for Baian's father and the landscape, is not maintained throughout.

A peculiar episode deals with a Chechen who is returning home by train but prefers to sit on the roof. At first, it seems that he is just a man from the mountains for whom the claustrophobic tightness of the wagon is unpleasant; indeed, he himself presents matters that way. But later, when the trusting and respectful grandfather approaches him and wants to know more, the Chechen reacts aggressively to his inquiry and threatens the Kazakh. The secret of this strange encounter is never spelled out, but it is hardly the rehabilitation of the deported Chechens that some wanted to see in this episode, something unthinkable at the time.[12] More likely, the episode represents a confirmation that certain members of national minorities were collaborators and had reason to hide and stay apart from the majority, in this case the group of travelers on the train.[13]

*Land of the Fathers* is rich in significant details and symbols, some of which are hard to recognize outside the context of the 1960s. A small but politically interesting episode concerns Lenin. When Baian asks the archeologist what Lenin was like as a person, the professor's unexpected answer is that he was awkward and uncommunicative as a youngster and had a speech impediment (*kartavil*). Surprisingly, this gross violation of all standards of the Soviet Lenin cult seems to have gone unnoticed by censors.

Philosophical relevance is indicated by the motif of water charged with a cleansing function that is emphasized by the camera (ritualized washing of the hands; washing and drinking in the wild river; crossing the Volga on a huge bridge).

The question of what remains after an individual's life has ended is a leitmotif, the variations of which provide the film with a cohesive ideational structure. Above all, *Land of the Fathers* praises unity: of the multinational Soviet homeland that had won an unprecedented war; of the Kazakh nation that had played a decisive part in achieving this victory; and of the family, whose cohesion remains intact even after one of its young members has perished. These facets of unity act in a complementary fashion rather than competing against each other. Thus, the reunion of Baian and his grandfather on Russian soil is a dramatic highpoint following the recognition that the remains of the grandfather's son/Baian's father should stay within the fraternal grave near Leningrad, the city that he defended.[14]

Despite audiences' underwhelming reactions, *Land of the Fathers* became a key work for the evolution of Kazakh cinema. Conspicuously, the film did not impact the latter's development primarily through audience response and positive remembrance (as was the case with *Our Dear Doctor*), but through the profound impression it left on other filmmakers and critics. From today's standpoint, the deep faith that guides the old Kazakh man appears even wiser and more in tune with the evolution of the nation than at the time of the film's making when the Soviet framework seemed eternal. *Land of the Fathers* is thus a visionary film that anticipates Kazakhstan's search for a viable national identity. It was insufficiently understood at the time because its approach to the theme of identity was dialectical and complex.

Of all Aimanov's pictures, *Land of the Fathers* is the one that brought him the closest to the status of an auteur filmmaker. This part of his legacy would become eminent when Kazakh cinema reinvented itself in the late 1980s and saw the emergence of a range of auteurs who would leave the land of their fathers, only to return to it eventually.

## BACK TO COMEDY

For Shaken Aimanov it was essential to reconnect with the millions of spectators that comprised his audience. In 1968, he expressed his frustration about *Land of the Fathers* in no uncertain terms in an article in the newspaper *Soviet Culture* titled "The Viewer Has the Last Word." Setting the standard of what it means for a Kazakh film to be considered successful, Aimanov writes, is his own *Our Dear Doctor* from more than a decade earlier. That comedy retained a presence on Kazakhstan's screens for years and attracted over 50 million viewers nationwide. In addition, it was sold to forty countries! *Land of the Fathers* did not even come close to such smashing success. "And I would like to believe that we were able to convey the main idea of the film: that the fatherland is not that narrow piece of land on which one is born, grew up, and aged. Fatherland—that's our entire country, from the Baltic Sea to Cape Dezhnev, from the Barents Sea to the heights of the Pamirs. Grandfather and grandson, searching for the grave of a soldier who died in the battles of the Great Patriotic War, acquired a fatherland—the very fatherland for which their son and father had died."[15] Aimanov calls the failure of *Land of the Fathers* to connect with viewers a catastrophe (*beda*). The State Prize of the Kazakh SSR that he won for the film in 1968 could not change that fact, as he openly states. In the article, Aimanov searched for the reasons that would explain the lack of a popular response to his latest work. "In some respects, the film is visually poor, boring. The passions are at times hidden so deeply that the viewer cannot see them: they remain outside the frame. Perhaps we have found some new approaches, but this novelty gives the viewer hardly anything."[16]

Without explicitly saying it, Aimanov rejects the notion of an *auteur* approach to filmmaking, for which the reactions of mass audiences are irrelevant. Indeed, his article reveals just how painful the lack of popularity of *Land of the Fathers* was for him. It is therefore not surprising that he followed the underappreciated somber reflectiveness of *Land of the Fathers* with a musical comedy.

Made ten years after the groundbreaking *Our Dear Doctor*, *Angel in a Cap* (Angel v tiubeteike, 1968) has all the necessary ingredients of a hit: a funny story, modern music, and fashionable costumes. Visibly inspired by the international lighthearted musicals that were released in the USSR in the late 1960s, having been imported from both the West and the Eastern bloc, Aimanov inventively transferred many of their characteristic elements onto Kazakh soil. But he did more: below its glitzy surface, *Angel in a Cap* contains a discourse about the essential features of the cultural evolution that had taken place in his homeland, the difference between genuine and faddish values, and the place that modern Kazakhstan could and should occupy within these parameters.

True to the laws of musical comedy, the plot is simple: Tana, a rural woman in her fifties (Amina Umurzakova), comes to Alma-Ata to visit her son Tailak (Atageldy Ismailov). She is concerned about his bachelor status, an anomaly at twenty-eight. Following rural customs, the mother addresses various young women on the bus or in the street and invites them to meet her son. After numerous amusing encounters and some degree of confusion, Tailak finally makes his choice and gets married.

Many comedic effects result from the mother's controlling nature, her inability to accept that Tailak is a grown-up, and the directness with which she applies rules of the countryside to the modern urban environment. "A man cannot live by himself," Tana states directly into the camera. "He needs his mother. Or at least a wife." The way in which Amina Umurzakova utters these words conveys such genuine conviction that the viewer cannot help but be amused. Indeed, the chemistry between the characters is a strong point of *Angel in a Cap*. Umurzakova gives one of her signature performances as a loving Kazakh matriarch, in this case offering its comical inversion, which is remarkable as it demonstrates both sensitivity and openness.[17] Her son maintains the right balance between respect for tradition and insistence on his own sovereignty as an adult man. The solid acting (remarkably, Ismailov was a nonprofessional!) compensates for the shortcomings of the musical revue: whenever there is a chance, the plot development is interrupted by a song.

As in previous films, Aimanov makes a point of featuring Kazakhstan's leading artists, including *Estrada* star Bibigul' and the opera singer Ermek Serkebaev. This justifies switching back and forth between the relatively realistic comedic episodes and the non-realistic show scenes with singing and dancing, such that it does not present a challenge for the viewer. Aimanov was fully aware that musical comedies are based on this conditionality and audiences' knowing how to handle it. To make the musical interludes more attractive, he added some erotic flair and, within the restrictions of the 1960s Soviet Union, risqué dresses: in two episodes, the female dancers appear in bikini-like costumes, quite daring for the time and a cause of horror for Tailak's mother who finds even ballet reprehensible ("You cannot marry that girl—the man had his hands all over her body!"). The constant clashes between time-honored traditions and modern life in Alma-Ata are arguably the most effective source of humor in *Angel in a Cap*.

Modern tunes and instruments accompany fashionably dressed people who are filmed against a backdrop of new buildings. As a matter of fact, Alma-Ata is exclusively presented as a modern city, its inhabitants living in neat interiors, getting information and buying soft drinks and beer in glass kiosks and riding in comfortable, sparkling clean cars and buses. The colors are bright, resembling travel catalogs; that, too, was an internationally accepted convention of the musical comedy genre. Still, the selectiveness of this imagery signifies that Aimanov wanted to show Kazakhstan as a country whose urbanites feel comfortable living in such conditions. The underlying sociopolitical agenda may not have pleased everybody at the time, when prudish attitudes with respect to physicality and sexuality were dominant both in Kazakhstan and in the Soviet Union at large. But in *Angel in a Cap*, Aimanov seems to be calling upon his countrymen not to fear modern times, to embrace new cultural trends, and to move courageously toward an urban future.

Particularly remarkable is the complete acceptance of the *Western* nature of modernity: it is not even debated but simply taken for granted! During one of the encounters between Tailak and a potential bride, the latter compares him to Marcello Mastroianni, while he likens her to Brigitte Bardot. The jazz and pop music in which the protagonists indulge and the fashionable clothes that they wear are clearly products not of Soviet culture but of Western consumerism. A liberal approach to consumerism was generally viewed as problematic at the time and was hotly debated in Soviet media by various ideological factions; the presence of these discussions can be sensed in the film, although they never take center stage. Indeed, whenever the clash of traditional and modern culture is shown, the native origins of the former and the Western origins of the latter remain unexplained. This was not a politically harmless approach. In reality, the Western provenance and assumed decadent potential of pop and rock was one of the strongest arguments of the Soviet proponents of cultural repression, who unceasingly pointed to the dangerous effects of these "cultural weapons of imperialism." Aimanov simply ignored the political and ideological dimensions of the debate. Perhaps this uncommon openness was also intended as a signal to the film's potential international audiences to recognize Kazakhstan as part of the rapidly modernizing world.

However, with respect to the issues of private life, marriage, and intimacy, he gives all sides the chance to present their case. The tension between traditional and modern culture is the central issue in a scene in which Tana and her son visit a well-known academic who performs a folklore tune. This tune is then picked up in classical rendition by the professor's son, accompanied first by a piano, then by an orchestra. The young man happens to be a famous singer who believes that the supreme musical form is opera. Then a younger son and his girlfriend dance to the same melody, now in jazz form. The professor is horrified, but the freshness and mobility of the performance are beyond doubt. And during the ensuing polemic, the son makes the case that jazz, too, is popular music, that is, its origins are found in the culture of the people. Aimanov seems to embrace the notion. While each character belongs to a different generation (the folklore traditionalist is in his late fifties, the opera singer in his thirties, and the jazz and pop fan in his early twenties) all three opinions are valid in their own way. A conspicuous visual comment is the large portrait of Abai in the background, signifying a foundational cultural consensus that none of the debating men challenges. Indeed, Abai himself was an outspoken modernizer, rendering him a crown witness to the proponents of change, but without ridiculing the more conservative voices. The film also points to the right of the older generation to find love later in life: the widowed professor takes a liking to Tana, cares for her when she is sick, and ultimately proposes to her.

Apart from its funny plot, *Angel in a Cap* features numerous inside jokes, beginning with the animated credits containing cartoon portraits of the crew. In a later scene, Aimanov himself is seen giving instructions to the cameraman. A number of scenes make caustic references to the pathetic state of Kazakh soccer that were surely met with approving laughter at the time of the film's release. There are a few serious touches as well: Tana mentions that her husband, the father of her five children, perished in the war and since her other four children are daughters, it is up to Tailak to continue the clan. A noteworthy exchange takes place in the Medeo area, where a foreign tourist, referring to the cold, exclaims "This is Russian winter!" to which a neighbor responds, "Kazakh winter!"

Stylistically important for the film is its visible affection for Alma-Ata, with its parks and flowerbeds and the snow-covered mountains in the background. This affection is expressed through a song, but also through sequences of picturesque shots of its streets and squares.

Despite the provocative inclusion of adapted elements of Western lifestyle, Aimanov made a deeply national film. Its humor is proof of the vitality of native culture, which should be secure in the legitimacy of its values when interacting with modern influences.

*Angel in a Cap* could easily have charmed audiences across the Soviet republics, not just in Kazakhstan. It is unabashedly entertaining, maintains a light and benevolent touch throughout, and presents its tolerant view of contemporary culture with remarkable confidence. But this explicitly pro-Western cultural stance rendered the film suspicious to the political establishment; as a result, it was never promoted as it should have been and remained unknown to most Soviet viewers. One critic objected to the scene in which Tana is confronted with dancing students: not only do they dance the Twist, but they do so barefoot! This, according to the critic, was not funny but brutal.[18] However, the film's humor has not aged, and it enjoyed a successful afterlife in the post-independence era when the cultural tensions between old and new lost their ideological significance.

After *Angel in a Cap*, Shaken Aimanov agreed to be cast in a project of his protégé, Kuat Abuseitov, *At the Foot of the Naizatas* (U podnozh'ia Naizatas, 1969), a made-for-TV production about life in a contemporary sovkhoz. Then, he devoted all his energies to the Eastern, *The End of the Ataman*, which would be the final film of his career.

## THE BIRTH OF KAZAKH ANIMATION

By the time the decade came to an end, there could be no doubt that many of the problems facing Kazakhstani cinema that were associated with the country's vastness had been overcome. About 7,000 film projectors were servicing the republic's citizens, six times as many as twenty years earlier! When the Union of Kazakhstani Film Workers took stock of the accomplishments and the lacunae of the 1960s, the chairman of the State Committee for Cinema, Aleksandr Fedulin,[19] proudly declared that in 1968, Kazakhfilm studio had, for the first time in its history, worked on eight full-length feature films simultaneously. He complained, however, that there were not enough problem-conscious movies about contemporary Kazakhstan.[20]

At the second Congress of Kazakhstani Film Workers, held on January 23–24, 1969, in Alma-Ata, Shaken Aimanov presented his official report to delegates and guests from the Central Committee of the Communist Party of Kazakhstan and from Moscow. At that time, preparations for the celebration of the 100th anniversary of Lenin's birth were dominating Soviet culture, and

Aimanov, first secretary of the Union of Kazakhstani Film Workers, spent much time emphasizing the importance of Lenin for Kazakhstan and particularly for its cinema. What he could not openly say was that Kazakh filmmakers had not delivered even one feature film that described Lenin's importance for their republic. Moreover, those films that dealt with the 1917–1923 period such as the ideologically provocative *A Worrisome Morning* were too problem-conscious and too deeply steeped in the peculiarities of national history to pass as contributions to the coming Lenin jubilee.

Among the studio's accomplishments, Aimanov mentioned his own *Land of the Fathers*, as well as the nascent production of animation and children's films. The latter genres had won over the hearts of Kazakhstani viewers in a manner that the more "mature" films could only dream of. Native audiences responded enthusiastically to Amen Khaidarov's debut,[21] the nine-minute animated fairy-tale *Why the Swallow's Tail Is Split in Half* (Pochemu u lastochki khvost rozhkami, 1967). Public approval was so overwhelming that the production of animated films at Kazakhfilm studio was made permanent. The fact that these films were narratively and stylistically rooted in folklore did not escape viewers' attention, making these little gems precious objects of national identification. The undisputed champion of Kazakhstani animation among film critics, Bauyrzhan Nogerbek, proudly pointed to the fact that leading performers and composers, among them Shaken Aimanov, Serke Kozhamkulov, Zamzagul Sharipova, and Nurgisa Tlendiev, were actively involved in the production of animated shorts.[22] Two years after the release of Kazakhstan's first animated films, at the 1969 film festival of the republics of Central Asia and Kazakhstan, the jury, headed by Aleksandr Zarkhi, awarded the prize for the best animated film to Amen Khaidarov's *Aksak Kulan*.

Despite the successful birth of Kazakhstani animation, the congress concluded that Kazakhfilm studio still owed its viewers a great deal: so far, not one feature film about the country's working class, geologists, shepherds, or farmers had been delivered. Interestingly, the report omitted Aimanov's own attempts in this regard, as well as those of Efim Aron's, whose successful 1966 border patrol drama *Where the Edelweiss Is Blooming* went completely unmentioned. Rather than focusing on undeniable genre-specific successes (e.g., Aimanov's delightful comedy *Angel in a Cap*), the stated priorities were utterly political and were mechanically applied to studio production. This was truly a self-assessment formula for failure.[23]

The number of members of the Union of Film Workers increased from 87 to 101; 19 of them were elected to the board, with Shaken Aimanov once again being approved as first secretary. Judging by the developments in Kazakh cinema that followed the second Congress, the real trajectories were discussed not from the pulpit but in smaller, unofficial meetings. Nothing in Aimanov's report gives any indication of the large-scale projects that had already been conceived, most importantly the Civil War spy thriller *The Death of the Ataman* and the mythological epic *Kyz-Zhibek*. These pictures, although developed in the late 1960s, would make their full impact during the following decade.

## NOTES

1. Aimanov got directly involved in other directors' projects, helping them to overcome professional difficulties. One such case was Kuat Abuseitov's first feature film, *The Road of Life* (Doroga zhizni, 1960). Despite his countless other duties, Aimanov would accompany the crew on location shots and train the director on the spot, thus saving the film that was facing a near-fiasco. Cf. Siranov, *Kinoiskusstvo sovetskogo Kazakhstana*, p. 129.

2. Cf. Siranov, *Kinoiskusstvo sovetskogo Kazakhstana*, pp. 308–9. In his discussion of Aimanov's speech, Siranov calls his statements "mistaken."

3. Aimanov, "Obrashchaias' k druz'iam," p. 18.

4. Ibid., p. 19.

5. *Murza* (also *Mirza*): powerful head of a clan in feudal nomad society.

6. Kabysh Siranov wrote that *Beardless Swindler* caused controversies among critics and historians, some of whom doubted the authenticity of the popular Aldar Kose as presented by Aimanov. Cf. Siranov, *Kinoiskusstvo sovetskogo Kazakhstana*, pp. 128–29.

7. Ainagulova, Alimbaeva. *Tendentsii razvitiia kinoiskusstva Kazakhstana*, p. 9.

8. Aimanov was painfully aware of the fact that his film "failed to capture the viewer"; cf. Ainagulova, Alimbaeva, *Tendentsii razvitiia kinoiskusstva Kazakhstana*, p. 17. He concluded that he had to make films that engage audiences by their exciting, colorful form. While this diagnosis may have been accurate, his blockbuster *The End of the Ataman* (1970) was certainly below the artistic level of *Land of the Fathers*.

9. In his analysis of *Land of the Fathers*, Stephen Norris devotes considerable attention to aspects of landscape; cf. Stephen M. Norris, "Landscape and Loss: World War II in Central Asian Cinema." In Michael Rouland, Gulnara Abikeeva, and Birgit Beumers (eds.), *Cinema in Central Asia*. London: I.B. Tauris, 2013, pp. 79–80.

10. The assessment in *Istoriia sovetskogo kino* (vol. 4, pp. 240–41) is positive and points to essential conceptual elements.

11. Murat Aimanov (1939–1993), Shaken Aimanov's son, was a cinematographer and director who graduated from the Soviet film school VGIK in Moscow in 1966. After *Land of the Fathers*, his debut, he switched to documentary cinema.

12. Cf. Stephen Norris, who quotes from the first encounter with the Chechen but does not discuss the disturbing conclusion, in "Landscape and Loss: World War II in Central Asian Cinema," pp. 79–80.

13. Gulnara Abikeeva interpreted the character of the old Chechen as tragic and mentions that he dies on the roof when the train enters a tunnel. F. Abikeeva, *Natsiostroitel'stvo v Kazakhstane*, pp. 88–9.

14. The film was reedited in 1978; this version was included in the jubilee DVD edition of Kazakh cinema that came out in 2011. It would be worthwhile to analyze what changes were made to the 1966 original and why.

15. Aimanov, Shaken, "Poslednee slovo za zritelem." *Sovetskaia kul'tura*, 17 April 1969.

16. Ibid.

17. Amina Umurzakova won the prize as best actress at the film festival of the Central Asian Republics and Kazakhstan in 1969.

18. Matskevich, Oleg, "A vse-taki smeshno." *Kazakhstanskaia pravda*, 22 January 1969.

19. Fedulin, Aleksandr Semenovich (1913–1999), Russian-Soviet politician and administrator. Fedulin studied at various Communist Party schools before being sent to the Kazakh SSR where he worked as a regional Komsomol and Party leader. In 1963, Fedulin was appointed head of the Kazakh Goskino (State Committee of the Council of Ministers of the Kazakh SSR for Cinema), a position he held until 1973. He is credited with overseeing the construction of the new Kazakhfilm Studio at Al-Farabi Avenue.

20. Fedulin, A.S., "Po bol'shomu puti." *Ogni Ala-Tau*, 23 January 1969.

21. Khaidarov (also: Khaidar), Amen (1923–2015), Kazakh animator, the founder of Kazakhstani animation. Khaidarov studied at the Alma-Ata Art School, graduating in 1950, and later at the Soviet State Film Institute (VGIK), graduating in 1965. After his 1967 debut, he made numerous animated shorts; his last film (*The Magic Carpet*) was released in 1982. He then taught animation at the Zhurgenov Institute in Alma-Ata.

22. Smailova, *Kinoentsiklopediia Kazakhstana*, p. 449.

23. See the official report in the Communist Party newspaper: "Pobuzhdat' vysokie pomysly i chuvstva." *Kazakhstanskaia pravda*, 29 January 1969.

*Chapter 8*

# Hits and Anti-Hits

The 1960s ended (or, rather, *culminated*) with the production of two major moving pictures that in many ways reflected the enormous progress made by Kazakhstani cinema in the 1960s: Sultan-Akhmet Khodzhikov's *The Silken Maiden* (Kyz-Zhibek) and Shaken Aimanov's *The End of the Ataman* (Konets atamana). Both were of epic proportions, had twice the running time of a regular feature film, boasted unprecedented production values, and were profoundly national in their outlook. And although both films premiered in 1970, they are the result of processes that unfolded during the preceding decade, with its daring search for thematic and aesthetic novelty.

## THE SILKEN MAIDEN (KYZ-ZHIBEK)

To this day, *The Silken Maiden* (Kyz-Zhibek) stands as one of Kazakhstan's most spectacular moving pictures and a veritable national classic. But its production was lengthy and complicated for logistical and aesthetic reasons. When Sultan-Akhmet Khodzhikov took on the project in the late 1960s, he had to consider a number of risk factors. First and foremost, the story of Kyz-Zhibek is part of Kazakh living folklore. Although the legend of lovers Tolegen and Zhibek, who belong to two different clans within the same *juz*,[1] dates back centuries,[2] for many Kazakhs, its screen adaptation was more than just a film project: it was an emotionally charged cause of national significance. In 1936, Evgenii Brusilovskii's opera *Kyz-Zhibek*, using Gabit Musrepov's libretto, was performed to great acclaim during the "dekada" (i.e., ten-day festival) of Kazakh culture in Moscow.[3] Back then, it signified the appearance of a legitimate and highly presentable national artifact and a worthy Kazakh part of the multinational family of Soviet cultures. Three decades later, the film adaptation had the potential to serve as another significant step in Kazakhstan's evolving cultural identity and self-representation—or else miss the mark and become a disappointment.

The scale of the production was unprecedented for Kazakhfilm studio: a two-part wide-screen epic with large numbers of extras and hundreds of expensive historical costumes. But even more daring was the aesthetic challenge of visualizing an ancient legend without making the film look archaic, let alone theatrical. The filmmakers' primary goal was to achieve national authenticity, creating a picture that would meet the high expectations of Kazakh audiences, a film that would matter to the Kazakh nation. The casting process was hotly debated, with Khodzhikov being attacked by Musrepov, who favored a different actress for the title role, among other conflicts. Yet, despite widespread skepticism, including naysayers within the intellectual establishment, the ultimate film was a triumph, a fact that was acknowledged even by its most vocal detractors.[4]

The opening images of *Kyz-Zhibek* signal violence and tragedy. Blood is spilled over the steppe ground; its source remains invisible. The appearance of white swans, agitated and crying in despair, conveys a sense of doom. In Kazakh mythology, swans are protected and must never be harmed, let alone killed. They also act as witnesses: in the original legend, it is the swans who expose one of the characters as the murderer. The water surrounding the swans is red, adding to their agitation, as if the majestic birds were trying to flee from the source of violence but were unable to. As the prologue to a love story, these images set a foreboding tone.

The next image, of a caravan, is accompanied by a song[5] about war and the miseries suffered by people in the past, mourning the loss of life and the fate of widows and orphaned children.

These images are interspersed with shots of swans running on the ground, leaving traces of blood on the soil in their wake. The ambitious warrior

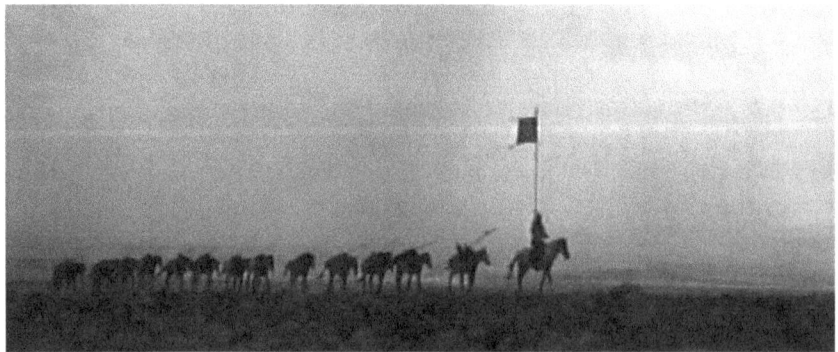

Figure 8.1   **The Toll of War.** *Kyz-Zhibek* (1970, Sultan-Akhmed Khodzhikov)

Bekezhan's announcement of victory is immediately tempered by shots of long lines of women standing in the mountains and waiting in vain for their husbands, brothers, and fathers to return. This poetic opening is characteristic of the film as a whole. It combines symbolic and realistic elements, seamlessly blending them to the point that the real and the surreal can no longer be distinguished and the myth is established as cinematic reality.

The ominous symbolism is not just a signal to the viewer, alluding to an underlying philosophical dimension, but is recognized by some of the characters in the film as well: they keenly search their surroundings for signs and omens. The system of signification implicitly proposed by *Kyz-Zhibek* is based on the assumption that reality cannot be approached by rational means alone.

The film's narrative structure is defined by an alternation between dramatic and lyrical episodes. Conceptually, it is built upon dichotomies: war versus peace, hatred versus love, distrust versus friendship, and adversity versus harmony. Episodes of war, aggressive enmity, and distrust mostly unfold against a backdrop of infertile, harsh mountains and are dominated by dark brownish colors, whereas the world of peace, song, love, and togetherness is placed in the fertile meadows near the river Yaik. The film's visual dynamism is complemented by a rich color spectrum dominated by red, blue, and green. Particularly during the scenes of harmony and joy, when the lovers and other members of the community frolic in the meadows, a harmonious relationship between these colors is established, promising, at least temporarily, a good world ruled by love and understanding.

From the very beginning, the importance of music is made obvious.[6] Characters express their feelings through songs, some of which are accompanied by a choir and others of which are performed a capella.

The main conflict arises when the victorious fighter Bekezhan (Asanali Ashimov) is granted a wish but chooses to wait.

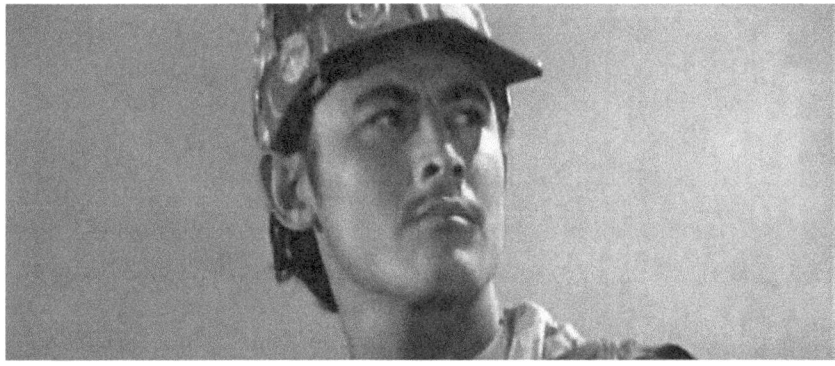

Figure 8.2 The Noble Hero. Kuman Tastanbekov in the Role of Tolegen. *Kyz-Zhibek* (1970, Sultan-Akhmed Khodzhikov)

220                        Chapter 8

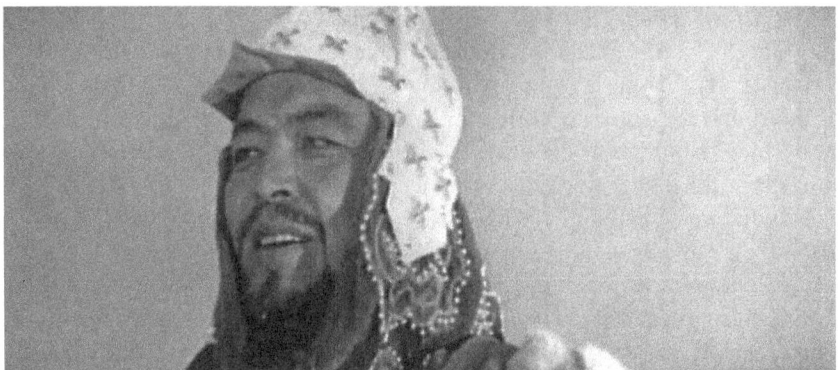

**Figure 8.3   The Aggressor. Asanali Ashimov in the role of Bekezhan.** *Kyz-Zhibek* (1970, Sultan-Akhmed Khodzhikov)

At this point, another young man from a different clan arrives: Tolegen (Kuman Tastanbekov). Young, dashing, and witty, he wins everybody's heart, much to the chagrin of the morose and vain Bekezhan.

The two men immediately engage in disputes: where was Tolegen when the people were in mortal danger? Why has he arrived so late, coming when the war is already over? To embarrass his opponent, Bekezhan suggests that all Tolegen is capable of is flirting with girls. But Tolegen, although prepared to defend his honor, is not interested in a fight with Bekezhan. As a matter of fact, he has come to talk about peace and unity among the Kazakh tribes, a message that the wise Adiar welcomes. Nevertheless, the verbal competition between Bekezhan and Tolegen continues and results in a duel, which is anxiously observed by the clan members, most of whom would have preferred to avoid bloodshed.

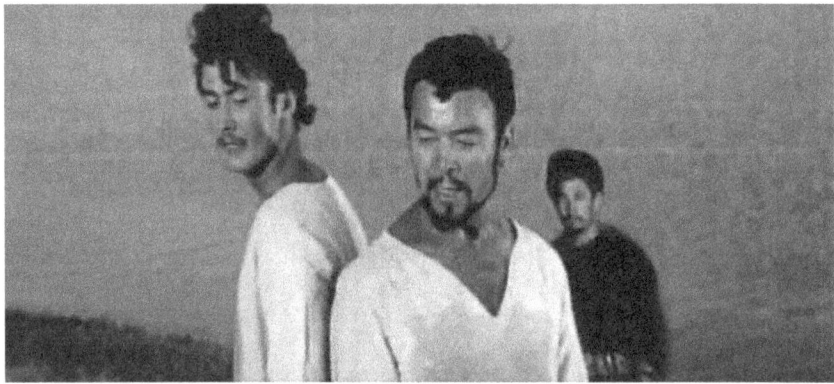

**Figure 8.4   Confrontation between Good and Evil.** *Kyz-Zhibek* (1970, Sultan-Akhmed Khodzhikov)

Within the film's narrative framework, the two men are depicted not as supermen but regular, down-to-earth characters. But they also stand for opposing worldviews. The aggressive Bekezhan embodies an unrelenting virility that goes far beyond the need to defend his honor and the safety of his homeland. Rather, he feels challenged by anybody who might be superior, whether physically or mentally. Bekezhan will not stop until he has proven his own superiority over that other man. His relentless need to fight is fundamentally irrational. Tolegen represents the opposite pole: reason and moderation. He is willing to fight when his country and its people are in danger and when his honor is threatened, but only then. In the absence of a threat, he would prefer to live in peace. Tolegen treats Bekezhan's loud aggressiveness with friendly irony, like horseplay, an attitude that only aggravates the other man's hostility. Tolegen's view of Bekezhan is naïve. He is simply unable to fathom the depth of his competitor's enmity. Instead, he keeps trusting Bekezhan; after all, he is a fellow Kazakh who faces the same external enemies and shares the same values and beliefs. Tolegen's benevolence will ultimately prove fatal, as will Bekezhan's irrational resentment.

Since its release in 1970, *Kyz-Zhibek* has been embraced by the Kazakh people as an authentic adaptation of a major national epic.[7] The audience's continuous enthusiastic response to the film, albeit mostly in Kazakhstan itself rather than in the Soviet Union at large or internationally, is understandable. The repeated message about the vital need for national unity, in particular, resonated with millions of viewers at home but not abroad. Interestingly, despite this nationally relevant message, the filmmakers avoided certain typical features of foundational epics such as grandiose, static shot compositions, a declarative tone, theatricality, and explicit didacticism encouraging self-sacrifice for the national cause. The story of *Kyz-Zhibek* is presented as a tragic romance within a historically turbulent epoch. Both the title heroine and her lover lose their lives in the end. But the tragedy is not caused by external enemies. Tolegen, the character who stands for decency, honesty, and national unity, is treacherously killed by a fellow Kazakh. In terms of historical orientation and viewer motivation, this is hardly an inspiring outcome, not least because no uplifting message is derived from the tragedy by any of the participants and observers. Indeed, *Kyz-Zhibek* does not engage in explicitly preaching national values. Instead, it mourns the tragedy of individual love that is destroyed by irrational forces from within the community. The lovers' sacrifice is not conveniently twisted into a contribution to the Kazakh cause; it is senseless and pessimistic. If the telos of a national epic is the ultimate triumph of the nation, whether real or as a vision for the future, the ending of *Kyz-Zhibek* is non-teleological and even anti-teleological. Nothing can bring back Kyz-Zhibek and Tolegen who were meant for each other, and no promise of national triumph can alleviate their tragedy. That is why the creators of the film were right to avoid loud visual or audial pathos. Khodzhikov's *Kyz-Zhibek* is a lyrical and tragic picture in concept and atmosphere.

In strong support of this approach, Askhat Ashrapov's cinematography subverts any potential for visual stability. It does not offer foundational pathos, although there were numerous opportunities to do so, including in the scenes featuring the court. Adiar speaks with solemn authority, his appearance is dignified and his decisions are just. But his court is not shown in grandiose symmetrical compositions or from awe-inspiring low-angle viewpoints. The implicitly relativist concept of the ruler is part of the overall worldview of *Kyz-Zhibek*. Adiar lacks the military might to fight competing clans or the intruding Dzhungars. Sultan Khodzhikov was aware of the story's ambiguity, arguing that Gabit Musrepov's screenplay had the potential to support different interpretations: it could be approached as a historical chronicle, as a lyrical poem, and as a heroic drama. As Kabysh Siranov stated, Khodzhikov managed to overcome this ambiguity by synthesizing all elements into a lyrical-epical picture.[8]

Thus, *Kyz-Zhibek* is not a national foundational epic in the conventional sense of the term because the paradigm of societal order around which it is structured is too weak to protect individuals from each other's destructiveness. Of course, the fact that *Kyz-Zhibek* is different from typical national epics does not diminish its artistic significance. On the contrary! The narrative focus is on the individual, not on overarching statehood and its representation.

Conceptually, the film is grounded in the assumption that political power has no tools to prevent the lovers' tragedy. In the episodes featuring Adiar, just as in most other scenes of the film, the camera has the dynamic mobility one would expect of a contemporary drama, not of a national legend. The prevailing visual restlessness conveys an atmosphere of instability, which also defines the story's conceptual core: the lovers have no one to turn to for their protection, and judging by the debates among clan leaders, neither does the Kazakh nation. There is no unity between the junior, median, and senior *Juzes*, nor between the clans, *Shekty* and *Zhagalbaily*. Thus, there can be no stability, only a never-ending series of personal and communal clashes and tragedies.

A specific feature of *Kyz-Zhibek* is the relationship between epical elements, defined by the macro framework of yearning for unity for the lovers *and* for the nation, on the one hand, and the poetic elements derived from the romance between Tolegen and the title heroine, on the other. While the epical and the poetic dimensions are logically and causally intertwined, greater weight is given to the love story. Tolegen is a hero: he can fight and is eager to do so when the motherland is threatened, but when he has a choice, he prefers private fulfillment and is more than happy to avoid antagonism.

This makes him a more natural character within the Kazakh context than Bekezhan, as the main existential principle for Kazakh nomadic communities was not expansion but survival. Little wonder, then, that the larger message of national unity did not resonate among these communities as much as within sedentary societies.

Tolegen and Bekezhan stand for two approaches to the prioritization of values among Kazakhs. To Bekezhan, war is the natural state of the world. Anything else is condemned as unmanly and unworthy. He is an aggressor on all levels, personal and social. For him, compromise is not an option; there is only winning or losing. Tolegen constantly attempts to prove to Bekezhan that such a worldview weakens the Kazakh people and threatens their very existence; Kazakhs, he argues, should save their fighting skills for their numerous external enemies and not waste them fighting each other. In part II of the film, it seems as if the competitors find at least some common ground when confronting the intruding Dzhungars. Indeed, on that occasion, both Bekezhan and Tolegen show exemplary courage and skill; their competition plays a positive role and leads to greater success for the community. But Bekezhan cannot accept Tolegen's happiness in his loving relationship with Zhibek. Thus, he kills him right after the jointly achieved victory. The manner in which he carries out his plan is particularly heinous: he encourages his resting comrade to return home to be with Zhibek. Then he shoots him in the back.

Was Tolegen naïve to trust Bekezhan? Certainly, to an extent. But this naïveté was a consequence of his personality and worldview; he lived by the principle of mutual trust, practicing unity and solidarity with his own people and expecting his comrade-in-arms to respond with the same trust. Only when Tolegen is dying does he fully grasp the profound evil that is driving his foe. Only then does he look Bekezhan in the eyes and utters: "So this is what a lowly human being you are!" Remarkably, Bekezhan himself realizes how despicable his behavior is. And yet he is unable to act differently. In a review, the writer Satimzhan Sanbaev generalized the meaning of Tolegen's death with a far-reaching conclusion, indicating that his murder comes across as something to be expected "simply because Tolegen is too graceful, lacks power, and cannot cope with the evil element of the steppe, which gave birth to him."[9] The animal symbolism used in the film may indicate that there can be no resolution to the conflict between Bekezhan and Tolegen and that it is rooted in instincts, in wild nature itself.

In Kazakhstan, *Kyz-Zhibek* triumphed on a scale that nobody could have foreseen. This success was not orchestrated. The picture was released with merely 330 copies, about a third of what was normal for Soviet feature films, which indicates that officials in Alma-Ata and Moscow may have distrusted the film's message, deeming it too nationally specific, or even nationalist.

Whatever the fears of culture hacks may have been, *Kyz-Zhibek* became truly popular, a hit whose longevity in Kazakhstan's cultural memory is unrivaled. In the long term, it gained the affection of millions of viewers who named it as their single favorite picture in Kazakhstani cinema.

Judged solely by its plot, *Kyz-Zhibek* is a Romeo-and-Juliet-style melodrama in historical garb, complemented by a seemingly simple message of national unity. But is this enough to explain its lasting popularity? The film's appeal was primarily national and specifically to Kazakh youths. This is not surprising since its main characters are young and attractive, and their emotions strong and uncompromising. But what truly defined the film's originality and secured its success was that, for the first time, a motion picture openly celebrated Kazakhstani traditions and customs. *Kyz-Zhibek* shows Kazakhstan in full bloom. Although the characters are engaged in life-and-death conflicts, their aesthetic appeal is profound: the costumes they wear are elegant and bright, the dances gracious, and the fights breathtaking. The interactions between men and women are utterly within the defined lines of national tradition and embraced by all characters.

Never before had Kazakhstan been presented on screen with such lavishness. Never before had the nation had a chance to recognize the beauty of its traditional lifestyle and its enduring potential for the future with such undivided enthusiasm. Never before had the private and the national, the natural and the social, been brought into such perfect balance on Kazakh screens. Most importantly, Gabit Musrepov's screenplay and Sultan-Akhmed Khodzhikov's direction remained loyal to the spirit of the original legend and did not, as had often been the case in Soviet cinema, compromise the source by introducing the Marxist concept of class struggle as the root of all antagonism.[10] Instead, the tragedy unfolds when the ethical principles of the ancestors are betrayed. This is what renders *Kyz-Zhibek* at once so authentically Kazakh and so hard for non-Kazakh audiences to appreciate. It made the film a powerful object of identification for native audiences, something no previous feature film had achieved to such an extent.

An assessment of the film's success based exclusively on box office results would be misleading. It was a huge hit in Kazakhstan but much less so in the Russian Federation and the other Soviet republics. *The End of the Ataman*, for example, was three times as successful by the sheer number of viewers (30 million viewers in the first year of release compared to 8 million for *Kyz-Zhibek*). However, success in this case is defined not by box office statistics, but by long-term national impact. The very fact that such a large-scale feature film with a distinctly non-Soviet message could be produced at all is astounding. It may also indicate that a certain faction in Kazakhstan's political leadership was interested in maintaining and developing a sense of national identity through cultural means and was willing to protect it against predictable accusations from Marxist-Leninist dogmatists and their internationalist agenda.

## THE END OF THE ATAMAN

Shaken Aimanov continued his searching for the kind of Kazakh film that would establish a genuine connection with viewers both at home and across the USSR. *Land of the Fathers* was a critical success but a relative failure with respect to the number of viewers it attracted.[11] *Angel in a Cap* was successful in Kazakhstan but was hardly seen outside the republic, most likely due to administrative restrictions. Which topic and what kind of approach would manage to square the circle and satisfy both critics and mass audiences, Kazakh and Soviet spectators?

The 1918–1920 Civil War, with its violent, decade-long aftermath, had always been a favorite subject of Soviet cinema, combining political propaganda and adventurous entertainment. Despite the millions of deaths, starvation, destruction, and indescribable cruelties that defined the Civil War, its popularity as a movie subject began as early as the silent period. Swashbucklers such as *The Gang of Father Knysh* (Banda bat'ki Knysha, 1922) turned the carnage into an exciting "goodies vs. baddies" spectacle in which the political and ideological aspects were secondary. *Little Red Devils* (Krasnye d"iavoliata, 1923), depicting the adventures of teenagers fighting an anti-Soviet gang, was made in Georgia by Russian director Ivan Perestiani and became the first Soviet box office hit, much more in demand than *Battleship Potemkin*, *The Mother*, or Vertov's *Film Truth*. Unlike dogmatic film critics who distrusted the light approach of adventure films, the Communist Party realized that the Civil War adventure genre had huge potential to inspire young Soviet fighters. It was primarily for that reason that the potboiler *Chapaev* (1934) was officially declared a template for the newly formulated doctrine of Socialist Realism: it demonstrated the required ideological commitment, showed recent history in accordance with Communist Party guidelines, and was understood and appreciated by "the people," that is, by millions of viewers. Furthermore, it featured a positive hero who could be embraced and emulated by young and old alike.

During the Thaw, the cinematic image of the Civil War became more complex. However, the mid-1960s marked a return to earlier adventure formulas in which the anti-Bolshevik enemy was shown to be not only on the wrong side of history, but also deplorable and downright stupid. The most spectacular box office hit of the decade was *The Uncatchable Avengers* (Neulovimye mstiteli, 1965), a remake of Perestiani's *Little Red Devils*, which featured "the Whites" and their leader being outfoxed by an international group of young people. This movie and its sequels once again ushered in an era of Civil War adventures that pleased both the communist establishment and millions of regular Soviet viewers.

The film studios of Central Asia contributed to this boom in their own way, combining clear ideological messages with action-centered plots. There were exceptions, however, such as Abdulla Karsakbaev's *A Worrisome Morning*. Its depiction of the Civil War was that of a national tragedy, foreshadowing the impending Stalinist purges.

Conspicuously, when Shaken Aimanov turned to the Civil War theme, he did not continue the path of historical-philosophical exploration begun by Karsakbaev, but emulated the linear model of the "Eastern," in which the ideology was in clear accordance with official guidelines, action was primary, and philosophical aspects secondary. This may have been precisely the formula of success, as Aimanov churned out one of the most spectacular hits of Kazakhstani cinema, indeed, one of the most exemplary "Easterns" of all time.

The screenplay of *The End of the Ataman* was written by Andrei Mikhalkov-Konchalovskii and Eduard Tropinin.[12] Mikhalkov-Konchalovskii had professional and personal ties to Central Asia. His debut, *The First Teacher* (Pervyi uchitel', 1965), adapted from a story by Kyrgyz author Chingiz Aitmatov, was recognized at the Venice film festival, winning Kazakh actress Natal'ia Arinbasarova the Volpi Cup as Best Female Lead. Mikhalkov-Konchalovskii had an eye for effective subject matter and supplied filmmakers in Central Asia with some excellent screenplays. Tropinin's contribution is harder to assess. As an active KGB officer, he dealt with Central Asia and Afghanistan in his line of work and had access to secret files. In the case of *The End of the Ataman* this privilege was essential, since its topic is a secret service operation the circumstances of which were never fully disclosed: the assassination of a White Army commander, Ataman Dutov, by Soviet agents in 1921.

Despite his decision to make a film in the framework of the mainstream Eastern, Aimanov's film is not purely action-oriented. The episodes preparing the viewer for the showdown are conceptually as significant as the assassination itself. Aimanov introduces his main character, the Bolshevik secret service agent Kasymkhan Chadiarov (Asanali Ashimov), in an intimate situation, sleeping at home, surrounded by his family. After quietly getting up, he tenderly kisses his child. This opening imbues the image of the secret agent with humanity and emotional vulnerability.[13] However, in the following episode, Chadiarov allows an anti-Soviet saboteur to escape, which undermines the viewer's trust in his honesty. We learn that he was an aristocrat by birth and had a bourgeois upbringing before joining the communists. Many of his comrades in the Special Commission (*Chrezvychainaia Komissiia*, *ChK*, or *Cheka*, the predecessor organization to the GPU and KGB) dislike him because of his pedigree. Their worst suspicions seem to come true when Chadiarov is arrested as an anti-Bolshevik agent, before managing to escape from his cell. Even his wife, to whom he bids farewell, curses him when she learns that he intends to cross the border. Only later does the viewer begin to realize that the whole story of arrest and escape was an elaborate cover-up, meant to provide Chadiarov with a believable narrative to win the trust of the nearby White Army units and their commander. There is just one other ChK official who knows the truth about Chadiarov's mission, and he is guarding this secret to ensure the success of the operation to assassinate Dutov. A secondary task is the unmasking of an agent of the Whites who is suspected of clandestinely working inside the local ChK office supplying the enemy with classified information.

Now on enemy territory, the stone-faced Chadiarov plays the role of a former prince who never really gave up his tsarist convictions, with chilling perfection. He demonstrates the intricacies of spying, sharing them with the viewer only in extreme close-ups, for example, when marking the doors of his closet with a hair.

For Soviet viewers, the underlying plot pattern of a Soviet, that is, "one of us," who is secretly infiltrating enemy structures, was always intriguing. In the 1970s, the television miniseries *Seventeen Moments of Spring* (Semnadtsat' mgnovenii vesny, 1973), featuring a Soviet agent within Nazi Germany's highest echelons of power, became one of the most popular television events of all time. Aimanov's film preceded *Seventeen Moments*: the filmmaker's ability to sense Soviet audiences' readiness for this type of plot put Kazakh-Soviet cinema in a pioneering position. The ambiguity of the main character, a man with highly developed skills in mimicry who impersonates a traitor, fooling both the enemy and, by necessity, his own comrades, produces an endless line of suspenseful situations and a high degree of psychological intrigue. After all, the viewer can never be sure whether the main character is for real or just faking his political convictions. The plot pattern thus indirectly reflected the reality of totalitarian society experienced daily by the audience. Moreover, such plots are cinematically efficient, placing great importance on minuscule gestures or mimics that the viewer must recognize while the enemy in the movie must not, inviting a clever kind of viewer identification.

In respect to historical complexity, though, *The End of the Ataman* marks a step back from *A Worrisome Morning* because the main character's ambiguity does not reflect the real dilemma of a patriotic Kazakh communist but is merely a trick to achieve success in an officially approved intelligence operation. Aimanov's Chadiarov has no doubts regarding the legitimacy of his spy work; he just pretends to have switched sides in order to convince the anti-Bolshevik forces of his loyalty toward their movement. Thus, what was an existential conflict for Baitenov, becomes for Chadiarov a mere pretext for a political assassination plot. In this regard, *The End of the Ataman* is much closer to the conventional "Easterns" than Karsakbaev's 1966 picture.

Besides being a solid example of Civil War adventure, Aimanov's film has elements of a docudrama, in which the reconstruction of the historical facts outweighs the conventions of genre and plot. While viewers, especially children, hardly worry about factual accuracy, the story of Chadiarov's assassination of ataman Dutov has acquired new relevance in independent Kazakhstan. The historical facts behind it are still debated.

General Aleksandr Dutov (1879–1921) was born into an Orenburg Cossack family; his ancestors had fought for the Russian Empire in Central Asia. Dutov's military career suggests that he was a courageous man who repeatedly volunteered for duty on the front lines and was severely wounded in action. Politically, he supported the February Revolution and the bourgeois provisional government.[14] Dutov was the first ataman to refuse to recognize the legitimacy of the October Revolution. He successfully led a Cossack campaign against Bolshevik troops, freeing the entire Orenburg region and endorsing the administration of Admiral Kolchak. Upon the defeat of his army, he withdrew to Suidun in China, where he was killed on February 21, 1921 by a group of special agents led by Kasymkhan Chanyshev, allegedly a Uighur or Tatar prince working for the ChK. Chanyshev is the historical prototype for the film's hero, Chadiarov. But whether it was really Chanyshev or a member of his group who killed the ataman in his office is still a matter of disagreement.[15] So is Chanyshev's life after accomplishing his mission and returning to Kazakhstan. The latter aspect of his biography, namely, that an erstwhile hero of Soviet intelligence could end up in the grinders of the 1930s purges, was conspicuously anticipated in Karsakbaev's *Worrisome Morning* but completely avoided in *The End of the Ataman*, which remains ideologically Orthodox from the first shot to the last.

As for the title hero, Soviet historians preferred to depict Ataman Dutov as a one-dimensional, negative figure, a militant enemy of the new communist order whose assassination was justified. The fact that Dutov opposed both the tsarist order and the communists (whom he regarded as German agents) was usually not mentioned. Nor was the character of Chadiarov's historical prototype discussed in any depth. One of the officially distributed versions described Kasymkhan Chanyshev as a pro-Bolshevik loyalist who led a local militia unit; later versions denied his alliance with the Bolsheviks, claiming that the real Chanyshev was trading opium for gold. In the film, Chadiarov's illegal trade is mentioned, but as a cover-up, that is, drug trafficking was an instrument cleverly used to help Chadiarov disguise his operation to assassinate Dutov. Most documents agree that the deadly shots were fired by a member of Chanyshev's group, the Uighur Khodzhamiarov. Why, then, did the film position Chanyshev/Chadiarov at the very center, making him the assassin and elevating him to the status of superhero?

This emphasis points to an implicit polemics against the traditional communist conviction that a person's class origins determine his political viewpoint. Indeed, if that dogmatic concept were true, a man like Chadiarov, that is, a prince whose family members suffered under the new regime and whose immediate family was possibly taken hostage by the secret service to force him to carry out the assault, could never have joined the Bolshevik intelligence community out of conviction. But in *The End of the Ataman*, Chadiarov's inner beliefs outweigh his class origins. That is why the screenplay, rather than picking one of the conflicting historical versions (drug dealer, secret service member, or hired killer), combines them into one, making a case for trust among likeminded people despite their appearance or class origins. For Mikhalkov-Konchalovskii, himself offspring of an aristocratic family, this circumstance was of principal significance. Issues of trust and distrust were likewise essential for Aimanov, who had to face them several times over the course of his career.

While *The End of the Ataman* is ideologically much more simple than other Kazakh Easterns, it would be inaccurate to categorize the film as pure propaganda fare. Rather, in a backhanded manner, the authors inserted some taboos into the film. For example, when Chadiarov tries to convince his wealthy Chinese uncle that his defection from the Bolsheviks was for real, he declares: "I changed my views when I saw the Bolsheviks executing forty-seven honest Kazakhs who wanted to see their homeland free." This is obviously an allusion to the Alash-Orda movement and their government, although neither is mentioned by name.

What is truly simplistic in the film is its depiction of the anticommunist forces, which exceeds even the usual clichés. It is noteworthy that the most off-putting character in the film is not Dutov himself, although he comes across as vain and buffoonish, but the head of his secret service. An archpriest (*protoierei*) by the name of Iona, he is depicted as a ruthless cynic who runs his highly efficient agency on both sides of the border. The film's portrayal of a man of the church as a cold-blooded killer and secret service operative reveals the aggressive anticlerical and anti-Orthodox line promoted by the Communist Party in the 1960s when the film was conceived. One reviewer insisted that Dutov was supported by this shady figure (described in the article as a monk-priest [hieromonachos/*ieromonakh*]), a man who tried to take over the command after Dutov's assassination.[16] The claim becomes downright insulting when "Father Iona" is shown conducting a religious service. In hindsight, given the available information on the corruption of numerous Orthodox officials by the *Communist* establishment, such a denunciation of the church as a haven for secret service activities acquires a bitterly ironic taste, although certainly not in the way in which the film's creators intended.

Upon its release, *The End of the Ataman* was viewed first and foremost through the prism of its genre, as a historical detective yarn and Civil War adventure, which also implied the status of an artistic lightweight.[17] This classification lowered critical expectations and rendered any artistic achievement in a film of that category a pleasant surprise. Indeed, Aimanov features several complex issues that are not always immediately obvious. These include the originality of the central character, a prince turned Bolshevik agent and assassin; the problem of weighing trust against distrust among Bolsheviks engaged in a war against the class enemy; and the legitimacy of resistance against imposed Bolshevization. Of course, the latter aspect is denounced rather than taken seriously. Dutov and his entourage are depicted as an anachronistic assembly of has-beens who simply cannot understand that their time is up; they are never given a chance to express any genuine political and ideological conviction. This is an unfortunate omission, since in reality, Dutov did write about mourning the disappearance of his homeland (referring both to the Orenburg region and to Russia at large) in emotionally charged statements. Moreover, the historical Dutov maintained a relatively consistent political worldview, rejecting both monarchism and Bolshevism. None of this is mentioned in the film. The only aspect that is verbalized, in a debate between Dutov and Chadiarov, is the issue of Kazakhstan's independence. The ataman makes it very clear that, upon victory, he does not intend to grant the people of Central Asia any form of political sovereignty and that Cossack rule will continue. That was indeed his viewpoint and may explain why the negative image of the ataman has not been revised in post-communist decades.

As for Aimanov's direction, his focus in *The End of the Ataman* is on the actors. The performances are brilliant, above all those of Asanali Ashimov in the role of Chadiarov and Vladislav Strzhelchik as Dutov. Chadiarov's encounter with Ataman Dutov quickly turns into a duel of two minds, in which the Bolshevik agent proves to be superior. Dutov is portrayed as a vainglorious poseur whose initial distrust vis-à-vis Chadiarov is dispersed precisely because the agent exploits the commander's vanity. In *The End of the Ataman*, Aimanov also managed to create a number of atmospherically intense episodes in the wilderness, for example, at the border river and in the desert. However, the many lengthy interior episodes reek of studio artificiality due to their unimaginative decoration and excessive lighting. For Aimanov, that represented a step back. Unlike *Land of the Fathers*, whose black-and-white images are richly textured, the visual plane in *The End of the Ataman*, filmed in color and widescreen, suffers from static staleness (Askhat Ashrapov was responsible for the cinematography).

Still, while the film can hardly be called a masterpiece, it represents solid genre fare within a stiff Soviet ideological framework. To this day, *The End of the Ataman* is Kazakhstan's most successful motion picture in terms of viewership, with over 30 million spectators in its first year of release. It also motivated other directors to try out the "Eastern" subgenre, although Aimanov's film remained somewhat exceptional due to its epical approach: with a two-and-a-half-hours running time, it was released in two parts, an anomaly for a thriller. Once the main plotline is clear, the narration slows down significantly. And, while *The End of the Ataman* is never boring, some episodes could have been condensed without any loss of narrative logic or psychological depth. On the positive side, Aimanov demonstrated that, as a distinct subgenre, the Civil War adventure is elastic enough to allow for individual variations, whether in respect to camera work or acting style.

And yet, when viewed as the swan song (inadvertent though it was) of Aimanov's remarkable career in cinema, this is a strange film. On the one hand, as a filmmaker Aimanov was finally able to reach a huge audience. On the other, the screenplay was ideologically reductionist and predictable, simplifying the real political situation in Central Asia to the point of falsification. However, just as in the case of *Amangeldy*, none of this mattered to regular viewers. Chadiarov was accepted and endorsed as a new type of *national superhero*. Unlike Amangeldy, his outspoken predecessor from three decades earlier, Chadiarov perfected the art of social mimicry while keeping a warm heart beneath his impenetrable surface. The Kazakh spy's ability to adjust his behavior for the purpose of survival and success won him millions of young and adult admirers.

Aimanov conveniently eliminated any differentiation within the White movement, let alone the Bolsheviks, suggesting that fellow Soviet agents' hostility toward Chadiarov was based on a misunderstanding. Thus, the film's political logic is entirely pro-Soviet. But historical accuracy was secondary for the tens of millions of viewers who adored a newborn super-agent.

The primary factor that made *The End of the Ataman* legendary was that its superhero was presented as an authentic *Kazakh*. Chadiarov's manliness and wit, his ability to completely control his reactions, his transitions from cold-blooded operator to loving father, husband, and loyal comrade established an image of unprecedented physical and psychological superiority, truly a *batyr* for the twentieth century. And, remarkably, the film features no Russian guide who would lead the Kazakh in the right direction: Chadiarov is sovereign and independent in his knowledge, precision, and decision-making. Thus, although the film's Soviet ideological framework was unquestionable, the elevation of a Kazakh secret agent to superhero status was Mikhalkov-Konchalovskii's, Aimanov's and Ashimov's true discovery.

Kazakhfilm studio produced three sequels to *The End of the Ataman*, all of them inferior to Aimanov's original. But they, too, were commercially successful, albeit not to the same extent as the first film. Since the time between the sequels was quite long and they were helmed by different directors, the lack of stylistic or conceptual consistency between them is not surprising. The only unifying element of the four Chadiarov films is their lead actor, Asanali Ashimov, for whom the franchise became the vehicle to all-Soviet stardom. Just as in the case of Aimanov's original, the sequels' popularity has nothing to do with historical verisimilitude, which became more questionable with every new installment.

Seven years after *The End of the Ataman*, *Trans-Siberian Express* (Transsibirskii ekspress, 1978) was made from a screenplay by Nikita Mikhalkov and Eldor Urazbaev; the latter also directed. The most obvious difference between Aimanov's film and its first successor is that *Trans-Siberian Express* gave up any epic ambitions. The new film was a historical thriller, running about half the time of the first installment. The narration is noticeably faster. Compared to Aimanov's deliberate pensiveness, Urazbaev preferred dynamic editing and relatively brief episodes. Moreover, the film is filled with action and violence, unlike *The End of the Ataman*, in which the violent culmination (the killing of Ataman Dutov) was prepared for with over two hours of relatively limited movement. In *Trans-Siberian Express*, the fast-paced narration is likely a response to the changing viewing habits of Soviet audiences, which were by then being shaped by hugely successful Western action imports to Soviet screens, but also due to a shift in genre: while the central character is still the spy Chadiarov, *Trans-Siberian Express* is not so much an "Eastern" as a political thriller. It reveals the influence of the Italian mafia flics that were en vogue in the 1970s, when directors such as Damiano Damiani became household names in the Soviet Union. Also, while the background of *Trans-Siberian Express* is historical, its political undertones clearly refer to the 1970s and the period of détente.

*Trans-Siberian Express* takes place in 1927. The influential Japanese industrialist Saito is the target of sinister Western secret service schemes occasioned by his announcement that he intends to establish business ties with the fledgling Soviet Union. A sniper shoots Saito's daughter who was on the verge of getting married. But this tragedy does not deter the aging businessman, whose suspicions regarding the reasons for the assassination are spot on. Chadiarov, who now lives under the name Kasymkhanov in Harbin, the center of White emigration to China, is chosen by anti-Soviet intelligence operatives to kill Saito on his way from the Far East to Moscow. Little do they know that this very Kasymkhanov, posing as a dimwitted Kazakh émigré who is wanted by the Soviets because he escaped from the Red Army, is the high-profile secret agent Chadiarov, the killer of Ataman Dutov six years earlier.

The White emigration is depicted as one gigantic mafia with close ties to global anticommunist intelligence networks and organized crime. Throughout the film, this denunciatory claim is complemented by another, more philosophical discourse on what it means to have a homeland. The patriotic discourse gives *Trans-Siberian Express* a certain poetic tone. For example, when the train taking Saito and his detractors to Russia moves into Soviet Kazakhstan, we see fascinating images of the steppe, with people running toward and waving at the passengers. These images are accompanied by dombra tunes, giving them an unusual intensity: this is Kazakhstan as seen through the eyes of Kasymkhanov/Chadiarov, who has not been able to visit his country for six years and dreams about his native *aul*, his wife and his child, the latter representing another visual motif that reappears at regular intervals. Deep in his soul, this stone-faced spy and skillful impersonator maintains an intense love for his homeland and her people, as well as for his mother tongue.

The same sinister intelligence operatives who conceived Saito's assassination force Kasymkhanov to take a "wife" with him on the train. This woman, Aleksandra, is an arrogant, cold, and blasé member of the White movement who flatly denies having any feelings for her Russian motherland or for anything or anyone else. However, at the end of the film, when she realizes both her personal loneliness and the fact that the operation has been a complete fiasco, she suddenly experiences an outburst of emotions triggered by the encounter with her native land. The Kasymkhanov-Aleksandra polarization represents the motivational gap between the film's positive and negative personae: the former are not just communists but also Kazakh and Russian patriots who work for the future of their Soviet homeland, while the latter have lost their roots forever.

The screenwriter of *The End of the Ataman*, Andrei Mikhalkov-Konchalovskii, also contributed to the script of *Trans-Siberian Express*. The nature of his work is not exactly discernible, but one may assume that it has to do with the character of Aizhan, a young Kazakh woman portrayed by Mikhalkov-Konchalovskii's then-wife, Natal'ia Arinbasarova. Aizhan is a member of the Komsomol communist youth organization who is traveling on the fateful train in a third-class compartment. Alas, the episodes involving Aizhan are utterly preposterous. Kasymkhanov, who addresses her in Kazakh and learns that she is from his native *aul*, asks her to perform an important task, helping him to expose who the anti-Soviet spies on the train are. Aizhan succeeds brilliantly. Later, she rides on a horse next to the fast-moving train, trying to tell Kasymkhanov about the danger he is in—a James-Bond-type stunt bordering on self-parody.

Despite such shortcomings, *Trans-Siberian Express* was a box office hit and to this day has its share of admirers among Kazakh viewers. It is easy to see why: the film is one of the few Soviet thrillers to truly be worthy of the name. Its dramatic tension is enhanced by the enclosed space of the train, where three quarters of the action takes place. The atmosphere on a Soviet train is captured realistically. For Kazakhfilm studio, delivering a hit that attracted over 15 million viewers across the Soviet Union, was a bright spot in the otherwise lackluster 1970s.

Following two major hits, namely, *Kyz-Zhibek* and *The End of the Ataman*, that raised the reputation of Kazakhfilm studio within Soviet cinema, the national film community had to reassess its achievements and determine the future trajectory of Kazakh cinema. The annual production volume of Kazakhfilm was too small to allow for much experimentation. The genres that viewers inside and outside the republic were sure to appreciate were historical action, comedies, and children's films. Contemporary dramas were a slippery slope, as Aimanov, Begalin, and Khodzhikov had learned in the early 1960s. Films about the Great Patriotic War with a specific Kazakh angle offered sufficient room for artistic and thematic innovation, as did the "Eastern," the Central Asian variety of Civil War adventure, although the latter was fraught with conceptual risks because of certain taboo aspects of Kazakhstan's history in the 1910s–1920s. The biopic had lost its significance as a national identity-defining genre altogether.

*Kyz-Zhibek* was an artistic and national triumph, while *The End of the Ataman* became an unprecedented all-Soviet box office hit, the largest Kazakhstani cinema had ever produced. But Aimanov's tragic passing on December 23, 1970, thrust the Kazakh film community into a state of shock. In the blink of an eye, it had lost its towering leadership figure whose authority and openness to artistic innovation had supplied the country's growing film industry with constructive energy as well as administrative and political protection. To some, Aimanov's death appeared to be an omen. The subsequent development of Kazakhstan's cinema in the 1970s seemed to justify those premonitions: it was a period in which indistinct movies constituted the majority and outstanding films were few and far between. Most importantly, the political pressures on filmmakers grew substantially.

Imagining how Kazakhstani cinema would have developed had Aimanov lived and remained actively involved is not fruitless speculation. After all, he had planned to adapt Mukhtar Auezov's multi-volume epic *The Path of Abai*. Shortly before his death, he directed the play *Abai* for the Theater of the Young Viewer in Almaty, an indicator of the consistency and seriousness of his intentions. The envisioned film had the potential to become an epical manifesto for Kazakh culture, likely as significant for Kazakhstan's national identity as *Kyz-Zhibek*. It is hard to imagine any other director taking over that project.

On April 13, 1971, the fourth plenum of the Union of Kazakhstani Film Workers took place. It elected Akim Tarazi (real name: Akim Ashimov)[18] to the position of first secretary, replacing Shaken Aimanov. Tarazi had made a name for himself as an excellent screenwriter, particularly with *The Traces Go Beyond the Horizon* (1964) and *A Shot at the Karash Passage* (1968). However, it was doubtful whether he would be able to fill Aimanov's shoes, first and foremost because Aimanov held enormous authority not just in Kazakhstan but throughout the Soviet Union and had influential friends in Moscow as well. Tarazi would hold the position of first secretary until 1980, overseeing a period of political repression and loss of quality in Kazakhstani cinema.

## BACKLASH

By the late 1960s, the grassroots democratic impulses of the Thaw were largely neutralized and the Soviet intelligentsia's hopes for the continued liberalization of Soviet society had been crushed. In lieu of genuine liberties, some cultural compromises offered by the CPSU establishment created convenient niches for dissatisfied intellectual groups that were accompanied by ongoing cat-and-mouse games between dissidents and the secret service. The Brezhnev administration prioritized détente stability externally and moderate consumerism internally.

For the cinema of Kazakhstan, this political framework was not beneficial. Already in the early 1970s, when it seemed that Kazakh filmmakers had gained a sure footing and might be on their way to continuous national and international significance, there were signals that the continuation of the paths begun with *Land of the Fathers*, *A Worrisome Morning*, *The Song of Manshuk*, and *Kyz-Zhibek* was not seen as desirable in some quarters of the communist establishment. It is not clear whether this was an outcome of the usual center-periphery constellation that guarded internationalist principles against any trends toward national cultural emancipation, or of a split within Kazakhstan's communist establishment, perhaps along ethnic lines, or both. The exact relationship between the Kazakhfilm studio administration, Communist Party factions (some of which may have been positively inclined toward a stronger emphasis on Kazakhstani cultural tradition) and other players is difficult to reconstruct fifty years later, especially since the relevant archives are largely inaccessible. What was obvious in the aftermath of Shaken Aimanov's tragic death was the power vacuum left by the loss of this most authoritative defender of Kazakh filmmakers' artistic ambitions. Whether the authority of Olzhas Suleimenov, Mazhit Begalin, Sultan Khodzhikov, and Abdulla Karsakbaev would be sufficient to maintain an atmosphere of aesthetic openness and growing national self-confidence, and to preserve the loyalty of a large native audience, was now an open question.

The decline in overall quality in Kazakhfilm studio's production indicates that some members of the political leadership and their representatives at the studio were willing to accept thematic boredom and aesthetic blandness instead of risking subversion of any kind; others, openly or quietly, disagreed with this opportunism. Assessing the output of Kazakhfilm studio after *Kyz-Zhibek* and *The End of the Ataman*, it is undeniable that official tolerance for thematically convenient, politically safe, and mediocre films increased. Aesthetic inertia marked the true "stagnation" in Soviet-Kazakh culture, whose regrettable effects could be observed not just in Kazakhstani but, to a varying degree, in all national film cultures of the Soviet Union in the 1970s and early 1980s.

Still, the situation was never simple. It is well known that Kazakhstan's powerful Communist Party leader, Dinmukhamed Kunaev, the highest arbiter in all controversial cases, tried to maintain amicable relations with the native intelligentsia, including the film community. But he, too, had to take into account signals coming from the center that demanded a more controlling and repressive attitude with respect to artistic innovation and thematic daring.

To understand the impact on Kazakhstani cinema of what was later called "stagnation," it is essential to look at the release history of specific films. In this regard, the 1970s were the first conflict-ridden decade in the history of national cinema, when a total of seven Kazakh feature films were banned. A somewhat milder category of censorship was the limited release granted to certain films, allowing them to be shown only in the Kazakh SSR but not in the USSR. Those films were also barred from export to other countries.[19]

Of all the shelved Kazakhstani films, *The Funeral Feast* (1972) was the first and arguably most prominent victim of the state's anti-liberal rollback strategy. Helmed by Turkmen director Bulat Mansurov,[20] it was adapted from a poem by Ilias Dzhansugurov, who had perished during the Stalinist repressions in the 1930s and who also happened to be an early Kazakh film pioneer.

*The Funeral Feast* is marked by several features indicating high artistic ambition: Its screenplay is based on a literary text that had been recognized as aesthetically exceptional; the picture is deeply national in spirit and style; and it has a parabolic substructure that allows for far-reaching philosophical and sociopolitical generalizations.

The film's working title was that of Dzhansugurov's original poem, *Kulager*, which is the name of the main character's favorite horse. That central character, famed poet Akan-Sery, was a real historical person. For Akan-Sery, the horse Kulager embodies the ideals of strength and beauty, which are as significant to him as are justice and truth. At the funeral feast for the powerful *bay* Sagynbai, Akan-Sery (Kargambai Sataev) appears as the maverick who breaks social and political taboos, utters inconvenient truths, and challenges the clans' upper stratum, demanding freedom and justice for the commoners. What appears like an unachievable goal suddenly seems in reach during the sacred rituals. An ancient rule stipulates that the owner of the horse that wins the race in honor of the deceased shall be granted a wish. Akan-Sery leaves no doubt that he will demand freedom for the people as the reward for his horse's victory. This is a prospect that horrifies those in power, so much so that they resort to an unspeakable crime, having the beautiful Kulager killed to prevent Akan-Sery from achieving victory.

At the beginning, the film's credits explicitly point to the year when this event took place: 1876. But the way in which Mansurov visualizes the story goes beyond historical concreteness, aiming to transcend history in pursuit of philosophical generalization. First and foremost, *The Funeral Feast* is a parable dealing with certain aspects of the human condition per se. In true parabolic fashion, each of the main characters stands for a larger concept. The new *bay* embodies ruthless ambition but also the fragility of power; the leader of a mutiny, who is about to be exiled, stands for the grassroots yearning for freedom; and the poet Akan-Sery embodies both the might and the impotence of art, which can engage with the powerful and voice the needs and desires of the disenfranchised but little more than that. Another symbolic character is the sycophant, a sellout artist whom Akan-Sery challenges. When provoked, this opportunist discloses his cynical worldview, based on the assumption that the people in whom Akan believes are in reality just a cowardly crowd and that the strict hierarchy, corrupt though it may be, is vital to a functioning order.

To be sure, Akan-Sery's worldview is not entirely rational; he appears to be yearning for self-sacrifice, driven by the desire to be not just a poet, but a grandiose hero. He risks the life of his famous horse to win the competition and even allows his little deaf-mute son to ride Kulager at the races, enhancing his chance to win due to the latter's light weight. The stakes are high and even existential for Akan, as if his sacrifice was intended to set an example for all to see, an act to be emulated by the people whose freedom he so cherishes.

Despite its strong parabolic dimension, the film's plot unfolds within a clearly defined cultural space, using a wealth of Kazakhstani specifics. The funeral feast resembles a festival. Characters address each other with songs, expressing their view on issues such as love, dignity, and freedom. There is always a crowd of spectators in the background ("the people") who are watching and reacting collectively, like the choir in a Greek tragedy. When speaking and singing, individual characters are mindful of those spectators' presence and reactions. But in parallel to the ritualized presentations, one can also detect an underlying discourse of realpolitik: For example, the widow of the deceased whispers schemes into the ear of the new bay, Batrashbay. As the prospect of another rebellion fills the air, the instigators of the previous mutiny lie tied up for all to see amid the somber festivities.

The real tension in the closed space of the feast results from the deep gap between the spoken and the unspoken, that is, the words and lyrics uttered and sung, on the one hand, and the unspeakable (the social taboos) on the other. It is Akan-Sery who acts as a mediator between these two spheres, and all sides respect him for his ability to do so. Yet, he, too, is fully aware that "He who speaks the truth gets chased from all homes." Akan-Sery symbolizes the glory and the misery of the great artist and his literal homelessness in a world rent by irreconcilable tensions.

Stylistically, *The Funeral Feast* is close to *Kyz-Zhibek*, a deeply national picture that demonstrated the enormous aesthetic potential of Kazakh traditional art for cinema and for evoking lively reactions from native audiences. Nurgisa Tlendiev, one of Kazakhstan's leading composers, wrote the scores for both films; dynamic and passionate, they rely on national musical patterns and instrumentation. A major cinematic inspiration for *The Funeral Feast* that has rarely been mentioned by critics was Sergei Paradjanov's *Shadows of Forgotten Ancestors* (Tini zabutykh predkiv/Teni zabytykh predkov, 1964), a radical eye-opener in the 1960s that had demonstrated to stunned Soviet and international audiences the degree to which the modern art of cinema could absorb folkloric and mythical impulses. No less of an influence appears to have been Paradjanov's maligned and mutilated *Color of Pomegranates* (Nran guyne/Tsvet granata, 1969), a picture that further tested the limits of Soviet film aesthetics. Devoted to a medieval artist, it explored the trials and tribulations of artistic and intellectual creativity in an unwelcoming environment.

Mansurov conceptualized *The Funeral Feast* in a reminiscent manner, insisting on the coexistence of realistic and artificial elements, regardless of how disturbing this might be for an unprepared viewer. Due to numerous editorial intrusions, the film's last redaction diminished these elements. However, even in the redacted version, Kazakh folklore visually and musically dominates most scenes.

After the groundbreaking success of *Kyz-Zhibek*, *The Funeral Feast* could have become the second in a potentially steady line of national mythological epics. Indeed, while *Kyz-Zhibek* brought out the beautiful and tragic richness of the Kazakh cultural tradition, *The Funeral Feast* exposed its subversive political potential. That subversion was authentic and not retroactively projected so as to establish an artificial parallel with modern dissident artists: subversion of the status quo had always been an integral element of Kazakhstani culture, be it the traveling minstrels who radically criticized the powers-that-be or the *aitys* competitions in which predecessors to modern-day standup comedians violated norms that in normal life had to be observed at all cost. Both politically and aesthetically, *The Funeral Feast* could have played a groundbreaking role in Kazakhstani cinema, similar to that of *Shadows of Forgotten Ancestors* in Ukrainian cinema (which, interestingly, was directed by a non-native just as *The Funeral Feast*). However, the film's eventual withdrawal from postproduction and shelving interrupted a development that seemed natural and desired both by filmmakers and by audiences. What had happened?

Russian film historian Valerii Fomin, who keenly followed the production of the erstwhile *Kulager* from its inception,[21] devoted a chapter in his book *Prohibited Films*[22] to *The Funeral Feast*. For Fomin, a major factor contributing to the difficulties was the personality of its director. Bulat Mansurov was known as a forthright and fearless man who was constantly striving for the ideal and never willing to compromise. In addition, his nonchalant way of dealing with Kazakh specifics made him vulnerable to accusations of acting like an arrogant foreigner who did not understand the peculiarities of the host country's culture.

Mansurov's debut, *The Contest* (Shukur-Bakshi/Sostiazanie, 1964), had catapulted him into the ranks of the most promising Central Asian filmmakers. *Kulager*'s subject matter seemed ideally suited for a worthy response to other Soviet films about uncompromising artists who had to define their mission in harsh times, most prominently Tarkovskii's *Andrei Rublev* (1966). However, in the early 1970s, Moscow censors had learned to decipher subversive subtexts in seemingly inoffensive genres such as myth and biopic. In a parallel manner, many educated viewers in the Soviet bloc had acquired a stunning refinement in detecting dissidence in all arts. Responding to this new situation, Soviet censorial authorities in the 1970s were stricter than ever in neutralizing such hidden political explosives. In *The Funeral Feast*, the role of the artist as the speaker of truth vis-à-vis an establishment guided solely by power considerations could easily be interpreted as a parable about contemporary Soviet dissidents facing a dictatorial establishment, while the despicable sellouts at the *bay*'s court could be identified as opportunistic intellectuals belonging to the communist establishment. To send dissidents into exile was an increasingly common practice in the USSR by the early 1970s, precisely as the Kazakh *bays* had handled inconvenient artists a century earlier. Thus, the political teeth of *The Funeral Feast* were sharp enough to awaken communist cultural watchdogs.

Fomin opines that Mansurov was so open in expressing his film's political agenda that his picture was no longer a parable but a head-on provocation. "Perhaps most horrifying in Akan-Sery's life was that the people, deformed and intimidated by those in power, did not support their poet and champion precisely in the moment when the poet-mutineer cast a direct challenge to the powerful."[23] In addition to the aforementioned points, critic and filmmaker

Serik Raibaev identified what he called "mistakes" that were found in *The Funeral Feast*, including the distortion of the physical appearance of the Kazakh people and their customs.[24] The film's peculiar aesthetics also made it an easy target for accusations of incomprehensibility, which are not altogether unfounded.

After viewing the raw cut, the Main Administration of Feature Films in Moscow (Goskino) issued a memorandum containing a list of critical demands and suggestions. Although they acknowledged that the unfinished film featured impressive color sequences and rich details showcasing the national traditional lifestyle (*byt*), the overall structure of the material was not considered cohesive with respect to plot and concept. Another point raised by the Moscow authorities was that the people in whose name the main character acts are depicted as a gray, faceless, and passive mass. The plot, they contended, was sometimes difficult to follow; the division into chapters[25] was unnecessary and should be abolished; there were naturalistic details[26] that had to be removed. The official assessment ended with an ultimatum, stating that the film could only be released when all these demands were met.[27]

Amid the turbulences surrounding *The Funeral Feast*, the Film Commission of the Kazakhstani SSR sent a new, modified version of the picture to Moscow for approval on March 27, 1972, revealing surprising stamina on behalf of the periphery vis-à-vis the Soviet center. It then took over a year of debates behind closed doors for the chief redactor of Goskino, Dal' Orlov, to sign a document giving permission for a limited release in Kazakhstan (March 28, 1973), but not in the USSR at large. However, the First Secretary of the Communist Party of Kazakhstan, Dinmukhamed Kunaev, personally disapproved of the film, which sealed its fate. In the late 1970s, Mansurov made an attempt to save his picture by agreeing to cuts, but to no avail. Only a decade later, in February 1987, did the premiere of *The Funeral Feast* take place at the Moscow House of Cinema. The event became part of the rehabilitation of a long line of previously shelved films. However, Mansurov's aesthetic and political radicalness, which would certainly have rendered his Kazakh picture an important event in the early 1970s, perhaps with international resonance, was no longer apparent in the context of glasnost liberalization. In the highly politicized atmosphere of perestroika, when breaking taboos of the Soviet past and present mattered more than aesthetic innovation, this extraordinary Kazakh film was now of mere historical interest.

Viewing *The Funeral Feast* in a post-Soviet context, its sophisticated usage of color is still fascinating and deserves thorough analysis. Similarly, comparing the film to other pictures about great artists that caused a "silent revolution" in Soviet cinema in the 1960s, followed by a turn toward reflectiveness and introversion in intellectual cinema (the aforementioned *Andrei Rublev* and *The Color of Pomegranate*, as well as Giorgi Shengelaia's

*Pirosmani* belong in this category), appears promising. Because *The Funeral Feast* was never fully included in the canon of Kazakh cinema (where, in my view, it belongs) even after it was released in 1987, it is also not present in the consciousness of modern Kazakh viewers. Its full critical and historical rehabilitation is still lacking.

## NATURAL NONCONFORMISM: *WHERE THE MOUNTAINS ARE WHITE*

While *The Funeral Feast* managed to achieve at least limited prominence during the perestroika period as belonging to the now honorable category of formerly shelved films, another extraordinary picture was largely forgotten: *Where the Mountains Are White* (Tam, gde gory belye,[28] 1973). Less politically subversive than *The Funeral Feast*, this story of an old man and his friendship with a white camel is a poetic gem with deep philosophical grounding. To understand the reasons for its shelving (permission for its release was only granted in 1991), it is essential to reconstruct the cultural context from which this film emerged.

Among the few areas that were open for limited critical discourse in the Soviet Union in the 1970s was environment protection. The catastrophic pollution of rivers, the reckless wasting of natural resources by inefficient Soviet agriculture, and out-of-control urbanization sounded the alarms among Soviet intellectuals. Interestingly, protecting the environment was also one of the few issues that united liberal and conservative factions within the intelligentsia, albeit for different reasons. The so-called village prose (*derevenskaia proza*), which emerged in Russia in the mid-1960s and was soon echoed in other national cultures, expressed widespread misgivings about the direction in which Soviet society was moving. Authors such as Vasilii Belov and Valentin Rasputin addressed the growing unease about the USSR's environmental recklessness, and increasingly associated it with fundamental concerns about the moral and cultural effects of modernization per se. As soon as the writings of village prose authors began to betray a degree of skepticism about the Soviet civilizational model, especially in respect to the violent 1920s collectivization of agriculture, the official censorial mechanisms were engaged. It was acceptable to lament the disappearance of natural habitats or the alienation of youth from nature, but questioning the legitimacy of the aggressive industrialization campaign of the 1920s and 1930s meant violating a communist taboo. The resulting frictions between the Soviet state and social, cultural, and intellectual trends provoked a political hypersensitivity that resulted in the prohibition, or mutilation, of literary texts. Such hypersensitivity had an impact on Soviet cinema, too: crackdowns on films both in the central studios and in the republics' characterized the heightened tensions between filmmakers and censors in the late 1960s and early 1970s. The parabolic nature of certain films challenged cultural administrators to suspect hidden heresy even in inconspicuous stories about animals.

*Where the Mountains Are White* reflects ecological sensitivities in a profoundly national manner. The film's main character, Mirzeke (Nurmukhan Zhanturin), is a retired worker who lives in an *aul* not far from the oil field to which he devoted his adult life. He and his wife (Baken Rimova) constantly quarrel, sometimes about their daughter who lives in the city with her little boy, but more often about the young camel that they keep in the barn. The camel often escapes and must be brought back over many miles. Named Aryana, it is of a rare breed: white with just one hump. To find a male counterpart that could impregnate it, Mirzeke is forced to travel to faraway places. His neighbor Shopak constantly reminds him of the need to do so; otherwise, how will Aryana ever become useful, producing milk and offspring? Mirzeke's discussions with Shopak reveal that the two men have been antagonists for many years. Although both fought in the Great Patriotic War, Shopak, who lost an arm, views the world in a crude manner, through the eyes of an accountant. Mirzeke's personality is completely different. For him, Aryana does not need to be profitable. He respects the white camel as a living being, a unique individual. And an individual it is: perceptive, intelligent, stubborn, and unpredictable. It seems as if Mirzeke recognizes himself in the animal. His own personality is complex and he has a reputation for being difficult; most of his conversations with family members and former colleagues end in fights. But when he is with Aryana, his peaceful and caring side comes to the fore. During the brutal insemination procedure, when Mirzeke hears the tormented animal moan and scream, he suffers no less than the camel herself. He also identifies with Aryana's yearning for freedom, which, despite his neighbor's predictions, does not disappear after giving birth. Rather, as soon as the baby camel can stand on its own legs, mother and child run away together.

Mirzeke's inner monologues reveal a high degree of empathy with all living creatures. He explains the camel's insatiable drive to be free by reference to its longing for home, namely, the white chalk mountains from which it comes (hence the film's title). The camel's whiteness and the white of its native mountains further point to a deep kinship in which Aryana's desire is grounded. Ultimately, Mirzeke accepts the animal's drive as legitimate and no longer attempts to catch it and bring it back to the *aul*. Shopak, on the other hand, refuses to give up and aggressively pursues mother and child, putting their lives in danger. Herein lies the film's deep subversiveness: the yearning for freedom is part of a living being's identity, whether that being is a human or an animal. Moreover, wanting free choice about one's life does not mean the rejection of social ties per se, but the need for a life in one's place of origin, in this case the white mountains that exercise such a powerful attraction over the camel. This aspect informs the story with a parabolic dimension: true freedom requires true identity, and vice versa. When applied to the Kazakh nation, the inevitable conclusion must be that Kazakhs cannot find fulfillment except as free people in their native land, and that no transnational experiments will ever change that.

Given the aforementioned political hypersensitivity in all cultural matters in the Soviet Union, the censors quickly accused *Where the Mountains Are White* of nationalism. This alone would explain the harsh treatment to which the film was subjected, worse even than that of *The Funeral Feast*. After all, its creators were never given an opportunity to make corrections, which even the director of *The Funeral Feast* was granted. Apparently, the censors recognized that the main violations of ideological rules in this film were at the very core of its plot and therefore could not be "corrected" by minor cuts. According to Serik Raibaev, the longing to return to one's native land was also seen as an allusion to the quest for Jewish immigration to Israel in the 1970s, a suspicion that may have contributed to the film's banning.[29]

In the oeuvres of screenwriter Satimzhan Sanbaev (who adapted his own novella), director Viktor Pusurmanov,[30] and cameraman Askhat Ashrapov, *Where the Mountains Are White* stands out as a singular achievement. The story itself reveals the influence of Kyrgyz author Chingiz Aitmatov, especially his novellas "Djamilia" and "Goodbye, Gulsary!" The latter describes the lifelong friendship of a man and his horse and is told retrospectively from the point when Gulsary is old and frail and about to die. The fascinating, albeit controversial, adaptation of "Farewell, Gulsary!" by Sergei Urusevskii (1968) had used a rich variety of camera techniques to convey meaning not through the narrative alone, but in purely visual terms. A similar approach was applied by Ashrapov, one of the most interesting Kazakhstani cinematographers, to include subjective shots that capture the world as seen through the eyes of the camel, mostly with the help of special lenses. On several occasions, close shots of Mirzeke are intercut with close shots of the camel Aryana, whose dark, shining eyes seem to express her suffering and longing. Most of these close shots are low-angle, conveying a deep respect for the animal. Equally impressive is the film's score by Gaziza Zhubanova.[31] Whenever Aryana is running toward the white mountains on the horizon, we hear a female choir singing a solemn, quasi-religious tune a capella. This motif enhances the significance of the shots, lending them symbolic weight.

## URALSK ON FIRE

The interpretation of history was one of the most sensitive aspects of filmmaking in the Soviet Union, reflecting shifts in ideological regulations more than any other element. Thus, the control mechanisms imposed during pre- and postproduction of historical films were particularly strict and could trigger lengthy and exhausting battles between filmmakers and various state agencies, delaying the release for months and years. This happened to Kazakh director Mazhit Begalin. In the 1970s, Begalin, who split his activities between Almaty and Moscow, continued to explore the complexities of Russian-Kazakh relations. After the critical success of *The Song of Manshuk*, he turned his attention to the Civil War era that followed the Bolshevik Revolution. Of the various aspects that were associated with Kazakhstan, he chose a lesser-known episode, the 1919 defense of the city of Uralsk, a theme that combined Kazakh-Soviet history with elements of adventure and action.

*Uralsk on Fire* (Ural'sk v ogne[32]) opens with a sequence of images of contemporary Paris. Its cityscapes (beautiful avenues and alleys shot from a car) display a blend of modern and historical architecture accompanied by pleasant modern tunes. At a cemetery, two men, one Kazakh, the other Russian, stand in front of the gravestone of general Viacheslav Tuchnov,[33] the Russian visitor's grandfather, who had died as an émigré in France. When the grandson mentions that kinship, he triggers a debate between the Soviet visitors and an old man in a wheelchair, apparently an émigré, who claims that Tuchnov never had a son. With one of Begalin's trademark sharp cuts, that statement is followed by a sudden switch to the year 1919, showing general Tuchnov furiously exclaiming "I no longer have a son." The person to whom he addresses this utterance is indeed his son, a history student serving as an ensign in the White Army. To the anger of his father, young Tuchnov had concluded that the cause for which he and his father were fighting had lost all meaning.

The following shot is an animated map illustrating the context of the debate between the Tuchnovs. The young Soviet republic is under attack from all sides. In the South, White Army commanders Denikin and Kolchak are striving to unite their forces and are closing in; only the city of Uralsk, held by Red Army units, stands between them. The commentary expresses how vital it was for the White Army to overcome the city's resistance in order to move toward Moscow and Petrograd and thereby defeat the Bolshevik revolution. Of course, this constellation precisely repeats that of *Behind Us Is Moscow*, when the combined Soviet-Kazakh military force decided the fate of the Soviet capital. *Uralsk on Fire* demonstrates how the White Army plan was prevented from succeeding by an alliance between Russian and Kazakh pro-Bolshevik forces.

Begalin's film was an officially approved, high-profile project with strong propaganda elements. Ideologically, it seemed safe; indeed, what disagreements could there be in showcasing the revolutionary struggle of Reds against Whites? However, from the beginning, *Uralsk on Fire* was more than a run-of-the-mill Civil War potboiler. For Begalin, it was essential to focus on the revolutionary fighting not as a purpose in itself but as part of a wider historical process, emphasizing the role of Kazakhs in the seventy-day-long siege of Uralsk, which ended in Bolshevik victory. At the same time, mindful of the tradition of Civil War adventures, he combined this lesson in history with popular genre elements. Most importantly, there is plenty of action. Thus, in an opening episode, Red Army horsemen chase a White Army officer and shoot him, discovering valuable information in his bag; these are drawings that outline how to conquer the besieged Uralsk, which are immediately taken to the revolutionary city council. Such action sequences appear throughout the film in a fairly organic manner. Secondly, there is a "bromance" that could appeal to young audiences, the friendship between two youthful characters, the Kazakh Bektai (portrayed by Nartai Begalin, the director's son) and general Tuchnov's idealistic son Aleksei. The latter had been sentenced to death by his own father but managed to escape together with the imprisoned Kazakh. Thirdly, there is the spy plot about White Army agents infiltrating Uralsk with the goal of unleashing an uprising against the Bolshevik administration. Preventing this uprising is the main challenge for the Extraordinary Commission, *ChK*. Initially, the ChK officials treat the young Tuchnov with caution, but when he proves his loyalty in practice, he is entrusted with teaching history to the children at the local school.

*Uralsk on Fire* has a number of features that betray its kinship with Soviet movies devoted to the Bolshevik revolution and the Civil War made in the early 1970s. Begalin's depiction of the White Army as a formidable, but brutal and arrogant force that did not shy away from sadistic acts against the civilian population resembles *The Escape* (aka *The Flight*/Beg, 1971), Aleksandr Alov and Vladimir Naumov's exemplary adaptation of a famous play by Mikhail Bulgakov in which the moral degradation of White Army officers features prominently. It is important to remember that earlier Soviet movies had treated anti-Bolshevik forces as buffoons who could easily be defeated even by children. This approach constituted a Soviet cinematic tradition that began in the 1920s, was continued throughout the Soviet era, and established a popular genre of its own. Begalin deviated from that tradition, following Alov and Naumov's earnestness in dealing with the White movement as an existential opponent and giving the Civil War theme more gravitas without undermining the official ideological line.

In *Uralsk on Fire*, the main dividing line between the Red and the White Army is clearly marked and allows for no ambiguities. Indeed, General

Tuchnov, portrayed by Mikhail Gluzskii, is a wooden brute whose service to the anti-Bolshevik cause suppresses any paternal feelings or Christian pity for the victims of this war. There can be no doubt that he is a dangerous enemy with whom no compromise is possible and any intellectual discussions are in vain. In stark contrast, the Soviet side is depicted as humane and erudite. Thus, in his first appearance on screen, Red Army commander Mikhail Frunze quotes a poem by Aleksandr Blok to his aide; the man, who happens to be Kazakh, responds with a story of how he was once present at one of Blok's public poetry readings. Such episodes indicate that Russia's rich cultural heritage will be safe with the Reds, not the Whites. To confirm this claim, young Aleksei Tuchnov implores members of the revolutionary council to preserve an important historical site for archeological excavations, a request to which they react with surprise but also with respect.

None of these episodes would have contradicted Soviet official historiography in any way, just the opposite: the enmity between White and Red forces is shown as value-based and irreconcilable. Why, then, was such an unambiguously pro-Soviet film prohibited?

One possible answer lies in its depiction of Kazakhs and the political divisions among them. After Karsakbaev's *Worrisome Morning*, *Uralsk on Fire* was the first feature film to depict the Alash-Orda movement as a significant political factor during the Civil War. Its members are part of the White forces, although General Tuchnov demonstrates with unabashed candor how he feels about these "allies" when he publicly humiliates a Kazakh dignitary by demonstrating downright colonial arrogance. As a consequence of Tuchnov's shortsighted attitude, one of the Kazakh leaders turns to the Bolsheviks, visiting commander Frunze and offering him the cooperation of Alash-Orda. In this key episode, the prominent Bolshevik rejects the nationalists' overtures, but for different reasons than Tuchnov, who regards the Kazakh people as inferior. Calmly and wittily, never violating the norms of military respect, Frunze outlines what he thinks about the goals of Alash-Orda: they are striving to achieve national independence in order to turn Kazakhstan into a supplier of natural resources to Western countries. This, Frunze states, would condemn the Kazakh people to eternal exploitation, which is not the kind of independence that the Bolsheviks have in mind.

It may well be that the mere mention of Alash-Orda, which was tabooed by Soviet officialdom after the organization's defeat in 1921, was viewed as undesirable by Goskino censors, who may have feared that these episodes could trigger inconvenient questions in the audience. After all, the entire leadership of Alash-Orda that had remained in the Soviet Union was executed during the 1937–1938 purges, along with any suspected sympathizer. A discussion of their goal to establish an independent Kazakhstan, even if presented from a loyal pro-Soviet viewpoint, could set in motion and legitimize a flow of inquiries that would be hard to keep under control. Another potentially objectionable aspect may have been the choice of Aleksei Tuchnov, a naïve intellectual, as the Russian counterpart for the Kazakh Bektai, an orphan who intuitively trusts him. Why not pick a revolutionary as the Kazakh's equal, a Russian proletarian or peasant lad of which Soviet cinema had so many examples?

However, the most substantial point of criticism, and the hardest to refute, came from the film's military consultant, an official representative of the Ministry of Defense of the USSR. He objected to the overall way in which the Uralsk siege was depicted, pointing out inaccuracies and downright mistakes, although none of them carried any ideological weight. This irritated Begalin, who, according to one account, retorted: "I'm not making a documentary but a feature film." However, as the officials at Goskino wanted to avoid a conflict with the Ministry of Defense at all costs, they decided not to release the picture.[34]

To be sure, the mere fact that a film was prohibited by Soviet authorities is not automatically an indication of political subversion.[35] Unlike other shelved Civil War pictures, such as Andrei Smirnov's *Angel* (1967), Larissa Shepitko's *The Homeland of Electricity* (Rodina elektrichestva, 1967), and Aleksandr Askol'dov's *The Commissar* (1967), Begalin's *Uralsk on Fire* never visualizes the brutality, fanaticism, or ineptitude of the Red Army. Rather, Begalin emphasizes the opposite: the communists defending Uralsk against the White Army onslaught are shown as humane, sacrificing their scarce food rations for the children. They are taken by surprise by sneaky enemy attacks, and they trust, rather than shoot, former White Army ensign Aleksei Tuchnov, who had defected under suspicious circumstances. Moreover, the Russian Bolsheviks stand side by side with Kazakh fighters; their alliance is shown as natural and unbreakable. Perhaps this forced idealization of Bolshevik internationalism, together with their strong intellectual disposition, went too far even for the Moscow censors. But would that have been enough to prohibit an entire high-profile movie?

Aesthetically, *Uralsk on Fire*, shot in color and widescreen, is not a remarkable picture in cinematic terms and represents a step back compared to Begalin's earlier work. Abiltai Kasteev's cinematography is indistinct, the dirty and bloody reality of the Civil War is largely avoided, and even the costumes and faces appear neat and squeaky clean. The acting is mostly bland; none of the characters are developed enough to encourage viewer identification. Furthermore, the combination of too many diverse genre elements creates confusion. And yet Begalin's film should also be remembered as a victim of the sharpening censorship during the early 1970s, when the atmosphere in the Soviet film industry grew increasingly unpleasant and suspicious and even the slightest ideological deviations were treated with heavy-handed vindictiveness. According to several sources, the never-ending frustrations experienced by Begalin during the production of *Uralsk on Fire* made him an outcast in some quarters and contributed to his untimely death.[36]

## NOTES

1. Zhibek is a member of the Shekte clan, while Tolegen belongs to the Zhagalbaily clan; both are parts of the junior *juz*.

2. The issue of when the legend came into being (in the eighteenth century or earlier) has been the cause of academic controversies. Khodzhikov decided to depict the Dzhungars as the external aggressors, which would place the legend in the 18th century. Cf. M. Sul'kin, "Segodniashnimi ochami. . ." In Chertok, S. (ed.), *Ekran 1972–1973*. Moskva: Iskusstvo, 1973, pp. 57–60.

3. *Kyz-Zhibek* was Gabit Musrepov's first libretto, adapted from a folk poem. Composed by Evgenii Brusilovskii, the opera (the first musical drama in Kazakh history) premiered on November 7, 1934 in the State Musical Theater of Kazakhstan; the director was Kanabek Baiseitov. It was shown to widespread acclaim in Moscow during the ten-day festival of Kazakhstani culture on May 17, 1936.

4. Rico Isaacs stated: "Perhaps the reason why the film has lived long in the imagination of Kazakhs is because of the extent to which Khodzhikov was able to re-create a believable and fully rounded 'Kazakh world'." Isaacs, *Film and Identity in Kazakhstan*, p. 86.

5. In the Russian version, which was distributed throughout the USSR, Kadyr Myrzaliev's lyrics are translated by a voiceover.

6. The score was written by the eminent composer Nurgisa Tlendiev.

7. With regard to the political context of the positive depiction of Kazakh nationality, Rico Isaac commented: "The greater confidence in Kazakh representation of identity mirrors the confidence with which Dinmukhamed Kunayev ruled the Kazakh Soviet Socialist Republic." Isaacs, *Film and Identity in Kazakhstan*, p. 64.

8. Siranov, Kabysh, "Proshloe—dalekoe i blizkoe," *Kazakhstanskaia pravda*, 16 July 1972.

9. Sanbaev, Satimzhan, "Neumiraiushchaia Kyz-Zhibek," *Kazakhstanskaia pravda*, 18 July 1971.

10. As the critic Bauyrzhan Nogerbek noted, there were those who rejected the film because it seemed operetta-like and costume-oriented, i.e., not an expression of a serious folkloric-historical approach. On the opposite end, those who preferred a more entertaining kind of cinema found the film to contain excessively long episodes. Cf. Nogerbek, *Na ekrane 'Kazakhfil'm*," p. 43.

11. The critic Mikhail Sul'kin wrote that *Land of the Fathers* enjoyed unanimous success both with viewers and critics. The fact that Aimanov was dissatisfied with the box-office results and wrote about his frustration in the weekly *Soviet Culture* led to controversies. According to Sul'kin, Aimanov was accused of taking into consideration the preferences only of those viewers to whom cinema was mere entertainment.

Cf. M. Sul'kin, "Poslednii fil'm Shakena Aimanova." In Golovskoi, V. (ed.), *Ekran 1971–1972*. Moskva: Iskusstvo, 1972, p. 28.

12. Mikhalkov-Konchalovskii wrote in his memoirs: "Eduard Tropinin—another wonderful person in my life—appeared when I was writing *The End of the Ataman*. Kolia Sishlin, who worked for the Central Committee, introduced him to me. Tropinin's real name was Makarov, he was a Chekist [a generic term referring to members of the Soviet secret service: Extraordinary Commission – *Chrezvychainaia Kommissiia*, i.e., *ChK*—P.R.], was active in foreign espionage as a specialist on the East and responsible for Afghanistan. (. . .) I recall how he once returned from a mission and said: 'We f. . .ed up Afghanistan. They ousted the king, these idiots.' Moscow had arranged a revolution and brought Taraki to power. Maybe, Edik had arranged it himself—not by his own wish, of course. In the 1980s he died of cancer." Konchalovskii, Andrei: *Vozvyshaiushchii obman*. Moskva: "Sovershenno sekretno," 1999, pp. 54–55.

13. Such humanity and hidden emotionality resemble another film spy, colonel Shtirlits from the legendary miniseries *Seventeen Moments of Spring* (1973), arguably the most lasting contribution to the romantic idealization of espionage in Soviet history.

14. Mikhail Sul'kin undeservedly denounces Dutov as "a Russian monarchist." Sul'kin, "Poslednii fil'm Shakena Aimanova," p. 29.

15. In the afore-mentioned article by M. Sul'kin, the prototype's name is spelled "Chanyshov;" he is called "a Chekist from Semirech'e" and listed with another secret agent, Kuzhamiiarov. Cf. Sul'kin, "Poslednii fil'm Shakena Aimanova," p. 31.

16. G. Aksel'rod, "Put' k vershine," *Kazakhstanskaia pravda*, 2 March 1971.

17. Kabysh Siranov discussed the film's genre, stating that from the point of view of its plot, *The End of the Ataman* is a detective movie (*kinodetektiv*); but the viewer perceives it as a historical revolutionary film, which, in Siranov's view, marks it as an artistic innovation. Siranov, "Proshloe—dalekoe i blizkoe."

18. Tarazi, Akim (real name: Akim Ashimov) (b. 1933), Kazakh author, screenwriter, and administrator; in 1971–1980, Tarazi served as the First Secretary of the Union of Film Workers of the Kazakh SSR.

19. Cf. Serik Raibaev, "Nevostrebovannaia zhizn'," *Novyi fil'm*, 9/1991, p. 8. Raibaev's list of prohibited Kazakhstani feature films includes *Jump into the Unknown* (Pryzhok v neizvestnost') by Iurii Piskunov, *Operation 'Wedding'* (Operatsiia 'Svad'ba') by Igor' Polovski, *Don Quixote of My Childhood* (Don Kikhot moego detstva) by Satybaldy Narymbetov, and *A Rainy Summer in a Southern City* (Dozhdlivoe leto v iuzhnom gorode) by Edige Bolysbaev, in addition to the films analyzed in this chapter. Raibaev also discusses a number of animated and documentary films that were shelved at the time.

20. Mansurov, Bulat (1937–2011), Turkmen director who made three films in Kazakhstan: *The Funeral Feast* (1972, released in 1987); the unremarkable pilot romance *Parable of Love* (Pritcha o liubvi, 1975); and the historical epic *Sultan Beibars* (1989).

21. The screenplay by Mansurov and Askar Suleimenov was granted permission for production on September 1, 1971.

22. V.I. Fomin, *Zapreshchennye fil'my* (*Polka*, Vypusk 2). Moskva: NT-Tsentr, 1993. Cf. the chapter on *The Funeral Feast* (Trizna), pp. 130–44.

23. Ibid., p. 131.

24. Raibaev, "Nevostrebovannaia zhizn," p. 8.

25. The division into chapters may have been inspired by *Andrei Rublev*.

26. In Soviet discourses, "naturalism" usually meant graphic violence, for which Tarkovskii's *Andrei Rublev* was chastised as well.

27. *Zapreshchennye fil'my* (*Polka*, Vypusk 2). Moskva: NT-Tsentr, 1993, pp. 137–39.

28. The film's original title was *The White Aruana* (Belaia aruana), adapted from a novella by Satimzhan Sanbaev.

29. Raibaev, "Nevostrebovannaia zhizn," p. 8.

30. Pusurmanov, Viktor (1937–2010), Kazakh director whose films are often based on mythological subjects.

31. Zhubanova, Gaziza (1927–1993), Kazakh composer who wrote a number of remarkable film scores.

32. The film was later renamed *Thunder of the Steppes* (Stepnye raskaty).

33. The name Tuchnov is fictitious; the character's real prototype was general Tolstov, but the censors insisted that this name be replaced. Cf. Ol'ga Khrabrykh, "Begalinskii svet." *Ekspress K*, 33 (16419), 22 February 2008.

34. Ibid.

35. *Uralsk on Fire*/*Thunder of the Steppes*, which became Begalin's last picture, was first shown on Kazakhstani TV in 2002 as part of the celebrations of the director's 80th birthday.

36. Khrabrykh, "Begalinskii svet."

*Chapter 9*

# The New Status Quo

In the history of Kazakhstani cinema, the 1970s are a difficult period to assess, be it from an aesthetic, a political, or an overall cultural standpoint. To provide a multifaceted and differentiated view of this decade, which started out with two triumphs but continued with confusion and contradictory trends, the following chapters will examine aspects of the development of Kazakhstani film under sociopolitical circumstances that differed substantially from those of the previous decade. Of course, cinema was just one of several cultural branches, but it did reflect the contradictory trends of Kazakh-Soviet society as a whole. Kazakhstan was not alone in its dilemma. The status quo that was established in the 1970s transformed Soviet society as such. To be sure, the historical evaluation of that transformation has undergone extreme changes as well. At the beginning of the perestroika period, the 1970s were retroactively and uniformly denounced as the "period of stagnation" (*zastoi*). Communist Party activists and journalists, inspired by Mikhail Gorbachev's campaign for the restauration of Soviet values, defined the Brezhnev years as a time in which societal development "slowed down" and many citizens, giving up on the ideals of socialism and communism, purportedly settled for a petit bourgeois lifestyle. Five years later, in the first post-Soviet decade, after the perestroika project itself had crumbled, the "stagnation" decade was revisited, this time being reframed as "not so bad after all." For many, the geopolitical détente, moderately satisfying consumerism, and socioeconomic stability of the 1970s had a certain appeal during the politically turbulent, divisive, and economically humiliating 1990s. Of course, such changing attitudes were often caused by selective memory, which likewise afflicted academic discourse, including film historians. To avoid emotionally charged extremes and arrive at a balanced assessment of the penultimate Soviet decade and its cultural output, it is necessary to look at the forces that were involved in cultural production and the factors that caused Kazakhstani cinema to lose the high status it had gained in the 1960s.

To this end, negative generalizations about this period that are routinely formulated as part of the common characterization of the 1970s as "stagnation," denoting the degeneration of Soviet society as a whole and its culture in particular, will be scrutinized by looking at the output of Kazakhstani cinema in detail. To do justice to both the accomplishments and the shortcomings of Kazakhfilm studio's production between 1970s and the early 1980s, it is vital to pay close attention to the actual films that were released in those years, the thematic and genre trends that can be discerned, and exceptional films that have stood the test of time. To be sure, most of the films from that decade have been forgotten; many are no longer even shown on television. But even flops and failures can fill the gaps in our understanding of film history, helping to tell a more complete story of Kazakh national cinema.

Is it true that Kazakhstan's cinematic legacy of the 1970s is a largely negligible quantity? Compared to the 1960s, it is hard to deny a downward trend, especially when measured against the triumph of *Kyz-Zhibek* and *The End of the Ataman* as the conclusion of the previous decade. The shelving of even mildly subversive pictures as part of the Communist Party's rollback strategy corroborates the overall bleak impression of the 1970s, which ended with an increasing number of lackluster productions giving Kazakhstani cinema a bad name. By the late 1960s, the country's film industry and film community had demonstrated the full range of their capabilities. However, these achievements were immediately followed by painful backlashes, particularly the official discrimination against artistically original projects, which sent a chilling signal to Kazakh filmmakers. The tragic death of Shaken Aimanov in 1970 was a blow the consequences of which would be felt for years to come; Sultan Khodzhikov's career was marred by long-term illness due to his war injuries; Aleksandr Karpov moved to Minsk; and Mazhit Begalin to Moscow. While the remaining directors at Kazakhfilm studio, including Abdulla Karsakbaev and Sharip Beisembaev, had proven their ability to direct noteworthy and sometimes outstanding pictures, their authority was inadequate to fill the gap left by those four who were no longer active parts of the Kazakh film community.

The most important fallout of the sudden loss of talent and authority was the ever-solidifying primacy of bureaucrats over artists. The struggle between these two categories of professionals within the film industry had been visible from the early 1960s, when a campaign against Aimanov was unleashed. Back then, however, artistic arguments, as opposed to bureaucratic and ideological ones, still won the day. By the early 1970s, the balance of that constellation had shifted toward the bureaucrats.

For the film cultures of the Soviet republics, the 1970s brought increased political pressures, but also, paradoxically, some welcome relaxation. The political parameters were narrowed in comparison to the early to mid-1960s, but morality in private life was handled with less prudishness and the need for ideologically unassuming mass entertainment was de facto recognized as legitimate. Commercial imports from the West, including comedies, musicals, Westerns, and even thrillers were watched by tens of millions of Soviet viewers just as eagerly as homegrown comedies and melodramas. Generally, material without explicit propaganda messages was preferred. In Kazakhstan, this trend was reflected by a turn toward clearly defined genre films: children's adventure, sports drama, and even detective mystery. Imports from India often became super hits and developed a following of their own.

The technical basis for making the film repertoire accessible to all, meanwhile, was in better shape than ever before. By 1979, the Kazakhstani SSR's distribution network was operating 14,733 film projectors, twice as many as just ten years earlier, with 10,700 of them serving the rural population. Between 1956 and 1979, 400 movie theaters were built, of which 62 were equipped with widescreen technology.[1]

It is noteworthy that during the 1970s, when the need for pure entertainment and visual spectacle was accepted and technically secured, the Soviet establishment also recognized a legitimate need for arthouse cinema, satisfying the cultural expectations of intellectual strata and enhancing the country's international prestige. In the 1920s, the split between mass entertainment and limited arthouse cinema had been an inevitable consequence of the emergence of the film avant-garde, but it was delegitimized in the 1930s and subsequently suppressed until the 1960s. In Kazakhstani cinema, attempts to enhance cinematic sophistication for more demanding viewer strata had historically been met by covert resistance. Thus, one of the most interesting Kazakhstani films, Begalin's *The Traces Go to the Horizon*, was barely released. For Shaken Aimanov, who would never accept a segmentation of audiences into ordinary viewers and cinephiles, the disconnect between regular viewers and his masterpiece *Land of the Fathers* was an aberration. However, in the 1970s, attempts were made to produce high-quality pictures that could represent the republic at national and international festivals without necessarily being popular among mass audiences.

Thus, in the early 1970s, an increasing bifurcation into highbrow and lowbrow segments of Soviet culture, especially in cinema, which was once declared to be the art of the masses, became apparent and was quietly accepted by most of the political establishment. Indeed, this segmentation became the basis for the repertoire of the major film studios. The underlying intention was to satisfy both the millions of viewers who expected movies to entertain and the minority of viewers who were looking for intellectual and aesthetic gratification. The ultimate goal of these and other cultural strategies was to stabilize society. This goal was largely achieved: Soviet cinema offered space for home-made comedy blockbusters and for highbrow productions that could be sent to international festivals. Only a few nonconformist artists refused to participate in the new Soviet status quo. The repressions against them pointed to the demarcations of how far intellectuals were allowed to go and where forbidden territory began. However, the majority of Soviet film workers accepted and internalized the new norms, which were politically uncompromising but more aesthetically elastic. Thus, while the international cineaste community was outraged over the trials and tribulations of Andrei Tarkovskii and Sergei Paradjanov and the cat-and-mouse games played by the communist establishment with dissidents, the filmmakers of republics such as Georgia and Kyrgyzstan were given the green light to continue their aesthetic and thematic explorations; indeed, artistically ambitious filmmakers could get away with some projects that would have been unthinkable in earlier periods. Kazakhstan also played a role in these developments, albeit a limited one.

Following the triumphs of *Kyz-Zhibek* and *The End of the Ataman*, the cinema of Kazakhstan entered the 1970s in a state of conceptual undecidedness, hampering the evolution of a truly national film culture. As the major authoritative filmmakers were no longer present in the decision-making councils at Kazakhfilm studio, aesthetically and politically harmless fare began to dominate the output. The emphasis in the repertoire was on lightweight movies that appealed to specific strata of the viewership and did not up the ante ideologically. Most of them were rendered with sufficient professionalism but reeked of conflict avoidance and opportunism. Aesthetic innovation and daring were reprimanded. Many Kazakhstani filmmakers chose the safest route and simply continued thematic lines that had been discovered in the 1960s. Without Aimanov, Begalin, Khodzhikov, and Karpov, artistic originality was increasingly difficult to find. However, for a differentiated and fair assessment, it is important to go beyond such broad generalizations and provide a detailed evaluation of each genre and individual filmmaker.

## CHILDREN, HORSES, LOVE

After the astonishing success of Abdulla Karsakbaev's *My Name Is Kozha*, movies for and about children became a mainstay of Kazakhstan's film production. Karsakbaev had managed to define the gold standard of the Kazakhstani children's film; after him, many tried to reach it, but few succeeded. Karsakbaev's most consistent successor in the children's film genre was Kanymbek Kasymbekov, who had a special gift for eliciting natural performances from children and for widening the framework of the genre to some degree.

A specific aspect of children's development and sensitivity as portrayed in Kasymbekov's films was their interaction with animals. Acquiring an identity grounded in national values is depicted as being linked to establishing a deep connection with living nature. Often, the plot of such films gains traction when the relationship between a child character and an animal causes hostile reactions from the world of adults, which also signifies a learning process for the young protagonists. The charm of these films is derived from the parallelism between the socialization and education of little human beings and the animals for whom they care.

In *Shok and Sher* (Shok i Sher, 1972[2]), Kasymbekov portrays a nine year old who might as well be Kozha's younger cousin. The boy Sher steals apples, avoids helping out around the house, and refuses to reveal who gave him a black eye. Sher's grandmother and chess partner is far from enthusiastic about his pranks, but his natural intelligence impresses her. Sher reads about a hero (*batyr*) on a flying horse, which immediately sparks his imagination. When a colt is born and named Shok, he takes it under his wing and gives it all his attention. Sher acts as Shok's mentor, shedding his own childish habits in the process. Vis-à-vis the pony, the boy displays an attitude of rightful ownership, waiting every evening for Shok to return from the pasture. It is remarkable that only with this perceived ownership does Sher develop a sense of responsibility: prior to "owning" Shok, he forgot to feed the horses and was generally oblivious to any kind of duty. A conflict with the adult world occurs when Sher's father sells Shok while the boy is in the hospital. Sher and his sister make a trip to Ålmaty to fetch the colt, finding it at a hippodrome. The children take "their" colt and bring it home. When three men arrive and demand it back, it is Sher's grandmother who testifies that the boy is the rightful owner, securing the film's triumphant finale.

Kasymbekov, who directed from a screenplay by Satybaldy Narymbetov, succeeded in creating the believable portrait of a children's micro-community with its own rules and ways of communicating. Most importantly, he was able to show how children in the countryside begin to understand existential aspects of life at an early age. Thus, little Galimzhan presses her ear to the womb of a pregnant horse to hear the baby horse inside; later, the children must cope with the fact that the mother horse died while her baby survived. Rather than framing it as a traumatic experience, the film treats the parallel appearance and disappearance of living beings as normal facets of life. Accordingly, while there can be no doubt that the bond between Sher and Shok is deep, the relationship is not sentimental. The boy behaves toward the horse in a manner that is caring but not tender. After all, his dream is to become a *batyr* like the one he heard about from his grandmother. The most interesting aspect of *Shok and Sher* is the sense of freedom experienced by the children when they interact with animals, particularly with horses. Spectacular dolly shots capture the ecstatic happiness of boys racing with their horses. While the national aspect of this experience of freedom is not verbalized, it is undeniably present. The final reunification of Shok and Sher is also shown as an act of regaining freedom and full identity.

As in many Kazakh films, the rural environment is depicted in fresh and shining colors, as a world of beauty and harmony, whereas the city is visualized as overwhelming, confusing, and obviously following other priorities than the home *aul*. In this regard, it is noteworthy that the children feel closer to their rural grandparents than to their parents: the parental generation is portrayed as having adopted urban values, as with Sher's father preferring a motorcycle, whereas his son and the other children want horses.

The integration of comedic elements also worked well in Kazakhstani children's films, appealing both to young viewers, who loved the "brat" adventures, and to adult audiences, who picked up on witty allusions addressed to them. A good example of this twofold approach is Bolat Shmanov's *A Bride for Brother* (Nevesta dlia brata, 1979).

When a young man named Baiterbek returns from the city without a university degree, he is reintegrated into the *aul* community in more ways than expected. In particular, his little brother, Ayan, does his best to arrange a marriage for him. Many comedic effects result from the precocious conversations of teenage boys about women, love, and the qualities that a bride needs to have to be a good wife. Ayan seems to know more about adults than the other kids; surprisingly, he is sure that the unsightly Fatimah is the right candidate for Baiterbek. However, while Fatimah is intelligent and perceptive, she is also physically clumsy. Furthermore, she is deeply in love with a painter from the city who is spending time in the *aul* working on a large mural (convincingly portrayed by Kuman Tastanbekov, who had become a national heartthrob after playing Tolegen in *Kyz-Zhibek*). Rather than waiting for his lackluster brother to take the initiative, the junior sibling writes romantic letters to Fatimah, transforming the girl into a real beauty who finally joins Baiterbek so that both can find happiness.

Besides being an enjoyable situational comedy, *A Bride for Brother* touches upon serious issues. Thus, an old man asks the teenager to write letters to his children who no longer visit him. The theme of old-age loneliness gained major importance in Soviet cinema in the 1970s, signaling the onset of the disintegration of social structures. Despite such sobering elements, the quasi-comedic treatment of sexual issues builds up to the film's lighthearted finale. Along the way, the viewer is amused by the children's curiosity about romantic love, their first infatuations, and their bragging about their "expertise" in matters of the heart. In this regard, *A Bride for Brother* is clearly a descendant of *My Name*

*Is Kozha* with its cheerfulness and goodhearted humor. Shmanov's direction features a rare inventiveness: even the credits are crafted in a witty manner.

An important element that most *Kozha* derivatives have in common is the view of the modern *aul* as representing a firm social foundation that can accommodate many different characters and has the potential to correct harmless deviations from behavioral norms. With this image of a settlement that combines modern and ancient features, the directors of children's films crafted an Ur-Kazakhstan on screen, a place in which individual, community, society, and nature live together in productive harmony. In *A Bride for Brother*, such stable social space provides the necessary peaceful framework for traditional comedic clichés such as fake love letters, youngsters meddling in adult relationships, and the Cinderella transformation of an unsightly girl. The *aul* is also a decisive factor that gives such films their local charm and a degree of national authenticity. It is no coincidence that many Kazakh films about children and youths open with a panorama shot of an *aul*, usually with shimmering mountains in the background. An interesting detail is the open-air discotheque featured in *A Bride for Brother*, where a local band named "Steppe Wolves" performs modern tunes on electric guitars. Quite an innovation in the Soviet context!

## KARSAKBAEV'S OWN *KOZHA* VARIATIONS

Throughout his career, Abdulla Karsakbaev consciously resisted being labeled a children's film director. Indeed, his second feature, *A Worrisome Morning*, is a mature picture, philosophically deep and tragic; it shares with Karsakbaev's debut, *My Name Is Kozha*, only a keenly national outlook. But over the twenty years of his active career, Karsakbaev did return to the genre of children's and youth film several times. One of the reasons for this was his rare gift of building cohesive ensembles of professional and nonprofessional performers and eliciting convincing interaction in psychologically and physically challenging scenes. Karsakbaev's trust in children's healthy intuition is detectable in all his pictures, including those that contain elements of political opportunism, which became the general norm in Kazakhstani cinema in the 1970s. An example is *Hey There, Cowboys!* (Ei vy, kovboi!, 1974), the story of an athlete, Gulia, who acts as a fearless leader in sports and games and is the head of a small children's gang. Her authority is only questioned by another youth gang, led by the arrogant Uzunture. The members of Uzunture's gang dress in Western-style costumes and try to patronize Gulia's group by all possible means, including unfair ones. For Gulia, whose grandfather Daulet was a well-known martial arts fighter who still practices with his granddaughter, such violations of the rules are completely unacceptable.

*Hey There, Cowboys!* adds a specific gender aspect to the joyful adventurous-comedic childhood reenactments that are typical of Soviet-Kazakh children's films. Gulia, both in appearance and behavior, is a tomboy. She prefers soccer and martial arts to gymnastics, regularly challenges the boys to one-on-one fights, and dreams of a career as the captain of a large ship. Her victories put the defeated boys in a difficult position: friends and family shake their heads in embarrassment, wondering how "a guy can be beaten up by a girl." Conspicuously, Gulia does not act in a brutal or vulgar way. Her leadership role is to a large degree based on her noble principles, which she never betrays, even at the price of physical pain. At the same time, Gulia cannot stand the loud posturing of her male antagonists and mocks them mercilessly. Her boyishness provides her with authority but also with a certain charm.

Decades later, in the post-Soviet period, several Kazakh films revisited the motif of the youthful amazon in pictures such as *Strizh* (2007) and *Seker* (2009). As an early exploration of transgressing traditional gender roles, *Hey There, Cowboys!* was a pioneer in its genre. It also reflected the atmosphere of détente in the mid-1970s. Thus, the kids repeatedly make positive references to the United States, for example, asking each other "Which state are you from?" followed by the response, "From Texas." Within this playful American framework, the mountains in which the Kazakh children frolic reveal an unexpected kinship with those in John Ford's movies and Gulia's self-confident insistence on the freedom to choose her identity acquires a remarkable non-Soviet tone.

Unlike in *My Name Is Kozha*, in *Hey There, Cowboys!* adults play only a marginal role: the real focus is on the inner dynamics of adolescent groups. However, the film is hardly subversive, since it reduces all conflicts to dramatic but harmless games. And despite her gender ambiguity, Gulia is socially well-adjusted and is presented as an exemplary juvenile whose leadership ambitions will likely result in a successful Soviet career.

The deliberate elimination of social conflict, which noticeably weakens the suspense of children's films, became typical of the 1970s and is evident in Karsakbaev's *Alpamys Goes to School* (Alpamys idet v shkolu, 1976). While the film reprises many of the accomplishments of the director's debut, the differences between the two are significant and worth pondering, as they shed light on the changes that took place in Kazakhstani cinema from the 1960s to the 1970s.

The character constellation in *Alpamys Goes to School* resembles that of *My Name Is Kozha*, featuring two friends, one of whom is curious and sensitive and the other of whom is a simple-minded slacker. The typical well-functioning rural community serves as the background. But the title hero is younger than Kozha, and he is anything but a misfit. Rather, the opposite is true: Alpamys is frustrated because his age does not allow him to attend school yet. He is eager to learn to read and to calculate, unlike his older buddy, Kalikhan, who would rather not go to school at all but must. Despite their fundamental differences in age and attitude, Alpamys and Kalikhan get along fabulously, and their joint pranks succeed without negative consequences, thanks to an empathetic teacher. Thus, when Kalikhan misunderstands a homework assignment to showcase live animals and brings a poisonous snake to the classroom, the teacher shows no anger and puts the dangerous animal in the appropriate cage, even lauding the boy. Alpamys likes to sit on a tree near the open classroom windows, picking up every word uttered by the teacher. As a result, he soon begins to read and multiply. In the finale, Kalikhan proudly presents his young preschool friend at a festival as the main attraction, a veritable wunderkind.

The film's title is ambivalent: Alpamys is officially too young to go to school. Instead, he regularly goes to the school building to learn on his own. Another semantic aspect of the title is "the school of life." Just as he cannot wait to read books, Alpamys is constantly asking questions, especially when talking to a sickly old man, Mynar-ata, who is respected by the entire village. When queried about his own education, the old man answers that his teachers were "the mountains and the steppe." However, this formulation is not meant to dismiss formal schooling. Mynar-ata only wants to point out that there are other sources of wisdom as well, an insight that Alpamys immediately adopts.

Not only is Alpamys younger than his predecessor Kozha, but he is also liked by everybody and praised as "cute." Most importantly, Alpamys is well-adapted, making him the exact opposite of Kozha. Moreover, unlike his older friend Kalikhan, Alpamys is intuitively able to distinguish right from wrong. Due to its title character's highly positive image, *Alpamys Goes to School* at first gives the impression of an idyll in which there can only be minor conflicts, if any. Nurgisa Tlendiev's tender and joyous tunes seem to confirm that perspective. However, the film does feature two powerful, albeit underlying, messages that were controversial at the time and remain so to this day. First, Karsakbaev demonstrates that children have different gifts and that society must be able to respond to their varying levels of intelligence and perceptiveness without denial or discrimination. The teacher provides superb examples of how to challenge young people while remaining inclusive. Second, Karsakbaev underlines the profound value of life lessons that are not, and cannot be, learned in school. The generational continuity expressed in the affectionate and respectful relationship between Alpamys and old Mynar demonstrates that traditional wisdom, including specific Kazakh values, is a vital inspiration for children even in the modern age. Mynar repeatedly calls Alpamys a *batyr*, regardless of his current small size, and tells him that he will have twelve sons who will all become extraordinary men. For Alpamys, these extracurricular lessons serve as a compass the accuracy of which he never questions. Other adults also quote from ancient wisdom so that the boy might remember those words forever. "When you are lost, always trust the horse, it will find the right path," advises his father. On another occasion, he tells Alpamys, "When you are in an alien country, always look for a fellow-countryman." One of the unique discoveries of *Alpamys Goes to School* is the character of the teacher. Young, awkward, and sometimes unintentionally funny, he overcomes all problems with his untiring enthusiasm, his trust in the positive nature of all children, and his inventiveness.

The prevailing harmony does not diminish the existential experiences that even a little boy must have. Varia, the beautiful young seamstress whom Alpamys adores, gets married and leaves for the city. Mynar-ata, the wise old man, dies. But he leaves Alpamys his saddle, and the boy speaks to him in his thoughts: "Mynar-ata, I am going to school now."

It must be underlined that the Soviet-Kazakh variety of children's films never trivialized the artistic discoveries of the picture from which they sprang, *My Name Is Kozha*. But in the 1970s, the constellation "outsider vs. majority of well-adjusted children" morphed into a different relationship, centering on well-adjusted main characters who stand out for their talents and achievements. This change significantly reduced the potential for personality friction and serious conflict in comparison to *Kozha*. The overall nature of such films became affirmative and no longer subversive.

## THE SPORTS DRAMA

Kazakhstani films about social emancipation usually focused on women and their empowerment as part of the new socialist society, with characters ranging from Raikhan and Botagoz in the 1940s and 1950s to Manshuk in the 1960s and Nesibeli in the 1980s. On the opposite pole, the normative depiction of male behavior and male maturation was a preferred subject of the sports drama and the thriller. The subgenre of sports drama, in particular, holds a special place in Kazakhstani cinema. Given the huge popularity of boxing, martial arts, and soccer among Kazakhs, it is not surprising that several Kazakhstani feature films deal with these disciplines. The sports drama underwent a first period of blooming in the 1970s and has remained a mainstay of Kazakhstani cinema ever since. From the point of view of gender concepts and as part of national identity formation and formulation, these films offer a wealth of insight, even though they are rarely distinguished by aesthetic originality or exceptional artistry. The fact that leading Kazakh actors such as Asanali Ashimov and Doskhan Zholzhaksynov agreed to be cast in such movies speaks to the respect that this subgenre commanded among rank-and-file audiences, if not critics. Sports dramas respond to deep-seated audience needs, ranging from an obsession with athletic looks to the yearning for protection from physical aggression.

The earliest example of Kazakh sports drama is Sharip Beisembaev's *The White Square* (Belyi kvadrat, 1970), the story of a boxer and his relationship with his coach, with women, and fame. The film demonstrates the serious potential of the genre, revealing social and psychological insights that are hard to come by elsewhere. *The White Square* also features the inspirational message that is typical of most movies about athletes: acquiring aptitude in a certain athletic discipline is presented as a process of self-empowerment, culminating in the acquisition of a positive social and gender identity.

In the beginning of Beisembaev's film, its main character, Kuat (Abdrashit Abdrakhmanov), is attacked by a group of aggressive young men. Kuat is shy and does not know how to fight back. Were it not for the help of an older man, he would have been beaten up badly. Kuat's rescuer, Zhulike (Mukhtar Bakhtygereev), takes him under his wing and promises to teach him boxing. It soon turns out that Kuat has genuine talent and is gifted enough to begin a boxing career.

The coach comes across as a somewhat mysterious character, and his complexity is one of the reasons why *The White Square* is an above-average picture. This aging retired athlete is a recovering alcoholic. Although he does have a family, he has made a conscious decision to live by himself. Zhulike speaks cynically about women and love, but the reasons for his bitterness are never explained. The burgeoning relationship between mentor and mentee gives the film a degree of psychological and social depth, as does the romance between Kuat and the young doctor Zauresh, who at some point puts pressure on the athlete by claiming that she is pregnant. Zhulike cares for Kuat like a substitute father; this role gives him a chance to make up for his own lost chances in life. As a coach, he is still well-known in the world of boxing. The respect of the younger for the older is deeply ingrained in Kuat's behavior. Whenever there are tensions, a simple reminder about Zhulike's seniority reestablishes the hierarchy. In turn, Kuat has a positive effect on the older man: the coach's newly acquired responsibility helps him overcome his addiction. This quasi-paternal relationship is a source of inspiration for Kuat and is corroborated by his ambition to become "a real djigit," just like his father was. However, backlashes do occur. At one point, when Kuat is already a national celebrity, he suffers a defeat in an important fight. To make things worse, Zauresh reveals that she lied about her pregnancy. As a result, the young athlete loses his interest in sports and in life altogether. Only when he meets another girl, who turns out to be the right match for him, does he return to the ring, ready to fight again.

In *The White Square*, boxing is depicted as a discipline that teaches a man how to be a man, especially how to protect himself and his loved ones. Only when boxing becomes a full-blown vocation is it accompanied by negative side effects. The potential for corruption is depicted early on. Following a failed entrance exam for medical school, one of the instructors argues for keeping Kuat because of his athletic skills. Thankfully, Kuat is spared such a humiliation. Zauresh is mainly impressed by Kuat's fame as an athlete and leaves him when his personality turns out to be more difficult than she expected. The challenges that come with success may also have caused Zhulike's personal crisis. Yet the aforementioned temptations do not diminish the widely shared belief in the educational and moral potential of sports. As one coach states: "I have done my best to raise beautiful people!" The film corroborates the belief that there is an intimate connection between good sports and ethics, demonstrating that only those athletes who adhere to the highest behavioral standards will be victorious. Kuat, too, is only able to give his best as a boxer when his social relations are intact. Indeed, victory is based not on ruthless competitiveness but on a noble disposition that requires constant work. This disposition is presented as specific for a man and an essential part of manliness. *The White Square* explicitly formulates this Kazakh ideal as being derived from age-old patriarchal tradition and points to the value of continuity: the highest goal for a son is to become a *djigit* like his father. The inherent discourse on manliness and its elements continued to occupy Kazakh cinema and became something of an obsession in times of societal crisis, especially in the early 2000s.

In *The White Square*, Abdrashit Abdrakhmanov, a real-life boxer, played the lead role in a sufficiently convincing manner; for him, the film marked the beginning of a successful career in cinema that ran parallel to his career as an athlete.[3]

Also during the 1970s, Sergei Shutov,[4] fresh out of film school, made his debut with a quality sports drama that is related to *The White Square* yet challenges the latter's assumption of an automatic connection between sports and ethics. The first episodes of Shutov's *A Decisive Fight* (Reshaiushchaia skhvatka, 1978) seem to cofirm the widespread view of the importance of sports for positive character formation. Alzhan Tulegenov (A. Suleev), a journalism student and well-known martial arts champion, projects confidence, strength, and elegance. He is friendly to all and ready to grant help, spontaneously allowing an impressionable ten year old from the neighborhood into his training center. Alzhan's mother (Amina Umurzakova) dotes on him; only his father (Nurmukhan Zhanturin) seems to be concerned about something in his personality, making a point of sending him to the faraway city of Pavlodar for an internship. In the offices of a local Pavlodar newspaper, Alzhan's personal qualities are put to the test. His first assignment is to follow up on a letter of complaint from a young worker who feels mistreated by his older colleagues. Alzhan visits the factory and quickly pens a critical article about the rampant corruption there. But instead of approval, he causes outrage among the workers: the article targeted the wrong people, including an old army friend of Alzhan's father. Instead of thoroughly researching the issue, Alzhan went for the easy effect.

At this point, the young man's athletic upbringing comes into the picture. Rather than participating in a championship, Alzhan rectifies his mistake as an aspiring journalist, meets with the old worker, and watches the missed tournament on TV, where the victory is automatically granted to Alzhan's opponent because he did not show up for the fight ... The film is filled with dramatic martial arts scenes, but also with effective shots of female gymnastics, a discipline in which Alzhan's sensitive girlfriend, Saule, excels. The unexpected finale points to the limitations of sports, proving that winning a championship is not worth sacrificing one's integrity. Alzhan ultimately makes the right choice, watching himself be disqualified but knowing that the injustice he caused has been rectified. Shutov's film, although without noticeable artistic ambition, features believable characters and some mild social criticism. Most importantly, it reveals skepticism regarding the effects of sports, especially of athletic stardom, and questions the domineering self-confidence that is so typical of athletes on screen.[5]

The sports drama clearly had the potential to provide a thematic framework for broader social and moral issues. Because of the popularity of sports, it was also used as a means to regain audience trust. Thus, *On the Field's Edge* (U kromki polia, 1982) features the attractive soccer milieu for a plot that follows a well-known pattern: a new coach, Askar Temirov (Talgat Nigmatulin), arrives in a provincial town, tasked with bringing the local soccer team up to speed. His methods do not sit well with all players who at some point threaten to revolt. Askar insists on relentless and hard exercise, bringing the team close to physical exhaustion. Moreover, he will only accept victories that are the result of fair play; preferential treatment by the referee is an abomination, and he openly rejects such outcomes. As resistance mounts, Askar's private life is in disarray, too: he loves a woman who has been promised to another. But at least on the soccer field his efforts pay off. Thanks to his willpower and untiring explanations, the team begins to grow and steadily improve its performance. Only when it is forced to play against a far superior team, defeat is inevitable, forcing the coach to leave. Finally, both the team administrator and the woman Askar loves ask him to stay, securing a happy ending.

What may appear like a trivial story does contain some sharper edges, as most Kazakh sports dramas do. For example, the regional political establishment, for whom soccer is a discipline to satisfy their personal ambitions, is shown in a rather negative light. There are even hints that in some cases the results of matches have been prearranged by politicians. In addition to corruption in the highest ranks, star players indulge in primadonna-like behavior and lack discipline and team spirit. But Askar sticks to his moral principles and refuses to compromise, ultimately winning over his opponents. This focus on the coach's struggles makes *On the Field's Edge* primarily a film about leadership and the qualities that a genuine leader must possess to gain authority, whether in soccer or elsewhere. Director Bolat Shmanov (Bolat Sharip)[6] elicited solid performances, with Nigmatulin's portrayal of Askar particularly standing out. But the film as a whole lacks tension, likely because the conflicts are insufficiently developed and the soccer episodes are not filmed intriguingly enough, something that is difficult in fictional films in the first place.

## VARIATIONS OF THE SPORTS THEME

In the 1970s, a time of tougher ideological control over cinema, the sports drama offered certain advantages: the conflicts at its center were real but non-political; characters possessed psychological depth, but their inner tensions were rarely socially determined; and the milieu itself inspired visual attractiveness. In addition, Kazakh sports films focused on commonly accepted standards of female and male beauty and noble character disposition, proposing their harmonious complementarity as a supreme ideal, suggesting to the viewer that this is an issue of national significance. Within this framework, several variations were tried out.

An example of an unusual Kazakh sports film is *The Throw, or It All Began on a Saturday* (Brosok, ili Vse nachalos' v subbotu, 1976). This peculiar blend of sports drama and science fiction questions the harsh competitiveness and the star cult that are characteristic of the lives of athletes, especially when mass media get involved. A thought experiment of some originality, *The Throw* features Asanali Ashimov in a brilliant performance as a diabolical scientist confronting a young architect, Temir (Esbolgan Zhaisanbaev), who looks and behaves like a couch potato. Embarrassed by his physical insufficiencies and the need to improve himself, the architect agrees to participate in the experiment, soon demonstrating extraordinary skills as a basketball player despite his average build and non-athletic disposition; among other detrimental factors, he remains a smoker. But as an athlete who throws the ball with utmost precision, he becomes the linchpin of the "Arman" team, without whom the others cannot win. Temir also becomes a media darling surrounded by journalists and elegant women competing for his attention.

The "What if?" plot was adapted from the short story "The Ability to Throw a Ball" by Russian sci-fi author Kir Bulychov and directed by the young Kazakh director Serik Raibaev.[7] While there is nothing nationally specific about the plot itself, the depiction of Kazakhstan's sports milieu is intriguing and largely believable. The professor, a Mephisthophelean character who even quotes from *Faust*, gives the film an unexpected intellectual whiff. One of the most interesting aspects of *The Throw* is how it captures society's obsession with normative physicality: when Temir first appears on the court, the fans laugh because he is chubby and looks distinctly different from the other team members. The most severe conflict occurs when the team itself begins to resent Temir since every success is owed to him, while the collective contributions no longer count and go unnoticed by the public. Temir himself does like his teammates, but he quickly becomes isolated, as the others cannot forgive him his extraordinary abilities. This interesting dialectical take on the relationship between exceptional talent and collective achievement also makes this film a noteworthy contribution to the sports subgenre.

Another genre blend, this time combining brat comedy and athlete drama, is *The Champion* (Chempion, 1979). Although a minor film, it nevertheless reveals a lot about the values of Kazakhstani society past and present, especially in the context of sports films for adults. *The Champion* tells the story of ten-year-old Murat, who is harassed by classmates and children in the courtyard because of his underdeveloped physical prowess. Murat hates sports, due not to any kind of a bad disposition but to simple laziness. Whenever he can find a convenient excuse, he misses class. The boy has accepted his lack of athletic skills and is even willing to "pay" sweets to a young neighborhood thug nicknamed Genghis Khan to avoid getting beaten (an early anticipation of school racketeering in Kazakh films of the 2000s). The principles on which Murat's upbringing is based are openly discussed by his family. While his father and grandmother speak out in favor of a rougher, more "manly" approach, his overprotective mother will have none of it.

The motivational trigger for change, as in many Kazakh sports dramas, is a girl. Murat is interested in the smart and sensitive Zhanat, who likes him, too. In a curious reversal of clichés, it is Zhanat who practices karate and generally takes the initiative: she is the one who proposes to Murat, "Let's be friends!" When Zhanat gives Murat an apple, he keeps it like a precious talisman. This inspires him, for the first time, to stand up to Genghis Khan who wants to "requisition" the gift. The other agent of change is the new sports teacher, Ilias (Doskhan Zholzhaksynov), who will not accept Murat's laziness. As luck would have it, he also happens to be Zhanat's father. When Ilias organizes a boxing club at school, Murat wants to join, but his parents are adamantly opposed. Conspicuously, rather than prohibiting it themselves, they ask the teacher to reject Murat, with the result that his girlfriend, Zhanat, begins to coach him, with his grandmother serving as the stand-in during training sessions. It all comes crashing down when Genghis Khan humiliates Murat in front of Zhanat, who is deeply disappointed and breaks up with him. At this point, Zhanat's father demonstrates his pedagogical skill. He disapproves of his daughter's decision to drop Murat and coaches the boy individually. As is typical of inspirational sports films featuring the transformation of a "loser" into a victor, Murat ends up winning a youth competition in the triumphant finale, with his parents, his girlfriend, and even Genghis Khan applauding.

*The Champion* was adapted from a children's story by the popular Berdybek Sokpakbaev, who also authored *My Name Is Kozha*, a classic of Kazakh youth literature.[8] In retrospect, the noteworthy aspects of *The Champion* are less the athletic but the pedagogical references, which explore the question of what it means to be a boy and to become a man; what role parents and grandparents play in the process; and how much of an impact school can have. Murat's attraction to Zhanat is his major motivation to get himself in shape and become a man who can stand up for his girlfriend. Thus, *The Champion* makes a case for clearly defined social roles and values. Zhanat, although trained in karate, expects Murat to fight for her; in other words, the adjustment of gender roles that is marked by her practicing martial arts will only go so far. Those who resist these values (e.g., the thoroughly urbanized mother) are depicted as violators of the natural order, whereas the traditionalist grandmother intuitively knows what is right and what is wrong for a boy by Kazakh standards. Murat's being bullied by another youngster is portrayed as a challenge that is normal and must be expected and confronted—an unfortunate but inevitable part of life. On the one hand, demanding payments in sweets appears harmless and even funny; on the other, such normalization points to more serious behavioral patterns that extend into the adult world. Sports marks the path to establishing justice and order.

Noteworthy, albeit a minor aspect, is the militant nature of communist education shown in *The Champion*. Guided by their teacher, the children participate in a paramilitary game of "summer lightning" (*zarnitsa*), using realistic model rifles. The fact that Zhanat courageously helps her team win the war game draws a connection with the women warrior characters that are a traditional trope of Kazakh culture and came to prominence in World War II with legendary fighters Manshuk Mametova and Aliia Moldagulova. Indeed, *The Champion* contains a noticeable dosage of national spirit, with the teacher Ilias as a role model. At home, the athlete-cum-teacher plays the dombra. His ideals aim at much more than mere success in athletic competition. At one point, Zhanat states that her father "wants all people to be strong, beautiful, and healthy," a formulation resembling the earliest Kazakh sports film, *The White Square*.

*The Champion* makes some explicit reference to national specifics. Murat is inspired by Ilias, but also by a book illustrated with pictures of Kazakh heroes, *batyrs*. The obstacle to achieving the ideal is the urban lifestyle, which threatens to alienate children from the values of the past. Thus, Murat's mother, a nurse in an ultramodern hospital, is completely detached from traditional male upbringing; her pedagogical principles are mocked because they are denationalized, whereas Murat's grandmother understands full well the desirable direction of her grandson's development. Murat's ultimate transformation from slacker into fighter is substantially enhanced by his discovery of his national roots. His goal is not only to be stronger than the bully Genghis Khan, but to protect other children from him—precisely in accordance with the ancient honor code of the noble warrior.

## BIRTH OF THE KAZAKH THRILLER

The detective film, or thriller, in Kazakhstani cinema did not emerge with the reintroduction of capitalism in the 1990s but first appeared in the 1970s. In its Soviet phase, the Kazakh film industry gained some experience with crime stories, although few of them demonstrated high narrative, let alone artistic qualities. For the most part, the studio and the makers of such movies hoped that the genre itself would be attractive enough to lure audiences to the movie theaters. Not surprisingly, in the 1980s, in a period of revision and reassessment, those films were critically panned as part of cineastes' and critics' frustration with Kazakh cinema.

The generally negative attitude toward the detective genre by Soviet critics and ideological authorities notwithstanding, an assessment of Soviet-Kazakhstani films that broadly fall into this category reveals a few movies that are of thematic and sociological interest. One such film is *The Choice* (Vybor, 1975), which may be categorized as an "ecological thriller." With the heightened environmental awareness across the USSR in the 1970s, this subgenre gained prominence throughout Soviet cinema, featuring poachers and ruthless administrators mindlessly endangering the ecological balance. The central character and positive hero of *The Choice*, Maken Iskakov (Dzhambul Khudaibergenov), is a wildlife guard (*eger'*) in a national park. Maken projects physical strength and calm when he fearlessly confronts reckless poachers and later the larger organized crime structures to which they belong. When Maken discovers an entrapped snow tiger, he has no doubt that this was the work of criminals. He manages to save the animal and keeps it in his research center, but the attacks on wildlife continue. The evil spirit behind them is an influential official, Kozhamkulov (Asanali Ashimov), a well-connected man who in public projects a different, cultured personality, fooling friends and family. A direct confrontation is inevitable when Kozhamkulov's poachers attack Maken after shooting a huge number of wild goats. During the subsequent car chase, the criminals throw the slaughtered animals from their truck one by one, finally injuring Maken himself.

Meanwhile, Kozhamkulov, who inhabits a luxurious city apartment filled with refined furniture, cynically justifies his passion for hunting and trapping to his wife, a surgeon. It is obvious that this is just a rationalization of his arrogant lawlessness. During the showdown at the wildlife support station, Kozhamkulov and his men mock Maken who states that he has made his choice to protect wildlife (hence the title), will stand by it, and will not close the case against them. In the end, militia men arrest the gang, and the rescued snow tiger is returned to his peaceful habitat.

Given the linearity of its plot and the psychological simplicity of its characters, *The Choice* primarily stands out for Ashimov's excellent portrayal of a corrupt urbanite whose attitude toward nature is one of reckless consumerism. His opponent, Maken, who often appears on horseback, is depicted as a noble cowboy. Maken is educated and cares about nature for deep reasons. The two opposing worldviews are irreconcilable and based on firm convictions. Thus, Maken asks a timberman why he has no pity for the countless huge trees he cuts: after all, these are rare Tian-Shan firs. His care extends far beyond animals and is much more ethically and, implicitly, nationally grounded than the attitude toward nature featured in *The Golden Horn* twenty-five years earlier. Obviously, priorities in Kazakhstani society have changed from efficient exploitation of nature to protection of precious resources.

The film's gender aspects are noteworthy as well. Maken represents a manliness that is both strong and educated. Remarkably, *The Choice* succeeds in making the lawful characters appear more attractive than the lawbreakers. This is no small achievement in a genre which often inspires viewers to side with criminals as long as they are good-looking and inventive. Indeed, the actor Dzhambul Khudaibergenov[9] would become one of the few exemplary "positive heroes" of the 1970s, a decade in which the societal atmosphere was increasingly marred by ethical relativism and cynicism. With his Kazakh hat, athletic build, and self-confident, generous disposition, he was cast as a believable reincarnation of legendary *batyrs*. Taking up the cause of protecting nature against those who greedily destroy it, Maken set a moral standard and an image of independent virility that complemented the Kazakhstani gallery of exemplary film athletes and could impress young audiences. (It must be pointed out that in the documentary genre, Viacheslav Belialov and Larisa Mukhamedgalieva pursued a similar goal, churning out numerous shorts about endangered species in Kazakhstan's mountains; interestingly, a decade later, they, too, turned to feature filmmaking with detective subplots.)

Apart from its subject-matter, *The Choice* represents the typical Soviet crime narrative, in which good and bad are contoured with excessive clarity and the forces of law are unquestionably superior on every scale. Within the proposed schematics, the social and moral order may be temporarily violated by perpetrators but is ultimately invariably reinstated through the efforts of an archetypal selfless hero. Still, the degree to which the forces of evil manage to advance in an otherwise stable society is disturbing. Perhaps unintentionally, clearly defined genre movies such as *The Choice* reveal negative aspects of Soviet-Kazakh society that no other genre would address.

## A SINGULAR MASTERPIECE: *THE FIERCE ONE*

Conspicuously, Kazakhstani cinema in the 1970s provided fertile ground for the exploration of genre variations. Alas, ideological opportunism and aesthetic mediocrity began to blossom during that decade as well. To be sure, such generalizations are not based on the elitist criteria that were often applied by film critics, especially some writing in the Soviet center judging productions of the national peripheries. The evolution of distinct genres during that period, including inspirational sports dramas and thrillers, was a legitimate development. But at the same time, the number of outstanding pictures striving for the highest artistic quality shrank dramatically. However, this does not mean that there were no masterpieces at all. A close look reveals that, despite the abundance of demoralizing control mechanisms and bureaucratic pressures, there was room for exceptional films. As long as artistically ambitious projects were politically safe, the administration of Kazakhfilm studio and the republic's *Goskino* were eager to promote them. Since some of the senior leading Kazakh directors were no longer active, it became common practice to invite directors from neighboring republics to helm artistic prestige projects; perhaps some in the studio administration feared that native directors would not be able to cope with the challenge. One outstanding picture to come out of Kazakhstan during that difficult period is *The Fierce One* (Liutyi, 1973), adapted by Kyrgyz director Tolomush Okeev from a short story by Mukhtar Auezov. The inclusion of this film in Kazakhstani film history even though its director, cameraman, and male lead are Kyrgyz, is justified because of its roots in Kazakh literature and its production at Kazakhfilm studio.

The plot of *The Fierce One* is relatively linear. The poor, unmarried shepherd Akhangul lives with his old mother and his nephew, Kurmash, in the steppe. When Akhangul pursues a she-wolf and kills three of her cubs, the little boy asks for the fourth cub to be spared. As it grows up, the wolf, named Koksen, displays increasingly aggressive behavior, but Kurmash defends him against all threats from his uncle. When the enraged Akhangul throws the animal into the wild river, the boy risks his own life to save it. For months, Kurmash and Koksen are left to themselves in the mountains guarding the family's sheep, some of which Akhangul stole from the rich *bay*. But when a pack of wolves attacks the herd, Koksen refuses to fight them and later escapes. Traumatized by this betrayal, Kurmash decides to live by himself in a cave, avoiding his uncle's fury. A fugitive political activist, Hassen Kenzhetaev, invites the starving boy into his hut and teaches him lessons about humanity and social injustice. Still, Kurmash wants to help his blind grandmother and leaves with his uncle, who had been searching for him. In the middle of winter, the hungry Koksen approaches Kurmash, but just as the boy tries to put a muzzle over his head, the wolf bites him severely. Akhangul shoots the animal, while Hassen, who was treating the boy's injuries, is arrested by tsarist police.

*The Fierce One* is an atmospherically tense picture, the complexity of which unfolds on two levels, one socio-historical and the other philosophical. The historical aspect is introduced at the beginning of the film through a text that clarifies that the story takes place before the 1917 revolution. In subsequent episodes, Okeev emphasizes the social hardships endured by Akhangul, his mother, and his little nephew, Kurmash. He does so with directness that sometimes appears excessive, so much so that some scenes resemble a Marxist pamphlet. However, the inherent philosophical discourse evolves from sociohistorical parameters, that is, the poverty and social injustice at the margins of the Russian Empire, that are based on fundamental Marxist assumptions, although the film ultimately transcends them. In other words, the retroactive criticism of tsarist society, which at first may appear as political opportunism in the Soviet 1970s, is necessary for a conceptual association with the film's deeper discourse on what defines humanity and human evolution in a world of natural and social wilderness.

The hunter Akhangul unabashedly espouses a "survival-of-the-fittest" approach to life. When he discovers the wolf cubs, he kills them without mercy, as these animals are his direct competitors for food. To Akhangul, his little nephew's pity for the tiny helpless creatures seems unnatural, and he chastises Kurmash for "crying like a girl." What follows are two counter-arguments against Akhangul's worldview, one ethical and one pragmatic. The ethical objection is expressed by Akhangul's friend, the convict Hassen, who says that any living being treated well will respond in kind. The pragmatic objection comes from Akhangul's old mother, who realizes that the she-wolf will now come to the *aul* every night looking for her offspring, disturbing and threatening the community. The ethical objection remains one of the film's inherent hypotheses, while the pragmatic one immediately proves to be accurate, demonstrating that when human society and wild nature exist in proximity to each other, a purely Darwinian approach such as Akhangul's will aggravate problems, not resolve them.

Arguably the most conceptually important character is the boy Kurmash. Endowed with precocious self-confidence and an inquisitive heart, he stands up for himself against all those who are stronger, including his uncle and the older children in the *aul*. Kurmash pities the young wolf because he can identify with him, as his own parents are dead and buried in a faraway place, a trauma to which he keeps returning.

The political convict Hassen represents a thoroughly humanist approach. In one of the first episodes, he gives Akhangul, whom he calls a friend, a valuable animal that he shot. Akhangul refuses the gift, claiming that he does not know how to reciprocate. But Hassen insists and Akhangul finally gives in, although such gestures of sharing clearly make him feel uncomfortable. Kurmash seems to have been born with a compassionate disposition similar to that of Hassen, sharing his food with Koksen as a matter of course, as if the instinct to share is innate and only eliminated later, in adulthood. Time and time again, Hassen voices his ideals of education and progress. Toward the end, when Kurmash escapes and tries to live on his own in a grave temple where he believes his parents are buried, Hassen convinces him that it is advantageous to live together, a lesson the boy quickly internalizes. He performs his share of labor, milling the grain and absorbing what Hassen tells him about railways and other miracles of the modern world.

Below its explicit Marxist surface, *The Fierce One* is a harshly realistic picture that raises the question of humankind's potential for moral evolution. This central question is posed but remains unanswered. Indeed, is the semi-domesticated title hero, the fierce young wolf, aggressive because he was victimized by Akhangul or would he have grown up aggressive regardless, because his behavior is genetically determined? In other words, were Kurmash's attempts to make the wolf a loyal friend and a member of the community doomed from the beginning? The film leaves room for both options: that wolves will always be wolves, or, had the boy been left alone with the animal, that the outcome might have been different. The main reason for this disquieting ambiguity is the impossibility of creating a pure experimental situation in which the fundamental question could be answered without external interference: the circumstances both of man's and wolf's education are determined by the society surrounding them. In the case of Kurmash and his wolf, it is the inhumane tsarist society that favors the likes of the *bay*'s son and punishes the humane Hassen. However, Akhankul's "beat first" approach does not help him either since society, with its brutal police force, is much stronger than even the strongest lone wolf, metaphorically or literally. Thus, the film's finale unites the perceptive child, the brutal uncle, and the loving grandmother in shared despair. This despair is caused not by the "cruelty" of living nature, but by the cruelty of human society.

Okeev's cameraman was one of the best in Central Asian cinema, Kadyrzhan Kydyraliev. His vision of wilderness alternates between tender, pastel-like landscapes and harshly shaped mountain images that seem to reflect the unforgiving nature of life, both the wild and the social. Most episodes are shot in color; some are black-and-white. Such alternation was popular in the 1970s, signaling the presence of a philosophical concept; however, it is hard to determine what exactly motivates the switch from one to the other. The film certainly gains greater harshness due to the introduction of black-and-white in some scenes.

*The Fierce One*, arguably Tolomush Okeev's greatest accomplishment thanks to its unsentimental truthfulness and philosophical depth, is also one of the best films made in Soviet Kazakhstan. The story unfolds at the beginning of the twentieth century. The aforementioned statement at the film's beginning makes it clear that "the described events take place prior to the October Revolution." But *The Fierce One* is also a timeless parable about the dim hopes for humane civilizational values in the face of the laws of nature, which extend into the depth of society. Remarkably, society's common cruelty and deeply ingrained injustice are also marked as the result of quasi-natural class structures. Indeed, the film displays unusual skepticism toward the effectiveness of enlightening and humanizing efforts as such, be it through education, empathy, or moral appeal. Within a Soviet context, which was based on the firm assumption of historical progress, this skepticism was particularly disturbing.

Just like the Auezov story from which it was adapted, *The Fierce One* is told in a stringent, energetic manner that leaves no room for romantic distraction or self-deception. Rather, the viewer is confronted with an inconvenient truth about the roots of human misery and its seemingly unstoppable self-reproduction. Little Kurmash, both sensitive and strong-willed, can empathize with the suffering of others; his faith in the power of loyalty and kindness marks the film's positive hypothesis. This attitude is rooted in Kazakh national tradition, which places great importance on compassion as a fundamental value. The view of the world as principally good, and the faith in nature in particular, are reinforced by the boy's frail grandmother, who embodies wisdom and unconditional love. The antithesis to this faith is represented by Kurmash's bitter, disenchanted uncle, who tries to turn the boy into a "real man" through systematic physical and psychological abuse.

This dichotomy of patriarchal upbringing, with male mercilessness and female forgiveness as extreme poles, marks the film's ethical discourse, and little Kurmash, armed solely with a courageous heart and will, sets out to test the limits of the ethical space that society affords. To him, the wolf cub is a fellow orphan, a brother in suffering, which explains the trust that he places in the animal as a kindred creature. To the very end, Kurmash cannot accept the wolf's inability to respond in kind. After all, did he not save it from drowning after Akhangul threw it into the river? However, to Koksen, survival is his sole purpose in life: the animal's instincts remain unaltered, and regardless of what acts of kindness come his way, he will respond to any perceived threat by attacking, even if this means harming his rescuer and only friend. Worse yet, Koksen becomes more dangerous than other wolves because he is familiar with humans, does not fear them, and has learned how to outwit them. This uncompromising stance on the stability of genetic predisposition makes *The Fierce One* a challenge to the cliché-filled melodramas about children and wildlife that are common in the history of Soviet and world cinema. Indeed, Okeev's drama is a powerful antithesis to sentimental indulgence in wild nature. And still, the film does not fall into the opposite extreme, promoting a Jack London-type mercilessness. Auezov did believe in civilizational advancement, and his story and its adaptation contain sufficient arguments in its favor.

In the context of Kazakhstani cinema, another aspect is relevant as well. The traditionally strong identification with the worldview and perception of children in Kazakh films finds a novel application in *The Fierce One*. Kurmash embodies an inborn sense of justice and empathy. Thus, he rejects the world of adults to the point that he completely isolates himself and makes a serious attempt to survive on his own. Unlike Kozha's carefree friend and tempter, Sultan, in *My Name Is Kozha*, this quest for solitude is not the result of failure in society, but of revulsion toward the rules that govern it. Kurmash is ethically superior to his environment. The child's inborn moral compass is incorruptible, and all attempts by his uncle to break that compass just make it stronger.

This Rousseauean view of children as bearers of moral values who find an ally in living nature, as opposed to the corrupt world of violent adults, is comparable to a film that went largely unnoticed in the United States but made a huge impression on many Soviet filmmakers: Stanley Kramer's *Bless the Beasts and the Children* (1971). Released at the time of the most profound debates about the Vietnam War and the moral state of US society, Kramer expressed his disagreement with a world of unforgiving brutality through a parable about young outsiders who save a herd of buffalos from slaughter. The screenwriter of *The Fierce One*, Andrei Mikhalkov-Konchalovskii, was certainly familiar with this film, which was shown in closed screenings at Moscow's House of Cinema, and Tolomush Okeev may also have seen it there. If *The Fierce One* was indeed a Kyrgyz-Kazakh response to *Bless the Beasts and the Children*, it is certainly less sermonic and sentimental, but it does share a faith in the original goodness of humans that regresses into beast-like evil because of repressive socialization.

Okeev elicited exemplary performances from the entire cast, particularly little Kambar Valiev as Kurmash and Suimenkul Chokmorov as his uncle, Akhangul. Dunchenbai Botbaev's darkly dramatic, folklore-inspired score powerfully supports the parabolic aspects of the plot. The community of herdsmen is depicted as fearful and disjointed, intimidated both by ruthless native *bays* and by the uniformed servants of Russian autocracy. The only adult character who offers at least some realistic hope is Hassen Kenzhetaev, the leftist intellectual with a deep understanding of the archaic, quasi-biological foundation of tribal laws, which he fights fearlessly. Like a messenger from utopia, Hassen believes in the power of education, mutual aid, and modernization. Indeed, his tales about the miraculous railroads serve as an inspiration to Kurmash. But the teacher's sad end, which coincides with the boy's agony and despair, may well leave the viewer to draw a sobering and pessimistic conclusion about the limited transformability of nature, including human nature.

## A SLEEPER HIT

While Okeev's *The Fierce One* was a prestige project for Kazakhfilm that became an international arthouse success, other pictures produced at the studio were predominantly appreciated by domestic audiences and eventually became part of an internal canon that has remained unrecognized and unknown elsewhere. *My Name Is Kozha* and *Kyz-Zhibek* served as impressive overtures to this phenomenon, which has not been critically assessed. While Kazakhfilm studio's former leading directors of the 1960s (Shaken Aimanov, Mazhit Begalin, and Sultan-Akhmet Khodzhikov) could no longer play a major role in the process of developing this internal Kazakh film canon, there were less recognized directors who created films that were modest in appearance but remarkable in the authenticity of their message and in their national staying power.

Sharip Beisembaev's *Protect Your Star* (Gauhartas/Khrani svoiu zvezdu, 1975) is such a "sleeper hit," that is, a film that at first was hardly noticed but over the years revealed its innate conceptual relevance and lasting charm. Indeed, this optimistic family drama, based on a screenplay by Dulat Isabekov, has been remembered and reviewed with increasing fondness in more recent decades. Just as in the case of *Kyz-Zhibek*, the absence of explicit communist messages therein is especially noteworthy.

The film's plot lacks excessively dramatic or tragic elements. Surprisingly and with disarming candor, the opening credits predict just that. The authors' focus on "normal" life was a deliberate choice. Indeed, *Protect Your Star* develops its narrative energy in part because of its implicit allusions to clichéd, overused dramatic devices. The main plotline is simple and unspectacular: Dastan, a young shepherd (Anuarbek Boranbaev), marries Saltanat (Zhannat Kuanysheva) and takes her to the family farm where his parents and his younger brother Kairken live. All family members work hard and closely together, maintaining a high standard of living and honoring traditional values. At the end, Kairken is drafted and leaves for service in the Soviet army.

This synopsis, however, reveals little of the film's unobtrusive originality. *Protect Your Star* gains its significance from numerous details embedded in it. The main source of the film's inspirational energy lies in its loving depiction of regular folks and their daily life. That does not mean that it promotes an artificially idyllic picture of Kazakh society—far from it. At the beginning, it may seem as if the family's wealth and their adherence to ancient tradition are causally connected. But that harmonious picture soon begins to crumble, and the tensions among various family members lead to a crisis. Kairken, who has internalized a deep sense of duty regarding his role as a man and a younger brother, is endowed with a poetic gift: he sings to the dombra with his own improvised lyrics and is proud of this talent. He also expresses a shy admiration for his beautiful sister-in-law. The two seem to connect in more ways than one: for example, Saltanat has a beautiful singing voice, which she initially denies. The family, however, cares little about artistry and poetic perceptions; what matters is work and work alone. Moreover, the clear definition of gender roles is strictly observed. At one point, Dastan tells his younger brother, "You have nothing manly in yourself!", hurting him deeply. While the mother, superbly portrayed by Amina Umurzakova, tries to smooth the tensions with love and care, the father sides with his older son's emphasis on patriarchal norms of behavior. The simmering conflict reaches a boiling point when Saltanat inadvertently oversteps these norms. Her husband is a proud horseman who has won many races. When his wife, who is no less experienced, dares to ride his favorite horse without asking for permission, he loses his self-control and slaps her. Saltanat is deeply shocked, develops a fever, and is taken to the hospital. At this point, even the father begins to realize that patriarchal rule, taken literally, has the potential to destroy the family.

This subplot of Saltanat and Dastan's marital woes suggests closeness to Mazhit Begalin's *The Traces Go Beyond the Horizon*. However, *Protect Your Star* arrives at a profoundly different conclusion, a conclusion that is in line with the atmosphere of the 1970s. As if to quietly polemicize with its predecessor, Beisembaev's film is not directed against patriarchal principles per se and does not advocate the kind of radical self-liberation that marked the ending of Begalin's film a decade earlier. Instead, what makes *Protect Your Star* so unusual is its characters' *voluntary* loyalty to their traditional lifestyle, a loyalty that is persistent but not blind, strong but not inflexible. There is no black-and-white scheme denouncing one side and arguing in favor of the other. Rather, the film's poetic imagery itself embraces the harmonious life in the middle of blooming nature, and the score underlines the warmth and love reigning in the family. The frictions and the estrangement are depicted as temporary and not insurmountable. The reason that this approach comes across as believable is the film's trust in common sense and love. Traditionalism is not conveyed in a polemical manner nor presented as vehemently anti-modern. After all, cutting-edge technology is part of this family's life, including modern machinery and a generator that produces electricity for the yurts and the water pump. The characters themselves seem to be unaware of their old-fashioned attitudes when it comes to internal hierarchy. Thus, after the incident with his horse, Dastan is deeply concerned about his wife and does his utmost to save her, albeit applying old standards once again. When he tries to reward the visiting physician with a valuable sheep, he is flabbergasted by the doctor's rejection: "The state pays me for my work." In this episode the patriarchal husband, who meant well and did what was common practice in the past, looks ridiculous because he has failed to notice how life around him has changed.

When pondering the reasons why *Protect Your Star* holds such lasting appeal for Kazakh viewers, one must take into consideration the film's context. In Soviet cinema, stories denouncing the traditional rural lifestyle and patriarchy were a mainstay. In the 1920s and 1930s, representatives of "the old world," unwilling to give up their values and beliefs, were described as fierce enemies of Soviet power who would rather set fire to the farm and kill their own kin than accept change, and therefore had to be eliminated. *Enemies' Paths* and *Raikhan*, signature films about class struggle and collectivization in Kazakhstan in the 1930s, are examples of that antagonistic approach. In those stories, a representative from the Soviet center would typically serve as the messenger of new, modern social relations to the backward periphery. *Protect Your Star*, made forty years later, has abandoned that scheme. As a matter of fact, the film implicitly rejects it: Dastan and his father are not the enemies, and there is no need to neutralize or leave them; Saltanat herself is the first to admit that. Instead, they just need to change their priorities, abandon prejudices, and adjust their behavior to a new age.

In Beisembaev's film, even the most headstrong men realize that they should adjust their ways to protect what is the most important value of all: family love. The family is the unit that will weather internal problems. Thus, the attraction felt between Saltanat and Kairken does not lead to adultery or a catastrophic resolution, nor does Dastan's one-time transgression.

This implicit anti-antagonistic message is distinctly Kazakh—and it is completely un-Soviet. Interestingly, the collectivist alternative to the family that had been propagandized for decades is also depicted in an unusual manner. When the head of the collective farm and other honored members of the community come to visit the family, which lives separately from the village, they invite Dastan and Saltanat to join their collective, but do so without the typical accusations of individualism and threats of dire consequences in the event of their refusal.

One night, Saltanat and her brother-in-law, Kairken, go to the village to dance. Both enjoy the occasion to spend quality time together (as luck would have it, Saltanat's husband cannot stand disco noise or loud television sets). To be sure, the evening is about music, not some potential erotic encounter. For Saltanat and Kairken, their interaction remains completely innocent; any ambiguity would be unthinkable. On their way home, a vain truck driver, who has been openly flirting with Saltanat, accompanies them, but Kairken cleverly keeps the pushy suitor away from his sister-in-law in an episode that radiates wonderful soft humor. Indeed, this is perhaps the most unusual and appealing feature of *Protect Your Star*: conflicts are resolved in a peaceful, benevolent manner; characters who would have become victims in the usual clichéd dramas possess enough self-confidence to take care of themselves, and their potential victimizers are able to change, based on their own insights and the forgiveness of their environment. The film shows that life has more to offer than a simple "either/or."[10]

Thus, *Protect Your Star* is most remarkable as a cliché-defying film. As mentioned earlier, this is explicitly stated at the very beginning: a narrator declares, with soft irony, that "the following story will not unfold in a typical manner." Beisembaev proves this at every point when a certain plot turn seems to suggest a predictable outcome (for example, Kairken and Saltanat could have begun an affair that would have ended badly, perhaps even in violent death; either of them could have left the oppressive family in protest to realize their artistic potential, etc.). If the film itself were not so mild, one could justifiably conclude that it promotes Kazakh values over Soviet ones, and it certainly does, albeit in a non-polemical manner. In *Protect Your Star*, the family as such is the supreme value for its members, superseding all seemingly inevitable conflicts. Indeed, the family is the star from the title that must be protected.

Ashkhat Ashrapov's carefully composed images, with the isolated yurts placed within softly contoured pastel landscapes, corroborate this positive attitude.[11] The fact that Dastan is an individual farmer (*edinolichnik*) is not once cited as a reason to condemn him. Instead, despite his temper and often grumpy outlook on life, his uncompromising work ethic is repeatedly commended. *Protect Your Star* shows that the conflict between tradition and modernity in Kazakhstan is not a simple one and that both sides have arguments in their favor. Furthermore, traditional values have enough elasticity to allow for reasonable adjustments. To be sure, the film leaves no doubt that modern culture can only grow and be appreciated in the communal realm; in other words, it does not advocate individualism or a reclusive lifestyle per se. But for Saltanat, Dastan, Kairken, and their parents, love and individual achievement emerge from their family and its adherence to traditional values. This worldview is depicted with fairness and patience, avoiding conventional judgment and convenient denunciation. In its social benevolence and tolerance, the film preempted the Soviet mega-hit *Moscow Does Not Believe in Tears* (Moskva slezam ne verit, 1979). In the words of Kabysh Siranov, after the fiasco of four Kazakhstani films (*The Funeral Feast*, *Where the Mountains Are White*, *Uralsk on Fire*, and *Jump into the Unknown*), *Protect Your Star* was perceived as the long-awaited event that could predict positive change in the trajectory of Kazakhfilm's work.[12] It is plausible to assume that censorial authorities were more generous to this film than was typical *because* of its deliberate conflict avoidance after so many difficult, controversial projects had been shelved. They missed, or conveniently overlooked, the subversive potential that is also inherent in this non-Soviet, humane, profoundly national picture. The constructive viewpoint embraced by *Protect Your Star* had the staying power to survive the destruction of the Soviet paradigm and would play a fundamental role in the redefinition of national identity after Kazakhstan gained its independence.

## KAZAKHS AND RUSSIANS AS FAMILY

The relationship between Kazakhs and Russians has been among the most complicated issues for citizens of Kazakhstan. Especially in the new millennium, aspects of language policy, cultural priorities, and a reevaluation of the Soviet past have made Kazakh-Russian issues a highly controversial subject. During the Soviet period, cinema was initially used to implement a mentor/ mentee relationship between center and periphery and between members of the two ethnic groups. Thus, in early Kazakh films such as *Daughter of the Steppes* (1954), Russian women and men appear as civilizational and political educators, providing orientation to Kazakhs in all professional and academic disciplines and assisting them in their appropriation of a modern urban lifestyle. Some films of the 1960s, such as Aimanov's *In One District* (1960), indicate the presence of frictions between Kazakh and Russian perceptions, based on their national peculiarities, while others, such as Begalin's *Song of Manshuk*, even demonstrate the moral superiority of exceptional Kazakh characters vis-à-vis their Russian environment. But in general, the relationship between the two ethnic groups was always presented in Kazakhstani cinema as a positive one. Because many ramifications of interethnic relations in the country remained taboo, the issue was touchy and rarely addressed explicitly.

One of the few films to deal directly with Russian-Kazakh relations was made in the 1970s: *The Son's Return* (Vozvrashchenie syna, 1977). Directed by Sharip Beisembaev from a screenplay by Valentin Chernykh and Saiyn Muratbekov, the film traces the roots of Kazakh-Russian togetherness to the Great Patriotic War. In the chaos of war, a Russian woman, Evdokia Mikhailovna (Lidiia Smirnova), handed her little son to her sister who was evacuated to Kazakhstan. But when the sister perished, the boy lost contact with his mother: he was raised by Kazakh foster parents. Thirty-five years later, that boy, Sergei (Vitalii Grishko), now a grown man and himself a father of five, manages to find the address of his birth mother and writes her a letter. The scene in which Evdokia receives her son's letter opens the film with a veritable emotional rollercoaster. When the aging mother, who is suffering from a heart ailment, visits Sergei in his *aul* in the mountains, she is welcomed with utmost respect, especially by Sergei's stepmother, Rabiga (Biken Rimova). The Kazakh mother insists, in a tone that allows no disagreement, that her stepson travel to Evdokia's native village and then make his decision whether to stay in Kazakhstan or move to Russia.

The plot may seem constructed for maximum melodramatic and internationalist effects. However, Kazakh society with its high level of trust within families, produced many such real-life stories, especially in the postwar period, when similar cases were regularly featured in newspapers. Besides its emotional impact, the plot of *The Son's Return* serves as an obvious vehicle to illustrate the reality of interethnic connections in the Soviet Union. The positive surface is interspersed with details pointing to a darker side. For one thing, not everybody is happy with the prospect of Sergei leaving the *aul*. His father-in-law angrily asks who would take care of him when he became frail and sick. For another, when Sergei takes his teenage son Sapar to Evdokia's village, the Russian male youths drop some nasty remarks about the "squint-eyed guy" and plan to beat him up, especially when he forms a strong bond with a local teenage girl. But such temporary dissonances remain minor, as the *aul* and the village share one quality: a strong sense of community order. Sergei decides to build a new house for his mother, and the entire village helps. This is depicted as one of the common features of Kazakh and Russian communities: the ability to integrate newcomers, be they native or "alien." The spirit of togetherness is verbalized, although with some restraint, as a human value, not a political slogan. Only during a celebration in the finale can one hear toasts such as "To our homeland, to our brotherhood!" and "The peoples of our country are one great family." Prior to these announcements, the political messages are largely dissolved in the film's melodramatic fabric.[13]

Valentin Chernykh, a screenwriter who would acquire huge fame two years later with another accommodational melodrama, *Moscow Doesn't Believe in Tears* (Moskva slezam ne verit, 1979), emphasizes the day-to-day benevolence of Soviet society, its everyday human warmth. Chernykh's avoidance of explicit propaganda and his ability to cleverly evoke a pro-Soviet mood from the popular genre of melodrama with comedic elements made him the signature screenwriter of the 1970s. His ability to capture the atmosphere of the time was unrivaled. It is no coincidence that the roots of Evdokia's story date back to the Second World War, which was won not by Russia alone but by the Soviet Union as one multiethnic entity that, according to its self-image, acted as the strongest advocate of peace in the world. The 1970s appear in *The Son's Return* (just like in *Moscow Doesn't Believe in Tears*) as a time of protected social peace in which past wounds have been healed and family love can blossom. Beisembaev's direction continues seamlessly the emphasis on harmony and fulfillment in Soviet private life successfully begun in *Protect Your Star* (1975), and extends it to a multinational subject. Among the film's specific Kazakh aspects are the country's openness to the integration of foreign ethnic groups (a theme that would be continued after independence) and the validity of ancient ethical rules such as respect for one's roots. A key moment in the film is Rabiga's stern decision that Sergei must join his aging mother, as she is the one who gave him life. This law outweighs all other considerations, and both Kazakhs and Russians acquiesce.

The status quo referred to in the title of this chapter is part of the subsequent characterization of the decade as the "age of stagnation." In reality, this status quo defined an unwritten agreement between Soviet society and its ruling establishment about fundamental values on which Soviet life could rest in relative stability. Kazakhstan's standard of living in the 1970s was considered high in comparison to other Soviet republics, which shaped the population's more sophisticated cultural needs. But underneath a positive surface, there was growing dissatisfaction with the state of Kazakhstani culture, especially cinema. The successful development of popular film genres could give the impression that all was well at Kazakhfilm studio. However, the general perception of the studio's output was predominantly negative. The shelved films were seen by many as a disgrace rather than as victims of repressive policies. The film community tried its best to keep the internal conflicts under wraps.

One of the few cases when internal problems reached the public took place in 1972. Technical personnel from Mosfilm had written to the central newspaper, *Pravda*, complaining about the untenable situation in the production of film stock. Soviet film stock often turned out to be defective after being developed, which meant that precious shooting time had gone to waste and the lost scenes had to be filmed again. The staff of Kazakhfilm studio added their opinion, stating that "for the costs of defect film stock one could build more than one film stock-producing factory. Unfortunately, the artistic losses cannot be expressed in rubles."[14] One can only imagine the frustration of crews when large investments and artistic concentration turned out to be in vain.

The Third Congress of the Union of Kazakhstani Film Workers took place on April 6–7, 1976. The number of union members was now 133, while its governing board had increased since the previous congress almost twofold, counting 27 members. Akim Tarazi was reelected as first secretary. Externally, therefore, Kazakh cinema seemed to be sailing in safe waters, and all official announcements suggested stability. But the quantitative and qualitative crisis of Kazakh cinema had already become a matter of public discussion, with an emphasis on the need to find solutions to the lack of quality screenplays and qualified directors. This, of course, was merely a repetition of the old adage that began three decades earlier.

Preparatory courses for film students that had been created under the auspices of the screenwriting studio seemed to yield a quantitative effect. Their impact on professional and artistic quality, however, is debatable. One of the directors who graduated from these courses later remembered that, to be admitted, he had to write a short story, an essay, a sketch, and a film review. Then, for one year, he was taught fundamental skills and basic knowledge in areas that would be required during the VGIK entrance exam in Moscow. The teachers coaching him were the most prominent film artists of Kazakhstan's national studio, including the director Sultan-Akhmet Khodzhikov, the cameraman Mark Berkovich, and the art director Pavel Zal'tsman. And still, it was not enough for Damir Manabaev to pass.[15] The most demanding part, according to his recollection, was a thorough oral examination in which the applicant's knowledge of art, literature, and politics was tested, before switching to issues of general education. The fact that even one full year of high-level training was not enough to bring Kazakh applicants up to speed is a sad testimony to general educational shortcomings in the country. As a result, the shortage of qualified directors remained the Achilles' heel of Kazakhfilm studio.

## NOTES

1. Cf. Smailova, *Kinoentsiklopediia Kazakhstana*, p. 449.

2. The screenplay was written by Satybaldy Narymbetov, who in later years expressed some dissatisfaction with Kasymbekov's handling of the story.

3. About Abdrashit Abdrakhmanov's film career see Khrabrykh, Ol'ga, "Belyi kvadrat Abdrakhmanova." *Leninskaia smena. Ekspress*, 23 May 2008; Sergei Railian, "Kino i boks." *Karavan*, 10 July 2009.

4. Shutov, Sergei Gennadievich (b. 1954), Kazakhstani film director who graduated from the Soviet State Film Institute in 1976, before directing several full-length feature films at Kazakhfilm Studio; the best among them is the social thriller *The Human Factor* (1984). Shutov emigrated to Canada in 1998.

5. The screenplay for *A Decisive Fight* was adapted by Feliks Frantsuzov from a story by A. Kuleshov; the film was made for TV and features leading performers, including Doskhan Zholzhaksynov and Mukhtar Bakhtygereev as coaches.

6. Shmanov, Bolat (later changed to Bolat Sharip) (b. 1941), Kazakhstani director. He worked at Kazakhfilm studio since 1967, assisting Sultan Khodzhikov on

*Kyz-Zhibek* and Shaken Aimanov on *The End of the Ataman*. In 1978, he graduated from the Leningrad State Institute for Theater, Music, and Cinema in 1978 and then embarked on a directing career that included children's and detective films, as well as literary adaptations and documentaries.

7. Raibaev, Serik (1948–2006), Kazakh director and screenwriter who graduated from the Soviet State Film Institute in 1972 and helmed four full-length feature films and a number of documentaries at Kazakhfilm studio.

8. The screenplay was authored by V. Malinovskaia; the film was directed by Sergei Shutov.

9. Khudaibergenov, Dzhambul (1949–1990), Kazakh actor who studied with legendary Boris Babochkin at the Soviet State Film School (VGIK), graduating in 1974. Khudaibergenov appeared in a wide variety of genres but gained the greatest popularity in action-oriented roles.

10. One of the reviews interpreted the film as the story of a transformation, with Saltanat entering a traditional shepherd's home (the critic uses the term '*domostroi*') and transforming it with her soft kindness. While this conventional approach is legitimate to some degree, the more unusual aspect of the film is its endorsement of basic elements of the patriarchal order, which is not mentioned by the reviewer. Makarova, A. "'Khrani svoiu zvezdu,'" *Zvezda Priirtysh'ia*, 6 July 1977.

11. Typical of both *Kyz-Zhibek* and *Protect Your Star* is that the steppe is filmed with exceptional tenderness; far from being artificially modelled as an idyllic place, it is visualized as a welcoming, light, and nourishing sphere.

12. Siranov, Kabysh, "Sstenarii – osnova fil'ma," *Kazakhstanskaia pravda*, 3 April 1976.

13. Some minuscule propaganda details include a slogan, "Glory to the USSR" (Slava SSSR) when Evdokia arrives at Almaty airport, and a portrait of Leonid Brezhnev in an administrative office in the Russian village.

14. Beliavskii, O., "Lezhat fil'my na polkakh." *Pravda*, 27 April 1972, p. 3.

15. Akhmetova, V. "Molodezh' – budushchee ‚Kazakhfil'ma'". *Novyi fil'm*, 3/1977, p. 14.

*Chapter 10*

# State Cinema and Its Subversion

In their own ways, *The Fierce One, The Funeral Feast, Where the Mountains Are White*, and *Protect Your Star* all demonstrated that it is simplistic to denounce the 1970s as a wasted decade for Kazakhstan's cinema. Exceptional films were produced, some of which found official recognition and others of which were prohibited. Children's films, sports dramas, and thrillers made a reasonable attempt to satisfy the need for genre fare in certain segments of viewership. Assessing Kazakhfilm's overall output, however, it is undeniable that the studio settled—voluntarily or under pressure—for a politically inconspicuous cinema that left less room for artistic ambition and was oriented toward an increasingly conformist society. The time of sociopolitical and aesthetic risk-taking was over. In hindsight, the 1970s thus appear as a period of enforced cultural stability dominated by nonantagonistic, mostly mediocre films. Unlike the 1960s, it was difficult for deep and original narratives to get approval, especially those that expressed essential national values. The shelving of seven full-length feature films within a few years was catastrophic for a national studio with limited production volume. Worse yet, it paralyzed the creative daring of younger directors.

Indeed, powerful impulses from the previous decade yielded only limited results, and the profile of Kazakhfilm studio became aesthetically indistinct, some exceptional pictures notwithstanding. Thus, the radical criticism launched in the mid-1980s retroactively against Kazakhstani cinema of "the Brezhnev period," or "the time of stagnation," does have a point. Besides some genuine gems and a flow of more or less solid genre fare, the 1970s saw the emergence of a new phenomenon: the so-called gray films (*serye fil'my*). The term refers to uninventive, lackluster, and unexciting movies some of which paid political lip service while others, paradoxically, were churned out with the specific goal of "entertainment," that is, these movies were using the very niche that the new internal policies of the communist establishment permitted. Shown both in cinemas and on television, these politically opportunistic and artistically faceless movies were the result of a cynical view of the medium and its recipients.

However, the criticism launched by the first secretary of the Communist Party of Kazakhstan, Dinmukhamed Kunaev, against Kazakhfilm studio and its homegrown productions was based either on hypocrisy or on a profound misunderstanding of the functioning of the cultural apparatus that he himself oversaw. Demanding artistic quality and originality while simultaneously stifling creative initiative, as Kunaev and his communist establishment did, could not help but confuse Kazakhstani filmmakers, encouraging opportunists and alienating genuine artists. The cinematic representations of the Soviet-Kazakh past that the status quo cinema turned out lacked much of the authenticity that they once had. Those movies that fully embraced the ideological program of the Communist Party and met all its ideological criteria were pseudo-historical, pseudo-idealistic, and pseudo-romantic. The screenwriters and directors who participated in such productions were usually unambitious, intimidated, or willing to sacrifice aesthetic standards for the chance to enjoy the privileges that came with belonging to the upper echelons of Soviet society. It is undeniable that such "gray" movies are part of the legacy of Kazakhstani cinema and must be included in its history, considering their political, cultural, and moral context. These films, which are mostly forgotten today, provide depressing evidence that progress on the path to grasping the complexity of Kazakhstani history, down which filmmakers had begun to tread so forcefully in the 1960s, had come to a halt.

## CLEANSED VERSIONS OF THE PAST

It cannot be emphasized enough that in the 1960s, Kazakhstani cinema was distinguished by an uncommon willingness to experiment thematically and cinematically. Compared to filmmakers in other Soviet republics, Kazakhstani screenwriters and directors provided images of their nation's past that were less ideologically adjusted. Karsakbaev's *A Worrisome Morning* demonstrated how much some native filmmakers were willing to risk in order to capture the painful truths of Kazakhstan's Sovietization in the 1920s and 1930s. Even a failed attempt such as Karpov's *The Path of One Thousand Miles* avoided cheap regurgitations of the generic Civil War fare produced by other studios. However, the 1970s saw more bellicose reactions to nonconformism by the communist establishment and a greater readiness of many filmmakers to produce the kind of narratives that respected official taboos regarding Kazakh history.

These "ideologically correct" films were approved, financed, produced, and released as the studio's tributes to the Communist Party establishment rather than as honest attempts to engage audiences in a cinematic discourse on historical issues. As a matter of fact, such films rarely attracted significant numbers of viewers, unless contingents of army units and high school classes were assigned to attend the screenings. The transition from conceptually original and daring films to opportunistic propaganda fare did not happen overnight, however. Historical films such as *In Those Days* (V te dni, 1970) can be viewed as transitory products, in which the path toward an ideologically cleansed version of Kazakhstan's history was not fully completed but already discernible.

Directed by Zhardem Baitenov,[1] whose debut *The Blue Route* had caused shrill controversies in the media and required its director to rehabilitate himself, *In Those Days* stayed in politically safe waters. This "historical-revolutionary film," as the genre was officially called, takes place in the milieu of coal miners right before the 1917 revolution, in the settlement of Ridder, where a British company owns the license for the exploitation of coal. But the foreign investors are still in doubt as to whether Kazakhs are willing and able to work underground. The native population has its own worries. What will happen to their camels? Is it permissible to violate the ancestors' sacred soil? For the main character, Zholat (Nurzhuman Ikhtymbaev), the first encounter with the "steel camel that eats black stones and gets strong" is an eye-opener, demonstrating the power of the new industrial age. Getting a job as a miner will help Zholat earn enough money to marry his beloved. His motivation is so strong that he shows up for work even when the other Kazakh and Russian miners go on strike. But Danila Sirotin, a Russian propagandist (Boris Goldaev), educates him politically, and when a Cossack unit shows up to break the miners' resistance, Zholat hides a record with a Lenin speech that made a deep impression on everybody. Then the inhabitants of Ridder hear about the revolution that took place in Petrograd. The foreign capitalists ponder flooding the mines that are about to be nationalized. The showdown comes when the miners take over political power in Ridder, and the owners and their minions are forced to escape.

*In Those Days*, made from a screenplay by the prominent communist author and administrator Dmitrii Snegin,[2] has undeniable qualities. Ikhtymbaev as the proto-proletarian and Numurkhan Zhanturin as his rich reactionary opponent perform their parts with the visible dedication and passion that had become a mainstay of Kazakh cinema. The mentality of the miners (a traditionally very active social stratum) is well captured, and the arguments in political debates of the day, including anti-Russian slogans, are presented with dramatic verve. Mikhail Aranyshev's camera work is superb as always, as is the dynamic score by Gaziza Zhubanova. But what could such a movie offer to contemporary viewers? Beginning with its uninventive title, *In Those Days* is little more than a standard history lesson in which everything leads to predictable conclusions, from the emergence of a working class in Kazakhstan to the natural solidarity between Kazakh and Russian miners, which overrides the national unity between members of the upper and lower classes. The learning process of a naïve rural dweller who becomes a class-conscious fighter had been illustrated in Soviet cinema countless times before, beginning with Pudovkin's classic *The End of St. Petersburg* (1927). However, the calculation of the studio and its supervisors in the Communist Party and the Ministry of Culture apparatuses was that films such as *In Those Days* were fulfilling a political obligation; audiences' indifference was an embarrassing but ultimately acceptable side effect and was increasingly taken for granted. The real addressee of such films was the Communist establishment, not regular audiences.

While Baitenov's movie featured at least some realistic situations and dramatic tension, another historical film shows the genre's rapid decline in quality in the 1970s. *Horizons* (Gorizonty, 1972) also deals with the history of mining in Kazakhstan, continuing where *In Those Days* left off. It depicts the 1930s as a time of exploration and struggle against backwardness and indifference but excludes even a hint at inconvenient truths such as the purges and the GULAG concentration camps. The film's central character, Tair Murzin, is a geologist who returns to Kazakhstan after six years of study in Leningrad. The members of his clan accuse him of selling their country's riches to the Russians, while he understands that exploration of Kazakhstan's mineral resources is only possible within the Soviet industrial framework and that ethnic notions are immaterial to this goal-oriented approach. His assignment to become the new boss at a drilling station is marred by clashes with foreign contractors, who are still permitted to work under Soviet rule but are only interested in short-term profits. Side by side with them are arrogant Russian bourgeois leftovers, who badmouth Murzin as an "Asian" behind his back, and lazy workers who are not used to order and discipline. For Murzin, finding precious minerals is a task of strategic importance for securing the future of Soviet Kazakhstan. The film concludes with documentary shots of World War II that demonstrate the vital importance of minerals to defending the USSR. History has proven Murzin right.

To understand the studio's intentions in producing a film such as *Horizons*, which is even more formulaic than *In Those Days*, it is crucial to know that Kazakhstan's highest communist official, Dinmukhamed Kunaev, was himself a geologist whose career had begun with the exploration of mineral sites in the 1930s. Thus, *Horizons* was an implicit homage to the country's leader and enjoyed priority status. At the same time, it was also subject to the strictest ideological control. Contradictory facts that could undermine the official historical doctrine were excluded. The resistance encountered by Murzin is shown to come from negative stock characters, never from the Soviet bureaucracy itself. His attempts to find support in Leningrad and Moscow are depicted as a smooth ride: once his old professor arranges an appointment with Politbureau member Ordzhonikidze, Murzin's problems magically disappear. The question of what such personal interference on the highest government level reveals about the functioning principles of the Soviet economic system is, of course, never posed. The only difference between the Muscovite *deus ex machina* and Stalinist falsifications of reality is that the decision-maker is not Stalin but Ordzhonikidze. Indeed, Stalin is never even mentioned, nor does his portrait appear anywhere—in a film dealing with the 1930s! The one instance of Russian nationalist hubris, when an engineer named Bukhanov speaks arrogantly about Murzin to the woman he loves (who happens to be Russian) is the film's hint at the presence of "enemies of the people," thus implicitly justifying the mass repressions, although the term *vrag naroda*, which was ubiquitous in the 1930s, is never used.

But the most revealing element of "grayness" in *Horizons*, and an inevitable effect of its ideological opportunism, is not the film's blatant omission of historical facts but the complete lack of artistic passion. A bland title, an uneventful plot, ahistorical costumes and hairstyles, and blindness vis-à-vis period atmosphere are typical of the tedious hackwork that defined a large part of the studios' output in the 1970s. Talented actors such as Bolot Beishenaliev in the role of Murzin can do little to save a film whose principal dishonesty about the Soviet past is matched only by its low-level narrative energy. Apparently, *Horizons*' limitations were understood even by the political hacks who initially supported the project. There are indications that the production was disrupted by serious disagreements. For example, prominent writer Gabit Musrepov is mentioned as coauthor in some sources, but not in the credits, while coauthor Eduard Volodarskii is listed as the only screenwriter at the beginning of the movie. For director Ararat Mashanov, *Horizons* was to be his sole attempt at feature filmmaking; thereafter, he switched to documentary films.

The fact that no senior director was willing to take on opportunistic prestige projects such as *In Those Days* and *Horizons* also sheds light on the increasing division between genuine artists and minor, or gullible, filmmakers that was taking place in Kazakhstani cinema and would become characteristic of the entire Soviet film industry. Pseudo-historical, lackluster propaganda fare proved that communist officialdom had completely lost its connection with the population. Such films were mere alibi productions, intended to show that the national studio was mindful of its "political responsibility," and little else. Still, the fact that *Horizons* was generally regarded a failure, which even *Kazakhstanskaia Pravda* had to admit, proves that artistic standards were still alive in some quarters and could not be completely neutralized by ideological correctness. *Horizons* was not even deemed good enough to be sent to the USSR film festival.³ While an analysis of the systemic reasons for the appearance of "gray films" was impossible at the time, the decline in the quality of the studio's output was clear for all to see.

## *BROTHER OF MINE*

Although he was one of the best Kazakhstani filmmakers, Abdulla Karsakbaev unfortunately also contributed to the line of bland historical movies that marred the 1970s. The subject he chose for *Brother of Mine* (Brat moi, 1972) was certainly promising: the life of one of the founders of Kazakhstani Communist Youth, Gani Muratbaev.⁴ Muratbaev's passionate activism, his unconditional faith in the communist cause, and his death of tuberculosis at the age of twenty-two made him an excellent choice for a youthful star, perhaps even a potential James Dean of the Kazakh Komsomol. Kuman Tastanbekov as the male lead delivered what was expected, creating the image of an eternally positive and optimistic young fighter with black curls and a dashing smile. Yet despite his and the director's efforts, the film turned out to be a disappointment.

The first half of the plot focuses on the 1921 campaign to help the starving people of the Volga region (Povolzh'e) following a cable from Lenin urgently requesting food donations. The second half describes Muratbaev's work in Moscow, in close proximity to Nadezhda Krupskaia, Lenin's wife. Neither subject offers much in terms of conflict or action, to say nothing of the moral choices that were the strength of Karsakbaev's *Worrisome Morning*. Unlike that historical film, *Brother of Mine* presents a sanitized version of the early Soviet period, the era of a cultural revolution that shook patriarchal Islamic societies to their foundations. The film shows no conceptual disagreements between Communist Party leaders; there is no mention of Trotskii or Stalin, nor of the inner torments of those Kazakhs who sided with the Bolsheviks. Amid numerous conflict-free episodes, only two stand out as evoking some human interest. In the first, the son of a *bay* is excluded from the Komsomol when it is discovered that his class background is not proletarian. On that occasion, Muratbaev utters some words of caution, asking his comrades to tame their radicalism and think whether exclusion is really the only method to keep their movement politically pure. In another episode, a young woman, Sholpan, attends the congress of the Central Asian Komsomol in a full burka. Rather than assaulting or shaming her for sticking to traditional law, Krupskaia tells the story of a repressed boy who becomes a teacher. This soft approach does the trick: the young woman who has listened carefully finally exposes her face, signaling her liberation. But even these episodes are far from the profound search for truth that characterized the same director's *Worrisome Morning* a mere five years earlier. Apparently, Karsakbaev was aware of the artistic failure he was about to deliver: changes were made to Leonard Tolstoi's screenplay even during the shooting process, but to no avail.[5]

A special plotline is devoted to Gani Muratbaev's care for a young juvenile delinquent whom he takes under his wing. However, the late echoes of *Road-to-Life* romanticism are sanitized as well: neither the language nor the behavior of the problem boy come across as authentic or colorful. Thus, *Brother of Mine* has more in common with *Horizons* and *In Those Days* than with the proud Kazakhstani tradition of problem-oriented historical pictures. One can only imagine how strong the pressure of political control mechanisms must have been in order to yield such a lamentable outcome.

Looking at the facts of Muratbaev's life, so much could have been achieved even within an ideologically strict framework: as a boy, Gani lost his father and had to care for his family; then, his hard-working mother and young sister died of typhoid fever; as a sixteen year old, he had already assumed a leading position in the communist youth movement, helping poor and homeless orphans get an education. After his untimely passing, Magzhan Zhumabaev and Ilias Dzhansugurov wrote songs about Muratbaev. What a source of cultural continuity this could have been in the film!

It is worth noting that nonfictional cinema could sometimes take greater political risks than feature films. Conspicuously, in 1972, the same year that *Horizons* was produced, Emir Faik made a documentary about the poet Ilias Dzhansugurov. While this short film did not address the historical context of Dzhansugurov's arrest and execution in 1937, the production of a 20-minute tribute to a victim of the Stalinist repressions was the de facto rehabilitation of an outstanding artist and thus sent an important signal. This, too, could only have happened with the agreement of the communist leadership and, most likely, Dinmukhamed Kunaev personally.

## THE DECLINE OF GENRE CINEMA

Whatever criticism may have been levied against Kazakhstan's national cinema in the 1960s, one merit is undeniable: its films were never boring. In the 1970s, that changed. An increasing number of Kazakhstani feature films demonstrated an embarrassing tediousness and lack of narrative cohesion. It is worthwhile to explore how so many professional lapses came about: as the result of badly conceived and insufficiently redacted screenplays; as the consequence of intrusions during the production process; or due to disagreements between the filmmakers and the studio, the Ministry of Culture, the Communist Party department of culture, or other administrative bodies. Whatever the underlying causes, the outcome in each case was a film lacking clear exposition, the logical development of conflicts and character constellations, a satisfactory conclusion, and narrative speed.

In the case of several projects, the initial idea was interesting, but the execution weak. Considerations of fulfilling the studio's annual plan could also play a role in rushing the production rather than ensuring professional standards. The financial system was set up in such a way that delivering a low-quality product was preferable to not delivering a film at all. Completing a film with a delay that would make its release within the current annual plan impossible was regarded impermissible. Quality arguments, charging that continued work on a project would secure a better outcome or that it was preferable to give a project extra time than to release a movie that nobody wanted to see, were less persuasive to the bureaucratic apparatus than the formal fulfillment of plan goals. Eyewitnesses tell numerous stories about the rush to finish a delayed film at any cost. Thus, Sharip Beisembaev became known as a specialist in bringing overdue projects to completion and securing the formal fulfillment of the annual production plan. These factors may also be responsible for the brevity of many Kazakh feature films, which often had a running time of just 65–75 minutes instead of the standard 90–100 minutes. The general acceptance of increasingly nonartistic priorities ultimately gave Kazakhstani cinema a bad reputation, which continued to decline well into the 1980s. It is particularly regrettable that genres and subgenres in which the studio had excelled just a few years earlier were now represented by substandard productions.

An example of this decline is the "Eastern" *Once and for an Entire Life* (Odnazhdy i na vsiu zhizn', 1977). Adapted from a story by Gabit Musrepov and directed by Viktor Pusurmanov, who had been reprimanded a few years earlier for *Where the Mountains Are White*, this movie could have become an exciting Civil War yarn with many national specifics and a tolerable dosage of communist propaganda. Instead, the film is incoherent and never establishes a suspenseful narrative dynamic, even though it contains all the ingredients for a solid movie: stars, adventures, and romance.

The main character, an errant poet named Erken (Dzhambul Khudaibergenov), has joined the Bolsheviks and travels from *aul* to *aul* persuading the skeptical local population to support the Reds against the anti-Bolshevik resistance. The year is 1918, when the Alash-Orda movement (the name of which is not explicitly mentioned) had established a Turkestani government of national independence. The difference from other Kazakh films with a similar conflict is Erken's vocation: several times, listeners demand that he recite his poems instead of making political speeches. Erken's authority as an artist is enormous, so much so that his enemies, although more numerous and better organized than the Bolsheviks, do not dare to kill him. A Russian White Army officer, an ally of the Kazakh nationalists, is befuddled by this respect, stating: "For you people in the steppe, a poet is like a saint." But this interesting theme remains undeveloped. Instead, Erken's talent as a horseman is shown ad nauseam in trivial, repetitive action scenes. While the poet's appearance (dressed in a white blouse and sporting long dark hair) could have become a popular cultural image, not even the episodes involving his love interest, the young Aklima (Gulnara Suleimenova), are filmed accordingly, leaving the viewer indifferent. Another episode, in which Kazakhs at a railway station watch a newsreel about Lenin, is rendered with the same lack of inventiveness. The most impressive elements of *Once and for the Entire Life* are the supporting performances by Raisa Mukhamediarova and Kauken Kenzhetaev, demonstrating the potential that was wasted by an incoherent direction.

To be clear, Musrepov's story was ideologically linear and offered few opportunities for subversion in the spirit of Abdulla Karsakbaev's *Worrisome Morning*. But it could at least have produced an exciting revolutionary adventure story with a national cult hero. Alas, the final product never even came close. This case also shows how hard it was for Kazakhstani filmmakers to establish a believable national Bolshevik lead, an endeavor in which Karpov had failed with *The Path of One Thousand Miles* and in which Azerbaidzhan Mambetov would fail a few years later with *Blood and Sweat*. Strangely, in each of the aforementioned ideologically formulaic movies, the anticommunist leaders always come across as more intriguing than those "positive heroes" who were supposed to be the center of attention.

## GRAY MOVIES ON BIG AND SMALL SCREENS

Some contemporary critics and quality-conscious film workers knew full well that a high percentage of Kazakhfilm studio's output during the 1970s was artistically substandard. However, rather than analyzing the reasons why there were so many "gray films," they often blamed this reality on too many films being made by artists from the outside. This proto-nationalist view first appeared in the 1950s and was usually discussed behind closed doors due to the sensitivity of ethnic issues. But the question of why it was necessary to "import" filmmakers and their projects to Kazakhstan was legitimate. Indeed, one might wonder why a film such as *My Love During Junior Year* (Moia liubov' na tret'em kurse, 1976) was produced in Kazakhstan and not in the Russian Federation or the Ukrainian SSR.

Mikhail Shatrov's screenplay follows a group of students in their early twenties who are being sent to a *sovkhoz* to build a pigsty. The youngsters approach this challenge in high spirits, frolicking, falling in love, and talking about their dream of building communism. To make the political idealism more palatable, several episodes feature pop music, dancing, and singing with guitar accompaniment. The wide variety of songs even includes the Beatles ("Yesterday"). But the film's faux romanticism never gains traction, for lack of an intriguing plot that could capture the viewer. Directed by Iurii Boretskii, with songs contributed by Komsomol darling Aleksandra Pakhmutova (a Muscovite just like Shatrov), the film is almost free of Kazakh elements: the national-cultural context was completely neutralized. Only the presence of a few native performers indicates that the story takes place in Kazakhstan.

Sports dramas, which sometimes featured a surprising degree of sociopolitical candor, also fell victim to this trend toward blandness and conflict avoidance. An example of a "gray" sports film is *Encounters at Medeo* (Vstrechi na Medeo, 1976). Its title refers to a famous ice rink (ice skating is to this day among the most beloved pastimes of Almaty residents). On the surface, the topic is athletic achievement, yet the film has little to do with the daily lives of athletes, which were marked by merciless competition, ambition, and stress. In *Encounters at Medeo*, Dzhambul Khudaibergenov plays a figure skating coach. He and a tough female colleague in a big fur hat (Lola Abdukarimova) are supposed to embody the kind of positive authoritarianism that youngsters were expected to look up to. Figure skating was, of course, hugely popular in the 1970s; its stars and coaches enjoyed tremendous media attention, and Soviet victories at international competitions were celebrated like geopolitical triumphs. Strange as it may seem, ice dancing was a field of confrontation between East and West, and the communist establishment invested considerable funds in maintaining a leading position in this discipline. Thus, the film's plot about an ice dancer who is paired with a woman he does not like is more than a simple story of athletic frustration since the characters' decisions have potential political consequences. But, as had become customary in the 1970s, the conflicts are only hinted at, while lengthy scenes of skating and dancing to moderately modern pop music attempt to compensate for the abysmal acting.

Colorless movies such as *Encounters at Medeo* were often produced for television. The calculation that Kazakhfilm studio could get away with gray movies more easily when they were made for the small screen was based on an opportunistic attitude toward TV audiences and was widespread within the film community. After all, in the USSR, viewers had so few choices that even the blandest products could pass muster. Many directors did not take TV feature film seriously and delivered second- and third-rate fare. The budget of a Soviet made-for-television movie was on average about one-third that of a full-length feature film: 150,000 rubles as opposed to 500,000 rubles.

This, too, explains the low rank of such productions in studio planning. Askhat Ashrapov, one of the leading Kazakhstani cameramen, agreed to direct *Encounters at Medeo* together with Sapargali Suleimenov. More than anything, Ashrapov's choice indicates a lack of other opportunities for gifted artists in that period.

However, the "made-for-television" label cannot take all the blame for the artistic fiasco that was *Encounters at Medeo*. This is demonstrated by another movie, also intended for "entertainment" and produced as a high-profile coproduction between Kazakhfilm studio and the national studio of Czechoslovakia, Barrandov. Despite the participation of first-rate performers such as Doskhan Zholzhaksynov, *Goodbye, Medeo!* (Do svidaniia, Medeo!, 1981) is little more than a lackluster revue with skating stars and pop singers from both countries, including Roza Rymbaeva and Helena Vondračkova. Compared to Aimanov's fresh and witty *Our Dear Doctor* and *Angel in a Cap*, *Goodbye, Medeo!* is boring and devoid of national specifics. It was precisely the increasing domination of such "gray films" in the repertoire of Kazakhfilm studio that a few years later inspired the fury and contempt of those young directors who would form the "Kazakh New Wave."

As the example of Ashrapov shows, sometimes even artists with high quality standards could be dragged into the mills of endless intrusions by redactors and censors, so that the result was an embarrassing, faceless product. This happened to Olzhas Suleimenov, who had delivered outstanding screenplays in the 1960s; to director Zhardem Baitenov, whose *Blue Route* (from Suleimenov's screenplay) had demonstrated undeniable talent; and to Viktor Pusurmanov, whose beautiful parable *Where the Mountains Are White* was prohibited, likely with a paralyzing effect on the director. In the 1970s, traumatized artists found it hard to recover from such blows: senior authorities such as Aimanov who could straighten out conflicts were gone, the competition from ambitious opportunists was fierce, and the rules of Party discipline were enforced with unforgiving vigor.

Lowered quality standards at Kazakhfilm studio added to this degenerative trend. Thus, even though studio officials knew that Suleimenov's screenplay of *Winter Is No Harvest Season* (Zima—ne polevoi sezon, 1972) and *A B in Singing* (Chetverka po peniiu, 1973), directed by Baitenov, were weak, they were given the green light anyway. A telling example of a gray film made by talented artists is Baitenov's *Snow-Drops* (Podsnezhniki, 1974), from a screenplay by Olga Bondarenko. It features children preparing for International Women's Day by going to the mountains to fetch snow-drops. Since they go on their journey without permission, their disappearance causes panic among the adults. But the runaways are found in no time and the bland idyll is complete again. Despite its running time of barely over one hour, the film is boring due to its utter predictability. Soviet reality is depicted in a completely sanitized manner; the highest priority of society is the protection of childhood, as parents, teachers, and the army cooperate to save the naïve ten year olds. Gone are the days of Kozha's freedom and irreverent wit.

A few articles published at the time, as well as internal documents, demonstrate that knowledgeable cultural administrators understood Kazakhstani cinema's dilemma: they state that the national studio was producing too many embarrassing pictures and too few solid ones. However, the convenient solution was to point fingers at the screenwriters (yet again!) and demand even more comprehensive control of the production process. Such "criticism," just like the ethnocentric bias against non-Kazakh artists, was disingenuous and part of a pointless blame game that avoided any analysis of the real factors that led to so many abysmal Kazakh films in the 1970s and early 1980s.[6]

## CINEMATIC OFFICIALDOM

Due to its high production costs and potential effects on mass viewership, cinema has always been an object of state interest, regardless of the political system in place. The state could offer both support and interference, not just by means of censorial control, but also through direct investments in prestige projects that promise to benefit it by increasing its legitimacy. The presence of such prestige films, whose primary purpose is the celebration of the state and the confirmation of its ideology, can be observed throughout the Soviet era. While the relative weight of different genres in Soviet cinema varied, depending on political circumstances and viewer demands, state prestige films always maintained a presence. In the 1920s, when there was still a degree of competition in the film market, commercial considerations had greater weight than in the 1930s, when the Soviet market was largely shut off. The political framework played a decisive role in the increase or decrease in the number of state prestige films. Thus, viewers' preferences influenced studio decision-making on a much larger scale in the 1960s than in the 1930s. Of course, the real competition between imposed political agendas and audience expectations was never publicly discussed. Only internally, in the studios, were the pressures coming from the Communist Party and its battalions of censors ("redactors"), critics, and agents, on the one hand, and the revenue plans of the powerful State Plan (Gosplan), on the other, weighed against each other. Eventually, a relative balance was established between feature films that were considered politically essential (such as films about Lenin and the 1917 revolution or about the contemporary working class) and those that promised solid box office results. The profits from the latter helped compensate for the losses that were inevitably incurred by the former.

As usual in the cultural sphere, there were contradictions and gray zones: some Lenin films turned out to entertain, break taboos, or offer surprising historical revelations. A film about the October revolution occasionally included daring aesthetic experimentation, whereas explicitly apolitical films made "for entertainment" could be uninventive and boring. But for regular viewers, the demarcation line between state prestige films and entertaining movies was usually obvious, and exceptions were too few and far between to make it worthwhile looking for them. Because audiences tended to ignore state prestige films in principle, even when they had genuine qualities, the box office results in the USSR were kept secret. All Soviet studios, whether located in the center or at the national peripheries, continued to include state prestige films in their plans, understanding full well that they would bring about substantial deficits.

In the 1970s, leading decision-makers in the Soviet film industry promoted state prestige projects that were elephantine both in running time and budget with barely hidden cynicism. As the status quo that emerged during that decade gave viewers a choice between quality entertainment and propaganda, including domestic products and Western imports, word-of-mouth became a decisive factor in a film's popularity. Lenin's calculation that the viewer had to sit through propagandistic hackwork prior to being able to enjoy the actual feature film, which had been the lifeblood for newsreels and documentary cinema for decades, was largely invalidated. During the Brezhnev period, grandiose propaganda epics that were celebrated by critics but ran in empty movie theaters became a common phenomenon. A notorious example was *Soldiers of Freedom* (Soldaty svobody, 1976), a stale epic about World War II that, among other "innovations," highlighted the contributions of Colonel Brezhnev to the Soviet victory. Only the official media pretended to take such movies seriously, while street folklore delightedly tore them apart in countless jokes. Soviet film administrators compensated for the lack of viewer interest by forcing military units and school children to attend morning and daytime screenings, thus achieving minimally presentable box office numbers.

In hindsight there can be little doubt that state prestige films[7] are predominantly of historical relevance and rarely have artistic interest, albeit that, due to their large budgets, they were in some cases visually spectacular. For an understanding of the evolution of Kazakhstani cinema, however, some of the most prominent state-sponsored prestige films deserve a closer look, not least as a backdrop for aesthetically worthy pictures.

To regular audiences, state prestige films were an inevitable nuisance that had to be endured on some occasions, especially during official celebrations such as the anniversary of the October Revolution or of Lenin's birth. This passive acceptance became the unofficial behavioral norm and a source of widespread mockery during the 1970s and early 1980s. This, too, was a symptom of the so-called period of stagnation. One of the characteristic features of state prestige films was that they were generally made with no regard for audience interest. There were, however, exceptions.

## THE TASTE OF BREAD

One of General Secretary Leonid Brezhnev's claims to fame was his involvement in the Virgin Lands (*tselina*) campaign in the mid-1950s. The twenty-fifth anniversary of that event became an official cause to celebrate the purported economic success story with a colossal movie, *The Taste of Bread* (Vkus khleba, 1979). With a running time of six hours, viewers were obliged to spend two evenings in the movie theater watching 1950s characters fight over agricultural production methods.

The film's central character, Stepan Sechkin (Sergei Shakurov), is a hands-on administrator who initially refuses to take part in the Virgin Lands campaign. A street-smart guy-next-door who always speaks his mind, Sechkin discusses the problems of Soviet grain production with his comrades first in the ministry's men's room and later in a rural bath-house and similar places that convey a sense of everyday normalcy. After Sechkin changes his mind, he recruits other administrators to the gigantic cause, which is supposed to solve the USSR's grain supply problem once and for all. The territory to be cultivated in Kazakhstan is half the size of the entire US land mass used for wheat production. On February 22, 1954, the first trains bearing hundreds of virgin lands activists leave Moscow. When they arrive in the steppe, the enthusiasts find themselves in an endless snow desert. Working in this environment is dangerous. Thus, a heavy bulldozer falls through the ice taking its driver to his death. Nothing has been prepared for the workers' arrival: no bread to eat and no money to be paid. People live in primitive tents and are expected to soldier on, nourished by slogans alone. Sechkin's willpower and practical disposition help resolve some of the most urgent problems, often through shouting and improvisation. But the film admits something that would have been unthinkable to show in the 1950s *tselina* films: that the campaign was incompetently designed and demanded huge sacrifices from all participants.

In 1956, Soviet-Kazakhstani cinema addressed the Virgin Lands campaign in movies by Aleksandr Medvedkin, Sultan Khodzhikov, Shaken Aimanov, and Iurii Pobedonostsev. Those films had been safely forgotten by the 1970s. Thus, the challenge for the filmmakers was to generate viewer interest in a topic that was clearly based on a state assignment (*gosudarstvennyi zakaz*). Screenwriters, director, and performers tried hard to deliver a state prestige film whose story and characters nevertheless had sufficient popular appeal to engage tens of millions of viewers. The strategy of the screenwriters (a team of four that included the experienced Valentin Chernykh) was not entirely determined by the inevitable propaganda agenda. To establish human interest, the cast of characters was first shown in trivial situations, often involving conflicts with their loved ones; this was followed by these characters' move to the Kazakhstani steppe to implement the goals set by the Communist Party. The cast includes an alcoholic, a two-faced schemer, a sensitive Komsomol functionary, and shortsighted Party functionaries; in other words, real human beings, warts and all. But most of the screen time of *The Taste of Bread* is devoted to passionate debates about the right way to tackle an unprecedented socioeconomic project, with skeptics warning of managerial recklessness and dogmatics claiming that there is no time for trials and experiments. This revival of the debate drama is remarkable for the 1970s, a time when cynical complacency had taken over society. Yet the dialogues' occasional challenges to historical taboos about the *tselina* campaign are insufficient to compensate for the lack of intrigue and dramatic plot turns.

Likely, many citizens who were pondering whether they should watch this huge Soviet epic asked themselves what its point was. To get to the film's essence, one needs to sit through several hours of controversies. Surprisingly, the reward is, to some degree, worth it: *The Taste of Bread* is a curious lesson in Soviet history that official textbooks hesitated to openly discuss. Predictably, very few people had the patience to find out.

Parts I and II of the four-part epic (*Our Daily Bread* and *Bread and Soil*) are fashioned as a chronicle of land cultivation and its countless heroic pioneers. However, part III (*Bread and People*) opens a polemical line that is directed against Nikita Khrushchev's policies of the early 1960s. One needs to take into consideration the fact that Khrushchev's name, let alone a discussion of his agricultural initiatives, was excluded from all Soviet discourses after his 1964 ouster. In this respect, the film explored new ground. It states that the initial enthusiasm that carried the virgin lands campaign in the 1950s had waned, wheat production had become less and less efficient, and the replacement of wheat with corn (Khrushchev's infamous brainchild) was ludicrous. As a result of incompetence and mismanagement at the very top of the government, the Soviet Union was forced to buy millions of tons of grain from Canada, and in 1962, even the citizens of Moscow and Leningrad experienced bread shortages. In the film, the common-sense administrator Sechkin is shown fighting against the highest echelons of power and is eventually stripped of all his positions and honors. Only at the end does a decision made directly in the Kremlin allows for a correction of the nation-wide economic insanity. Thus, *The Taste of Bread* turns out to be an apologia for Brezhnev's coup against Khrushchev, purportedly carried out to save the country's economy from complete fiasco. This depiction of recent history would normally have caused a sensation. Only the fact that it was part of a state prestige film, which regular audiences did not trust, prevented it from being recognized for what it was: a rare piece of truth in a genre not usually known for truthfulness.

From the beginning, close cooperation between the Mosfilm and Kazakhfilm studios was regarded as a fundamental condition for the logistical and ideological success of *The Taste of Bread*. This meant that Kazakhstan had to be given its due, from plot development to official recognition. While the screenplay emphasized the role of the Moscow center in making the decision to start the virgin lands campaign, it was essential to pay sufficient attention to Kazakhstanis' contribution in order to make the coproduction between the two studios work. Thus, leading Kazakh performers such as Idris Nogaibaev, Asanali Ashimov, and especially Natal'ia Arinbasarova were given significant screen time. There was not much to play, though: unlike the Russian characters, the Kazakhs were designed in linear fashion, and the fact that the abovementioned performers were awarded a State Prize of the USSR was more political gesture than recognition of artistic merit.

*The Taste of Bread* was showered with praise in the Soviet press. Kazakhstani film critics and historians devoted many pages to its "analysis," celebrating the Russian-Kazakh epic as an exemplary achievement. However, the film was immediately hidden after Brezhnev's passing in 1982. As a large-scale prestige project, it represents an important aspect of Kazakhstan's film industry in the 1970s, when substantial financial and logistical resources were wasted on films that nobody wanted to see.

## BLOOD AND SWEAT

The late 1970s witnessed the production of another state-sponsored prestige film, *Blood and Sweat*, the large-scale adaptation of a Soviet-Kazakh revolutionary epic.

In the 1960s, Kazakhfilm studio, with its small production volume of three to five full-length pictures per year, was unable to finance the costly reenactments of revolutionary events that were a mainstay of the central studios and were screened ad nauseam on official holidays for high school and army audiences. The peculiar genre of the Eastern, the Civil War thriller that was firmly established in the mid-1960s and came to full bloom in the 1970s, offered a viable compromise between Soviet state demands and audience wishes. Those films could even test the limits of ideological dogma by nuancing the characterizations of the enemy, as Abdulla Karsakbaev's *Worrisome Morning* (1966) proved. Aimanov's *The End of the Ataman* (1970), while more ideologically simple, demonstrated that Kazakh subject matter within the Civil War thriller genre could appeal to large audiences both inside and outside Kazakhstan. However, that newfound compromise between ideological norms, official recognition, and viewer appreciation failed to hold together in *Blood and Sweat* (Krov' i pot, 1978), a state prestige film par excellence.

Adapted from a canonical three-volume novel by Abujamal Nurpeisov that was published in 1961–1970 and was awarded a USSR State Prize in 1974, *Blood and Sweat* describes the impact of the Bolshevik revolution on the Kazakh people on an epic scale. The novel was one of the central texts in the Soviet-Kazakh literatury canon and was immediately proclaimed a classic, highly praised but little read. Its adaptation for the screen became one of the grand national projects of the 1970s, intended as a demonstration of Kazakhfilm's ideological awareness and prestige film potential. The project's inception, realization, and ultimate failure are rooted in its official representational purpose, which outweighed all artistic considerations.

Categorizing *Blood and Sweat* as a state prestige film is justified for several reasons. First, Nurpeisov was a leading representative of Socialist Realism and one of Kazakhstan's most visible writer-functionaries; therefore, this novel (his major literary accomplishment) almost inevitably had to be adapted for the screen at some point, just like the other socialist-realist epics of Soviet literature. True, the adaptability of such a heavy narrative text was limited. Today, a television miniseries would likely be the genre of choice for capturing the various involved plotlines. Second, as in all Soviet prestige films, the validity of the Leninist class theory had to be demonstrated, no matter how predictable this rendered the film's characters. And third, there was no need to worry about audience interest: given the distribution practices common for prestige films, the real box office results would never be disclosed or discussed in the media. All these aspects are typical of state prestige films, the direct cinematic tributes of the Soviet film industry to the communist system at a time when fewer and fewer people believed in the practicability of the underlying ideology and the achievability of the communist utopia.

In the Soviet era, Nurpeisov's epic was praised for its realism and ideological correctness. With epic breadth, the author used an approach that was first applied by Mikhail Sholokhov in *And Quiet Flows the Don* (Tikhii Don, 1928–1940) and later adapted in other Soviet national literatures, embedding a passionate love story in the tumults of class warfare before and after the October revolution. Nurpeisov's intimate knowledge of the life of Aral Sea fishermen supplied his novel with the required amount of verisimilitude, while the plot evolved precisely in line with Leninist assumptions of how social progress was supposed to unfold. The film adaptation was to emulate the canonized epic, demonstrating Kazakhstan's adherence to official Soviet norms and its studio's ability to produce a large-scale revolutionary epic that included certain national peculiarities. Just as *Amangeldy* four decades earlier proved to the Soviet leadership and to native and Soviet audiences that Kazakhstan could boast the same kind of exemplary leader of the national liberation struggle as the Russian Chapaev, *Blood and Sweat*, directed by the influential theater director Azerbaizhan Mambetov (supported by Iurii Matsiugin), was to prove the similarity of historical developments in Kazakhstan to those in other countries. These goals set the film in diametrical opposition to the revisionist Kazakh Eastern, which emphasized the peculiarities of the country's culture and historical development.

The screenwriters, Andrei Mikhalkov-Konchalovskii and Rodion Tiurin, rearranged the convoluted plot of *Blood and Sweat* to make it suitable for the screen, putting greater emphasis on the novel's love triangle than on the socioeconomic reality experienced by the fishermen. Mikhalkov-Konchalovskii, who had played a crucial role in the formation of the adventurous "Eastern" both as a screenwriter and as a director in the 1960s, created a logical structure by introducing a frame narrative. Each of the film's two parts opens with the frame narrative, followed by flashbacks that constitute the main plotline.

The overarching theme is the birth of class consciousness among Kazakhstani fishermen who rise against both branches of the ruling class: the native *bays* and the Russian bourgeoisie. The frame narrative is introduced by an explanatory text describing how, in 1919, remnants of Admiral Kolchak's White Army moved to the Caspian Sea to unite with Western allied troops. Guided by a respected and wealthy Kazakh, Tanibergen, the White troops cross the desert, hoping to reach the promised sea, while being closely watched by Red Army units under the command of Elaman, one of Tanibergen's former farmhands. Adding to the tension between Tanibergen and Elaman is their mutual love of the beautiful Akbala. Due to an agreement between her father and Elaman, Akbala had to marry the poor man. In search of a better life, the couple had left the steppe and settled near the Aral Sea. However, their move ended in disaster: when the greedy entrepreneur Fedorov forced the fishermen to work during a snowstorm on the brittle ice and several men lost their lives, Elaman killed the exploiter and was exiled to Siberia. In Elaman's absence, Akbala became Tanibergen's second wife, living in luxury, but also in disrespect due to her past.

Tanibergen and Elaman are designed as representatives of their respective classes, the haves and the have-nots. Such a tightly defined conceptual framework allows for only limited psychological differentiation. However, *Blood and Sweat* is not primitive in its evocation of pre-Soviet-Kazakh society: the many shades between the two social poles, featuring a variety of opportunists, traitors, and cowards, do complicate the character constellation, while the Kazakh traditions and beliefs are shown as keeping the social fabric together. But the degree of exploitation, the constant injustice experienced by the poor, and the lack of any positive outlook make the class divide ever sharper. World War I, when Kazakh men for the first time had to serve in the tsar's army, followed by the Russian revolutions in February and October 1917, ultimately blew up the traditional order even in the remote steppe. Tanibergen supports the White Army, while Elaman, radicalized during the war, joins a Red Army unit. The conflicting loyalties that emerge in the class struggle affect various supporting characters and are repeatedly touched upon. As a theme, they remained important for Kazakh cinema for years to come.

Adapting a voluminous epic for the screen, even with sufficient funding for a two-part version, presented numerous challenges. *Blood and Sweat* failed to meet most of them, primarily due to the conditions imposed by the prestige film category itself. First and foremost, the narrative order is incoherent because of how the flashbacks were inserted. It is often hard for the viewer to discern which episode takes place where, when, and why. The incoherent causality also weakens the evolutionary aspect, that is, the depiction of a developing class consciousness, which was one of the major purposes of all Soviet historical prestige films dealing with the communist takeover. Defying the film's own mission, the political insight into its characters remains largely the same as determined by their birth into the upper or lower class. Elaman immediately seems to know everything required of a dedicated class fighter. Thus, instead of an evolution of the mind, the film's focus is on the lifelong duel between two rivals, Tanibergen and Elaman. This narrative emphasis on two opposing characters bound together by history resembles the then-fashionable *1900* (Novecento, 1976) by Bernardo Bertolucci, a Euro-communist attempt to revive the communist spirit in a cinematically spectacular manner that impressed many Soviet filmmakers when it was shown in closed screenings. Considering that the screenwriter of *Blood and Sweat*, Mikhalkov-Konchalovskii, risked a Soviet answer to Bertolucci in his *Siberiade* (1979), the likelihood of such direct influence is not too farfetched.

Still, *Blood and Sweat*, while undoubtedly conceived and perceived as an expression of Soviet officialdom and a Kazakhstani prestige film, does possess artistic qualities that lift it above the average. Askhat Ashrapov's camera work is superb in the exterior episodes, especially those taking place in the Aral region (unfortunately, the interior scenes reek of studio decoration, are excessively lit, and never come to life). But the most important quality, and a deviation from the norms of official prestige film, was impossible to foresee: the actor Tungyshbai Dzhamankulov, portraying Tanibergen, created a character of such color and complexity that his work outshone that of all others.[8] Given the film's dichotomous structure, with Tanibergen and Elaman standing for their respective classes, this was particularly precarious for Anuar Moldabekov, whose stone-faced fisherman-turned-revolutionary never even comes close to Dzhamankulov's powerful expressiveness. While Tanibergen, with catlike intelligence and refined facial features, exudes a natural aristocratic superiority, Elaman remains wooden and predictable throughout. Tanibergen is torn between his clear understanding of the unjust exploitation system from which he is profiteering, a system that alienates the Kazakhs from each other, and the impossibility to transcend it. He is further torn between his passionate love for Akbala and his obedience vis-à-vis traditional clan rules of morality and between his siding with the White Army and his protection of his own *aul*, which is ultimately raided as a result of his opportunism.[9] Tanibergen, in Dzhamankulov's portrayal, is a truly tragic character whose death in the sand of the desert appears to be the logical outcome of his conflicted behavior. In his historical-psychological complexity, he is akin to Zharasbai in Shamshiev's 1968 *The Shot at the Karash Pass*. Tanibergen's respect for his people and, simultaneously, his contempt for them, together with his air of superiority reflect an identity problem of the Kazakh elites that goes beyond the concrete historical case depicted in *Blood and Sweat*.

Notwithstanding the exceptional complexity of Tanibergen, the ideologically required dogmatic equation at the center of *Blood and Sweat* ensures that all the characters eventually get what they deserve: Akbala, who betrayed her poor husband and preferred the rich life, is kicked out of Tanibergen's house, losing her baby and ultimately her life; Tanibergen, who puts class loyalty above justice, is betrayed by his Russian allies and likewise perishes; Tanibergen's first wife, who mercilessly evicted Akbala, is gang-raped by White Army troops. On the other side, Elaman, who had endured so much pain and humiliation and was deprived of his wife and son, triumphantly rides with his comrades across the steppe toward a grandiose communist future.[10]

Conspicuously, this saga of class divide also brings to life traditional Kazakh beliefs about guilt and redemption, which coincide with aspects of communist class determinism, giving *Blood and Sweat* an authentic, albeit underplayed, national flavor. It is possible that Dzhamankulov's masterful performance and the epic scope of *Blood and Sweat* might someday bring about a critical and popular rediscovery of the film; however, at the time of its release, it flopped badly and has not since been included in any of the DVD compilations of the best Kazakhstani films. Thus, *Blood and Sweat* shared the fate of all prestige films, whether possessing intrinsic qualities or not: they are touted as great events before their release, are awarded state prizes, and then, rather quickly, fall into oblivion without leaving a trace in viewers' or filmmakers' memories.

## HITS BY DESIGN

Although box office results were usually not made public during Soviet times, viewers themselves had a well-developed instinct of which movies were hits and which were flops. These instincts enhanced the success of a film by word-of-mouth propaganda, whereas official film reviews played an insignificant role. As a result, the tens of millions of Soviet viewers had at least some leverage over production and distribution plans—less so than in market economies, but still enough to influence thematic and genre trends. Of course, economists at the Soviet center clearly understood that a working-class drama would most likely attract fewer spectators than a thriller and a Lenin film would bring less revenue than a musical comedy. However, despite this knowledge, projects that were hopelessly out of touch with audience wishes were regularly included in annual plans as a matter of course. Indeed, for a significant segment of the repertoire, political agenda trumped economic efficiency. Only when the split between costly propaganda and state prestige projects, on the one hand, and viewer-oriented films, on the other, reached a grotesque dimension, creating a serious budgetary disbalance and jeopardizing the financial goals set for the Soviet film industry, which did play a role on the macro-level and could sometimes be reached only with the help of Western imports, did this also become a political matter. Thus, the more entrepreneurially inclined among Soviet administrators, screenwriters, and directors began to push select film projects that indulged viewers with Western-style genre attributes, sometimes combined with Soviet subject matter.

The unhealthy imbalance between ideological requirements and audience wishes was a side effect of the 1970s' status quo. Now it became obvious how right Shaken Aimanov was in the 1950s and 1960s to remain mindful of maintaining a trusting partnership with native audiences: he knew early on what viewers wanted and always made meeting their expectations his top priority. At the same time, he never went for cheap popularity: his comedies and adventures were conscientiously crafted, a far cry from the openly imitative, faux-commercial products that began to emerge from Soviet studios in the 1970s in the form of "gray films."

Most Soviet film critics understood full well the financial pressures that underlay the production of thrillers (by the way, a specialty of the three Baltic studios), musicals, and slapstick comedies, but on the surface these critics continued to perform ideological cat-and-mouse games, taking studios and filmmakers to task for producing movies whose focus was primarily on entertainment and box office returns.

From time to time, Kazakhfilm studio opened its doors to deliberate imitations of foreign genre fare. A particularly prominent (and eventually notorious) example was *The Shield of the City* (Shchit goroda, 1979). Written and directed by Muscovite Leonid Agranovich, this well-publicized project transplanted the Western *disaster movie* to Kazakhstan. It was obvious even to unsophisticated viewers that *The Shield of the City* followed in the footsteps of such US blockbusters as *The Towering Inferno* and *Earthquake* (both 1974), neither of which were released in the USSR but which made worldwide headlines that somehow reached attentive Soviet viewers, too.

Agranovich's screenplay was structured similarly to the master plot of the Western disaster movie, opening with idyllic images right before the catastrophe hits. While unsuspecting people are frolicking at a lake, a huge torrent descends from the mountains with mortal power, killing the little daughter of engineer Kasym Batyrov (Anuarbek Moldabekov). After the initial shock, the question arises of whether such disasters can be prevented. The urgent task to build a dam strong enough to stop avalanches becomes Batyrov's personal and professional cause. If he fails, the city (which is obviously Almaty, although its name is never mentioned) could easily become the victim of another avalanche. Because time is of the essence, Batyrov suggests a radical solution: an explosion that would fill the valley with debris and cut off the path of a potential new avalanche. As in all disaster movies, this is where the hard part begins, as the main character must fight numerous skeptics among administrators and scientists who do not believe in the feasibility of such an approach. However, the chairman of the government's national security committee (Idris Nogaibaev) supports the project, the success of which marks the film's culmination. When another avalanche occurs, the dam holds, protecting the city.

Disaster movies are only as good as their special effects, and considering the international standards of the time, *Shield of the City* does not disappoint. Typical of the genre is the stark contrast between idyllic civilian everyday life and clandestine dangerous operations. Again, the Soviet-Kazakh variation meets genre standards. Furthermore, the story's emphasis on the victory of human reason over the wild forces of nature (a common feature of most Western disaster movies) generates certain pathos. In this respect, the Soviet clone can even legitimately hark back to the communist tradition of "fighting nature" that was prominent in the 1930s. Agranovich followed yet another principle of Western disaster movies: an all-star cast, with many of the best-known Kazakh actors in lead and supporting roles, including the venerable Kapan Badyrov in the cameo of an old general. Moldabekov as the male lead excellently conveys the severe burden of responsibility of an innovator who believes in his solution, fighting against offices filled with bureaucratic naysayers. Particularly impressive is Nogaibaev's portrayal of a dignified government leader.[11]

The aforementioned elements made *The Shield of the City* a solid, entertaining movie within its genre. And yet it caused serious controversies. Rather than accepting the film for what it was, namely, a professionally rendered Soviet-Kazakh replica of a popular genre that originated in the capitalist West, critics applied stern aesthetic criteria, charging that the plot was schematic (how could it be otherwise in a disaster movie?!), that there was neither an imaginative worldview nor any artistic individuality, and so on.[12] As if the filmmakers had foreseen such objections, they took every possible political precaution, true to the spirit of 1970s status quo cinema. For example, the heavy infighting between proponents and opponents of the dam project, which was based on a real case, was toned down. But anything else would have hampered the production from the beginning, as the true severity of conceptual disagreements among major Soviet political players in that period was simply not admitted onto screens. However, critics did not appreciate such caution nor the demonstrative patriotic spirit underlying many scenes. They diagnosed the manipulative intentions of the film's politics and remained unforgiving in their judgment. Thus, Kazakhfilm had to pay a high price for its commercial opportunism: *The Shield of the City* was torn apart by all major Soviet newspapers.

Reassessing the critical battles of the 1970s and early 1980s, it seems fair to conclude that even modest attempts to establish a feedback-based relationship between audiences and filmmakers were risky. While countless "gray films" managed to fly under the radar of official critics, the instincts of some studio administrators to produce at least some films that would respond to viewers' preferences were nipped in the bud in the name of politically and aesthetically "correct" approaches, box office numbers be damned. Instead, studios both at the Soviet center and on the peripheries were forced to produce formulaic, ideologically opportunistic fare. Tendencies of national self-exploration were monitored with enormous distrust and countered with films that projected Soviet political priorities into the past. An example of such projection is *Heralds Hurry* (Gontsy speshat, 1980), a prestige film about the struggle of Kazakh tribes against Dzhungar intruders. Based on a novel by Anuar Alimzhanov and helmed by theater director Azerbaizhan Mambetov, who had just won laurels, if not popularity, with *Blood and Sweat*, this project was part of a series of historical narratives undertaken by several Soviet republics that claimed that the multinational Union of Soviet Socialist Republics was the result of a quasi-natural development that emerged long before communism. For Georgia, Armenia, and Kazakhstan, these films were intended as proof that the colonization of their territories was based on a vital need for protection and national survival, to which tsarist Russia had responded by sensibly incorporating these nations into its empire. *Heralds Hurry* was supposed to lead viewers to the conclusion that only unification with the Russian Empire could guarantee the safety of the Kazakh people, resulting in the signing of an official document in October 1731.

However, the film failed to deliver its message. Although it featured leading stars of Kazakhstani cinema, including Dzhambul Khudaibergenov, Asanali Ashimov, Tungyshbai Dzhamankulov, and Idris Nogaibaev, audiences reacted with indifference. The production was expensive, as evidenced by the number of extras involved in battle scenes as well as the use of helicopter shots, which in the 1970s was a sure sign that this was a prestige project, a "state film" in the literal sense of the word. The opening episodes depicting the barbarity of the Dzhungars, who kill babies and burn yurts, could have been a powerful point of departure for a patriotic action yarn with appeal to young and old. In time-honored adventure fashion, the plot juxtaposes the goodies and the baddies and later has the female lead (Almira Ismailova) dramatically kill the main traitor. However, a believable reconstruction of the period is missing. The cinematography's overreliance on close-ups prevents the establishment of period authenticity, which is vital for a historical picture regardless of its ideological tendency. The plot, showcasing a captured Russian as the loyal friend of the Kazakh rebels, is too ideologically transparent to evoke audience identification.

To be sure, the subject of Kazakh-Russian "historical brotherhood" has always been a complex one. Suffice it to say that Anuar Alimzhanov wrote all his prose in Russian and was a proponent of state unity; after all, he occupied some of the highest official positions in the Soviet *nomenklatura*. The same is true of Azerbaizhan Mambetov, a celebrated stage director and darling of the Soviet-Kazakh cultural establishment who also brought to Kazakhstani cinema a certain stylistic staleness that must be viewed as symptomatic of the 1970s. Oleg Osetinskii, the maverick Russian screenwriter whose reputation was based on the fine Decemberist drama *Star of Capivating Happiness* (Zvezda plenitel'nogo schast'ia, 1975) but who then squandered it with dubious prestige fare such as *The Start* (Vzlet, 1979), leaves no doubt that he fully backed the novel's pro-Russian agenda. As a result, *Heralds Hurry* became a hack job whose flop demonstrated yet again the degree to which Kazakh cinema had lost viewers' trust within a mere decade.

## THE KAZAKH REVISIONIST EASTERN I: *CHASE IN THE STEPPE*

Along with the growing number of "gray" films and ideologically driven prestige projects, a characteristic feature of Kazakhstani cinema in the 1970s was the simultaneity of opportunism and courage, of formulaic tediousness and aesthetic inventiveness. One of the filmmakers who fought hard to maintain a high level of artistry was Abdulla Karsakbaev. It took him years after *A Worrisome Morning* to be able to return to the Civil War theme. Karsakbaev's artistic originality was undiminished in his last historical films, which are also a part of the legacy of the "decade of stagnation" that must not be forgotten. Indeed, whenever Karsakbaev addressed topics that had become clichéd in Soviet cinema, such as the Civil War in the "Eastern" or World War II, his films offered unexpected perspectives within the subgenres of revolutionary and war film and transcended their narrow ideological framework.

Karsakbaev's *Chase in the Steppe* (Pogonia v stepi, 1979) stands out as one of the best films of the decade. It opens with an episode that belies its trivial-sounding title and was unprecedented in Kazakhstan's cinema. A group of horsemen approaches an *aul* in the evening hours. Their leader unceremoniously enters a yurt and threatens the men who have gathered for dinner. The intruder is about to shoot the only Bolshevik among the guests when the host, a village elder named Akan, implores him to honor the law of hospitality and not murder a guest inside his yurt.

The unusual aspect of this episode is the cowardly reaction of the threatened Bolshevik. This man in uniform, Seisembaev, is so scared that he begins to weep and beg for his life. In the framework of the regular Eastern, where gun-happy communists in dark leather jackets were invariably portrayed as fearless and both physically and intellectually superior, Seisembaev's behavior is an anomaly on the Soviet screen: a Bolshevik coward. The intruder, a self-proclaimed anarchist named Kudre, gains deep satisfaction from his opponent's humiliation and leaves the yurt without killing Seisembaev. News of this incident spreads across the steppe at the speed of lightning: a ranking functionary of the new communist power behaved in a shameful way in front of other Kazakhs! If, for a regular man, such behavior would destroy his honor once and for all, the effect is twice as severe for a representative of Bolshevism.

This unusual scene opens a film that on the surface seemed to be little more than another adventurous historical thriller. For a Soviet movie, the episode, which sets the tone for the entire story, and its reverse representation of friend and foe comes as a surprise, since it turns the established genre formula on its head. In its subsequent episodes, *Chase in the Steppe* demonstrates how many sacrifices the other communists were compelled to make to compensate for the failure of one. The film's central character, the Bolshevik Khamid, is the exact opposite of Seisembaev: courageous, selfless, and stoic. His supervisor even asks him: "When was the last time you cried? When was the last time you smiled?"

Central Asian Bolsheviks' quasi-samurai stoicism was a traditional feature of Easterns, most impressively embodied by Kyrgyz actor Suimenkul Chokmorov. In *Chase in the Steppe*, Doskhan Zholzhaksynov in the role of Khamid builds on that tradition, but, in line with Karsakbaev's original directorial strategy also subverts it. Khamid acts as the Bolshevik punisher and protector and is mostly in control of dangerous situations. However, unlike his predecessors in other Easterns, his emotions do at times shine through his stone-faced façade: when he craves revenge and when he yearns for love.

At first, his main antagonist also appears to possess unusual caliber. Kudre, who describes himself as a man who only respects his own laws and fears nobody, rules his gang with strategic intelligence, cynicism, and ruthlessness. But here, too, Karsakbaev deviates from established genre conventions. In several episodes, it seems that Khamid, the righteous communist fighter, is a hothead who sometimes shoots from the hip, at his own and his comrades' peril. Thus, he appears inferior to the calculating Kudre, whose ultimate plan is to lead a massive escape of Kazakhs, along with their herds, across the Soviet border. Only toward the end of the film do we realize that Khamid's spontaneity and thoughtlessness were part of a mask that misled his enemies—and us, the audience. His motionless features conceal relentless analytical work, the results of which are never verbalized, but his plans are carried out with flawless precision, quietly.

Listening to Akan, who claims to be frail and indifferent toward worldly affairs and political fights, Khamïd realizes early on that the old man is behind the anti-Bolshevik operations, supplying Kudre with ideological justifications ("I obey no laws") that the uneducated bandit parrots verbatim. To mislead Akan and Kudre, Khamid cleverly spreads false news about a powerful Red Army unit that will soon arrive and put an end to the bandits' rule. This "deadline" allows him to impose a timeline on Kudre and his men and guide them toward a cleverly constructed trap. As a result, he manages to neutralize the dangerous gang, even though his own forces are inferior. The viewer is thus entrapped as well: outraged by the seeming naïveté of Khamid, who allows Kudre to escape, we only begin to fully grasp the Bolshevik's masterful plan when it succeeds. Karsakbaev, once again going against genre clichés, does not turn Kudre's death into the film's culmination, but shows it rather unspectacularly: the gangster is shot like a lowly creature, without any chance to display qualities beyond mere physicality. In hindsight, it turns out that Kudre was never an equal opponent for Khamid; his quasi-anarchist slogans were not part of a developed worldview, but a cheap pose adapted from the cunning elder Akan. Kudre's power was only temporary.

Aside from the cowardly Bolshevik featured at the beginning, *Chase in the Steppe* contains another unusual element: love, presented in a restrained yet erotically powerful manner. At one point, the daughter of a slaughtered Bolshevik comes to Khamid's rescue, after which he acts as her protector. This character constellation was introduced by Andrei Mikhalkov-Konchalovskii in *The First Teacher* (Pervyi uchitel', 1965) and then reproduced, with slight variations, in other Easterns. In *Chase in the Steppe*, the girl, Aigiren (Gulnara Dusmatova), is a teenager looking no older than fifteen. Tender and impressionable, she suffers after having shot one of the bandits. But when it comes to her feelings, she is not shy at all, asking Khamid directly: "Do you love me?" When the Bolshevik replies in the affirmative, the viewer cannot help but be baffled: after all, the age difference between the two is considerable, and Aigiren has the looks of a child. Yet the film questions neither the erotic bond between the mature Bolshevik fighter and the teenage steppe girl nor the legitimacy of the feeling, which is shown to be mutual. This constellation likely raised eyebrows in some quarters. But Karsakbaev is unapologetic in presenting the love between the stern, mature Khamid and the tender juvenile Aigiren as legitimate and a reward for the main character's heroism and selflessness.

As usual in Karsakbaev's oeuvre, the national dimension is omnipresent. Both Khamid and Aigiren belong to Kazakh culture and follow Kazakh traditions. Although they fully embrace Communism and Soviet power, they remain part of their nation. This approach can also serve as the definition of Karsakbaev's own worldview and artistic approach: his films are principally pro-Soviet, yet they never betray their Kazakh roots. In Karsakbaev's historical films, revolution, Civil War, and Great Patriotic War unfold within an authentic Kazakhstan, not a construction springing from ideological wishful thinking. More distinctly than Aimanov in *The End of the Ataman*, Karsakbaev captured this national spirit in a manner that is both fundamental and affectionate, yet also thoroughly realistic. That makes his films valuable beyond ideological and pedagogical surface messages, which were inevitable in the framework of Soviet cinema. Thus, the first episode of *Chase in the Steppe* is remarkable not only because it features a communist coward, but also because it illustrates the catastrophic consequences of such cowardice in *Kazakh* society, where news of the shameful act travels quickly across the steppe and undermines the efforts to legitimize the new Soviet system.

Kudre, the clever enemy, is fully aware of the power of symbolic acts and indulges in them himself. When he captures Khamid, he drags the tied-up Bolshevik by the nose, to the laughter of his gang and bystanders. The physical pain caused by this act is secondary; what matters is the dishonoring effect. Not surprisingly, the bandit refers to it shortly before his own demise: "I dragged you by the nose, red scum!" It is telling for Karsakbaev's directorial position that the Bolshevik Khamid is more loyal to genuine Kazakh tradition than his antagonist. For example, Kudre prohibits the burial of Bolsheviks, letting their remains rot in the sun, whereas Khamid immediately begins to dig a grave when he discovers such violation of Kazakh laws, and even utters words of mourning.

Several dialogues in *Chase in the Steppe* have a philosophical dimension that goes far beyond the film's adventurous surface. Unlike other Easterns, the lead characters are thinking and reflecting about the events in which they are involved. It would thus be justified to call Karsakbaev's variety of the Civil War adventure genre "a thinking viewer's Eastern." Thus, when old Akan states "Soviet power is alien to the steppe," this is meant as a direct challenge to Khamid, who is giving his all to persuade the frightened and skeptical native population of the opposite. From a post-Soviet standpoint, Akan's statement sounds different yet again. Indeed: strangely prophetic.

## THE KAZAKH REVISIONIST
## EASTERN II: *THE LAST PASSAGE*

The subgenre of Eastern culminated in the late 1970s and early 1980s, finally tapering off with the beginning of the perestroika period. Due to their narrative energy and solid performances, some of these movies belong to the positive part of Kazakhfilm studio's Soviet legacy. From a post-Soviet standpoint, Easterns reveal a wealth of insights into the process of Kazakhstani identity formation.

In its final years, the Eastern came up with a few more noteworthy pictures, such as *The Last Passage* (Poslednii perekhod, 1981), which shows similarities to *Chase in the Steppe* in several subversive aspects. As a matter of fact, Abdulla Karsakbaev was initially supposed to direct *The Last Passage*, before being removed from the project by the author of the screenplay, Olzhas Suleimenov, without official explanation.[13]

Whatever the reasons for replacing Karsakbaev with a lesser director may have been,[14] *The Last Passage* in its final form nevertheless presents another noteworthy rearrangement of Eastern conventions. First and foremost, the usual point of view has been reversed: the main character of *The Last Passage* is not a brave Bolshevik samurai but an "enemy," the leader of a group of anti-Soviet mutineers, Oraz Mergen. His gang steals horses from the newly established Soviet farms in Southern Kazakhstan, selling them across the border to China to sustain themselves. Oraz is horrified when he learns that the Soviet government plans to build a railway line across his native region and implores old Dosmukhambet, a former *bay*, to help him recruit a military unit that can stop the construction, which, as he puts it, "will change our way of life forever." But the *bay* is no longer interested in forging an alliance of the rich and the mutineers: the people are tired of blood; they appreciate the stability established by the new power and the peace and the land that have been given to them. Soon thereafter, Oraz Mergen and his fighters are captured, apparently because the *bay* betrayed them. Paradoxically, the viewer is inclined to side with the betrayed class enemy!

Tied up, the prisoners sit on a cart and endure humiliations from the Soviet troops, especially one Cossack who views the native population as alien heathens (*basurmany*). But the prisoners are clever, managing to free themselves and kill most of the guards. At this point, *The Last Passage* displays its first unexpected plot turn: the gang members do not kill the remaining two Soviets (one of them the cruel Cossack) who were tied up during the scuffle. For viewers familiar with the Eastern, this is unprecedented: how can anti-Soviet mutineers follow a code of honor if the very absence of honor has always been one of their defining traits? Furthermore, when two of Oraz Mergen's fighters kidnap a teenage girl to serve as a hostage, the commander is outraged by this grave violation of national tradition: Kazakhs do not capture girls as hostages. He shoots one of these fighters and only pardons the other because the gun malfunctions, thus obeying another tradition. This adherence to ancient rules, which are viewed as rooted in eternal order, ultimately becomes Oraz Mergen's undoing. He returns the hostage girl, Ainazh, who was treated with utter respect and even fatherly care, to her home *aul*. The Soviet commander expected him to do just that. Oraz Mergen naïvely assumes that no harm will be done to him and his men—after all, they are guests in the *aul*. However, Dosmukhambet shoots the three honorable enemies, over the protests of his granddaughter, who has formed a bond with the anti-Soviet mutineers.

The main plotline of *The Last Passage* represents yet another shift from the typical Eastern pattern of "Red goodies chase White baddies." The film depicts the tragedy of a man who is sincerely unable to accept the new communist order because it negates everything he believes in. This goes even further than Karsakbaev's *A Worrisome Morning* and makes Oraz Mergen a new type of enemy, one who insists on his anti-Soviet and anticommunist views because of his and his ancestors' *moral* values. Oraz Mergen's tragedy is twofold: he does not understand that his value-based conservatism is no longer shared by all Kazakhs, turning him into a lone defender of tradition; and he cannot believe that the Soviets have managed to establish a stable order that offers more advantages than disadvantages to the majority. The year is 1926, after all! Rather than becoming a heroic resistance leader, Oraz is a quixotic leftover from a battle whose outcome has long since been decided. One of the film's reoccurring visual motifs—the majestic white summits, too far away to be reached—thus acquires symbolic significance, representing the purity of the national ideal that Oraz Mergen yearns to protect.

The character of Oraz Mergen, a man who stoically overcomes the pain caused by his injured left arm, is arguably the most important novelty in *The Last Passage*. Brilliantly portrayed by Tungyshbai Dzhamankulov, who had just delivered a similar, although politically more linear, performance of a class enemy in *Blood and Sweat*, this noble mutineer embodies nomadic ethics in his resistance against militant Soviet modernization. The film's title, interpreted metaphorically, points to the transition from the traditional lifestyle and way of thinking to an epoch that follows modern, non-Kazakh rules.[15] A major change compared to earlier films about the 1920s is the ambiguity of the Kazakh rank-and-file. Previously, they were shown as victims of anti-Soviet terror, since any resistance to Bolshevik power was denounced as "terrorism" purportedly promoted by an alliance of former exploiters and militant thugs and financed by ominous foreign powers. In *The Last Passage*, the simple folks are passive and confused, but not because of the mutineers' struggle. Oraz Mergen's reasoning makes sense to them, yet they no longer have the will to resist the onslaught of social, political, and industrial modernization that the Soviets have begun. Because of regular Kazakhs' confusion, Oraz Mergen can still be tactically successful; strategically, however, he is doomed, a man of the past, not of the future. The *bay* Dosmukhambet, who gave away his herds but still holds considerable authority in the community, views resistance as an illusion. He is pragmatic and sides with the Soviets to the point that he rats out those fighting for the old order. This, too, is an unusual take on the former ruling class: rather than resisting, its members adjust and make accommodations with the new communist order.

The young generation is yet another separate stratum. Represented by the innocent Ainazh, the young enter Soviet life with the traumatic memory of the antagonistic clash between the militant victors and the defeated representatives of noble rules, while the community to which they belong is caught in the middle. Rather than siding with the Soviets and looking forward to a bright future, as was the norm in mainstream Eastern movies, they are traumatized and must find a path of their own.

Like other revisionist Easterns, *The Last Passage* deemphasizes the action elements that had made the genre so popular and a welcome propaganda tool for the Soviet establishment in the 1960s and 1970s. Neither side kills with ease, let alone enjoyment. The Soviet commander of the OGPU unit that chases Oraz Mergen's gang even calls upon his men not to shoot; alas, that is an order they regularly disobey. The only scene in which fighting skills are prominently featured is the mutineers' self-liberation, where the Soviet troopers look rather hapless and pitiful, compared to Oraz Mergen's fast and agile men. The showdown seems more like slaughter than an honest fight; there is nothing heroic in this victory over the anti-Bolshevik mutineers. Very unusual, too, is the depiction of pro-Soviet troops as arrogant toward the native population, their culture and habits. The aforementioned Cossack, who goes so far as to force prisoners to drink water from an unknown well to see whether it is poisonous, admits his shortsightedness after he has been pardoned by them: the mutineers clearly display moral superiority. These anti-Soviet forces are depicted as politically wrong and misguided, but not evil. As a result, *The Last Passage* becomes more than an original variation of the Eastern genre conventions; it represents a conceptual subversion. As such, the film anticipates the historical revisionism of the era of national independence and the rehabilitation of traditional values in the twenty-first century, although that post-Soviet revisionism avoided the genre of the Eastern. Interestingly, the film, although bilingual, is heavily dominated by Kazakh language, which appears as the genuine, authentic means of communication.

Director Amangeldy Tazhbaev achieved an atmospheric authenticity and psychological differentiation that protects the screenplay's main contrasts. In some respects, *The Last Passage* also anticipates Akan Sataev's thrillers of the 2010s in which traditional Kazakh values, which were making a spectacular comeback after independence, clash with harsh new socioeconomic demands.

Karsakbaev's *Chase in the Steppe* and Tazhbaev's *The Last Passage* represent a powerful conclusion to the probing of painful traumas of Kazakh-Soviet history of the 1920s. Furthermore, these films demonstrate that an undifferentiated characterization of the 1970s and early 1980s as a period of utter decline is too simple. These years obviously had room for interesting approaches, both continuing concepts that had begun in the 1960s and deploying concepts that went much further than previous Easterns. That subgenre would prove its conceptual elasticity and depth in exploring national values one more time before concluding its evolution.

## BETWEEN REALITY AND IDYLL

The crisis of Soviet-Kazah cinema, which reached its low point in the late 1970s, was aggravated by an increasing alienation between the film industry and native audiences. Prestige films such as *The Taste of Bread* and *Blood and Sweat* only deteriorated the situation, destroying the trust between Kazakh filmmakers and native viewers that had been established in the 1950s and 1960s and had culminated in the massive endorsement of *Kyz-Zhibek* and *The End of the Ataman*. The economic consequences were severe: instead of the 10–15 million viewers on average that Kazakhstani pictures regularly attracted even in the late 1950s, the new normal was 2–4 million viewers per film in the first year of release. Many films were marred by a chronic fear of showing Soviet reality, with its everyday frustrations and widespread existential dissatisfaction. Strictly monitored from conception to release, filmmakers often took the easy way out and delivered harmless narratives about contemporary life, which was shown to be stable, secure, and reasonably happy for those who fit in. Interestingly, television sometimes offered an alternative, allowing frustrated film directors to work on modestly budgeted but more realistic films with contemporary subject matter.

Viktor Pusurmanov, who had both noteworthy pictures, such as the prohibited *Where the Mountains Are White*, and weak fare under his belt, specialized for some time in "small" stories that approached Kazakhstani reality in a moderately honest manner while avoiding an overly critical edge. For traumatized filmmakers like him, this was perhaps the only way to maintain a modicum of artistic integrity in a society that rewarded blatant opportunism and witnessed the degeneration of basic professional standards. Pusurmanov's made-for-television films were about one hour long and often contained some unexpected gems in their performances and in the camerawork. *We Are Adults* (My—vzroslye, 1980), which the director helmed with

Askhat Ashrapov behind the camera, resembles the ill-fated *Blue Route* from a decade before in its conflict structure. Two young men become friends on a train and together look for work. Both are educated but alienated from their families. Now, they must learn how to deal with the rough tone and manners of the working class, which they temporarily join. Girl trouble and adventures in the wild steppe cement their friendship and teach them valuable lessons about the underlying complexity of milieus that seem primitive and brutal on the surface. *We Are Adults* lacks the polemical edge of the erstwhile *Blue Route* but shares its trust in the decency of young people and youth culture. Episodes of anti-intellectual mobbing, as well as images of godforsaken, backward *auls* shed a light on Soviet reality that was rarely allowed onto the big screen.

From a post-Soviet point of view, the idealistic foundation of such modest but honest films appears quixotic and sometimes touchingly naïve. But such movies remain watchable because of the human interest generated by their characters. Surprisingly charming in the context of the late Soviet status quo period is *The Melon* (Dynia, 1982), adapted for television by Pusurmanov from a story by Gabit Musrepov. This comedy's most intriguing aspect is its main character, Bulat Musaev, an unmarried fashion designer with a fear of flying. Doskhan Zholzhaksynov portrays Bulat, whose characteristic trusting chivalry and awkwardness are the opposite of the qualities typically expected of a Kazakh man. While the aforementioned attributes might indicate a self-aware, perhaps effeminate outsider, Bulat is the opposite: a strong believer in ideals, he clashes with cynical society on account of his principles. A dedicated uncle, he is bossed around by his sister and used by women whom he encounters on a train and whose every whim he tries to fulfill. This serious and endearing Don Quixote stubbornly refuses to join the materialistic status quo. The melon, which he is carrying around because he wants to please the woman who ordered it, stands for the burden of goodness that accompanies him everywhere. His behavior is so out of the ordinary that an irritated man shouts, "What's wrong with you, are you insane [literally: abnormal—*nenormal'nyi*] or what?!" To which Bulat replies, "No, I am normal."

The question of what defines a real man, a question that has been a concern of Kazakh cinema in both its Soviet and post-Soviet period, is at the center of this genuinely funny comedy. Clearly, this is a fundamental cultural issue: to what degree can virile aggressiveness and competitiveness, which are integral parts of the traditional Kazakh normative manliness, go together with reason, compromise, empathy, forgiveness, and chivalry? Why is a man such as Bulat ridiculed and treated as an outsider violating behavioral norms? Why is he the only one who helps others in need, and consequently must hurry all the time, while the vast majority of Soviet citizens could not care less about the problems of others and has all the time in the world? To be sure, *The Melon* demonstrates trust in rank-and-file people. A truck driver, for example, values Bulat's dependability and becomes a friend. But Bulat never manages to get the woman of his dreams, no matter how hard he fights for her. The fact that he is worried about others catching their train while he misses his own is emblematic of a man whose solidarity with his fellow humans has become an anachronism and the subject of laughter.

Despite its general softness and forgiving sense of humor, *The Melon* signals certain unease about the state of public morality in Soviet Kazakhstan. Kindness and mutual support should not be viewed as grotesque exceptions in a society that still calls itself communist or socialist, and yet they are. Other Kazakhstani films of the early 1980s were less critical of contemporary society and, rather than questioning it in a comedic or dramatic manner, embraced its norms in full. A prominent example of this kind of affirmative cinema is *Sweet Juice Inside the Herb* (Sladkii sok vnutri travy, 1984). As was typical in status quo movies, Soviet Kazakhstan appears as a country populated by members of a mature middle class who enjoy all-around socioeconomic stability as a matter of course; indeed, this stability is viewed as everyday *normalcy*. Their offspring may be caught in slight turbulences, undergoing the regular processes of puberty and emotional growth, but these problems seem dramatic and unique only to them. The film's main character, Siuirik, whose name means "sweet juice inside the herb," is a sensitive teenager. She cares for her siblings and adores her parents, hangs out with a crowd of like-minded youngsters, and spends much of her time at the river, swimming and singing. Siuirik is in love with Marat, but she can only express her feelings shyly, with her eyes. Marat is a generous guy who gives other kids rides on his bicycle and is nice to everybody, but he does not return Siuirik's feelings. When a new girl, Sasha, joins the class and displays self-confident femininity, Marat falls for her head over heels, inadvertently causing Siuirik to suffer and eventually making her seriously ill. Apparently unaware of the effects of his behavior, the boy remains passive, and Siuirik is too embarrassed to disclose her emotions.

*Sweet Juice Inside the Herb*, directed by Aman Alpiev[16] with support from Sergei Bodrov who also contributed to Zauresh Ergalieva's screenplay,[17] is visibly inspired by idyllic youth romances that became fashionable after Sergei Solov'ev's *One Hundred Days After Childhood* (100 dnei posle detstva, 1975). The aesthetic indulgence of those movies was a significant element of the cultural status quo in the 1970s. But the Kazakh film possesses qualities that distinguish it from other Soviet teen movies of that period. For one, it captures the charming atmosphere of Alma-Ata, its blend of old and new architecture, streetcars, and trees, an atmosphere that has become the object of nostalgic recollections in the decades since. For another, the film never vulgarizes its subject: the relations within the groups of teenagers, on the one hand, and between teenagers and family members, on the other. Both are described with tact and respect. That is why the harmony dominating the film, which at times seems oppressive, is still psychologically plausible. The featured characters cherish love and friendship above all else and try not to let jealousy or depression destroy this vital foundation of their lives. That is one of the reasons why *Sweet Juice Inside the Herb* has been remembered fondly in the post-Soviet decades. Its near-perfect family frame is held together by an understanding mother and a tender father who even brings a pony to the window of Siuirik's hospital room to help her get well soon. It is also significant that the values of family and group cohesion are never verbalized and preached: they permeate the characters' lives as the societal norm, as a consensus that goes without saying. Only the precocious newcomer Sasha is an exception to this internal harmony, acting brashly and hurting the feelings of others without thinking twice. In the end, when she leaves for another city, her departure also means that the wounds she caused will soon begin to heal and harmony will be reestablished.

It would be easy to point out the many social problems facing Kazakh society in the early 1980s that the film simply ignores. Its excessive idealization of contemporary Soviet Kazakhstan is beyond question, and its sole focus on bashfully emerging erotic perceptions is at times saccharine. As a matter of fact, the love story is related in such tender tones that some of its elements may be lost on the viewer. The young Gulshad Omarova portrays Siuirik with shy sweetness, carefully avoiding verbalization, expressing herself through a beautifully pure smile and innocent eyes in whose dreaminess Fedor Aranyshev's camera indulges, albeit perhaps too frequently (to be fair, Siuirik's face in its changing states is indeed the film's most arresting visual element). The appeal of *Sweet Juice Inside the Herb* for certain viewer segments is rooted in its preference for a predominantly aesthetic, harmony-driven approach to reality, and its deliberate avoidance of the serious social issues of life that even an affluent area of Kazakhstan's capital was facing. But such selectiveness in subject matter and reduction of cinematic reality to an idyll was precisely what some desired in a movie at a time when the symptoms of the approaching systemic crisis of Soviet life could no longer be ignored. Viewers who expect an embellishment of reality regard the resulting sociopolitical blindness[18] not as a weakness but as an accomplishment. Films such as *Sweet Juice Inside the Herb* were on the opposite pole from "kitchen-sink" realism (a British equivalent for the Russian "*chernukha*," a term still used for films that indulge in focusing on the ugly sides of life). In *Sweet Juice Inside the Herb*, the world is filled with well-wishing, compassionate Soviet citizens; no action or utterance is ever drastic, and a little joke is the most intrusive gesture one can expect from a neighbor. Soviet society is depicted as one that firmly protects its individuals. Indeed, the atmosphere of all-around protection is one of the important messages implicitly conveyed by this film.

One of the few curious aspects of *Sweet Juice Inside the Herb* is its handling of ethnic issues. Siuirik and her family are Kazakh; the girl's father is working on a book titled *The Role of Space in the Culture of Nomads*, which is a noteworthy detail, however minor. Sasha, the competitor girl, appears to be Russian, although no inter-ethnic tension is explicitly stated. When Siuirik overcomes her lung infection, she meets Ahmad, a young man from the Caucasus, who immediately falls for her. Ahmad's attempts to impress Siuirik by playing chess (and always losing) and gathering a group of musicians to perform for her, culminate in his proposal to get married as soon as she is old enough (as a student in the eighth grade, Siuirik can be no older than fifteen). In these episodes, the film displays stark ethno-cultural contours that stand in contrast to the mild-mannered, Russified Kazakhs. Conspicuously, it is Ahmad who is the first to ask Siuirik about her ethnicity. His passionate directness elicits some comical effects but can also provoke some consideration of the different degrees of assimilation of ethnic groups within Soviet society.

## FURTHER DECLINE OF THE GENRE FILM

The connection between sports and national self-consciousness is essential for *Don't Mess with Our Kind!* (Znai nashikh!, 1985), the last picture directed by Sultan-Akhmet Khodzhikov, of *Kyz-Zhibek* fame. Martial arts had been extremely popular throughout the Soviet Union for a long time, but mostly as an underground phenomenon. In Soviet movies, the martial arts cult came into public awareness in the late 1970s, when Boris Durov's *Pirates of the 20th Century* (Piraty 20ogo veka, 1979) took movie theaters by storm and became one of the greatest box office hits of all time. But Soviet cultural officials were on the alert, making sure that the violent thrill and suspense of martial arts were not exploited as aims in themselves. Fighting skills could only be legitimately endorsed when they were based on high moral principles within a clearly designed patriotic framework. Khodzhikov, who also coauthored the screenplay for *Don't Mess with Our Kind!*, certainly shared that view. In his film, the only characters who display high fighting skills are those who happen to be the most decent human beings.

The film takes place at the beginning of the twentieth century, showcasing the evolution of Kazakhstani sports and its close connections with Russia. In other words, the story was suitable for strengthening national pride but also met Soviet ideological standards. In 1904, the fighter Hodja Mukan (other spellings: Kazhymukan, Khodzha Mukan, or Khadzhimukan) Munaitpasov[19] is introduced to the legendary Russian athlete Ivan Poddubnyi, marking the beginning of a long friendship in which the Kazakh and the Russian come to each other's aid in the most challenging of situations. *Don't Mess with Our Kind!* describes both the wild popularity and the corruption that are characteristic of martial arts. In the first episode, a ruthless entrepreneur uses dirty tricks to ensure that Ivan Poddubnyi is late for an important fight so that his much weaker opponent, Kurbas, will win the championship on technical grounds. To save the great athlete from public humiliation, the Kazakh Hodja Mukan volunteers to take his place and fight in his stead. But Kurbas arrogantly declares that he will only accept a "Grand Russian" (*velikoross*) as his opponent, not "an Asian."

Despite their different backgrounds, Poddubnyi and Mukan share similar values: both despise trickery and greed and refuse to fight for money. The commercialization of sports is one of the film's central themes, especially when Poddubnyi, Mukan, and a third fighter, the physically imposing peasant Grigorii Kashcheev, are officially sent to Paris to represent Russia at the world championship in "French martial arts." While the film depicts the decadent bourgeois culture of Can-Can and champagne in a relatively positive manner, the destructive role of money in sports is pointed out time and time again. Thus, when it becomes clear that the French world champion may lose either to one of the Russians or to the Kazakh, the administration introduces a new rule stipulating that only fighters who pay a "bond" of 5,000 francs will qualify for the competition. It takes a stroke of luck and an enormous amount of willpower for the three friends to overcome that obstacle.

*Don't Mess with Our Kind!* obviously targeted juvenile audiences and in many ways delivered what those viewer segments expected from a martial arts movie. It is a story of noble strength and solidarity among buddies who together overcome adversity. The plot itself had sufficient appeal to make up for the lack of acting skills (only Dmitrii Zolotukhin in the role of Poddubnyi was a professional, whereas Aleukhan Bekbulatov, who portrayed Hodja Mukan, was a simple tractor driver[20]). But the film is marred by several irritating weaknesses, including the cameraman's inability to effectively capture fights, making the drama in the ring often visually incomprehensible. Ahistorical music and an excessive emphasis on the negotiation of rules and technicalities during the tournaments are unnecessary distractions as well. Likely for all these reasons, the film was initially not very popular, attracting barely 2 million viewers despite its topic and the scarcity of martial arts movies on Soviet screens.

However, many Kazakh viewers remember it fondly today, perhaps due to the theme of national pride that distinguishes *Don't Mess with Our Kind!* from other sports films. Hodja Mukan is shown as a self-conscious Kazakh who repeatedly faces ethnic bias from tsarist officials. Thus, in one episode, when the fighter sings to the dombra, a government official expresses his displeasure. During the selection of the Russian delegation for the championship in Paris, another official demandes that Hodja Mukan, as an "alien" (*inorodets*), takes the last position in the lineup. But like many Kazakhstani films, this historical sports drama is not simplistic in its approach to national issues. For example, the Grand Prince, who is present at the selection, does not object to a Kazakh athlete being one of three representatives of the Russian Empire sent to Paris. Interestingly, when Mukan is asked why he is shouting during fights, his answer is remarkable: he is calling on his ancestors' spirits for support—and on Allah, too!

Hodja Mukan has remained a legendary name in the history of Kazakh sports. He is also remembered for his interest in the stage: in 1926 in Kyzyl-Orda, he cofounded the first professional theater of Kazakhstan, in which the great actor Kalibek Kuanyshpaev, among others, began his career.

*Don't Mess with Our Kind!* is clearly marked as part of the status quo period in Kazakhstani cinema that began in the 1970s and lasted well into the 1980s. Compared to Khodzhikov's previous picture, *Kyz-Zhibek*, it is artistically disappointing. The deliberate simplification of its subject and its lack of depth and cinematic sophistication demonstrate the effect that a national cinema in decline can have on a talented director.

The time of the Civil War was not tackled by subversive Easterns alone but was also the subject of rather conformist children's movies, for example, *The Red Yurt* (Krasnaia iurta, 1982) by Kanymbek Kasymbekov. With its simple division into good and evil characters this late Eastern reverses the trend toward differentiation and complexity in the non-formulaic Civil War dramas initiated by Abdulla Karsakbaev's *Worrisome Morning*. *The Red Yurt* portrays a phenomenon that was commonplace in the 1920s: Bolshevik propaganda units moving across the steppe to spread communist ideology. In Kasymbekov's film, the ideological mission is linked to an educational and medical one: members of the revolutionary team talk and sing about the revolution, but also immunize the children against typhoid fever and other infectious diseases. These activists are depicted as young, clean, and handsome; they are carriers of culture and modernity, as opposed to the *bays*, mullahs, and their underlings, who use violence and intimidation to win back lost ground. Kasymbekov was generally a fine filmmaker, and this movie about the communist takeover in Central Asia is certainly not primitive; rather, it can be called a romantic ballad praising the selfless idealism of a generation of believers in the new system. But *The Red Yurt* is historically selective and naïve, conveying a version of history that unconditionally legitimized the communist system for millions of Kazakhs during the Soviet period.

Films such as *Don't Mess with Our Kind!*, *Sweet Juice Inside the Herb*, and *The Red Yurt*, while produced in the early 1980s, are direct extensions of the dominant conformist trend of the 1970s. Praised by the official media and at national festivals, they only attracted a few million viewers and had no healing effect on the crisis of trust between the Kazakhstani film industry and native and Soviet-wide audiences, notwithstanding their moderate references to national pride.

Given the rather gloomy picture that national film production presented in the 1970s, it may come as a surprise that at the end of that decade, Kazakhstan boasted the second highest movie attendance per capita in the USSR, with only the Russian Federation ahead of it. In rural areas, the Kazakh SSR was the world leader, with every Kazakh in the countryside going to the movies an average of twenty times a year. However, these numbers are somewhat misleading, since the statistics do not differentiate between Kazakhstani, Soviet, and imported films. Most likely, Western imports and especially films from India attracted the largest numbers of viewers. But, as the poet and screenwriter Olzhas Suleimenov stated, when it came to its own film production and the quality of its films, Kazakhstan occupied one of the last positions in the world. He added: "It is not Kazakhstan, but us, the film workers of 'Kazakhfilm,' who are occupying the last place. The republic has nothing to do with it. It cannot be blamed for our miseries. All necessary conditions for our creative development have been established for us. We have not been able to make use of them."[21]

Indeed, despite some exceptional pictures, the 1970s profoundly harmed the reputation of Kazakhfilm studio. Its output was generally perceived as bland and boring. The national and internal debates about the reasons for this dilemma and possible ways to overcome it were conducted in a passionate but, alas, insufficiently objective and analytical manner. Kazakhstan's film community was divided into clans that fought for influence and position. When the First Secretary of the Union of Kazakhstani Film Workers, Akim Tarazi, who had held this position since 1971, stepped down "due to his transition to creative work" (the official formulation) on June 12, 1980, it was clear that major changes were in store. The election of Olzhas Suleimenov, a personal confidante of Communist Party leader Dinmukhamed Kunaev, as Tarazi's successor had symbolic significance. Suleimenov remained in the first secretary's chair for less than a year, until April 1981, when he was appointed head of the powerful State Film Board (*Goskino*), which held direct administrative power. The fights determining these decisions remained behind closed doors, of course, but their effects were visible when it came to the assignment of new projects, casting decisions, and public criticism. Specific national factors further complicated the crisis of Kazakhstani cinema, which for the most part reflected USSR-wide trends. There was no solution in sight.

## NOTES

1. Baitenov, Zhardem (b. 1932), Kazakh film director who worked both in feature and documentary cinema.
2. Dmitrii Snegin (1912–2001) was an influential journalist and prose writer who was named People's Writer of the Kazakh SSR in 1984.
3. Siranov, Kabysh, "Radosti i ogorcheniia," *Kazakhstanskaia pravda*, 17 June 1973.
4. Muratbaev was the First Secretary of the Komsomol of Turkestan from 1921–24.
5. Cf. Siranov, *Ocherki istorii kazakhskogo kino*, p. 96.
6. Siranov, Kabysh, "Stsenarii—osnova fil'ma," *Kazakhstanskaia pravda*, 3 April 1976.
7. State prestige films have been produced both before and after Kazakhstan's independence. This continuity as such would merit a closer analysis. However, in respect to Soviet Kazakhstan, the term does not primarily refer to the source of funding, since until 1991, all Kazakh films were state financed and thus can legitimately be called state prestige films; even after the introduction of free market conditions in 1991, the majority of Kazakh films still is produced with the state as the main investor. In the Kazakhstani context, the proposed term has to do with the message and spirit of a certain film, when it illustrates (explicitly or implicitly) the very values that are declared to be of fundamental importance for the Kazakh state. The term may evoke negative connotations such as "propaganda" and "cult," but only if the conflation of state and art is considered negative per se and under any circumstances. My intention in using the term, however, is to objectively describe a situation when the government solicits a feature film on a certain topic, to be rendered in a manner entirely consistent with political officialdom. To be sure, a number of filmmakers create such films out of personal conviction, without taking direct instructions from state representatives, or out of a sense of civic duty. But whether the motivation was an individual agreement with the state or is the result of a deal of convenience, the important part is the consequence, i.e., the film itself.
8. For Katesh Alimbaeva, this anomaly was a conscious decision made both by the screenwriters and the two directors, who viewed the contrast between the handsome looks and the unprincipled behavior of Tanibergen as the real object of interest, whereas Elaman only appears as a code. However, it seems more likely that the resulting dominance of the "negative" character happened unintentionally—after all, one can easily imagine more convincing performances of Tanibergen's communist opponent and his beautiful wife that would have prevented the imbalance. Cf. Ainagulova, Alimbaeva, *Tendentsii razvitiia kinoiskusstva Kazakhstana*, pp. 35–37.
9. The highly perceptive Tanibergen begins to notice a difference between the internationalist Communists and the Whites with whom he has allied himself. When some of the White Army officers humiliate him and repeatedly express their distrust because he is a Kazakh, he utters: "The Reds have faith in the poorest Kazakhs, while you don't even believe in me, one of the wealthiest!" In other words, while the class solidarity that he expected to run across national divides is just a sham for the Russian

bourgeoisie and aristocracy, it does work for the exploited. However, this insight comes too late to make any difference for Tanibergen. He embodies an upper class that is at odds with itself and resigns under pressure from a self-confident antagonist.

10. The repeated meetings between Elaman and Tanibergen point to an invisible destiny that ties them together. Of course, destiny is a concept incompatible with Marxist-Leninist dialectical materialism, but it could be justified from an aesthetic point of view as symbolism, that is, the two men symbolize the fate of their respective social strata that are tied together in antagonism. The parallelism is curious, though. For example, both characters at different points spare each other's lives; however, when Tanibergen argues for letting the captured Elaman free, the latter attacks him and shouts that he will kill him whereever he can find him. Later, when Tanibergen is captured by the Reds, Elaman, whom his adversary insulted as a "slave," lets him go, too, saying "You have chosen your own destiny." During an improvised meeting, when Elaman tries to convince members of his village community to join the Red Army, one man replies that "this is just a Civil War among Russians; why should we have a part in it?!"

11. Only Farida Sharipova as the engineer's wife gets little opportunity to develop her character and remains rather pale. In her case, talent was wasted.

12. For a good survey of the criticism that was launched against the film, cf. Ainagulova, Alimbaeva, *Tendentsii razvitiia kinoiskusstva Kazakhstana*, pp. 56–57. The authors agree with the outrage over this film's artistic flaws.

13. Suleimenov was first credited under a pseudonym, Olzhas Karakulov, and then had his name removed altogether, for reasons unknown.

14. Cf. a critical assessment of that decision in Raibaev, "Nevostrebovannaia zhizn'," p. 8.

15. The original title was *Blood of the Drake* (Krov's seleznia).

16. Alpiev, Aman (1942–2007), Kyrgyz director of documentary and feature films who mainly worked in Kazakhstan; his best-known picture is *Sweet Juice Inside the Herb* (1984, codirected with Sergei Bodrov).

17. Ergalieva, Zauresh (b. 1944), Kazakh screenwriter.

18. One critic noticed an underlying conflict between the girl's parents: the father was depicted as an idealistic intellectual, while the mother pursued materialistic goals and tried to influence her daughter (the father's gift to Siuirik is a pony, while the mother's is a porcelain service). Katesh Alimbaeva correctly pointed out that such a juxtaposition was not previously motivated and that a critique of a phenomenon called "hailaphism" (i.e., consumerism) in the film is unconvincing. One might add that the juxtaposition between the charaters is handled so timidly that the viewer may be excused for missing it. Ainagulova, Alimabeva. *Tendentsii razvitiia kinoiskusstva Kazakhstana*, p. 59.

19. Hodja Mukan Munaitpasov (1871 [?]–1948) was born into the ancient clan Altybas. His physical prowess was legendary. For many years, he participated in national and international competitions and worked as a circus artist. Numerous facts of his life are still debated, including the exact year of his birth and the time and place of his martial arts education. Better documented is his international career that took him to Europe, Asia, and North and South America, following his victory at a

martial arts tournament in Goteborg in 1909. However, the two major fights featured in *Znai nashikh!* (one in Kazan and one in Paris) are not historically documented. Interestingly, the film does not mention the honors bestowed upon Hodja Mukan during the Soviet period. Thus, in 1927 he was named "Batyr of the Kazakh People" by the Central Executive Committee of Kazakhstan. In Astana, a stadium has been named after Kazhymukhan (i.e., Hodja Mukan).

20. Aleukhan Bekbulatov (1954–2015) was cast because of his physical strength and his likeness to Hodja Mukan. According to some sources, he was later offered other roles but refused to continue his movie career, working as a businessman instead.

21. Suleimenov, Olzhas, "Ot mirosozertsaniia—k mirovozzreniiu. Dialog s korrespondentom 'IK' Katesh Alimbaevoi," *Iskusstvo kino*, 3/1982, p. 34.

## Chapter 11

# Crisis and Reconstruction

While officially endorsed films such as *Sweet Juice Inside the Herb* displayed the purity and naïveté of a high school essay, some films in the early 1980s gave indications that Soviet-Kazakh society was not well at all. For various reasons, none of these films received the attention they deserved, either because the studio and the cultural administration deliberately limited their distribution or because audiences no longer expected anything honest and original to come out of Kazakhfilm studio.

However, the studio's abysmal reputation was not solely the fault of its creative personnel. Repressive control mechanisms that were installed in the 1970s led to the prohibition of seven full-length feature films and to increased internal self-censorship, a psychological reaction known to be detrimental to creativity.

The impact of censorship extended to all branches of filmmaking. Besides feature films, the studio continued to churn out dozens of short and full-length documentaries every year. In this domain, too, strict controls were implemented so that inconvenient truths could not get out into the open. An example is Sergei Azimov's 20-minute-long *The Interval* (Interval, 1982), which soberly depicts the irresponsible manner in which livestock were treated in Soviet Kazakhstan. Films such as this were shelved and remained hidden from viewers, who eventually lost all hope of seeing their own experiences reflected on screen, whether in fictional or nonfictional cinema. Indeed, a major symptom of the impending crisis in Kazakhstani cinema was the loss of trust between filmmakers and audiences, a trust that had been established in the 1950s and 1960s but was squandered in the following decade. However, the evaporation of cultural trust was not unique to Kazakhstan. One of the signs that Soviet society was approaching breakdown was the growing alienation between the Soviet film industry and mass audiences. Still, the consequences for Kazakhstani cinema were particularly severe.

## PERESTROIKA FILM CRITICISM: LOOKING BACK IN ANGER

The 1980s have justly been called "the most contradictory phase" in the history of Kazakhstan's cinema.[1] What were the contradictions that defined the last Soviet-Kazakh decade and what factors were decisive in the evolving crisis of society at large and of its film industry in particular? On the one hand, Soviet-Kazakhstani society was shaped by strata that implicitly accepted the Brezhnev era's sociopolitical and cultural status quo, the agreement within the communist establishment to pursue ideological goals more formally than substantively and otherwise leave Soviet citizens to their private lives, within certain limitations, creating a sense of protection and stability but also of frustrating social immobility. As a result, countless Kazakhstani citizens, including intellectuals, increasingly sought fulfillment outside the workplace. Private consumption and family happiness became solidified as supreme values, indirectly expressed by cinema through highly successful melodramas and lyrical comedies. Work-related problems or societal issues at large were treated with a sense of distance or mildly cynical complacency. As such, the stability of the Brezhnev era led to arrested societal development, which the communist reformers of the mid-1980s would eventually denounce as "stagnation." In all cultural spheres, complacency became the most widespread attitude—which could hardly serve as inspiration for genuine artistry. Little wonder, therefore, that great filmmakers such as Andrei Tarkovskii and Otar Ioseliani left the USSR and settled in the West.

The cinema of Kazakhstan reflected the tension between the ideals of the past and the convenience of the status quo in the present, albeit often indirectly. This was particularly obvious in state prestige films such as *The Taste of Bread* and *Blood and Sweat*, on the one hand, and in aesthetically lackluster "entertainment" products, that is, the so-called gray films, on the other. These were interspersed with the occasional artistic exception that was either officially accepted, such as *The Fierce One*, or condemned, such as *The Funeral Feast*. One aspect of film production in republics such as Kazakhstan that remained under tight control and was keenly monitored by the Moscow center was the search for national identity, usually denounced as "nationalism."

In Soviet cinema, most of the pictures addressing contemporary issues were thematically and aesthetically unremarkable. Comedies featuring moderate social awareness, such as the super hit *Moscow Does Not Believe in*

*Tears* (Moskva slezam ne verit, 1980), reflected the consequences of evolving gender roles in Soviet society; its worldwide success was rooted in the benevolently compromising spirit that carried the film. The societal paradigm was depicted as functioning smoothly, while tensions emerged as the result of private conflicts that were considered part of the human condition and deemed to have nothing to do with the specifics of socialism/communism per se: adultery, intergenerational miscommunication, or unrequited love. Conspicuously, millions of viewers appreciated that type of apolitical drama or comedy. Soviet society seemed to have grown tired of never-ending revolutionary impatience, preferring secure civility and consumerism, corrupt though the consequences may have been.

In the early 1980s, numerous reforms were attempted, but these yielded only mixed results. In light of this, critics of the Brezhnev period undertook a radical reassessment of the years from 1970 to 1985, including its cultural output. With the beginning of perestroika, regional periodicals for the first time opened their pages to genuinely critical voices on Kazakhstani cinema. In many articles, the reevaluation of Kazakhstani feature films was formulated in a radically negative tone.

Thus, the journalist Viacheslav Kuvshinnikov diagnosed in Kazakhstani cinema an underlying, consciously designed system that was opposed to true artistry. This he identified as the main impediment to the improvement of Kazakh films. Instead of complaining about the huge number of mediocre movies, Kuvshinnikov opined, the time had come to recognize the body of ideas that carried those worthless films.[2] Among its elements, he singled out the absence of real conflicts that was meant to suggest the absence of problems in reality itself. Kuvshinnikov also observed a lowering of aesthetic standards that went along with a superficial ethnographic masking of reality, hiding the absence of a genuine understanding of Kazakhs' way of life and of their moral values.[3] As an alternative, Kuvshinnikov pointed to the non-Kazakh director Bulat Mansurov, whose *Funeral Feast*, in his view, possessed the very qualities that the Kazakh mainstream was lacking. On the opposite end, the critic identified productions that on the surface seemed to add to Kazakhfilm's prestige but were in reality scarcely veiled commercial vehicles that could easily have been shot elsewhere. However, Kuvshinnikov's main target was not state prestige films, but genre fare: the detective thrillers *The Secrets of Madame Wong* (Tainy Madam Vong, 1986), an infamous potboiler directed by Stepan Puchinian from a screenplay by Stanislav Govorukhin, and Bolat Shmanov's *The Victims Have No Complaints* (Poterpervshie pretenzii ne imeiut, 1986), from a script by two of the leading Soviet authors of detective stories, brothers Georgii and Arkadii Vainer. A viable alternative to these (in Kuvshinnikov's view) unacceptable movies was *The Alien White and Checkered One* (Chuzhaia belaia i riaboi,

1986), Sergei Solov'ev's postwar drama, which cleverly combined arthouse and popular features. However, he had to admit that neither Solov'ev's picture nor Aman Alpiev and Sergei Bodrov's *Sweet Juice Inside the Herb* nor Bodrov's *The Non-Professionals*, all of which were made at Kazakhfilm studio, added much to the reputation of Kazakh cinema. According to Kuvshinnikov, they were "author's films," that is, they belonged to the filmography of Russian directors Sergei Solov'ev and Sergei Bodrov rather than to Kazakhstan, where they were made.

Kuvshinnikov's article represents the type of radical assault on the cultural legacy formulated in a "looking-back-in-anger" mode that was characteristic of the perestroika discourses of the mid-1980s. While such analyses of recent history were certainly healthy, their unforgiving maximalism and lack of differentiation were problematic. Analyses such as Kuvshinnikov's operated on the surface of socioeconomic and cultural reality, interpreting negative phenomena as the result of some "system" that forced individuals to make "wrong" moral choices. The implication of this criticism was that once the incompetent and corrupt individuals were removed, the system itself would transform as well. In radical perestroika film criticism, the underlying socioeconomic and administrative realities of cultural production were generally not taken into consideration. The harshness of these critics' judgment was based on their own unrealistic expectations: films were supposed to be of high artistic quality *and* attract millions of viewers. In the end, such criteria could not help but make the entire production of Kazakhfilm studio look unsatisfactory. In the long run, this type of maximalist film criticism was unsustainable, revealing the reform-oriented intelligentsia's lack of knowledge about contemporary Soviet society.

When looking back at the output of Kazakhstani cinema in the 1970s and 1980s, the unrealistic evaluative standards that were commonly applied by perestroika-era media should not simply be embraced and repeated. A fair and even-handed assessment of pre-perestroika cinema can only be accomplished by considering the studio output with all its elements in light of the multiple internal and external factors influencing film production, to the extent that they are known. Furthermore, it is important to recognize that the entire system of production, distribution, and publicity was based on ideological assumptions discussed earlier: Communist Party demands were met with ideologically clean prestige films that regular audiences did not want to see, while intellectuals were provided with a few arthouse pictures that were shown in small studio theaters. As a result of this division of labor within culture, the statistical goals of the plan (i.e., box office numbers) were accomplished through commercial imports (thrillers, comedies, Bollywood dramas), as well as domestic import-substitutions such as the notorious *Secrets of Madame Wong*. The latter category of films deserves a thorough analysis to lay open the mechanisms by which Soviet-Kazakhstani cinema functioned prior to its final demise at the end of the decade.

## STUDIO TROUBLE

Kazakhfilm was officially honored with the name "Shaken Aimanov" in 1984. From an economic point of view, the so-called period of stagnation had established the studio as a significant factor in the republic's cultural production. Of its 1,130 employees, 360 were occupied in creative professions. They had at their disposal 3,000 square meters of office space and 20 hectares of studio space.[4] In other words, the material conditions for making movies left little to be desired. However, the real technical functionality of the studio was far from secure. Of the twelve Party meetings that the studio held between January 1982 and October 1983, seven were devoted to technical malfunctions, production disruptions, and organizational problems. Closely connected with these issues were the many shortcomings in the artistic sphere. For example, in 1983, not one of the studio's feature films was selected for the annual USSR film festival in Leningrad! The critic Bauyrzhan Nugerbek claimed that the studio did not employ a single reputable director and there was no sign of new ones.[5]

This perception was shared by Olzhas Suleimenov and Murat Auezov,[6] both of whom were exceptionally harsh in their judgments of the achievements of the filmmakers working at Kazakhfilm studio, going so far as to claim that the goal of radically reforming Kazakhstani cinema could not be achieved with the directors presently working at the studio. Thus, according to them, the entire creative personnel had to be replaced, although not by "imported" directors as had often been done in the past, but by newly educated native ones. This assessment is precisely the reason for the administrative implementation of what would later be coined the "Kazakh New Wave," which was the result of planning, not spontaneous development. However, once beneficial conditions were created, the work of individual directors and the further development of Kazakhstani cinema were no longer under the control of the very bodies that were supposed to oversee and regulate them.

On April 7–8, 1981, the Fourth Congress of the Union of Kazakhstani Film Workers took place. Since the previous congress, the number of full members had increased to 190; interestingly, at 17 members, the governing board was half the size of its predecessor. A real sensation, preempting developments at the Moscow center, was the election of Bulat Gabitov-Dzhansugurov, the son of the poet Ilias Dzhansugurov (a pioneer of Kazakhstani cinema in the 1920s and 1930s and a victim of the Stalinist terror) to the post of first secretary, which he held until 1984.[7] As in similar situations in previous years, the state reacted to widespread criticism by making administrative adjustments. Thus, in 1985, the "Shaken Aimanov Kazakhfilm Studio" was renamed the "Republican Creative-Industrial Association Shaken Aimanov Kazakhfilm"—an awkward construct indeed. At the height of perestroika, on June 2, 1988, the Supreme Soviet of the Kazakh SSR issued a decree dissolving the State Film Committee (*Goskino*), which had existed since 1963. It was replaced by the Main Film Administration of the Council of Ministers of the Kazakh SSR, an entity that would survive for barely four years.

All these bureaucratic changes were attempts to stop a decline that had begun in the early 1970s and continued into the 1980s and whose outcome and ultimate dimensions were hard to predict. Most administrative measures proved to be inefficient from a production point of view. But some of the films made at Kazakhfilm studio were much better than the studio's overall reputation. These films managed to capture reality to a surprising degree, indicating to anybody who was willing to see and listen that a deep crisis of Soviet-Kazakh society was imminent. Indeed, some of Kazakhstan's filmmakers sensed the profound unease spreading in society earlier than the republic's governing bodies. In hindsight, it is obvious that the harsh words that perestroika-era film critics hurled at Kazakhstani filmmakers were often based on a lack of awareness and unfair generalizations.

## SUBVERSION OF THE STATUS QUO I

Kazakhstani cinema in the early 1980s was far from the bleak picture painted by Auezov, Suleimenov, and those who agreed with their uncompromising condemnation of Kazakhfilm studio's production. As outlined in the previous chapter, along with opportunistic "gray" films, artistically unremarkable genre fare, and little-seen state prestige films, the studio continued to produce ideologically subversive Easterns and quality films made for television. Although hardly noticed by critics, those years also saw the release of realistic films, signaling a quiet, qualitative shift away from imposed celebratory officialdom and mindless entertainment. None of these films became hits, but when analyzed retrospectively in the context of Soviet-Kazakh history, they stand out for their thematic novelty, sincerity, and humanism. These include films about national minorities (*The Year of the Dragon*), the Great Patriotic War (*The Salty River of Childhood*, *The Long Milky Way*), and contemporary society (*Atone for Your Guilt*, *The Human Factor*, *The Nonprofessionals*, *Nesibeli*), as well as the late Easterns that were analyzed in the previous chapter (*Chase in the Steppe*, *The Last Passage*). Most of these films possess considerable critical and subversive potential that is not so much anti-Soviet or anti-communist as it is moralist, mildly nationalist, and spiritual. The subsequent critical discourses of perestroika (1985–1990) largely neglected these films, an attitude that is unjustified from a historical point of view.

The First Secretary of the Communist Party of Kazakhstan, Dinmukhamed Kunaev, took a personal interest in the state of Kazakhstani cinema. Thus, at the XIV Party congress, he suggested that given the absence of qualified native screenwriters and directors, Kazakhstan had no choice but to hire outside specialists. One of Kunaev's most vocal supporters, the famed poet Olzhas Suleimenov, commented that this suggestion was made with "bitter irony."[8] Suleimenov, the First Secretary of the Union of Kazakhstani Filmmakers, was appointed head of Kazakhstan's Goskino in April 1981, clearly with the support of his protector, Kunaev, whom he praised on various occasions. Of course, Suleimenov had many years of experience working in Kazakh cinema; after all, he was the author of two of the most interesting screenplays of the 1960s, *Land of the Fathers* and *The Blue Route*. As an exceptional poet and a loyal member of the Communist Party, he tried to use the powers that his new position gave him to improve the quality of both Kazakhstani feature films and documentaries. His assessment of the 1970s was devastating, and he did not shy away from personal attacks, for example against Sharip Beisembaev, stating that every new film directed by this veteran of Kazakh cinema looked like the work of a rookie.[9] One can only imagine the effects of these harsh words on a director whose filmography included such superb works as *Protect Your Star!*[10]

Judging by the films that were released in the early 1980s, a fair assessment would appreciate the *coexistence* of negative and positive trends within Kazakhstani cinema, as well as the ups and downs in individual careers such as Beisembaev's. Moreover, as the following sections will show, there were films produced at Kazakhfilm studio in the early 1980s that had distinct subversive potential, setting them apart from the status quo cinema that had emerged in the 1970s and continued to exert influence. The realization of thematically and artistically interesting films belies the claim that Kazakhstani cinema had nothing to offer prior to the arrival on the scene of the New Wave filmmakers at the end of the decade.

Among Kazakhstani feature films of the early 1980s, *The Year of the Dragon* (God drakona, 1982) was unique. It dealt with a politically sensitive issue: the persecution of the Uyghur people in China. The screenplay was written by the well-known bard and actor Iurii Vizbor, from a novel by Uyghur author Zia Samadi, *Maimkhan*. It tells the story of Uyghurs' national mobilization against the Chinese empire in the first half of the nineteenth century.

The opening scenes describe Chinese atrocities against the Uyghur population, including a brutal attack on a wedding celebration. Yet the barbaric method used by the Manchurian-Chinese administration to suppress the resistance of a small but proud people yields the opposite of the intended effect, strengthening the Uyghurs' will to sacrifice everything to achieve liberation. A young woman, Maimkhan (Tamara Iandieva), joins the gang of Akhtam (Iusup Saitov), with whom she soon falls in love. Akhtam's fighters manage to defeat a Chinese unit. When Maimkhan is captured and used as a hostage to force Akhtam to surrender, he seems to acquiesce but plays a trick on the captors and defeats them again. However, treason within his own ranks ultimately prevents Akhtam from achieving victory.

The topic of *The Year of the Dragon* was subversive for two reasons. Firstly, the USSR-Chinese relations had been severely strained since the 1960s, and a feature film with a clear anti-Chinese agenda could be viewed as a provocation with potential international consequences. Secondly, the story of the oppression of small nations located on the margins of the Chinese empire could legitimately be understood as an allusion to oppressive Soviet nationality policies. To avoid the former accusation, the depiction of the Chinese is somewhat differentiated. Thus, Akhtam states, "There are different kinds of Chinese people;" on another occasion, somebody utters, "We are not at war with the Chinese people." Maimkhan's father, a teacher, emphasizes that "all peoples are great," opposing nationalist slogans. The second suspicion, namely, of using the history of the Uyghurs in China as a metaphor for Soviet national discrimination, was more difficult to refute and may be one of the reasons why the film disappeared from theaters relatively quickly. Be that as it may, to this day, Uyghurs all over the world remember *The Year of the Dragon* with gratitude as arguably the only feature film dedicated to their plight. Codirected by Asanali Ashimov and the Korean-Kazakh Guk In Tsoi,[11] the film combines historical action with romance, borrowing some approaches from films about Native Americans (then called Indians) as bearers of freedom and independence. *The Year of the Dragon* stands out for its thematic daring, if not so much for its artistic originality. The fact that it was Kazakhfilm studio that produced a feature film about national liberation and the fight for equal rights was connected to the large Uyghur minority living in the republic and with Kazakhstan's own tolerant nationalities policy. Such a production was certainly an honorable gesture and was rewarded with a diploma at the fifteenth Soviet Film Festival in Tallin in 1982.

One of the strengths of Soviet-era Kazakhstani cinema was its ability to give an unexpected national outlook to a theme whose normative, mainstream treatment had been established at the center of the USSR film industry, an outlook that ultimately subverted the normative approach. This ability became obvious in the 1960s with the films of Abdulla Karsakbaev and Mazhit Begalin; it was artificially suppressed in the 1970s with the prohibition of Mansurov's *Funeral Feast* and Pusurmanov's *Where the Mountains Are White*, and quietly continued with variations of the Eastern in the late

1970s and early 1980s. During the latter period, Karsakbaev decided to address the topic of the Great Patriotic War.

What on the surface appeared to be a children's film became in reality a serious revision of the normative interpretation of the war experience. *The Salty River of Childhood* (Solenaia reka detstva, 1983), from a screenplay by Bulat Mansurov, describes the sojourn of three children on the river Syrdaria in 1943. Their boat is primitive and may turn over at any moment; the places they visit, delivering salt, flour, and letters to isolated communities on faraway islands, are dangerous, and the news they bring to the people are tragic. In the beginning, an elderly man, Zeinolla (Nurmukhan Zhanturin) accompanies them, but after an accident at night he disappears. Now, the girl Dariga and the boys Mukhtar and Amir must face all dangers, including a criminal gang, by themselves. At the end, after saving several forlorn old women from a flood, the three children find Zeinolla and visit him at the hospital.

The film's plot could not be simpler; its entire magic lies in Abdulla Karsakbaev's direction. First, the relations between the shy yet morally strong Dariga and the cousins Mukhtar and Amir undergo a transformation, from show-offy competition to sincere sympathy and mutual support. Old Zeinolla seems to understand what is going on between the kids and does not interfere, instead observing their interactions from afar. Two factors shape the traveling children more profoundly than anything else: nature and coming into contact with communities of strangers. The three kids are exceptionally attuned to all living creatures: birds, hares, foxes, wolves, and fish. A long, dark snake that lives with them on the boat protects their precious cargo from rats and later scares away thugs. They recognize in the wilderness a wisdom at work that maintains life everywhere. This recognition helps them overcome their own fears of not fitting into adult society.

The children must also act as the harbingers of tragic news, for example, to an old woman living on a tiny island: she had already lost both of her sons in the war, and now her only daughter, Amina, has been killed in action, too. Time and time again, as if in disbelief, the camera zooms in on the little photo on the wall showing Amina and her disturbingly serious gaze.

During the flood, the boat becomes a veritable Noah's Ark on which people find safety for themselves and their belongings. One woman collects jewelry, to be sold to help the war effort, and even the poorest make a sacrifice. The only exceptions are three thugs who attempt to rob the travelers, but thanks to Dariga, who threatens them with a rifle, they flee in horror.

Karsakbaev's film is somber and yet, in a modest and almost shy manner, life-affirming. Its overarching dichotomy is, on the one hand, the human world of war, which itself remains invisible but which affects all people, and, on the other, the natural world of life, to which the children are drawn. This is not so much a juxtaposition but an analogy: the war is a catastrophe with universal impact, just like the flood that threatens young and old. In both cases, victory is won because of the strong communal spirit uniting all decent people. On another level, the film captures the flow of time as such, symbolized by the broad, mostly peaceful, then suddenly wild and deadly river. *The Salty River of Childhood* shows war not as a political but as an existential phenomenon. Experiencing the effects of war in the hinterlands, the three children undergo a rite of passage.

Arguably the most provocative deviation from Soviet cinematic norms, marking the film's subversive dimension, takes place in the beginning. At an old harbor, where the boat is loaded with staples to be distributed during the trip, people work selflessly. They even continue to do so as the loudspeakers announce the latest news about the front. This stands in contrast to classical Soviet war films, in which this moment is usually among the most pathos-filled: once the anchor's solemn declamation begins, the crowd freezes and listens. In Karsakbaev's film, meanwhile, everybody continues to work, as if the people were oblivious to the radio announcements. Unlike many previous Soviet films, *The Salty River of Childhood* never romanticizes war. Its effects are so horrendous that any political slogan would sound utterly false.

With a running time of just sixty-four minutes, Karsakbaev's picture seems like a sketch or a study, the equivalent of a short story. In its existential seriousness and assignation of precocious roles to children, it resembles the worldview of Andrei Platonov. The result is an unspectacular masterpiece.

This was Karsakbaev's last film. He died, at the age of fifty-six, a few months after its premiere. While *The Salty River of Childhood* is one his finest pictures, the director's untimely passing is yet another case of a disrupted artistic evolution in Kazakh cinema. Had Karsakbaev lived for just another decade, what might he have accomplished? If *The Salty River of Childhood* is any indication, he could have created a deep, genuinely realistic depiction of the catastrophic collectivization of the early 1930s, or captured, perhaps through the eyes of children, the extreme ups and downs of perestroika, which affected Kazakhstan's national evolution in a very peculiar way. Karsakbaev's untimely death contributed to the discontinuity in the evolution of Kazakhstani cinema, just like that of Shaken Aimanov and Mazhit Begalin before him.

It took many years before Kazakhstani viewers and film historians recognized the true caliber of Karsakbaev's legacy. It is remarkable how he managed not only to use the early years of relative creative freedom in the 1960s to the maximum, but also to withstand the pressures of opportunism and dogmatism that crushed so many others during the 1970s. Even during that decade of status quo cinema, he made films that have stood the test of time with their quiet truthfulness and unpretentious aesthetic mastery.

*The Long Milky Way* (Dolgii mlechnyi put', 1983), produced at the same time as *The Salty River of Childhood*, has many similarities with Karsakbaev's film in its sad and melancholic recreation of the effects of the World War on rank-and-file Kazakhs.[12] *The Long Milky Way* also takes place in the hinterlands, describing the hardships that the civilian population had to endure. Adapted from a story by the popular Berdybek Sokpakbaev by screenwriters Bolat Gabitov-Dzhansugurov[13] and Sergei Bodrov, the film portrays a little-known episode of the war when a group of shepherds herded livestock from Kazakhstan to Ukraine, which had just been liberated from Nazi troops. Transporting 500 cows to the Donbass on foot was easier ordered than done: in 1944, the Soviet infrastructure was in tatters, and all resources were directed toward the fighting troops.

Lieutenant Khangeldin (Dzhambul Khudaibergenov), who is entrusted with this unusual task, would rather be sent to the front. A former translator, he is soft-hearted and must learn to act like a commander. Among the rank-and-file Kazakh civilians, he struggles to gain authority. This is especially trying when it turns out that he is an inexperienced horseman, cannot swim, and does not even have a wife. But during weeks of walking hundreds of miles under severe conditions, Khangeldin and his men grow together and begin to understand the higher meaning of their assignment. Thus, disobeying strict orders, they bring milk to starving children at a train station. Marauding gangs of criminals and deserters present a constant danger. Nor does the herd attract only thieves, as kolkhoz directors need cattle for their farms, too. It turns out that cows are a precious commodity, and Khangeldin cannot afford to lose even one of them. Reconciling empathy and common sense with heartless military rules is his main challenge. Thus, the entire caravan is arrested when Khangeldin risks taking a shortcut, leading the herd across a defunct airport.

Four decades after the World War, *The Long Milky Way* offered viewers a valuable lesson in altruism from a time when many people were engaged in sheer struggle for survival. Director Amangeldy Tazhbaev consistently went against the trivialized war image that had become so common, especially in Soviet television miniseries. Without the slightest sensationalism, he not only shows the daily suffering experienced by millions of regular Soviet people, including double amputees, but also focuses on human details of everyday life: from sleeping toddlers protected by their mothers to the baking of bread in the middle of the steppe and the methods of treating cows so that the herd is kept together and healthy.

At the film's conceptual center is the necessity to maintain social and moral order. War and its consequences are understood as the most extreme form of disorder, whose dangerous ramifications quickly spread everywhere in the hinterlands. Although these territories were not directly affected by warfare, soldiers and officers must do their utmost to resist the process of elementary norms falling apart. To be sure, most people continue to act as decent human beings. The adults even tell their children not to play war games. Mutual help, not Communist Party leadership, is shown to be the main factor that keeps society together and morally sound. The meaning of the film's title goes beyond a simple pun about herding cows to a faraway land. One night, the guards of the herd look at the stars in deep thought, as though the night sky reminded them of the inherent order ruling the universe.

Another distinct message is the cooperation between nations against naysayers who question the mission as such ("Aren't you sorry to give away such great cows to the miners?" asks one negatively disposed Kazakh). *The Long Milky Way* indicates the existence of a special relationship between Kazakhstan and Ukraine; not coincidentally, the film was recognized for this aspect at the All-Soviet film festival in Kiev in 1984.

## SUBVERSION OF THE STATUS QUO II

One of the critically underrated films of the early 1980s that deserves a closer look is *Atone for Your Guilt* (Iskupi vinu, 1983). Adapted from a story by Tolen Abdikov and directed by Serik Zharmukhamedov,[14] the film features an intriguing plot.

Sultan, an only son, has died in a car accident. At the funeral, many good words are spoken about the young man, until the Imam asks the ceremonial question, "Does the deceased owe any debt to anyone?" While this question is part of the religious ritual, the essential truth to which it points becomes the subject of the ensuing story. Whenever old Kozhabek (Anuarbek Moldabekov) rides his horse on the shore of the river, he remembers his late Sultan. The memories are accompanied by a melancholic song about the relationship between fathers and sons. One day, a driver arrives from Almaty and reports that Sultan may be the father of a little boy in the city. Or is this mere gossip? To find out the truth and offer help to his unknown grandchild, Kozhabek takes the bus to Almaty. He first looks for Sultan's friend, Nurlan (Doskhan Zholzhaksynov), who lives with his girlfriend in an apartment spacious enough to host the visitor from the countryside. In a café, Kozhabek meets a woman who was apparently intimately involved with Sultan but denies having had his child. Another woman was Sultan's love interest when both were students, but he abandoned her when she got pregnant; now, she lives with her little boy, whom Sultan did not even know. At one point, Nurlan plays a tape of Sultan singing a romantic song about another woman he loved, Saya. Although Saya's mother is angry and outspoken when she meets Kozhabek, the beautiful, tender, and very young Saya does admit that she and Sultan had been about to get married. In heavy rain, the old man returns to his *aul* and asks Allah's forgiveness for his son's sins and for his own.

*Atone for Your Guilt* is remarkable first and foremost for the religious framing of its narrative, to which the title explicitly alludes. Indeed, the film opens and ends with a prayer, which, needless to say, is highly unusual for Soviet cinema. As a deeply moralistic narrative, *Atone for Your Guilt* reflects a profound unease about socio-cultural trends in contemporary (and at that point still solidly Soviet) Kazakhstan. The more the father learns about his son, the more he realizes how little he knew him. Old Kozhabek is guided by rural tradition (in one episode, he is shown working in the field with a scythe) and is completely unaware of the profound changes in moral standards that had taken place in Kazakh society, with women expecting something different than what tradition had previously granted them. *Atone for Your Guilt* also reflects the catastrophic miscommunication between countryside and city, including their radically different moral standards. Although the café where Nurlan takes the old man features Kazakh folklore music, it is perceived with a superficial, consumerist attitude, as mere exotic entertainment.

The filmmaker's position vis-à-vis the diagnosed moral-cultural transformation of his nation can be defined as enlightened skepticism, pointing toward existential contradictions within modern urban trends. As Kozhabek observes, on the one hand, Nurlan's girlfriend is demonstratively independent and visibly annoyed when her partner puts the tradition of hosting a senior guest above their plan to go out that night. On the other hand, she is irritated that Nurlan has still not proposed to her. Conspicuously, the one character who undergoes a genuine transformation from interacting with the old father is Nurlan himself: pondering his late friend Sultan's brief life, he begins to realize the consequences of instability and undecidedness in personal relationships, and finally decides to get married.

Nurlan changing his mind represents the film's constructive, albeit simple alternative to the diagnosed moral crisis; it is the only openly didactic element. Remarkably, such a conclusion is the opposite of earlier Soviet social didacticism. The original communist attitude, established in the 1920s and only slightly adjusted during subsequent decades, introduced precisely the carefree ways in which young people got married and divorced, had abortions, and gave up children for adoption, practices that defined typical aspects of the Soviet way of life. *Atone for Your Guilt* advocates a viewpoint that is unabashedly traditionalist, in effect signaling a return to *pre-Soviet* moral notions. The film never preaches those values; it allows viewers to draw their own conclusions. Yet it does display a quiet, tragic tonality. Conspicuously, no fully formulated alternative moral concept is offered (except for Nurlan's change of mind). *Atone for Your Guilt* explores the legacy of a life tragically interrupted and arrives at a negative conclusion, signified by the guilt of the title, ending with the stated need for atonement. The dombra tunes, which add a peculiar pensiveness to several episodes, seem to underline the national specificity of this moral view.

To arrive at a fair and differentiated assessment of Kazakhfilm, it is important to emphasize the *simultaneity* of films produced by the studio in the early 1980s that feature an entire spectrum of worldview components. The state expressed its preferences but could not direct the artistic processes completely—nor influence audience reactions. Thus, on the one hand, *Sweet Juice Inside the Herb*, a film that poeticized the Soviet societal status quo, attracted a mere 1.2 million viewers in its first 15 months of release but won prizes at prestigious festivals and enjoyed official endorsement of its idyllic image of Soviet-Kazakh reality. *Atone for Your Guilt*, which was conceived outside the parameters of the ideological status quo, was hardly noticed by critics. Yet it was the latter, outwardly unassuming picture that accurately foreshadowed the impending deep transformations in Kazakh society. One proposed indulging in self-deception, while the other signaled the coming abandonment of Soviet norms.

The Soviet model of civilization that had brought social and technical modernization to Kazakhstan, appeared increasingly unsustainable, in part because it was incompatible with traditional moral values. The fact that these values and their underlying religious foundation had survived at all, despite the complete removal of Islamic institutions from public life, demonstrated that the core of Kazakh culture had not been fundamentally replaced during the Soviet decades. Paradoxically, both the benevolently opportunistic *Sweet Juice Inside the Herb* and the subversive *Atone for Your Guilt* prove that the quest for a stable traditional value system had remained intact even in an urban environment.

## SUBVERSION OF THE STATUS QUO III

A direct assault on the "stagnation" status quo, both on the moral and on the social level, was Sergei Shutov's *The Human Factor* (Chelovecheskii factor, 1984). Shutov's interest in sharply contoured social conflicts was already obvious in his earlier work *A Decisive Fight*, although the frame of a didactic sports drama limited that film's polemical energy. In *The Human Factor*, Shutov took no prisoners. Among Kazakhstani feature films, it was arguably the most fearless exposure of widespread corruption.

The film's main character is a young accountant, Dariia (Gulnara Dusmatova), who gives her life to defend the law against brutal criminal structures permeating the Soviet economy like a cancerous growth. The factory in which she works produces clothes. But under the surface of a regular socialist enterprise, expensive jeans are made and then illegally sold, a highly profitable shadow business whose main players inhabit the gray zone between legality and the criminal world. To hide the large-scale theft, the factory's books are systematically cooked, something that Dariia discovers almost immediately. The godfathers of this mafia have friends in high places and international connections as well; they live in lavish villas and resort to murder when they see their shady business threatened. Dariia is a modern woman, educated, elegant, and incorruptible. Still, she is not immune to the advances of a young show-off, Alik, who tries to impress her with his newest acquisition, a Ford Capri (a truly exotic sight on the streets of Soviet Almaty!). But when it comes to matters of law and workplace ethics, Dariia knows no doubts and can be neither bought off nor intimidated.

*The Human Factor* begins by laying out the crime that has been committed. Black-and-white photographs show the fatal injuries sustained by Dariia with graphic accuracy. Step by step, the investigator (Doskhan Zholzhaksynov) analyzes the victim's milieu and the conflicts caused by her forthrightness. Weak and morally ambivalent characters such as Alik soon admit their guilt, whereas the hardened head of the gang, Aldiiar (Nurzhuman Ikhtymbaev), who is officially the director of the warehouse, does not give up without a fight.

Overall, the plot follows one of the patterns of French and Italian "message" thrillers, which were en vogue in the 1970s and in which primary importance was given to social analysis rather than suspense per se. The ending is didactic in a Soviet way: decent workers and law-abiding administrators from the textile factory confront the criminals, and the militia arrests them. But this conclusion cannot make up for the preceding revelations about the state of law in Soviet society. The events of the film are depicted not as an isolated instance, but as a systemic ill, even though the underlying economic conditions that make corruption and crime possible in the first place are never verbalized. A logical question would be: why is the legal economy unable to produce enough quality jeans, which would obviate the need for illegal production and black markets? But such questions are avoided because they would lead to the very heart of Soviet economic absurdities. The film operates on a moral level and avoids systemic analysis. The murder of a naïve young woman comes as a shock, pointing to the existential seriousness of the economic dilemma, but it also turns the economic issue into a judicial problem. However, the cynicism of those administrators who are involved in the grand scheme and personally benefit from it is terrifying. While *The Human Factor* is a film of limited artistic ambition, its call for civic activism is remarkable, making it an authentic predecessor of perestroika cinema. With 4.9 million viewers, it was Kazakhfilm's most successful release in 1985.

Bolat Shmanov (Bolat Sharip) likewise used the genre of crime drama to analyze social ills. Working from a screenplay by the popular crime fiction authors Arkadii and Georgii Vainer, Shmanov delivered a sharp social study that belongs to the best examples of Soviet genre cinema. *The Victims Have No Complaints* (Poterpevshie pretenzii ne imeiut, 1986) features an intriguing plot resembling Western investigative thrillers. The case of a young man who was killed during a nighttime brawl in Alma-Ata seems to be simple; one of the suspects has confessed to the crime. However, the investigator, Ilias Sadykov (Doskhan Zholzhaksynov), stumbles upon contradictions in the testimonies of various witnesses and decides over the objections of his supervisor to reopen the case. With utmost thoroughness, he reconstructs the context and prehistory of a crime in which the victim was beaten and then hit by a car. Step by step, Sadykov discovers a wide-ranging conspiracy of smugglers who illegally sell large amounts of meat to restaurant administrators. The deadly outcome (punishing one of those who no longer wanted to play along) is more accidental than intentional; the real perpetrator turns out to be the brother of the man who confessed to the crime and, although innocent, is serving time in jail.

While the work of the police is shown in realistic detail, the investigation itself merely defines the film's surface. The real revelation is the existence of a shadow economy that has been functioning for many years and has brought its participants obscene wealth. This social aspect, which increasingly becomes the film's focus, points to the same phenomenon as *The Human Factor*. In both cases, innocent young people are drawn into shady businesses and lose their lives. Moreover, in both films, cowardly friends and relatives act as bystanders whose silence enables the perpetrators. Finally, in *The Human Factor* as well as in *The Victims Have No Complaints*, the police (*militsiia*) acts as a potent corrective to socioeconomic ills. Zholzhaksynov's character appears like a modern-day *batyr*: calm, strong-willed, fearless, perceptive, and tenacious. He also boasts a highly developed analytical mind that allows him to question seemingly flawless explanations and to see through the characters' deceptive mimicry.

By Western standards, Shmanov's film contains insufficient action as it consists mostly of conversations, interrogations, and debates among the investigators. To maintain some degree of suspense using such an approach requires quality acting, and indeed, the performances are solid throughout, keeping the viewer guessing as to what might actually have happened.[15] *The Victims Have No Complaints* continues the development of a distinct genre cinema that began in the 1970s, satisfying the massive need for quality entertainment with elements of social criticism; the latter attribute distinguishes it from formulaic status quo cinema.

An important issue in evaluating Shmanov's film from a post-Soviet viewpoint is its "Kazakhness." Neither relations within the criminal structures, nor the attitudes of the policemen have any national specifics. *The Victims Have No Complaints* could equally well take place in any other Soviet republic, since meat was in short supply everywhere and schemes to distribute such "deficit" goods illegally were common in the Russian Federation just as much as in Central Asia or Belarus. Shmanov's social thriller exemplifies an approach to reality in which national specifics are absent and the origins of the crime plot lie in the economic conditions that were common to all Soviet republics. This denationalized concept of crime fiction puts Shmanov's film in a similar category to the popular thrillers produced at the three Baltic studios, which regularly attracted between 15 and 40 million viewers. However, there is one minor caveat. On both sides of the law, Kazakhs and Russians form functioning communities in which ethnicity is not an issue. And yet, the fact that Ilias Salykov resists the urging of his *Russian* supervisor (Anatolii Romashin) to close the investigation makes viewers more likely to identify with the *Kazakh* investigator.

It is doubtful that a single investigator was really able to stand up against a powerful mafia whose success is enabled by systemic flaws in the communist economy. But Shmanov's direction deliberately emphasizes the moral aspects of the story, leaving no doubt about the distinction between right and wrong. It is interesting to note that a similar ethical firmness reappeared in Akan Sataev's innovative thrillers of the 2000s (e.g., *The Liquidator*, 2011) and in one of the blockbusters of 2017, *Arman: When the Angels Are Asleep*. These post-Soviet films, too, showcase the material and social advantages of a lawless life but ultimately lead their main characters to severe punishment or an understanding that such lawlessness can never be the basis for a meaningful individual life. Hedonism and moral relativism are depicted as unacceptable in Soviet-Kazakh films *and* in independence-era thrillers. Thus, there is a conceptual continuity between Soviet-style and post-Soviet thrillers that would reward further critical and scholarly attention.

An interesting example of social criticism that was released around the beginning of perestroika and featured high subversive potential without using the framework of a thriller is Sergei Bodrov's *The Nonprofessionals* (Neprofessionaly, 1985), whose dark images of contemporary Soviet Kazakhstan breathe hopelessness and fatigue.

The story of a group of amateur musicians touring the countryside and finally bringing joy to the inhabitants of a retirement home to some degree compensates for the depressing effect of its general visual bleakness. The young members of the "vocal-instrumental ensemble Rainbow" dream of becoming professional musicians and are willing to make sacrifices to reach that goal. Their daily life is miserable. Not only do the hosting factories and kolkhozes refuse to pay them an honorarium, but they do not even give the young artists anything to eat, making it painfully obvious that nobody really needs their performances. When the musicians accept an invitation from a retirement home, the film's second plotline comes to life, describing the preparations of the retirees, who plan to reward their young guests with their own songs, which they have already begun to rehearse.

The musicians idolize the Beatles, constantly listening to their music and identifying themselves with Paul McCartney. But soon, reality intrudes on their dream world. In the retirement home, a strange woman is caring for a cow, protecting it from the cook who would like to slaughter it. Unknowingly, the musicians are the ones who make the unthinkable happen: they force the cow into their bus and kill it with a sledgehammer. They then threaten the old woman, who witnessed their attempt to hide the remains, and only let her go when she swears to keep quiet. The youngsters' sudden violent behavior is never fully explained; it seems unmotivated, brutal, and out of character. Perhaps Bodrov meant to point to the young generation's moral degradation, which lay hidden behind a façade of romantic artistry; however, these aspects of the characters are neither foreshadowed nor developed any further.

References to Kazakhstan in Bodrov's film are few and far between, as *The Nonprofessionals* deals with Soviet reality in general rather than with life in this country per se.[16] The band members are completely indifferent to the republic in which they live and travel; they might equally well be touring Russia, Ukraine, or Armenia. The main dichotomy within their perception is not Kazakh versus Russian, but Soviet versus Western. This is a major subversive element and valid for Kazakhstani urban youth, who chose their cultural orientation from Western sources. Their encounter with a community of elderly people whose cultural experiences were utterly Soviet reveals the profound transformation that urban society has undergone.

*The Nonprofessionals* manages to capture the sadness and the chaos of the last phase of Soviet history. It does so through its imagery rather than its timidly optimistic conclusion that brings two generations together. While the plot is structured in a way that suggests sources of hope and potential reform, the sheer weight of the depressing atmosphere is such that these arguments, voiced by aging people looking back at their lives, and by their garrulous doctor, ring hollow and pretentious. Whether the compromise position is the result of genuine respect for these characters or simple opportunism that allowed the film to be released is now a moot question. The diagnosis regarding Soviet life in the mid-1980s could not have been more devastating. *The Nonprofessionals* shows a society at its wit's end. The cultural disconnect between the young and the old[17] is one of the symptoms that may be repaired for a moment, but the fundamental lack of societal cohesiveness can no longer be overcome by good will or mere communication. Metaphorically, just as the band falls apart, so does Soviet society.

Subversion of the status quo cinema that had been established in the 1970s came through feature films with a strong national dimension, including the aesthetically superior *The Salty River of Childhood*, the sincere and touching *Long Milky Way*, and the revisionist and openly spiritual *Atone for Your Guilt*. But the crisis in the relationship between Kazakhstani cinema and native viewers was already beyond repair; serious and honest films were too few to bring about a fundamental improvement in audience attitudes. The same must be said about crime dramas with a strong dosage of social criticism, such as *The Human Factor* or *The Victims Have No Complaints*, which also subverted the stability of the status quo, albeit in an all-Soviet legal framework. Such films were important because they pointed to social ills, but they could not overcome the skepticism of native viewers toward Kazakhstani cinema as such. To overcome the external side of the crisis (that is, the lack of viewers), cultural officials tried another strategy: directly adapting Western genres, with the goal of exploiting their attractiveness to Soviet viewers. The results of this import-replacement were disastrous.

## IMITATIONS OF WESTERN GENRE FILMS

Kazakhfilm's most scandalous film of the decade was *The Secrets of Madam Wong* (Sekrety Madam Vong, 1986). More than any other movie, it was cited as proof of the deep crisis in which the studio was caught. Its production model resembled that of *Shield of the City* six years earlier. The screenplay by a Moscow author (Stanislav Govorukhin) was offered to Kazakhfilm studio, then slightly adjusted to local needs by making one of the lead characters Kazakh; to add insult to injury, it was helmed by a director from another studio (Stepan Puchinian). Regarding its plot, *The Secrets of Madam Wong* was conceived in the same way as Mosfilm studio's *Pirates of the 20th Century* (Piraty dvadtsatogo veka, 1980), the greatest box office success of Soviet cinema, which had also been written by Govorukhin and which attracted tens of millions of mostly young viewers with its unusual focus on action and martial arts. To be sure, the ideological framework of both films is ultra-patriotic, praising the loyalty of the crews of Soviet ships that are under attack from Asian pirates and drug lords, respectively. Thus, from a political viewpoint, communist watchdogs had no reason to object. But the film's aesthetics were so obviously borrowed from Bruce Lee potboilers that Soviet film critics reacted with unanimous outrage.

The uncompromising official rejection of movies such as *Pirates of the 20th Century* and *The Secrets of Madam Wong* revealed a widening split between normative official film criticism and mass popularity. It indicated that the ideological standards that had held the socialist realist paradigm together for six decades, were increasingly difficult to sustain. Soviet cinema was no longer able to cope with the challenge of making a film that met Soviet aesthetic requirements while simultaneously appealing to millions of viewers. On a larger scale, that split signaled the approaching end of communist society and its major cultural pillar, cinema.

*The Secrets of Madam Wong* virtually rehashed all plot elements of *Pirates of the 20th Century*, but in even less believable ways. The title character, the infamous "queen of pirates," Madam Wong (Irina Miroshnichenko), uses the services of a large Soviet vessel, the "Ivan Bunin," to travel incognito to Hong Kong. She and her gang have kidnapped the grandson of an honest investigator, Mr. Thompson (Armen Dzhigarkhanian), who has been pursuing them for thirty years. When Bulat, a Soviet navy officer (Serik Konakbaev), witnesses a murder carried out on the ship by members of Madam Wong's gang, he is himself attacked and thrown into the ocean. However, Bulat survives and finds refuge on a yacht that Mr. Thompson stole to go looking for the treasures that Madame Wong has hidden on a mysterious island. Together, the Soviet officer and the Hong Kong detective manage to find Madam Wong's gold bars and overwhelm the criminals who temporarily captured them.

What about this movie was Kazakh? Nothing, except the character of Bulat, whose ethnic identity is announced early on. He is an all-around admirable hero and martial arts fighter who at one point sings an Okudzhava song while accompanying himself on the guitar; waits for news from home, where his wife is about to give birth; and performs breathtaking stunts both aboveground and underwater. He also displays exemplary reliability and generosity, for example, when Mr. Thompson abandons him twice (!) with the excuse that he is after the gold, which he needs as a ransom to save his grandson. However, at no point is the Soviet-Kazakh superman's ethnicity developed any further. Instead, on the treasure island, when Thompson asks Bulat, "Are you from Russia?" the officer replies, "Yes." In an improbable coincidence, it turns out that Thompson's grandfather was a White Army officer who had immigrated to Shanghai. Thus, the two men can communicate in Russian, saving them from displaying their knowledge of English and the viewer from the inconvenience of having to read subtitles. Conspicuously, Bulat does not disclose anything about his hometown, family, or culture: he views himself as Soviet, and throughout the movie, all ethnic differences are neglected.

The screenplay was a primitive imitation of Western action movies with a clear commercial agenda. Of course, within the confines of the genre, there is nothing objectionable about that. However, the rendition is so hapless that the plot, with its countless absurdities, becomes an insult to the viewer's intelligence.[18] Predictably, the movie starts with establishing shots of an ultramodern city skyline (in this case Hong Kong), just like in any Western thriller.

But the characters are so wooden and humorless as to make Charles Bronson or Chuck Norris seem like paragons of psychological nuance in comparison. Most action scenes are directed in a cumbersome manner, with little sense of rhythm or physical logic. The reason for this lackluster treatment of subject matter designed to attract mass audiences was a long-held disdain for entertainment genres, an attitude that permeated the entire Soviet film industry for decades. The performers do not even try to create believable characters and appear completely detached from the action. This makes audience identification impossible. After all, what kind of viewer would be thrilled to see two "goodies" treating each other with silent indifference before defeating moronic "baddies" and their bored bosses? And still, with 27 million tickets sold, *The Secrets of Madam Wong* was one of the most successful Soviet films of the year, outperforming all other Kazakhfilm productions by far.

In the critical discourses, however, it became an embarrassment for the studio. Not only was this thematically non-Kazakh movie repeatedly cited as evidence of how low the artistic level of Kazakhstani cinema had sunk, but it also showed that the republic's film studio had lost any serious connection with quality-conscious native audiences and seemed to be unable to come up with nationally meaningful themes. Just as Kazakhstan's territory had been used for decades for all-Soviet economic campaigns and dangerous military tests, its national film studio was abused as a playground for dubious commercial exercises.

*The Secrets of Madam Wong* also shows that viewer-oriented Soviet cinema had arrived at a dead end. The exploitation of foreign plot formulas was rendered in a manner disrespectful of the audience, while the constant display of Western cars, clothes, and alcohol to viewers who had no access to such goods was shameless. Most importantly, the employment of reputable performers such as Dzhigarkhanian and Miroshnichenko[19] as stars, including in the Western-style credits, could never cover up the fact that these actors and the director did not take the *genre* seriously. The professional imperfection of this and other Soviet quasi-commercial imitations was also a predictor of the severe problems into which the first attempts at for-profit filmmaking would run after the breakdown of the communist system. While Soviet critics' snobbishness regarding entertainment genres per se was misguided, their rejection of primitive imitations of Western commercial cinema was justified.

## STANDALONE FILMS ABOUT THE WILDERNESS

Far from the grand political battles about the right direction for Kazakhstani cinema, a barely noticed phenomenon was developing: feature films about children and wildlife. This theme had already been addressed by Kazakh children's films in the 1970s, but *The Leopard Returns* (Gepard vozvrashchaetsia, 1985) and *The Snow Tiger* (Tigr snegov, 1987) approached it from a completely different angle than, say, *Shok and Sher*. The films were conceived and directed by two filmmakers who had won prominence in the documentary genre, Viacheslav Belialov and Larissa Mukhamedgalieva.[20] Belialov studied cinematography at VGIK, worked for Kazakhstani television, and specialized early on in shorts documenting Kazakhstani wildlife. He and his wife maintained a close relationship with leading biologists throughout their career; their supreme goal was to help preserve the life of species that were in danger of extinction. In 1982, Belialov and Mukamedgalieva were honored for their nonfictional oeuvre, which comprised several dozen documentaries, with a State Prize of the Kazakhstani SSR. This opened the door to feature filmmaking.

Larissa Mukhamedgalieva, who had studied screenwriting in Moscow, developed two stories in which a city boy (portrayed by the couple's son, Ali, appearing under his own name) encounters wildlife in the mountains and becomes a defender of animals. In *The Leopard Returns*, Ali spends his summer vacation at his grandparents' farm in the mountains. His grandfather Temirkhan (Akyl Kulanbaev) is a passionate wildlife guard who teaches him climbing. Together, they catch a falcon and train it for hunting. The wiry, energetic old man is also on the lookout for poachers. When two such perpetrators injure a leopard, Ali and his grandfather bring the animal to their farm and give it a chance to heal. In the finale, the leopard, who seems to have grown attached to these humans, returns for one final visit, as if to bid farewell before returning to life in freedom.

*The Leopard Returns* contains many excellent documentary sequences of wildlife, including goats and birds of prey. Among the most intriguing scenes are those in which the recovering leopard interacts with the dogs, the horse, and the chicken on the farm. Ali shows no fear of the dangerous beast. Trusting in the goodness of nature, he feeds and pets it, just as he did with the tamed falcon. And the animals return his goodwill. This is the most important educational aspect of Belialov/Mukhamedgalieva's narrative films: just like in their documentaries, they present wildlife as having a moral core that, if respected by humans, will allow for the two to have a harmonious relationship. Grandfather Temirkhan also teaches Ali that animals will always strive for freedom and that nobody should interfere with this drive. But he conveys to the boy a more general philosophy of nature as well. "Each landscape has its own soul," he says. "It must be loved to be understood." Interestingly, while there can be no doubt about his disgust with the poachers, the old man risks his life to rescue theirs when they face doom for their recklessness. He is not out to kill the criminals but to teach them a lesson by example, for even a poacher's life must be respected.

The great Kyrgyz director Tolomush Okeev served as the artistic supervisor of Belialov/Mukhamedgalieva's feature film debut, clearly a sign of respect for their talent and cause. According to one source, Belialov was accused of misrepresenting the Kazakh people as primitive in his 1970s documentaries, after which he purportedly stopped filming humans and focused exclusively on animals.[21] However, *The Leopard Returns* proves that he and Mukhamedgalieva were far from escapism and remained interested in the wider social implications of environmental protection. Their second feature, *The Snow Tiger* (Tigr snegov, 1987), clearly demonstrates that interest, adding a psychological dimension to the ecological issues. The film tells the story of a trapper named Akhan (Abdrashid Abdrakhmanov) and his son (Ali Belialov). The father, a muscular and grumpy man who had to give up his boxing career, now makes a living by catching rare animals for zoos. His current assignment, to find a leopard for a Dutch zoo, promises a sizable bonus. But Ali is outraged by his father's businesslike attitude toward nature and angrily destroys his traps.

The film opens with spectacular extreme long shots of an avalanche going down into a valley, cutting to the close-up of a leopard listening to the approaching noise. But unlike *The Leopard Returns*, in *The Snow Tiger* human conflicts are central. The father-son tensions echo the relationship between the uncle and little Kurmash in Okeev's *The Fierce One* (1973), only under Soviet conditions. Akhan dislikes his son's affection and compassion for humans and animals. His own image of manliness is based on rejection, stoicism, and discretion. Ali, however, would prefer to live with his father than in the city dorm and would rather forsake a career than be without his family. The teenager is depicted as a carrier of healthy natural instincts, including a yearning for togetherness and mutual care, a disposition that makes it easy for him to appreciate nature. His father clashes with a surgeon from the city (Tungyshbai Zhamankulov) who is spending his vacation with his wife in a nearby tent: the urbanites make a case for young Ali's humane behavior, but their words fall on deaf ears. The father has a view of nature that is completely different from Ali's. For example, for the trapper it is absurd to heal an injured goat. Only when Ali himself gets caught in one of his father's traps does Akhan swear to give up his business. He then sets the snow tiger free.

The radical character of young Ali is an indicator of the strong ecological sensitivities that had evolved in the USSR, reflecting a global trend as well. While earlier Kazakh films such as *The Choice* (1975) emphasized the illegality of poaching, *The Snow Tiger* expresses the reprehensiveness of any violent interference with nature, legal or not. The fact that the son wins the duel with his traditionalist father suggests that a profound transformation in values has taken place in Soviet society.

The 1987 feature film has a curious prehistory. In 1970, Belialov was the cinematographer of a 10-minute documentary also titled *The Snow Tiger* (Tigr snegov). Comparing the two films of the same name makes it possible to elucidate the evolution that took place in Belialov/Mukhamedgalieva's (and, arguably, society's) views on nature over the course of nearly two decades. In the documentary, the narrator-in-the-first-person also catches animals. As if to defend himself, he states, "The word 'hunter' is too severe. I do not shoot; I am a catcher and hope to bring joy to people who cannot observe animals in freedom." In the nonfictional short, the leopard is filmed as a being of dignity, not an object of pursuit, which defines Belialov/Mukhamedgalieva's nonintrusive view of ideal human relations with wildlife. However, while catching animals for display in zoos was still an acceptable practice in 1970, by 1987 it no longer was, as the feature film clearly states.

In the 1990s, Viacheslav Belialov's extraordinary experience in nature cinematography found international recognition when he was hired by the BBC and German television as a member of camera teams filming the Kazakhstani wilderness. However, only in the new millennium was his and his wife's *artistic* work recognized as groundbreaking. In the 1980s, their two feature films were so marginal that even the voluminous reference work *Film Encyclopedia of Kazakhstan* (Kinoentsiklopediia Kazakhstana, 2010) pays barely any attention to them.[22]

## A STUDIO IN CRISIS

The 1970s and early 1980s, a time of superficial stability in Soviet society and culture, held insufficient potential for the artistic growth of Kazakhstani cinema. To many observers it was clear that Kazakhstani cinema was in a state of crisis, never mind the exceptions discussed earlier, and no matter how this crisis was officially denied. Maybe it seemed to some opportunistic administrators and film professionals that the time-honored approaches of bland entertainment, self-imposed conflict avoidance (the opposite of the ironic subversion of clichéd conflicts in *Protect Your Star*), and moderate thematic experimentation could be continued ad infinitum. But behind the stable façade, an increasing sense of frustration was discernible.

However, the existential crisis that Kazakh cinema had entered in the early 1980s was hardly debated in the open, nor was the impact of the few realistic and subversive films made during that period assessed. The major political impulse for dismantling the façade of faux civility and harmony came from the Soviet center: reform-oriented factions within the Communist Party decided to take the initiative and encourage an economic, social, and cultural self-renewal of unprecedented radicalness. Soviet cinema was to play a central role in these reforms, which would have major effects on the national periphery, although, alas, not as intended.

When Kazakhstan's film workers were summoned to their fifth Congress on March 20–21, 1986, *Atone for Your Guilt* was not even mentioned in the reports they heard. Instead, *Sweet Juice Inside the Herb* was cited as a success and praised as the winner of the jury prize at the Moscow Film Festival. The meeting's political framework was defined by the XXVII Congress of the Communist Party, at which the new strategy of acceleration (*uskorenie*) had been announced. Among other aspects, the responsibility of cinema and television for a "healthy moral climate" in Soviet society was emphasized. Earlier, the Communist Party of Kazakhstan had bemoaned that the country's cinema had not overcome its "backwardness," without defining exactly what that meant.

At the time of the congress, the union had 230 members, 35 of whom belonged to the governing board. The re-election of Kaltai Mukhamedzhanov,[23] who had been elected at the plenary session of the Union of Kazakhstani Film Workers in April 1984 to replace Gabitov-Dzhansugurov, was obviously intended as a signal of stability and continuity. However, such opportunistic decisions were based on wishful thinking and could only temporarily mask the widespread dissatisfaction looming underneath. To be sure, the official criticism voiced at the congress rang hollow and was largely pro forma. Moscow authorities had expressed the need for socioeconomic and political reforms, and the Communist Parties of the republics dutifully echoed those statements. Hardly anyone in the Soviet-Kazakhstani establishment could grasp that the current crisis was an existential one for the system in its entirety and foreshadowed the beginning of the end of communist society and the USSR as its carrier. The official reform proposals addressed symptoms on the surface, including issues in the various spheres of culture. Cinema, long defined as the most important of the arts because of its propagandistic potential and mass appeal, could no longer satisfy the needs of Soviet audiences. These audiences were fractured in a manner that anticipated the coming turbulences. Russian urban audiences preferred French, American, and Italian imports, whereas Central Asian viewers generally adored Indian films. Soviet youths were increasingly oriented toward a Western consumerist, libertarian lifestyle, while the revolutionary heroes and warriors of yesteryear were good for sultry jokes at best. The few box office hits produced by Soviet studios imitated Western thrillers, slapstick comedies, and martial arts movies. Soviet society was in a state of fundamental unease with itself and its own culture, and the state of its cinema was symptomatic of that unease. The crisis in Kazakhstani cinema was among the worst in the Soviet republics.

In his report, Kaltai Mukhamedzhanov mentioned Kazakhfilm studio's increased genre diversity as one of its accomplishments, citing psychological drama, films on moral-ethical themes, biographical and historical-revolutionary films, and pictures about the heroism of the Great Patriotic War, among others.[24] But he could not name one example of a Kazakh film that had truly connected with audiences. Indeed, with unprecedented candor, the first secretary of the Kazakhstani Union of Film Workers voiced concerns about the lack of viewers in the republic's movie theaters: according to Mukhamedzhanov, on average, half of the seats remained empty.

The direct influence of the nascent perestroika discourse can be detected in Mukhamedzhanov's remark about the lack of films taking a stance against corruption, bureaucracy, and consumerism. However, this criticism, just like that of the lack of moviegoers, was mainly an expression of the speaker's opportunism, echoing Moscow guidelines rather than genuine concern. Just a few years earlier, even mentioning such issues as important topics would have been unthinkable. Now, Mukhamedzhanov, as one of the chief administrators of Kazakhstani cinema and an indirect censorial authority, blamed insufficient "thematic planning" for the absence of films reflecting the country's socioeconomic transformations, rather than pointing a finger at the intrusiveness and paranoia of the cultural control mechanisms that he himself represented and that had discouraged any attempts to engage audiences in an honest dialogue about the country's ills. Mukhamedzhanov also criticized Kazakh filmmakers' indulgence in children's films which, according to him, were a way to gloss over problematic reality, as well as the excessive number of detective movies.

Because of the political limitations of his position, the first secretary only pointed out symptoms; any systematic, let alone systemic, analysis of the reasons for the malaise in Kazakhstani cinema was, predictably, missing. From the report it is not clear how much the leading cultural hacks really knew, or wanted to know, about the situation in Kazakhstan's cinema. For example, Mukhamedzhanov discussed the fact that Kazakhfilm studio produced three to four made-for-TV films per year but cited only *Shok and Sher* (a children's film made fifteen years earlier!) after which, according to the speaker, things had gone downhill. This assessment clearly ignores some truly worthwhile productions that addressed precisely the topics that were declared to be missing from the national cinema: corruption and moral disorientation. After all, was the high number of thrillers not itself an indicator of moral degradation? But neither *The Human Factor* nor *The Victims Have No Complaints* was cited in this framework. The signs of an emerging constructive approach to Soviet reality in artistically viable films of the early 1980s were completely ignored. Nothing in the report indicates a deeper understanding of the structural factors that were stifling not only Kazakhstani cinema but Soviet cinema as a whole. Nothing indicated that the cultural establishment realized what fundamental changes the film industry was about to undergo, changes that would start in the same year, 1986. The congress demonstrated one last time how destructive the election of obedient bureaucrats to governing positions had been for Kazakhstan's culture, particularly cinema.

However, amid underappreciated realistic films and disingenuous administrative criticism, one decision was taken the long-term ramifications of which would only become visible after the demise of perestroika and Soviet Kazakhstan. It began with the idea of creating a special Kazakhstani master class at the Soviet State Film School in Moscow.

## THE CONCEPTION AND EDUCATION OF THE "KAZAKH NEW WAVE"

The 1950s had shown that one promising method of energizing Kazakhstan's film production was the systematic grooming of young filmmakers. In the 1980s, this solution once again became an officially approved strategy. The Central Committee of the Communist Youth (Komsomol) of Kazakhstan, together with the Union of Kazakhstani Film Workers, announced "professional-artistic education" as one of its priorities and organized a biannual film competition, "Bastau."[25] According to several sources, the initiative came from Olzhas Suleimenov, the Kazakh poet and one-time head of the Kazakh State Film Committee, Goskino, who also conducted master classes in Almaty's House of Cinema.[26] Shortly thereafter, in 1984, Russian director Sergei Solov'ev arrived in Alma-Ata on assignment from the central Soviet State Cinema Administration. Solov'ev discussed with Suleimenov and Murat Auezov, then chief redactor of the screenplay committee of Kazakhfilm studio, the possibility of organizing a special Kazakh masterclass under his own leadership. Calls for application were published in Kazakh newspapers, and in July 1984, Solov'ev conducted a four-step selection process, at the end of which a group of seven young men was admitted to the Soviet State Film School (VGIK).[27]

Auezov, a highly respected public intellectual, had diagnosed the situation of Kazakhstan's cinema as being so dismal that any solution would by sheer necessity appear brilliant, a statement that has often been quoted in later years. The idea of a Kazakhstani master class to be conducted in the Moscow film school seemed to fit the bill. Nor did the selected seven students have to start from scratch. Indeed, they boasted an impressive array of educational and professional backgrounds: Ardak Amirkulov had studied philology, Darezhan Omirbaev mathematics, Bakhyt Kilibaev Arabic, and Abai Karpykov history; Rashid Nugmanov was a young architect already in his third year at VGIK; Amir Karakulov was a poet, and Aleksandr Baranov a playwright.²⁸ Another student of Solov'ev at VGIK was Talgat Temenov, who had enrolled two years prior.²⁹

What effect did VGIK have on them? Was it really the film school itself that gave the group the right impetus for the "creation of a Kazakh national cinema," as some critics have retroactively claimed? The artistic education practiced in the Soviet center primarily enabled students to overcome their specific brand of provinciality, be it regional or social, and broaden their horizon with respect to world culture. Both the curriculum and the vast extracurricular opportunities systematically exposed students to the masterpieces of world cinema past and present and put them in the midst of the most highly qualified community of film experts that the Soviet Union could offer. In addition, the atmosphere in the Soviet metropolis of the mid-1980s was not only politically refreshing but also aesthetically dynamic and open-minded. The budding filmmakers from Kazakhstan could not have arrived at a better time.

Unlike other director-pedagogues teaching at VGIK, Solov'ev encouraged his students to make developing their own aesthetic approach the supreme goal, above a sense of answerability to society, let alone Marxist-Leninist dogma. Solov'ev's priorities were those of an individualist, not a collectivist. As a result, when the VGIK graduates returned to Almaty, their first short films demonstrated a remarkable diversity of styles. It was obvious that they had thrown off the baggage of traditional, de-individualized Soviet normative approaches (including that of Kazakhstan's own "gray films") and taken inspiration from international auteur cinema, with influences ranging from Truffaut and Bresson to Kurosawa and Bergman.³⁰ Their films were not made with native mass audiences or societal demands and obligations in mind; instead, they were conceived as part of an ongoing dialogic process within a framework of global, innovative artistic cinema. Thus, sending this group of students to VGIK may not have yielded exactly the results that officials had hoped for: Aprymov, Amirkulov, Karpykov, and the others did not create their films primarily as artists representing their nation, but as budding *auteurs*, that is, individualists with a sharpened, liberated vision of life and of cinema's function therein.³¹

Solov'ev also had the right instinct when he decided to complete his Kazakh masterclass with an actual film project at Kazakhfilm studio. That picture, *The Alien White and Checkered One* (Chuzhaia belaia i riaboi, 1986), was both aesthetically ambitious and thematically innovative. As a critical revision of the Soviet postwar period, it breathes the pathos of perestroika but avoids simplistic political or moral schemes and conclusions. The film demonstrates Solov'ev's continued fascination with the joys and traumas of childhood and youth, which coincided with the preoccupations of his Kazakhstani students.

## MASTER CLASS CINEMA

The main character of *The Alien White and Checkered One* is Vanya Naidenov, a Russian boy who was evacuated to Kazakhstan during World War II. When his father, a painter, returns from the war as an invalid, having lost an arm, relations between him and his son change and grow emotionally tense. Among other problems, Vanya gets involved in his father's affair with an evacuated actress, a frail beauty who struggles to protect her classical nineteenth-century ideals against a vulgar and brutalized environment. The boy is obsessed with pigeons, like all men young and old in his milieu. The birds are guarded, groomed, traded, and sometimes sold, representing a rare commodity in a society of hungry have-nots. To catch, steal, or regain a precious pigeon, the men are willing to risk a lot, even their lives, as Vanya learns the hard way. Dealing with pigeons marks his and his gang's peculiar path to adulthood by affirming one's self-worth and strength and, if need be, fighting for it. Of course, pigeons flying high in the sky make for a wonderful poetic motif, signaling the desire for freedom and self-realization, a motif that this visually inventive film uses to maximum effect.

Solov'ev's Kazakh students worked on this coproduction[32] as interns. What artistic lessons could they take from it? Firstly, *The Alien White and Checkered One* strives hard to convey a sense of verisimilitude: exteriors and interiors are seamlessly connected, and the atmosphere of postwar Soviet Kazakhstan is captured with a consistently high degree of authenticity. Indeed, the depiction of postwar manners and speech patterns is one of the film's major strengths; the fact that political aspects of that period are underemphasized may have to do with Solov'ev's general lack of interest in such themes and his preoccupation with youthful romantic yearning rather than analytical thoroughness. Thus, his film never comes across as accusatory toward the system, but empathetic toward the characters who have adjusted to it. Secondly, the plot is less important than the atmosphere. This impressionistic approach, which includes select dramatic episodes but ignores the rules of stringent storytelling, points to a mode of narration more typical of arthouse than mainstream. Thirdly, and in deliberate contrast to its lowlife milieu, the film overflows with high culture. Solov'ev opens on a high note with an explicit reference to classical literature (a Dostoevskii quote about the significance of childhood for any human life) and maintains this loftiness by using non-diegetic classical music, from Mozart to Bartok. The musical motifs form a productive contrast against the imagery of postwar poverty, a contrast that, together with frequent transitions from black-and-white to color and vice versa, imbues the whole picture with an air of aesthetic gravitas.

Fourth, the director employs literary elements ranging from a first-person narrator (the adult Vanya Naidenov recollecting his childhood) to numbered chapters (1. "My Father," 2. "The White," etc.) and inscriptions that establish a motif structure of their own ("This was the 484th day of peace and every single day was a day of bliss"). The continuous tension between text and image is a productive element as well, referring to early silent cinema, when intertitles were not merely a necessity to make up for the lack of sound but also commented on the moving images, producing expectations and evaluative reactions. The textual-literary dimension gives the film structure and rhythm, preventing it from falling apart. Finally, in *The Alien White and Checkered One*, Solov'ev largely avoids the narcissistic nostalgia that hampers so many films about the postwar period, with their focus on clothes, cars, and scratchy gramophone period music. Instead, he openly shows the widespread crude materialism that forced educated people to sell their few commodities to ensure survival. Interestingly, it is Vanya who explains to the much older actress Ksenia that life is governed by the rules of commerce, while she chooses to go to church instead of the black market. Solov'ev evokes the image of a harsh, merciless society whose members are engaged in a struggle for survival. His film engages in a kind of realism that is not normative socialist, but neorealist and humanist. At the time of its release, this approach to Soviet history gave the picture an element of mild subversiveness.

Such were the lessons that Solov'ev's Kazakh assistants could take away from the production of *The Alien White and Checkered One*. The Russian filmmaker succeeded in demonstrating *ad oculo* how a Soviet artist in the mid-1980s could walk the fine line between self-conscious (and self-confident) auteur aesthetics and general accessibility, at least for the implied educated viewer. This approach to filmmaking obviously made a lasting impression on Solov'ev's students. While their subsequent aesthetic searches went in vastly different directions, the films of Abai Karpykov, Ardak Amirkulov, and Serik Aprymov display a non-commercial individualism without being elitist or narcissistically avant-gardist. Solov'ev the artist-pedagogue taught the students of his Kazakh masterclass ways in which quality filmmaking could be combined with a sufficient dose of individualism without sacrificing general appeal. It was a lesson that his students would not forget.

To be sure, *The Alien White and Checkered One* does have its share of shortcomings, especially a lack of psychological subtlety in the performances. The film emphasizes that all its characters have been traumatized by the war and that each character is trying to recover in their own way. However, the resulting behavioral patterns are not always convincing. Some situations in which characters find themselves are extreme, but instead of establishing believable intonations, they fall into hysteria. This may have been a price the director was willing to pay for the pathos he chose as an antidote to the cynicism underlying his characters' motivations. The narrative pace, which over the course of the film regularly increases and decreases without any logical reason, at times loses energy altogether. Most significantly, though, the Kazakh national motifs featured prominently in the film's opening later fade away completely, with Vanya's friend Murad being one of the few reminders of the film's location. Indeed, its neglect of Kazakhstan is a regrettable squandering of potential in an otherwise outstanding picture.

But whatever its shortcomings, the production itself became a genuine university for its artistic crew and had a lasting impact on Kazakh cinema, also influencing filmmakers who did not belong to the New Wave generation. To wit, both Satybaldy Narymbetov's *Memories of a Young Accordion Player* (1994) and Rustem Abdrashev's *The Island of Resurrection* (2004) reveal a stylistic and conceptual indebtedness to *The Alien White and Checkered One*.

It is no exaggeration to say that with the various innovative impulses encompassed by the term "Kazakh New Wave," Kazakhstani cinema was reborn again: a fourth time, if we apply Shaken Aimanov's formula. According to Ludmila Pruner, the first Western scholar to attempt to critically analyze the phenomenon, the term "New Wave" was initially applied to Kazakh cinema at the 1989 Moscow Film Festival.[33] The term itself, coined by critics who sought to capture the phenomenon in its entirety, was a useful choice on several levels. It pointed to the aesthetic freshness of these directors' pictures, which began to appear in the late 1980s; it suggested that, beyond individual styles, the group shared certain values; and, by association with the French Nouvelle vague, it emphasized the international influences that could be detected in the fabric of these films. Whether the directors subsumed under the term "Kazakh New Wave" really "converged on a common film language," as Gönül Dönmez-Colin claimed in 1997, is doubtful.[34] However, the association with the Nouvelle vague of the late 1950s and early 1960s expressed critical respect for the newcomers from Kazakhstan, including a new respect of the former center for the previously controlled periphery. Connecting these directors with a prestigious phenomenon in world cinema paved the way for Kazakh cinema to be accepted on the international festival circuit. With equally surprising ease, the members of the Kazakh New Wave were declared living classics of cinema by some critics. However, not all their careers maintained their initial promise.

## PERESTROIKA HOPES AND STUDIO TURMOIL

There can be no doubt that the successful education of a new generation of Kazakh filmmakers had a profound impact on national cinema. However, the often-heard claim that nothing worthwhile came from Kazakhstan's cinema in the 1980s prior to the New Wave is effective but unfair. Equally missing the mark is the reduction of the New Wave itself to the members of Solov'ev's Kazakh masterclass: directors such as Edyge Bolysbaev and Ermek Shinarbaev made superb innovative pictures in the second half of the 1980s as soon as they were given the green light by the studio administration. Indeed, years before the VGIK graduates returned to Almaty, several Kazakh films had revealed a heightened sense of social and moral perceptiveness and had offered their viewers an honest image of Kazakh-Soviet reality. These films were not sufficient in number to form a trend, but they did present an alternative to the status quo movies released in the late 1970s and early 1980s that were artistically unremarkable and politically opportunistic. Along with previously discussed subversive films such as *The Salty River of Childhood* and *Atone for Your Guilt*, these exceptions must be included in a balanced assessment of Kazakhstani cinema of the last Soviet decade. The political context of perestroika and glasnost must be taken into account as well.

The perestroika pathos as expressed in cinema was, first and foremost, a pathos of truth as opposed to the dishonest opportunism and cynicism justifiably attributed to the preceding period, which was associated with the name of Leonid Brezhnev and the accusatory term "stagnation." The critical probes of the Soviet present and past that contributed to the perestroika discourses rapidly became more principled and historically deep. Over the previous seven decades, the Soviet establishment had accumulated so many taboos that the slightest loosening of cultural controls was fraught with unleashing a flood of revelations. It is important to keep in mind, though, that in the beginning of perestroika, the positions taken by critical filmmakers remained principally pro-communist and only select aspects of society were questioned, without doubting, or delegitimizing, the system as such. In their relatively conciliatory attitude and constructive social criticism, many perestroika films resembled the films of the Thaw years.

Perestroika has generally been defined as a reform attempt from above, but the impulses that came from Mikhail Gorbachev and his supporters beginning in 1985 almost immediately triggered strong grassroots reactions. An increasing number of Soviet citizens dared to speak out about inefficiency and incompetence at work, the frustrations of daily life, and the difficulties in obtaining truthful notions of the past. Kazakhstani cinema reflected such attitudes. However, the center-periphery mechanisms established in the 1920s were still in place: political signals originating from the Soviet-Russian capital were understood in the national republics first and foremost as calls *to reform film production* as such, which was in bad need of streamlining. Fewer and fewer competent administrators were put in charge of vital production segments. Consequently, Kazakhfilm studio was often unable to complete the number of projects dictated by the annual plan. The connections between the creative and the business levels of film production had become increasingly dysfunctional, such that sometimes no film was shot on the studio premises for several months. Various supervisory committees of the Communist Party and the Kazakhstani government repeatedly issued critical memos, with negligible effect. In early 1987, Kazakhfilm studio owed over 2 million rubles to the State Bank.[35]

One of the direct effects of perestroika on Kazakhstani cinema was the attempt to apply democratic methods to the management of film production. The strictly hierarchical administrative approach of the 1930s–1970s was subverted by grassroots initiatives. Sometimes, democratic trends were mixed with symptoms of a struggle between clans. As a result, Kazakhfilm studio found itself in a state of turmoil. The divisions between different generations and groups with distinct views on political and ethnic issues were deep, and the infighting loud and unpleasant. At a Party meeting, the studio staff decided to vote on its administration. Several high-ranking bureaucrats were relieved of their duties, while the iconoclast Murat Auezov was elected the studio's chief redactor. This seemed to open the doors to new initiatives, both economic and artistic.

A plenary session of the Union of Kazakhstani Film Workers in 1987 revealed continuing widespread frustration with the state of Kazakhstani cinema. The four films released by the studio in 1985 had attracted a mere 8.3 million viewers in the entire USSR—an embarrassment. Of course, the annual production plan only measured the quantitative output of films as units. As long as Kazakhfilm studio completed four feature films and four made-for-TV films, the plan goals were met and the expected bonuses were paid out. The number of viewers watching these films was considered much less relevant. Only when the plan's production goals were not met did the studio's more than 1,000 employees receive no bonus pay. Thus, the last months of every year resembled a feverish race to complete the minimum number of required films, no matter their quality. This explains why so many Kazakhstani feature films are relatively short, running between 70 and 80 minutes. Neither their artistic level nor their popularity at the box office had a comparable impact on the payout; at most, the artistic level determined the quality category assigned to every film, which in turn influenced the seize of individual bonuses. But the notion of "artistic level" was a relative one: state prestige films were given the First Category, with the highest bonuses, as a matter of course. The need to balance artistic reputation, plan fulfillment, and box office returns was one of the reasons why the studio accepted two films on opposite ends of the quality spectrum in its plan for 1986: Sergei Solov'ev's artistically ambitious *The Alien White and Checkered One* and the openly commercial *Secrets of Madam Wong*. One was a prestige project that could even be sent to the Venic film festival, the other a crowd pleaser. Both were controversial, albeit for different reasons.

At the 1987 plenary session of the Union of Kazakhstani Film Workers, emotions ran high. Members attacked each other with personal insinuations, accusing their opponents of acting like "*mankurts*" (people deprived of their memory) and "thieves." According to Murat Auezov, at the time the studio officially employed a whopping thirty-four feature film directors. Because of the limited production volume, only very few of them could be assigned any projects at all, causing envy and enmity.[36]

When the Moscow film critic Mikhail Sul'kin, a longtime observer of the developments in Kazakhstani cinema, visited Alma-Ata in the fall of 1987, he was horrified. Sul'kin's subsequent article in *Iskusstvo kino* demonstrates that he fully identified with the traditional role of the emissary from the Soviet center who was sent to the national periphery to inspect the situation on-site and report about it. However, this time the assessment criteria for the studio had changed from communist doctrinaire to perestroika liberalization. With the glasnost candor that had become the new mark of Soviet media, Sul'kin's article revealed numerous facts and scandals, shedding new light on the precarious situation at Kazakhfilm. One prominent example of the ongoing calamities at the studio was that of the screenwriter Zauresh Ergalieva, whose *Sweet Juice Inside the Herb* had been celebrated as an artistic success. Her new screenplay, *A Rainy Summer in a Spa City*, described the romance between a young Kazakh woman and a Russian man from Odessa, focusing on both the psychological and the social repercussions the couple was experiencing. According to Sul'kin, the screenplay had been accepted and production had already begun when the First Secretary of the Union of Kazakh Film Workers, Kaltai Mukhamedzhanov, sent a letter to the Central Committee of the Communist Party and to Kazakhstan's Sate Cinema Committee; the latter ordered that production be halted. The visiting Moscow critic regarded such administrative interference as unacceptable and in violation of the new spirit of perestroika.

Ergalieva's case was particularly curious because it demonstrated how the traditional roles of center and periphery had been suddenly reversed by reform efforts from above: The Soviet center, represented by Elem Klimov, who had just been elected First Secretary of the Soviet Film Workers Union, came to the defense of Ergalieva's project, whereas the periphery, representing the old power structures of the Kazakhstani SSR, resisted the decrees from Moscow. In the end, the local powers prevailed: Ergalieva's screenplay was stopped and taken out of the production plan. In a last-minute effort to fulfill the annual plan goals, Asanali Ashimov agreed to direct a new feature film, completing *Wormwood* (Polyn') in a record-setting thirteen days of shooting ... This tour de force enabled the studio to pay out the annual bonuses, while the film's artistic quality was not even discussed.

Interestingly, Sul'kin interpreted the disagreement between Kazakhstani administrative structures and Moscow reformers as part of the general resistance of this republic's political establishment to perestroika. For the Moscow journalist, this was one symptom among many others, including the demonstrations against the replacement of Dinmukhamed Kunaev with a Russian Communist Party functionary in December 1986, demonstrations that were violently suppressed and that Sul'kin denounced as nationalist.

Despite its many revelations, Sul'kin's bleak report about the situation in Kazakh cinema was not accurate in several respects. A number of films released both before and after Kunaev's ouster were fully in tune with the anti-corruption campaign that accompanied perestroika, and in some cases even preceded what was produced at Mosfilm or Lenfilm studios. However, in an effort to prove his charge that the ruling "conservatives" in Alma-Ata were resisting the reforms coming from Moscow, Sul'kin failed to mention any of those films.

## REBUILDING THE SOVIET-KAZAKH HOME: *SHANYRAK*

Again, it cannot be emphasized enough that Kazakhstani quality cinema did not begin with the Kazakh New Wave, as charged by some cinephiles. The remarkable pictures of Shaken Aimanov, Mazhit Begalin, Abdulla Karsakbaev, and others, made within the Soviet framework of the 1960s and 1970s, refute that claim. Likewise, the early films of Ermek Shinarbaev, who did not belong to the New Wave generation, demonstrated a unique artistic quality. Regarding social truthfulness, several Kazakh films challenged the opportunistic status quo prior to the New Wave. Moreover, Kazakhstani cinema responded to the political perestroika signals with feature films that revised socialist-realist clichés. The hopes for renewed efforts that would reform the socialist present and take inspiration from the past may seem naïve when assessed from a post-Soviet viewpoint. But the sincerity of these films can hardly be doubted.

The motif of injustice experienced by a nonconformist who sticks to his principles is one of the fundamental tropes of social-critical cinema that came to the fore during perestroika in all Soviet republics, including Kazakhstan. The drama *Shanyrak* (1987) by Edige Bolysbaev approaches Kazakh-Soviet reality through the prism of a nonconformist with unprecedented candor. The film's main character, Erlan, is a young man who has just returned from army service to his village in Southern Kazakhstan. He loves Maira, a woman from a more affluent family than his own. Erlan's intentions are serious, as his observance of the traditional customs when asking for Maira's hand proves. However, Maira's parents demand 9,000 rubles for their daughter—an enormous dowry that is far beyond Erlan's means. He decides to use another route allowed by Kazakh tradition, namely, "to steal" (i.e., kidnap) the bride; if she agrees and the operation is successful, the relatives have no choice but to accept the marriage. However, police arrest Erlan, and Maira, pressured by her parents, signs a document stating that the bride kidnapping was carried out against her will. Following a humiliating trial, Erlan is sentenced, according to §106 of Kazakhstani law, to three years of hard labor. What began as an amusing, quasi-folkloric comedy suddenly turns into an existential drama.

For Erlan, the injustices he experiences become part of his own rite of passage. From the beginning, he is portrayed as a courageous and incorruptible man. For example, when he discovers that workers at the lumber factory where he works are stealing wood, he interferes and threatens to report the perpetrators to the police. His respect for customs, however outlandish they may seem, also shows him to be an utterly decent, principled young man. But the late Soviet environment is either corrupt or complacent and unwilling to tolerate his forthrightness.

In *Shanyrak*, the central character's honesty on the job makes him stand out in the daily routine of accepted corruption, but it does not threaten his existence. It is his adherence to traditional rules that spells his downfall. Thus, Bolysbaev challenges the romantic depiction of national traditions that was typical of some films of the 1970s. All Erlan wants is to build a home for himself and his girl. That is the *shanyrak* of the film's title, but he is prevented from achieving his dream by the materialism of his bride's family, who would rather bend the law than allow Maira to be married without a sizable payment.[37] *Shanyrak* continues the line of anti-materialist and anti-consumerist films that began to emerge from Kazakhfilm studio in the early 1980s. Its underlying concept, pointing to the need to renew a tradition that has been corrupted by widespread materialism, is confirmed in the film's conclusion, when Erlan destroys his parents' house with a bulldozer after his mother's death and begins to erect a new home for himself.

The aspect of reconstruction and renewal shown in *Shanyrak* was another central trope of the perestroika spirit in cinema. This constructive approach assumes that it is not communist society itself that should be blamed for corruption and injustice, but despicable attitudes such as greed. Once those habits are overcome, a new and better society can be created *within the existing Soviet paradigm*. Indeed, it was typical of the pathos of such films that, while demonstrating formerly taboo aspects of Soviet reality, analysis of the roots of the problem remained on the surface and the remedy for improvement was seen in the characters' individual moral views, not societal structures.

The candor of *Shanyrak* extended to another aspect: juxtaposing old and new attitudes toward ethnicity. Erlan serves his prison sentence in a Siberian city, where he meets a compassionate Russian woman. Not only do they fall in love, but Irina even follows Erlan to his village, where the two get married. This unexpected turn gives the film an additional edge, calling for a modern, non-traditional attitude toward family and marriage, a variation of the ethnic plotline in Aimanov's *We Live Here* from thirty years earlier. This was particularly relevant in 1987, the year of the film's release: the scandal following the appointment of the Russian Gennadii Kolbin as First Secretary of the Communist Party of Kazakhstan had led to unprecedented social unrest in December 1986 that brought the strong anti-Russian and anti-Kazakh sentiments of opposing strata of the population out into the open. *Shanyrak* makes a case for a tolerant approach toward ethnicity, but without presenting Russians as bringing a solution to native corruption or idealizing them per se. Indeed, in an earlier scene, Erlan is severely beaten by local Russian men who dislike the fact that he is courting a Russian woman.[38] Such honesty in a film addressing issues of ethnic tension would have been unthinkable a few years earlier; the depiction of bias in a film such as Beisembaev's *The Son's Return* is mild compared to that in *Shanyrak*. This openness, too, was a symptom of perestroika and glasnost. Interestingly, the film embraces candor in Russian-Kazakh matters in practice, being bilingual itself: the first half and the finale are in Kazakh without subtitles, whereas the prison episodes are entirely in Russian. Switching from one language to the other is never addressed as a problem, even in the village scenes.

On the conceptual level, in contrast to Bodrov's ethnically indistinct *Nonprofessionals* and Shutov's *Human Factor*, *Shanyrak* is Kazakh through and through, from title to plot. This national dimension includes the film's deeply rooted faith that truth and justice will prevail. Even certain underlying beliefs, such as the karma-induced punishment haunting Maira for her betrayal and rewarding Erlan for his decency, are directed against the disillusionment that became a trademark of later perestroika films. Erlan, rather than giving up or becoming a cynic, accepts his destiny and believes that the forces of good will ultimately help him—as indeed they do. Regarding general social aspects, one can justifiably state that the shocking depiction of Soviet reality in *The Nonprofessionals* and *Shanyrak* to a certain extent prepared the ground for some films of the Kazakh New Wave, for example, Aprymov's *The Last Stop*. However, the element of positive agency that is so typical of constructive perestroika cinema and features prominently in *Shanyrak* was not accepted by the young iconoclast auteurs. It would soon disappear, replaced by total bleakness.

## THE LAST PRO-SOVIET FILMS

The last film directed by the undervalued Sharip Beisembaev was *Nesibeli* (aka *The Story of a Weak Woman*/Istoriia slaboi zhenshchiny, 1986). While it failed to make an impact in its day, *Nesibeli* deserves a serious reappraisal.

This story about the daily life of a middle-aged professional in Almaty provides a knowing and unsentimental account of Kazakhstani urban society in the last phase of its Soviet development. Nesibeli (the name literally means "the lucky one") serves on a jury where she is faced with petty criminals; she visits her husband's grave and meets a pilot-cum-cabdriver who shows a lively interest in her; she interacts with pushy family members; and she tries to resolve as many problems of her colleagues at work where she is a supervisor. The entire film refutes its alternative title: Nesibeli is not weak at all, and her social engagement is based on a genuine sense of responsibility. Beisembaev portrays a modern Kazakh woman who is actively engaged with her environment without verbalizing her situation or discussing it with others. Being there for other people is her natural inclination, conveying an unobtrusive sense of leadership. This sovereignty is depicted as one of the positive achievements of Soviet-Kazakhstani society. It continues the line of outstanding female characters from the 1950s onwards, beginning with Aimanov's *Daughter of the Steppes* and *The Intersection*. The unspectacular nature of this film should not deceive the viewer: *Nesibeli* has depth and substance, just as its title character, and is conceptually connected to such quietly optimistic films of the late 1980s as *Shanyrak*.

In its heyday, perestroika particularly energized those intellectuals who were eager to explore formerly taboo aspects of Soviet history. Kazakhstani cinema contributed to this trend a revised version of the legendary construction of the Turksib railway, this time in fictionalized form. The screenplay for *On the Pass* (Asuda/Na perevale, aka *Turksib*, 1987) was written by Bolat Gabitov-Dzhansugurov, whose father's name and poetry gained new prominence during perestroika and glasnost, processes that initiated the rediscovery of the victims of the Stalinist purges. The film, which takes place in 1928, assumes the audience's knowledge of the industrial project and its significance. The focus is on individuals involved in the construction, including the Kazakh engineer Dzhungarov (Tungyshbai Zhamankulov) and his Russian colleague, Klimov (Evgenii Zharikov). Together with these fictional characters, *On the Pass* features Tungar Ryskulov (Anvar Boranbaev), an influential communist leader whose name was eliminated from official Soviet historiography after his execution in 1938. *On the Pass*, then, is a gesture of rehabilitation. It was also intended as a corrective vis-à-vis the cleansed historical dramas of the early 1970s, with their factual selectiveness and opportunism.

The directors, Serik Zharmukhamedov and Kadyr Dzhetpisbaev, made a strong effort to reconstruct the hardships that had to be overcome to establish the railway line between Siberia and Turkestan, including weak work ethics and widespread alcoholism among the workers and the starvation of the native population following collectivization. Regrettably, the attempt to personify and juxtapose the forces of the Old and the New in the characters of Dzhungarov and his opponent, the *bay* Sarybura (Asanali Ashimov), largely fails. The latter is not provided with sufficient screen time to develop his complex, dignified character. Nor does the love intrigue add to the film's human depth, although the all-star cast is impressive, as is the cinematography of the accomplished Askhat Ashrapov. Most importantly, though, the pathos of communist construction can no longer serve as an authentic source of inspiration: symbolic images such as that of a sculptor who creates a huge bas-relief of Lenin on the rock above the construction site appeared anachronistic in the last years of Soviet Kazakhstan, when the decline of communist spirit was unstoppable. These critical remarks notwithstanding, *On the Pass* must be viewed as the last feature film produced at Kazakhfilm studio that attempted to portray the history of communist construction in Kazakhstan in a *positive* light. Its revisionist honesty about that history is unquestionable, but its message came too late for the disillusioned audiences of the late 1980s.

In constructive perestroika films such as *Shanyrak*, *Nesibeli*, and *On the Pass*, the harsh and honest depiction of Soviet-Kazakhstani reality was intended as an instrument to encourage improvement and pride in communist achievements, not systemic discreditation. A mere few years later, these hopes would themselves be dismantled and discredited.

## NOTES

1. Viacheslav Kuvshinnikov, "Vsmatrivaias' v vos'midesiatye," *Novyi fil'm*, 6/1990, p. 14.
2. Ibid., p. 15.
3. Ibid., p. 21.
4. Ivanova, V., "Kazakhfil'm – pogoda na zavtra," *Sovetskaia kul'tura*, 5 January 1984.
5. Nugerbekov, B., "Prikosnovenie k istokam," *Prostor*, 10/1985, p. 172.
6. Auezov, Murat (b. 1943), Kazakhstani critic, literary scholar, film administrator, and political activist. In 1982-1989, Auezov worked as the chief redactor and artistic director of Kazakhfilm studio.
7. However, three years later, at a plenum 12 June 1984, Gabitov was replaced by Kaltai Mukhamedzhanov.
8. Suleimenov, Olzhas, "Ot mirosozertsaniia – k mirovozzreniiu. Dialog s korrespondentom 'IK' Katesh Alimbaevoi," *Iskusstvo kino*, 3/1982, p. 42.
9. Ibid.
10. For a fair assessment of Beisembaev's career and films see Nogerbek, *Na ekrane 'Kazakhfil'm*," pp. 83–86.
11. Guk In Tsoi was born in North Korea in 1926. In 1951, he was officially delegated to the USSR to study film direction at the Soviet State Film School, VGIK,

which he finished in 1958. Tsoi decided to stay in the USSR, where he was naturalized in 1976. As a second director, he made considerable contributions to several films helmed by actors Nurmukhan Zhanturin and Asanali Ashimov. With the latter, he codirected the four-part miniseries *Legendary Chokan* (1984), for which he received a State Prize of the Kazakh SSR.

12. Another high-profile feature film about World War II was *Snipers* (Snaipery, 1985), directed by the accomplished Kyrgyz filmmaker Bolotbek Shamshiev. However, its portrayal of the legendary Kazakh sniper Aliia Moldagulova impressed neither viewers nor critics, arguably due to its emotionally detached depiction of the war. Cf. Kalgatina, Larisa, "O pol'ze samodistsipliny," *Iskusstvo kino*, 12/1986, pp. 52–54.

13. Gabitov-Dzhansugurov (1937–2004), the son of Ilias Dzhansugurov, was a screenwriter, documentary film director, and film administrator.

14. Zharmukhamedov, Serik (b. 1937), Kazakh director.

15. Liudmila Kairbaeva wrote a thorough and very positive review of Shmanov's film, in which the legitimacy of the "detective" genre in Soviet cinema is explicitly stated. She also praises the performances and the direction. Kairbaeva, L. "Poterpevshie pretenzii ne imeiut," *Novyi fil'm*, 5/1986, pp. 4–5.

16. Murat Auezov insists that *The Nonprofessionals* is a Kazakh film, stating that this is "a typical Alma-Ata story, which could happen only here. Furthermore, one can rightly say that Bodrov was born here as a director (...)." Abikeeva, *Natsiostroitel'stvo v Kazakhstane*, p. 109.

17. This disconnect, marked by musical tastes that were not appreciated by the older generation, was the theme of other perestroika films as well, including Valerii Ogorodnikov's *Intruder* (Vzlomshchik, 1986) and Vasilii Pichul's *Little Vera* (Malen'kaia Vera, 1988).

18. One episode showing a police raid on one of Madame Wong's villas was clearly inspired by Brian de Palma's *Scarface* and even rendered in acceptable quality. However, later scenes, such as one in which a crocodile that is about to attack Bulat is shot by Dzhigarkhanian, cross the line to self-parody.

19. Other first-rate actors in supporting roles are Bolot Beishenaliev and Aleksandr Abdulov.

20. Belialov, Viacheslav (1936–2004), Kazakhstani documentary and feature filmmaker who specialized on subjects of native wildlife. Mukhamedgalieva, Larisa (1938–2006), Kazakhstani screenwriter; lifelong creative partner of Viacheslav Belialov.

21. Cf. the documentary *Viacheslav Belialov* (2003) by Baian Kyzylova-Aristanova from the series *Liniia sud'by* on Khabar TV chanel.

22. The entry on Belialov (pp. 70–71) only mentions *The Leopard Returns*, while the entry on Mukhamedgalieva (p. 151) does not list either feature film. Cf. Smailova, *Kinoentsiklopediia Kazakhstana*, 2010.

23. Mukhamedzhanov, Kaltai (1928–2001), Kazakh playwright and film administrator.

24. Cf. the official report about the congress, "Za fil'my, dostoinye sovremennosti," *Kazakhstanskaia pravda*, 22 March 1986.

25. Cf. Gulnara Abikeeva in an interview with Ol'ga Malakhova, "Novaia volna: dvadtsat' let spustia," *Kazakhstanskaia pravda*, 8 August 2008.

26. Pruner, "The New Wave in Kazakh Cinema," p. 795; Nogerbek, *Na ekrane 'Kazakhfil'm,'* p. 67, 81.

27. For a lively, albeit highly subjective account of these events, see Solov'ev, Sergei, "Natsiia i mir. Aziia," *Druzhba narodov*, 2/2001, pp. 170–82.

28. Pruner, "The New Wave in Kazakh Cinema," p. 795.

29. For another account of the origins of the Kazakh New Wave, see Shimyrbaeva, Galiia, "Tak nachinalas' 'Kazakhskaia novaia volna.'" *Kazakhstanskaia pravda*, August 3, 2012.

30. Bauyrzhan Nogerbek formulated what was arguably the most radical view of the lack of continuity between Soviet-Kazakh cinema and late Soviet/post-Soviet cinema: "There is no visible connection between the oeuvres of the masters of Kazakh cinema of the 1950s and 1960s and the modern "new wave"—neither are there artistic-stylistic nor intellectual-spiritual links, the same way as there is no intersection between the Kazakh SSR and the Republic of Kazakhstan." Nogerbek. *Na ekrane 'Kazakhfil'm,'* p. 45.

31. Gulnara Abikeeva emphasized that the group of young filmmakers represented an independent Kazakhstan at international festivals at a time when the country itself was not yet independent. Cf. Malakhova, "'Novaia volna': dvadtsat' let spustia."

32. *The Alien White and the Checkered One* was produced by Kazakhfilm studio with participation of Mosfilm.

33. Pruner, "The New Wave in Kazakh Cinema," p. 791. She credits Rashid Nugmanov as having been the first to use the term. Nugmanov himself made the same claim. Cf. "Kak Rashid Nugmanov pridumal termin 'kazakhskaia novaia volna', i chto bylo potom." *Iia-Khkha*, January 17, 2009 (http://www.yahha.com/print.php?sid =371), accessed 11/20/2015.

34. Another formulation may be more to the point, namely, that the young directors abandoned "the epic tradition and Orientalism for a more Western outlook (…)." Dönmez-Colin, "Kazakh 'new wave,'" p. 115.

35. S. Taukelov quoted in Mikhail Sul'kin, "O chem nel'zia molchat'," *Iskusstvo kino*, 8/1987, p. 45.

36. Ibid., p. 41.

37. An ironic, albeit somewhat didactic plot turn is Maira's marrying a man in Erlan's absence on the advice of her family; but she is abused and must escape, which means that her parents now have to pay back the dowry to the groom.

38. When Irina is warned by her (otherwise well-meaning) boss about the risks of moving to another culture, she replies: "But Erlan is a real djigit," pointing to the young man's chivalry that she apparently misses in her own environment.

## Chapter 12

# From Perestroika to Katastroika

Perestroika, designed by the Communist Party as a top-down process of accelerated social reform, did not yield the miraculous results that the Soviet establishment and many ordinary citizens had hoped for. But the failure to produce economic bloom did not slow down the increasingly candid self-assessment of Soviet society. For its part, Kazakhstan made some noteworthy cinematic contributions to perestroika and glasnost discourses that brought renewed significance to the documentary genre.

One of the most eye-opening Kazakh documentaries was *I Will Be My Own Defense Attorney* (Budu zashchishchat'sia sam, 1987) by the young director and poet Vladimir Tiul'kin. At a half-hour running time, it tells the story of an extortionist who blackmailed corrupt citizens whose fortunes came from illegal business transactions. The film touched a raw nerve. This curious case of a modern Robin Hood and his gang revealed the degree to which the Soviet economy had lost its legitimacy. The fact that a criminal felt confident enough to defend himself in court because he had robbed those who themselves had stolen from society also pointed to the degeneration of all notions of right and wrong. The documentary made it obvious that Soviet-Kazakh society was rotten to the core: ironically, this film received a diploma as the best documentary at the USSR festival "Multinational Soviet Cinema Honoring the 70th Anniversary of the Great October Revolution" in Volgodonsk in 1987.

At the same festival, another Kazakh documentary, *Kumshagal Story* (Kumshagalskaia istoriia, 1987), was rewarded with a diploma for its civic courage. Directed by Igor' Vovnianko, a cinematographer by training, it is a shocking report about the life of thirty-two families of railway workers in the Dzhambul (Zhambyl) region. For decades, these people were forced to live in old railway cars at Kumshagal station, a fact that the local administration regarded with utter indifference. After the documentary was screened for the leadership of the Kazakhstani Communist Party, immediate measures were taken and the families were provided with apartments. But how many similar cases remained without media attention?

To some, it seemed that the truthfulness of a documentary could remedy an outrageous social malady, proving the effectiveness of glasnost in a socialist society. Could feature films play a similarly constructive role? Looking at the best Kazakhfilm studio productions of the late 1980s, it is obvious that Kazakh-Soviet reality was reflected with increasing honesty in a number of Kazakhstani pictures. Often enough, dark and depressing tones prevailed in them. Compared to the "gray" films of a decade earlier, these pictures indicated a radical reversal in the direction of Kazakhstani cinema, with respect both to social awareness and aesthetic daring.

## CHILDREN IN TWILIGHT, OR THE DISINTEGRATION OF THE SOCIAL FABRIC

Variants of the self-confident national and pro-modern approach toward Soviet-Kazakh society established by Abdulla Karsakbaev in *My Name Is Kozha*[1] were deployed in numerous subsequent films, an indication that viewers could not get enough of optimistic, life-affirming childhood narratives. It can be assumed that the makers of later *Kozha* variations were not only aware of this tradition, which had spontaneously emerged from within Kazakh cinema, but were consciously continuing it, adding their own facets to the genre. It is important to keep this inner dialogue between filmmakers and the relationship between later and earlier films in mind, as it shows the degree of continuity while also revealing new developments in the perception of social values. For the late perestroika period, this dialogue turned into a disturbing trend toward axiologixal discontinuity and increasing social pessimism.

An outstanding picture about children and their place in the stern world of adult rules is Kanymbek Kasymbekov's *Fly, Little Crane* (Leti, zhuravlik, 1985). On the surface, this story of a maladjusted boy who constantly gets in trouble both in his family and in school seems to rehash the basic constellation of *My Name Is Kozha*.[2] But Tuiak's situation is more precarious than that of his legendary predecessor. Proud and stubbornly independent in his attitudes, he is not liked by other children, nor even by his grandmother, the usual ally of young non-conformists in previous films. In Kasymbekov's story, Grandma prefers Tuiak's older brother. The boy's conflicts at school become so serious that he is not admitted to the Pioneers' organization and is publicly stigmatized during the school ceremony. Tuiak's only supporter is his grandfather with whom he rides horses. Both love the beauty and freedom of nature; they care for a young crane whose life they have saved.

Paradoxically, the boy's transformation comes from observing wildlife, not from societal institutions. He learns that when a crane stays alone, it is not able to reach Africa. Once Tuiak internalizes this lesson, he reaches out to his teachers and to his brother in a faraway dorm, asking the latter to rejoin the family. In turn, Tuiak's environment learns how to accept his individualism: the biology teacher no longer chastises the boy but characterizes him as "unusual" (*nestandartnyi*), which in this context is a compliment. The misfit is finally integrated into the social fabric without clipping his wings (to stay within the title metaphor) and gets his red Pioneer tie as a reward. Thus, the film ends on a harmonious note, inspired by the inherent harmony of nature itself. It demonstrates how vital it is to overcome sources of conflict such as fraternal competition or generational incomprehension in order to create spaces of social cohesion. The fact that Tuiak sets the rescued crane free in the end is also symbolic.

*Fly, Little Crane* is Kasymbekov's variation on the misfit/outsider trope of previous Kazakh children's films, to which he adds some new and serious aspects. While the film's ending is constructive, the initial situation had the potential for an antisocial outcome, an outcome that would be demonstrated most drastically (albeit in a post-communist framework) in Emir Baigazin's *Harmony Lessons* (2014), a qualitatively new variation of the same trope.

Arguably the most artistically serious of the childhood films during the late Soviet period is *Together* (Vmeste, 1988), directed by Leila Aranysheva from a screenplay by Aleksandr Baranov and Bakhytzhan Kilibaev. It features a six-year-old boy, Akhan, who lives in the countryside with his grandfather, Zhumangali. At first, their world seems perfectly harmonious and coordinated. The two share various household duties, assigning those types of work that neither of them likes (such as going to the store) with the help of funny games. The dialogues reveal the tragic background of the togetherness in the film's title: Akhan's mother died, and she never revealed the identity of his father. Akhan is an orphan. Thus, the older and frailer grandfather Zhumangali grows, the more fearful he becomes about his grandson's future. He discusses his health worries with other people and finally decides to give Akhan up for adoption.

At this point it becomes clear that the film is neither playful nor uplifting, as previous *Kozha* variations were. Instead, *Together* offers a serious exploration of the existential issues of life and society. Most admirably, it does so without lecturing. Life is depicted as having its own rules, which can easily cause plans to fall apart. For example, when grandfather Zhumangali sells the cow that gave him and Akhan nourishment over many years, the loyal animal stubbornly returns to the barn that it knows rather than staying with the new owner. But despite such humorous interludes, Zhumangali must reveal to Akhan his decision to send him to the city. This cannot be done without touching on the topic of his own death. Following a funeral, Zhumangali tells the naïve boy that the dead are flushed through water channels to the sea after burial. There, they are transformed into children again and return to the world of the living. Such a mythological construct makes perfect sense to little Akhan and subsequently shapes the imagery of the finale.

When their last trip together begins, Zhumangali takes Akhan to a huge Ferris wheel. Although it is closed, the grandfather finds it so important to show Akhan the world from high up that he bribes the operator to turn it on for them. As they ascend to the heights of the Ferris wheel, grandfather and grandson can see the whole world. This experience is meant to give the boy a sense of the freedom and choices that life will offer him. Then, Zhumangali takes his grandson to what appears to be the couple that adopted Akhan. After leaving the boy with them, the grandfather strolls through the streets by himself. Finally, he enters a tunnel, which is depicted as leading to the channels of the underworld that were part of his story about the path of the dead.

*Together* shares several features with *Kozha* and its successors, such as images of bucolic country life; gorgeous landscapes, including the familiar green pastures and snow-covered mountains of earlier children's films; and funny observations of children's behavior. Yet it elevates the habitual grandparent/grandchild constellation to a fundamentally different philosophical dimension, showing that sometimes there is no good solution to an existential dilemma. This change in tonality from exuberance to pensiveness makes it obvious that times have changed: the spirit of optimism that had carried the "brat films" of the 1960s and 1970s has evaporated. In *Together*, the sojourn undertaken by grandfather and grandson does not lead to a new sense of togetherness but to a separation that is final. The root of the story's tragic tonality is the fact that the boy grew up without parents and had to rely solely on his grandfather, pointing to an absence of functioning family networks. A film such as *Together* would have been unimaginable a decade earlier, let alone in the 1960s. It reveals the maturation of a core theme of Kazakhstani cinema to the point where it is better suited to adult audiences who can fully understand its implications.

In the late 1980s, many positive assumptions stemming from traditions that had shaped Soviet-Kazakhstani cinema were replaced by a sense of imminent crisis. *A Wolf Cub Among Humans* (Volchonok sredi liudei, 1988),[3] a heartbreaking story about a boy and his struggle to integrate a wild animal into his environment, can be viewed as a response to the earlier, predominantly harmonious Kazakh films about children and animals. The fact that the film's beginning so strongly resembles the typical idyllic scheme that had obviously satisfied a deep-seated need among Kazakh viewers for years, makes the contrast to that scheme in its finale all the sharper.

In *A Wolf Cub Among Humans*, the urge to explore living nature that is typical of children in Kazakhstani films is embodied in two boys who steal a cub from a wolf's cave. The grandmother of one of the boys is outraged, as she can find nothing cute about these predators, who have been the enemy of nomads since times immemorial. But several close-ups of the cub visually refute her angry words: the animal's eyes are big and innocent. The boy, Samat, is about twelve years old but appears much more thoughtful than his predecessor Kozha a quarter of a century earlier, and certainly more mature than little Kurmash from *The Fierce One*. After some reflection, Samat decides to hide the cub, whom he names "White Fang," inspired by the popular Jack London story.

Samat is an outsider among his fellow teenagers but is perfectly capable of standing his ground: he knows how to fight back when attacked, and even when a bully publicly humiliates him, he maintains his dignity and calls the bully a thief, regardless of the kicks it earns him. Samat has a sense of freedom that resembles that of Sher from Kasymbekov's *Shok and Sher*. Conspicuously, he sets White Fang free after his father puts the animal in a cage.

Director Talgat Temenov,[4] who made his debut with this poetic film, demonstratively discontinues the tradition of previous animal/children movies, in which frictions between adults and juveniles were depicted as temporary and were ultimately resolved harmoniously. In Temenov's picture, the world of adults is depicted as persistently harsh and unforgiving. Animals are no longer tolerated, not because they might inflict harm on children but because parents and other relatives no longer feel any connection with living nature. Temenov's direction is soberly realistic, a clear indication that the film was produced in the heyday of perestroika, when many Soviet filmmakers transitioned from the half-truths of *socialist* realism to the inconvenient truths of *social* realism and ceased to engage in the normative cover-up of unsightly reality.

But there is another conceptual element that distinguishes Temenov's film from its predecessors: the wolf responds positively to the boy's kindness. Samat's expectation regarding his partnership with the animal is not obedience but mutual respect. Unlike Koksen in *The Fierce One*, this wolf seems to appreciate that: when on a windy, dusty day, Samat sets the cub free, it returns and keeps following him. Thus, the incompatibility diagnosed by Temenov is not so much between wilderness and civilization as between nature (including positive human nature, as represented by the boy) and modern society, which is dominated by industrial production and consumption. Interestingly, pedagogy no longer serves as a constructive mediator between children/nature and adult society, as it did in several *Kozha* successor films. One example of this is a teacher in *A Wolf Cub Among Humans* who tells children that she finds camels "ridiculous;" her attitude is complemented by images of these graceful animals being taken to a slaughterhouse. Temenov demonstrates that in a modern urban civilization, most adults no longer understand nor need nature.

Temenov's film, a coproduction between Kazakhfilm and Mosfilm studio, comes close to an all-out denunciation of modernity. The hunter (Nurzhuman Ikhtymbaev) who saves Samat's life when he falls into the river insists that a wolf cub cannot be transformed into a dog. His killing and stuffing of the animal is a barbaric and offensive act, and the boy's outrage, which almost turns him into a murderer, is emotionally understandable.[5]

Compared to previous Kazakh pictures about children, Temenov's film tried out new approaches. However, it did echo certain perestroika-era debates featured in major media outlets, which addressed human alienation from nature. That theme emerged in Soviet literature and cinema in the 1970s, when Kyrgyz author Chingiz Aitmatov pointed to the ecological and ethical consequences of such alienation. Aitmatov's novel *The White Steamship* and its prize-winning 1975 adaptation by Bolotbek Shamshiev became influential contributions to a societal discourse that helped pave the way for the reform attempts of the mid-1980s. The peculiar tragic pathos of *A Wolf Cub Among Humans* has much more in common with Aitmatov's narrative than with *My Name Is Kozha* and its good-natured embrace of Soviet modernization.[6] In purely Kazakh terms, Temenov's film is a curious continuation of the wolf trope: the totemic animal of the Turkic people is depicted not as an eternal enemy but as a mythical kindred being, preempting a line of thought that would be continued in signature films of the 2000s, such as Serik Aprymov's *The Hunter* and Ermek Tursunov's *Kelin* and *Shal*. The needless, brutal destruction of this kindred creature symbolizes human alienation from nature and from other deep layers of identity.

The inconsolable melancholy and twilight atmosphere that were characteristic of Kazakhstani films about children of the mid-to-late 1980s presaged the sad end of optimism about perestroika and, perhaps subconsciously, the inglorious end of the entire Soviet epoch.

## *MUTANTS*

In the late 1980s, Kazakhfilm studio contributed to the wave of critical youth films that quickly became a signature phenomenon of perestroika. A number of these films approached the youth theme as symptomatic of intergenerational alienation: the young can find neither understanding nor support from parents, teachers, or administrators. Their culture is perceived as dangerous and provocative, including their hairstyles, their clothes, and especially their music. Kazakh rock music was similar to its Russian counterpart in the emphasis it put on the lyrics, which often conveyed messages of hopelessness, world-weariness, and aggressive rejection of any officialdom. Gone was the optimistic spirit of the organized youth movement. Its slogans were no longer taken seriously; its cultural representatives were ridiculed and dismissed.

The Kazakhstani drama *Mutants* (Mutanty, aka *Men before 16*/Muzhchiny do 16, 1988) made a serious if somewhat heavy-handed attempt to engage this generation.

*Mutants* is far from idealizing the young generation of the 1980s or endorsing it as a whole: the gangs from various regions of Almaty are depicted as brutal and mean-spirited. The focus of Zauresh Ergalieva and Ardak Amirkulov's screenplay is on the artistically gifted members of that generation who are harassed from all sides, by adults and fellow youths alike. Even these intellectual nonconformists drink, sometimes heavily, and are willing to risk minor criminal offenses such as stealing the front windshield of a car in order to finance their rock band. Mirzhan (Talgat Nauryzbaev) is a fifteen-year-old poet, while Takedo (Akan Suiunshalin) is a rock singer. The two meet when Mirzhan comes to Daken's defense in a street brawl. But they respect genuine creativity and have a deep-seated sense of honor. *Mutants* does not address political aspects of this generation's life at all, nor does the film bring out any national specifics of its protagonists. Instead, the film emphasizes their cultural isolation, for which there seems to be no remedy.

The adolescents featured in *Mutants* are younger than the characters in Rashid Nugmanov's *The Needle*, which was made around the same time. Mirzhan and Takedo do not interact with hard criminals and have not arrived at an alternative worldview; they and their friends are searching for a secure place and for orientation. One of the places that seems to provide answers is a martial arts school that the friends attend. The cultural foundations of Eastern martial arts and the rituals seem to meet the juveniles' need for order and structure. Interestingly, the best of them are rather chaste; even their dialogues are free of vulgarisms. Only when they clash with the youth gangs in the street does a rough side come out, and when it does, it brings about the end of their martial arts education: when their revered teacher learns that his students have used the skills he taught them for violent street fights, he closes the school.

Director Rustem Tazhibaev, son of the once-influential socialist-realist writer Abdilda Tazhibaev, captured the slang and some of the behavioral peculiarities of Kazakh perestroika-era teenagers and did his best to generate atmospheric authenticity. Indeed, when the band members meet in a dirty basement and rehearse their songs, this comes across as very realistic. The heartfelt friendship between Mirzhan and Takedo and their vow to be blood brothers is believable, too, as is Mirzhan's seriousness about protecting his girlfriend, a young ballet student. But the acting is, for the most part, rushed and awkward, and the camera work indistinct. Most importantly, *Mutants* fails to establish stylistic coherence, which was one of the strengths of *The Needle*. Thus, *Mutants* did not become the cinematic manifesto of a generation that it might have.

However, there is one episode that suggests truly innovative potential. As the high school arts teacher chastises the class about their inadequate reaction to a Renoir nude, the students, one by one, jump against the wall and fly out of the classroom into open space, moving around as though weightless. Had this surreal plotline been developed further and fortified with the necessary rock tunes, the film could have become an eye-opener, adding a dose of welcome fantastic humor to an otherwise morose story. Instead, this episode is but a brief interlude, after which the melodrama moves toward its inevitable tragic ending (in which Mirzhan is accidentally shot by a self-made gun). It would have taken visual daring to express the escapism of this generation's creative core, their naïve beauty and self-destructive doom. Perhaps such an excursion into uncharted territory was beyond the range of the filmmakers, who may not even have known these juveniles particularly well (focusing solely on certain attributes of clothing and motorcycles is insufficient to get at the heart of this generation's yearning). The abovementioned episode could have secured this now-forgotten film a degree of originality, distinguishing it from the well-known, and much more pedestrian, *Burglar* (Vzlomshchik, 1987) and similar perestroika films.

*Mutants* was Rustem Tazhibaev's last work in cinema; the film quickly disappeared both from the big screen and from television. Ardak Amirkulov later returned to the youth theme, already under neo-capitalist conditions, in his minimalist *Diary of Rustem with Pictures* (1997).

## DOING JUSTICE TO THE SOVIET PAST

Besides the many Kazakhstani pictures of the 1980s that went virtually unnoticed (sometimes deservedly so, sometimes not) that decade also saw the appearance of films that made a deep impression on Kazakh viewers. The relaxation of censorship in the mid-1980s allowed for the exploration of unique features of Kazakhstan's relationship with the past. One film that became a veritable national hit was Kalykbek Salykov's *The Balcony* (Balkon, 1988), a poetic evocation of the late Stalin period in Soviet Kazakhstan. Conspicuously, its probing of the past is rendered with a post-Soviet sensitivity, even though, at the time of the film's conception and release, the Soviet Union was still intact, at least on the surface.

*The Balcony* revisits the early 1950s, but, unlike the Russian revisionist dramas of the perestroika period, this is not a look back in anger but a more investigative and empathetic revision. The questions it asks point to the impact that this period had on those people who were coming of age at the time. With its sharply contoured yet even-handed approach, *The Balcony* can also be regarded as a forerunner and, preemptively, an alternative to other revisionist films that negatively assessed the postwar epoch.

*The Balcony* avoids one-dimensional answers to the question of moral choices in a harshly totalitarian society. Its depiction of the Soviet-Kazakh experience is less verbal than atmospheric. It is also distinctly Kazakh in its outlook, although this is an *urban* Kazakhness that grew from the experience of evolving Soviet modernity. The probing of layers of historical epochs is visualized in the film's opening, a graphic scene of surgery taking place in a present-day hospital. The surgeon notices a small tattoo on the patient's hand showing the number 20, a sign that the doctor carries as well. He asks himself which of the kids from his court gang may be lying on the operating table in front of him.

The film's central character, Aidar, is a self-confident teenager whose posture signifies aggressiveness and willpower. Aidar, who goes by the nickname "Sultan," is a natural-born leader. His position of superiority is accepted by the other boys in the courtyard due to his physical and mental superiority. Aidar also has the gift of improvising poetry. He creates verses on any occasion; these usually feature a witty conclusion that exposes his targets and turns them into laughing stocks. The young man is unimpressed by the authorities and stands up for what he believes are the basic principles of justice and fairness, whether in the communal apartment that he and his sister inhabit, at school, or in the courtyard.

Aidar's youth has been overshadowed by severe traumas. His father was arrested by the secret police; on the family photo, his face has been cut out. Aidar's mother has died, and his sister, Zhanna, is mentally ill. Zhanna is obsessed with their third sibling, Serik, who perished in the Great Patriotic War. No matter how much Aidar tries to convince Zhanna of the futility of her efforts, she keeps sending inquisitive letters to Marshall Zhukov and other officials, insisting that Serik may be alive. Her obsession becomes dangerous when she begins to write to Marshall Montgomery. A neighbor in uniform, Kirikulov, intercepts that letter, planning to use it against Aidar and Zhanna so that their room in the communal apartment will be transferred to him.

If that informer were the only representative of the Soviet state, *The Balcony* would fall squarely into the category of revisionist perestroika films that radically reassessed the country's Stalinist past, such as Aleksandr Proshkin's *Cold Summer of 53* (Kholodnoe leto 53ego, 1986). But the Kazakh film also features uncle Misha, a silver-haired, rotund local policeman in a white uniform, whose authority is so enormous that he can force two large youth gangs preparing for a street battle to stop and surrender their weapons.

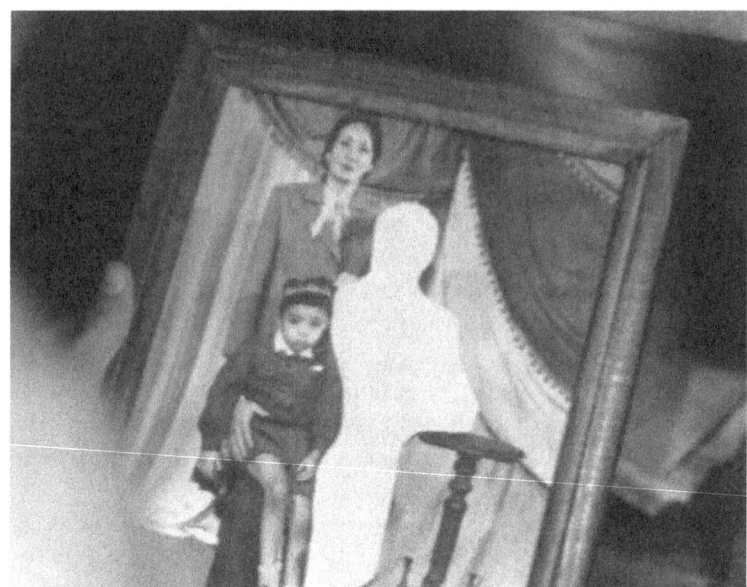

**Figure 12.1 Family Portrait with Cutout Father.** *The Balcony* (1988, Kalykbek Salykov)

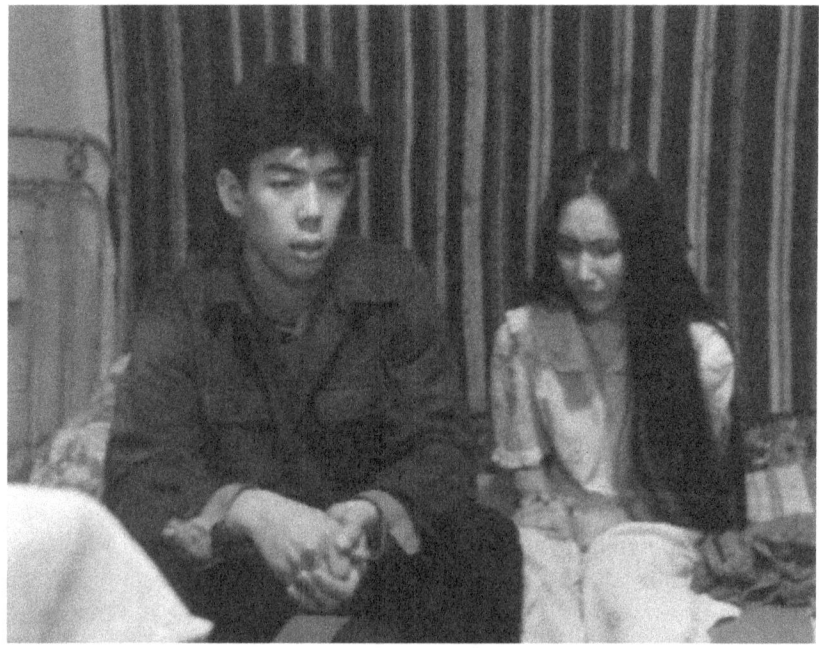

**Figure 12.2 Protective brother and disturbed sister.** *The Balcony* (1988, Kalykbek Salykov)

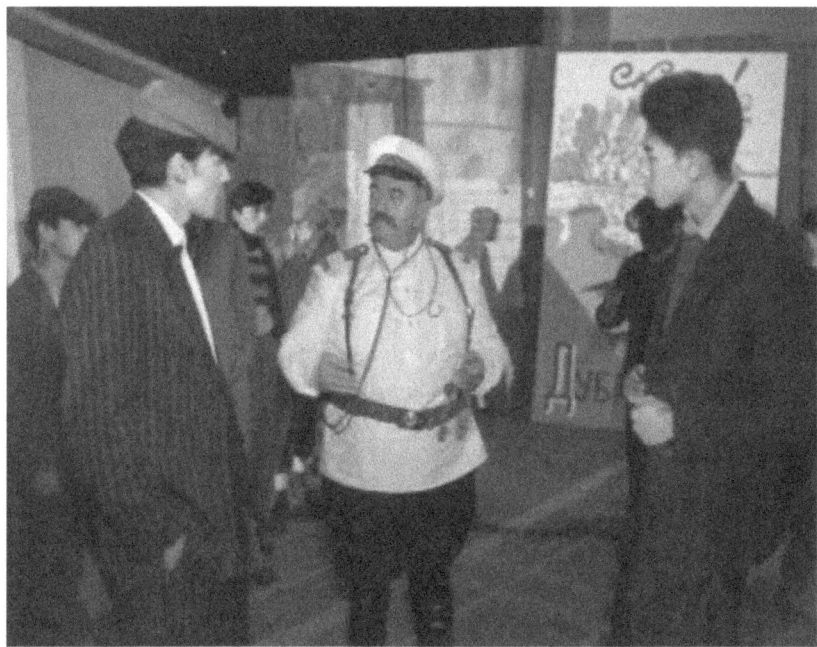

**Figure 12.3** State authority between youth gangs. *The Balcony* (1988, Kalykbek Salykov)

Likewise, the teacher who chastises Aidar for his erotic curiosity: while she enforces the prudish norms of that era, she is not a dogmatic authoritarian, but a beautiful woman who often empathizes with her students. The city, too, is filled not just with images of Lenin and Stalin, but also with statues of Abai and Pushkin.

This deliberately dialectical view of the Soviet period carefully avoids black-and-white characterizations, favoring a more complex, multifaceted, mosaic-type portrayal of Soviet-Kazakh society. The most interesting character in this regard is the father of Aidar's friend Zhenia, uncle Boria (Anatolii Ravikovich). Although disenchanted with the Stalinist present, this intellectual nonetheless maintains his faith in the ideals of communism. With quixotic stubbornness, he keeps sending food packages to the Congo and to India. Uncle Boria also comes to Zhanna's rescue, confronting the obnoxious informer and literally swallowing the girl's letter to Marshall Montgomery. The film implies that it is because of men like uncle Boria that the communist ideals are still respected, despite their utter distortion by the Soviet state. While the threatening presence of the secret police is explicitly addressed, people are shown to be paralyzed by it. Only a few resist quietly, and even fewer resist fiercely.

However, Aidar's closest and most loyal friend, Zhenia, uncle Boria's son, no longer shares his father's communist ideals. Increasingly elitist, Zhenia

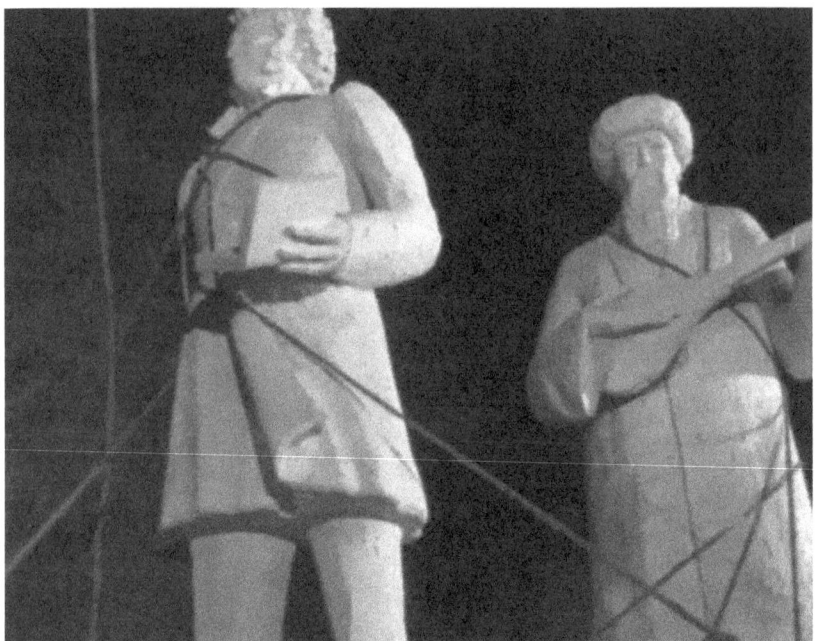

**Figure 12.4 Russian-Kazakh togetherness—Pushkin and Abai.** *The Balcony* (1988, Kalykbek Salykov)

despises the vulgarity of "the crowd" and ultimately distances himself from Aidar, too. A split between the two friends is inevitable: Aidar's path will be different from Zhenia's. Although Aidar is a born leader and stands out from the rank-and-file, he nevertheless remains an integral part of it.

The screenplay of *The Balcony* was adapted by Shakhimarden Kusainov from poems by Olzhas Suleimenov, the most famous Kazakh author of the 1960s–1980s. Many motifs are autobiographical, including the death of Aidar's father in the Stalinist purges. Aidar's ultimate choice of a life among ordinary people over an intellectual existence in an ivory tower is one that Suleimenov could also claim to have made. His poetry, while aesthetically original and passionately inventive, was never written for the chosen few. Suleimenov's sensational linguistic-historical explorations of the 1970s led to the birth of a new self-consciousness in Kazakhstan and Central Asia at large and made the poet a cult figure. However, after 1986, his status became more controversial.[7]

Films adapted from poetry are rare. A noteworthy example in Soviet cinema was Evgenii Evtushenko's *Kindergarten* (Detskii sad, 1984), in which lines of poetry recited by the author accompany several key episodes and the imagery is often lofty and pathos-filled. In this respect, *The Balcony* is different: except for Aidar's own provocative improvisations, Suleimenov's poetry is never cited verbatim, but is completely dissolved into the film's plot. Furthermore, the cinematography only rarely indulges in distinctly poetic images, for example, when the first snow falls at night. Beyond that, the reality of the early 1950s is reconstructed with sober care and without a hint of nostalgia, except for the music, which features Soviet and American period tunes.

However, reviewers such as Elena Ostrovskaia emphasized the nostalgic emotions that the recreation of old Alma-Ata evoked in the audience.[8] How can one explain this nostalgic response, and why have Kazakhstani viewers embraced *The Balcony* with such lasting loyalty? Apparently, this is one of those rare films that manages to respond to specific national sensitivities. Reflecting widespread sentiments, *The Balcony* neither idealized nor condemned the Kazakh-Soviet past, which is shown as a time in which the differences among various ethnic groups (Kazakhs, Russians, Jews, and Germans) were largely immaterial. Conspicuously, this past, as poeticized by Suleimenov and visualized by cinematographer Aubakir Suleev, is exclusively urban: there is no mention of *auls*, steppes, mountains, or mythical heroes. Aidar seems unaware of the ancient tradition from which his talent for poetic improvisation comes. *The Balcony* depicts a self-sufficient world of street gangs, their inner hierarchies and outer clashes, as well as of Soviet historical traumas, including the purges, the Great Patriotic War, and the Cold War, which are repeatedly brought up in conversations. In *The Balcony*, Russian language and culture exist in harmonious symbiosis with all elements of Kazakhstani urbanity, reflecting a historical experience, that is, the late 1940s and early 1950s, that was shared by millions of Kazakhstanis but rarely featured in cinema.

One of the film's major focuses is the macho youth culture that permeated the daily lives of Aidar and his gang far more than any political factors. From the beginning, militant virility is introduced as an important motif. These groups, which include children, teenagers, and young men, are in constant fighting mode. This is not just a posture, let alone a joking matter. The seriousness of these macho attitudes is demonstrated by the violent death of one gang member, a crime that is covered up by friend and foe but ultimately avenged by Aidar. A noteworthy detail is the presence of drugs and drug addiction: witnessing the torments of an addict in the hospital, Aidar rejects forever the temptation of drug use. Thus, while *The Balcony* evokes a past in which community, friendship, and loyalty play a major role, the film does not shy away from harsh aspects of that reality, implicitly addressing certain social problems that acquired a catastrophic dimension in the late 1980s.

*The Balcony* appealed to many intellectual viewers because it captured a situation in which the Kazakh-Soviet intelligentsia was fundamentally at peace with itself and its mission, despite frictions with the authoritarian state. Uncle Boria represents the quintessential intellectual idealist: egalitarian, open to great ideas, empathetic to all who suffer in the world. This distinguishes Salykov's film from those of the Kazakh New Wave that focus on antagonism and principally reject conciliatory attitudes.[9] An interesting (and very poetic) complementary motif is the episodic character of a weird old man in the streets, who is dressed in exotic clothes and crosses Aidar's path several times throughout the film, bowing to the monuments of Pushkin and Abai when a streetcar carries their sculptures through the avenues at night. The man seems to be homeless, a forlorn intellectual who is treated like a bum and comes across as a grotesque yet proud outsider to mainstream society. This, in addition to the leadership role within the young crowd, may be another facet of the poet's archetypal self-image.

A thematically complementary picture to *The Balcony* is *Higher Than the Mountains* (Vyshe gor, 1988). Taking stock of the entire Soviet period in Kazakh history, it uses a similar flashback technique to Salykov's film. Even the opening scene is similar. An old forester, Abdurakhman Beigembaev (Tasbulat Omarov), is undergoing surgery. Just like in *The Balcony*, this serves as the point of departure for a look back at the man's youth in the 1930s, when he was tasked with cutting trees in dense forests high in the mountains. The work is sheer drudgery, but Abdurakhman is tenacious and does not mind carrying out the strenuous assignment with his bare hands. In 1937, when he and his wife (Gulziia Belbaeva) encounter a writer and his family who are trying to escape from persecution, they help them hide from the secret police. The writer encourages Abdurakhman to not just cut trees, but to plant new ones as well. This turns out to be a noble but excruciating task due to the severe weather conditions: any storm can easily uproot the young plants, and torrential rain washes them down into the valley. In an eerie parallel, the couple's children keep dying one by one. The sheer repetitiveness of the humble couple burying their children and then continuing to raise more while also planting trees makes for tormenting viewing. But Abdurakhman's tenacity also instills in the viewer a sense of admiration for these modest, quiet people and their impeccable sense of duty. Meanwhile, the thoughtlessness and arrogance of the administrators who arrive by car every few years to inspect the forester's work are nothing less than insulting.

Time and time again, the film returns to the present, where the doctors are unable to locate the wound causing Abdurakhman's internal bleeding. The medical condition can be seen as analogous with the state of the nation: even with hundreds of thousands of nameless Kazakhs toiling for their country, it cannot get well. However, there is an invisible source of energy inside Abdurakhman that keeps him alive and that kept him and his wife moving forward, just as their country keeps growing despite endless historical tragedies and abuses. *Higher Than the Mountains* thus is a film about the selflessness of rank-and-file people who soldier on, ignoring the corrupt elites that exploit their natural sense of social duty.

What are the origins of Abdurakhman's strength? The film points to one major source, namely, the close companionship between husband and wife, which functions almost without words. One shot in particular stands out: the spouses hovering together under a raincoat, seeking protection from the heavy rain. Even when the wife claims in despair that it is the mountains themselves that are killing one child after another, she stands by Abdurakhman, until the first fruits of their decades-long labor emerge and their family, like the forest, grows in strength. However, in the 1970s and 1980s, poachers abuse the carefully groomed wilderness and brutally attack Abdurakhman; one of them sets the forest on fire, almost killing the increasingly frail man.

In a fascinating manner, *Higher Than the Mountains* complements *The Balcony* in that it reviews the Soviet-Kazakh experience from a micro- and a macro-perspective that allow for an overall assessment of the twentieth century. The unusual quality of this film is that it focuses on people outside the city: those whose existence is unknown to those inhabitants of Soviet Alma-Ata who care about issues of global injustice. Conspicuously, Abdurakhman and his wife speak Kazakh with each other, in contrast to the Russian-speaking urbanites in *The Balcony*. Moreover, the inhabitants of the mountains are politically naïve and follow ancient principles of decency. The film can legitimately be interpreted as a parable about the survival of the Kazakh nation in the twentieth century thanks to the rank-and-file citizens, who did their daily work despite suffering systematic abuse and asked for little in return. The film's historical conclusions are serious, but not bitter.

*Higher Than the Mountains* also contains elements of perestroika universalism, which was widespread in the late 1980s, when the fate of the Soviet Union was regularly interpreted in eschatological terms, as a portent of mankind's impending doom. The motif of an asteroid moving toward Earth points to this universalist dimension. The year 1937 is mentioned as a "lucky year" because an asteroid on a collision course with Earth, which would have ended all life, passed by our planet. The film ends with an asteroid approaching the Earth but missing it again, avoiding a global catastrophe. This motif underlines the humble approach that characterizes the film. Even a fateful year such as 1937, which signifies a high point of state terror in the USSR, is seen to pale in comparison to a potentially cosmic catastrophe.

The film, directed by Bolat Omar (formerly Omarov)[10] from a screenplay by Gennadii Bocharov, did not gain the cult status of *The Balcony* and has largely been forgotten in the post-Soviet period. Likely, its message of self-sacrifice for the good of the nation was perceived as anachronistic in the late 1980s; the complete absence of nostalgic motifs or quotes from popular culture also diminished its popularity. However, within a post-Soviet framework, Omar's film does reward careful viewing. Its atmospheric authenticity and philosophical severity preempted Ermek Tursunov's explorations of Kazakh national history twenty-five years later, particularly in *The Alien* (2015).

The fundamental social optimism permeating perestroika-inspired films such as *Shanyrak* and their underlying teleological worldview suggested that the emerging clannish and petit bourgeois mentality could be overcome if sufficient enlightened individuals fought for original Soviet values and the non-materialist Kazakh traditions that were more important than greed and consumerism. Films that took stock of Soviet-Kazakh history, such as *The Balcony* and *Higher Than the Mountains*, upheld a similarly optimistic spirit, despite the tragic facts that they revealed about the recent past. However, that historical optimism became rarer toward the end of perestroika and almost disappeared from Kazakhstani films in the early 1990s.[11]

## UNION TURMOIL

In March 1988, the leadership of the Union of Kazakhstani Film Workers met for a plenary session titled "Problems and Perspectives of the Cinema of Kazakhstan in Light of the Demands of Perestroika." At this meeting, the growing tensions within the Kazakh film community reached boiling point. Murat Auezov, who had worked as chief redactor of Kazakhfilm studio since 1982, had been denied membership of the Union of Kazakhstani Film Workers. At the same time, his expertise was constantly used in his capacity as head of the production unit "Alem." Known as a fearless speaker, Auezov declared that he did not recognize the authority of the current union leadership and nominated himself as first secretary. After the plenary session, Auezov was finally admitted to the union; several younger filmmakers were elected to the board (secretariat).[12]

The debates themselves were reminiscent of the scandalous congress of the Union of Soviet Film Workers in Moscow in December 1986, when the entire establishment of the USSR film industry was stripped of its positions. Admittedly, letting off steam was a healthy side effect of the rhetorical clashes, but one fundamental question remained unanswered: Would the profound changes in Kazakhstan's Union of Film Workers enable it to absorb the iconoclastic energies that were unleashed by perestroika and glasnost yet remain unscathed in its traditional shape? Was there a constructive solution for Soviet-Kazakh cinema's profound problems that would enable it to survive the growing turbulences?

On April 14–15, 1989, the Union of Kazakhstani Film Workers met for its sixth Congress. The timing was unusual: the next congress was supposed to take place in 1991. But the dissatisfaction with the state of cinema in Kazakhstan could no longer be ignored. The 249 union members elected Rashid Nugmanov, who had just gained USSR-wide notoriety with his drug drama *The Needle*, as its first secretary. Then, barely half a year later, on November 28, 1989, Nugmanov took "creative leave," never to return to his prominent post. His replacement, the documentary filmmaker Oraz Rymzhanov, showed more staying power. It was he who would navigate the union through the even more economically and politically turbulent 1990s.

## DARKNESS

During the perestroika years, from the mid- to late 1980s, the societal framework surrounding Kazakhstani cinema changed beyond recognition. Soviet values, which had been a major stabilizing factor in the self-reproduction of the socialist/communist order, were increasingly denounced by media discourses, and fewer and fewer people were willing to come to their defense or that of their underlying ideological platform. The growing lack of philosophical and moral consensus had an impact on the entire Soviet cinema. While some of its workers soldiered on in a traditional way, others tried out commercial or auteur modes. With the relaxation of censorship, by the mid-1980s genuine reality checks were possible in contemporary films. These did not reveal a pretty picture. In the context of the loyalist and traditionalist films that were still offered to Soviet viewers, the raw images of unpresentable facts were even more disturbing.

Members of Sergei Solov'ev's workshop were among the first to create entirely dark, shockingly realistic films about contemporary Kazakhstan. To be sure, it would be a simplification to claim that only they exposed the formerly hidden side of Soviet-Kazakhstani reality. Likewise, it is unfair to accuse these directors of indulging in "kitchen-sink realism," in analogy to British films of the early 1960s. After all, for Serik Aprymov, Rashid Nugmanov, and other directors, capturing the unpresentable aspects of life was not primarily a voyeuristic tool or a political cause. Nor was this done to discredit the Soviet social model as such or to call for its reformation, even though the latter mode of interpretation was prevalent among film critics discussing the first films of the New Wave. Rather, the depressing images of the late 1980s and early 1990s that began to emerge from Kazakhfilm studio redefined the background of stories that were of general human relevance. For the genuinely daring filmmakers, ridding their films of any underlying or covert ideological purpose was an act of self-liberation, allowing them to focus on the human condition per se.

## THE NEEDLE

The most famous of the "dark films" of the late 1980s is *The Needle* (*Igla*, 1988). As a matter of fact, it was the first film made in Kazakhstan since *The End of the Ataman* that achieved impressive box office results throughout the Soviet Union (with the exception of *The Secret of Madame Wong*, which should not be taken into consideration since it was not perceived as a Kazakhstani movie). Furthermore, *The Needle* was the first Kazakh film to be noticed on the international arthouse circuit. Whether David Cook's claim that "its success inspired three other Soloviev students to produce offbeat, low-budget features in 1989" is accurate or, rather, a retroactive simplification needs to be clarified in more detail.[13] None of the films listed by Cook as Nugmanov's direct successors (Aprymov's *Last Stop*, Baranov/Kilibaev's *The Three*, and Karpykov's *Little Fish in Love*) are thematically or stylistically close to *The Needle*; moreover, *The Last Stop* was shot almost simultaneously with *The Needle* and can hardly be called a variation of the former.[14] But what is certainly true is that Nugmanov's sensational success opened the door for new realistic Kazakh films that were suddenly welcomed by international festivals and distributors.[15]

The box office results deserve a closer look. In the 1980s, fewer and fewer Soviet feature films could compete with Western imports. Movies that managed to attract more than 30 million viewers (i.e., genuine blockbusters) were either satirical comedies such as those directed by Leonid Gaidai or imitations of Western genre movies. Especially toward the end of the decade, when a general disappointment in perestroika ideals gained ground, only a few films that exposed the horrors of the Soviet past (*The Cold Summer of 53*, 1986) or the societal degeneration of the Soviet present (*Little Vera*, 1988; *Intergirl*, 1989) could reach such spectacular numbers. *The Needle*, with a respectable 16 million viewers in its first year of release, belongs thematically to the second group, as it shows the heretofore taboo world of drug addicts and dealers. But the social aspects per se would not have been enough to secure a strong box office showing, particularly given the complexity of Nugmanov's narrative style. The film's most important attraction was its male lead, legendary rock musician Viktor Tsoi. His participation gave *The Needle* the value of a unique document, to be revered for as long as the cult surrounding Tsoi and his rock group, "Kino," was alive.

It can be argued that *The Needle* would have been just as successful had it been shot not in Kazakhstan but in Moscow or Tashkent, and by a different director with another, perhaps more mainstream stylistic approach. But Rashid Nugmanov, who belonged to Solov'ev's masterclass and had previously made an original short in which rock music played a substantial role, deliberately focused the entire picture on Tsoi and his inimitable persona;

hence many devotees of the singer went to see *The Needle* not just once but several times, making it a late Soviet cult film. Yet it would be shortsighted to attribute the film's success exclusively to the presence of Tsoi and his songs. After all, Aleksandr Baranov[16] and Bakhytzhan Kilibaev's screenplay provided an intriguing plot and sharp dialogues, while the director and the cameraman (Murat Nugmanov) created an atmosphere that made Tsoi's subversive performance highly effective.

The story focuses on a young man named Moro who returns to Almaty. Visiting his former girlfriend Dina (Marina Smirnova), Moro realizes that during his absence she has become a drug addict. He takes Dina to a quiet place on the Aral Sea and helps her overcome the addiction, but after they return to the city, the dealers prevail and kill Moro.

Drug usage is depicted graphically in one close shot of an intravenous injection; otherwise, the visualization of the physical effects of abuse remains moderate. The film's most intriguing aspect is the development of the relationship between Moro and Dina. Moro, as portrayed by Tsoi, presents a kind of male strength that was unprecedented in Soviet cinema: with his long dark mane, Western clothes, and relaxed body language, he fits the cliché of an "antisocial element," a cultural outsider that conformist Soviet society would reject, or at least regard with suspicion. At the same time, he is surprisingly neat, brushing his teeth and washing himself and the dishes as a matter of course, thus conveying an image of orderliness. Moreover, Moro is physically healthy, trained in martial arts, and able to defend himself and his girl from both petty street criminals and the corrupt doctor who participates in the drug business. Moro rejects drugs and those who profit from them. Thus, he does represent an image of male decency, but one situated *outside Soviet norms*.

Moro's decisions and actions are based on individual inner values. Despite (or perhaps because of) his status as an outsider, he acts as a source of social correction and stabilization. He does so almost wordlessly and with seeming indifference to Soviet society and its absurd, all-pervasive media environment. This is one of the reasons why Moro's image impressed so many youths and why its effect was so lasting: Moro/Tsoi projects a strength that is proudly independent of societal influences, a kind of manliness that will survive and maintain its integrity in every society, whether communist, capitalist, or otherwise. Thus, the Tsoi cult could legitimately embrace the character of Moro and *The Needle* as a film because the rock singer's public image seemed to coincide completely with the fictitious lead character: Moro was Tsoi, and Tsoi was Moro.

A controversial issue from the very beginning was the film's national identity, in other words, the "Kazakhness" of *The Needle*. Bauyrzhan Nogerbek,[17] a critic who was particularly sensitive to national issues, pointed to one episode in which an old man speaks to Moro in Kazakh, but no dialogue ensues; however, that episode is marginal and was likely not even noticed by many viewers. It is hard to deny that the plot of *The Needle* could easily be transplanted to any major Soviet city. But there is at least one organic connection between Moro and the Kazakh setting. Regardless of Moro's ethnicity, his personality has a nomadic foundation: he is a proud loner who moves from place to place and can survive anywhere. He appears on the screen like an alien, out of nowhere, and visibly feels uncomfortable in the gray, joyless city. The archaic environment at the seaside does not bother him in the slightest. Rather, it is this elementary, ultra-primitive environment that secures his girlfriend's healing. The abandoned vessel rusting at the drained sea symbolizes the faux grandiosity of past Soviet projects; its meaning can legitimately be extrapolated to point to the fiasco of the socialist/communist utopia as a whole. Climbing onto the ship, Moro asks with flippant naïvete, "And where is the crew?", indicating that for him, such metallic projections of human power hold little meaning.

*The Needle* ends with a sarcastic dedication "to Soviet television." Indeed, the film conveys deep disgust with the hypocritical media reality, in which the alienation expressed by cold, gloomily lit spaces and their cynical inhabitants is furthered by a pseudo-cheerful sound potpourri. The only constructive counterforce to common decay is the outsider Moro, whose calm demeanor, paradoxically paired with physical agility and fearlessness, resembles a Western action hero, a samurai, or a young *batyr*. Even though he is murdered in the finale, Moro/Tsoi's voice, both speaking and singing, creates an alternative to the falsity of the Soviet media cacophony. His body movements are fast and concentrated and easily deflate the postures of his criminal opponents. The fact that he is often rough but never cynical indicates that he has substantial reserves of inner goodness, perhaps even spirituality, that allow him to withstand fatalism and disorientation.

*The Needle* has been called "a manifesto of the New Wave cinema," a "postmodernist synthesis of different genres," combining "western with everyday life [*bytovoi*] film, thriller with tragicomedy, drama with light comedy, social fiction with a musical."[18] This interpretive framework was suggested by critics who were eager to shed the restrictive armor of socialist realism and to adopt the latest in critical theory. But does such a framework do justice to the picture's peculiar poetry or is it itself restrictive and misleading?

Rashid Nugmanov made only one other feature film and then abandoned filmmaking altogether, which seems to suggest that cinema and artistry were not foundational for his creative personality. In the history of Kazakh cinema, he remained the director of a single groundbreaking picture that not only came at the right moment but also possessed the necessary qualities, including an irreverent worldview and stylistic cohesion. Among the films of the

Kazakh New Wave, *The Needle* is the only one that managed to reach a mass audience. While the reasons for this success are manifold, Nugmanov's ability to bring together diverse elements and form a cohesive artifact is certainly one of them.

## Final Stop

Among Kazakhstani directors, Serik Aprymov was the most uncompromising in breaking away from the stifling legacy of Soviet filmmaking, including its artificial, ideologically forced social optimism. Aprymov's *Final Stop* (Konechnaia ostanovka, 1989) captured Kazakhstan in a raw state, without the crutches of active social engagement or timeless parables. Its unadorned realism confronted audiences with unsightly provincial reality, featuring young people without purpose or direction. Most shocking of all was the characters' complete lack of moral orientation. Owing to its radicalness, the film became a cultural symbol and a watershed in the transition from Soviet to post-Soviet cinema.

*Final Stop* first introduces its four protagonists, Arman, Erken, Takgat, and Murat, all born in 1964 in Aksuat. The introduction is rendered like a police protocol, with a typewriter mercilessly hammering the facts onto paper. What follows are episodes of one day in the lives of these young men. Erken returns home from military service, greets friends and family, speaks to a former girlfriend, and joins his buddies for drinks. Another young man keeps interfering, demanding to take a seemingly disturbed woman named Dina with him. His attacks grow more and more aggressive, finally triggering a deadly crime.

On the surface, Aprymov depicts a lackluster, unproductive milieu that holds no potential for any kind of future. People live without permanent jobs, inhabiting primitive huts and talking only about the most basic matters. Family structures seem to be the final barriers against total social disintegration. The married men are among the few to express a sense of responsibility; the bachelors run around in a senseless search for excitement that never materializes. But all the men react to their purposeless lives in a strangely accepting manner: "Times are getting hard now. Let's drink to that!" is one of their key utterances. The unbearable living conditions activate not social anger but individual aggression, expressed in a constant desire to engage in fights. Indeed, fights are shown to break out at any moment, disrupting a wedding and leading to injury and death. The attitude of the police is calmly cynical: they perform their assigned regulatory function with a stoic indifference akin to that of the population they monitor. Love is reduced to mechanical sex: if a woman indicates readiness, this is a chance for a man to use her without consequence; the arrangements are discussed in businesslike fashion.

Turning to national tradition does not offer a way out; a festival of horse races and other sports is depicted as moderately exciting but ultimately just another meaningless event.

In *Final Stop*, the title of which is openly metaphorical, Aprymov tests the state of Kazakh-Soviet society shortly before its final breakdown. He does so with unprecedented candor. The most shocking aspect at the time of the film's release was its lack of accusatory verbalization: it points fingers neither at the corruption of the Soviet state, nor at the broken promises of communism, nor at Russia and the Russians. Aprymov simply states the facts, as indicated in the opening sequence.

An awareness of the film's context, which was still Soviet at the time of its release, makes it possible to appreciate its profound effect on contemporary audiences. Primarily, many viewers were outraged by Aprymov's breaking of aesthetic taboos. *Final Stop* was the first film to show all the bleakness of Kazakhstani reality, which had heretofore been kept out of cinema. Within Soviet society, in whose continuing sustainability millions of people still believed (despite or because of the revelations of glasnost), this uncompromising assessment of life in Kazakhstan had to come as a shock. To be sure, Aprymov was not alone with this approach, although *Final Stop* takes even fewer prisoners than similar films like the Russian blockbuster *Little Vera* (1988), chiefly because it avoids melodramatic plot structures. Those film critics who were perestroika optimists defended what they perceived as a necessary turn toward social truthfulness, which they hoped would ultimately prove constructive for Soviet society. One critic wrote: "The truth about the 40 million people in the USSR who live below the existential minimum is no longer a secret and is revealed with great evidence [*s bol'shoi ochevidnost'iu*] in films such as *Final Stop*, thanks to the civic courage and humanity of their creators. Therefore, it is not the demonstration of the people's poverty on screen that should cause public outrage but the real poverty itself, a consequence of which is the absence of spirituality [*bezdukhovnost'*]." Obviously, the critic completely missed that Aprymov's film did not contain any call for reform but rather presented an assessment of reality that left no room for salvation within the Soviet paradigm. Aprymov also resisted any nationalist temptations that might have suggested that salvation would come through returning to the past. Conspicuously, he shared this sober attitude with fellow New Wave members.[19]

*Final Stop* is so convincing because it was rendered as a stylistic tour de force. Aprymov's directorial mastery is evidenced by the thoroughness with which all effects are calculated and then carried out in a manner that appears unrehearsed. The film itself seems to wander around in search of purpose, just like its characters. The casualness of the narrative adds to its realism, giving the impression of being quasi-unintentional. *Final Stop* is one of the earliest attempts of Kazakh cinema to give the agonizing Soviet-Kazakh society an authentic form. In this, it opened the door for many other film directors. Its effects could be felt well into the 2010s.

## *MY DEAR*

An example of the atmosphere of widespread resignation that took over Soviet-Kazakh cinema at the end of the 1980s is *My Dear* (Ainalaiyn/Milyi moi, 1990), a lyrical study of teenagers looking for orientation in a world that treats them with complete indifference. The film displays the sharp contrast between aggressive modernity coming from the center and immobile provincial reality, but without offering any constructive solution. The visual juxtaposition of jets taking off, on the one hand, with herds of camels walking along the same paths as they have for millennia, on the other hand, indicates that there are contradictions in Kazakhstan that represent its core and will shape its evolution regardless of the societal framework. In one episode, a teacher formulates such inconvenient truths, talking about the country's economic backwardness, poverty, and lack of a "healthy culture." But nobody is paying attention. The boys are more interested in sneaking peeks at a girl showering in a primitive barn than in the complexities of national history. The society's crisis may be deepening, but youngsters want to flirt with each other (however shyly) and dance at night, enjoying their first sexual experiences.

The film's central character, Alisher, is an orphan who lives with his frail grandfather. The old man speaks in a manner very different from the disillusioned school teacher, praising the beauty of Kazakhstan and its culture; pointing to the sacredness of the swan, whose shape once inspired the dombra; and calling upon Alisher to become like a bird himself. This is the best message he can give to a boy who is on his way to adulthood in a society where unsightly crowds in front of a liquor store angrily fight for their daily share of booze.

If *Shanyrak* showed a corrupt but still corregible Kazakhstan, *My Dear*, which was made a mere three years later, is set in a society of hopeless stasis, a milieu of near-medieval poverty. The village in which Alisher lives consists of shacks and huts that lack any modern amenities. A gigantic nuclear power plant is located nearby, and the lake in which Alisher and his friend swim is filled with lead from a polluted river. The environment is in a catastrophic state, yet few people seem to care. While the poverty in which the characters live may have a certain poetic air to it, the industrial pollution is shown as both repulsive and scary. For Alisher's grandfather, the nearby refinery is an object of resentment that he wants to blow up, and in one surreal episode it seems that this is precisely what is happening, with the grandfather dying in the explosion. The last image shows Alisher walking with a camel along the railway tracks.

In *My Dear*, resignation is downright palpable. It is verbalized by the sickly teacher who is constantly rambling about the pitiful state of the nation but concludes his sermons with the words, "Don't pay attention to what I am saying," which is the only advice that his students follow. Alisher's grandfather seconds this pessimism, exclaiming: "Poor Earth, poor people, the orphaned land of our ancestors," adding that he no longer has any dreams. The past is as much an object of destruction as is the present. At the cemetery where Alisher speaks to his late parents, a bulldozer is removing graves. The love scene between Alisher and his girlfriend takes place in open nature, resembling *The Blue Lagoon*, but the reality experienced by these teenagers is the opposite of idyllic. The director expressed this sentiment in several interviews, stating that "the young have lost their faith," and "There is no love, no friendship, no humanity."[20]

In its depiction of the severe legacy of the Soviet era, *My Dear* anticipates Satybaldy Narymbetov's *Leila's Prayer* (2002), although the latter makes the interaction between the local population and the nearby nuclear test site more explicit. Narymbetov's drama also uses the viewpoint of a teenager and spiritual references to express some hope for the future, no matter how small. Its finale connects this hope to the country's president. *My Dear*, however, was made a decade before *Leila's Prayer* and is still a Soviet film: one of the last in Kazakhstani cinema. It avoids any kind of pathos, and its disillusionment is only tempered by the natural strength and inner health of its young main character, Alisher, who seems to be endowed with the attributes necessary to face the future whatever it may bring. Shot in alternating black-and-white and color, *My Dear* was the directorial debut of actor Bolat Kalymbetov.[21] As the Kazakh film industry was in such disarray during that period, his film did not receive the critical and viewer attention it deserved.[22] Alas, it was hardly alone in this neglect.

Another late Soviet-Kazakh film that captured the disillusionment of the end of perestroika and the ensuing demise of the Soviet system in its entirety is *Running Target* (Begushchaia mishen', 1991). Arguably its most sensational aspect is the casting of Nonna Mordiukova, one of the all-time stars of Soviet cinema, in the role of Sima, an aging signalwoman who is trying to survive in a crude and unforgiving society. The male protagonist, a student, is the "running target" of the title, with state police as the hunter. The film opens with documentary footage of the 1986 December (*Zheltoksan*) turmoil in Alma-Ata, when students protesting the installation of a Russian Communist Party hack as the new leader of Kazakhstan were beaten, arrested, and abused by police.

The student, one of the participants in the demonstration, is traumatized by the events and forced to go into hiding after a search for him is announced on television. But the people he encounters during his attempts to find shelter and avoid persecution turn his involuntary sojourn into a gruesome rite of passage. Memories of the violence experienced on the squares of Alma-Ata keep haunting him. Aunt Sima, the grumpy elderly lady who reluctantly takes him in, has likewise been through harsh times; she reacts with distrust toward the entire world. Corrupt Soviet railway administrators regularly use her little house next to the railway lines for orgies with plenty of vodka and easy women, threatening Sima, who does her utmost to please them.

Director Talgat Temenov artfully parallels the process of ordinary people learning about the essence of the Soviet system with the maturation of a teenager who must realize that this system will not allow him to escape, and he will have to confront it directly. Remarkably, Temenov avoids any nationalist tones in his depiction of the 1986 events. It would have been easy to put all blame on "the Russians" for the corruption and destruction of the country. But the main culprit who ultimately causes Aunt Sima's death is Alibek, a Kazakh hack and ruthless alcoholic. The Kazakh student and the Russian woman alike are victims of the communist system; their ethnicity is irrelevant for an understanding of Kazakhstan's miseries.

*Running Target* is carried by the accusatory pathos and moral outrage that were so common during the perestroika years. But Temenov's film is more radical than previous dramas in its implicit diagnosis that the communist system can no longer be reformed: it must be abolished. Visually, the film is dominated by gray, foggy, thoroughly off-putting landscapes crossed by railway lines that convey an atmosphere of pure hopelessness. Rarely had the moral corruption and the lawlessness of the Soviet system been described in a Kazakh film with such directness as in *Running Target*. Just as in the case of *My Dear*, due to the breakdown of the distribution system, this film did not receive the attention it should have. Nor was it given a second chance in post-communist Kazakhstan, despite its outstanding cast and suspenseful plot. Nonetheless, it still has the potential to play an enlightening role for new generations of Kazakhs.

## THE SEARCH FOR ROOTS I: *SULTAN BEIBARS*

Turkmen filmmaker Bulat Mansurov gained recognition when his *Funeral Feast*, thanks to perestroika liberalization, was finally released in 1987. He used his increased status to renew his working relationship with Kazakhfilm studio and undertake a megaproject, the historical epic *Sultan Beibars*. Released in two parts in 1988/1989, the film reconstructs an ancient epoch whose relevance for the late 1980s was not immediately apparent. For Mansurov, it was the continuation of historical-philosophical explorations he had begun in the 1960s.

Beibars (other spelling: Baybars) was a thirteenth-century Egyptian ruler of extraordinary strategic talent who managed to defeat both the Crusaders and the Mongols. Mansurov adapted the screenplay from the historical novel *Emshan* (1966) with the help of its author, Moris Simashko. For the coauthors, the key aspect of Beibars's story was his birth in the steppe, which is said to have endowed him with particular gifts that enabled his rapid ascent to power. According to legend, which became the foundation of the novel and the film, Beibars was born into a Kipchak family, sold into slavery by the Mongols, and joined the Mamluk troops. He eventually became the sultan of Egypt, ruling from 1260 to 1277.

The fact that a proto-Kazakh reached the heights of world history at a time when his own people were barely able to survive the onslaught of neighboring tribes could serve as a source of national pride. But for Mansurov, the portrayal of a Kazakh warrior at the center of grand history was more than a hard-to-prove claim of significance from an otherwise barely documented ethnic group. Beibars' career trajectory—from slave to absolute ruler, from victim to victimizer—served as a parable of the potential for individual power within the maelstroms of history. With the decline of the Soviet empire in plain sight, Mansurov brought to the screen a *Game-of-Thrones*-type of story in which Beibars schemes his way to the top without regard for allies, friends, or loved ones. While he is still a mamluk, someone asks Beibars about his friends and the notion of friendship in general. "I don't know what that word means," he replies. The same is true of the word "trust": a meaningless notion in the world as Beibars sees it.

The film's second part is structured as a monologue in which Beibars ponders his career. His voice is that of an exhausted, disillusioned man who looks at human nature with disdain. Humans need *a leader* more than anything else and will give up their freedom and dignity to be led. At the same time, Beibars realizes that he himself fundamentally depends on those whom he leads. Thus, the sultan's absolute power turns out to be an illusion: the ruler and the ruled are bound together inextricably and in deadly mutual dependence.

For his concept of medieval reality, Mansurov developed a style radically different from conventional historical drama or biopic. The characters are mostly quiet; their faces remain expressionless. Thus, conflicts are not verbalized through dialogues nor even through gazes, as the characters keep their thoughts and feelings to themselves until the moment they act. This is a consequence of universal distrust: revealing one's attitudes, let alone plans, can mean death. Thus, *Sultan Beibars* comes across as a strange combination of wordless action, including lengthy rituals and sudden attacks, and the inner voice of the title character. The visual and the audial levels are logically connected, but this connection is not communicated or explicated by the characters involved to the viewer or to each other. The film's imagery is deliberately two-dimensional, almost flat, albeit with saturated colors; its stylization resembles illustrations in medieval chronicles.

Physically and mentally, Beibars is maximally suited to succeed in the chess games of power. Fighting to win seems to be the key trait he inherited through his Kipchak genes. His only weak spots are the memories of his childhood in the steppe, especially the aromas, and his doubts about the durability of his power and of power per se. Toward the end of the film, Beibars gives orders to open a grave in the pyramids. There, he discovers that the power of yesteryear leaves behind nothing but dust, despite the grandiose trappings of golden masks and armor. This ultimate proof of the futility of human efforts convinces Beibars that it is time for him to abandon his throne and return to the land of his birth (an instinct that is described as omnipotent in an earlier Kazakh film, *Where the Mountains Are White*). Now an aged man in beggar's clothes, Beibars finds an *aul* and a playing toddler who is lovingly protected by his young father, just as he himself was half a century ago. But suddenly, the image of harmony is destroyed by attacking warriors who kill the peaceful nomads and burn their yurts. As Beibars watches in tired wisdom, a new deadly circle of history begins...

*Sultan Beibars* is a difficult film, overburdened with philosophical ambition and visibly marred by a meager budget. A lot can be said about its shortcomings. As a commentary at the beginning admits, the historical documents concerning Beibars are scarce and contradictory, which means that many historical statements are based on mere speculation, and Beibars's Kipchak background is far from established by historians. Furthermore, the film's length and slowness are excessive and unnecessary; its philosophical claims and endless historiosophical musings in the voice-over sometimes appear pretentious. But there are doubtless achievements, too. First and foremost, Nurmukhan Zhanturin's portrayal of Beibars is unique in its near-total identification with the title character, a crowning achievement of one of the most remarkable acting careers in Kazakhstani cinema. Zhanturin's severe features and heavy eyelids bear all the marks of a long and hard life, conveying a profound knowledge of the hopelessness of human striving.

For Mansurov, *Sultan Beibars* was the continuation of his exploration of the East and its significance for Europe and the world, a significance that, from his point of view, had been downplayed or denied. Because the nomadic peoples of the steppe were unable to document their history, their contributions were ignored, if not suppressed, by the Western historians who wrote the chronicles. But the film goes beyond historical correction and rehabilitation.

Just like in his debut, *The Contest* (1964), Mansurov kept his focus on a universal question about the origins of violence in all human societies and the chances of overcoming it. The filmmaker's philosophical searches outweigh any cinematic considerations per se. That is why the two-dimensional shot compositions sometimes render the imagery flat, while the secondary characters lack any psychological nuance, making them cardboard illustrations of theses verbalized in the voice-over. This subjugation of aesthetic norms to the necessities of conceptual superstructures is radical in its own way. It no doubt alienated mass audiences who were expecting an exciting historical spectacle. Yet *Sultan Beibars* aimed at something deeper than entertainment. It is a work of active mythmaking, delivered by a monomaniacal filmmaker who resisted compromise throughout his career. The film's universalism is typical of the perestroika period, when Marxist-Leninist teleology was replaced by other constructs that could provide historical orientation, whether Eurasianism or pan-Turkism.

## THE SEARCH FOR ROOTS II: *SURZHEKEI, THE ANGEL OF DEATH*

One of the strictest taboos of Soviet Kazakhstan was the collectivization campaign of the late 1920s and early 1930s. The communist state's brutal assault on the traditional nomadic lifestyle and the scale of human losses were of such magnitude that this topic could only be whispered about. Although the liberalization with respect to historical themes initiated by Gorbachev's perestroika steadily decreased the number of taboos, the history of collectivization remained one of the last themes that could not be addressed in Soviet Kazakhstan. Breaking that taboo alone made *Surzhekei, the Angel of Death* (Surzhekei—angel smerti, 1991) a milestone in Kazakhstani cinema.

In his two-part film, Damir Manabaev,[23] who coauthored the screenplay with Smagul Elubaev, visualized the onslaught of Soviet power as an endless nightmare, creating a long string of unprecedented images of violence and destruction (the film's cinematographer was Bolat Suleev). The object of the communists' wrath is the traditional *aul* as such, in other words, the center of the world order in which Kazakhs had lived for centuries. Two brothers, Asbergen (Meirman Nurekeev) and Pakhridin (Nurmukhan Zhanturin), differ in their attitudes toward the intruding Soviets: the former advocates a massive escape of the community, taking their livestock across the border, while the latter is more deeply rooted in native soil and wants to wait and see how things unfold. Both the active and the passive approach fail tragically. The leader of the Soviet troops, an illiterate commissar who calls himself

"Surzhekei, the Angel of Death" (Zh. Abdykadyrov), carries out his mission to radically transform the *aul* with nihilistic contempt for age-old values and elementary civility. Surzhekei is helped by opportunists hoping to strike it rich by robbing the "class enemy." But in the end, even they lose everything. Communism is depicted not as a viable alternative to the traditional social order, but as a catastrophe that brings disorder, against which all appeals to reason and humanity are futile. While killing and burning, Surzhekei utters political slogans that were common at the time but sound preposterous in the context of the chaos that he unleashes. The population quickly realizes what his words are worth. Thus, when the commissar turns to a local woman and says, "Greetings, liberated woman!" she angrily replies, "To hell with your liberty!"

The film's nightmarish atmosphere is partially the result of most scenes taking place at night, with sharp chiaroscuro evoking apocalyptic associations. To make his moral concept visually clear, Manabaev shot the interiors of the yurts in color, whereas the exteriors were kept in black-and-white. As the yurts, the symbols of domestic safety and familial dignity, are violated by the intruding communists and then destroyed altogether, the screen turns from color to black-and-white, indicating the death of the *shanyrak* and the stable lifestyle it represented.

*Surzhekei, the Angel of Death* is an explicitly anti-communist film, arguably the first in the history of Kazakhstani cinema. With a 140-minute running time, it approaches epic proportions. However, the plot itself is essentially dramatic, unfolding within the same limited space and featuring a relatively small number of characters over a short period of time. Because of its deliberate narrative slowness, which is used to emphasize the scenes' inherent symbolism, the plot at times loses cohesion and falls apart.

The contradiction between epic breadth, dramatic plot, and symbolic signification overburdens the film for the viewer and, to a certain degree, undermines its persuasiveness. The accusatory pathos of the unfolding historical tragedy is mostly expressed through powerful images rather than through the relations between the characters, which are predominantly conveyed by grand emotions and gestures. Since the film was breaking new thematic ground, its makers likely wanted to achieve too many goals at once, resulting in constant meandering between the realistic and the symbolic dimensions. Likewise, the ongoing friction between epic and dramatic elements seriously diminishes the film's ability to engage the viewer beyond the mere horror of witnessing the intentional destruction of a civilization. Had the pathos of surreal images and symbolic actions been complemented by a factual and documentary framework, the film's argumentative prowess and effectiveness would have been considerably increased. In this respect, *Surzhekei, the Angel of Death*, shares some of the problems of Tengiz

Abuladze's anti-totalitarian parable *Repentance* (Monanieba/Pokaianie, 1984), which became *the* groundbreaking historical picture of the entire perestroika period and made headlines worldwide upon its 1986 release. However, because *Repentance* was the first Soviet film of its kind, its considerable aesthetic complexity and narrative imbalances, which left many viewers puzzled, were outweighed by the sheer sensation of its thematic radicalness.

Manabaev's film, which was produced by the independent studio "Katarsis," came a few years too late to cause the same sensation as its Georgian predecessor. Still, its honesty and artistic effort are beyond doubt. The topic of collectivization and mass starvation, with its millions of deaths continues to represent a challenge to Kazakhstani filmmakers that has not been adequately dealt with in the decades since Manabaev's courageous first attempt.

## ARTHOUSE

One of the unforeseen but intellectually significant effects of perestroika was the emergence of a legitimate arthouse cinema both in the Russian Federation and in the national republics. The interactions between the Soviet center and the peripheries in this regard were intense and, in the best case, mutually stimulating. In the late 1980s, the emergence of auteur films intended for a limited circle of cognoscenti indicated the presence of a growing space for creative self-realization and social acceptance of self-conscious artistic strata whose legitimacy was no longer denounced and attacked by the communist ideological apparatus. Indeed, because the economic framework was still Soviet, that is, box office expectations were of negligible importance for production, the last years of perestroika were ideal for arthouse cinema that could satisfy elitist tastes and groups of critics who applauded the homegrown auteurs. "Box office" had not yet become a meaningful concept.

The undisputed idol of the 1980s auteur filmmakers was Andrei Tarkovskii, whose stance against aesthetic and ideological control by the state defined the ethical maximalism of a generation of directors. The other side of the coin, the incomprehension or indifference of ordinary viewers toward arthouse films, was generally seen as a badge of honor; it was not yet realized that such an attitude would inevitably lead to the disappearance of arthouse cinema's first wave as soon as genuine capitalist conditions, with their non-negotiable criterion of profitability, set in.

A Kazakh filmmaker whose distinct arthouse profile emerged at the end of perestroika is Amanzhol Aituarov.[24] His debut, *The Touch* (Prikosnovenie, 1989), displays many of the characteristics of Soviet arthouse productions of the late 1980s. The film begins with a 360-degree panoramic shot of an ordinary room in which a woman is talking to a man. The next shot takes the viewer to a mountainous region, showing a blind young woman walking cautiously. She drinks eagerly from a cow's udder until a young man pushes her away. This young man, a beggar, later saves the blind woman from an errant warrior who tries to rape her. The two outcasts join forces, supporting each other in the art of survival on a path that takes them through a war-torn land in an undefined age. The young man, a former slave, dreams of wealth, although a fortune-teller predicts that he will have an untimely death. When two warriors overwhelm him and tie him up, it is the woman's turn to kill the attackers; she then patiently tends to her new partner's wounds, saving his life. The man and the woman share a bond even deeper than that of intimacy. Thus, when a powerful ruler captures the two, first feeding them and then threatening to have them killed, the beggar refuses to give up his lover, gaining the ruler's respect. However, when the stakes are raised, the man does betray the woman.

The influence of both Tarkovskii and Japanese historical drama (Kaneto Shindo and Akira Kurosawa, among others) on *The Touch* is hard to miss. Similarities include the deliberately ascetic mise-en-scène; laconic dialogues;[25] mysterious characters whose background and motivation remain unclear; and witchcraft mysticism that exercises real or imagined power over the characters. The world is described as filled with omnipresent violence that leaves individuals in constant danger, forcing them to remain on guard at all times and reducing them to an animal state, with their humanity constantly challenged. Many episodes focus on elementary urges such as hunger and the need for shelter. Water, plants, mud, and the burning sun define the enigmatic reality of the film, in which the characters can barely survive. The barrennness of the environment leaves ample room for spiritual presences and miracles: the young woman lost her eyesight when she witnessed the brutal killing of her parents by warriors; she regains it when she and her companion become sexually intimate for the first time.

Reminiscent of the moralistic debates of the perestroika years is the beggar's ultimate corruption by power (which constitutes a link to Mansurov's *Sultan Beibars*): he withstands all temptations of wealth until he is offered the chance to succeed the current ruler. At this point, he gives up the woman whom he loved and who had saved him. This conclusion demonstrates deep skepticism with regard to human moral potential, suggesting the supremacy of power and material values over individual bonds and loyalty.

Like many arthouse films, *The Touch* was intended as an atemporal parable, without any specific references to Kazakh history or contemporaneity, although the historical decorum is Kazakh. In its last episode, *The Touch* comes full circle, with the main heroine now living in present-day urban Kazakhstan. The implication may be quasi-Jungian: humans carry with them a subconscious knowledge of the past that awakens in dreams and fantasies.

On the one hand, these may be "real" emanations of the subconsciousness, sometimes called "genetic memory"; on the other hand, the film's subtitle is "A Fantasy," relativizing any claim to verisimilitude. However, the contemporary frame comes across as too direct in trying to enhance the story's philosophical gravitas.

Arguably, the film's arthouse ambitions are also too obvious. Nevertheless, Aituarov's picture was, without a doubt, a result of the newly gained freedom of artistic expression and found sufficient national and international recognition. *The Touch* was selected by several festivals and won prizes, among others in Sverdlovsk (conspicuously at the last All-Soviet film festival in 1990) and Nantes. Indeed, the film displays a narrative originality that rewards attentive viewing. As a parable of love and loyalty, it has indubitable potential. Had it been more decisive in its stylistic and conceptual development, the result could have been magnificent. Interestingly, the film's redactor was Darezhan Omirbaev, soon to become the master of Kazakh arthouse, which allows for some speculation as to the extent of his influence on the final picture.

Aituarov's next project, *A Voyage to Nowhere* (Puteshestvie v nikuda, 1992), was another arthouse experiment. It was completed right after Kazakhstan gained independence, but conceptually it still belongs to the category of "dark" films, such as *The Needle* and *My Dear*. As in many late Soviet and early post-Soviet arthouse films, the genre is dystopian: Aituarov made a curious attempt to capture the state of contemporary Kazakh youth in a partly dystopian framework. A group of young outcasts, among them rockers and Hara Krishna adherents, help an alcoholic pilot to rescue his institutionalized young son. In exchange, he promises to fly them to America. While the first part of the adventure succeeds, the second ends in disaster when the hijacked propeller plane proves to be in too poor a condition for the long voyage. The trip ends with a premature crash landing before it can even take the group out of the country. The youngsters who are dressed for hip San Francisco, find themselves instead in the middle of the desert, on a secretive military testing ground. Barely keeping their sanity, they try to help the local population while saving their own lives. But the pilot and his son are killed, and the merciless logic of the military leaves the adventurers no solution to their existential dilemma. Hippie dreams of Western freedom turn out to be dangerous illusions: there is no such thing as an escape to a better world.

Aituarov is an ambitious filmmaker. In *A Voyage to Nowhere*, he aptly diagnosed the disorientation of Kazakhstani youth after the breakdown of all Soviet certainties. Moreover, whether consciously or not, he correctly predicted the sad fate of a generation that was raised on dreams about a new world yet found itself stuck in the same brutal reality from which it was determined to escape. The young people's America-ready outfits are exposed as grotesquely inadequate for the rough conditions in the native desert. The story is fascinating, and so is the direction in several episodes. However, even more than in *The Touch*, Aituarov's ambition exceeds his ability to control the material. Thus, *A Voyage to Nowhere* can be viewed as an interesting experiment, although it comes, just like its protagonists, to a dead end.

## A RUSSIAN-KAZAKH TEAM: BARANOV/KILIBAEV

Aleksandr Baranov and Bakhyt Kilibaev belonged to the Kazakh New Wave.[26] In many ways, they embodied the Kazakh-Russian symbiosis that was typical of the film milieu of Kazakhstan from the beginning. When the crisis of Soviet cinema gave them a sudden chance to direct their own projects, they began with a genre experiment, the parable *The Three* (Troe, 1988). It takes place on a film set, a nationally indistinct modern space. Were it not for the fact that two of the main characters are Kazakh, the film's connection to Kazahstan would be impossible to grasp. The film, showing three outsiders who are trying to find a legitimate place for themselves amid chaos and cynicism, bears many marks of the theater of the absurd. This, too, was a popular phenomenon during late perestroika, when the formerly taboo *Waiting for Godot* and the plays of Eugene Ionesco became household notions. The three main characters from the title are homeless, intelligent, and willing to do something useful, yet society's response is one of indifference and rejection, an attitude experienced by millions of intellectuals in the late Soviet and early post-Soviet period. Human beings, no longer part of the previous societal paradigm that secured them a meaningful position in exchange for their self-realization, are in catastrophic free-fall and no longer able to define their own or each other's value.

On a deeper level, *The Three* also reflects the dilemma of cinema on the verge of systemic commercialization. This is an intriguing theme, especially in hindsight, from the viewpoint of fully established capitalism. The film set and its personnel are portrayed as shameless, undignified, and vain. When the homeless men propose a dangerous stunt in exchange for money, they are mocked by the actors and producers. In the end, they manage to get a reasonable amount of dollars, but they do not really know what to do with the money and immediately waste it. While the characters' behavior often seems unbelievable, the film's point is to showcase their priorities: the three test their newly commercialized environment with respect to its reliability and ability to accommodate them; they also test themselves and their ability to survive under these new conditions.[27]

## A HARVEST OF MASTERPIECES

Despite the unstable conditions during the last years of perestroika and the beginning breakdown of Soviet society, several filmmakers managed to create superb pictures. The harvest of masterpieces that marks the end of Soviet-Kazakh cinema will be highlighted with specific focus on the new aesthetic freedom that was also a product of deep transformations within Kazakhstani society.

Although the Soviet Union and the KazakhSoviet Socialist Republic were still intact as political entities, the late 1980s were, both atmospherically and thematically, a time of transition from Soviet to post-Soviet cinema. Within the Kazakhstani context, widespread ideological uncertainty enabled the creation of several moving pictures that are among the best in the nation's film history. These pictures, whose artistic caliber was not always recognized at the time of their release, are part of the lasting legacy of Kazakhstani cinema.[28]

During the late perestroika years, the Soviet film industry was still state-funded. Yet the relaxation of censorial control opened up a heretofore unseen range of creative opportunities that some filmmakers seized upon immediately, as if they could tell that such conditions would only last for a short time. The political liberalization had strong effects in the Soviet center and in selected parts of the periphery, that is, in some, but not all, national republics. Among the film cultures that profited the most from the transitory state was that of Georgia. Some of Kazakhstan's ambitious film artists, too, used these opportunities wisely. For such filmmakers, both members of the nascent New Wave and directors who belonged to earlier generations, the new situation allowed them to experience an aesthetic liberation that seemed miraculous. The most fruitful period in this respect were the three years prior to official independence (1988–1991), when state funding was still secure but the iron laws of free-market capitalism had not set in. Now, filmmakers yearning for unbridled artistic expression were able to take their chance.

The long-term significance of the high-caliber films that were created under these unique circumstances is more aesthetic than sociopolitical. This distinguished late Soviet-Kazakhstani cinema from the film cultures of other Soviet republics and from that of the Russian Federation itself. Freedom was most relevant for the aesthetic dimension of cinema. Each of the masterpieces created during this period deployed an individual aesthetic approach that was unprecedented in Kazakh and in Soviet film history. Conspicuously, these extraordinary pictures were hardly seen by native audiences, who were preoccupied with more existential concerns than their native film industry. But to stunned festival spectators at home and abroad, the release of these Kazakhstani films signified the emergence of a new, muscular national film culture endowed with self-confidence and ambition.

## Exiting the Forest and Entering a Meadow

Among the most aesthetically remarkable pictures to come out of Kazakhfilm studio during the late Soviet period was Ermek Shinarbaev's *Exiting the Forest and Entering a Meadow* (Vyiti iz lesa na polianu, 1988), adapted from stories by Anatolii Kim. Shinarbaev, who did not belong to the New Wave, had surprised Russian audiences with his poetic yet harshly realistic postwar drama *My Sister, Liusia* (Sestra moia, Liusia, 1987), likewise based on a screenplay by Kim, a Korean-Russian author who was born in Kazakhstan.[29] Compared to Shinarbaev's debut, however, *Exiting the Forest and Entering a Meadow* is a far more complex picture, a genuine philosophical study. Its radical visual and audial concentration and narrative minimalism are nothing short of stunning.

The film describes the encounter between a mathematician (Aleksei Zharkov) and an ailing recluse (Nikolai Grinko), who engage in a long philosophical dialogue while walking through a deep forest. Both men are at critical junctures in their lives. The mathematician is experiencing an existential crisis, having concluded that there is no hope for humankind in its drive toward self-destruction. He is suffering from severe depression, which was caused by his having recently killed a man in a car accident. The old teacher is awaiting the end of his life and reminisces about an abandoned love and his subsequent encounter with a woman who apparently had magical powers and pointed him in the direction of a fulfilled life following his service in World War II. During the walk, the teacher suddenly dies from a heart attack. Yet shortly thereafter, he reappears and talks to the mathematician about the powerlessness of death.

The dominant motif of *Exiting the Forest and Entering a Meadow*, both in the plot and the overall philosophical concept, is disorientation. The mathematician has lost all sense of certainty and literally gets lost in the forest, only to be found by the teacher the next morning. When the film was conceived, an overall sense of philosophical disorientation was widespread among Soviet intellectuals, reflecting the waning spirit of the last phase of perestroika, when the promises of successful reform turned out to be illusions and the formerly stable, albeit disdained, societal framework began to crumble. Atheism, materialism, and science were unable to provide answers in an atmosphere of widespread despair. In this situation, Anatolii Kim's prose gained unusual popularity due to its spiritual intensity and aesthetic originality. His narratives offered spiritually valid answers to existential questions at a time when the official ideological framework of dialectical materialism had been completely discredited. Kim's pantheistic metaphysics made no attempt to compete with rationalist world models but gave the reader a polyphonic narrative, in which authentic human voices arrived at a mature, positive acceptance of spiritual openness to the world. Mystical experiences, among others, were treated as legitimate as long as they were authenticated by real life and not imposed as dogma. It is essential for Kim's poetics that, while his narratives have a palpable philosophical dimension, they are not treatises: the narrator never preaches.

*Exiting the Forest and Entering a Meadow* is deeply infused with the peculiarities of Kim's prose. But it is also a highly poetic picture in which cinematography (Georgii Gidt, Sergei Kosmanev) creates a visual poetic dimension of its own. With its motifs of decay and danger, such as dying trees and deadly swamps, the visual dimension is clearly inspired by Andrei Tarkovskii. The Kazakh film's closeness to the oeuvre of the Russian director, who had reached the status of a quasi-prophet by the 1980s, comes across in other ways as well: Nikolai Grinko was one of Tarkovskii's favorite actors and often embodied ascetic paternal wisdom (for example, in *Ivan's Childhood* and *Solaris*), whereas Aleksei Zharkov evokes the features of other ascetic Tarkovskian actors such as Anatolii Solonitsyn and Aleksandr Kaidanovskii. The motif of the philosophical journey resembles *Andrei Rublev*, *Stalker*, and *Nostalghia*. Still, Shinarbaev's picture is far from imitative. Philosophically, it decisively moves away from the Russian director's Orthodox master tropes. From the viewpoint of film history, though, one can call *Exiting the Forest and Entering a Meadow* a legitimate cinematic response to Tarkovskii.

First and foremost, in Ermek Shinarbaev's film, the sources of positive energy that have the potential to overcome darkness and despair are original, not epigonal. The title itself points to a path toward clarity and purity after chaos and confusion: leaving the disorienting thicket of the forest behind and entering the wide, sun-filled airiness of a green meadow is a metaphor for the process of acquiring spiritual vision, for which the music of Haydn is the perfect audial representation.[30] As a work of cinematic art, *Exiting the Forest and Entering a Meadow* is characterized by exemplary structural stringency. Every element of the picture is carefully crafted. Shinarbaev's film represents a farewell to an epoch. The concluding phase of that epoch overwhelms the people entangled in it with deep angst. That angst, the film suggests, does not predict destruction but is the prelude to the spiritual liberation of the individual.

## *A Little Fish in Love*

Abai Karpykov, a historian by training and a member of Solov'ev's Kazakhstani masterclass at VGIK, debuted with three shorts that brought him recognition in film circles. Then came his first full-length feature film, which turned out to be truly groundbreaking: *A Little Fish in Love* (Vliublennaia rybka, 1989) displays a lightness of touch, a high caliber, fatalistic wit, and a cinematic playfulness that were unprecedented in Kazakh cinema.

Young Zhaken (Bopesh Zhandaev) sells his cow and goes to the city to visit his brother. Through chance encounters, he gets involved with a femme fatale (Natal'ia Novikova) and her cheating husband, a high-ranking government official. Through his older brother (Abai Karpykov), he meets more colorful characters, including Assan (Assan Kuiatte), an African musician who speaks perfect Russian. After a number of absurd adventures, including amorous ones, Zhaken returns to his *aul*.

Strangely, most critics interpreted the film on a sociological level, as a depiction of the confrontation between the rural and urban worlds in Kazakhstan. Apparently, this was the only available interpretive approach to an innovative, clever, but also confusing picture, forcing *A Little Fish in Love* into a long line of stories dealing with a common theme of Kazakh cinema and thus neglecting its uniqueness. For, Karpykov is far more original than his film's sociological frame may suggest, although the latter probably offered the easiest explanations to viewers who were baffled by the irreverent humor and the illogical plot.

Looking at the film from the distance of three decades, its most winsome quality is its manner of capturing the absurdity of a new civilization emerging from the ruins of communism. As the regulations of Soviet society are defunct, Kazakhstan has turned into a country in which people live by their egotistic ambitions and instincts, engaging in promiscuous relationships and using violence as a matter of course. Zhaken hurries toward the city together with countless others who seem to expect a huge feast but end up finding trivial consumerism at an eerie vanity fair. In this new world, people "consume" each other in crude utilitarian ways, whether it is husbands and wives, mothers and daughters, or friends and colleagues. Soviet society is still in place, albeit in name only. It has left no visible traces, except monstrous administrative buildings such as the "Council of Ministers," where one of the flaky characters relentlessly pursues his career.

In a manner distinct from the other members of the Kazakh New Wave, Karpykov developed a "cinema of the absurd" in which the fast-paced plot is pushed ahead by coincidences. Only occasionally do dialogues provide insights into the characters' background, as when the flirtatious wife of the government official screams at him about his indebtedness to her.

*A Little Fish in Love* describes Kazakhstan as a country in disarray. The disappearance of rules forces people to constantly improvise. Violence, including gun violence and rape, is experienced as normal, a casual occurrence that nobody takes too seriously. Karpykov made a post-Soviet film in a Soviet setting, with an attitude of ironic and blasé superiority toward Kazakh-Soviet reality, ignoring the usual moralizing that dominated perestroika discourses at the time. The film's characters have set down the baggage of the past and rush into the future both blindly and confidently, just as the musician and his African buddy inadvertently destroy the inherited Soviet car "Pobeda" (victory): their regret about the loss lasts for a minute at most. The characters' optimism is mindless and borderline psychotic; they act on impulses and little else. The film ends on the statement "Now we are going to live like real human beings." Truly an absurd conclusion.

Karpykov derives aesthetic pleasure from chaos. Conspicuously, there is one motif that can be traced throughout and provides structure: the power of women. Zhaken obsessively follows various females, although he never manages to get really close to any of them; as a matter of fact, the government official's wife, who finds Zhaken interesting, later denies knowing him at all. Zhaken's attraction to women is restricted to the purely physical, culminating in a scene at a pool in which a large group of female swimmers rehearse water ballet, with only their legs showing above the surface. Zhaken is not alone in his sexual helplessness: all men in *A Little Fish in Love* fail to establish meaningful relationships, and the women they are attracted to remain elusive.

Aesthetically, Karpykov aimed at transcending Soviet cinematic norms at a time when they were still in place. Karpykov's main instruments for achieving aesthetic sovereignty are irony and sarcasm, and he applies them with cruel coldness. Of course, the film's playfulness is amusing, beginning with the prologue, which uses select features of silent cinema: the barking of a dog is the only sound, while human utterances are conveyed through intertitles. *A Little Fish in Love* is a completely unpredictable film. Since it has deliberately abandoned the traditional paradigm of story-telling (including the stereotypical narratives about the alienation between country and city) it is never clear what turn the events will take in the next moment and how the characters will react to them. This unpredictability also reflects the inner freedom that Karpykov and other young Kazakh filmmakers had achieved before external freedom was granted to them.

## *July. Kairat*

Darezhan Omirbaev is often listed among the members of the Kazakh New Wave. However, he distanced himself from that group very early on. After a year of studying in Solov'ev's masterclass at VGIK, Omirbaev, a mathematician by training, realized that this was not the kind of cinema he had in mind and began to search for cinematic approaches more in tune with his sensitivities. Ever since, Omirbaev's oeuvre has been a standalone phenomenon.

*July* (Shilde, 1988), a 23-minute study of stasis and motion, causality and coincidence, signaled the emergence of a new kind of cinematic language in Kazakhstani film. No longer does the plot dictate narrative speed, imagery, and selective sound; instead, the plot itself is born out of a flow of images and sounds that maintain their primacy until the film's end. *July* is the story of a chance encounter that fails to lead to a successful connection. Images of the family of an officer on a train moving across the vast steppe are cross-cut with images of a young boy and his buddy who are selling two stolen melons at a railway station. When the train stops, the officer takes the melons and returns to his compartment to fetch money, but the door is locked from the outside and he cannot exit on his own. The boys wait in vain for their three rubles, which they needed to go to the movies.

The anecdotal incident can be interpreted on a symbolic level as a failed encounter between countryside and city, in which the latter abuses the former, although without malicious intent. It can also be read as a psychological sketch about a boy and his discovery of the adult world, which has the power to give or withhold. These and other aspects are significant for the film, but they are not what makes it exceptional. For Omirbaev, capturing the changing atmosphere in the sleepy, half-empty, slow-moving *aul* is the real focus, as is the perception of the boy: his fascination with an Indian movie, his attraction to a girl sitting next to him whose bare arm he touches, and his daydream about playing the piano in a concert when a horse suddenly walks on stage. *July* captures the world of a Kazakh *aul* in high summer, the sensual awakening of its main character, and the paradoxes of destiny, which often remain hidden to the protagonists involved. The alternation between objective and subjective reality, motion and motionlessness, darkness and light, and small restrained spaces (the train compartment, a bedroom) and the wide steppe express the film's exploration of inner causality. At any given point, the viewer is allowed to know more than the protagonists do, yet the film does not generalize, let alone verbalize, this advanced knowledge. The acceptance of life, both in the way that it unfolds "naturally" and in the way that it is perceived and conceptualized by the human beings involved, defines the magic of Omirbaev's cinema. Film is a means to establish a relationship with the world. To Omirbaev, this relationship is observational rather than proactive, tactful and nonintrusive rather than analytical, and visual rather than verbal. It indicates humility both toward life and toward the artistic medium.

Nobody had ever made a film like *July* in Kazakhstan before. Its artistry oriented it away from mass audiences and toward a sophisticated cineaste community that hardly existed in the country. Thus, it is not surprising that Darezhan Omirbaev became a household name on the international festival circuit but remains little known in his homeland. This is regrettable in that his films do not require viewers to have any specialist knowledge; indeed, they are not deliberately opaque. Omirbaev's full-length feature debut proves that: it is a masterpiece that remained inaccessible to regular viewers not because of any intrinsic complexity but due to viewers' general consumerist expectations vis-à-vis cinema, which had developed in the late Soviet period.

In a similar vein to *July*, *Kairat* (1991) deals with transitions from one sphere to another, defining borderlines and connections between them. The constellation in the first episode of *Kairat* resembles *July*: a boy in an *aul* is drawing a line on a white wall, while a young man is sitting in a compartment of a train that is moving toward the city. The boy is engulfed in the endless, motionless steppe, while the same steppe moves by fast in the window of the rushing train. A connection between the two is suddenly established: the boy picks up a stone and throws it at the train; it hits the window of the young man's compartment, cracking it; the young man freezes in shock.

Then, following the credits, *Kairat* embarks on a more conventional narrative. The young title hero is kicked out of an entrance exam because he naïvely passes a cheating note to a female applicant. He then passes a driver's exam; in a movie theater, where he watches an old German picture, he approaches a girl named Indira and begins a relationship with her; in his dorm, where he shares a room with two other guys, Kairat is threatened by a notorious aggressor; he realizes that Indira is cheating on him with another man; he provokes a fight with the dorm aggressor in which he is seriously injured; back in the dorm room, night is seen through the window as snow falls outside.

The synopsis of external events that *Kairat* depicts may indicate that the film is an episodic, impressionist portrait of a young man, a newcomer to a contemporary city. Indeed, the title character defines the film's center, although not exclusively, as there are other points of gravity. Thus, Kairat is unaware of the little country boy who threw the stone at his train and therefore of the reason for this potentially catastrophic event, the origins of which only the viewer witnesses. The viewer also knows about Indira's unfaithfulness before Kairat does. At the same time, neither the viewer nor Kairat can see the reasons for the dorm aggressor's attacks: the young man's ultraviolent demeanor remains unexplained, just like the boy's act of aggression against the train and its passengers at the beginning. Omirbaev does not attempt a social or psychological explanation of aggression and violence. However, he does hint at the presence of male rituals, which include aggressive acts and individual or collective defense against them. Regarding its main protagonist, *Kairat* tells the story of a rite of passage, which includes his integration into the community of a big city, as well as his establishment of a firm masculine identity by systematically looking for female companionship and self-assertion as a man who can physically defend his honor.

A particularly fascinating aspect of *Kairat* are the transitions from "real" to "virtual" reality. These transitions can have a disturbing effect, since they are not clearly marked. The first instance is when Kairat sits in the driver's seat of a training bus with a screen in front of him suggesting a virtual street, and the viewer shares his subjective point of view. A similar thing happens when the film that Kairat watches in the movie theater becomes indistinguishable from reality; we only realize later that this has occurred when he is talking to a friend about the jealousy drama and identifies deeply with the murderer. In these instances, the virtual world becomes reality for the main character and, at least temporarily, for the viewer as well.

*Kairat* offers a complexity of associations that can prove highly enriching to an open-minded spectator. It further develops the poetics of *July*, adding social and psychological concreteness while remaining true to the basic assumptions of Omirbaev's debut. Omirbaev's stylistic consistency, including the casting of nonprofessional performers who appear under their own names, leaves no doubt as to the exceptional artistic willpower at work in both films. With Omirbaev, Kazakhstani cinema acquired an auteur in the truest sense of the word.

## *The Homewrecker*

Amir Karakulov's *The Homewrecker* (Razluchnitsa, 1991), a darkly realistic jealousy drama, is also a parable revealing a fundamentally apolitical (or rather *transpolitical*) worldview. While it is certainly among the most original Kazakhstani films of the late Soviet period, no visible markers of the sociopolitical context are discernible. A triangle story of elementary power, *The Homewrecker* describes the love of two brothers for the same woman, which ends in her violent death. The brothers, Adil (Adil Turkbenbaev) and Rustem (Rustem Turkbenbaev), are young and display a strong male ego. Rustem dominates Adil, constantly forcing him to do things in this or that manner. Since they are the only members of the household (a circumstance that remains unexplained), there are no correctives to their peculiar relationship of domination and imitation. Rustem invites his girlfriend Elya (Dana Kairbekova) to move in with them, although it later turns out that he clearly foresaw Elya's attempts to initiate an affair with his brother during his own absence.

Even more intriguing than the story itself is the atmosphere evoked and maintained by *The Homewrecker* throughout. Inside the brothers' house, the light is dim; some scenes take place in near-darkness. This corresponds to the enigmatic nature of the triangle relationship, on which the sparse dialogues shed little light, since the brothers and the girl they pursue hardly ever verbalize their feelings. Instead, Adil and Rustem stare at each other for minutes under water in a pool or confront each other violently, making threats with a knife. The film's narrative rhythm is slow, supported by a free-jazz-inspired score, but under this relaxed surface lurk explosive passions.

*The Homewrecker* is, first and foremost, a two-faceted love story: about the love between men and women, and about the love between siblings. The violent removal of the one person who disturbs the peace in the brothers' home seems to happen with the quiet approval of both Adil and Rustem. This gives the story, which for two-thirds of the film resembles a late 1950s' French nouvelle vague picture, an unexpected edge. Even the title appears in a paradoxical light: normally, the word "*razluchnitsa*" refers to a woman who is loved by a married man who then leaves his wife and family to be with her (thus the English translation "homewrecker.") But the young woman in Karakulov's film threatens a home by trying to destroy the close relationship between two siblings. For the viewer, it is impossible to grasp the emotional depth of the brothers, since both habitually hide all emotions behind a stone-faced exterior; as a matter of fact, in several scenes Adil's face is made to look like an ancient bronze mask. For the audience, a highly level of focus is vital due to the irrelevance of dialogues and the importance of minutiae: if the viewer misses even a small detail, an essential element of the story may go missing as well.

In the two opening episodes, Rustem teaches Adil rhythmic movements. They are in the middle of nowhere, an unspecified wilderness, and their movements are accompanied by a drumbeat. Then, Rustem teaches his brother an exotic-sounding song, obviously pointing to some deep-seated urge. The complex chemistry between family bond and erotic passion, between kin loyalty and sexual drive, is presented as a clash of two elementary powers: Elya was playing with fire without realizing it.

*The Homewrecker*'s score brings together three types of music: exotic drums, opera arias (particularly Bellini, sung by Maria Callas), and Free Jazz (mostly trumpet and saxophone), i.e., a primordial, a classical, and a modern dimension. A similar combination would be featured in Ermek Shinarbaev's *Spot on a Grey Tripod* just a few years later; classical music, meanwhile, would play an even more essential role in Karakulov's own *Don't Cry* (2002). The blend of such different tunes signifies the quasi-eternal validity of the conflict: since the relationships are so elementary the story could take place anywhere.

In *The Homewrecker*, society as such is absent. The few encounters with outside people (an Afghan war veteran and two young men who provoke Adil to a fistfight) are inconsequential. This emphasis on the individual, who is mainly driven by primordial passions, signals a new view of human nature, one that is less determined by social or ethnic factors than by archetypes.

Karakulov created a masterpiece with an underlying anthropological focus, an unprecedented experiment in Kazakhstani cinema.

## The Revenge

The perestroika processes that had begun in the mid-1980s made it easier for both sociopolitical taboo-breakers and more aesthetically refined pictures with limited mass appeal to get funding and ensure at least minimal distribution: the film industry's losses and profits evened each other out on a national scale. Thus, Kazakhfilm studio could risk the production of a large-scale epic with a foreseeably minimal financial return. The project was entrusted to Ermek Shinarbaev, a director who has always maintained an aesthetic position of his own. Shinarbaev continued his collaboration with Korean-Russian writer Anatolii Kim; their first two pictures, *My Sister, Liusia* and *Exiting the Forest and Entering a Meadow*, were considerable critical successes, albeit limited to the arthouse circuit. Their third joint project, *The Revenge* (Mest', 1989, aka *The Red Flute*), was arguably the most ambitious.

The prose of Anatolii Kim gained prominence among Russian readers in the late 1970s and found growing international appreciation in the 1980s. Kim was born into a Korean family exiled to Kazakhstan in 1939. His childhood was overshadowed by the hardships associated with the Korean minority's forced resettlement from Sakhalin, which resulted in thousands of deaths from starvation and disease. Many Koreans felt deep gratitude to Kazakhstan, which had given them shelter amid rampant state terror. Kim's early prose artfully transcended the crudeness of historical reality, enchanting the reader by weaving into narratives a tenderly magical symbolism that imbued the most ordinary phenomena with mysteriousness and spiritual depth. As Eastern philosophy attracted more and more Soviet intellectuals, Kim's short stories and novellas satisfied a widespread need for meaning, especially with respect to individual life, that could compensate for the waning hollow formulas of socialist materialism.

In the early 1980s, Kim found a congenial partner in budding director Ermek Shinarbaev, who admired his prose and was sufficiently flexible to allow the text to determine the adaptations' narrative framework, being unafraid to directly transfer literary devices to the cinematic fabric. Kim was so pleased with the results of their work together that he entrusted the young filmmaker with ever more daring projects. *The Revenge* was their third and last film, completed before the breakdown of the moribund Soviet system. The screenplay, written by Kim himself, is based on the short story "The Revenge" but also contains motifs from other stories, among them "The Bride of the Sea." Thus, it is not accurate to view the film as a literary adaptation in the conventional sense. Rather, *The Revenge* is the product of an ongoing dialogue between literary texts and the medium of cinema, or, in a wider sense, between the literary and the cinematic imagination. *The Revenge* can justifiably be regarded as Kim's and Shinarbaev's joint crowning achievement.

The film consists of seven novellas, a prologue, and an epilogue. The central plot is relatively simple. The teacher Yan, enraged by his eviction from the house of the farmer Tsay, punishes his host's little daughter in class and, losing his mind, kills her. Tsay swears revenge and pursues Yan, who flees to China. When the pursuit fails, Tsay conceives a son with a mute young woman with the sole purpose of having someone to carry out revenge when he himself no longer can. After years of searching, this son, Sungu, finds Yan's wife, who reveals to him that the perpetrator died just a short while ago.

The main plotline is enriched by several subordinate narratives. The film opens with the image of a turtle crawling through deep grass toward the sea from whence she came. A Korean ruler, surrounded by members of his court, ponders the turtle's life and its direction; he then orders the commander of his guard to educate the crown prince with the aim of turning him into a fearless warrior. In the process, the crown prince becomes increasingly harsh and ultimately loses his closest friend, a poet. . . . The prologue signals that the subsequent story is a parable, even though an intertitle informed the viewer of the year: 1915. But it is obvious from the prologue's philosophical scope that the concrete historical time must be correlated with a higher level of meaning that transcends time. The story thus acquires a significance far beyond the horrific crime of infanticide committed by a mentally unstable and morally reprehensible man. Rather, it suggests that the issue at stake is the question of how such unspeakable act is possible in the first place. How can such evil go unpunished? Tsay's entire life is redefined by the crime and, from that point onwards, devoted to rectifying the fatal transgression, to bring justice to the perpetrator and thus *reinstate universal order*.

The fact that Yan, who comes across as both a coward and a cynical braggart, manages to escape justice, is deeply frustrating to the victim's father and to the viewer. However, the humble woman who helps Yan escape justice, despite herself being a victim of his endless drunken harassment, seems to possess a mystical understanding of what lies beneath the seeming breakdown of universal order. She is the one who in the end heals Tsay's son, Sungu, and accepts a violent death in an accident, a death that she foresaw.

*The Revenge* suggests the presence of an existential dimension beyond the visible but refrains from expanding on this concept or formulating an entire philosophy of justice. The film's main characters are driven by the search for meaning assigned to their lives, which becomes tormenting as soon as evil intrudes on their ordinary existence and causes chaos. It also suggests that, while human beings have no choice but to look for meaning and justice, the dimension where true meaning and justice can be found is inaccessible to them. Search they must, but the ultimate findings are far from what they expected or were able to fathom. Not just violent evil, but regular human interference turns people away from their original mission. Such is the case of the ruler in the prologue, who wants his sensitive son to be transformed into a merciless warrior, or of old Tsay, who wants his son, Sungu, to carry out revenge, even though he was born to be a poet. The assumption of an underlying order that makes the turtle wander toward the sea and the victims of evil seek justice is metaphysical, as is the belief that the grand design will always ensure the victory of justice in the end, albeit in ways unknowable to the participants in this process.

To be sure, *The Revenge* is not a film that proposes a fully fleshed-out worldview. It is, first and foremost, a work of poetic notions, subtlety, and enigma. Its concepts and conclusions are part of the aesthetic design, not a philosophical or religious construct. The epilogue, in particular, demonstrates that the film in its entirety cannot be condensed into one parable, although it does contain parabolic substructures that suggest otherwise. One example is a scene at the end when two aged women gathering seaweed talk about the burden of life. Suddenly, one of them, known as "Bride of the Sea," decides to free herself from it all; she throws her heavy burden back into the waves, and walks away. This decision to unburden herself of destiny and duty when the weight of life becomes too heavy is a curious ending for a film whose internal discourse deals with the individual's mission and the higher obligations derived from it. Freedom of choice is granted to all human beings: a liberating conclusion.

Most importantly, and poetic beauty notwithstanding, *The Revenge* establishes a rare balance between the literary and the cinematic text in which the former is given an unusual power. Several direct quotes grant the original text conceptual authority, making it, to a certain extent, an explanation to the viewer. This device harks back to silent cinema when explanatory intertitles were an essential part of any film. It is also an acknowledgment of this picture's unique status, its exceptionality in the context of Soviet, and global, mainstream cinema.

On the one hand, the makers of *The Revenge* were lucky that such a picture could be produced in the first place, with generous state funding enabling Shinarbaev to deliver lavish arthouse without any visible constraints regarding sets, costumes, and talent. On the other hand, the malaise that had befallen the Soviet film industry made a commercially efficient release impossible. A film with this level of sophistication stood no chance in terms of box office returns. But was it conceptually relevant for its time? Given the severe turbulences in which Soviet society, including Kazakhstan, found itself, was *The Revenge* not the product of aesthetic narcissism? Was the film not essentially escapist? A closer look at the historical context from which it emerged demonstrates that its central issues were intimately related to its time.

Perestroika and glasnost had enabled Soviet society to take a disillusioned look at its own past and present. The issue of justice for the countless systemic and individual transgressions over the past seven decades was essential to society's process of coming to terms with itself: its moral self-cleansing. But how could Soviet society, which during the serious moral discourses of perestroika had just acquired a new awareness of massive transgressions, deal with the subject of evil, in both spiritual and legal terms? One of the widely debated responses was Christian in nature: forgiveness and mercy (*miloserdie*) became key terms in public discourses even in Communist Party publications, signifying an approach that would allow for both truth-seeking and closure, thereby preventing society from becoming entangled in a cold civil war. Kim and Shinarbaev's response to the question of guilt and redemption originated in a culture profoundly different from the Soviet one. In *The Revenge*, universal design and human intentions are connected in a way that defies Western rational approaches. This is the justification for a mysterious intertitle that follows the prologue: "200 years before Gutenberg, book printing existed in Korea." The statement relativizes Western unilateralism and Eurocentrism, pointing to a kind of knowledge whose depth is yet to be discovered. The main plotline dealing with guilt and redemption is humane, yet also profoundly different from notions such as universal forgiveness.

In 1991, *The Revenge* was shown at the Cannes film festival in the "Un Certain Regard" section; thereafter, it was virtually forgotten. Inadvertently, the attitude of humility and patience expressed in the film found a stunning confirmation in its own destiny: twenty years after its barely noticed release, *The Revenge* received new international recognition when it was restored by the World Cinema Foundation and later included in the prestigious Criterion Collection as part of Martin Scorsese's *World Cinema Project*. It is the first and, so far, only Kazakhstani picture to be honored in this manner.

## *The Death of Otrar*

The production of *The Death of Otrar* in 1989–1991 represented an unprecedented challenge for the Kazakhstani film industry. At a time when the euphoria around perestroika reform was waning and the economic consequences of the impending self-abolition of the communist system were beginning to emerge, this two-part historical epic required logistical sophistication on a scale incomparable to Kazakhfilm's earlier projects, with the exception of *Kyz-Zhibek*. As if the risks of such a super-production were not great enough, this was the first major project of its director, Ardak Amirkulov, who had just graduated from VGIK as a member of Sergei Solov'ev's masterclass. To be sure, the final years of the Soviet Union created many opportunities for entrepreneurial minds that were unimaginable just a few years prior, and Kazakhstani cinema was no exception. But would the lessons learned in Moscow prove to be applicable to a large-scale studio production in Almaty?

In the context of general disorientation and societal turbulence, Kazakhfilm studio was willing to take the risk, first and foremost because this project promised a much-needed gain in prestige. Based on a screenplay by Russian maverick filmmaker Aleksei German and his wife, Svetlana Karmalita, *The Death of Otrar* explored unchartered territory in almost every respect. Most importantly, it offered a new, non-Marxist approach to Kazakhstan's history, looking far beyond the twentieth century and the Marxist-Leninist modernization framework. With respect both to practical realization and conceptual daring, the dangers were considerable. But so, too, were the potential spoils: if rendered in a persuasive manner, the underlying historical-philosophical concept could become the foundation for a new understanding of the nation's past at a time when it was experiencing a growing desire for independence. The historical constellation for Amirkulov's uniquely ambitious project could not have been more advantageous.

Otrar was once a wealthy urban center located in an oasis in Southern Kazakhstan, part of the empire of Khorezm (Khwarezm) along the Silk Road. In 1218, Genghis Khan sent a caravan of 450 merchants to Otrar. The motives of the Mongols are not entirely clear. According to the film, the delegation had the task of clandestinely mapping the city, figuring out the strenghts of its fortifications, and preparing an invasion. Kairkhan (other spelling: Ghayir-Khan), the city's governor, followed the instructions of the Shah of Khorezm, Muhammad II, and ordered the arrest of the merchants-cum-spies. Genghis Khan reacted with outrage, demanding that those responsible for the assault be held responsible, which Muhammad proudly refused to do. The refusal was used as the pretext for war: the Mongolian ruler sent an army to Otrar and began a siege that lasted five months. He also attacked other cities, all of which were unprepared for the massive onslaught. Eventually, Genghis Khan brought the entire empire of Khorezm to its knees.

The story of the catastrophe that befell the blossoming Khorezm Empire in the thirteenth century had previously been told in popular form by the eminent Russian author V. Ian (real name Vasilii Ianchevitskii, 1874–1954) in a trilogy that was rich in facts and conceptualized in accordance with Soviet-Russian mainstream historiography. However, there was an undeniable anti-Mongolian strain in that officially approved narrative, derived from the Russian Orthodox point of view: Ian described a decadent Khorezm being destroyed by savage Mongols. Aleksei German and Svetlana Karmalita chose a different conceptual focus for their screenplay. Completely ignoring the juxtaposition of Russian Orthodox civilization with Mongolian "barbaric" expansionism as described by Ian, they aimed for a kind of historical generalization that focused on the mechanism of empires collapsing, a process for which the blind arrogance of the ruling elites is of crucial importance. In *The Death of Otrar*, Khorezm signifies the hubris of a brutal superpower that mercilessly oppresses its own population, challenges its neighbors, and arrogantly ignores any sign of impending doom.

To establish a contrast with the reckless self-confidence of Khorezm's hegemon, the screenplay introduces a fictitious character by the name of Unzhu. He is the film's lead character, one of the few men who fully understand the empire's precarious situation. At the beginning, Unzhu returns from a secret assignment that took him to Mongolia, where he rose from slave to unit commander in charge of one thousand warriors. For seven years, Unzhu had studied the peculiarities of the Mongol nomadic civilization, reaching the conclusion that if Khorezm wanted to survive the inevitable Mongolian aggression, it had to mobilize all its resources. However, Unzhu's testimony is not taken seriously at Muhammad's court. At best, the ruler and his influential mother use the messenger of doom for their own petty schemes; at worst, they consider simply executing him. But under no circumstances will they listen to his advice.

*The Death of Otrar* is a cinematic epic about the laws of geopolitics and the inability of any individual, even the strongest and most intelligent, to prevent the downfall of a civilization. The Mongols are shown to be clever and quietly persistent; their endurance will overcome all walls and constructions erected by other civilizations, no matter how sophisticated. The fact that the more advanced civilization of Khorezm underestimates the Mongols is to the latter's advantage. Empires die and disappear, the film demonstrates, without understanding the factors causing their demise. Warnings are useless because the politicians in charge of protecting the empire are narcissists hypnotized by grandiose images of their own might and entangled in petty internal and external schemes. The politicians of Khorezm are convinced that the greatest danger is their rival, Baghdad, failing to see that doom is coming from the opposite direction and in plain sight. The administrative officials are unteachable by definition, which renders anyone who points to the danger a lone voice in the wilderness.

What is specifically Kazakh about this film, apart from the fact that some historians view Otrar as the "cradle of Kazakh civilization"? Arguably, the most intriguing accomplishment of *The Death of Otrar* as a narrative is not its historical concept and parabolic meaning, but the character of Unzhu. Dokhdurbek Kydyraliev's performance, displaying fearless virility and dangerous impenetrability, creates a character who is closely related to

Suimenkul Chokmorov's enigmatic fighters of the 1970s–1980s. Amirkulov's film allowed Kydyraliev to deepen that outstanding actor's warrior image, creating an archetype of Kipchak-Kazakh manly endurance. Making sense of his actions is a constant challenge, since Unzhu's face is mostly a mask and he chooses to stay alone, never opening himself up to anybody. The viewer is thus left unable to guess what this errant warrior is going to do next and what exactly motivates him.

This samurai-like Kipchak is fiercely intelligent and strong-willed, yet also surprisingly rational and humane, which becomes a source of conflict since the surrounding Khorezm civilization lacks any humane notions as such. Thus, at the beginning, guards point to slowly dying victims of the shah's wrath, their bodies hanging in the sun and eaten alive by flies. When Unzhu sees this, he first pours water onto one of those martyrs and later stabs him to end his torments. For this act of mercy, Unzhu is beaten unconscious . . . Only rarely is his intellectual and spiritual superiority shown directly. In one episode, he sits, completely nude like primordial man, at a lake and ponders that this is how Allah must have created the world: as a natural paradise without weapons. At the same time Unzhu, a warrior-cum-thinker capable of profound reflection, calls himself "Allah's Arrow," maintaining an inner sense of self-worth even in moments of complete outward subjugation.

Of all the characters in the picture, Unzhu is the only one to *see* what is coming, while his environment is blind to its own impending demise. Eyesight and blindness are recurring motifs. There are several references to weakening eyesight, one of them in respect to Muhammad's mother, who saves Unzhu's life with the purpose of using him for her shady schemes. When Unzhu tells her that the Chinese have invented crystals that help people to see better, she replies that nobody is allowed to even discuss her eyes except she herself. The film's gruesome finale also refers to eyesight: after Otrar's ruler, Kairkhan, is captured, following another month of resistance, the Mongols pour melted silver into his eyes and ears, carrying out an execution with a symbolic dimension that serves as a punishment for his previous figurative blindness and deafness in the face of repeated warnings. It is Genghis Khan himself who orders this didactic method of killing and tells the executioners not to be stingy with the silver.

The episode in which the legendary Mongolian ruler (portrayed by Bolot Beishenaliev[31] in one of his last roles) appears in person shows him to be an extraordinary despot whose overarching goal is to conquer the universe. In their screenplay, German and Karmalita conceived Genghis Khan in a manner akin to a twentieth-century despot. He is meant to resemble Iosif Stalin, from the yellow color of his eyes to his detailed instruction of how to treat enemy rulers to his keen interest in the secrets of longevity.[32] *The Death of Otrar* thus culminates with a vision of a new type of despot whose skills allow him to defeat and replace the more sophisticated elites of Khorezm and all culturally superior but decadent empires.

Amirkulov's direction is aesthetically surefooted, betraying an awareness of the great historical epics of world cinema. As with other members of the Kazakh New Wave, his primary target audience was cineastes and intellectuals, not fans of period adventure, even though the film's historical framework and the nature of the main character would have provided plenty of opportunities to create an exciting blockbuster. Instead, Amirkulov carefully avoids showing breathtaking stunts, exotic colors, and erotically charged love intrigues. Authenticity and accuracy are of primary importance, systematically eliminating any kind of modern romantic projections and commercial speculation. Recognizable allusions to world cinema range from shady court schemes unfolding in claustrophobic interiors in Eizenshtein's *Ivan the Terrible* to bleak rainy exteriors in Fritz Lang's second part of *Die Nibelungen*, the metaphysics of Kurosawa's early medieval parables, and the hopelessness of the dark ages in Tarkovskii's *Andrei Rublev*. The geopolitical catastrophes of yester-year are not recreated in architectural splendor and shining costumes; they unfold in dark tunnels, mud, poverty, ignorance, and humiliation. The images have brownish and grayish tones; at times, it is hard to tell whether a scene was shot in black-and-white or in color. Thus, stylistically Amirkulov's film also follows the direction defined by the classics of world cinema, for whom the genre of historical film was a pretext for exploring the human condition per se.

*The Death of Otrar* exudes a type of universal historical pessimism regarding humanity's prospects that is characteristic of screenwriter Aleksei German's own directorial oeuvre. However, such pessimism is not typical of Kazakhstani culture. Prior to Amirkulov's film, several Kazakh writers had dealt with the history of the mysterious city of Otrar, its disappearance and later reemergence. Their depiction of the reasons for Otrar's demise differ from Amirkulov's concept in significant ways. Most importantly, Otrar's destruction was interpreted as a national, proto-Kazakh tragedy that set the development of the emerging nation back centuries.

When Amirkulov's picture was released, it impressed international audiences. But it did not become an epochal cultural event whose celebration could unite the Kazakh nation by providing an illuminating and inspiring vision of its past and, implicitly, its future. The fact that a Kazakh director had made a film based on a screenplay by one of the most internationally recognized Russian-Soviet filmmakers could certainly be interpreted as a gain in prestige, especially for a studio whose reputation had suffered many blows since the mid-1970s. Given its aesthetic prowess, the film unsurprisingly did well on the festival circuit. It also won a 1992 State Prize of the now-independent Republic of Kazakhstan. But *The Death of Otrar*, certainly a masterpiece in its own right, was never a national favorite that would be warmly remembered and praised by generations of audiences, as its narrative is too involved and its cinematic style too self-consciously opaque.

The question of why Kazakhfilm studio, in a time of economic and political crisis, engaged in the production of such a costly epic goes to the very heart of Kazakhstan's situation at the end of its communist period and the beginning of its independence. The Soviet era had rendered the country a fully integrated, but also peripheral, exploited, and abused part of a multinational empire. When the Soviet empire's demise neared, the values guiding Kazakhstani society had to be revised. Which of them had outlived their day, and which were able to serve the nation in an uncertain future? Viewed in this context, *The Death of Otrar* can offer important insights.

First and foremost, it demonstrates that the nation and her culture are not identical with the state that hosts them. Empires come and go, but the nation can survive them, if she so chooses. Secondly, Amirkulov's picture encourages national self-reliance and self-orientation. Unzhu the *Kipchak* (conceptualized as the ancestor of modern Kazakhs) has a better grasp of geopolitical realities than the educated imperial establishment. In other words, the periphery can attain a deeper understanding of the empire's real situation than its center. Thirdly, the character of Unzhu is shown as the guarantor of survival: his strength lies in the depth and endurance of his personality, and, arguably, in his silence. Whenever he talks, he endangers himself and others; whenever he quietly follows his insights and instincts, he wins. Deliberate or not, this endorsement of Kazakh mentality is a positive message, regardless of the film's overall gloom and doom. But unlike films that established themselves over the years as key elements in the identity formation of Kazakhstan, *The Death of Otrar* did not achieve that popular status. As a matter of fact, none of Amirkulov's films did. While the philosophical significance of this epic for the nation in a time of disorientation, when Kazakhstan ceased to be part of a larger empire and began to build a state of its own, is beyond doubt, the messages addressing aspects of national survival are implicit. The viewer is forced to make a conscious effort to reach them. For that reason, Amirkulov's film did not and could not become a *foundational epic* with an assigned political-propagandistic role. As a tool for political officialdom, it is too aesthetically independent and irreverent. Its historical outlook is too grim and its message too ambivalent and enigmatic to inspire patriotic pride. Yet, despite the film's problems in finding a passionate native audience, *The Death of Otrar* proved the logistical and artistic capacities of Kazakhstani cinema, refuting pessimists and naysayers. Moreover, the proud individualism of its maker encouraged other Kazakh directors to dream big: no small achievement indeed! Amirkulov's appointment as the General Director of Kazakhfilm in 1992 was obviousy a consequence of the artistic and international festival success of *The Death of Otrar*. It remained to be seen if this success could also serve as a compass for the studio under the new free-market conditions in independent Kazakhstan.

## TOWARD A POSTSOVIET KAZAKH CINEMA

By the late 1980s and early 1990s, Kazakhstani filmmakers had won several prizes at international festivals. This was an unprecedented phenomenon. But the disintegration of the Soviet state and its socialist economy, including its nationwide noncommercial film industry and distribution system, made it difficult to capitalize on the unexpected success. One of the first responses of the state was to establish a state trust (*gosudarstvennyi kontsern*) "Kazakhkino." It addressed many pressing issues that came with independence. As the rights to all Kazakhstani films produced in the USSR belonged to the center, i.e., Goskino in Moscow, the new trust had to find a way to return them to Kazakhstan. Furthermore, the privatization of the film industry had led to the selling of signature movie theaters in the capital such as "Udarnik" and "Mir"; preventing any further loss of assets was vital. The trust planned to fund children's films and culturally valuable pictures, creating a counterweight to the cheap imports in genres such as thrillers and sexploitation that were flooding the country. Last but not least, the abysmal living conditions of Kazakh filmmakers (especially the young) had to be improved.[33]

Solov'ev's masterclass, which formally graduated in 1989 but had begun to make full-length features the year before, gave Kazakhstani cinema powerful impulses. It demonstratively separated itself from the Soviet-Kazakh tradition and arrived on the international festival scene with novel approaches. However, the euphoria did not last very long. Rashid Nugmanov followed the sensational success of *The Needle* with the uninspired *Wild East* (Dikii vostok, 1992), a postmodern absurdist thriller, after which he abandoned filmmaking altogether and focused on political activities and producing, splitting his activities between France, Russia, and Kazakhstan. Abai Karpykov's *He Who Is More Tender* (Tot, kto nezhnee, 1996), while stylistically more coherent than *The Wild East*, also shows a rapid loss of narrative energy. Following the entertaining comedy *Fara* (1999), Karpykov focused on television work. Aleksandr Baranov made a melancholic farewell film about the old Alma-Ata (*Shanghai*, 1996) and then moved to Moscow to direct indistinct television serials. The most consistently productive filmmakers of the Kazakh New Wave were Darezhan Omirbaev, who technically did not even belong to the group; Ardak Amirkulov; and Serik Aprymov.

What might explain the petering-out of a highly promising movement after just a few years of innovative work? Could it be that the disappearance of the stiff Soviet socio-cultural framework, from which the "Kazakh Wild Boys" had so beautifully liberated themselves, also took away a major source of productive friction? Was making films for festival audiences ultimately insufficient as a source of inspiration? Each individual case is different, of course. But it is noteworthy that, unlike the directors of the French New Wave of the 1950s–1960s (among them Truffaut, Chabrol, Godard, and Rivette, whose productivity remained undiminished for decades), the Kazakh New Wave directors of the late 1980s—early 1990s did not have such staying power.

The undeniable achievement of the Kazakh New Wave was that it brought the notion of auteur cinema to Kazakhstan. Conspicuously, it was not only the New Wave directors who discovered their "inner auteur": Ermek Shinarbaev did not belong to the group, nor did Talgat Temenov, although the latter was trained by Sergei Solov'ev. What united these directors was the fact that their films won prizes at national and international festivals but never recouped their costs. This did not bode well for the future of Kazakhstan's cinema as a cultural industry. In this context, the aptitude of several New Wave directors for business is paradoxical; after all, a few of them made a fortune after putting cinema to the side for a while or for good. In the new millennium, when the New Wave had become a phenomenon of film history, several of its directors agreed to make television series, few of which were distinguished by artistic ambition or originality. Arguably, the most noble part of these filmmakers' legacy, besides their early masterpieces, is their engagement in teaching: at one point or another, various New Wave members inspired budding directors at the Zhurgenov Academy of the Arts, preparing the ground for another reemergence of Kazakh cinema.

## NOTES

1. I prefer to call Karsakbaev's method in *My Name Is Kozha* an approach, not a formula, because each of the "brat" films is somewhat different and was not just mechanically repeated, except that it focuses on a boy's life.

2. One sign of continuity is the dynamic score composed by Nurgisa Tlendiev.

3. *A Wolf Cub Among Humans* was produced at Mosfilm studio. However, the critic Bauyrzhan Nogerbek insists on counting this film as Kazakh: "For me, Talgat Temenov's film was certainly created on the cultural backdrop of Kazakh cinema." (Nogerbek, Bauyrzhan Ramazanuly, *Kino Kazakhstana*. Almaty: Natsional'nyi prodiuserskii tsentr, 1998, p. 209).

4. Temenov, Talgat (b. 1954), Kazakh director and author.

5. Nogerbek views Temenov's film as being connected with earlier Kazakh children's films and even speculates that its inclusion in Mosfilm's production plan

was "the result of the recognition of the achievements of Kazakhstan's children's cinema and an expression of trust toward the Kazakh model of children's cinema." Cf. Nogerbek, *Kino Kazakhstana*, pp. 209–12. However, a close look at the parameters that characterized the films of Karsakbaev and Kasymbekov reveals that Temenov distances himself from their largely optimistic worldview. His film is revisionist in the creative sense of the term.

6. *Together* and *A Wolf Cub Among Humans*, just like *The Fierce One* and *The White Steamship*, are pictures about children, not for children. In such films, children symbolize purity and generational continuity.

7. Elena Ostrovskaia does not mention the Suleimenov connection at all, perhaps because the poet was considered an ally of the ousted Kazakhstani leader Kunaev. Cf. her review "Deti 'Broda'" in *Novyi fil'm*, 10/1988, p. 16.

8. Ostrovskaia devotes a large portion of her text to the nostalgic atmosphere which supposedly connected her own generation to that of her parents who lived through the 1950s. She uses the term "retro" for these kinds of film. Ostrovskaia. "Deti 'Broda'," p. 16.

9. Kalykbek Salykov (1954–1995) made only two feature films, *The Balcony* and *December Lovers* (Liubovniki dekabria, 1991); the latter deals with the tragic events in December 1986 in Almaty. For a sensitive assessment of Salykov's films cf. Nogerbek. *Na ekrane 'Kazakhfil'm,'"* pp. 67–68.

10. Bolat Omar (b. 1947) began to work as a driver at Kazakhfilm before being admitted to the department of screenwriting at the Soviet State Film School VGIK in 1967. He worked in documentary cinema and animation and made his first feature film, *The House Under the Moon*, in 1983.

11. The critic Kulshara Ainagulova gave an optimistic assessment of Kazakhfilm productions of the late 1980s, including *Higher than the Mountains*, *The Balcony*, *The Needle*, and complex philosophical films such as *Leaving the Forest and Entering the Meadow*. She pointed out that "the formerly forbidden topics now had become fashionable," indicating an element of opportunism as part of the national studio's strategies. However, the survey is overly cautious in defining the artistic innovations that differentiated them from the conventional mainstream of previous years. Cf. Ainagulova, K., "Chtoby ne rabotat' na polku." *Kazakhstanskaia pravda*, 14 April 1989.

12. V. Maricheva, "Takie vot igry," *Sovetskaia kul'tura*, 19 March 1988.

13. David Cook, *A History of Narrative Film*. Fourth edition. New York and London: W.W. Norton & Company, 2004, p. 715. Of the three photos illustrating the four-page section on Kazakhstani cinema, two are from *The Needle*.

14. Rashid Nugmanov's first film, the half-hour *Ya-Ha* (Ya-khkha, 1986), is an interesting portrait of the Leningrad rock music scene, featuring Konstantin Kinchev, Viktor Tsoi, and the legendary rock groups Alisa, Zoopark, and Kino. Stylistically, Nugmanov managed to evoke a gloominess supplemented by laid-back irony. That film is still of importance as a cultural document of the 1980s, capturing the atmosphere of semi-legal rock concerts, punk clothes, and unsightly back yards.

15. However, Hal Erickson wrote in his review that "*The Needle* has yet to receive the widespread U.S. release it deserves." Erickson, Hal, "The Needle (1989)." *The New York Times*, November 3, 2012.
16. Baranov, Aleksandr (b. 1955), Russian-Kazakhstani director.
17. Nogerbek, Bauyrzhan (1948–2017), Kazakh critic.
18. Pruner, "The New Wave in Kazakh Cinema," p. 799.
19. Ludmila Pruner wrote: "New Wave film directors make no attempt to lament a lost national cultural heritage nor do they try to resurrect traditions (. . .)." Cf. Pruner, "The New Wave in Kazakh Cinema," p. 795.
20. Quoted in Dönmez-Colin, "Kazakh 'new wave,'" p. 117.
21. Kalymbetov, Bolat (b. 1955), Kazakh actor and director.
22. *My Dear* was produced by Kazakhfilm studio for television.
23. Manabaev (Manabai), Damir (b. 1946), Kazakh director and screenwriter.
24. Aituarov, Amanzhol (b. 1957), Kazakh director.
25. The screenplay was authored by Aituarov and Baian Sarygulov.
26. Gulnara Abikeeva rightly pointed out that their contributions to the new Kazakhstani cinema have been undeservedly forgotten. Abikeeva, *Natsiostroitel'stvo v Kazakhstane*, p. 112.
27. Alimbaeva does not limit her assessment to the film's civic relevance but also points out its aesthetic refinement. See chapter 2 in K. Ainagulova, Alimbaeva, *Tendentsii razvitiia kinoiskusstva Kazakhstana*, p. 69.
28. Ermek Shinarbaev emphasized the creative achievements of Kazakhstani cinema that began in the mid-1980s. His brief article was polemically titled "We have no crisis" and stated that, what was being called "the Kazakh phenomenon," was an expression of the new opportunities used by the young generation of directors raised by Sergei Solov'ev. Cf. Sinarbaev, Ermek, "U nas net krizisa," *Sovetskaia kul'tura*, 9 June 1990.
29. Pruner, "The New Wave in Kazakh Cinema," p. 794.
30. Tarkovskii preferred Bach, of course; it would be interesting to explore this difference and its consequences for the aesthetics of particular pictures.
31. This is yet another link to Tarkovskii; it was young Beishenaliev who contributed an impressive performance as the Mongol khan conquering and looting the city of Vladimir in *Andrei Rublev*.
32. For educated viewers in 1991, such allusions were unmistakable, since the features of Stalin's personality had been discussed in the media with great intensity throughout perestroika.
33. S. Mustafina, "Blesk i nishcheta kazakhskogo kino," *Tselinogradskaia Pravda*, 14 March 1992.

# Conclusion

The cinema of Soviet Kazakhstan evolved in the context of communist cultural construction and regulation. The administrative model of Soviet cinema was profoundly centralist. Since cinema was considered an ideologically and economically significant part of the Soviet cultural sphere, the government regulated it directly, and the film administration networks were branches of the complex governmental hierarchy and its *nomenklatura*. The hierarchical relationship between center and periphery was a guiding and controlling one. What "Moscow" decided could not be overridden by a national republic; it was the law for the entire multinational film industry. This relationship was maintained until the end of the Soviet system, albeit with certain temporary modifications. The centralist model of cultural governance also implied constant personal interferences of the highest echelons of leadership in all matters concerning the film industry, ranging from the macro- to the micro-level. The simultaneity of numerous levels of decision-making and answerability rendered the administration of Soviet cinema clumsy, distrustful of individual creativity, and prone to political and personal schemes.

The centralist structures were reflected in the emerging film branches in the Soviet republics. The mentor-mentee relationships between the Moscow center and the national peripheries were indeed primarily *structural*, although their subjective perception was often *national* and *ethnic*. In other words, the many difficulties caused by the centralist system of administration were sometimes interpreted as the result of Russian domination of other ethnic groups in the USSR, even though their causality was organizational and managerial, not necessarily prejudicial. The undeniably advanced position of the film industry of the Russian Federation was another factor contributing to the long-term mentor-mentee relationship between central and national studios, including the cinema of Kazakhstan. This relationship was reinforced by the education of the creative personnel at the Soviet State Film School VGIK in Moscow, from which almost all filmmakers of the national cinemas graduated until the 1950s. The cinema of Kazakhstan had to struggle with centralist attitudes throughout its Soviet phase. Only during World War II did the relationship undergo an unexpected reversal.

Due to geographic and historical factors, Kazakhstan was sometimes treated as a nationally undefined territory, a wide-open space for socioeconomic construction, a tabula rasa without any obstacles for building a communist society as soon as the class enemy has been eliminated. Films taking place in Kazakhstan without the slightest reference to its national parameters were produced in Almaty in the 1930s–1980s. The question of how these narratives mesh with Kazakh tradition and cultural values was never even posed. The occasional inclusion of a few Kazakh elements served a mere apologetic function. The fact that to many Kazakhs Russian was a foreign language and their customs and costumes were different added an exotic color at best, but mainly painted them as in need of education, that is, learning better Russian. While this may have been an expression of the filmmakers' unconscious, quasi-colonial condescension, their negligent attitude was also fully in line with the communist establishment's goals, by which ethnic differences had to be deemphasized because they all would eventually dissolve in the communist melting pot. There was a whole series of Soviet feature films that use Kazakhstan as mere background with almost no national specifics: *Kazakhstan without Kazakhs*. No other Central Asian republic was treated that way by the Soviet center. This nonchalant attitude toward a country as a culturally and historically undefined space is in itself significant and worth pondering.

The inner workings of the studio during the Soviet decades are difficult to assess. Documents shedding light on the production process, decision-making, and Party meetings have yet to be unearthed.

In the late 1950s, within a relatively short time span, Kazakhstani cinema had acquired the ability to produce blockbuster comedies, historical epics, and biopics that could stand up to competition from other Soviet studios and even pursue pioneering aesthetic approaches. Such rapid development was nothing short of astonishing. The Soviet central cultural institutions would *de jure* maintain a mentor/mentee attitude in dealing with the rapidly growing filmmaking community in Kazakhstan, but the cultural periphery was de facto set to continue on its path toward national cinematic emancipation. Shaken Aimanov's strategy of actively engaging in a native film culture turned out to have been the right choice. The dynamically developing national cinema, which included both feature films and documentaries, became a factor within Kazakh culture that had to be taken seriously. However, Soviet critics at the center continued to view Kazakhstani films as works of *regional* importance, as products of a fledgling culture with little relevance for Soviet cinema as a whole, and even less international significance.

In the 1950s, Kazakhstani film comedies began building a relationship of trust with Kazakh audiences and establishing a positive reputation for Kazakhstani cinema with viewers throughout the Soviet Union. These comedies for the first time placed Kazakhstan on the map of Soviet cinema, bringing its people and culture to the attention of millions of viewers.

The early 1960s were marked by Kazakhstani cinema's continuing fast maturation. Shaken Aimanov as the country's first native filmmaker opened the door for younger talents such as Mazhit Begalin, Sultan Khodzhikov, and Abdulla Karsakbaev. Non-Kazakh directors, such as Aleksandr Karpov, found a new home at the quickly growing Kazakhfilm studio. An increasing number of performers became skilled screen actors and gained prominence as movie stars, including Farida Sharipova and Asanali Ashimov. Cinematographers such as Mikhail Aranyshev and Askhat Ashrapov brought visual brilliance to Kazakhstani pictures. These positive achievements were countered, however, by an increasing resistance of segments of Kazakhstan's political establishment against filmmakers' thematic daring, making it clear that addressing contemporary social problems would be met by repressive measures such as limited release and negative media campaigns. As a result, the second half of the 1960s shows a decrease in contemporary drama and a focus on history. During their relatively short careers, neither Shaken Aimanov nor Sultan-Akhmet Khodzhikov nor Mazhit Begalin were able to fully realize their artistic potential. But their oeuvres contain examples of artistic experimentation that justify considering these directors as emerging auteurs. The process of serious critical recognition of their best pictures would begin only after their passing, when Kazakhstan gained its national independence. In this sense, their time, too, would come.

A number of Kazakhstani films contain strong elements of imitation, as conventional and politically safe themes were transplanted from mainstream Russian-Soviet cinema to a Kazakhstani environment. The imitative approach was caused by political caution in the highest ranks of the cultural leadership, just as the thematic daring of other films often reflected reform-minded trends in Kazakhstan's establishment. There are indications that some factions in Kazakhstan's political leadership were opposed to convenient imitations and were instead interested in maintaining and developing a sense of national identity through cultural means and were willing to protect it against predictable accusations from Marxist-Leninist dogmatists and their internationalist agenda.

Since the founding of the Kazakh National Theater in Kzyl-Orda in January 1926, the national school of acting was the strongest supplier of authenticity and realism to the country's cinema. However, the leadership of the Kazakhstani film industry paid insufficient attention to this asset. The main problem was the virtual absence of stardom-building strategies within the national film administration and the lack of screenplays that would focus on popular actresses and actors. Arguably, only Shaken Aimanov fully understood what a unique treasure his best performers represented, especially in building a Kazakh national identity. Thus, he regularly cast certain actors and actresses, even if only in supporting roles, throughout his career.

The concept of the *Soviet homeland* conveyed in Aimanov's *Land of the Fathers* became a key element for the evolution of Kazakh cinema. Conspicuously, the film did not impact the latter's development primarily through audience response and positive remembrance (as was the case with *Our Dear Doctor*), but through the profound impression it left on other filmmakers and critics. From today's standpoint, the deep faith that guides the old Kazakh man appears even wiser and more in tune with the evolution of the nation than at the time of the film's making when the Soviet framework seemed eternal. *Land of the Fathers* is thus a visionary film that anticipates Kazakhstan's search for a viable national identity. It was insufficiently understood at the time because its approach to the theme of identity was dialectical and complex.

The peculiar triumph of *Kyz-Zhibek* demonstrated that there was a deep need for profoundly Kazakh pictures among Kazakhstani audiences. Never before had Kazakhstan been presented on screen with such lavishness. Never before had the nation had a chance to recognize the beauty of its traditional lifestyle and its enduring potential for the future with such undivided enthusiasm. Never before had the private and the national, the natural and the social, been brought into such perfect balance on Kazakh screens. Most importantly, Gabit Musrepov's screenplay and Sultan-Akhmet Khodzhikov's direction remained loyal to the spirit of the original legend and did not, as had often been the case in Soviet cinema, compromise the source by introducing the Marxist concept of class struggle as the root of all antagonism. Instead, the tragedy unfolds when the ethical principles of the ancestors are betrayed. This is what renders *Kyz-Zhibek* at once so authentically Kazakh and so hard for non-Kazakh audiences to appreciate. It made the film a powerful object of identification for native audiences, something no previous feature film had achieved to such an extent. The very fact that such a large-scale feature film with a distinctly non-Soviet message could be produced at all is astounding.

Aimanov's tragic passing on December 23, 1970, thrust the Kazakh film community into a state of shock. In the blink of an eye, it had lost its towering leadership figure whose authority and openness to artistic innovation had supplied the country's growing film industry with constructive energy as well as administrative and political protection. The subsequent development of Kazakhstan's cinema in the 1970s seemed to justify widespread fears: it was a period in which indistinct movies constituted the majority and outstanding films were few and far between. Most importantly, the political pressures on filmmakers grew substantially.

The most important fallout of the sudden loss of talent and authority in the early 1970s was the ever-solidifying primacy of bureaucrats over artists. The struggle between these two categories of professionals within the film industry had been visible from the early 1960s, when a campaign against Aimanov was unleashed. Back then, however, artistic arguments, as opposed to bureaucratic and ideological ones, still won the day. By the early 1970s, the balance of that constellation had shifted toward the bureaucrats. Moreover, in the early 1970s, an increasing bifurcation into highbrow and lowbrow segments of Soviet culture, especially in cinema, which was once declared to be the art of the masses, became apparent and was quietly accepted by most of the political establishments. Indeed, this segmentation became the basis for the repertoire of the major film studios. The underlying intention was to satisfy both the millions of viewers who expected movies to entertain and the minority of viewers who were looking for intellectual and aesthetic gratification. The ultimate goal of these and other cultural strategies was to stabilize society. This goal was largely achieved: Soviet cinema offered space for home-made comedy blockbusters and for highbrow productions that could be sent to festivals.

The cinema of Kazakhstan entered the 1970s in a state of conceptual undecidedness, hampering the evolution of a truly national film culture. As the major authoritative filmmakers were no longer present in the decision-making councils at Kazakhfilm, aesthetically and politically harmless fare began to dominate the studio output. The emphasis in the repertoire was on lightweight movies that appealed to specific strata of the viewership and did not up the ante ideologically. Most of them were rendered with sufficient professionalism but reeked of conflict avoidance and opportunism. Aesthetic innovation and daring were reprimanded. Many Kazakhstani filmmakers chose the safest route and simply continued thematic lines that had been discovered in the 1960s. Without Aimanov, Begalin, Khodzhikov, and Karpov, artistic originality was increasingly difficult to find. However, for a differentiated and fair assessment, it is important to go beyond such broad generalizations and provide a detailed evaluation of each genre and individual filmmaker.

Conspicuously, Kazakhstani cinema in the 1970s provided fertile ground for the exploration of genre variations. Children's films, sports dramas, and thrillers made a reasonable attempt to satisfy the need for genre fare in certain segments of viewership. Alas, ideological opportunism and aesthetic mediocrity began to blossom during that decade as well. To be sure, such generalizations are not based on the elitist criteria that were often applied by film critics, especially some writing in the Soviet center judging productions of the national peripheries. The evolution of distinct genres during that period, including inspirational sports dramas and thrillers, was a legitimate development. But at the same time, the number of outstanding pictures striving for the highest artistic quality shrank dramatically. This does not mean, however, that there were no masterpieces at all. A close look reveals that, despite the abundance of demoralizing control mechanisms and bureaucratic pressures, there was room for exceptional films. As long as artistically ambitious projects were politically safe, the administration of Kazakhfilm studio and the republic's *Goskino* were eager to promote them. Since some of the senior leading Kazakh directors were no longer active, it became common practice to invite directors from neighboring republics to helm artistic prestige projects; perhaps some in the studio administration feared that native directors would not be able to cope with the challenge.

Assessing Kazakhfilm's overall output in the 1970s and early 1980s, it is undeniable that the studio settled (voluntarily or under pressure) for a politically inconspicuous cinema that left less room for artistic ambition and was oriented toward an increasingly conformist society. The time of sociopolitical and aesthetic risk-taking was over. In hindsight, the 1970s thus appear as a period of enforced cultural stability dominated by non-antagonistic, mostly mediocre films. Unlike the 1960s, it was difficult for deep and original narratives to find approval, especially those that expressed essential national values. The shelving of seven full-length feature films within a few years was catastrophic for a national studio with limited production volume.

Reassessing the 1970s and early 1980s, it seems fair to conclude that even modest attempts to establish a feedback-based relationship between audiences and filmmakers were risky. While countless "gray films" managed to fly under the radar of official critics, the instincts of some studio administrators to produce at least some films that would respond to viewers' preferences were nipped in the bud in the name of politically and aesthetically "correct" approaches, regardless of embarrassing box office numbers. Instead, studios both at the Soviet center and on the peripheries were forced to produce formulaic, ideologically opportunistic fare. Tendencies of national self-exploration did continue but were monitored with enormous distrust. However, these years also had room for unconventional and even subversive approaches, continuing concepts that had begun in the 1960s and deploying concepts that went much farther than previous Easterns. That subgenre would prove its conceptual elasticity and depth in exploring national values one more time before concluding its evolution.

A major symptom of the impending crisis in Kazakhstani cinema was the loss of trust between filmmakers and audiences, a trust that had been established in the 1950s and 1960s but was squandered in the following decade. However, the evaporation of cultural trust was not unique to Kazakhstan. One of the signs that Soviet society was approaching breakdown was the growing alienation between the Soviet film industry and mass audiences. Still, the consequences for Kazakhstani cinema were particularly severe, as some of the films made at Kazakhfilm studio were much better than the studio's overall reputation. These films managed to capture reality to a surprising degree, indicating to anybody who was willing to see and listen that a deep crisis of Soviet-Kazakh society was imminent. Indeed, some of Kazakhstan's filmmakers sensed the profound unease spreading in society earlier than the republic's governing bodies. In hindsight, it is obvious that the harsh words that perestroika-era film critics hurled at Kazakhstani filmmakers were often based on a lack of awareness and unfair generalizations. Judging by the films that were released in the early 1980s, a fairer assessment would appreciate the *coexistence* of negative and positive trends within Kazakhstani cinema, as well as the ups and downs in individual careers such as Sharip Beisembaev's. Moreover, there were films produced at Kazakhfilm studio in the early 1980s that had distinct subversive potential, setting them apart from the status quo cinema that had emerged in the 1970s and continued to exert influence. The realization of thematically and artistically interesting films belies the claim that Kazakhstani cinema had nothing to offer prior to the arrival on the scene of the New Wave filmmakers at the end of the decade. The untimely passing of director Abdulla Karsakbaev came as another blow to the creative potential of Kazakh cinema. Had he lived just a few more years, Karsakbaev could have created a deep, genuinely realistic depiction of the catastrophic collectivization of the early 1930s, or captured, perhaps through the eyes of children, the extreme ups and downs of perestroika, which affected Kazakhstan's national evolution in a very peculiar way. Without him, the discontinuity in the evolution of Kazakhstani cinema became even more severe, similar to the negative effect of Shaken Aimanov's and Mazhit Begalin's premature passing.

The uncompromising official rejection of pseudo-commercial movies such as *The Secrets of Madam Wong* revealed a widening split between normative official film criticism and mass popularity. It indicated that the ideological standards that had held the socialist realist paradigm together for six decades, were increasingly difficult to sustain. Soviet cinema was no longer able to cope with the challenge of making films that met Soviet aesthetic requirements while simultaneously appealing to millions of viewers. On a larger scale, that split signaled the approaching end of communist society and its major cultural pillar, cinema. In the critical discourses, commercial imitations of Western genre fare became an embarrassment for the studio. Not only was this thematically non-Kazakh movie repeatedly cited as evidence of how low the artistic level of Kazakhstani cinema had sunk, but it also showed that the republic's film studio had lost any serious connection with quality-conscious native audiences and seemed unable to come up with nationally meaningful productions. Just as Kazakhstan's territory had been used for decades for all-Soviet economic campaigns and dangerous military tests, its national film studio was abused as a playground for dubious commercial exercises.

The aspect of reconstruction and renewal was a central trope of the perestroika spirit in Kazakh cinema. This constructive approach assumes that it is not communist society itself that should be blamed for corruption and injustice, but despicable attitudes such as greed. Once those habits are overcome, a new and better society can be created *within the existing Soviet paradigm*. Indeed, it was typical of the pathos of such films that, while demonstrating formerly taboo aspects of Soviet reality, analysis of the roots of the problem remained on the surface and the remedy for improvement was seen in the characters' individual moral views, not societal structures. However, the inconsolable melancholy and twilight atmosphere that were characteristic of Kazakhstani films about righteous loners and children of the mid- to late 1980s presaged the sad end of optimism about perestroika and, perhaps subconsciously, the inglorious end of the entire Soviet epoch.

During the perestroika years, from the mid- to late 1980s, the societal framework surrounding Kazakhstani cinema changed beyond recognition. Soviet values, which had been a major stabilizing factor in the self-reproduction of the socialist/communist order, were increasingly denounced by media discourses, and fewer and fewer people were willing to come to their defense and that of their underlying ideological platform. The growing lack of philosophical and moral consensus had an impact on the entire Soviet cinema: while some of its workers soldiered on in a traditional way, others tried out commercial or auteur modes. With the relaxation of censorship, by the mid-1980s genuine reality checks were possible in contemporary films. In the context of the loyalist and traditionalist films that were still offered to Soviet viewers, the raw images of unpresentable facts were even more disturbing. In the late 1980s, the emergence of auteur films intended for a limited circle of cognoscenti indicated the presence of a growing space for creative self-realization and social acceptance of self-conscious artistic strata whose legitimacy was no longer denounced and attacked by the communist ideological apparatus. Indeed, because the economic framework was still Soviet, that is, box office expectations were of negligible importance for production, the last years of perestroika were ideal for arthouse cinema that could satisfy elitist tastes and groups of critics who applauded the homegrown auteurs. "Box office" had not yet become a meaningful concept. It would emerge as the fundamental issue for the survival of the Kazakhstani film industry at the end of the Soviet-Kazakh epoch and thus, the end of Soviet-Kazakh cinema.

# Glossary

| | |
|---|---|
| *Adat* | System of laws |
| *Aitys* | Public poetry and song contest |
| *Aksakal* | Honored older man; clan elder |
| *Akyn* | Traveling singer and poet |
| *Aul* | Village |
| *Batyr* | Accomplished fighter; hero warrior |
| *Bay* | A wealthy man |
| *Bii* | Judge within the Adat system of laws |
| *Djigit* | Warrior |
| *Dzhungars* | A tribe in Western China |
| *Kalym* | Price paid to the family of the bride by the family of the groom |
| *Kishlak* | Village in Kazakhstan |
| *Kumys* | Refreshing alcoholic drink made from horse milk |
| *Kurgan* | Grave monument |
| *Madrasah* | Moslem secondary high school |
| *Sal* | Privileged traveling singers accompanied by an entourage |
| *Toi* | Kazakh wedding |
| *Uezd* | Administrative district |
| *Volost* | Administrative district, part of an *uezd* |

# Bibliography

Abdukarimova, L. "Nagrada – ulybka zritelia." *Novyi fil'm*, 16/1980, pp. 8–9.
Abdulakhatova, R.K. "K voprosu sozdaniia zhenskikh obrazov v kazakhskikh fil'makh." *Izvestiia Akademii nauk Kazakhskoi SSR*, seriia obshchestvennykh nauk, 1/1969, pp. 88–92.
Abdulakhatova, R.K. "Istoriko-biograficheskii fil'm 'Amangel'dy.'" *Izvestiia Akademii nauk Kazakhskoi SSR*, seriia obshchestvennykh nauk, 3/1973, pp. 23–27.
Abdysalimova, A. "Segodnia i zavtra kazakhstanskogo kino." *Kazakhstanskaia pravda*, 22 April 1992.
Abikeeva, G. "Belye piatna istorii..." *Novyi fil'm*, 9/1991, pp. 4–5.
Abikeeva, G. *Natsiostroitel'stvo v Kazakhstane i drugikh stranakh Tsentral'noi Azii i kak etot protsess otrazhaetsia v kinematografe*. Almaty: TSTSAK [Tsentr Tsentral'no-aziatskoi kinematografii], 2006.
Abikeyeva, Gulnara. *The Heart of the World: Films from Central Asia*. Almaty: Kazakhfilm National Company Shaken Aimanov, 2003.
Abyzov, V. "Zhizn' Kazakhstana na ekrane." *Kazakhstanskaia Pravda*, 15 January 1956.
Aimanov, Shaken. "Kak ia rabotal nad obrazom Dzhambula." *Sovetskii Kazakhstan*, 7/1953, p. 90.
Aimanov, Shaken. "Po vole partii." *Iskusstvo kino*, 9/1958a, p. 3.
Aimanov, Shaken. "Novye vozmozhnosti, novye zadachi." *Kazakhstanskaia pravda*, 19 June 1958b.
Aimanov, Shaken. "Glavnoe – sovremennost'." *Sovetskaia kul'tura*, 27 August 1959.
Aimanov, Shaken. "Obrashchaias' k druz'iam." *Iskusstvo kino*, 10/1965, pp. 17–19.
Aimanov, Shaken. "Tri rozhdeniia (Iz istorii kazakhskoi kinematografii)." *Novyi fil'm*, 1/1969, p. 5.
Ainagulova, K. "Kak sozdavalas', Belaia roza.'" *Kazakhstanskaia Pravda*, 13 April 1975.
Ainagulova, K. "Fol'klor i kino." *Vecherniaia Alma-Ata*, 24 June 1985.
Ainagulova, K. "Kulager v puti." *Kazakhstanskaia Pravda*, 4 February 1988.

Ainagulova, K. "Chtoby ne rabotat' na polku." *Kazakhstanskaia Pravda*, 14 April 1989.
Ainagulova, Kul'shara, and Katesh Alimbaeva. *Tendentsii razvitiia kinoiskusstva Kazakhstana*. Alma-Ata: Gylym, 1990.
Akhmetova, V. "Molodezh' – budushchee 'Kazakhfilma'." *Novyi fil'm*, 3/1977, p. 14.
Alimbaeva, K. "Problema geroia v kazakhskom khudozhestvennom kino." *Izvestiia Akademii nauk Kazakhskoi SSR*, seriia filologii, 2/1979, pp. 26–30.
Alimzhanov, Anuar. "'Ego vremia pridet.' Zametki o kinofil'me." *Kazakhstanskaia pravda*, 23 November 1958.
Antonov, S. "V perelomnyi moment istorii." *Sovetskaia kul'tura*, 13 December 1958.
Arkus, Liubov' (ed.). *Noveishaia istoriia otechestvennogo kino 1986–2000. Kinoslovar'*. 3 vls. St. Petersburg: SEANS, 2001.
Ashimov, A. "Detishche soiuza narodov-brat'ev." *Iskusstvo kino*, 12/1972, pp. 41–46.
Ashimov, A. "Vozvrashchenie k teme." *Iskusstvo kino*, 3/1979, pp. 78–79.
Ashimov, A. "Pafos utverzhdeniia." *Iskusstvo kino*, 11/1980, pp. 49–51.
Ashrapov, A. "Lenta pamiati." *Novyi fil'm*, 3/1988, pp. 18–19.
Auezov, M. "Nachalo." *Iskusstvo kino*, 4/1989, pp. 23–32.
Auezov, M.M. "Vremia natiagivaet tetivu." *Ogni Alatau*, 16 August 1988, p. 12.
Badyrov, K. "Vremia trevozhnoe, schastlivoe (Vospominaniia o TsOKSe)." *Novyi fil'm*, 7/1975, p. 3
Baiderin, V. "Dva arbuza v odnoi ruke." *Izvestiia*, 13 September 1961; cf. the response to this article in *Izvestiia*, 4 December 1961.
Baimuratova, A.T. (ed.). *Kinoiskusstvo Kazakhstana. Ukazatel' literatury*. Almaty: Natsional'naia biblioteka Respubliki Kazakhstan, 1994.
Bekkulova, S. "Strannyi kazakhskii fil'm." *Novoe pokolenie*, 15/1993, p. 11.
Bekmakhanov, E. "Razdum'ia o geroiakh." *Novyi fil'm*, 9/1978, p. 2.
Bekmakhanov, E. "Slavnyi put' kazakhskogo kino." *Novyi fil'm*, 4/1980, p. 14.
Berkovich, Mark. *Kadry neokonchennoi lenty*. Alma-Ata: Oner, 1984.
Beumers, Birgit. "Growing Up: Children in Central Asian Cinema." In: Michael Rouland, Gulnara Abikeyeva, and Birgit Beumers (eds) *Cinema in Central Asia: Rewriting Cultural Histories*. London and New York: I.B. Tauris, 2013, pp. 187–198.
Bikbaev, M. "Puteshestvie v kollektivizatsiiu." *Vecherniaia Alma-Ata*, 23 September 1993.
Blagin, N. "Kazakhstan ne imeet eshche svoei kinematografii." *Sovetskaia step*, 9 July 1931.
Bleiman, S. "Bez skidok." *Iskusstvo kino*, 7/1958, pp. 90–93.
Bodrov, S. "Vstrechi v puti (O rabote studii ‚Kazakhfil'm' v gody Velikoi Otechestvennoi voiny i v nastoiashchee vremia)." *Sovetskii ekran*, 14/1982, pp. 4–5.
Bogatenkova, L. *Nurmukhan Zhanturin*. Alma-Ata: Zhasushy, 1975.
Bondarchuk, S. "Obraz narodnogo pevtsa." *Pravda*, 2 June 1953.
Bragin, A. "Kinopoema o narode i ego pevtse." *Kazakhstanskaia Pravda*, 9 July 1944.
Buketov, E. "Zhizneradostnaia kinokomediia." *Kazakhstanskaia Pravda*, 6 July 1955.

Bulatova, T. "Kto zhe poterpevshii?" *Leninskaia smena*, 2 October 1986.
Butenko, M. "Dzhambul na ekrane." *Sovetskii Kazakhstan*, 7/1953, pp. 86–90.
Cherkesov, V. "Povest' o schast'e kazakhskoi zhenshchiny. Volnuiushchaia Pravda." *Kazakhstanskaia pravda*, 23 April 1955.
Darimbetov, B. "Kniga na ekrane." In: *Iskusstvo Kazakhstana*. Alma-Ata, 1982, pp. 66–69.
Davletbekov, Kh. "Eto bylo tak." *Novyi fil'm*, 12/1972, p. 4.
Dönmez-Colin, Gönül. "Kzakh 'new wave': post-perestroika, post-Soviet Union." *Central Asian Survey*, 16(1)/1997, pp. 115–118.
Dönmez-Colin, Gönül. *Cinemas of the Other*. Bristol and Chicago: Intellect, 2012.
Drieu, Cloé (ed.). *Écrans d'Orient. Propagande, innovation et resistance dans les cinémas de Turquie, d'Iran et d'Asie central (1897–1945)*. Paris: Éditions Karthala, 2014.
Dunaev, V. "Geroi teleekrana – nash sovremennik." *Vecherniaia Alma-Ata*, 15 March 1982.
Dzholdasova, A. "Razvitie vsestoronnego dvuiazychiia i mnogoiazychiia v sfere kazakhskogo kino." In: *Iazykovaia politika v Kazakhstane i puti ee realizatsii*. Tezisy respublikanskoi nauchno-issledovatel'skoi konferentsii. Chast' II, pp. 81–83.
Eniseeva, L. "Problemy golubogo ekrana." *Novyi fil'm*, 4/1974, pp. 2–3.
Eniseeva, L. "Vozvrashchaias' k bylomu." *Vecherniaia Alma-Ata*, 27 November 1981.
Eniseeva, L. "Fil'm-pamiat'." *Tselinogradskaia Pravda*, 1 May 1985.
Eniseeva, L. "Trizna." *Novyi fil'm*, 4/1987, pp. 4–5.
"Eshche raz o kazakhskoi kinodramaturgii." *Novyi fil'm*, 3/1988, pp. 18–19.
Fomin, Valerii. *Polka*. Vypusk 3. Moscow: Materik, 2006.
Fomin, Valerii, et al. (eds) *Letopis' rossiiskogo kino. 1863–1929*. Moscow: Materik, 2004; vol. 2: *1930–1945* (2007); vol. 3: *1946–1965* (2010).
Gabitov, B.I. "S trevogoi i nadezhdoi." *Novyi fil'm*, 12/1986, pp. 14–15.
Galiev, A. "Stranitsy istorii." *Kazakhstanskaia Pravda*, 12 February 1959.
Galimzhanova, L. "God iubileinyi (Iz istorii kazakhskogo kino)." *Novyi fil'm*, 14/1979, p. 3.
Gennad'ev, N. "Pervye kinos"emki v Kazakhstane." *Novyi fil'm*, 9/1970, p. 14.
Gerasimov, Sergei. "Vazhen protsess poiska." *Sovetskaia kul'tura*, 25 December 1984, p. 4.
German, A. "Tol'ko perezhivaia strakh…" *Novyi fil'm*, 4/1989, pp. 11, 14–15.
Giricheva, T. "Izgoi." *Novyi fil'm*, 6/1991, pp. 8–9.
Golovskoi, V. (ed.). *Ekran 1966–1967*. Moskva: "Iskusstvo," 1967.
Golovskoi, V. (ed.). *Ekran 1971–1972*. Moskva: "Iskusstvo," 1972.
Gorshkov, M.K. "Gluboko poznavaia zhizn'." *Ogni Alatau*, 20 March 1986.
"Griaz' i temnota." *Kino*, 33(205)/1927, p. 1.
Grigor'ev, A. "Amangel'dy." *Pravda*, 15 November 1938.
Grigor'ev, V. "Put' k dobroi pravde." *Iskusstvo kino*, 3/1964, pp. 23–25.
Ibraev, B. "Pustyni – tozhe nasha Rodina (O liubopytnykh aspektakh vliianiia kazakhskogo kino na nekotorye storony zhizni)." *Novyi fil'm*, 11/1987, pp. 10–11.

Ibragimov, R. "Bol'shoi ekran Kazakhstana." *Agitator Kazakhstana*, 15/1983, pp. 30–31.
Idrisov, A. "Shirokie vozmozhnosti." *Izvestiia*, 22 December 1970.
"Igla: Neskol'ko mnenii ob odnoimennom khudozhestvennom fil'me." *Sovetskaia kul'tura*, 5 January 1989, p. 4.
Ignat'eva, E. "Eti dni ne zabyt'." *Novyi fil'm*, 14/1979, pp. 11–12.
Ignat'eva, E. "Solenaia reka detstva." *Novyi fil'm*, 8/1983, pp. 2–3.
Isaacs, Rico. "Nomads, Warriors and Bureaucrats: Nation-Building and Film in Post-Soviet Kazakhstan." *Nationalities Papers*, 43(3)/2015, pp. 399–416.
Isaacs, Rico. *Film and Identity in Kazakhstan*. London, New York: I.B. Tauris, 2018.
Ismailova, G. "Novye zadachi, novye zamysly." *Iskusstvo kino*, 6/1959, p. 121.
*Istoriia sovetskogo kino*. 4 vls. Moscow: Iskusstvo, 1969–1978.
Iutkevich, Sergei (ed.). *Kinoslovar'*. 2 vls. Moscow: Sovetskaia entsiklopediia, 1966–1970.
Iutkevich, Sergei (ed.). *Kinoslovar'*. Moscow: Sovetskaia entsiklopediia, 1987.
"Iz biografii Kazakhfil'ma." *Novyi fil'm*, 12/1986, pp. 5, 7, 16.
Kairbaev, Amangeldy. *Vstrechi na ekrane. Rasskazy o kazakhskom kino*. Alma-Ata: Zhalyn, 1979.
Kairbaeva, L. "Poterpevshie pretenzii ne imeiut." *Novyi fil'm*, 5/1986, pp. 4–5.
"Kak molody my byli…" *Novyi fil'm*, 9/1988, pp. 4–5.
Kalashnikova, T. "Perekrestok." *Zapadnyi Kazakhstan*, 4 August 1963.
Kalgatina, L. "O pol'ze samodistsipliny." *Iskusstvo kino*, 12/1986, pp. 52–54.
Kaliev, M. "O fenomene ponaslyshke." *Vecherniaia Alma-Ata*, 24 December 1992.
Kanakhin, U. "Zhivoe dykhanie eposa." *Novyi fil'm*, 11/1972, p. 14.
Kanapin, A., and L. Varshavskii. *Kul'tura sovetskogo Kazakhstana*. Alma-Ata: Kazgisizdat, 1958.
Kausova, G. "Igla." *Novyi fil'm*, 1/1988, p. 3.
Khan, E. "Bez skidki na molodost'." *Leninskii put'*, 15 June 1959, p. 3.
Kharchenko, I. "Tikho! Idet s"emka…" *Kazakhstanskaia pravda*, 4 February 1960.
Khasanov, B.Kh. "Problemy dvuiazychiia v sfere kino, radio i televideniia (na materiale kazakhskogo iazyka)." In: *Iazyk i massovaia kommunikatsiia: Sotsiologicheskie issledovaniia*. Moskva, 1984, pp. 111–124.
Khlopliankina, T. "Put' k perevalu." *Iskusstvo kino*, 5/1969, pp. 71–77.
Khodzhikov, S. "Kazakhfil'm: vchera, segodnia, zavtra." *Ogni Alatau*, 30 December 1982.
*Kino Kazakhstana: Kto est' kto*. Almaty: Zhibek Zholy, 2003.
Kosenko, P. "Rozhdenie stilia?" *Kazakhstanskaia pravda*, 27 July 1960.
Kosenko, P. "Konflikty ‚Perekrestka'." *Kazakhstanskaia pravda*, 9 March 1963a.
Kosenko, P. "Mat' soldata." *Kazakhstanskaia Pravda*, 11 August 1963b, p. 3.
Kovalev, N. "Pervyi tsvetnoi." *Alma-Atinskaia pravda*, 14 September 1956.
"Krepit' sviaz' s zhizn'iu naroda, sozdavat' vysokokhudozhestvennye proizvedeniia." *Kazakhstanskaia Pravda*, 11 January 1963.
Kuvshinnikov, V. "Vsmatrivaias' v vos'midesiatye." *Novyi fil'm*, 6/1990, pp. 14–15, 21.
Lebedeva, E. "Sila dolzhna byt' dobroi." *Put' Lenina*, 20 October 1985.

Lednev, A. "Dostoinstvo pamiati." *Novyi fil'm*, 12/1989, pp. 2–3, 8.
Levin, M. "Zdravstvui, molodoe kazakhskoe kino-iskusstvo." *Kazakhstanskaia Pravda*, 28 January 1939, p. 3
Levin, M. "Kak sozdavalas' kartina 'Amangel'dy'." *Novyi fil'm*, 14/1978, p. 12.
Leyda, Jay. *Kino: A History of Russian and Soviet Film*. Princeton, NJ: Princeton University Press, 1983.
Lim, K. "Balkon." *Novyi fil'm*, 2/1988, p. 3.
Lyndina, E. *Suimenkul Chokmorov*. Moskva: Iskusstvo, 1985.
Lyndina, L. "Vgliadyvaias' v den' zavtrashnii." *Novyi fil'm*, 12/1987, pp. 4–5.
Macheret, Aleksandr, and Nina Glagoleva (eds) *Sovetskie khudozhestvennye fil'my. Annotirovannyi katalog Gosfil'mofonda SSSR*. 5 vls. Moscow: Iskusstvo, 1961–1979.
Makarova, A. "Khrani svoiu zvezdu." *Zvezda Priirtysh'ia*, 6 July 1977.
Maksimova, L. "Vazhnaia tema v tvorchestve." *Novyi fil'm*, 14/1979, pp. 12–14.
Maksimova, L. "Gontsy speshat." *Novyi fil'm*, 6/1980, pp. 6–7.
Manabaev, D. "Vsegda nakhodiatsia podletsy, kotorye…" *Novyi fil'm*, 12/1991, pp. 10–11.
Maricheva, A. "Takie vot igry (Zametki s VI plenuma pravleniia Soiuza kinematografistov Kazakhstana)." *Sovetskaia kul'tura*, 19 March 1988.
Maricheva, V. "Snimaiutsia poslednie kadry." *Leninskaia smena*, 28 May 1960.
Markov, S. "Mir Abaia na ekrane." *Literaturnaia gazeta*, 16 February 1946.
Matskevich, O. "Bez skidki na trudnosti zhanra." *Kazakhstanskaia pravda*, 13 March 1958.
Mordiukova, N. "Chtoby serdtsa bylo mnogo." *Gorizont*, 26 January 1991, p. 10.
Mukanova, A. "Pervye stranitsy." *Novyi fil'm*, 22/1971, p. 2.
Mukhamedzhanov, K. "V trud moei respubliki." *Iskusstvo kino*, 12/1970, pp. 1–4.
Mustafin, A. "Tvorcheskii pod"em kazakhskogo kino." *Ogni Alatau*, 29 December 1971.
Mustafina, S. "Blesk i nishcheta kazakhskogo kino." *Tselinogradskaia Pravda*, 14 March 1992.
Nazarov, A.S. *Pervenets kazakhskogo kino*. Alma-Ata: Өner, 1980.
Nikolaev, K. "Na podstupakh k znachitel'noi teme." *Kazakhstanskaia pravda*, 13 August 1959.
Nogerbek, Bauyrzhan. *Kino Kazakhstana*. Almaty: Natsional'nyi prodiuserskii tsentr, 1998.
Nogerbek, Bauyrzhan. *Na ekrane 'Kazakhfil'm*. Almaty: RUAN, 2007.
Nogerbek, Bauyrzhan. "Cherez klassiku – k sovremennosti." *Kinoforum*, 2/2008, pp. 11–15.
Norris, Stephen. "Nomadic Nationhood: Cinema, Nationhood, and Remembrance in Post-Soviet Kazakhstan." *Ab Imperio*, 2/2012, pp. 378–402.
Novozhilov, G. "Pervye kinos emki v Kazakhstane." *Kazakhstanskaia pravda*, 19 April 1960.
Novozhilov, G. "Kino v Turkestane." *Novyi fil'm*, 8/1989, p. 9.
Nugerbekov, B. "Prikosnovenie k istokam." *Prostor*, 10/1985, pp. 169–172.
Nugerbekov, B. "Pervenets li kazakhskogo kino fil'm 'Amangel'dy'?" *Izvestiia Akademii nauk Kazakhskoi SSR. seriia filologii*, 4/1990, pp. 63–67.

Nugerbekov, B. "Skol'ko let kazakhskomu kino?" *Novyi fil'm*, 11/1991a, pp. 4–5.
Nugerbekov, B. "Novaia volna i natsional'noe... " *Novyi fil'm*, 4/1991b, pp. 2–4.
Nugmanov, A. "Podarok kinematografistov." *Kazakhstanskaia pravda*, 29 December 1957.
Nurmagambetova, O. "Verno i ubeditel'no." *Kazakhstanskaia pravda*, 23 April 1955.
*Ocherki istorii kazakhskogo kino*. Alma-Ata: Nauka, 1980.
Oganian, D. "Legkoe dykhanie." *Iskusstvo kino*, 7/1985, pp. 88–90.
Omarov, I. "Kinoiskusstvo Kazakhstana – na novye vysoty." *Kazakhstanskaia pravda*, 3 June 1959.
Omirbaev, Darezhan. "Iazyk kino – sistema koordinat." *Kinoforum*, 2/2008, pp. 16–19.
Ospanova, M. "Printsipy ekranizatsii." *Izvestiia Akademii nauk Kazakhskoi SSR*, seriia filologii; 2/1977, pp. 47–50.
Ostrovskaia, E. "Deti 'Broda'." *Novyi fil'm*, 10/1988, p. 16.
Paramonova, K. "Nepovtorimoe i trafaretnoe." *Iskusstvo kino*, 11/1953, pp. 76–88.
Pavlova, Marina (ed.). *Sovetskie khudozhestvennye kinofil'my. Annotirovannyi katalog, 1966–1987*. 11 vls. Moscow: Gosfil'mofond Rossii, 1995–2001.
Payne, Matthew. "Viktor Turin's *Turksib* (1929) and Soviet Orientalism." *Historical Journal of Film, Radio, and Television*, 21(1)/2001a, pp. 37–62.
Payne, Matthew. *Stalin's Railroad: Turksib and the Building of Socialism*. Pittsburgh: Pittsburgh University Press, 2001b.
Piastolov, V. "Pravdu zhizni – na ekran." *Kazakhstanskaia pravda*, 27 March 1962.
Pinchukova, L. "Fil'm o krasivykh liudiakh." *Alma-Atinskaia Pravda*, 12 August 1959.
Piotrovskii, K. "Obraz Chokana Valikhanova." *Iskusstvo kino*, 7/1958, pp. 83–87.
"Pobuzhdat' vysokie pomysly i chuvstva." *Kazakhstanskaia Pravda*, 29 January 1969.
Proskurin, V., and S. Duvanov. "Volshebnyi fonar' Vernogo." *Vecherniaia Alma-Ata*, 18 August 1979.
Pruner, Ludmilla. "The New Wave in Kazakh Cinema." *Slavic Review*, 51(4)/1992, pp. 791–801.
Radvanyi, Jean. *Le Cinéma d'Asie centrale soviétique*. Paris: Éditions du Centre Georges Pompidou, 1991.
Raibaev, S. "Zapiski na khlopushke epokhi zastoia." *Novyi fil'm*, 8/1989, pp. 10–11.
Raibaev, S. "Seks i kazakhskoe kino – znak voprosa?" *Novyi fil'm*, 7/1991a, pp. 6–7.
Raibaev, S. "Nevostrebovannaia zhizn'." *Novyi fil'm*, 9/1991b, p. 8.
Ramazanuly, B. "Natsional'no li kazakhskoe kino?" *Madeniet*, 31 July 1992a, pp. 14–15.
Ramazanuly, B. "Kto pervyi kazakhskii rezhisser?" *Madeniet*, 18/1992b, pp. 10–11.
Rollberg, Peter. *Historical Dictionary of Russian and Soviet Cinema* (2nd, expanded edition) Lanham, Boulder, New York, Toronto, Plymouth: Rowman & Littlefield, 2016.
Rollberg, Peter. "Rascals, Misfits, Patriots: Youth in Kazakhstani Cinema." In: Marlene Laruelle (ed.) *The Nazarbayev Generation: Youth in Kazakhstan*. Lanham et al.: Lexington Books, 2019, pp. 191–212.

Roshal', G. "Pristal'nym vzgliadom." *Iskusstvo kino*, 6/1959, pp. 108–118.
Rouland, Michael, Gulnara Abikeyeva, and Birgit Beumers (eds). *Cinema in Central Asia: Rewriting Cultural Histories*. London, New York: I.B. Tauris, 2013.
"S pozitsii poiskov i trebovatel'nosti." *Novyi fil'm*, 11/1981, pp. 3–5.
Shandybin, G. "Slovo ob Eizenshteine." *Gorizont*, 23 April 1988.
Sharipov, A. "K fil'mu ,Liutyi'." *Novyi fil'm*, 7/1974, p. 12.
Shcherbakov, K. "Posle debiuta." *Komsomol'skaia Pravda*, 6 May 1971.
Shemiakin, A. "Novaia volna v kontse sezona tumanov." *Novyi fil'm*, 4/1991, p. 5.
Shinarbaev, E. "U nas net krizisa." *Sovetskaia kul'tura*, 9 June 1990.
Shnaider, A. "Pervenets natsional'nogo kino." *Turgaiskaia nov'*, 2 April 1983.
Siranov, K. *Kinoiskusstvo sovetskogo Kazakhstana*. Izdatel'stvo "Kazakhstan," Alma-Ata, 1966.
Siranov, K. *Shaken Aimanov – kinorezhisser i akter kino*. Alma-Ata: Zhazushi, 1970.
Siranov, K. "Proshloe – dalekoe i blizkoe." *Kazakhstanskaia Pravda*, 16 July 1972.
Siranov, K. *Kino. Gody. Mysli* (edited by B. Darimbetov). Alma-Ata: Oner, 1983.
Siranov, Kabysh. *Kazakhskoe kinoiskusstvo*. Alma-Ata: Kazakhskoe Gosudarstvennoe Izdatel'stvo, 1958.
"Slovo za kinoprokatom." *Vecherniaia Alma-Ata*, 3 February 1989.
Smailov, K. "Geroi – v zhizni i na ekrane." *Novyi fil'm*, 8/1972a, p. 13.
Smailov, K. "Kazakhstanskoe kino – sversheniia i zamysly." *Prostor*, 5/1972b, pp. 99–102.
Smailov, K. "S pozitsii sovremennosti." *Kazakhstanskaia Pravda*, 6 April 1976.
Smailov, K. "Problemy i perspektivy ekrannogo iskusstva." *Prostor*, 12/1982, pp. 138–143.
Smailova, Inna. "Kazakhskaia 'Novaia volna:' Izobrazitel'noe reshenie fil'mov." *Prostor*, 5/2010a, pp. 165–168.
Smailova, Inna. "Problema izobrazheniia v sovremennom kazakhskom kino." *Vestnik Kazakhskogo Natsional'nogo Universiteta*, 2010b (https://articlekz.com/article/8335; accessed 17 April 2017).
Smailova, T.K. (ed.). *Kinoentsiklopediia Kazakhstana*. Almaty: Kazakfil'm, 2010.
"Sozdavat' fil'my, dostoinye epokhi." *Kazakhstanskaia Pravda*, 10 April 1976.
"Sozdavat' fil'my, sozvuchnye vremeni." *Kazakhstanskaia Pravda*, 10 April 1981.
Stishova, Elena (ed.). *Territoriia kino: Postsovetskoe desiatiletie*. Moscow: Pomatur, 2001.
Suleimenov, Olzhas. "Iskat' v obydennom vechnoe." *Sovetskaia kul'tura*, 15 May 1981.
Suleimenov, Olzhas. "Ot mirosozertsaniia k mirovozzreniiu. Dialog s korrespondentom 'IK'
Katesh Alimbaevoi. *Iskusstvo kino*, 3/1982, pp. 34–52.
Sul'kin, M. "Poslednii fil'm Shakena Aimanova." In: V. Golovskoi (ed.) *Ekran 1971–1972*. Moskva: "Iskusstvo," 1972, pp. 28–32.
Sul'kin, M. "Segodniashnimi ochami…" In: S. Chertok (ed.) *Ekran 1972–1973*. Moskva: "Iskusstvo," 1973, pp. 57–60.
Sul'kin, M. "O chem nel'zia molchat'." *Iskusstvo kino*, 8/1987, pp. 41–54.
Tarazi, A. "Samoe molodoe." *Kazakhstanskaia pravda*, 27 August 1969.

Tasbulatova, D. "I eto – zhizn'?" *Leninskaia smena*, 26 August 1989.
Taurbaeva, S. "Dumaite, patsany!" *Ogni Alatau*, 7 April 1989.
Tiurin, Iu. "Vremia – epicheskoe." *Iskusstvo kino*, 9/1979, pp. 42–49.
Tkachenko, O. "Semnadtsat' let spustia." *Vecherniaia Alma-Ata*, 18 December 1987.
Toguzakov, Kasym. "Pervyi kazakhskii fil'm." *Kazakhstanskaia pravda*, 17 May 1938.
Toguzakov, Kasym. "Voprosy razvitiia kinoiskusstva." *Kazakhstanskaia pravda*, 4 March 1939.
"Trudnosti rosta." *Novyi fil'm*, 6/1988, pp. 4–5.
"Tsentral'nomu komitetu Kommunisticheskoi Partii Sovetskogo Soiuza: Obrashchenie uchastnikov 1 uchreditel'nogo s"ezda kinematografistov Kazakhstana." *Kazakhstanskaia pravda*, 12 January 1963.
Umbetbaev, A., and Kh. Kikymbaev. "Kazakhskii Chapaev." *Sotsialisticheskaia Alma-Ata*, 26 January 1939.
Umurzakov, Eleubai. "Rabota nad rol'iu." *Sotsialisticheskaia Alma-Ata*, 22 August 1937.
Undasynov, N. "Pervyi kazakhskii fil'm." *Iskusstvo kino*, 5/1939, p. 20.
Varshavskii, L. "Tri problemy kazakhskogo kino." *Kazakhstanskaia Pravda*, 27 May 1965.
Vereshchagin, I. "Kinopoema o sovremennosti." *Vecherniaia Alma-Ata*, 16 December 1980.
"Za fil'my, dostoinye sovremennosti." *Kazakhstanskaia Pravda*, 22 March 1986.
"Za rastsvet kazakhskogo kino." *Kazakhstanskaia pravda*, 12 January 1963.
Zhezhelenko, L. "Kazakhskie aktery v fil'me 'Raikhan'." *Iskusstvo kino*, 11/1940, pp. 53–54.
Zhienkulova, Sh. "Amangel'dy – vechnaia molodost'." *Novyi fil'm*, 11/1985, p. 3.

# Index

Abai Kunanbaev, 59–63, 74, 143, 378
Abdikov, Tolegen, 336
Abdrakhmanov, Abdrashit, 261, 262, *281*, 347
Abdrashev, Rustem, 355
Abdukarimova, Lola, 93, 98, *117*, 133, 292
Abdulakhatova, Roza, *81*, *118*
Abdykadyrov, Zh., 394
Abikeeva, Gulnara (Gulnar), *83*, *189*, *214*, *365*, *421*
Abishev, Oraz, 13, *28*
Abrikosov, Andrei, 14
Absaliamov, Faizulla, 13, 43, 54
Abuladze, Tengiz, 396
Abuseitov, Kuat, 113, *119*, 212, *214*
Abyzov, Vladimir, 90, 96, *116*
Adilova, Gulbakhram, 142
Agranovich, Leonid, 303, 304
Aimanov, Murat, 207, *214*
Aimanov, Shaken, 12, 17, 24, *28*, 35, 48, 60, 64, 65, 70, 73, 74, 77, 80, 85, 90–94, 97–101, 111, 115, 116, *118*, 121–30, 133–37, 154–57, *159*, *160*, 163, 186, 191–217, 225–34, 252–54, 274, 278, *282*, 296, 298, 309, 334, 355, 359, 361, 362, 425–27, 429
Ainagulova, Kulshara, 73, 77, *420*
Aitmatov, Chingiz, 172, 226, 243, 372

Aituarov, Amanzhol, 396–99, *421*
Alash-Orda, 19, 21, 105, 166, 186, 229, 246, 290
Aleksandr II, 107, 109
Aleksandrov, Grigorii (director), 41, 87, 98, 100
Aleksandrov, Grigorii (politician), 57
Alimbaeva, Katesh, *117*, 158, *162*, *321*, *421*
Alimzhanov, Anuar, 107, 110, *118*, 305
Alov, Aleksandr, 245
Alpiev, Aman, 315, *322*, 328
Amangeldy. *See* Imanov, Amangeldy
Amirkulov, Ardak, 351, 352, 354, 373, 374, 413–18
animation, 213, *215*
Aprymov, Serik, 352, 354, 372, 383, 384, 387–88, 418
Aranyshev, Fedor, 316
Aranyshev, Mikhail, 73, 76, 78, *82*, 96, 115, 131, 135, 146, 163, 187, 285, 425
Aranysheva, Laila, 369–70
Argimbekov, T., 77
Arinbasarova, Natalia, 181, 226, 233, 298
Aron, Efim, 9, *30*, 48, 49, 53, 58, 59, 65, 67–69, 101–11, 114, 115, 126, 152–55, 192, 213

Ashimov, Asanali, 110, 127, 137, 139, 163, 165, 185, 219, 220, 226, 230, 231, 260, 264, 267, 268, 298, 305, 332, 358, 362, *363*, 425
Ashrapov, Askhat, 105, *117*, 133, 139, 140, 163, 176, 222, 230, 243, 277, 293, 301, 314, 363, 425
Askol'dov, Aleksandr, 247
Auezov, Mukhtar, 32, 33, 37, 49, 52, 53, 59, 62, 64, 70, 74, 80, 142, 143, 149, 169, 193, 234, 269
Auezov, Murat, 329, 330, 351, 357, 358, *363*, *364*, 382
Azimov, Sergei, 325

Babochkin, Boris, *282*
Badyrov, Kapan, 22, 45, 47, 48, 60, 71, 100
Baigazin, Emir, 369
Baikadamov, Bakhitzhan, 88
Baiseitov, Kanabek, 22, 110, 132, *248*
Baiseitova, Kuliash, 74
Baitenov, Zhardem, 158, 285, 293, 321
Baizakov, Isa, 186
Bakhtygireev, Mukhtar, 261, *281*
Baranov, Aleksandr, 351, 369, 384, 385, 399, 418, *421*
Bardot, Brigitte, 210
Bartashevich, Konstantin, 92
Bartok, Bela, 353
Begalin, Mazhit, 44, 73, 106–10, 112, 114, 116, 124, 130, 138–41, 154–58, *161*, 163, 176–85, *190*, 234, 235, 244–48, 252–54, 274, 275, 278, 332, 334, 359, 425, 427, 429
Begalin, Nartai, 245
Beibars, 391–93
Beisekov, Nurgali, 43, 54
Beisembaev, Sharip, 149, 151, *162*, 252, 261, 274, 277, 278, 280, 290, 331, 361, *363*, 429
Beishenaliev, Bolotbek, 415, *421*
Bekbulatov, Aleukhan, 318, *322*
Belbaeva, Gulziia, 380
Belialov, Ali, 346, 347

Belialov, Viacheslav, 268, 346–48, *364*
Bellini, Vincenzo, 408
Belov, Vasilii, 241
Bergman, Ingmar, 352
Berkovich, Mark, 116, 125, 186, 281
Bertolucci, Bernardo, 301
Bleiman, Mikhail, 90, 107
Blekhman, E.E., 5
Blinov, Boris, 42
Blok, Aleksandr, *190*, 246
Bocharov, Gennadii, 381
Bodrov, Sergei, 315, 328, 335, 341–42, 361
Bogoliubov, Pavel, 98, 114
Bokin, Tokash, 168
Bol'shakov, Ivan, 32, 38, 40, 42, 57, 63
Bolysbaev, Edige, *249*, 356, 359
Bondarchuk, Fedor, 172, 176, *189*
Bondarenko, Olga, 293
Boranbaev, Anvar, 362
Boretskii, Iurii, 292
Botbaev, Dunchenbai, 273
Brecht, Bertolt, 51
Bresson, Robert, 352
Brezhnev, Leonid, 251, *282*, 283, 295, 296, 326, 356
Bronson, Charles, 345
Brusilovskii, Evgenii, 49, 78, 88, 96, 115, *117*, 217, *248*
Budennyi, Semen, 5
Bukeeva, Hadisha, 34–36, 38, 71, 100, 111, 137, 139
Bulgakov, Mikhail, 245
Bulychov, Kir, 264

Callas, Maria, 408
Carter, Huntly, 9
Central United Film Studio (TsOKS), 41, 52
Chabrol, Claude, 419
Chanyshev, Kasymkhan, 228
Chapaev, Vasilii, 17, 19
Cherkasov, Nikolai, 44
Chernykh, Valentin, 278, 279, 297
Chernyshevskii, Nikolai, 61

Chirkov, Boris, 41
Chokmorov, Suimenkul, 169, 171, *189*, 273, 307, 415
Chukhrai, Grigorii, 131, 135, 164, 172, *189*
cinefication (*kinofikatsiia*), 3, 13
collectivization, 11
Cook, David, 384

Damiani, Damiano, 232
Darwin, Charles, 61, 270
Davletbekov, Hakim, 7, 10, 14, *27*, 186
De Palma, Brian, *364*
Denikin, Anton (General), 244
Diordiev, Evgenii, 99
Dönmez-Colin, Gönül, 355
Donskoi, Mark, *118*, 131, 186
Dostoevskii, Fedor, 107, 109, 353
Dovzhenko, Aleksandr, 57, 86
Dubrovskii, Aleksandr, 10
Dubrovskii-Eshke, Boris, 41, 54
Duganov, Marat, 157
Durov, Boris, 317
Dusmatova, Gulnara, 308, 338
Dutov, Aleksandr (Ataman), 193, 226, 228, 232
Dvoretskii, Ignatii, 130
Dzhamankulov, Tungyshbai, 301, 302, 305, 311, 347, 362
Dzhambul Dzhabaev, 49, 71–82
Dzhandarbekov, Kurmanbek, 22
Dzhandarbekova, Sholpan, 77
Dzhangeldin, Alibi, 1, 2, *25*, 187
Dzhansugurov, Ilias, 7, 11, *26*, 236, 289, 329
Dzhetpisbaev, Kadyr, 362
Dzhigarkhanian, Armen, 344, 345
Dzhumadylov, Sovetbek, 169
Dzigan, Efim, 71–73, 192

"Eastern," 163–87, 306–13, 330
Eizenshtein (Eisenstein), Sergei, 6, 39, 41, 42, 44, 45, 52, 56, 86, 416
El-Registan, 10, *27*
Elubaev, Smagul, 394

Ergalieva, Zauresh, 315, *322*, 358, 373
Erguzhinova, Amina. *See* Umurzakova, Amina
Ermler, Fridrikh, 51, 52, 64, 67
Ermolinskii, Sergei, 10, 44, 54, 107
Esenberlin, Ilias, 70, *82*
Evtushenko, Evgenii, 378

fabri (entrepreneur), 2
Faik, Emir, *117*, *161*, 289
famine, 11
Fatuev, Roman, 78
Fedorovskii, F., 23
Fedulin, Aleksandr, 212, *214*
Fomin, Valerii, 239
Ford, John, 258
Frantsuzov, Feliks, *281*
Frunze, Mikhail, 6, 246
Furmanov, Dmitrii, 6, 23

Gabitov-Dzhansugurov, Bulat, 329, 335, 349, 362, *363*, *364*
Gaidar Arkadii, 146, 147
Gakkel, Karl, 55, 77, 78, *83*
Galiev, A., 123
Galimzhanova, Liailia, 67, 113, 125
Gardin, Vladimir, 10
Gel'man, Aleksandr, 130
Gelovani, Mikheil, 73
Genghis Khan, 415
Gerasimov, Sergei, 44, *118*, 138, *161*
German, Aleksei, 413–16
Gidt, Georgii, 402
Gintsburg, A., *161*
Gitlevich, Isaak, 103
Glotov, Ivan, 40
Gluzskii, Mikhail, 246
Gnesin, Mikhail, 22
Godard, Jean-Luc, 419
Goldaev, Boris, 285
Goldblatt, Moisei, 75
Gor'kii, Maksim, *29*, 186
Gorbachev, Mikhail, 251, 356, 394
Goskino (State Committee for Cinema), 188, 193, 212, 269, 320, 330

Govorukhin, Stanislav, 327, 343
Grinko, Nikolai, 401
Grishko, Vitalii, 279
Guk In Tsoi, 332, *363*
GULAG, 44, 286
Gurzo, Sergei, 87, 88

Haydn, Joseph, 402
Hodja Mukan, 317–19, *322*

Iakubov, Valiia, 58
Ian, V., 413
Iandieva, Tamara, 332
Ikhtymbaev, Nurzhuman, 285, 339, 372
Imanov, Amangeldy, 1, 16–19, 22, *29*, 102
Iofis, Evsei, 44, 55
Isaacs, Rico, *30*, *248*
Iskakov, Kalikhan, 187
Ismailov, Adilbek, 157
Ismailov, Atageldy, 187, 209
Ismailova, Almira, 306
Ismailova, Gulfairus, 103, *118*, 187
Iudin, Konstantin, 152
Iurenev, Rostislav, 21, *29*
Iurtsev, Boris, 53, 56, 58
Iutkevich, Sergei, *119*
Ivanov, Vsevolod, 17, 21, *30*

Kadochnikov, Valentin, 42, 54
Kaidanovskii, Aleksandr, 402
Kairbaeva, Liudmila, *364*
Kairbekova, Dana, 407
Kairkhan, 413, 415
Kalatozov, Mikheil, 8, 171, 172
Kalymbetov, Bolat, 390
Karakulov, Amir, 351, 407–8
Karmalita, Svetlana, 413–15
Karmen, Roman, 50
Karnovich-Valua, Grigorii, 104
Karostin, Mikhail, 10, *27*
Karpov, Aleksandr, 96, 124, 126, 130–32, 138, 155, 156, *160*, 163, 172–76, 187, 252, 254, 284, 425, 427

Karpykov, Abai, 351, 352, 354, 384, 402–4, 418
Karsakbaev, Abdulla, 45, 98, 124, 144–49, 151, 155, 157, 163, 165–88, 206, 226, 228, 235, 246, 252, 254, 257–59, 284, 288, 289, 291, 298, 306–10, 313, 319, 332–34, 359, 368, *419*, 425
Karsakbaev, Idris, *190*
Kasteev, Abiltai, 168, 247
Kasymbekov, Kanymbek, 254–55, 319, 368, 371
"Kazakh New Wave," 329, 351–55, *365*, 380, 383, 399, 403, 416, 418
Kenzhetaev, Kauken, 100, 177, 185, 291
Khaidarov (Khaidar), Amen, 213, *215*
Khamdamov, Rustam, 50
Kheifits, Iosif, 34, 135
Khodzhikov, Sultan-Akhmet, 76, 89, 106, 114, 116, 124, 132–34, 140–42, 154–59, 163, 186, *190*, 217–25, 234, 235, *248*, 252, 254, 274, 281, 296, 317, 425–27
Khrushchev, Nikita, 127–29, 168, 197, 205, 297
Khudaibergenov, Dzhambul, 267, 268, *282*, 290, 292, 305, 335
Khusainov, Shakhmet, 74, *82*, 96
Khutsiev, Marlen, 131
Kilibaev, Bakhyt, 351, 369, 384, 385, 399
Kim, Anatolii, 402, 409–10
Kimyagarov, Bension, 192
Klimov, Elem, 358
Koichubaeva, Rakhia (Raisa), 34, 67, 135
Kolbin, Gennadii, 361
Kolchak, (Admiral), 244, 300
Konakbaev, Serik, 344
Kosenko, Petr, *160*, *161*, 189
Kosmanev, Sergei, 402
Kozhabekov, Kenenbai, 98, 104, 122
Kozhamkulov, Serke, 7, 10, *27*, 49, 75, 213

Kozintsev, Grigorii, 35, 42, 52, 57
Kramer, Stanley, 273
Krupskaia, Nadezhda, 288
Kuanyshpaev, Kalibek, 22, 49, 60, 62, 71, 191, 319
Kuiatte, Assan, 403
Kulanbaev, Akyl, 346
Kuleshov, Lev, 5
Kulidzhanov, Lev, *160*
Kunaev, Dinmukhamed, 236, 240, *248*, 284, 286, 289, 320, 331, 359, *420*
Kurkina, Raisa, 95
Kurosawa, Akira, 352, 397, 416
Kuvshinnikov, Viacheslav, 327–28
Kuzmichev, Sergei, 2
Kydyraliev, Dokhdurbek, 414, 415
Kydyraliev, Kadyrzhan, 271

Lang, Fritz, 416
Lanza, Mario, 196
Lavrenev, Boris, 164
Lee, Bruce, 343
Lemberg, Aleksandr, 9
Levin, Moisei, 18–21, *29*, 32, 34–37, 39, 53, 70
Lenin, Vladimir, 5, 21, 67, 126, 150, 207, 213, 285, 288, 291, 295, 377
Lenin Prize, 143
Linder, Max, 3
Lindgren, Astrid, *161*
Lukashev, 43
Lukov, Leonid, 63
Lumumba, Patrice, 150
Lyndina, El'ga, *189*

Macheret, Aleksandr, *27*
machismo, 143
Magarill, Sofia, 42
Mailin, Beimbet, 17, 21, 22, *29*
Makarova, Tamara, 80
Mambetov, Azerbaijan, 185–87, *190*, 291, 300, 305, 306
Mametova, Manshuk, 180, 182, 266
Manabaev (Manabai), Damir, 156, 281, 394–96, *421*

Mansurov, Bulat, 236–40, 327, 332, 391–94, 397
Maretskaia, Vera, 42, 80
Marx, Karl, 14
Mashanov, Ararat, 287
Mastroianni, Marcello, 210
Matsiugin, Iurii, 300
McCartney, Paul, 342
Medvedkin, Aleksandr, 50, 86–90, 125, 296
Metal'nikov, Budimir, 94
Mifune, Toshiro, 171
Mikhalkov, Nikita, 181, 232
Mikhalkov, Sergei, 45
Mikhalkov-Konchalovskii, Andrei, 183, 226, 229, 233, *249*, 273, 300, 308
Minkin, Adol'f, 49
Miroshnichenko, Irina, 344, 345
Moldabekov, Anuar, 185, 301, 304, 336
Moldagulova, Aliia, 266, *364*
Molotov, Viacheslav, 32
Momysh-uly, Bauyrzhan, 177, *189*
Montgomery (Marshall), 375, 377
Mordiukova, Nonna, 390
Morozov, Valentin, 48
Mozart, Wolfgang Amadeus, 353
Muhammad II, 413
Mukanov, Sabit, 6, *26*, 102
Mukhamedgalieva, Larisa, 268, 346–48, *364*
Mukhamediarova, Raisa, 196, 291
Mukhamedzhanov, Kaltai, 349, 350, 358, *363*, *364*
Mukhamedzhanov, Sydyk, 135, 199
Munaitpasov. *See* Hodja Mukan
Muratbaev, Gani, 288, 289, *321*
Muratbekov, Saiyn, 278
Musrepov, Gabit, 17, 21, 22, *29*, 45, 64, 73, 74, 76, 122, 191, 217, 222, 224, *248*, 287, 290, 291, 314, 426
Musser, Charles, 9
Mustafin, Gabit, 113
Myrzaliev, Kadyr, *248*

Nabatov, Il'ia, 155

Narokov, Mikhail, 14
Narymbetov, Satybaldy, *249*, 255, *281*, 355, 390
Naumov, Vladimir, 245
Nauryzbaev, Talgat, 373
Nazariants, Khecho, 36, 53
New Economic Policy (NEP), 4
Nigmatulin, Talgat, 263
Nogaibaev, Idris, 92, 122, 142, 165, 298, 304, 305
Nogerbek (Nugerbekov), Bauyrzhan, 22, *28*, 53, *81*, *83*, 110, *161*, *188*, *189*, *190*, 213, *248*, 329, *365*, 385, *419*, *421*
Norris, Chuck, 345
Norris, Stephen, *214*
Novikova, Natal'ia, 403
Novozhilov, Gennadii, 12, 13, *28*
Nugmanov, Marat, 385
Nugmanov, Rashid, 351, *365*, 383–87, 418
Nurekeev, Meirman, 394
Nurmakhanov, A., 157
Nurpeisov, Abujamal, 299

Ogorodnikov, Valerii, *364*
Oguzbaev, Zhagda, 47, 48, 78
Okeev, Tolomush, 269, 347
Okudzhava, Bulat, 344
Omar (Omarov), Bolat, 381, *420*
Omarov, Tasbulat, 380
Omarova, Gulshad, 316
Omirbaev, Darezhan, 116, 351, 398, 404–7, 418
Ordzhonikidze, Sergo, 287
Orlov, Dal', 240
Osetinskii, Oleg, 306
Ostrovskaia, Elena, 379, *420*

Pakhmutova, Aleksandra, 292
Panfilov, Ivan (General), 177, 178, *189*
Paradjanov, Sergei, 238, 254
Pentslin, Eduard, 58
Perestiani, Ivan, 5, 225
performance film (*fil'm-spektakl'*), 76

Petrov, Aleksandr, 65
Pichul', Vasilii, *364*
Piskunov, Iurii, *249*
Platonov, Andrei, 134
Pobedonostsev, Iurii, 94, *117*, 296
Poddubnyi, Ivan, 318
Pogodin, Nikolai, 72
Polikarpov, Dmitrii, 39
Polonskii, Konstantin, 42
Polovskii, Igor', *249*
Pomerantsev, Iurii, 99, 100, 202, 207
Popov, Gavriil, 51
Popov, S., 142
populism (*narodnost'*), 61
Posel'skii, Iakov, 50, 86
Pravov, Ivan, 13
Preobrazhenskaia, Ol'ga, 13
Proshkin, Aleksandr, 375
Protazanov, Iakov, 164
Pruner, Ludmila, 355
Prut, Iosif, 45
Ptushko, Aleksandr, 48, 52
Puchinian, Stepan, 343
Pudovkin, Vsevolod, *28*, 39, 41, 43, 45, 51, 52, 286
Pushkin, Aleksandr, 378
Pusurmanov, Viktor, 243, *250*, 290, 293, 313
Pyr'ev, Ivan, 41, 45, 52, 87, 98, 100

Raibaev, Serik, 240, *249*, 264, *282*
Raizman, Iulii, 41, 125, 135
Rakhmadiev, Erkegali, 206
Ramazanuly, B., *30*
Rappaport, Gerbert, 39, 45, 51
Rasputin, Valentin, 241
Ravikovich, Anatolii, 377
Riazanov, El'dar, 96, *117*
Rimova, Biken, *82*, 242, 279
Rivette, Jacques, 419
Romashin, Anatolii, 341
Romm, Mikhail, 42, 52
Room, Abram, 64, 67
Roshal', Grigorii, *30*, 44, 45, 48, 52, 59–61, 63, 192

Rossini, Gioachino, 196
Rymbaeva, Roza, 293
Rymzhanov, Oraz, 383
Ryskulov, Turar, 6

Sagimbaev, Maulutkhan, 13, *28*
Saitov, Iusup, 332
Salykov, Kalykbek, 374–80, *420*
Samadi, Zia, 331
Sanaev, Vsevolod, 178
Sanbaev, Satimzhan, 187, 223, 243
Sandler, Oskar, 49
Sataev, Akan, 76, 159, 312, 341
Sataev, Kargambai, 236
Satpaev, Kanysh, 74
Savvin, I., 168
Scorsese, Martin, 412
Segel', Iakov, *160*
Segisbaev, Nurlan, 145
Semenov Tian-Shanskii, Petr, 108, *118*
Serkebaev, Ermek, 100, *117*, 196, 210
Shakurov, Sergei, 296
Shamiev, Ahmed, 104, 132
Shamshiev, Bolotbek, 169, 188, 302, *364*, 372
Sharip (Shmanov), Bolat, 256, 257, 264, *281*, 327, 340–41
Sharipova, Farida, 134, 137, 139, *161*, 163, *322*, 425
Sharipova, Zamzagul, 45, 78, 137, 213
Shashkin, Zinovii, 168
Shatrov, Mikhail, 292
Sheinin, Semen, 46
Shengelaia, Giorgi, 196, 240
Shepit'ko, Larisa, *118*, 247
Shinarbaev, Ermek, 356, 359, 401–2, 408–12, 419, *421*
Shindo, Kaneto, 139, 397
Shirokov, G., 44
Shmanov, Bolat. *See* Sharip (Shmanov), Bolat
Sholokhov, Mikhail, *118*, 299
Shukhov, Ivan, 13, *29*, 73
Shumiatskii, Boris, 33
Shutov, Sergei, 262, *281*, *282*, 338, 361

Siglov, B., 103
Siranov, Kabysh, 4, 10, 11, 21, 26, 42, 43, 48, 49, 55, 58, 70, 80, *82*, 93, 94, 99, 110, 111, 114, 115, 122, *160*, *214*, 222, *249*, 278
Smirnov, Andrei, 247
Smirnov, Iakov, 13, *28*
Smirnova, Lidiia, 279
Smirnova, Marina, 385
Snegin, Dmitrii, *83*, 105, 285, *321*
Socialist Realism, 102
Sokpakbaev, Berdybek, 144, 151, *161*, 266, 335
Solonitsyn, Anatolii, 402
Solov'ev, Sergei, 315, 328, 351–54, 356, 357, 383, 384, 402, 413, 418, 419
Solov'ev, Vasilii, *189*
Solov'ev-Sedoi, Vasilii, 99
Stalin, Iosif, 21, 43, 57, 67, 70, 73, 80, 287, 377
Stalin Prize, 37, 70, 74
Stanislavskii, G., 23
State Prize of the Kazakhstani SSR, 176, 187, *214*, 346, *364*
Stepanova, Lidiia, 73, *82*
Stolper, Aleksandr, 44
Stroeva, Vera, 45, 53, 55, 72
Strzhelchik, Vladislav, 230
Suiunshalin, Akan, 373
Sul'kin, Mikhail, *248*, 358–59
Suleev, Bolat, 394
Suleimenov, Askar, *249*
Suleimenov, Olzhas, 155, 157, 168, 192, 204, 205, 235, 293, 310, 320, *322*, 329–31, 351, 378, *420*
Suleimenov, Sapargali, 293
Suleimenova, Gulnara, 291
Svilova, Elizaveta, 50

Tarazi, Akim, 149, 234, *249*, 281, 320
Tarkovskii, Andrei, 183, 184, 239, 254, 396, 397, 402, 416, *421*
Tastanbekov, Kuman, 219, 220, 256
Tastanova, A., 135

Tazhbaev, Amangeldy, 312, 313, 335
Tazhibaev, Abdilda, 48, 72, 74, *82*, 112, 373
Tazhibaev, Rustem, 373
Tchaikovsky, Petr, 196
Temenov, Talgat, 352, 371, 391, 419
Tetkin, B., *94*
Tikhonov, 43
Timoshenko, Semen, 6, 49
Tiul'kin, Vladimir, 367
Tiurin, Rodion, 300
Tlendiev, Nurgisa, 146, *161*, 168, 213, 238, *248*, 259
Tokhtarov, Tulegen, 48
Tokmagambetov, A., 132
Tolchan, Iakov, 5, 26
Tolstoi, Leonard, 289
Topalova, Nursulu, 48
Trauberg, Leonid, 35, 49, 52
Tropinin, Eduard, 226, *249*
Truffaut, Francois, 135, 352, 419
*tselina*. See Virgin Lands Campaign
Tsoi, Viktor, 384–86
TsOKS. See Central United Film Studio (TsOKS)
Tulegenova, Bibigul, 100, *117*
Turabekov, M., 171
Turin, Viktor, 7, 27
Turkbenbaev, Adil, 407
Turkbenbaev, Rustem, 407
Tursunov, Ermek, 372, 382
Tynyshpaev, Iskander, 7, 11, *27*, 105

Ulanovskii, S., 105, 113
Umuraliev, Asanbek, 178
Umurzakov, Eleubai, 17, 18, 34–36, 67, 78, 202, 205, 207
Umurzakova, Amina, 43, 54, 60, 173, 175, 176, 209, *215*, 262, 275
Undasynov, Nurtas, *30*, 43
Union of Kazakh Film Workers, 123–26, 159, 197, 212–13, 280–320, 329–30, 349, 357, 382
Ural'skii, Viktor, 170
Urazbaev, Eldor, 232

Urusevskii, Sergei, *118*, 243

Valiev, Kambar, 273
Valikhanov, Chokan, 106–10, 140
Varshavskii, Lev, 155, 156
Vasil'ev, Dmitrii, 152
Vasil'ev brothers, 16, 41, 52
Vertov, Dziga, 50–52, 115, 225
VGIK (Soviet State Film School), 32, 114, *119*, 138, 156, 351–413, 424
Virgin Lands Campaign (*tselina*), 85–96, *117*, 296–98
Vizbor, Iurii, 331
Volchek, Boris, 41, 43
Volodarskii, Eduard, 287
Volodarskii, Matvei, 116
Vondračkova, Helena, 293
Vovnianko, Igor,' 367

*War Film Almanac*, 40, 45, 46

Žalakevičius, Vytautas, 164
Zal'tsman, Pavel, 281
Zarkhi, Aleksandr, 34, 213
Zhaisanbaev, Esbolgan, 264
Zhakov, Oleg, 45, 46
Zhambyl. See Dzhambul Dzhabaev
Zhandaev, Bopesh, 403
Zhanturin, Nurmukhan, 75, 77, 79, 109, *118*, 122, 142, 156, 188, 242, 262, 285, 333, *364*, 393, 394
Zharikov, Evgenii, 362
Zharkov, Aleksei, 401
Zharmukhamedov, Serik, 336, 362, *364*
Zhdanov, Andrei, 39, 57
Zhezhelenko, Leonid, 48
Zhienkulova, Shara, 18, 22, 100
Zholzhaksynov, Doskhan, 260, 265, *281*, 293, 314, 336, 339, 340
Zhubanov, Akhmet, 22, *30*
Zhubanova, Gaziza, 186, 243, *250*, 285, 307
Zhukov, Georgii (Marshall), 375
Zhumabaev, Magzhan, 289
Zolotukhin, Dmitrii, 318

# About the Author

**Peter Rollberg** is professor of Slavic languages, film studies, and international affairs at the George Washington University (GWU). He earned his PhD in 1988 from the University of Leipzig and came to GWU in 1991 after teaching at Duke University. He published the *Historical Dictionary of Russian and Soviet Cinema* in 2008; the second, expanded edition appeared in 2016.